THE ART OF COMPUTER PROGRAMMING

VOLUME 4, FASCICLE 0

Introduction to Combinatorial Algorithms and Boolean Functions

DONALD E. KNUTH *Stanford University*

ADDISON–WESLEY

Upper Saddle River, NJ · Boston · Indianapolis · San Francisco
New York · Toronto · Montréal · London · Munich · Paris · Madrid
Capetown · Sydney · Tokyo · Singapore · Mexico City

The author and publisher have taken care in the preparation of this book, but make no expressed or implied warranty of any kind and assume no responsibility for errors or omissions. No liability is assumed for incidental or consequential damages in connection with or arising out of the use of the information or programs contained herein.

For sales outside the U.S., please contact:

> International Sales
> international@pearsoned.com

Visit us on the Web: www.awprofessional.com

Library of Congress Cataloging-in-Publication Data
Knuth, Donald Ervin, 1938-
  The art of computer programming / Donald Ervin Knuth.
  xii,216 p. 24 cm.
  Includes bibliographical references and index.
  Contents: v. 4, fascicle 0. Introduction to combinatorial
algorithms and Boolean functions.
  ISBN 0-321-53496-4 (pbk. : alk. papers : volume 4, fascicle 0)
1. Computer programming. 2. Computer algorithms. I. Title.
  QA76.6.K64 2005
  005.1--dc22

      2005041030

Internet page http://www-cs-faculty.stanford.edu/~knuth/taocp.html contains current information about this book and related books.

See also http://www-cs-faculty.stanford.edu/~knuth/sgb.html for information about *The Stanford GraphBase*, including downloadable software for dealing with the graphs used in many of the examples in Chapter 7.

And see http://www-cs-faculty.stanford.edu/~knuth/mmix.html for basic information about the MMIX computer.

ISBN 0-321-53496-4

Text printed in the United States, on recycled paper, at the Courier Corporation plant in Stoughton, Massachusetts

First printing, April 2008

PREFACE

To put all the good stuff into one book is patently impossible,
and attempting even to be reasonably comprehensive
about certain aspects of the subject is likely to lead to runaway growth.
— GERALD B. FOLLAND, "Editor's Corner" (2005)

La dernière chose qu'on trouve en faisant un ouvrage
est de savoir celle qu'il faut mettre la première.
— BLAISE PASCAL, *Pensées* 740 (c. 1660)

THIS BOOKLET is Fascicle 0 of *The Art of Computer Programming*, Volume 4: *Combinatorial Algorithms*. As explained in the preface to Fascicle 1 of Volume 1, I'm circulating the material in this preliminary form because I know that the task of completing Volume 4 will take many years; I can't wait for people to begin reading what I've written so far and to provide valuable feedback.

To put the material in context, this fascicle contains the opening sections intended to launch a long, long chapter on combinatorial algorithms. Chapter 7 is planned to be by far the longest single chapter of *The Art of Computer Programming*; it will eventually fill at least three volumes (namely Volumes 4A, 4B, and 4C), assuming that I'm able to remain healthy. Like the second-longest chapter (Chapter 5), it begins with pump-priming introductory material that comes before the main text, including dozens of exercises to get the ball rolling. A long voyage lies ahead, and some important provisions need to be brought on board before we embark. Furthermore I want to minimize the shock of transition between Chapter 6 and the new chapter, because Chapter 6 was originally written and published more than thirty years ago.

Chapter 7 proper begins with Section 7.1: Zeros and Ones, which is another sort of introduction, at a different level. It dives into the all-important topics that surround the study of Boolean functions, which essentially underly everything that computers do. Subsection 7.1.1, "Boolean basics," attempts to erect a solid foundation of theoretical and practical ideas on which we shall build significant superstructures later; subsection 7.1.2, "Boolean evaluation," considers how to compute Boolean functions with maximum efficiency.

The remaining parts of Section 7.1 — namely 7.1.3, "Bitwise tricks and techniques," and 7.1.4, "Binary decision diagrams" — will be published soon as Volume 4, Fascicle 1. Then comes Section 7.2, Generating All Possibilities; the fascicles for Section 7.2.1, "Generating basic combinatorial patterns," have already appeared in print. Section 7.2.2 will deal with backtracking in general.

And so it will go on, if all goes well; an outline of the entire Chapter 7 as currently envisaged appears on the `taocp` webpage that is cited on page ii.

These introductory sections have turned out to have more than twice as many exercises as I had originally planned. In fact, the total number of exercises in this fascicle (366) is almost unbelievable. But many of them are quite simple, intended to reinforce the reader's understanding of basic definitions, or to acquaint readers with the joys of *The Stanford GraphBase*. Other exercises were simply irresistible, as they cried out to be included here — although, believe it or not, I did reject more potential leads than I actually followed up.

I would like to express my indebtedness to the late Robert W Floyd, who made dozens of valuable suggestions when I asked him to look over the first draft of this material in 1977. Thanks also to Robin Wilson of the Open University for his careful reading and many detailed suggestions; and to hundreds of readers who provided fantastic feedback on early drafts that circulated on the Internet.

I shall happily pay a finder's fee of $2.56 for each error in this fascicle when it is first reported to me, whether that error be typographical, technical, or historical. The same reward holds for items that I forgot to put in the index. And valuable suggestions for improvements to the text are worth 32¢ each. (Furthermore, if you find a better solution to an exercise, I'll actually reward you with immortal glory instead of mere money, by publishing your name in the eventual book:–)

Notations that are used here and not otherwise explained can be found in the Index to Notations at the end of Volumes 1, 2, or 3. Those indexes point to the places where further information is available. (See also the entries under "Notation" in the present booklet.) Of course Volume 4 will some day contain its own Index to Notations.

Machine-language examples in all future editions of *The Art of Computer Programming* will be based on the MMIX computer, which is described in Volume 1, Fascicle 1.

Cross references to yet-unwritten material sometimes appear as '00' in the following pages; this impossible value is a placeholder for the actual numbers to be supplied later.

Happy reading!

Stanford, California   D. E. K.
January 2008

Preface to Volume 4

THE TITLE of Volume 4 is *Combinatorial Algorithms*, and when I proposed it I was strongly inclined to add a subtitle: *The Kind of Programming I Like Best.* My editors have decided to tone down such exuberance, but the fact remains that programs with a combinatorial flavor have always been my favorites.

On the other hand I've often been surprised to find that, in many people's minds, the word "combinatorial" is linked with computational difficulty. Indeed, Samuel Johnson, in his famous dictionary of the English language (1755), said that the corresponding noun "is now generally used in an ill sense." Colleagues tell me tales of woe, in which they report that "the combinatorics of the situation defeated us." Why is it that, for me, combinatorics arouses feelings of pure pleasure, yet for many others it evokes pure panic?

It's true that combinatorial problems are often associated with humongously large numbers. Johnson's dictionary entry also included a quote from Ephraim Chambers, who had stated that the total number of words of length 24 or less, in a 24-letter alphabet, is 1,391,724,288,887,252,999,425,128,493,402,200. The corresponding number for a 10-letter alphabet is 11,111,111,110; and it's only 3905 when the number of letters is 5. Thus a "combinatorial explosion" certainly does occur as the size of the alphabet grows from 5 to 10 to 24 and beyond.

Computing machines have become tremendously more powerful throughout my life. As I write these words, I know that they are being processed by a "laptop" whose speed is more than 100,000 times faster than the trusty IBM Type 650 computer to which I'm dedicating these books; my current machine's memory capacity is also more than 100,000 times greater. Tomorrow's computers will be even faster and more capacious. But these amazing advances have not diminished people's craving for answers to combinatorial questions; quite the contrary. Our once-unimaginable ability to compute so rapidly has raised our expectations, and whetted our appetite for more — because, in fact, the size of a combinatorial problem can increase more than 100,000-fold when n simply increases by 1.

Combinatorial algorithms can be defined informally as techniques for the high-speed manipulation of combinatorial objects such as permutations or graphs. We typically try to find patterns or arrangements that are the best possible ways to satisfy certain constraints. The number of such problems is vast, and the art of writing such programs is especially important and appealing because a single good idea can save years or even centuries of computer time.

Indeed, the fact that good algorithms for combinatorial problems can have a terrific payoff has led to terrific advances in the state of the art. Many problems that once were thought to be intractable can now be polished off with ease, and many algorithms that once were known to be good have now become better. Starting about 1970, computer scientists began to experience a phenomenon that we called "Floyd's Lemma": Problems that seemed to need n^3 operations could actually be solved in $O(n^2)$; problems that seemed to require n^2 could be handled in $O(n \log n)$; and $n \log n$ was often reducible to $O(n)$. More difficult problems saw a reduction in running time from $O(2^n)$ to $O(1.5^n)$ to $O(1.3^n)$, etc. Other problems remained difficult in general, but they were found to have important special cases that are much simpler. Many combinatorial questions that I once thought would never be answered have now been resolved, and these breakthroughs are due mainly to improvements in algorithms rather than to improvements in processor speeds.

By 1975, such research was advancing so rapidly that a substantial fraction of the papers published in leading journals of computer science were devoted to combinatorial algorithms. And the advances weren't being made only by people in the core of computer science; significant contributions were coming from workers in electrical engineering, artificial intelligence, operations research, mathematics, physics, statistics, and other fields. I was trying to complete Volume 4 of *The Art of Computer Programming*, but instead I felt like I was sitting on the lid of a boiling kettle: I was confronted with a combinatorial explosion of another kind, a prodigious explosion of new ideas!

This series of books was born at the beginning of 1962, when I naïvely wrote out a list of tentative chapter titles for a 12-chapter book. At that time I decided to include a brief chapter about combinatorial algorithms, just for fun. "Hey look, most people use computers to deal with numbers, but we can also write programs that deal with patterns." In those days it was easy to give a fairly complete description of just about every combinatorial algorithm that was known. And even by 1966, when I'd finished a first draft of about 3000 handwritten pages for that already-overgrown book, fewer than 100 of those pages belonged to Chapter 7. I had absolutely no idea that what I'd foreseen as a sort of "salad course" would eventually turn out to be the main dish.

The great combinatorial fermentation of 1975 has continued to churn, as more and more people have begun to participate. New ideas improve upon the older ones, but rarely replace them or make them obsolete. So of course I've had to abandon any hopes that I once had of being able to surround the field, to write a definitive book that sets everything in order and provides one-stop shopping for everyone who has combinatorial problems to solve. It's almost never possible to discuss a subtopic and say, "Here's the final solution: end of story." Instead, I must restrict myself to explaining the most important principles that seem to underlie all of the efficient combinatorial methods that I've encountered so far. At present I've accumulated more than twice as much raw material for Volume 4 as for all of Volumes 1–3 combined.

This sheer mass of material implies that the once-planned "Volume 4" must actually become several physical volumes. You are now looking at Volume 4A. Volumes 4B and 4C will exist someday, assuming that I'm able to remain healthy; and (who knows?) there may also be Volumes 4D, 4E, ...; but surely not 4Z.

My plan is to go systematically through the files that I've amassed since 1962 and to tell the stories that I believe are still waiting to be told, to the best of my ability. I can't aspire to completeness, but I do want to give proper credit to all of the pioneers who have been responsible for key ideas; so I won't scrimp on historical details. Furthermore, whenever I learn something that I think is likely to remain important 50 years from now, something that can also be explained elegantly in a paragraph or two, I can't bear to leave it out. Conversely, difficult material that requires a lengthy proof is beyond the scope of these books, unless the subject matter is truly fundamental.

OK, it's clear that the field of Combinatorial Algorithms is vast, and I can't cover it all. What are the most important things that I'm leaving out? My biggest blind spot, I think, is geometry, because I've always been much better at visualizing and manipulating algebraic formulas than objects in space. Therefore I don't attempt to deal in these books with combinatorial problems that are related to computational geometry, such as close packing of spheres, or clustering of data points in n-dimensional Euclidean space, or even the Steiner tree problem in the plane. More significantly, I tend to shy away from polyhedral combinatorics, and from approaches that are based primarily on linear programming, integer programming, or semidefinite programming. Those topics are treated well in many other books on the subject, and they rely on geometrical intuition. Purely combinatorial developments are easier for me to understand.

I also must confess a bias against algorithms that are efficient only in an asymptotic sense, algorithms whose superior performance doesn't begin to "kick in" until the size of the problem exceeds the size of the universe. A great many publications nowadays are devoted to algorithms of that kind. I can understand why the contemplation of ultimate limits has intellectual appeal and carries an academic cachet; but in *The Art of Computer Programming* I tend to give short shrift to any methods that I would never consider using myself in an actual program. (There are, of course, exceptions to this rule, especially with respect to basic concepts in the core of the subject. Some impractical methods are simply too beautiful and/or too insightful to be excluded; others provide instructive examples of what *not* to do.)

Furthermore, as in earlier volumes of this series, I'm intentionally concentrating almost entirely on *sequential* algorithms, even though computers are increasingly able to carry out activities in parallel. I'm unable to judge what ideas about parallelism are likely to be useful five or ten years from now, let alone fifty, so I happily leave such questions to others who are wiser than I. Sequential methods, by themselves, already test the limits of my own ability to discern what the artful programmers of tomorrow will want to know.

The main decision that I needed to make when planning how to present this material was whether to organize it by problems or by techniques. Chapter 5 in Volume 3, for example, was devoted to a single problem, the sorting of data into order; more than two dozen techniques were applied to different aspects of that problem. Combinatorial algorithms, by contrast, involve many different problems, which tend to be attacked with a smaller repertoire of techniques.

I finally decided that a mixed strategy would work better than any pure approach. Thus, for example, these books treat the problem of finding shortest paths in Section 7.3, and problems of connectivity in Section 7.4.1; but many other sections are devoted to basic techniques, such as the use of Boolean algebra (Section 7.1), backtracking (Section 7.2), matroid theory (Section 7.6), or dynamic programming (Section 7.7). The famous Traveling Salesrep Problem, and other classic combinatorial tasks related to covering, coloring, and packing, have no sections of their own, but they come up several times in different places as they are treated by different methods.

I've mentioned great progress in the art of combinatorial computing, but I don't mean to imply that all combinatorial problems have actually been tamed. When the running time of a computer program goes ballistic, its programmers shouldn't expect to find a silver bullet for their needs in this book. The methods described here will often work a great deal faster than the first approaches that a programmer tries; but let's face it: Combinatorial problems get huge very quickly. We can even prove rigorously that a certain small, natural problem will *never* have a feasible solution in the real world, although it is solvable in principle (see the theorem of Stockmeyer and Meyer in Section 7.1.2). In other cases we cannot prove as yet that no decent algorithm for a given problem exists, but we know that such methods are unlikely, because any efficient algorithm would yield a good way to solve thousands of other problems that have stumped the world's greatest experts (see the discussion of NP-completeness in Section 7.9).

Experience suggests that new combinatorial algorithms will continue to be invented, for new combinatorial problems and for newly identified variations or special cases of old ones; and that people's appetite for such algorithms will also continue to grow. The art of computer programming continually reaches new heights when programmers are faced with challenges such as these. Yet today's methods are also likely to remain relevant.

Most of this book is self-contained, although there are frequent tie-ins with the topics discussed in Volumes 1–3. Low-level details of machine language programming have been covered extensively in those volumes, so the algorithms in the present book are usually specified only at an abstract level, independent of any machine. However, some aspects of combinatorial programming are heavily dependent on low-level details that didn't arise before; in such cases, all examples in this book are based on the MMIX computer, which supersedes the MIX machine that was defined in early editions of Volume 1. Details about MMIX appear in a paperback supplement to that volume called *The Art of Computer Programming*, Volume 1, Fascicle 1; they're also available on the Internet, together with downloadable assemblers and simulators.

Another downloadable resource, a collection of programs and data called *The Stanford GraphBase*, is cited extensively in the examples of this book. Readers are encouraged to play with it, in order to learn about combinatorial algorithms in what I think will be the most efficient and most enjoyable way.

Incidentally, while writing the introductory material at the beginning of Chapter 7, I was pleased to note that it was natural to mention some work of my Ph.D. thesis advisor, Marshall Hall, Jr. (1910–1990), as well as some work of *his* thesis advisor, Oystein Ore (1899–1968), as well as some work of *his* thesis advisor, Thoralf Skolem (1887–1963). Skolem's advisor, Axel Thue (1863–1922), was already present in Chapter 6.

I'm immensely grateful to the hundreds of readers who have helped me to ferret out numerous mistakes that I made in early drafts of this volume, which were originally posted on the Internet and subsequently printed in paperback fascicles. But I fear that other errors still lurk among the details collected here, and I want to correct them as soon as possible. Therefore I will cheerfully pay $2.56 to the first finder of each technical, typographical, or historical error. The taocp webpage cited on page ii contains a current listing of all corrections that have been reported to me.

Stanford, California   D. E. K.
April 2008

> *Naturally, I am responsible for the remaining errors—*
> *although, in my opinion, my friends could have caught a few more.*
> — CHRISTOS H. PAPADIMITRIOU, *Computational Complexity* (1995)

A note on references. References to *IEEE Transactions* include a letter code for the type of transactions, in boldface preceding the volume number. For example, '*IEEE Trans.* **C-35**' means the *IEEE Transactions on Computers*, volume 35. The IEEE no longer uses these convenient letter codes, but the codes aren't too hard to decipher: '**EC**' once stood for "Electronic Computers," '**IT**' for "Information Theory," '**SE**' for "Software Engineering," and '**SP**' for "Signal Processing," etc.; '**CAD**' meant "Computer-Aided Design of Integrated Circuits and Systems."

*The author is especially grateful to the Addison–Wesley Publishing Company
for its patience in waiting a full decade for this manuscript
from the date the contract was signed.*

— FRANK HARARY, *Graph Theory* (1968)

Bitte ein Bit!
— Slogan of Bitburger Brauerei (1951)

x

CONTENTS

Chapter 7 — Combinatorial Searching   1

7.1. Zeros and Ones   47
    7.1.1. Boolean Basics   47
    7.1.2. Boolean Evaluation   96

Answers to Exercises   134

Index and Glossary   201

Hommage à Bach.

COMBINATORIAL SEARCHING

You shall seeke all day ere you finde them,
& when you have them, they are not worth the search.

— BASSANIO, in *The Merchant of Venice* (Act I, Scene 1, Line 117)

Amid the action and reaction of so dense a swarm of humanity,
every possible combination of events may be expected to take place,
and many a little problem will be presented which may be striking and bizarre.

— SHERLOCK HOLMES, in *The Adventure of the Blue Carbuncle* (1892)

The field of combinatorial algorithms is too vast to cover
in a single paper or even in a single book.

— ROBERT E. TARJAN (1976)

While jostling against all manner of people
it has been impressed upon my mind that the successful ones
are those who have a natural faculty for solving puzzles.
Life is full of puzzles, and we are called upon
to solve such as fate throws our way.

— SAM LOYD, JR. (1927)

COMBINATORICS is the study of the ways in which discrete objects can be arranged into various kinds of patterns. For example, the objects might be $2n$ numbers $\{1, 1, 2, 2, \ldots, n, n\}$, and we might want to place them in a row so that exactly k numbers occur between the two appearances of each digit k. When $n = 3$ there is essentially only one way to arrange such "Langford pairs," namely 231213 (and its left-right reversal); similarly, there's also a unique solution when $n = 4$. Many other types of combinatorial patterns are discussed below.

Five basic types of questions typically arise when combinatorial problems are studied, some more difficult than others.

i) Existence: Are there any arrangements X that conform to the pattern?
ii) Construction: If so, can such an X be found quickly?
iii) Enumeration: How many different arrangements X exist?
iv) Generation: Can all arrangements X_1, X_2, ... be visited systematically?
v) Optimization: What arrangements maximize or minimize $f(X)$, given an objective function f?

Each of these questions turns out to be interesting with respect to Langford pairs.

For example, consider the question of existence. Trial and error quickly reveals that, when $n = 5$, we cannot place $\{1, 1, 2, 2, \ldots, 5, 5\}$ properly into ten positions. The two 1s must both go into even-numbered slots, or both into odd-numbered slots; similarly, the 3s and 5s must choose between two evens or two odds; but the 2s and 4s use one of each. Thus we can't fill exactly five slots of each parity. This reasoning also proves that the problem has no solution when $n = 6$, or in general whenever the number of odd values in $\{1, 2, \ldots, n\}$ is odd.

In other words, Langford pairings can exist only when $n = 4m-1$ or $n = 4m$, for some integer m. Conversely, when n does have this form, Roy O. Davies has found an elegant way to construct a suitable placement (see exercise 1).

How many essentially different pairings, L_n, exist? Lots, when n grows:

$$
\begin{aligned}
L_3 &= 1; & L_4 &= 1; \\
L_7 &= 26; & L_8 &= 150; \\
L_{11} &= 17{,}792; & L_{12} &= 108{,}144; \\
L_{15} &= 39{,}809{,}640; & L_{16} &= 326{,}721{,}800; \\
L_{19} &= 256{,}814{,}891{,}280; & L_{20} &= 2{,}636{,}337{,}861{,}200; \\
L_{23} &= 3{,}799{,}455{,}942{,}515{,}488; & L_{24} &= 46{,}845{,}158{,}056{,}515{,}936.
\end{aligned}
\tag{1}
$$

[The values of L_{23} and L_{24} were determined by M. Krajecki, C. Jaillet, and A. Bui in 2004 and 2005; see *Studia Informatica Universalis* **4** (2005), 151–190.] A seat-of-the-pants calculation suggests that L_n might be roughly of order $(4n/e^3)^{n+1/2}$ when it is nonzero (see exercise 5); and in fact this prediction turns out to be basically correct in all known cases. But no simple formula is apparent.

The problem of Langford arrangements is a simple special case of a general class of combinatorial challenges called *exact cover problems*. In Section 7.2.2.1 we shall study an algorithm called "dancing links," which is a convenient way to generate all solutions to such problems. When $n = 16$, for example, that method needs to perform only about 3200 memory accesses for each Langford pair arrangement that it finds. Thus the value of L_{16} can be computed in a reasonable amount of time by simply generating all of the pairings and counting them.

Notice, however, that L_{24} is a *huge* number — roughly 5×10^{16}, or about 1500 MIP-years. (Recall that a "MIP-year" is the number of instructions executed per year by a machine that carries out a million instructions per second, namely 31,556,952,000,000.) Therefore it's clear that the exact value of L_{24} was determined by some technique that did *not* involve generating all of the arrangements. Indeed, there is a much, much faster way to compute L_n, using polynomial algebra. The instructive method described in exercise 6 needs $O(4^n n)$ operations, which may seem inefficient; but it beats the generate-and-count method by a whopping factor of order $\Theta((n/e^3)^{n-1/2})$, and even when $n = 16$ it runs about 20 times faster. On the other hand, the exact value of L_{100} will probably never be known, even as computers become faster and faster.

We can also consider Langford pairings that are *optimum* in various ways. For example, it's possible to arrange sixteen pairs of weights $\{1, 1, 2, 2, \ldots, 16, 16\}$ that satisfy Langford's condition and have the additional property of being "well-balanced," in the sense that they won't tip a balance beam when they are placed in the appropriate order:

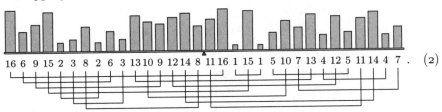

$$16\ 6\quad 9\ 15\ 2\quad 3\quad 8\quad 2\quad 6\quad 3\ 13\ 10\ 9\quad 12\ 14\ 8\quad 11\ 16\quad 1\quad 15\ 1\quad 5\ 10\ 7\ 13\ 4\ 12\ 5\ 11\ 14\ 4\ 7\ . \qquad (2)$$

In other words, $15.5 \cdot 16 + 14.5 \cdot 6 + \cdots + 0.5 \cdot 8 = 0.5 \cdot 11 + \cdots + 14.5 \cdot 4 + 15.5 \cdot 7$; and in this particular example we also have another kind of balance, $16 + 6 + \cdots + 8 = 11 + 16 + \cdots + 7$, hence also $16 \cdot 16 + 15 \cdot 6 + \cdots + 1 \cdot 8 = 1 \cdot 11 + \cdots + 15 \cdot 4 + 16 \cdot 7$.

Moreover, the arrangement in (2) has *minimum width* among all Langford pairings of order 16: The connecting lines at the bottom of the diagram show that no more than seven pairs are incomplete at any point, as we read from left to right; and one can show that a width of six is impossible. (See exercise 7.)

What arrangements $a_1 a_2 \ldots a_{32}$ of $\{1, 1, \ldots, 16, 16\}$ are the *least* balanced, in the sense that $\sum_{k=1}^{32} k a_k$ is maximized? The maximum possible value turns out to be 5268. One such pairing — there are 12,016 of them — is

$$2\ 3\ 4\ 2\ 1\ 3\ 1\ 4\ 16\ 13\ 15\ 5\ 14\ 7\ 9\ 6\ 11\ 5\ 12\ 10\ 8\ 7\ 6\ 13\ 9\ 16\ 15\ 14\ 11\ 8\ 10\ 12. \qquad (3)$$

A more interesting question is to ask for the Langford pairings that are smallest and largest in lexicographic order. The answers for $n = 24$ are

$$\{ \mathtt{abacbdecfgdoersfpgqtuwxvjklonhmirpsjqkhltiunmwvx,} \atop \mathtt{xvwsquntkigrdapaodgiknqsvxwutmrpohljcfbecbhmfejl} \} \qquad (4)$$

if we use the letters a, b, ..., w, x instead of the numbers 1, 2, ..., 23, 24.

We shall discuss many techniques for combinatorial optimization in later sections of this chapter. Our goal, of course, will be to solve such problems without examining more than a tiny portion of the space of all possible arrangements.

Orthogonal latin squares. Let's look back for a moment at the early days of combinatorics. A posthumous edition of Jacques Ozanam's *Recreations mathematiques et physiques* (Paris: 1725) included an amusing puzzle in volume 4, page 434: "Take all the aces, kings, queens, and jacks from an ordinary deck of playing cards and arrange them in a square so that each row and each column contains all four values and all four suits." Can you do it? Ozanam's solution, shown in Fig. 1 on the next page, does even more: It exhibits the full panoply of values and of suits also on both main diagonals. (Please don't turn the page until you've given this problem a try.)

By 1779 a similar puzzle was making the rounds of St. Petersburg, and it came to the attention of the great mathematician Leonhard Euler. "Thirty-six officers of six different ranks, taken from six different regiments, want to march in a 6×6 formation so that each row and each column will contain one officer of each rank and one of each regiment. How can they do it?" Nobody was able to

Fig. 1. Disorder in the court cards: No agreement in any line of four. (This configuration is one of many ways to solve a popular eighteenth-century problem.)

find a satisfactory marching order. So Euler decided to resolve the riddle — even though he had become nearly blind in 1771 and was dictating all of his work to assistants. He wrote a major paper on the subject [eventually published in *Verhandelingen uitgegeven door het Zeeuwsch Genootschap der Wetenschappen te Vlissingen* **9** (1782), 85–239], in which he constructed suitable arrangements for the analogous task with n ranks and n regiments when $n = 1$, 3, 4, 5, 7, 8, 9, 11, 12, 13, 15, 16, ...; only the cases with $n \bmod 4 = 2$ eluded him.

There's obviously no solution when $n = 2$. But Euler was stumped when $n = 6$, after having examined a "very considerable number" of square arrangements that didn't work. He showed that any actual solution would lead to many others that look different, and he couldn't believe that all such solutions had escaped his attention. Therefore he said, "I do not hesitate to conclude that one cannot produce a complete square of 36 cells, and that the same impossibility extends to the cases $n = 10$, $n = 14$ ... in general to all oddly even numbers."

Euler named the 36 officers $a\alpha$, $a\beta$, $a\gamma$, $a\delta$, $a\epsilon$, $a\zeta$, $b\alpha$, $b\beta$, $b\gamma$, $b\delta$, $b\epsilon$, $b\zeta$, $c\alpha$, $c\beta$, $c\gamma$, $c\delta$, $c\epsilon$, $c\zeta$, $d\alpha$, $d\beta$, $d\gamma$, $d\delta$, $d\epsilon$, $d\zeta$, $e\alpha$, $e\beta$, $e\gamma$, $e\delta$, $e\epsilon$, $e\zeta$, $f\alpha$, $f\beta$, $f\gamma$, $f\delta$, $f\epsilon$, $f\zeta$, based on their regiments and ranks. He observed that any solution would amount to having two *separate* squares, one for Latin letters and another for Greek. Each of those squares is supposed to have distinct entries in rows and columns; so he began by studying the possible configurations for $\{a, b, c, d, e, f\}$, which he called *Latin squares*. A Latin square can be paired up with a Greek square to form a "Græco-Latin square" only if the squares are *orthogonal* to each other, meaning that no (Latin, Greek) pair of letters can be found together in more than one place when the squares are superimposed. For example, if we let $a = \mathtt{A}$, $b = \mathtt{K}$, $c = \mathtt{Q}$, $d = \mathtt{J}$, $\alpha = \clubsuit$, $\beta = \spadesuit$, $\gamma = \diamondsuit$, and $\delta = \heartsuit$, Fig. 1 is equivalent to the Latin, Greek, and Græco-Latin squares

$$
\begin{pmatrix} d & a & b & c \\ c & b & a & d \\ a & d & c & b \\ b & c & d & a \end{pmatrix}, \quad
\begin{pmatrix} \gamma & \delta & \beta & \alpha \\ \beta & \alpha & \gamma & \delta \\ \alpha & \beta & \delta & \gamma \\ \delta & \gamma & \alpha & \beta \end{pmatrix}, \quad \text{and} \quad
\begin{pmatrix} d\gamma & a\delta & b\beta & c\alpha \\ c\beta & b\alpha & a\gamma & d\delta \\ a\alpha & d\beta & c\delta & b\gamma \\ b\delta & c\gamma & d\alpha & a\beta \end{pmatrix}. \tag{5}
$$

Of course we can use *any* n distinct symbols in an $n \times n$ Latin square; all that matters is that no symbol occurs twice in any row or twice in any column. So we might as well use numeric values $\{0, 1, \ldots, n-1\}$ for the entries. Furthermore we'll just refer to "latin squares" (with a lowercase "l"), instead of categorizing a square as either Latin or Greek, because orthogonality is a symmetric relation.

Euler's assertion that two 6×6 latin squares cannot be orthogonal was verified by Thomas Clausen, who reduced the problem to an examination of 17 fundamentally different cases, according to a letter from H. C. Schumacher to C. F. Gauss dated 10 August 1842. But Clausen did not publish his analysis. The first demonstration to appear in print was by G. Tarry [*Comptes rendus, Association française pour l'avancement des sciences* **29**, part 2 (1901), 170–203], who discovered in his own way that 6×6 latin squares can be classified into 17 different families. (In Section 7.2.3 we shall study how to decompose a problem into combinatorially inequivalent classes of arrangements.)

Euler's conjecture about the remaining cases $n = 10$, $n = 14$, ... was "proved" three times, by J. Petersen [*Annuaire des mathématiciens* (Paris: 1902), 413–427], by P. Wernicke [*Jahresbericht der Deutschen Math.-Vereinigung* **19** (1910), 264–267], and by H. F. MacNeish [*Annals of Math.* **23** (1922), 221–227]. Flaws in all three arguments became known, however; and the question was still unsettled when computers became available many years later. One of the very first combinatorial problems to be tackled by machine was therefore the enigma of 10×10 Græco-Latin squares: Do they exist or not?

In 1957, L. J. Paige and C. B. Tompkins programmed the SWAC computer to search for a counterexample to Euler's prediction. They selected one particular 10×10 latin square "almost at random," and their program tried to find another square that would be orthogonal to it. But the results were discouraging, and they decided to shut the machine off after five hours. Already the program had generated enough data for them to predict that at least 4.8×10^{11} hours of computer time would be needed to finish the run!

Shortly afterwards, three mathematicians made a breakthrough that put latin squares onto page one of major world newspapers: R. C. Bose, S. S. Shrikhande, and E. T. Parker found a remarkable series of constructions that yield orthogonal $n \times n$ squares for all $n > 6$ [*Proc. Nat. Acad. Sci.* **45** (1959), 734–737, 859–862; *Canadian J. Math.* **12** (1960), 189–203]. Thus, after resisting attacks for 180 years, Euler's conjecture turned out to be almost entirely wrong.

Their discovery was made without computer help. But Parker worked for UNIVAC, and he soon brought programming skills into the picture by solving the problem of Paige and Tompkins in less than an hour, on a UNIVAC 1206 Military Computer. [See *Proc. Symp. Applied Math.* **10** (1960), 71–83; **15** (1963), 73–81.]

Let's take a closer look at what the earlier programmers did, and how Parker dramatically trumped their approach. Paige and Tompkins began with the following 10×10 square L and its unknown orthogonal mate(s) M:

$$
L = \begin{pmatrix}
0 & 1 & 2 & 3 & 4 & 5 & 6 & 7 & 8 & 9 \\
1 & 8 & 3 & 2 & 5 & 4 & 7 & 6 & 9 & 0 \\
2 & 9 & 5 & 6 & 3 & 0 & 8 & 4 & 7 & 1 \\
3 & 7 & 0 & 9 & 8 & 6 & 1 & 5 & 2 & 4 \\
4 & 6 & 7 & 5 & 2 & 9 & 0 & 8 & 1 & 3 \\
5 & 0 & 9 & 4 & 7 & 8 & 3 & 1 & 6 & 2 \\
6 & 5 & 4 & 7 & 1 & 3 & 2 & 9 & 0 & 8 \\
7 & 4 & 1 & 8 & 0 & 2 & 9 & 3 & 5 & 6 \\
8 & 3 & 6 & 0 & 9 & 1 & 5 & 2 & 4 & 7 \\
9 & 2 & 8 & 1 & 6 & 7 & 4 & 0 & 3 & 5
\end{pmatrix}
\quad \text{and} \quad
M = \begin{pmatrix}
0 & \llcorner & \llcorner & \llcorner & \llcorner & \llcorner & \llcorner & \llcorner & \llcorner & \llcorner \\
1 & \llcorner & \llcorner & \llcorner & \llcorner & \llcorner & \llcorner & \llcorner & \llcorner & \llcorner \\
2 & \llcorner & \llcorner & \llcorner & \llcorner & \llcorner & \llcorner & \llcorner & \llcorner & \llcorner \\
3 & \llcorner & \llcorner & \llcorner & \llcorner & \llcorner & \llcorner & \llcorner & \llcorner & \llcorner \\
4 & \llcorner & \llcorner & \llcorner & \llcorner & \llcorner & \llcorner & \llcorner & \llcorner & \llcorner \\
5 & \llcorner & \llcorner & \llcorner & \llcorner & \llcorner & \llcorner & \llcorner & \llcorner & \llcorner \\
6 & \llcorner & \llcorner & \llcorner & \llcorner & \llcorner & \llcorner & \llcorner & \llcorner & \llcorner \\
7 & \llcorner & \llcorner & \llcorner & \llcorner & \llcorner & \llcorner & \llcorner & \llcorner & \llcorner \\
8 & \llcorner & \llcorner & \llcorner & \llcorner & \llcorner & \llcorner & \llcorner & \llcorner & \llcorner \\
9 & \llcorner & \llcorner & \llcorner & \llcorner & \llcorner & \llcorner & \llcorner & \llcorner & \llcorner
\end{pmatrix}. \quad (6)
$$

We can assume without loss of generality that the rows of M begin with 0, 1, ..., 9, as shown. The problem is to fill in the remaining 90 blank entries, and the original SWAC program proceeded from top to bottom, left to right. The top left $\llcorner$ can't be filled with 0, since 0 has already occurred in the top row of M. And it can't be 1 either, because the pair $(1, 1)$ already occurs at the left of the next row in (L, M). We can, however, tentatively insert a 2. The digit 1 can be placed next; and pretty soon we find the lexicographically smallest top row that might work for M, namely 0214365897. Similarly, the smallest rows that fit below 0214365897 are 1023456789 and 2108537946; and the smallest legitimate row below them is 3540619278. Now, unfortunately, the going gets tougher: There's no way to complete another row without coming into conflict with a previous choice. So we change 3540619278 to 3540629178 (but that doesn't work either), then to 3540698172, and so on for several more steps, until finally 3546109278 can be followed by 4397028651 before we get stuck again.

In Section 7.2.3, we'll study ways to estimate the behavior of such searches, without actually performing them. Such estimates tell us in this case that the Paige–Tompkins method essentially traverses an implicit search tree that contains about 2.5×10^{18} nodes. Most of those nodes belong to only a few levels of the tree; more than half of them deal with choices on the right half of the sixth row of M, after about 50 of the 90 blanks have been tentatively filled in. A typical node of the search tree probably requires about 75 mems (memory accesses) for processing, to check validity. Therefore the total running time on a modern computer would be roughly the time needed to perform 2×10^{20} mems.

Parker, on the other hand, went back to the method that Euler had originally used to search for orthogonal mates in 1779. First he found all of the so-called *transversals* of L, namely all ways to choose some of its elements so that there's exactly one element in each row, one in each column, and one of each value. For example, one transversal is 0859734216, in Euler's notation, meaning that we choose the 0 in column 0, the 8 in column 1, ..., the 6 in column 9. Each transversal that includes the k in L's leftmost column represents a legitimate way to place the ten k's into square M. The task of finding transversals is, in fact, rather easy, and the given matrix L turns out to have exactly 808 of them; there are respectively $(79, 96, 76, 87, 70, 84, 83, 75, 95, 63)$ transversals for $k = (0, 1, \ldots, 9)$.

Once the transversals are known, we're left with an exact cover problem of 10 stages, which is much simpler than the original 90-stage problem in (6). All we need to do is cover the square with ten transversals that don't intersect — because every such set of ten is equivalent to a latin square M that is orthogonal to L.

The particular square L in (6) has, in fact, exactly one orthogonal mate:

$$
\begin{pmatrix}
0 & 1 & 2 & 3 & 4 & 5 & 6 & 7 & 8 & 9 \\
1 & 8 & 3 & 2 & 5 & 4 & 7 & 6 & 9 & 0 \\
2 & 9 & 5 & 6 & 3 & 0 & 8 & 4 & 7 & 1 \\
3 & 7 & 0 & 9 & 8 & 6 & 1 & 5 & 2 & 4 \\
4 & 6 & 7 & 5 & 2 & 9 & 0 & 8 & 1 & 3 \\
5 & 0 & 9 & 4 & 7 & 8 & 3 & 1 & 6 & 2 \\
6 & 5 & 4 & 7 & 1 & 3 & 2 & 9 & 0 & 8 \\
7 & 4 & 1 & 8 & 0 & 2 & 9 & 3 & 5 & 6 \\
8 & 3 & 6 & 0 & 9 & 1 & 5 & 2 & 4 & 7 \\
9 & 2 & 8 & 1 & 6 & 7 & 4 & 0 & 3 & 5
\end{pmatrix}
\perp
\begin{pmatrix}
0 & 2 & 8 & 5 & 9 & 4 & 7 & 3 & 6 & 1 \\
1 & 7 & 4 & 9 & 3 & 6 & 5 & 0 & 2 & 8 \\
2 & 5 & 6 & 4 & 8 & 7 & 0 & 1 & 9 & 3 \\
3 & 6 & 9 & 0 & 4 & 5 & 8 & 2 & 1 & 7 \\
4 & 8 & 1 & 7 & 5 & 3 & 6 & 9 & 0 & 2 \\
5 & 1 & 7 & 8 & 0 & 2 & 9 & 4 & 3 & 6 \\
6 & 9 & 0 & 2 & 7 & 1 & 3 & 8 & 4 & 5 \\
7 & 3 & 5 & 1 & 2 & 0 & 4 & 6 & 8 & 9 \\
8 & 0 & 2 & 3 & 6 & 9 & 1 & 7 & 5 & 4 \\
9 & 4 & 3 & 6 & 1 & 8 & 2 & 5 & 7 & 0
\end{pmatrix}. \tag{7}
$$

The dancing links algorithm finds it, and proves its uniqueness, after doing only about 1.7×10^8 mems of computation, given the 808 transversals. Furthermore, the cost of the transversal-finding phase, about 5 million mems, is negligible by comparison. Thus the original running time of 2×10^{20} mems — which once was regarded as the inevitable cost of solving a problem for which there are 10^{90} ways to fill in the blanks — has been reduced by a further factor of more than $10^{12}(!)$.

We will see later that advances have also been made in methods for solving 90-level problems like (6). Indeed, (6) turns out to be representable directly as an exact cover problem (see exercise 17), which the dancing links procedure of Section 7.2.2.1 solves after expending only 1.3×10^{11} mems. Even so, the Euler–Parker approach remains about a thousand times better than the Paige–Tompkins approach. By "factoring" the problem into two separate phases, one for transversal-finding and one for transversal-combining, Euler and Parker essentially reduced the computational cost from a product, $T_1 T_2$, to a sum, $T_1 + T_2$.

The moral of this story is clear: Combinatorial problems might confront us with a huge universe of possibilities, yet we shouldn't give up too easily. A single good idea can reduce the amount of computation by many orders of magnitude.

Puzzles versus the real world. Many of the combinatorial problems we shall study in this chapter, like Langford's problem of pairs or Ozanam's problem of the sixteen honor cards, originated as amusing puzzles or "brain twisters." Some readers might be put off by this emphasis on recreational topics, which they regard as a frivolous waste of time. Shouldn't computers really be doing useful work? And shouldn't textbooks about computers be primarily concerned with significant applications to industry and/or world progress?

Well, the author of the textbook you are reading has absolutely no objections to useful work and human progress. But he believes strongly that a book such as this should stress *methods* of problem solving, together with mathematical ideas and *models* that help to solve many different problems, rather than focusing on the reasons why those methods and models might be useful. We shall learn many beautiful and powerful ways to attack combinatorial problems, and the elegance of those methods will be our main motivation for studying them. Combinatorial challenges pop up everywhere, and new ways to apply the techniques discussed in this chapter arise every day. So let's not limit our horizons by attempting to catalog in advance what the ideas are good for.

For example, it turns out that orthogonal latin squares are enormously useful, particularly in the design of experiments. Already in 1788, François Cretté de Palluel used a 4×4 latin square to study what happens when sixteen sheep — four each from four different breeds — were fed four different diets and harvested at four different times. [*Mémoires d'Agriculture* (Paris: Société Royale d'Agriculture, trimestre d'été, 1788), 17–23.] The latin square allowed him to do this with 16 sheep instead of 64; with a Græco-Latin square he could also have varied another parameter by trying, say, four different quantities of food or four different grazing paradigms.

But if we had focused our discussion on his approach to animal husbandry, we might well have gotten bogged down in details about breeding, about root vegetables versus grains and the costs of growing them, etc. Readers who aren't farmers might therefore have decided to skip the whole topic, even though latin square designs apply to a wide range of studies. (Think about testing five kinds of pills, on patients in five stages of some disease, five age brackets, and five weight groups.) Moreover, a concentration on experimental design could lead readers to miss the fact that latin squares also have important applications to coding and cryptography (see exercises 18–24).

Even the topic of Langford pairing, which seems at first to be purely recreational, turns out to have practical importance. T. Skolem used Langford sequences to construct Steiner triple systems, which we have applied to database queries in Section 6.5 [see *Math. Scandinavica* **6** (1958), 273–280]; and in the 1960s, E. J. Groth of Motorola Corporation applied Langford pairs to the design of circuits for multiplication. Furthermore, the algorithms that efficiently find Langford pairs and latin square transversals, such as the method of dancing links, apply to exact cover problems in general; and the problem of exact covering has great relevance to crucial problems such as the equitable apportionment of voter precincts to electoral districts, etc.

The applications are not the most important thing, and neither are the puzzles. Our primary goal is rather to get basic concepts into our brains, like the notions of latin squares and exact covering. Such notions give us the building blocks, vocabulary, and insights that *tomorrow's* problems will need.

Still, it's foolish to discuss problem solving without actually solving any problems. We need good problems to stimulate our creative juices, to light up our grey cells in a more or less organized fashion, and to make the basic concepts familiar. Mind-bending puzzles are often ideal for this purpose, because they can be presented in a few words, needing no complicated background knowledge.

Václav Havel once remarked that the complexities of life are vast: "There is too much to know... We have to abandon the arrogant belief that the world is merely a puzzle to be solved, a machine with instructions for use waiting to be discovered, a body of information to be fed into a computer." He called for an increased sense of justice and responsibility; for taste, courage, and compassion. His words were filled with great wisdom. Yet thank goodness we do also have puzzles that *can* be solved! Puzzles deserve to be counted among the great pleasures of life, to be enjoyed in moderation like all other treats.

Of course, Langford and Ozanam directed their puzzles to human beings, not to computers. Aren't we missing the point if we merely shuffle such questions off to machines, to be solved by brute force instead of by rational thought? George Brewster, writing to Martin Gardner in 1963, expressed a widely held view as follows: "Feeding a recreational puzzle into a computer is no more than a step above dynamiting a trout stream. Succumbing to instant recreation."

Yes, but that view misses another important point: Simple puzzles often have generalizations that go beyond human ability and arouse our curiosity. The study of those generalizations often suggests instructive methods that apply to numerous other problems and have surprising consequences. Indeed, many of the key techniques that we shall study were born when people were trying to solve various puzzles. While writing this chapter, the author couldn't help relishing the fact that puzzles are now more fun than ever, as computers get faster and faster, because we keep getting more powerful dynamite to play with. [Further comments appear in the author's essay, "Can toy problems be useful?", originally written in 1976; see *Selected Papers on Computer Science* (1996), 169–183.]

Puzzles do have the danger that they can be *too* elegant. Good puzzles tend to be mathematically clean and well-structured, but we also need to learn how to deal systematically with the messy, chaotic, organic stuff that surrounds us every day. Indeed, some computational techniques are important chiefly because they provide powerful ways to cope with such complexities. That is why, for example, the arcane rules of library-card alphabetization were presented at the beginning of Chapter 5, and an actual elevator system was discussed at length to illustrate simulation techniques in Section 2.2.5.

A collection of programs and data called the Stanford GraphBase (SGB) has been prepared so that experiments with combinatorial algorithms can readily be performed on a variety of real-world examples. SGB includes, for example, data about American highways, and an input-output model of the U.S. economy; it records the casts of characters in Homer's *Iliad*, Tolstoy's *Anna Karenina*, and several other novels; it encapsulates the structure of Roget's *Thesaurus* of 1879; it documents hundreds of college football scores; it specifies the gray-value pixels of Leonardo da Vinci's *Gioconda* (Mona Lisa). And perhaps most importantly, SGB contains a collection of five-letter words, which we shall discuss next.

The five-letter words of English. Many of the examples in this chapter will be based on the following list of five-letter words:

aargh, abaca, abaci, aback, abaft, abase, abash, ..., zooms, zowie. (8)

(There are 5757 words altogether — too many to display here; but those that are missing can readily be imagined.) It's a personal list, collected by the author between 1972 and 1992, beginning when he realized that such words would make ideal data for testing many kinds of combinatorial algorithms.

The list has intentionally been restricted to words that are **truly** part of the English language, in the sense that the author has encountered them in actual use. Unabridged dictionaries contain thousands of entries that are much more esoteric, like `aalii`, `abamp`, ..., `zymin`, and `zyxst`; words like that are useful primarily to Scrabble® players. But unfamiliar words tend to **spoil** the fun for anybody who doesn't know them. Therefore, for twenty years, the author systematically took note of all **words** that seemed **right** for the expository **goals** of *The Art of Computer Programming*.

Finally it was necessary to freeze the collection, in order to have a **fixed point** for reproducible experiments. The English language will always be evolving, but the 5757 SGB words will therefore always stay the same — even though the author has been tempted at times to add a few words that he didn't know in 1992, such as `chads`, `stent`, `blogs`, `ditzy`, `phish`, `bling`, and possibly `tetch`. No; **noway**. The time for any changes to SGB has long since **ended**: `finis`.

> *The following Glossary is intended to contain all well-known English words*
> *... which may be used in good society, and which can serve as Links.*
> *... There must be a stent to the admission of spick words.*
> — LEWIS CARROLL, *Doublets: A Word-Puzzle* (1879)
>
> *If there is such a verb as to tetch, Mr. Lillywaite tetched.*
> — ROBERT BARNARD, *Corpse in a Gilded Cage* (1984)

Proper names like `Knuth` are not considered to be legitimate words. But `gauss` and `hardy` are `valid`, because "gauss" is a unit of magnetic induction and "hardy" is hardy. In fact, SGB words are composed entirely of ordinary lowercase letters; the list contains no hyphenated words, contractions, or terms like `blasé` that require an accent. Thus each word can also be regarded as a vector, which has five components in the range $[0 \, .. \, 26)$. In the vector sense, the words `yucca` and `abuzz` are furthest apart: The Euclidean distance between them is

$$\|(24, 20, 2, 2, 0) - (0, 1, 20, 25, 25)\|_2 = \sqrt{24^2 + 19^2 + 18^2 + 23^2 + 25^2} = \sqrt{2415}.$$

The entire Stanford GraphBase, including all of its programs and data sets, is easy to download from the author's website (see page ii). And the list of all SGB words is even easier to obtain, because it is in the file '`sgb-words.txt`' at the same place. That file contains 5757 lines with one word per line, beginning with '`which`' and ending with '`pupal`'. The words appear in a default order, corresponding to frequency of usage; for example, the words of rank 1000, 2000, 3000, 4000, and 5000 are respectively `ditch`, `galls`, `visas`, `faker`, and `pismo`. The notation '`WORDS`(n)' will be used in this chapter to stand for the n most common words, according to this ranking.

Incidentally, five-letter words include many plurals of *four-letter words*, and it should be noted that no Victorian-style censorship was done. Potentially offensive vocabulary has been expurgated from *The Official Scrabble® Players Dictionary*, but not from the SGB. One way to ensure that semantically unsuitable terms will not appear in a professional paper based on the SGB wordlist is to restrict consideration to WORDS(n) where n is, say, 3000.

Exercises 26–37 below can be used as warmups for initial explorations of the SGB words, which we'll see in many different combinatorial contexts throughout this chapter. For example, while covering problems are still on our minds, we might as well note that the four words 'third flock began jumps' cover 20 of the first 21 letters of the alphabet. Five words can, however, cover at most 24 different letters, as in {becks, fjord, glitz, nymph, squaw} — unless we resort to a rare non-SGB word like waqfs (Islamic endowments), which can be combined with {gyved, bronx, chimp, klutz} to cover 25.

Simple words from WORDS(400) suffice to make a *word square*:

$$
\begin{array}{l}
\text{class} \\
\text{light} \\
\text{agree} \;. \\
\text{sheep} \\
\text{steps}
\end{array}
\qquad (9)
$$

We need to go almost to WORDS(3000), however, to obtain a *word cube*,

$$
\begin{array}{lllll}
\text{types} & \text{yeast} & \text{pasta} & \text{ester} & \text{start} \\
\text{yeast} & \text{earth} & \text{armor} & \text{stove} & \text{three} \\
\text{pasta} & \text{armor} & \text{smoke} & \text{token} & \text{arena} \;, \\
\text{ester} & \text{stove} & \text{token} & \text{event} & \text{rents} \\
\text{start} & \text{three} & \text{arena} & \text{rents} & \text{tease}
\end{array}
\qquad (10)
$$

in which every 5×5 "slice" is a word square. With a simple extension of the basic dancing links algorithm (see Section 7.2.2.2), one can show after performing about 390 billion mems of computation that WORDS(3000) supports only three symmetric word cubes such as (10); exercise 36 reveals the other two. Surprisingly, 83,576 symmetrical cubes can be made from the full set, WORDS(5757).

Graphs from words. It's interesting and important to arrange objects into rows, squares, cubes, and other designs; but in practical applications another kind of combinatorial structure is even *more* interesting and important, namely a *graph*. Recall from Section 2.3.4.1 that a graph is a set of points called *vertices*, together with a set of lines called *edges*, which connect certain pairs of vertices. Graphs are ubiquitous, and many beautiful graph algorithms have been discovered, so graphs will naturally be the primary focus of many sections in this chapter. In fact, the Stanford GraphBase is primarily about graphs, as its name implies; and the SGB words were collected chiefly because they can be used to define interesting and instructive graphs.

Lewis Carroll blazed the trail by inventing a game that he called Word-Links or Doublets, at the end of 1877. [See Martin Gardner, *The Universe in a Handkerchief* (1996), Chapter 6.] Carroll's idea, which soon became quite popular, was to transform one word to another by changing a letter at a time:

$$
\text{tears} — \text{sears} — \text{stars} — \text{stare} — \text{stale} — \text{stile} — \text{smile}. \qquad (11)
$$

The shortest such transformation is the shortest *path* in a graph, where the vertices of the graph are English words and the edges join pairs of words that have "Hamming distance 1" (meaning that they disagree in just one place).

When restricted to SGB words, Carroll's rule produces a graph of the Stanford GraphBase whose official name is $words(5757, 0, 0, 0)$. Every graph defined by SGB has a unique identifier called its *id*, and the graphs that are derived in Carrollian fashion from SGB words are identified by *id*s of the form $words(n, l, t, s)$. Here n is the number of vertices; l is either 0 or a list of weights, used to emphasize various kinds of vocabulary; t is a threshold so that low-weight words can be disallowed; and s is the seed for any pseudorandom numbers that might be needed to break ties between words of equal weight. The full details needn't concern us, but a few examples will give the general idea:

- $words(n, 0, 0, 0)$ is precisely the graph that arises when Carroll's idea is applied to WORDS(n), for $1 \le n \le 5757$.
- $words(1000, \{0, 0, 0, 0, 0, 0, 0, 0, 0, 0\}, 0, s)$ contains 1000 randomly chosen SGB words, usually different for different values of s.
- $words(766, \{0, 0, 0, 0, 0, 0, 0, 0, 1, 0\}, 1, 0)$ contains all of the five-letter words that appear in the author's books about TeX and METAFONT.

There are only 766 words in the latter graph, so we can't form very many long paths like (11), although

$$\text{basic} \longrightarrow \text{basis} \longrightarrow \text{bases} \longrightarrow \text{based}$$
$$\longrightarrow \text{baked} \longrightarrow \text{naked} \longrightarrow \text{named} \longrightarrow \text{names} \longrightarrow \text{games} \qquad (12)$$

is one noteworthy example.

Of course there are many other ways to define the edges of a graph when the vertices represent five-letter words. We could, for example, require the Euclidean distance to be small, instead of the Hamming distance. Or we could declare two words to be adjacent whenever they share a subword of length four; that strategy would substantially enrich the graph, making it possible for **chaos** to yield **peace**, even when confined to the 766 words that are related to TeX:

$$\text{chaos} \longrightarrow \text{chose} \longrightarrow \text{whose} \longrightarrow \text{whole} \longrightarrow \text{holes} \longrightarrow \text{hopes} \longrightarrow \text{copes} \longrightarrow \text{scope}$$
$$\longrightarrow \text{score} \longrightarrow \text{store} \longrightarrow \text{stare} \longrightarrow \text{spare} \longrightarrow \text{space} \longrightarrow \text{paces} \longrightarrow \text{peace}. \qquad (13)$$

(In this rule we remove a letter, then insert another, possibly in a different place.) Or we might choose a totally different strategy, like putting an edge between word vectors $a_1 a_2 a_3 a_4 a_5$ and $b_1 b_2 b_3 b_4 b_5$ if and only if their dot product $a_1 b_1 + a_2 b_2 + a_3 b_3 + a_4 b_4 + a_5 b_5$ is a multiple of some parameter m. Graph algorithms thrive on different kinds of data.

SGB words lead also to an interesting family of *directed* graphs, if we write $a_1 a_2 a_3 a_4 a_5 \to b_1 b_2 b_3 b_4 b_5$ when $\{a_2, a_3, a_4, a_5\} \subseteq \{b_1, b_2, b_3, b_4, b_5\}$ as multisets. (Remove the first letter, insert another, and rearrange.) With this rule we can, for example, transform **words** to **graph** via a shortest oriented path of length six:

$$\text{words} \to \text{dross} \to \text{soars} \to \text{orcas} \to \text{crash} \to \text{sharp} \to \text{graph}. \qquad (14)$$

Theory is the first term in the Taylor series of practice.
— THOMAS M. COVER (1992)

The number of systems of terminology presently used in graph theory
is equal, to a close approximation, to the number of graph theorists.
— RICHARD P. STANLEY (1986)

Graph theory: The basics. A graph G consists of a set V of vertices together
with a set E of edges, which are pairs of distinct vertices. We will assume that
V and E are *finite* sets unless otherwise specified. We write u — v if u and v
are vertices with $\{u, v\} \in E$, and $u \not\!\!-\!\!- v$ if u and v are vertices with $\{u, v\} \notin E$.
Vertices with u — v are called "neighbors," and they're also said to be "adjacent"
in G. One consequence of this definition is that we have u — v if and only if
v — u. Another consequence is that $v \not\!\!-\!\!- v$, for all $v \in V$; that is, no vertex is
adjacent to itself. (We shall, however, discuss multigraphs below, in which loops
from a vertex to itself are permitted.)

The graph $G' = (V', E')$ is a *subgraph* of $G = (V, E)$ if $V' \subseteq V$ and $E' \subseteq E$.
It's a *spanning* subgraph of G if, in fact, $V' = V$. And it's an *induced* subgraph
of G if E' has as many edges as possible, when V' is a given subset of the
vertices. In other words, when $V' \subseteq V$ the subgraph of $G = (V, E)$ induced by
V' is $G' = (V', E')$, where

$$E' = \big\{\, \{u, v\} \mid u \in V', \, v \in V', \text{ and } \{u, v\} \in E \,\big\}. \tag{15}$$

This subgraph G' is denoted by $G \mid V'$, and often called "G restricted to V'." In
the common case where $V' = V \setminus \{v\}$, we write simply $G \setminus v$ ("G minus vertex v")
as an abbreviation for $G \mid (V \setminus \{v\})$. The similar notation $G \setminus e$ is used when
$e \in E$ to denote the subgraph $G' = (V, E \setminus \{e\})$, obtained by removing an edge
instead of a vertex. Notice that all of the SGB graphs known as *words*(n, l, t, s),
described earlier, are induced subgraphs of the main graph *words*$(5757, 0, 0, 0)$;
only the vocabulary changes in those graphs, not the rule for adjacency.

A graph with n vertices and e edges is said to have *order* n and *size* e. The
simplest and most important graphs of order n are the *complete graph* K_n, the
path P_n, and the *cycle* C_n. Suppose the vertices are $V = \{1, 2, \ldots, n\}$. Then

- K_n has $\binom{n}{2} = \frac{1}{2}n(n-1)$ edges u — v for $1 \leq u < v \leq n$; every n-vertex
  graph is a spanning subgraph of K_n.
- P_n has $n - 1$ edges v — $(v{+}1)$ for $1 \leq v < n$, when $n \geq 1$; it is a path
  of length $n{-}1$ from 1 to n.
- C_n has n edges v — $((v \bmod n){+}1)$ for $1 \leq v \leq n$; it is a graph only when
  $n = 0$ or $n \geq 3$ (but C_1 and C_2 are multigraphs).

We could actually have defined K_n, P_n, and C_n on the vertices $\{0, 1, \ldots, n{-}1\}$,
or on *any* n-element set V instead of $\{1, 2, \ldots, n\}$, because two graphs that differ
only in the names of their vertices but not in the structure of their edges are
combinatorially equivalent.

Formally, we say that graphs $G = (V, E)$ and $G' = (V', E')$ are *isomorphic*
if there is a one-to-one correspondence φ from V to V' such that u — v in G if

and only if $\varphi(u) \relbar \varphi(v)$ in G'. The notation $G \cong G'$ is often used to indicate that G and G' are isomorphic; but we shall often be less precise, by treating isomorphic graphs as if they were equal, and by occasionally writing $G = G'$ even when the vertex sets of G and G' aren't strictly identical.

Small graphs can be defined by simply drawing a diagram, in which the vertices are small circles and the edges are lines between them. Figure 2 illustrates several important examples, whose properties we will be studying later. The Petersen graph in Figure 2(e) is named after Julius Petersen, an early graph theorist who used it to disprove a plausible conjecture [L'*Intermédiaire des Mathématiciens* **5** (1898), 225–227]; it is, in fact, a remarkable configuration that serves as a counterexample to many optimistic predictions about what might be true for graphs in general. The Chvátal graph, Figure 2(f), was introduced by Václav Chvátal in *J. Combinatorial Theory* **9** (1970), 93–94.

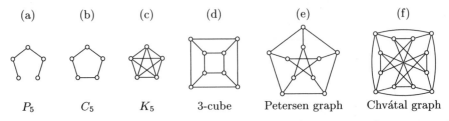

(a)	(b)	(c)	(d)	(e)	(f)
P_5	C_5	K_5	3-cube	Petersen graph	Chvátal graph

Fig. 2. Six example graphs, which have respectively $(5, 5, 5, 8, 10, 12)$ vertices and $(4, 5, 10, 12, 15, 24)$ edges.

The lines of a graph diagram are allowed to cross each other at points that aren't vertices. For example, the center point of Fig. 2(f) is *not* a vertex of Chvátal's graph. A graph is called *planar* if there's a way to draw it without any crossings. Clearly P_n and C_n are always planar; Fig. 2(d) shows that the 3-cube is also planar. But K_5 has too many edges to be planar (see exercise 46).

The *degree* of a vertex is the number of neighbors that it has. If all vertices have the same degree, the graph is said to be *regular*. In Fig. 2, for example, P_5 is irregular because it has two vertices of degree 1 and three of degree 2. But the other five graphs are regular, of degrees $(2, 4, 3, 3, 4)$ respectively. A regular graph of degree 3 is often called "cubic" or "trivalent."

There are many ways to draw a given graph, some of which are much more perspicuous than others. For example, each of the six diagrams

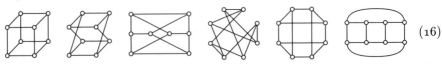   (16)

is isomorphic to the 3-cube, Fig. 2(d). The layout of Chvátal's graph that appears in Fig. 2(f) was discovered by Adrian Bondy many years after Chvátal's paper was published, thereby revealing unexpected symmetries.

The symmetries of a graph, also known as its *automorphisms*, are the permutations of its vertices that preserve adjacency. In other words, the permutation φ is an automorphism of G if we have $\varphi(u) \relbar \varphi(v)$ whenever $u \relbar v$ in G. A well-chosen drawing like Fig. 2(f) can reveal underlying symmetry, but a single diagram isn't always able to display all the symmetries that exist. For example, the 3-cube has 48 automorphisms, and the Petersen graph has 120. We'll study algorithms that deal with isomorphisms and automorphisms in Section 7.2.3. Symmetries can often be exploited to avoid unnecessary computations, making an algorithm almost k times faster when it operates on a graph that has k automorphisms.

Graphs that have evolved in the real world tend to be rather different from the mathematically pristine graphs of Figure 2. For example, here's a familiar graph that has no symmetry whatsoever, although it does have the virtue of being planar:

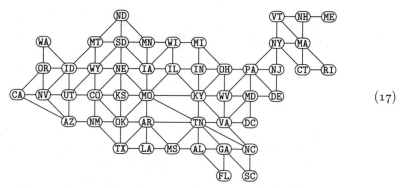

$$(17)$$

It represents the contiguous United States of America, and we'll be using it later in several examples. The 49 vertices of this diagram have been labeled with two-letter postal codes for convenience, instead of being reduced to empty circles.

Paths and cycles. A spanning path of a graph is called a *Hamiltonian path*, and a spanning cycle is called a *Hamiltonian cycle*, because W. R. Hamilton invented and sold a puzzle in 1859 whose goal was to find such paths and cycles on the edges of a dodecahedron. T. P. Kirkman had independently studied the problem for polyhedra in general, in *Philosophical Transactions* **148** (1858), 145–161. [See *Graph Theory 1736–1936* by N. L. Biggs, E. K. Lloyd, and R. J. Wilson (1998), Chapter 2.] The task of finding a spanning path or cycle is, however, much older — indeed, we can legitimately consider it to be the oldest combinatorial problem of all, because paths and tours of a knight on a chessboard have a continuous history going back to ninth-century India (see Section 7.3.3). A graph is called *Hamiltonian* if it has a Hamiltonian cycle. (The Petersen graph, incidentally, is the smallest 3-regular graph that is neither planar nor Hamiltonian; see C. de Polignac, *Bull. Soc. Math. de France* **27** (1899), 142–145.)

The *girth* of a graph is the length of its shortest cycle; the girth is infinite if the graph is acyclic (containing no cycles). For example, the six graphs of Fig. 2 have girths $(\infty, 5, 3, 4, 5, 4)$, respectively. It's not difficult to prove that a graph of minimum degree k and girth 5 must have at least $k^2 + 1$ vertices. Further analysis shows in fact that this minimum value is achievable only if $k = 2$ (C_5), $k = 3$ (Petersen), $k = 7$, or perhaps $k = 57$. (See exercises 63 and 65.)

The *distance* $d(u,v)$ between two vertices u and v is the minimum length of a path from u to v in the graph; it is infinite if there's no such path. Clearly $d(v,v) = 0$, and $d(u,v) = d(v,u)$. We also have the triangle inequality

$$d(u,v) + d(v,w) \;\geq\; d(u,w). \tag{18}$$

For if $d(u,v) = p$ and $d(v,w) = q$ and $p < \infty$ and $q < \infty$, there are paths

$$u = u_0 - u_1 - \cdots - u_p = v \quad \text{and} \quad v = v_0 - v_1 - \cdots - v_q = w, \tag{19}$$

and we can find the least subscript r such that $u_r = v_s$ for some s. Then

$$u_0 - u_1 - \cdots - u_{r-1} - v_s - v_{s+1} - \cdots - v_q \tag{20}$$

is a path of length $\leq p + q$ from u to w.

The *diameter* of a graph is the maximum of $d(u,v)$, over all vertices u and v. The graph is *connected* if its diameter is finite. The vertices of a graph can always be partitioned into connected *components*, where two vertices u and v belong to the same component if and only if $d(u,v) < \infty$.

In the graph $words(5757,0,0,0)$, for example, we have $d(\texttt{tears},\texttt{smile}) = 6$, because (11) is a shortest path from `tears` to `smile`. Also $d(\texttt{tears},\texttt{happy}) = 6$, and $d(\texttt{smile},\texttt{happy}) = 10$, and $d(\texttt{world},\texttt{court}) = 6$. But $d(\texttt{world},\texttt{happy}) = \infty$; the graph isn't connected. In fact, it contains 671 words like `aloof`, which have no neighbors and form connected components of order 1 all by themselves. Word pairs such as `alpha` —— `aloha`, `droid` —— `druid`, and `opium` —— `odium` account for 103 further components of order 2. Some components of order 3, like `chain` —— `chair` —— `choir`, are paths; others, like $\{\texttt{getup},\texttt{letup},\texttt{setup}\}$, are cycles. A few more small components are also present, like the curious path

$$\texttt{login} - \texttt{logic} - \texttt{yogic} - \texttt{yogis} - \texttt{yogas} - \texttt{togas}, \tag{21}$$

whose words have no other neighbors. But the vast majority of all five-letter words belong to a giant component of order 4493. If you can go two steps away from a given word, the odds are better than 15 to 1 that your word is connected to everything in the giant component.

Similarly, the graph $words(n,0,0,0)$ has a giant component of order $(3825, 2986, 2056, 1198, 224)$ when $n = (5000, 4000, 3000, 2000, 1000)$, respectively. But if n is small, there aren't enough edges to provide much connectivity. For example, $words(500,0,0,0)$ has 327 different components, none of order 15 or more.

The concept of distance can be generalized to $d(v_1, v_2, \ldots, v_k)$ for any value of k, meaning the minimum number of edges in a connected subgraph that contains the vertices $\{v_1, v_2, \ldots, v_k\}$. For example, $d(\texttt{blood},\texttt{sweat},\texttt{tears})$ turns out be 15, because the subgraph

$$
\begin{array}{l}
\texttt{blood} - \texttt{brood} - \texttt{broad} - \texttt{bread} - \texttt{tread} - \texttt{treed} - \texttt{tweed} \\
\hspace{11.7em} | \hspace{3.5em} | \\
\texttt{tears} - \texttt{teams} - \texttt{trams} - \texttt{trims} - \texttt{tries} - \texttt{trees} \hspace{1em} \texttt{tweet} \hspace{2em}(22)\\
\hspace{18em} | \\
\hspace{13.5em} \texttt{sweat} - \texttt{sweet}
\end{array}
$$

has 15 edges, and there's no suitable 14-edge subgraph.

We noted in Section 2.3.4.1 that a connected graph with fewest edges is called a *free tree*. A subgraph that corresponds to the generalized distance $d(v_1, \ldots, v_k)$ will always be a free tree. It is misleadingly called a *Steiner tree*, because Jacob Steiner once mentioned the case $k = 3$ for points $\{v_1, v_2, v_3\}$ in the Euclidean plane [*Crelle* **13** (1835), 362–363]. Franz Heinen had solved that problem in *Über Systeme von Kräften* (1834); Gauss extended the analysis to $k = 4$ in a letter to Schumacher (21 March 1836).

Coloring. A graph is said to be k-*partite* or k-*colorable* if its vertices can be partitioned into k or fewer parts, with the endpoints of each edge belonging to different parts — or equivalently, if there's a way to paint its vertices with at most k different colors, never assigning the same color to two adjacent vertices. The famous Four Color Theorem, conjectured by F. Guthrie in 1852 and finally proved with massive computer aid by K. Appel, W. Haken, and J. Koch [*Illinois J. Math.* **21** (1977), 429–567], states that *every planar graph is 4-colorable.* No simple proof is known, but special cases like (17) can be colored at sight (see exercise 45); and $O(n^2)$ steps suffice to 4-color a planar graph in general [N. Robertson, D. P. Sanders, P. Seymour, and R. Thomas, *STOC* **28** (1996), 571–575].

The case of 2-colorable graphs is especially important in practice. A 2-partite graph is generally called *bipartite*, or simply a "bigraph"; every edge of such a graph has one endpoint in each part.

Theorem B. *A graph is bipartite if and only if it contains no cycle of odd length.*

Proof. [See D. König, *Math. Annalen* **77** (1916), 453–454.] Every subgraph of a k-partite graph is k-partite. Therefore the cycle C_n can be a subgraph of a bipartite graph only if C_n itself is a bigraph, in which case n must be even.

Conversely, if a graph contains no odd cycles we can color its vertices with the two colors $\{0, 1\}$ by carrying out the following procedure: Begin with all vertices uncolored. If all neighbors of colored vertices are already colored, choose an uncolored vertex w, and color it 0. Otherwise choose a colored vertex u that has an uncolored neighbor v; assign to v the opposite color. Exercise 48 proves that a valid 2-coloring is eventually obtained. ∎

The *complete bipartite graph* $K_{m,n}$ is the largest bipartite graph whose vertices have two parts of sizes m and n. We can define it on the vertex set $\{1, 2, \ldots, m+n\}$ by saying that $u \mathrel{—} v$ whenever $1 \le u \le m < v \le m + n$. In other words, $K_{m,n}$ has mn edges, one for each way to choose one vertex in the first part and another in the second part. Similarly, the *complete k-partite graph* $K_{n_1, \ldots, n_k}$ has $N = n_1 + \cdots + n_k$ vertices partitioned into parts of sizes $\{n_1, \ldots, n_k\}$, and it has edges between any two vertices that don't belong to the same part. Here are some examples when $N = 6$:

$$\underset{K_{1,5}}{\text{⬦}} \; ; \quad \underset{K_{3,3}}{\text{⬦}} \cong \text{⬦} \; ; \quad \text{⬦} \cong \underset{K_{2,2,2}}{\text{⬦}} \, . \tag{23}$$

Notice that $K_{1,n}$ is a free tree; it is popularly called the *star graph* of order $n+1$.

From now on say "digraph" instead of "directed graph."
It is clear and short and it will catch on.
— GEORGE PÓLYA, letter to Frank Harary (c. 1954)

Directed graphs. In Section 2.3.4.2 we defined *directed graphs* (or *digraphs*), which are very much like graphs except that they have *arcs* instead of edges. An arc $u \longrightarrow v$ runs from one vertex to another, while an edge $u \longrightarrow v$ joins two vertices without distinguishing between them. Furthermore, digraphs are allowed to have self-loops $v \longrightarrow v$ from a vertex to itself, and more than one arc $u \longrightarrow v$ may be present between the same vertices u and v.

Formally, a digraph $D = (V, A)$ of order n and size m is a set V of n vertices and a multiset A of m ordered pairs (u, v), where $u \in V$ and $v \in V$. The ordered pairs are called arcs, and we write $u \longrightarrow v$ when $(u, v) \in A$. The digraph is called *simple* if A is actually a set instead of a general multiset — namely, if there's at most one arc (u, v) for all u and v. Each arc (u, v) has an initial vertex u and a final vertex v, also called its "tip." Each vertex has an *out-degree* $d^+(v)$, the number of arcs for which v is the initial vertex, and an *in-degree* $d^-(v)$, the number of arcs for which v is the tip. A vertex with in-degree 0 is called a "source"; a vertex with out-degree 0 is called a "sink." Notice that $\sum_{v \in V} d^+(v) = \sum_{v \in V} d^-(v)$, because both sums are equal to m, the total number of arcs.

Most of the notions we've defined for graphs carry over to digraphs in a natural way, if we just insert the word "directed" or "oriented" (or the syllable "di") when it's necessary to distinguish between edges and arcs. For example, digraphs have subdigraphs, which can be spanning or induced or neither. An isomorphism between digraphs $D = (V, A)$ and $D' = (V', A')$ is a one-to-one correspondence φ from V to V' for which the number of arcs $u \longrightarrow v$ in D equals the number of arcs $\varphi(u) \longrightarrow \varphi(v)$ in D', for all $u, v \in V$.

Diagrams for digraphs use arrows between the vertices, instead of unadorned lines. The simplest and most important digraphs of order n are directed variants of the graphs K_n, P_n, and C_n, namely the *transitive tournament* $\vec{K_n}$, the *oriented path* $\vec{P_n}$, and the *oriented cycle* $\vec{C_n}$. They can be schematically indicated by the following diagrams for $n = 5$:

$$\vec{K_5} \; ; \qquad \vec{P_5} \; ; \qquad \vec{C_5}. \tag{24}$$

There's also the *complete digraph* J_n, which is the largest simple digraph on n vertices; it has n^2 arcs $u \longrightarrow v$, one for each choice of u and v.

Figure 3 shows a more elaborate diagram, for a digraph of order 17 that we might call "expressly oriented": It is the directed graph described by Hercule Poirot in Agatha Christie's novel *Murder on the Orient Express* (1934). Vertices correspond to the berths of the Stamboul–Calais coach in that story, and an arc $u \longrightarrow v$ means that the occupant of berth u has corroborated the alibi of the person in berth v. This example has six connected components, namely $\{0, 1, 3, 6, 8, 12, 13, 14, 15, 16\}$, $\{2\}$, $\{4, 5\}$, $\{7\}$, $\{9\}$, and $\{10, 11\}$, because connectivity in a digraph is determined by treating arcs as edges.

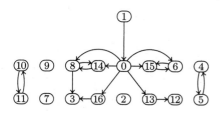

2: Samuel Edward Ratchett, the deceased American
3: Caroline Martha Hubbard, the American matron
4: Edward Henry Masterman, the British valet
5: Antonio Foscarelli, the Italian automobile salesman
6: Hector MacQueen, the American secretary
7: Harvey Harris, the Englishman who didn't show up
8: Hildegarde Schmidt, the German lady's maid
9: (vacancy)
10: Greta Ohlsson, the Swedish nurse
11: Mary Hermione Debenham, the English governess
12: Helena Maria Andrenyi, the beautiful countess
13: Rudolph Andrenyi, the Hungarian count/diplomat
14: Natalia Dragomiroff, the Russian princess dowager
15: Colonel Arbuthnot, the British officer from India
16: Cyrus Bettman Hardman, the American detective

LEGEND
0: Pierre Michel, the French conductor
1: Hercule Poirot, the Belgian detective

Fig. 3. A digraph of order 17 and size 18, devised by Agatha Christie.

Two arcs are *consecutive* if the tip of the first is the initial vertex of the second. A sequence of consecutive arcs $(a_1, a_2, \ldots, a_k)$ is called a *walk* of length k; it can be symbolized by showing the vertices as well as the arcs:

$$v_0 \xrightarrow{a_1} v_1 \xrightarrow{a_2} v_2 \cdots v_{k-1} \xrightarrow{a_k} v_k. \tag{25}$$

In a simple digraph it's sufficient merely to specify the vertices; for example, $1 \longrightarrow 0 \longrightarrow 8 \longrightarrow 14 \longrightarrow 8 \longrightarrow 3$ is a walk in Fig. 3. The walk in (25) is an oriented path when the vertices $\{v_0, v_1, \ldots, v_k\}$ are distinct; it's an oriented cycle when they are distinct except that $v_k = v_0$.

In a digraph, the directed distance $d(u, v)$ is the number of arcs in the shortest *oriented* path from u to v, which is also the length of the shortest walk from u to v. It may differ from $d(v, u)$; but the triangle inequality (18) remains valid.

Every graph can be regarded as a digraph, because an edge $u \,$—$\, v$ is essentially equivalent to a matched pair of arcs, $u \longrightarrow v$ and $v \longrightarrow u$. The digraph obtained in this way retains all the properties of the original graph; for example, the degree of each vertex in the graph becomes its out-degree in the digraph, and also its in-degree in the digraph. Furthermore, distances remain the same.

A *multigraph* (V, E) is like a graph except that its edges E can be any *multiset* of pairs $\{u, v\}$; edges $v \,$—$\, v$ that loop from a vertex to itself, which correspond to "multipairs" $\{v, v\}$, are also permitted. For example,

$$\text{①—②—③} \tag{26}$$

is a multigraph of order 3 with six edges, $\{1,1\}$, $\{1,2\}$, $\{2,3\}$, $\{2,3\}$, $\{3,3\}$, and $\{3,3\}$. The vertex degrees in this example are $d(1) = d(2) = 3$ and $d(3) = 6$, because each loop contributes 2 to the degree of its vertex. An edge loop $v \,$—$\, v$ becomes *two* arc loops $v \longrightarrow v$ when a multigraph is regarded as a digraph.

Representation of graphs and digraphs. Any digraph, and therefore any graph or multigraph, is completely described by its *adjacency matrix* $A = (a_{uv})$, which has n rows and n columns when there are n vertices. Each entry a_{uv} of this matrix specifies the number of arcs from u to v. For example, the adjacency matrices for $\vec{K_3}$, $\vec{P_3}$, $\vec{C_3}$, J_3, and (26) are respectively

$$\vec{K_3} = \begin{pmatrix} 011 \\ 001 \\ 000 \end{pmatrix}, \quad \vec{P_3} = \begin{pmatrix} 010 \\ 001 \\ 000 \end{pmatrix}, \quad \vec{C_3} = \begin{pmatrix} 010 \\ 001 \\ 100 \end{pmatrix}, \quad J_3 = \begin{pmatrix} 111 \\ 111 \\ 111 \end{pmatrix}, \quad A = \begin{pmatrix} 210 \\ 102 \\ 024 \end{pmatrix}. \tag{27}$$

The powerful mathematical tools of matrix theory make it possible to prove many nontrivial results about graphs by studying their adjacency matrices; exercise 65 provides a particularly striking example of what can be done. One of the main reasons is that matrix multiplication has a simple interpretation in the context of digraphs. Consider the square of A, where the element in row u and column v is

$$(A^2)_{uv} = \sum_{w \in V} a_{uw} a_{wv}, \qquad (28)$$

by definition. Since a_{uw} is the number of arcs from u to w, we see that $a_{uw} a_{wv}$ is the number of walks of the form $u \longrightarrow w \longrightarrow v$. Therefore $(A^2)_{uv}$ is the total number of walks of length 2 from u to v. Similarly, the entries of A^k tell us the total number of walks of length k between any ordered pair of vertices, for all $k \geq 0$. For example, the matrix A in (27) satisfies

$$A = \begin{pmatrix} 2 & 1 & 0 \\ 1 & 0 & 2 \\ 0 & 2 & 4 \end{pmatrix}, \qquad A^2 = \begin{pmatrix} 5 & 2 & 2 \\ 2 & 5 & 8 \\ 2 & 8 & 20 \end{pmatrix}, \qquad A^3 = \begin{pmatrix} 12 & 9 & 12 \\ 9 & 18 & 42 \\ 12 & 42 & 96 \end{pmatrix}; \qquad (29)$$

there are 12 walks of length 3 from the vertex 1 of the multigraph (26) to vertex 3, and 18 such walks from vertex 2 to itself.

Reordering of the vertices changes an adjacency matrix from A to $P^- A P$, where P is a permutation matrix (a 0–1 matrix with exactly one 1 in each row and column), and $P^- = P^T$ is the matrix for the inverse permutation. Thus

$$\begin{pmatrix} 210 \\ 102 \\ 024 \end{pmatrix}, \quad \begin{pmatrix} 201 \\ 042 \\ 120 \end{pmatrix}, \quad \begin{pmatrix} 012 \\ 120 \\ 204 \end{pmatrix}, \quad \begin{pmatrix} 021 \\ 240 \\ 102 \end{pmatrix}, \quad \begin{pmatrix} 402 \\ 021 \\ 210 \end{pmatrix}, \quad \text{and} \quad \begin{pmatrix} 420 \\ 201 \\ 012 \end{pmatrix} \qquad (30)$$

are all adjacency matrices for (26), and there are no others.

There are more than $2^{n(n-1)/2}/n!$ graphs of order n, when $n > 1$, and almost all of them require $\Omega(n^2)$ bits of data in their most economical encoding. Consequently the best way to represent the vast majority of all possible graphs inside a computer, from the standpoint of memory usage, is essentially to work with their adjacency matrices.

But the graphs that actually arise in practical problems have quite different characteristics from graphs that are chosen at random from the set of all possibilities. A real-life graph usually turns out to be "sparse," having say $O(n \log n)$ edges instead of $\Omega(n^2)$, unless n is rather small, because $\Omega(n^2)$ bits of data are difficult to generate. For example, suppose the vertices correspond to people, and the edges correspond to friendships. If we consider 5 billion people, few of them will have more than 10000 friends. But even if everybody had 10000 friends, on average, the graph would still have only 2.5×10^{13} edges, while almost all graphs of order 5 billion have approximately 6.25×10^{18} edges.

Thus the best way to represent a graph inside a machine usually turns out to be rather different than to record n^2 values a_{uv} of adjacency matrix elements. Instead, the algorithms of the Stanford GraphBase were developed with a data structure akin to the linked representation of sparse matrices discussed in Section 2.2.6, though somewhat simplified. That approach has proved to be not only versatile and efficient, but also easy to use.

The SGB representation of a digraph is a combination of sequential and linked allocation, using nodes of two basic types. Some nodes represent vertices, other nodes represent arcs. (There's also a third type of node, which represents an entire graph, for algorithms that deal with several graphs at once. But each graph needs only one graph node, so the vertex and arc nodes predominate.)

Here's how it works: Every SGB digraph of order n and size m is built upon a sequential array of n vertex nodes, making it easy to access vertex k for $0 \le k < n$. The m arc nodes, by contrast, are linked together within a general memory pool that is essentially unstructured. Each vertex node typically occupies 32 bytes, and each arc node occupies 20 (and the graph node occupies 220); but the node sizes can be modified without difficulty. A few fields of each node have a fixed, definite meaning in all cases; the remaining fields can be used for different purposes in different algorithms or in different phases of a single algorithm. The fixed-purpose parts of a node are called its "standard fields," and the multipurpose parts are called its "utility fields."

Every vertex node has two standard fields called NAME and ARCS. If v is a variable that points to a vertex node, we'll call it a *vertex variable*. Then NAME(v) points to a string of characters that can be used to identify the corresponding vertex in human-oriented output; for example, the 49 vertices of graph (17) have names like CA, WA, OR, ..., RI. The other standard field, ARCS(v), is far more important in algorithms: It points to an arc node, the first in a singly linked list of length $d^+(v)$, with one node for each arc that emanates from vertex v.

Every arc node has two standard fields called TIP and NEXT; a variable a that points to an arc node is called an *arc variable*. TIP(a) points to the vertex node that represents the tip of arc a; NEXT(a) points to the arc node that represents the next arc whose initial vertex agrees with that of a.

A vertex v with out-degree 0 is represented by letting ARCS$(v) = \Lambda$ (the null pointer). Otherwise if, say, the out-degree is 3, the data structure contains three arc nodes with ARCS$(v) = a_1$, NEXT$(a_1) = a_2$, NEXT$(a_2) = a_3$, and NEXT$(a_3) = \Lambda$; and the three arcs from v lead to TIP(a_1), TIP(a_2), TIP(a_3).

Suppose, for example, that we want to compute the out-degree of vertex v, and store it in a utility field called ODEG. It's easy:

$$\text{Set } a \leftarrow \text{ARCS}(v) \text{ and } d \leftarrow 0.$$
$$\text{While } a \ne \Lambda, \text{ set } d \leftarrow d+1 \text{ and } a \leftarrow \text{NEXT}(a). \qquad (31)$$
$$\text{Set ODEG}(v) \leftarrow d.$$

When a graph or a multigraph is considered to be a digraph, as mentioned above, its edges $u \longrightarrow v$ are each equivalent to two arcs, $u \longrightarrow v$ and $v \longrightarrow u$. These arcs are called "mates"; and they occupy two arc nodes, say a and a', where a appears in the list of arcs from u and a' appears in the list of arcs from v. Then TIP$(a) = v$ and TIP$(a') = u$. We'll also write

$$\text{MATE}(a) = a' \qquad \text{and} \qquad \text{MATE}(a') = a, \qquad (32)$$

in algorithms that want to move rapidly from one list to another. However, we usually won't need to store an explicit pointer from an arc to its mate, or to have a utility field called MATE within each arc node, because the necessary link can be deduced *implicitly* when the data structure has been constructed cleverly.

The implicit-mate trick works like this: While creating each edge $u — v$ of an undirected graph or multigraph, we introduce *consecutive* arc nodes for $u \longrightarrow v$ and $v \longrightarrow u$. For example, if there are 20 bytes per arc node, we'll reserve 40 consecutive bytes for each new pair. We can also make sure that the memory address of the first byte is a multiple of 8. Then if the arc node a is in memory location α, its mate is in location

$$\left\{ \begin{array}{ll} \alpha + 20, & \text{if } \alpha \bmod 8 = 0 \\ \alpha - 20, & \text{if } \alpha \bmod 8 = 4 \end{array} \right\} \; = \; \alpha - 20 + \big(40 \mathbin{\&} ((\alpha \mathbin{\&} 4) - 1)\big). \qquad (33)$$

Such tricks are valuable in combinatorial problems, when operations might be performed a trillion times, because every way to save 3.6 nanoseconds per operation will make such a computation finish an hour sooner. But (33) isn't directly "portable" from one implementation to another. If the size of an arc node were changed from 20 to 24, for example, we would have to change the numbers 40, 20, 8, and 4 in (33) to 48, 24, 16, and 8.

The algorithms in this book will make no assumptions about node sizes. Instead, we'll adopt a convention of the C programming language and its descendants, so that if a points to an arc node, '$a + 1$' denotes a pointer to the arc node that follows it in memory. And in general

$$\text{LOC(NODE}(a + k)) \; = \; \text{LOC(NODE}(a)) + kc, \qquad (34)$$

when there are c bytes in each arc node. Similarly, if v is a vertex variable, '$v + k$' will stand for the kth vertex node following node v; the actual memory location of that node will be v plus k times the size of a vertex node.

The standard fields of a graph node g include $\text{M}(g)$, the total number of arcs; $\text{N}(g)$, the total number of vertices; $\text{VERTICES}(g)$, a pointer to the first vertex node in the sequential list of all vertex nodes; $\text{ID}(g)$, the graph's identification, which is a string like words(5757,0,0,0); and some other fields needed for the allocation and recycling of memory when the graph grows or shrinks, or for exporting a graph to external formats that interface with other users and other graph-manipulation systems. But we will rarely need to refer to any of these graph node fields, nor will it be necessary to give a complete description of SGB format here, since we shall describe almost all of the graph algorithms in this chapter by sticking to an English-language description at a fairly abstract level instead of descending to the bit level of machine programs.

A simple graph algorithm. To illustrate a medium-high-level algorithm of the kind that will appear later, let's convert the proof of Theorem B into a step-by-step procedure that paints the vertices of a given graph with two colors whenever that graph is bipartite.

Algorithm B (*Bipartiteness testing*). Given a graph represented in SGB format, this algorithm either finds a 2-coloring with $\text{COLOR}(v) \in \{0, 1\}$ in each vertex v, or it terminates unsuccessfully when no valid 2-coloring is possible. Here COLOR is a utility field in each vertex node. Another vertex utility field, $\text{LINK}(v)$, is a vertex pointer used to maintain a stack of all colored vertices whose neighbors have not yet been examined. An auxiliary vertex variable s points to the top of this stack. The algorithm also uses variables u, v, w for vertices and a for arcs. The vertex nodes are assumed to be $v_0 + k$ for $0 \le k < n$.

B1. [Initialize.] Set COLOR$(v_0 + k) \leftarrow -1$ for $0 \le k < n$. (Now all vertices are uncolored.) Then set $w \leftarrow v_0 + n$.

B2. [Done?] (At this point all vertices $\ge w$ have been colored, and so have the neighbors of all colored vertices.) Terminate the algorithm successfully if $w = v_0$. Otherwise set $w \leftarrow w - 1$, the next lower vertex node.

B3. [Color w if necessary.] If COLOR$(w) \ge 0$, return to B2. Otherwise set COLOR$(w) \leftarrow 0$, LINK$(w) \leftarrow \Lambda$, and $s \leftarrow w$.

B4. [Stack $\Rightarrow u$.] Set $u \leftarrow s$, $s \leftarrow$ LINK(s), $a \leftarrow$ ARCS(u). (We will examine all neighbors of the colored vertex u.)

B5. [Done with u?] If $a = \Lambda$, go to B8. Otherwise set $v \leftarrow$ TIP(a).

B6. [Process v.] If COLOR$(v) < 0$, set COLOR$(v) \leftarrow 1 -$ COLOR(u), LINK$(v) \leftarrow s$, and $s \leftarrow v$. Otherwise if COLOR$(v) =$ COLOR(u), terminate unsuccessfully.

B7. [Loop on a.] Set $a \leftarrow$ NEXT(a) and return to B5.

B8. [Stack nonempty?] If $s \ne \Lambda$, return to B4. Otherwise return to B2. ∎

This algorithm is a variant of a general graph traversal procedure called "depth-first search," which we will study in detail in Section 7.4.1. Its running time is $O(m + n)$ when there are m arcs and n vertices (see exercise 70); therefore it is well adapted to the common case of sparse graphs. With small changes we can make it output an odd-length cycle whenever it terminates unsuccessfully, thereby proving the impossibility of a 2-coloring (see exercise 72).

Examples of graphs. The Stanford GraphBase includes a library of more than three dozen generator routines, capable of producing a great variety of graphs and digraphs for use in experiments. We've already discussed *words*; now let's look at a few of the others, in order to get a feeling for some of the possibilities.

• *roget*$(1022, 0, 0, 0)$ is a directed graph with 1022 vertices and 5075 arcs. The vertices represent the categories of words or concepts that P. M. Roget and J. L. Roget included in their famous 19th-century *Thesaurus* (London: Longmans, Green, 1879). The arcs are the cross references between categories, as found in that book. For example, typical arcs are water $\longrightarrow$ moisture, discovery $\longrightarrow$ truth, preparation $\longrightarrow$ learning, vulgarity $\longrightarrow$ ugliness, wit $\longrightarrow$ amusement.

• *book*("jean", $80, 0, 1, 356, 0, 0, 0)$ is a graph with 80 vertices and 254 edges. The vertices represent the characters of Victor Hugo's *Les Misérables*; the edges connect characters who encounter each other in that novel. Typical edges are Fantine — Javert, Cosette — Thénardier.

• *bi_book*("jean", $80, 0, 1, 356, 0, 0, 0)$ is a bipartite graph with $80+356$ vertices and 727 edges. The vertices represent characters or chapters in *Les Misérables*; the edges connect characters with the chapters in which they appear (for instance, Napoleon — 2.1.8, Marius — 4.14.4).

- *plane_miles*$(128, 0, 0, 0, 1, 0, 0)$ is a planar graph with 129 vertices and 381 edges. The vertices represent 128 cities in the United States or Canada, plus a special vertex INF for a "point at infinity." The edges define the so-called *Delaunay triangulation* of those cities, based on latitude and longitude in a plane; this means that $u \text{ --- } v$ if and only if the smallest circle that passes through u and v does not enclose any other vertex. Edges also run between INF and all vertices that lie on the convex hull of all city locations. Typical edges are Seattle, WA — Vancouver, BC — INF; Toronto, ON — Rochester, NY.

- *plane_lisa*$(360, 250, 15, 0, 360, 0, 250, 0, 0, 2295000)$ is a planar graph that has 3027 vertices and 5967 edges. It is obtained by starting with a digitized image of Leonardo da Vinci's *Mona Lisa*, having 360 rows and 250 columns of pixels, then rounding the pixel intensities to 16 levels of gray from 0 (black) to 15 (white). The resulting 3027 rookwise connected regions of constant brightness are then considered to be neighbors when they share a pixel boundary. (See Fig. 4.)

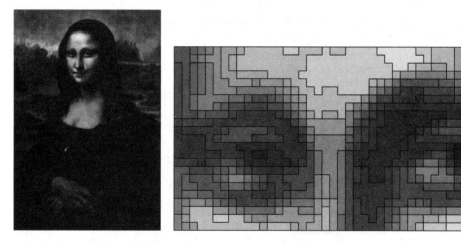

Fig. 4. A digital rendition of *Mona Lisa*, with a closeup detail (best viewed from afar).

- *bi_lisa*$(360, 250, 0, 360, 0, 250, 8192, 0)$ is a bipartite graph with $360 + 250 = 610$ vertices and 40923 edges. It's another takeoff on Leonardo's famous painting, this time linking rows and columns where the brightness level is at least $1/8$. For example, the edge r102 — c113 occurs right in the middle of Lisa's "smile."

- *raman*$(31, 23, 3, 1)$ is a graph with quite a different nature from the SGB graphs in previous examples. Instead of being linked to language, literature, or other outgrowths of human culture, it's a so-called "Ramanujan expander graph," based on strict mathematical principles. Each of its $(23^3 - 23)/2 = 6072$ vertices has degree 32; hence it has 97152 edges. The vertices correspond to equivalence classes of 2×2 matrices that are nonsingular modulo 23; a typical edge is (2,7;1,1) — (4,6;1,3). Ramanujan graphs are important chiefly because they have unusually high girth and low diameter for their size and degree. This one has girth 4 and diameter 4.

• $raman(5, 37, 4, 1)$, similarly, is a regular graph of degree 6 with 50616 vertices and 151848 edges. It has girth 10, diameter 10, and happens also to be bipartite.

• $random\_graph(1000, 5000, 0, 0, 0, 0, 0, 0, 0, s)$ is a graph with 1000 vertices, 5000 edges, and seed s. It "evolved" by starting with no edges, then by repeatedly choosing pseudorandom vertex numbers $0 \le u, v < 1000$ and adding the edge $u \text{---} v$, unless $u = v$ or that edge was already present. When $s = 0$, all vertices belong to a giant component of order 999, except for the isolated vertex 908.

• $random\_graph(1000, 5000, 0, 0, 1, 0, 0, 0, 0, 0)$ is a digraph with 1000 vertices and 5000 arcs, obtained via a similar sort of evolution. (In fact, each of its arcs happens to be part also of $random\_graph(1000, 5000, 0, 0, 0, 0, 0, 0, 0, 0)$.)

• $subsets(5, 1, -10, 0, 0, 0, {}^\#1, 0)$ is a graph with $\binom{11}{5} = 462$ vertices, one for every five-element subset of $\{0, 1, \ldots, 10\}$. Two vertices are adjacent whenever the corresponding subsets are disjoint; thus, the graph is regular of degree 6, and it has 1386 edges. We can consider it to be a generalization of the Petersen graph, which has $subsets(2, 1, -4, 0, 0, 0, {}^\#1, 0)$ as one of its SGB names.

• $subsets(5, 1, -10, 0, 0, 0, {}^\#10, 0)$ has the same 462 vertices, but now they are adjacent if the corresponding subsets have four elements in common. This graph is regular of degree 30, and it has 6930 edges.

• $parts(30, 10, 30, 0)$ is another SGB graph with a mathematical basis. It has 3590 vertices, one for each partition of 30 into at most 10 parts. Two partitions are adjacent when one is obtained by subdividing a part of the other; this rule defines 31377 edges. The digraph $parts(30, 10, 30, 1)$ is similar, but its 31377 arcs point from shorter to longer partitions (for example, $13+7+7+3 \longrightarrow 7+7+7+6+3$).

• $simplex(10, 10, 10, 10, 10, 0, 0)$ is a graph with 286 vertices and 1320 edges. Its vertices are the integer solutions to $x_1 + x_2 + x_3 + x_4 = 10$ with $x_i \ge 0$, namely the "compositions of 10 into four nonnegative parts"; they can also be regarded as barycentric coordinates for points inside a tetrahedron. The edges, such as $3,1,4,2 \text{---} 3,0,4,3$, connect compositions that are as close together as possible.

• $board(8, 8, 0, 0, 5, 0, 0)$ and $board(8, 8, 0, 0, -2, 0, 0)$ are graphs on 64 vertices whose 168 or 280 edges correspond to the moves of a knight or bishop in chess.

And zillions of further examples are obtainable by varying the parameters to the SGB graph generators. For example, Fig. 5 shows two simple variants of *board* and *simplex*; the somewhat arcane rules of *board* are explained in exercise 75.

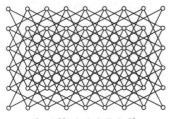
$board(6, 9, 0, 0, 5, 0, 0)$
(Knight moves on a 6×9 chessboard)

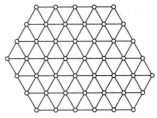
$simplex(10, 8, 7, 6, 0, 0, 0)$
(A truncated triangular grid)

Fig. 5. Samples of SGB graphs related to board games.

Graph algebra. We can also obtain new graphs by operating on the graphs that we already have. For example, if $G = (V, E)$ is any graph, its *complement* $\overline{G} = (V, \overline{E})$ is obtained by letting

$$u \text{—} v \text{ in } \overline{G} \qquad \Longleftrightarrow \qquad u \neq v \text{ and } u \text{—}\!\!\!/\; v \text{ in } G. \tag{35}$$

Thus, non-edges become edges, and vice versa. Notice that $\overline{\overline{G}} = G$, and that $\overline{K_n}$ has no edges. The corresponding adjacency matrices A and $\overline{A}$ satisfy

$$A + \overline{A} = J - I; \tag{36}$$

here J is the matrix of all 1s, and I is the identity matrix, so J and $J - I$ are respectively the adjacency matrices of J_n and K_n when G has order n.

Furthermore, every graph $G = (V, E)$ leads to a *line graph* $L(G)$, whose vertices are the edges E; two edges are adjacent in $L(G)$ if they have a common vertex. Thus, for example, the line graph $L(K_n)$ has $\binom{n}{2}$ vertices, and it is regular of degree $2n - 4$ when $n \geq 2$ (see exercise 82). A graph is called k-*edge-colorable* when its line graph is k-colorable.

Given two graphs $G = (U, E)$ and $H = (V, F)$, their *union* $G \cup H$ is the graph $(U \cup V, E \cup F)$ obtained by combining the vertices and edges. For example, suppose G and H are the graphs of rook and bishop moves in chess; then $G \cup H$ is the graph of queen moves, and its official SGB name is

$$gunion(board(8, 8, 0, 0, -1, 0, 0), board(8, 8, 0, 0, -2, 0, 0), 0, 0). \tag{37}$$

In the special case where the vertex sets U and V are disjoint, the union $G \cup H$ doesn't require the vertices to be identified in any consistent way for cross-correlation; we get a diagram for $G \cup H$ by simply drawing a diagram of G next to a diagram of H. This special case is called the "juxtaposition" or *direct sum* of G and H, and we shall denote it by $G \oplus H$. For example, it's easy to see that

$$K_m \oplus K_n \cong \overline{K_{m,n}}, \tag{38}$$

and that every graph is the direct sum of its connected components.

Equation (38) is a special case of the general formula

$$K_{n_1} \oplus K_{n_2} \oplus \cdots \oplus K_{n_k} \cong \overline{K_{n_1, n_2, \ldots, n_k}}, \tag{39}$$

which holds for complete k-partite graphs whenever $k \geq 2$. But (39) fails when $k = 1$, because of a scandalous fact: The standard graph-theoretic notation for complete graphs is inconsistent! Indeed, $K_{m,n}$ denotes a complete 2-partite graph, but K_n does *not* denote a complete 1-partite graph. Somehow graph theorists have been able to live with this anomaly for decades without going berserk.

Another important way to combine disjoint graphs G and H is to form their *join*, $G \text{——} H$, which consists of $G \oplus H$ together with all edges $u \text{—} v$ for $u \in U$ and $v \in V$. [See A. A. Zykov, *Mat. Sbornik* **24** (1949), 163–188, §I.3.] And if G and H are disjoint *digraphs*, their *directed join* $G \longrightarrow H$ is similar, but it supplements $G \oplus H$ by adding only the one-way arcs $u \longrightarrow v$ from U to V.

The direct sum of two matrices A and B is obtained by placing B diagonally below and to the right of A:

$$A \oplus B = \begin{pmatrix} A & O \\ O & B \end{pmatrix}, \tag{40}$$

where each O in this example is a matrix of all zeros, with the proper number of rows and columns to make everything line up correctly. Our notation $G \oplus H$ for the direct sum of graphs is easy to remember because the adjacency matrix for $G \oplus H$ is precisely the direct sum of the respective adjacency matrices A and B for G and H. Similarly, the adjacency matrices for $G{-\!\!-}H$, $G \longrightarrow H$, and $G \longleftarrow H$ are

$$A{-\!\!-}B = \begin{pmatrix} A & J \\ J & B \end{pmatrix}, \qquad A \longrightarrow B = \begin{pmatrix} A & J \\ O & B \end{pmatrix}, \qquad A \longleftarrow B = \begin{pmatrix} A & O \\ J & B \end{pmatrix}, \tag{41}$$

respectively, where J is an all-1s matrix as in (36). These operations are associative, and related by complementation:

$$A \oplus (B \oplus C) = (A \oplus B) \oplus C, \qquad A{-\!\!-}(B{-\!\!-}C) = (A{-\!\!-}B){-\!\!-}C; \tag{42}$$

$$A \longrightarrow (B \longrightarrow C) = (A \longrightarrow B) \longrightarrow C, \qquad A \longleftarrow (B \longleftarrow C) = (A \longleftarrow B) \longleftarrow C; \tag{43}$$

$$\overline{A \oplus B} = \overline{A}{-\!\!-}\overline{B}, \qquad \overline{A{-\!\!-}B} = \overline{A} \oplus \overline{B}; \tag{44}$$

$$\overline{A \longrightarrow B} = \overline{A} \longleftarrow \overline{B}, \qquad \overline{A \longleftarrow B} = \overline{A} \longrightarrow \overline{B}; \tag{45}$$

$$(A \oplus B) + (A{-\!\!-}B) = (A \longrightarrow B) + (A \longleftarrow B). \tag{46}$$

Notice that, by combining (39) with (42) and (44), we have

$$K_{n_1, n_2, \ldots, n_k} = \overline{K_{n_1}}{-\!\!-}\overline{K_{n_2}}{-\!\!-} \cdots {-\!\!-}\overline{K_{n_k}} \tag{47}$$

when $k \geq 2$. Also

$$K_n = K_1 {-\!\!-} K_1 {-\!\!-} \cdots {-\!\!-} K_1 \quad \text{and} \quad \vec{K}_n = K_1 \longrightarrow K_1 \longrightarrow \cdots \longrightarrow K_1, \tag{48}$$

with n copies of K_1, showing that $K_n = K_{1,1,\ldots,1}$ is a complete n-partite graph.

Direct sums and joins are analogous to addition, because we have $\overline{K_m} \oplus \overline{K_n} = \overline{K_{m+n}}$ and $K_m {-\!\!-} K_n = K_{m+n}$. We can also combine graphs with algebraic operations that are analogous to multiplication. For example, the *Cartesian product* operation forms a graph $G \,\square\, H$ of order mn from a graph $G = (U, E)$ of order m and a graph $H = (V, F)$ of order n. The vertices of $G \,\square\, H$ are ordered pairs (u, v), where $u \in U$ and $v \in V$; the edges are $(u, v){-\!\!-}(u', v)$ when $u{-\!\!-}u'$ in G, together with $(u, v){-\!\!-}(u, v')$ when $v{-\!\!-}v'$ in H. In other words, $G \,\square\, H$ is formed by replacing each vertex of G by a copy of H, and replacing each edge of G by edges between corresponding vertices of the appropriate copies:

$$\tag{49}$$

As usual, the simplest special cases of this general construction turn out to be especially important in practice. When both G and H are paths or cycles, we get "graph-paper graphs," namely the $m \times n$ *grid* $P_m \square P_n$, the $m \times n$ *cylinder* $P_m \square C_n$, and the $m \times n$ *torus* $C_m \square C_n$, illustrated here for $m = 3$ and $n = 4$:

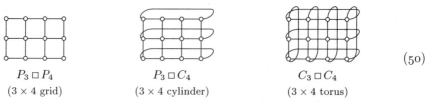

$$P_3 \square P_4 \qquad\qquad P_3 \square C_4 \qquad\qquad C_3 \square C_4 \tag{50}$$
$$(3 \times 4 \text{ grid}) \qquad (3 \times 4 \text{ cylinder}) \qquad (3 \times 4 \text{ torus})$$

Four other noteworthy ways to define products of graphs have also proved to be useful. In each case the vertices of the product graph are ordered pairs (u, v).

- The *direct product* $G \otimes H$, also called the "conjunction" of G and H, or their "categorical product," has $(u, v) \longrightarrow (u', v')$ when $u \longrightarrow u'$ in G and $v \longrightarrow v'$ in H.

- The *strong product* $G \boxtimes H$ combines the edges of $G \square H$ with those of $G \otimes H$.

- The *odd product* $G \triangle H$ has $(u, v) \longrightarrow (u', v')$ when we have either $u \longrightarrow u'$ in G or $v \longrightarrow v'$ in H, but not both.

- The *lexicographic product* $G \circ H$, also called the "composition" of G and H, has $(u, v) \longrightarrow (u', v')$ when $u \longrightarrow u'$ in G, and $(u, v) \longrightarrow (u, v')$ when $v \longrightarrow v'$ in H.

All five of these operations extend naturally to products of $k \geq 2$ graphs $G_1 = (V_1, E_1)$, ..., $G_k = (V_k, E_k)$, whose vertices are the ordered k-tuples $(v_1, \ldots, v_k)$ with $v_j \in V_j$ for $1 \leq j \leq k$. For example, when $k = 3$, the Cartesian products $G_1 \square (G_2 \square G_3)$ and $(G_1 \square G_2) \square G_3$ are isomorphic, if we consider the compound vertices $(v_1, (v_2, v_3))$ and $((v_1, v_2), v_3)$ to be the same as (v_1, v_2, v_3). Therefore we can write this Cartesian product without parentheses, as $G_1 \square G_2 \square G_3$. The most important example of a Cartesian product with k factors is the k-cube,

$$K_2 \square K_2 \square \cdots \square K_2; \tag{51}$$

its 2^k vertices $(v_1, \ldots, v_k)$ are adjacent when their Hamming distance is 1.

In general, suppose $v = (v_1, \ldots, v_k)$ and $v' = (v'_1, \ldots, v'_k)$ are k-tuples of vertices, where we have $v_j \longrightarrow v'_j$ in G_j for exactly a of the subscripts j, and $v_j = v'_j$ for exactly b of the subscripts j. Then we have:

- $v \longrightarrow v'$ in $G_1 \square \cdots \square G_k$ if and only if $a = 1$ and $b = k - 1$;
- $v \longrightarrow v'$ in $G_1 \otimes \cdots \otimes G_k$ if and only if $a = k$ and $b = 0$;
- $v \longrightarrow v'$ in $G_1 \boxtimes \cdots \boxtimes G_k$ if and only if $a + b = k$ and $a > 0$;
- $v \longrightarrow v'$ in $G_1 \triangle \cdots \triangle G_k$ if and only if a is odd.

The lexicographic product is somewhat different, because it isn't commutative; in $G_1 \circ \cdots \circ G_k$ we have $v \longrightarrow v'$ for $v \neq v'$ if and only if $v_j \longrightarrow v'_j$, where j is the minimum subscript with $v_j \neq v'_j$.

Exercises 91–102 explore some of the basic properties of graph products. See also the book *Product Graphs* by Wilfried Imrich and Sandi Klavžar (2000), which contains a comprehensive introduction to the general theory, including algorithms for factorization of a given graph into "prime" subgraphs.

*Graphical degree sequences. A sequence $d_1 d_2 \ldots d_n$ of nonnegative integers is called *graphical* if there's at least one graph on vertices $\{1, 2, \ldots, n\}$ such that vertex k has degree d_k. We can assume that $d_1 \geq d_2 \geq \cdots \geq d_n$. Clearly $d_1 < n$ in any such graph; and the sum $m = d_1 + d_2 + \cdots + d_n$ of any graphical sequence is always even, because it is twice the number of edges. Furthermore, it's easy to see that the sequence 3311 is not graphical; therefore graphical sequences must also satisfy additional conditions. What are they?

A simple way to decide if a given sequence $d_1 d_2 \ldots d_n$ is graphical, and to construct such a graph if one exists, was discovered by V. Havel [*Časopis pro Pěstování Matematiky* **80** (1955), 477–479]. We begin with an empty tableau, having d_k cells in row k; these cells represent "slots" into which we'll place the neighbors of vertex k in the constructed graph. Let c_j be the number of cells in column j; thus $c_1 \geq c_2 \geq \cdots$, and when $1 \leq k \leq n$ we have $c_j \geq k$ if and only if $d_k \geq j$. For example, suppose $n = 8$ and $d_1 \ldots d_8 = 55544322$; then

$$
\begin{array}{r} 1 \\ 2 \\ 3 \\ 4 \\ 5 \\ 6 \\ 7 \\ 8 \end{array}
\qquad\qquad (52)
$$

is the initial tableau, and we have $c_1 \ldots c_5 = 88653$. Havel's idea is to pair up vertex n with d_n of the highest-degree vertices. In this case, for example, we create the two edges 8 — 3 and 8 — 2, and the tableau takes the following form:

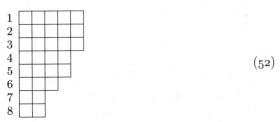

$$(53)$$

(We don't want 8 — 1, because the empty slots should continue to form a tableau shape; the cells of each column must be filled from the bottom up.) Next we set $n \leftarrow 7$ and create two further edges, 7 — 1 and 7 — 5. And then come three more, 6 — 4, 6 — 3, 6 — 2, making the tableau almost half full:

$$(54)$$

We've reduced the problem to finding a graph with degree sequence $d_1 \ldots d_5 = 43333$; at this point we also have $c_1 \ldots c_4 = 5551$. The reader is encouraged to fill in the remaining blanks, before looking at the answer in exercise 103.

Algorithm H (*Graph generator for specified degrees*). Given $d_1 \geq \cdots \geq d_n \geq d_{n+1} = 0$, this algorithm creates edges between the vertices $\{1, \ldots, n\}$ in such a way that exactly d_k edges touch vertex k, for $1 \leq k \leq n$, unless the sequence $d_1 \ldots d_n$ isn't graphical. An array $c_1 \ldots c_{d_1}$ is used for auxiliary storage.

H1. [Set the c's.] Start with $k \leftarrow d_1$ and $j \leftarrow 0$. Then while $k > 0$ do the following operations: Set $j \leftarrow j + 1$; while $k > d_{j+1}$, set $c_k \leftarrow j$ and $k \leftarrow k - 1$.

H2. [Find n.] Set $n \leftarrow c_1$. Terminate successfully if $n = 0$; terminate unsuccessfully if $d_1 \geq n > 0$.

H3. [Loop on j.] Set $i \leftarrow 1$, $t \leftarrow d_1$, and $r \leftarrow c_t$. Do step H4 for $j = d_n, d_n - 1, \ldots, 1$; then return to H2.

H4. [Generate a new edge.] Set $c_j \leftarrow c_j - 1$ and $k \leftarrow c_t$. Create the edge $k \mathbin{\text{---}} n$, and set $d_k \leftarrow d_k - 1$, $c_t \leftarrow k - 1$. If $k = i$, set $i \leftarrow r + 1$, $t \leftarrow d_i$, and $r \leftarrow c_t$. (See exercise 104.) ∎

When Algorithm H succeeds, it certainly has constructed a graph with the desired degrees. But when it fails, how can we be sure that its mission was impossible? The key fact is based on an important concept called "majorization": If $d_1 \ldots d_n$ and $d'_1 \ldots d'_n$ are two partitions of the same integer (that is, if $d_1 \geq \cdots \geq d_n$ and $d'_1 \geq \cdots \geq d'_n$ and $d_1 + \cdots + d_n = d'_1 + \cdots + d'_n$), we say that $d_1 \ldots d_n$ *majorizes* $d'_1 \ldots d'_n$ if $d_1 + \cdots + d_k \geq d'_1 + \cdots + d'_k$ for $1 \leq k \leq n$.

Lemma M. *If $d_1 \ldots d_n$ is graphical and $d_1 \ldots d_n$ majorizes $d'_1 \ldots d'_n$, then $d'_1 \ldots d'_n$ is also graphical.*

Proof. It is sufficient to prove the claim when $d_1 \ldots d_n$ and $d'_1 \ldots d'_n$ differ in only two places,

$$d'_k = d_k - [k = i] + [k = j] \qquad \text{where } i < j, \tag{55}$$

because any sequence majorized by $d_1 \ldots d_n$ can be obtained by repeatedly performing mini-majorizations such as this. (Exercise 7.2.1.4–55 discusses majorization in detail.)

Condition (55) implies that $d_i > d'_i \geq d'_{i+1} \geq d'_j > d_j$. So any graph with degree sequence $d_1 \ldots d_n$ contains a vertex v such that $v \mathbin{\text{---}} i$ and $v \mathbin{\text{--\!/--}} j$. Deleting the edge $v \mathbin{\text{---}} i$ and adding the edge $v \mathbin{\text{---}} j$ yields a graph with degree sequence $d'_1 \ldots d'_n$, as desired. ∎

Corollary H. *Algorithm H succeeds whenever $d_1 \ldots d_n$ is graphical.*

Proof. We may assume that $n > 1$. Suppose G is any graph on $\{1, \ldots, n\}$ with degree sequence $d_1 \ldots d_n$, and let G' be the subgraph induced by $\{1, \ldots, n-1\}$; in other words, obtain G' by removing vertex n and the d_n edges that it touches. The degree sequence $d'_1 \ldots d'_{n-1}$ of G' is obtained from $d_1 \ldots d_{n-1}$ by reducing some d_n of the entries by 1 and sorting them into nonincreasing order. By definition, $d'_1 \ldots d'_{n-1}$ is graphical. The new degree sequence $d''_1 \ldots d''_{n-1}$ produced by the strategy of steps H3 and H4 is designed to be majorized by every such $d'_1 \ldots d'_{n-1}$, because it reduces the largest possible d_n entries by 1. Thus the new $d''_1 \ldots d''_{n-1}$ is graphical. Algorithm H, which sets $d_1 \ldots d_{n-1} \leftarrow d''_1 \ldots d''_{n-1}$, will therefore succeed by induction on n. ∎

The running time of Algorithm H is roughly proportional to the number of edges generated, which can be of order n^2. Exercise 105 presents a faster method, which decides in $O(n)$ steps whether or not a given sequence $d_1 \ldots d_n$ is graphical (without constructing any graph).

Beyond graphs. When the vertices and/or arcs of a graph or digraph are decorated with additional data, we call it a *network*. For example, every vertex of *words*$(5757, 0, 0, 0)$ has an associated rank, which corresponds to the popularity of the corresponding five-letter word. Every vertex of *plane_lisa*$(360, 250, 15,$ $0, 360, 0, 250, 0, 0, 2295000)$ has an associated pixel density, between 0 and 15. Every arc of *board*$(8, 8, 0, 0, -2, 0, 0)$ has an associated length, which reflects the distance of a piece's motion on the board: A bishop's move from corner to corner has length 7. The Stanford GraphBase includes several further generators that were not mentioned above, because they are primarily used to generate interesting networks, rather than to generate graphs with interesting structure:

• *miles*$(128, 0, 0, 0, 0, 127, 0)$ is a network with 128 vertices, corresponding to the same North American cities as the graph *plane_miles* described earlier. But *miles*, unlike *plane_miles*, is a complete graph with $\binom{128}{2}$ edges. Every edge has an integer length, which represents the distance that a car or truck would have needed to travel in 1949 when going from one given city to another. For example, 'Vancouver, BC' is 3496 miles from 'West Palm Beach, FL' in the *miles* network.

• *econ*$(81, 0, 0, 0)$ is a network with 81 vertices and 4902 arcs. Its vertices represent sectors of the United States economy, and its arcs represent the flow of money from one sector to another during the year 1985, measured in millions of dollars. For example, the flow value from Apparel to Household furniture is 44, meaning that the furniture industry paid $44,000,000 to the apparel industry in that year. The sum of flows coming into each vertex is equal to the sum of flows going out. An arc appears only when the flow is nonzero. A special vertex called Users receives the flows that represent total demand for a product; a few of these end-user flows are negative, because of the way imported goods are treated by government economists.

• *games*$(120, 0, 0, 0, 0, 0, 128, 0)$ is a network with 120 vertices and 1276 arcs. Its vertices represent football teams at American colleges and universities. Arcs run between teams that played each other during the exciting 1990 season, and they are labeled with the number of points scored. For example, the arc Stanford $\longrightarrow$ California has value 27, and the arc California $\longrightarrow$ Stanford has value 25, because the Stanford Cardinal defeated the U. C. Berkeley Golden Bears by a score of 27–25 on 17 November 1990.

• *risc*(16) is a network of an entirely different kind. It has 3240 vertices and 7878 arcs, which define a *directed acyclic graph* or "dag" — namely, a digraph that contains no oriented cycles. The vertices represent gates that have Boolean values; an arc such as Z45 $\longrightarrow$ RO:7~ means that the value of gate Z45 is an input to gate RO:7~. Each gate has a type code (AND, OR, XOR, NOT, latch, or external input); each arc has a length, denoting an amount of delay. The network contains the complete logic for a miniature RISC chip that is able to obey simple commands governing sixteen registers, each 16 bits wide.

Complete details about all the SGB generators can be found in the author's book *The Stanford GraphBase* (New York: ACM Press, 1993), together with dozens of short example programs that explain how to manipulate the graphs and networks that the generators produce. For example, a program called LADDERS shows how to find a shortest path between one five-letter word and another. A program called TAKE_RISC demonstrates how to put a nanocomputer through its paces by simulating the actions of a network built from the gates of $risc(16)$.

Hypergraphs. Graphs and networks can be utterly fascinating, but they aren't the end of the story by any means. Lots of important combinatorial algorithms are designed to work with *hypergraphs*, which are more general than graphs because their edges are allowed to be *arbitrary* subsets of the vertices.

For example, we might have seven vertices, identified by nonzero binary strings $v = a_1a_2a_3$, together with seven edges, identified by bracketed nonzero binary strings $e = [b_1b_2b_3]$, with $v \in e$ if and only if $(a_1b_1 + a_2b_2 + a_3b_3) \bmod 2 = 0$. Each of these edges contains exactly three vertices:

$$[001] = \{010, 100, 110\}; \quad [010] = \{001, 100, 101\}; \quad [011] = \{011, 100, 111\};$$
$$[100] = \{001, 010, 011\}; \quad [101] = \{010, 101, 111\};$$
$$[110] = \{001, 110, 111\}; \quad [111] = \{011, 101, 110\}. \tag{56}$$

And by symmetry, each vertex belongs to exactly three edges. (Edges that contain three or more vertices are sometimes called "hyperedges," to distinguish them from the edges of an ordinary graph. But it's OK to call them just "edges.")

A hypergraph is said to be *r-uniform* if every edge contains exactly r vertices. Thus (56) is a 3-uniform hypergraph, and a 2-uniform hypergraph is an ordinary graph. The complete r-uniform hypergraph $K_n^{(r)}$ has n vertices and $\binom{n}{r}$ edges.

Most of the basic concepts of graph theory can be extended to hypergraphs in a natural way. For example, if $H = (V, E)$ is a hypergraph and if $U \subseteq V$, the subhypergraph $H \mid U$ induced by U has the edges $\{e \mid e \in E \text{ and } e \subseteq U\}$. The complement $\overline{H}$ of an r-uniform hypergraph has the edges of $K_n^{(r)}$ that aren't edges of H. A k-coloring of a hypergraph is an assignment of colors to the vertices so that no edge is monochromatic. And so on.

Hypergraphs go by many other names, because the same properties can be formulated in many different ways. For example, every hypergraph $H = (V, E)$ is essentially a *family of sets*, because each edge is a subset of V. A 3-uniform hypergraph is also called a *triple system*. A hypergraph is also equivalent to a matrix B of 0s and 1s, with one row for each vertex v and one column for each edge e; row v and column e of this matrix contains the value $b_{ve} = [v \in e]$.

Matrix B is called the *incidence matrix* of H, and we say that "v is incident with e" when $v \in e$. Furthermore, a hypergraph is equivalent to a *bipartite graph*, with vertex set $V \cup E$ and with the edge $v \!\!-\!\! e$ whenever v is incident with e. The hypergraph is said to be *connected* if and only if the corresponding bipartite graph is connected. A *cycle* of length k in a hypergraph is defined to be a cycle of length $2k$ in the corresponding bipartite graph.

For example, the hypergraph (56) can be defined by an equivalent incidence matrix or an equivalent bipartite graph as follows:

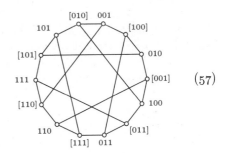

$$(57)$$

It contains 28 cycles of length 3, such as

$$[101] \!\!-\!\! 101 \!\!-\!\! [010] \!\!-\!\! 001 \!\!-\!\! [100] \!\!-\!\! 010 \!\!-\!\! [101]. \tag{58}$$

The *dual* H^T of a hypergraph H is obtained by interchanging the roles of vertices and edges, but retaining the incidence relation. In other words, it corresponds to transposing the incidence matrix. Notice, for example, that the dual of an r-regular graph is an r-uniform hypergraph.

Incidence matrices and bipartite graphs might correspond to hypergraphs in which some edges occur more than once, because distinct columns of the matrix might be equal. When a hypergraph $H = (V, E)$ does not have any repeated edges, it corresponds also to yet another combinatorial object, namely a *Boolean function*. For if, say, the vertex set V is $\{1, 2, \ldots, n\}$, the function

$$h(x_1, x_2, \ldots, x_n) = \big[\{ j \mid x_j = 1 \} \in E \big] \tag{59}$$

characterizes the edges of H. For example, the Boolean formula

$$\begin{aligned}
&(x_1 \oplus x_2 \oplus x_4) \wedge (x_2 \oplus x_3 \oplus x_5) \wedge (x_3 \oplus x_4 \oplus x_6) \wedge (x_4 \oplus x_5 \oplus x_7) \\
&\wedge (x_5 \oplus x_6 \oplus x_1) \wedge (x_6 \oplus x_7 \oplus x_2) \wedge (x_7 \oplus x_1 \oplus x_3) \wedge (\bar{x}_1 \vee \bar{x}_2 \vee \bar{x}_3)
\end{aligned} \tag{60}$$

is another way to describe the hypergraph of (56) and (57).

The fact that combinatorial objects can be viewed in so many ways can be mind-boggling. But it's also extremely helpful, because it suggests different ways to solve equivalent problems. When we look at a problem from different perspectives, our brains naturally think of different ways to attack it. Sometimes we get the best insights by thinking about how to manipulate rows and columns in a matrix. Sometimes we make progress by imagining vertices and paths, or by visualizing clusters of points in space. Sometimes Boolean algebra is just the thing. If we're stuck in one domain, another might come to our rescue.

Covering and independence. If $H = (V, E)$ is a graph or hypergraph, a set U of vertices is said to *cover* H if every edge contains at least one member of U. A set W of vertices is said to be *independent* (or "stable") in H if no edge is completely contained in W.

From the standpoint of the incidence matrix, a covering is a set of rows whose sum is nonzero in every column. And in the special case that H is a graph, every column of the matrix contains just two 1s; hence an independent set in a graph corresponds to a set of rows that are mutually orthogonal — that is, a set for which the dot product of any two different rows is zero.

These concepts are opposite sides of the same coin. If U covers H, then $W = V \setminus U$ is independent in H; conversely, if W is independent in H, then $U = V \setminus W$ covers H. Both statements are equivalent to saying that the induced hypergraph $H \mid W$ has no edges.

This dual relationship between covering and independence, which was perhaps first noted by Claude Berge [*Proc. National Acad. Sci.* **43** (1957), 842–844], is somewhat paradoxical. Although it's logically obvious and easy to verify, it's also intuitively surprising. When we look at a graph and try to find a large independent set, we tend to have rather different thoughts from when we look at the same graph and try to find a small vertex cover; yet both goals are the same.

A covering set U is *minimal* if $U \setminus u$ fails to be a cover for all $u \in U$. Similarly, an independent set W is *maximal* if $W \cup w$ fails to be independent for all $w \notin W$. Here, for example, is a minimal cover of the 49-vertex graph of the contiguous United States, (17), and the corresponding maximal independent set:

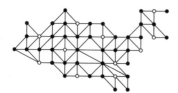 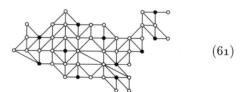

(61)

Minimal vertex cover,
with 38 vertices

Maximal independent set,
with 11 vertices

A covering is called *minimum* if it has the smallest possible size, and an independent set is called *maximum* if it has the largest possible size. For example, with graph (17) we can do much better than (61):

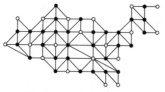 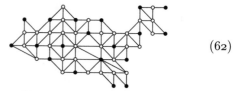

(62)

Minimum vertex cover,
with 30 vertices

Maximum independent set,
with 19 vertices

Notice the subtle distinction between "minimal" and "minimum" here: In general (but in contrast to most dictionaries of English), people who work with combinatorial algorithms use '-al' words like "minimal" or "optimal" to refer to combinatorial configurations that are *locally* best, in the sense that small changes don't improve them. The corresponding '-um' words, "minimum" or "optimum," are reserved for configurations that are *globally* best, considered over all possibilities. It's easy to find solutions to any optimization problem that are merely optimal, in the weak local sense, by climbing repeatedly until reaching the top of a hill. But it's usually much harder to find solutions that are truly optimum. For example, we'll see in Section 7.9 that the problem of finding a maximum independent set in a given graph belongs to a class of difficult problems that are called *NP-complete*.

Even when a problem is NP-complete, we needn't despair. We'll discuss techniques for finding minimum covers in several parts of this chapter, and those methods work fine on smallish problems; the optimum solution in (62) was found in less than a second, after examining only a tiny fraction of the 2^{49} possibilities. Furthermore, special cases of NP-complete problems often turn out to be simpler than the general case. In Section 7.5.1 we'll see that a minimum vertex cover can be discovered quickly in any bipartite graph, or in any hypergraph that is the dual of a graph. And in Section 7.5.5 we'll study efficient ways to discover a maximum *matching*, which is a maximum independent set in the line graph of a given graph.

The problem of maximizing the size of an independent set occurs sufficiently often that it has acquired a special notation: If H is any hypergraph, the number

$$\alpha(H) \;=\; \max\big\{|W| \;\big|\; W \text{ is an independent set of vertices in } H\big\} \qquad (63)$$

is called the *independence number* (or the stability number) of H. Similarly,

$$\chi(H) \;=\; \min\{k \mid H \text{ is } k\text{-colorable}\} \qquad (64)$$

is called the *chromatic number* of H. Notice that $\chi(H)$ is the size of a minimum covering of H by independent sets, because the vertices that receive any particular color must be independent according to our definitions.

These definitions of $\alpha(H)$ and $\chi(H)$ apply in particular to the case when H is an ordinary graph, but of course we usually write $\alpha(G)$ and $\chi(G)$ in such situations. Graphs have another important number called their *clique number*,

$$\omega(G) \;=\; \max\big\{|X| \;\big|\; X \text{ is a clique in } G\big\}, \qquad (65)$$

where a "clique" is a set of mutually adjacent vertices. Clearly

$$\omega(G) \;=\; \alpha(\overline{G}), \qquad (66)$$

because a clique in G is an independent set in the complementary graph. Similarly we can see that $\chi(\overline{G})$ is the minimum size of a "clique cover," which is a set of cliques that exactly covers all of the vertices.

Several instances of "exact cover problems" were mentioned earlier in this section, without an explanation of exactly what such a problem really signifies. Finally we're ready for the definition: Given the incidence matrix of a hypergraph H, an *exact cover* of H is a set of rows whose sum is $(1\,1\,\ldots\,1)$. In other words, an exact cover is a set of vertices that touches each hyperedge exactly once; an ordinary cover is only required to touch each hyperedge *at least* once.

EXERCISES

1. [*25*] Suppose $n = 4m - 1$. Construct arrangements of Langford pairs for the numbers $\{1, 1, \ldots, n, n\}$, with the property that we also obtain a solution for $n = 4m$ by changing the first '$2m-1$' to '$4m$' and appending '$2m-1\ 4m$' at the right. *Hint:* Put the $m - 1$ even numbers $4m-4$, $4m-6$, $\ldots$, $2m$ at the left.

2. [*18*] For which n can $\{0, 0, 1, 1, \ldots, n-1, n-1\}$ be arranged as Langford pairs?

3. [*22*] Suppose we arrange the numbers $\{0, 0, 1, 1, \ldots, n-1, n-1\}$ in a *circle*, instead of a straight line, with distance k between the two k's. Do we get solutions that are essentially distinct from those of exercise 2?

4. [*M20*] (T. Skolem, 1957.) Show that the Fibonacci string $S_\infty = babbabababbabba\ldots$ of exercise 1.2.8–36 leads directly to an infinite sequence $0012132453674\ldots$ of Langford pairs for the set of *all* nonnegative integers, if we simply replace the a's and b's independently by 0, 1, 2, etc., from left to right.

▶ **5.** [*HM22*] If a permutation of $\{1, 1, 2, 2, \ldots, n, n\}$ is chosen at random, what is the probability that the two k's are exactly k positions apart, given k? Use this formula to guess the size of the Langford numbers L_n in (1).

▶ **6.** [*M28*] (M. Godfrey, 2002.) Let $f(x_1, \ldots, x_{2n}) = \prod_{k=1}^{n}\left(x_k x_{n+k} \sum_{j=1}^{2n-k-1} x_j x_{j+k+1}\right)$.
a) Prove that $\sum_{x_1,\ldots,x_{2n}\in\{-1,+1\}} f(x_1, \ldots, x_{2n}) = 2^{2n+1} L_n$.
b) Explain how to evaluate this sum in $O(4^n n)$ steps. How many bits of precision are needed for the arithmetic?
c) Gain a factor of eight by exploiting the identities

$$f(x_1, \ldots, x_{2n}) = f(-x_1, \ldots, -x_{2n}) = f(x_{2n}, \ldots, x_1) = f(x_1, -x_2, \ldots, x_{2n-1}, -x_{2n}).$$

7. [*M22*] Prove that every Langford pairing of $\{1, 1, \ldots, 16, 16\}$ must have seven uncompleted pairs at some point, when read from left to right.

8. [*23*] The simplest Langford sequence is not only well-balanced; it's *planar*, in the sense that its pairs can be connected up without crossing lines as in (2):

$$2\ 3\ 1\ 2\ 1\ 3.$$

Find all of the planar Langford pairings for which $n \leq 8$.

9. [*24*] (*Langford triples.*) In how many ways can $\{1, 1, 1, 2, 2, 2, \ldots, 9, 9, 9\}$ be arranged in a row so that consecutive k's are k apart, for $1 \leq k \leq 9$?

10. [*M20*] Explain how to construct a *magic square* directly from Fig. 1. (Convert each card into a number between 1 and 16, in such a way that the rows, columns, and main diagonals all sum to 34.)

11. [*20*] Extend (5) to a "Hebraic-Græco-Latin" square by appending one of the letters $\{\aleph, \beth, \gimel, \daleth\}$ to the two-letter string in each compartment. No letter pair (Latin, Greek), (Latin, Hebrew), or (Greek, Hebrew) should appear in more than one place.

▶ **12.** [*M21*] (L. Euler.) Let $L_{ij} = (i+j) \bmod n$ for $0 \leq i, j < n$ be the addition table for integers mod n. Prove that a latin square orthogonal to L exists if and only if n is odd.

13. [*M25*] A 10×10 square can be divided into four quarters of size 5×5. A 10×10 latin square formed from the digits $\{0, 1, \ldots, 9\}$ has k "intruders" if its upper left quarter has exactly k elements ≥ 5. (See exercise 14(e) for an example with $k = 3$.) Prove that the square has no orthogonal mate unless there are at least three intruders.

14. [*29*] Find all orthogonal mates of the following latin squares:

(a)	(b)	(c)	(d)	(e)
3145926870	2718459036	0572164938	1680397425	7823456019
2819763504	0287135649	6051298473	8346512097	8234067195
9452307168	7524093168	4867039215	9805761342	2340178956
6208451793	1435962780	1439807652	2754689130	3401289567
8364095217	6390718425	8324756091	0538976214	4012395678
5981274036	4069271853	7203941586	4963820571	5678912340
4627530981	3102684597	5610473829	7192034658	6789523401
0576148329	9871546302	9148625307	6219405783	0195634782
1730689452	8956307214	2795380164	3471258906	1956740823
7093812645	5643820971	3986512740	5027143869	9567801234

15. [*50*] Find three 10×10 latin squares that are mutually orthogonal to each other.

16. [*48*] (H. J. Ryser, 1967.) A latin square is said to be of "order n" if it has n rows, n columns, and n symbols. Does every latin square of odd order have a transversal?

17. [*25*] Let L be a latin square with elements L_{ij} for $0 \le i, j < n$. Show that the problems of (a) finding all the transversals of L, and (b) finding all the orthogonal mates of L, are special cases of the general exact cover problem.

18. [*M23*] The string $x_1 x_2 \ldots x_N$ is called "n-ary" if each element x_j belongs to the set $\{0, 1, \ldots, n-1\}$ of n-ary digits. Two strings $x_1 x_2 \ldots x_N$ and $y_1 y_2 \ldots y_N$ are said to be *orthogonal* if the N pairs (x_j, y_j) are distinct for $1 \le j \le N$. (Consequently, two n-ary strings cannot be orthogonal if their length N exceeds n^2.) An n-ary matrix with m rows and n^2 columns whose rows are orthogonal to each other is called an *orthogonal array* of order n and depth m.

Find a correspondence between orthogonal arrays of depth m and lists of $m - 2$ mutually orthogonal latin squares. What orthogonal array corresponds to exercise 11?

▸ **19.** [*M25*] Continuing exercise 18, prove that an orthogonal array of order $n > 1$ and depth m is possible only if $m \le n + 1$. Show that this upper limit is achievable when n is a prime number p. Write out an example when $p = 5$.

20. [*HM20*] Show that if each element k in an orthogonal array is replaced by $e^{2\pi k i/n}$, the rows become orthogonal vectors in the usual sense (their dot product is zero).

▸ **21.** [*M21*] A *geometric net* is a system of points and lines that obeys three axioms:
   i) Each line is a set of points.
   ii) Distinct lines have at most one point in common.
   iii) If p is a point and L is a line with $p \notin L$, then there is exactly one line M such that $p \in M$ and $L \cap M = \emptyset$.
If $L \cap M = \emptyset$ we say that L is *parallel* to M, and write $L \parallel M$.
   a) Prove that the lines of a geometric net can be partitioned into equivalence classes, with two lines in the same class if and only if they are equal or parallel.
   b) Show that if there are at least two classes of parallel lines, every line contains the same number of points as the other lines in its class.
   c) Furthermore, if there are at least three classes, there are numbers m and n such that all points belong to exactly m lines and all lines contain exactly n points.

▸ **22.** [*M22*] Show that every orthogonal array can be regarded as a geometric net. Is the converse also true?

23. [*M21*] (*Error-correcting codes.*) The "Hamming distance" $d(x, y)$ between two strings $x = x_1 \ldots x_N$ and $y = y_1 \ldots y_N$ is the number of positions j where $x_j \ne y_j$. A *b-ary code with n information digits and r check digits* is a set $C(b, n, r)$ of b^n strings $x = x_1 \ldots x_{n+r}$, where $0 \le x_j < b$ for $1 \le j \le n+r$. When a codeword x is transmitted and the message y is received, $d(x, y)$ is the number of transmission errors. The code is called *t-error correcting* if we can reconstruct the value of x whenever a message y is received with $d(x, y) \le t$. The *distance* of the code is the minimum value of $d(x, x')$, taken over all pairs of codewords $x \ne x'$.

a) Prove that a code is t-error correcting if and only if its distance exceeds $2t$.

b) Prove that a single-error correcting b-ary code with 2 information digits and 2 check digits is equivalent to a pair of orthogonal latin squares of order b.

c) Furthermore, a code $C(b, 2, r)$ with distance $r+1$ is equivalent to a set of r mutually orthogonal latin squares of order b.

▶ **24.** [*M30*] A geometric net with N points and R lines leads naturally to the binary code $C(2, N, R)$ with codewords $x_1 \ldots x_N x_{N+1} \ldots x_{N+R}$ defined by the parity bits

$$x_{N+k} = f_k(x_1, \ldots, x_N) = \left(\sum \{x_j \mid \text{point } j \text{ lies on line } k\}\right) \bmod 2.$$

a) If the net has m classes of parallel lines, prove that this code has distance $m + 1$.

b) Find an efficient way to correct up to t errors with this code, assuming that $m = 2t$. Illustrate the decoding process in the case $N = 25$, $R = 30$, $t = 3$.

25. [*27*] Find a latin square whose rows and columns are five-letter words. (For this exercise you'll need to dig out the big dictionaries.)

▶ **26.** [*25*] Compose a meaningful English sentence that contains only five-letter words.

27. [*20*] How many SGB words contain exactly k distinct letters, for $1 \le k \le 5$?

28. [*20*] Are there any pairs of SGB word vectors that differ by ± 1 in each component?

29. [*20*] Find all SGB words that are *palindromes* (equal to their reflection), or mirror pairs (like **regal lager**).

▶ **30.** [*20*] The letters of **first** are in alphabetic order from left to right. What is the lexicographically *first* such five-letter word? What is the last?

31. [*21*] (C. McManus.) Find all sets of three SGB words that are in arithmetic progression but have no common letters in any fixed position. (One such example is {**power, slugs, visit**}.)

32. [*23*] Does the English language contain any 10-letter words $a_0 a_1 \ldots a_9$ for which both $a_0 a_2 a_4 a_6 a_8$ and $a_1 a_3 a_5 a_7 a_9$ are SGB words?

33. [*20*] (Scot Morris.) Complete the following list of 26 interesting SGB words:

about, bacon, faced, under, chief, ..., pizza.

▶ **34.** [*21*] For each SGB word that doesn't include the letter **y**, obtain a 5-bit binary number by changing the vowels {**a, e, i, o, u**} to 1 and the other letters to 0. What are the most common words for each of the 32 binary outcomes?

▶ **35.** [*26*] Sixteen well-chosen elements of WORDS(1000) lead to the branching pattern

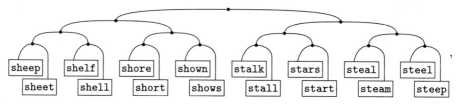

which is a complete binary trie of words that begin with the letter s. But there's no such pattern of words beginning with a, even if we consider the full collection WORDS(5757).

What letters of the alphabet can be used as the starting letter of sixteen words that form a complete binary trie within WORDS(n), given n?

36. [*M17*] Explain the symmetries that appear in the word cube (10). Also show that two more such cubes can be obtained by changing only the two words {stove, event}.

37. [*20*] Which vertices of the graph *words*(5757, 0, 0, 0) have maximum degree?

38. [*22*] Using the digraph rule in (14), change tears to smile in just three steps, *without computer assistance*.

39. [*M00*] Is $G \setminus e$ an induced subgraph of G? Is it a spanning subgraph?

40. [*M15*] How many (a) spanning (b) induced subgraphs does a graph $G = (V, E)$ have, when $|V| = n$ and $|E| = e$?

41. [*M10*] For which integers n do we have (a) $K_n = P_n$? (b) $K_n = C_n$?

42. [*15*] (D. H. Lehmer.) Let G be a graph with 13 vertices, in which every vertex has degree 5. Make a nontrivial statement about G.

43. [*23*] Are any of the following graphs the same as the Petersen graph?

44. [*M23*] How many symmetries does Chvátal's graph have? (See Fig. 2(f).)

45. [*20*] Find an easy way to 4-color the planar graph (17). Would 3 colors suffice?

46. [*M25*] Let G be a graph with $n \geq 3$ vertices, defined by a planar diagram that is "maximal," in the sense that no additional lines can be drawn between nonadjacent vertices without crossing an existing edge.

a) Prove that the diagram partitions the plane into regions that each have exactly three vertices on their boundary. (One of these regions is the set of all points that lie outside the diagram.)

b) Therefore G has exactly $3n - 6$ edges.

47. [*M22*] Prove that the complete bigraph $K_{3,3}$ isn't planar.

48. [*M25*] Complete the proof of Theorem B by showing that the stated procedure never gives the same color to two adjacent vertices.

49. [*18*] Draw diagrams of all the cubic graphs with at most 6 vertices.

50. [*M24*] Find all bipartite graphs that can be 3-colored in exactly 24 ways.

▶ **51.** [*M22*] Given a geometric net as described in exercise 21, construct the bipartite graph whose vertices are the points p and the lines L of the net, with $p \longrightarrow L$ if and only if $p \in L$. What is the *girth* of this graph?

52. [*M16*] Find a simple inequality that relates the diameter of a graph to its girth. (How small can the diameter be, if the girth is large?)

53. [*15*] Which of the words world and happy belongs to the giant component of the graph *words*(5757, 0, 0, 0)?

▶ **54.** [*21*] The 49 postal codes in graph (17) are AL, AR, AZ, CA, CO, CT, DC, DE, FL, GA, IA, ID, IL, IN, KS, KY, LA, MA, MD, ME, MI, MN, MO, MS, MT, NC, ND, NE, NH, NJ, NM, NV, NY, OH, OK, OR, PA, RI, SC, SD, TN, TX, UT, VA, VT, WA, WI, WV, WY, in alphabetical order.

    a) Suppose we consider two states to be adjacent if their postal codes agree in one place (namely AL — AR — OR — OH, etc.). What are the components of this graph?

    b) Now form a directed graph with XY ⟶ YZ (for example, AL ⟶ LA ⟶ AR, etc.). What are the *strongly connected components* of this digraph? (See Section 2.3.4.2.)

    c) The United States has additional postal codes AA, AE, AK, AP, AS, FM, GU, HI, MH, MP, PW, PR, VI, besides those in (17). Reconsider question (b), using all 62 codes.

55. [*M20*] How many edges are in the complete k-partite graph $K_{n_1,\ldots,n_k}$?

▶ **56.** [*M10*] True or false: A multigraph is a graph if and only if the corresponding digraph is simple.

57. [*M10*] True or false: Vertices u and v are in the same connected component of a directed graph if and only if either $d(u, v) < \infty$ or $d(v, u) < \infty$.

58. [*M17*] Describe all (a) graphs (b) multigraphs that are regular of degree 2.

▶ **59.** [*M23*] A *tournament* of order n is a digraph on n vertices that has exactly $\binom{n}{2}$ arcs, either $u \longrightarrow v$ or $v \longrightarrow u$ for every pair of distinct vertices $\{u, v\}$.

    a) Prove that every tournament contains an oriented spanning path $v_1 \longrightarrow \cdots \longrightarrow v_n$.

    b) Consider the tournament on vertices $\{0, 1, 2, 3, 4\}$ for which $u \longrightarrow v$ if and only if $(u - v) \bmod 5 \geq 3$. How many oriented spanning paths does it have?

    c) Is $K_n^{\rightarrow}$ the only tournament of order n that has a unique oriented spanning path?

▶ **60.** [*M22*] Let u be a vertex of greatest out-degree in a tournament, and let v be any other vertex. Prove that $d(u, v) \leq 2$.

61. [*M16*] Construct a digraph that has k walks of length k from vertex 1 to vertex 2.

62. [*M21*] A *permutation digraph* is a directed graph in which every vertex has out-degree 1 and in-degree 1; therefore its components are oriented cycles. If it has n vertices and k components, we call it *even* if $n - k$ is even, *odd* if $n - k$ is odd.

    a) Let G be a directed graph with adjacency matrix A. Prove that the number of spanning permutation digraphs of G is per A, the permanent of A.

    b) Interpret the determinant, det A, in terms of spanning permutation digraphs.

63. [*M23*] Let G be a graph of girth g in which every vertex has at least d neighbors. Prove that G has at least N vertices, where

$$N = \begin{cases} 1 + \sum_{0 \leq k < t} d(d - 1)^k, & \text{if } g = 2t + 1; \\ 1 + (d - 1)^t + \sum_{0 \leq k < t} d(d - 1)^k, & \text{if } g = 2t + 2. \end{cases}$$

▶ **64.** [*M21*] Continuing exercise 63, show that there's a *unique* graph of girth 4, minimum degree d, and order $2d$, for each $d \geq 2$.

▶ **65.** [*HM31*] Suppose graph G has girth 5, minimum degree d, and $N = d^2 + 1$ vertices.

    a) Prove that the adjacency matrix A of G satisfies the equation $A^2 + A = (d-1)I + J$.

    b) Since A is a symmetric matrix, it has N orthogonal eigenvectors x_j, with corresponding eigenvalues λ_j, such that $Ax_j = \lambda_j x_j$ for $1 \leq j \leq N$. Prove that each λ_j is either d or $(-1 \pm \sqrt{4d - 3})/2$.

    c) Show that if $\sqrt{4d - 3}$ is irrational, then $d = 2$. *Hint:* $\lambda_1 + \cdots + \lambda_N = \text{trace}(A) = 0$.

    d) And if $\sqrt{4d - 3}$ is rational, $d \in \{3, 7, 57\}$.

66. [*M30*] Continuing exercise 65, construct such a graph when $d = 7$.

67. [*M48*] Is there a regular graph of degree 57, order 3250, and girth 5?

68. [*M20*] How many different adjacency matrices does a graph G on n vertices have?

▶ **69.** [*20*] Extending (31), explain how to calculate both out-degree ODEG(v) and in-degree IDEG(v) for *all* vertices v in a graph that has been represented in SGB format.

▶ **70.** [*M20*] How often is each step of Algorithm B performed, when that algorithm successfully 2-colors a graph with m arcs and n vertices?

71. [*26*] Implement Algorithm B for the MMIX computer, using the MMIXAL assembly language. Assume that, when your program begins, register v0 points to the first vertex node and register n contains the number of vertices.

▶ **72.** [*M22*] When COLOR(v) is set in step B6, call u the *parent* of v; but when COLOR(w) is set in step B3, say that w has no parent. Define the *ancestors* of vertex v, recursively, to be v together with the ancestors of v's parent (if any).

   a) Prove that if v is below u in the stack during Algorithm B, the parent of v is an ancestor of u.

   b) Furthermore, if COLOR(v) = COLOR(u) in step B6, v is currently in the stack.

   c) Use these facts to extend Algorithm B so that, if the given graph is not bipartite, the names of vertices in a cycle of odd length are output.

73. [*15*] What's another name for *random_graph*(10, 45, 0, 0, 0, 0, 0, 0, 0, 0)?

74. [*21*] What vertex of *roget*(1022, 0, 0, 0) has the largest out-degree?

75. [*22*] The SGB graph generator *board*($n_1, n_2, n_3, n_4, p, w, o$) creates a graph whose vertices are the t-dimensional integer vectors $(x_1, \ldots, x_t)$ for $0 \le x_i < b_i$, determined by the first four parameters (n_1, n_2, n_3, n_4) as follows: Set $n_5 \leftarrow 0$ and let $j \ge 0$ be minimum such that $n_{j+1} \le 0$. If $j = 0$, set $b_1 \leftarrow b_2 \leftarrow 8$ and $t \leftarrow 2$; this is the default 8×8 board. Otherwise if $n_{j+1} = 0$, set $b_i \leftarrow n_i$ for $1 \le i \le j$ and $t = j$. Finally, if $n_{j+1} < 0$, set $t \leftarrow |n_{j+1}|$, and set b_i to the ith element of the periodic sequence $(n_1, \ldots, n_j, n_1, \ldots, n_j, n_1, \ldots)$. (For example, the specification $(n_1, n_2, n_3, n_4) = (2, 3, 5, -7)$ is about as tricky as you can get; it produces a 7-dimensional board with $(b_1, \ldots, b_7) = (2, 3, 5, 2, 3, 5, 2)$, hence a graph with $2 \cdot 3 \cdot 5 \cdot 2 \cdot 3 \cdot 5 \cdot 2 = 1800$ vertices.)

   The remaining parameters (p, w, o), for "piece, wrap, and orientation," determine the arcs of the graph. Suppose first that $w = o = 0$. If $p > 0$, we have $(x_1, \ldots, x_t) \longrightarrow (y_1, \ldots, y_t)$ if and only if $y_i = x_i + \delta_i$ for $1 \le i \le t$, where $(\delta_1, \ldots, \delta_t)$ is an integer solution to the equation $\delta_1^2 + \cdots + \delta_t^2 = |p|$. And if $p < 0$, we allow also $y_i = x_i + k\delta_i$ for $k \ge 1$, corresponding to k moves in the same direction.

   If $w \ne 0$, let $w = (w_t \ldots w_1)_2$ in binary notation. Then we allow "wraparound," $y_i = (x_i + \delta_i) \bmod b_i$ or $y_i = (x_i + k\delta_i) \bmod b_i$, in each coordinate i for which $w_i = 1$.

   If $o \ne 0$, the graph is directed; offsets $(\delta_1, \ldots, \delta_t)$ produce arcs only when they are lexicographically greater than $(0, \ldots, 0)$. But if $o = 0$, the graph is undirected.

   Find settings of $(n_1, n_2, n_3, n_4, p, w, o)$ for which *board* will produce the following fundamental graphs: (a) the complete graph K_n; (b) the path P_n; (c) the cycle C_n; (d) the transitive tournament $K_n^{\rightarrow}$; (e) the oriented path $P_n^{\rightarrow}$; (f) the oriented cycle $C_n^{\rightarrow}$; (g) the $m \times n$ grid $P_m \square P_n$; (h) the $m \times n$ cylinder $P_m \square C_n$; (i) the $m \times n$ torus $C_m \square C_n$; (j) the $m \times n$ rook graph $K_m \square K_n$; (k) the $m \times n$ directed torus $C_m^{\rightarrow} \square C_n^{\rightarrow}$; (l) the null graph $\overline{K_n}$; (m) the n-cube $P_2 \square \cdots \square P_2$ with 2^n vertices.

76. [*20*] Can *board*($n_1, n_2, n_3, n_4, p, w, o$) produce loops, or parallel (repeated) edges?

77. [*M20*] If graph G has diameter ≥ 3, prove that $\overline{G}$ has diameter ≤ 3.

78. [*M26*] Let $G = (V, E)$ be a graph with $|V| = n$ and $G \cong \overline{G}$. (In other words, G is *self-complementary*: There's a permutation φ of V such that $u \relbar v$ if and only if $\varphi(u) \not\relbar \varphi(v)$ and $u \neq v$. We can imagine that the edges of K_n have been painted black or white; the white edges define a graph that's isomorphic to the graph of black edges.)

   a) Prove that $n \bmod 4 = 0$ or 1. Draw diagrams for all such graphs with $n < 8$.

   b) Prove that if $n \bmod 4 = 0$, every cycle of the permutation φ has a length that is a multiple of 4.

   c) Conversely, every permutation φ with such cycles arises in some such graph G.

   d) Extend these results to the case $n \bmod 4 = 1$.

▶ **79.** [*M22*] Given $k \geq 0$, construct a graph on the vertices $\{0, 1, \ldots, 4k\}$ that is both regular and self-complementary.

▶ **80.** [*M22*] A self-complementary graph must have diameter 2 or 3, by exercise 77. Given $k \geq 2$, construct self-complementary graphs of both possible diameters, when (a) $V = \{1, 2, \ldots, 4k\}$; (b) $V = \{0, 1, 2, \ldots, 4k\}$.

81. [*20*] The complement of a simple digraph without loops is defined by extending (35) and (36), so that we have $u \to v$ in $\overline{D}$ if and only if $u \neq v$ and $u \not\to v$ in D. What are the self-complementary digraphs of order 3?

82. [*M21*] Are the following statements about line graphs true or false?

   a) If G is contained in G', then $L(G)$ is an induced subgraph of $L(G')$.

   b) If G is a regular graph, so is $L(G)$.

   c) $L(K_{m,n})$ is regular, for all $m, n > 0$.

   d) $L(K_{m,n,r})$ is regular, for all $m, n, r > 0$.

   e) $L(K_{m,n}) \cong K_m \,\square\, K_n$.

   f) $L(K_4) \cong K_{2,2,2}$.

   g) $L(P_{n+1}) \cong P_n$.

   h) The graphs G and $L(G)$ both have the same number of components.

83. [*16*] Draw the graph $\overline{L(K_5)}$.

▶ **84.** [*M21*] Is $L(K_{3,3})$ self-complementary?

85. [*M22*] (O. Ore, 1962.) For which graphs G do we have $G \cong L(G)$?

86. [*M20*] (R. J. Wilson.) Find a graph G of order 6 for which $\overline{G} \cong L(G)$.

87. [*20*] Is the Petersen graph (a) 3-colorable? (b) 3-edge-colorable?

88. [*M20*] The graph $W_n = K_1 \relbar C_{n-1}$ is called the *wheel* of order n, when $n \geq 4$. How many cycles does it contain as subgraphs?

W_8

89. [*M20*] Prove the associative laws, (42) and (43).

▶ **90.** [*M24*] A graph is called a *cograph* if it can be constructed algebraically from 1-element graphs by means of complementation and/or direct sum operations. For example, there are four nonisomorphic graphs of order 3, and they all are cographs: $\overline{K_3} = K_1 \oplus K_1 \oplus K_1$ and its complement, K_3; $\overline{K_{1,2}} = K_1 \oplus K_2$ and its complement, $K_{1,2}$, where $K_2 = \overline{K_1 \oplus K_1}$.

Exhaustive enumeration shows that there are 11 nonisomorphic graphs of order 4. Give algebraic formulas to prove that 10 of them are cographs. Which one isn't?

▶ **91.** [*20*] Draw diagrams for the 4-vertex graphs (a) $K_2 \square K_2$; (b) $K_2 \otimes K_2$; (c) $K_2 \boxtimes K_2$; (d) $K_2 \mathbin{\triangle} K_2$; (e) $K_2 \circ K_2$; (f) $\overline{K_2} \circ K_2$; (g) $K_2 \circ \overline{K_2}$.

92. [*21*] The five types of graph products defined in the text work fine for simple digraphs as well as for ordinary graphs. Draw diagrams for the 4-vertex digraphs (a) $\vec{K_2} \square \vec{K_2}$; (b) $\vec{K_2} \otimes \vec{K_2}$; (c) $\vec{K_2} \boxtimes \vec{K_2}$; (d) $\vec{K_2} \mathbin{\triangle} \vec{K_2}$; (e) $\vec{K_2} \circ \vec{K_2}$.

93. [15] Which of the five graph products takes K_m and K_n into K_{mn}?

94. [10] Are the SGB *words* graphs induced subgraphs of $P_{26} \square P_{26} \square P_{26} \square P_{26} \square P_{26}$?

95. [M20] If vertex u of G has degree d_u and vertex v of H has degree d_v, what is the degree of vertex (u, v) in (a) $G \square H$? (b) $G \otimes H$? (c) $G \boxtimes H$? (d) $G \triangle H$? (e) $G \circ H$?

▶ **96.** [M22] Let A be an $m \times m'$ matrix with $a_{uu'}$ in row u and column u'; let B be an $n \times n'$ matrix with $b_{vv'}$ in row v and column v'. The *direct product* $A \otimes B$ is an $mn \times m'n'$ matrix with $a_{uu'}b_{vv'}$ in row (u, v) and column (u', v'). Thus $A \otimes B$ is the adjacency matrix of $G \otimes H$, if A and B are the adjacency matrices of G and H.

Find analogous formulas for the adjacency matrices of (a) $G \square H$; (b) $G \boxtimes H$; (c) $G \triangle H$; (d) $G \circ H$.

97. [M25] Find as many interesting algebraic relations between graph sums and products as you can. (For example, the distributive law $(A \oplus B) \otimes C = (A \otimes C) \oplus (B \otimes C)$ for direct sums and products of matrices implies that $(G \oplus G') \otimes H = (G \otimes H) \oplus (G' \otimes H)$. We also have $\overline{K_m} \square H = H \oplus \cdots \oplus H$, with m copies of H, etc.)

98. [M20] If the graph G has k components and the graph H has l components, how many components are in the graphs $G \square H$ and $G \boxtimes H$?

99. [M20] Let $d_G(u, u')$ be the distance from vertex u to vertex u' in graph G. Prove that $d_{G \square H}((u, v), (u', v')) = d_G(u, u') + d_H(v, v')$, and find a similar formula for $d_{G \boxtimes H}((u, v), (u', v'))$.

100. [M21] For which connected graphs is $G \otimes H$ connected?

▶ **101.** [M25] Find all connected graphs G and H such that $G \square H \cong G \otimes H$.

102. [M20] What's a simple algebraic formula for the graph of *king moves* (which take one step horizontally, vertically, or diagonally) on an $m \times n$ board?

103. [20] Complete tableau (54). Also apply Algorithm H to the sequence 866444444.

104. [18] Explain the manipulation of variables i, t, and r in steps H3 and H4.

105. [M34] Suppose $d_1 \geq \cdots \geq d_n \geq 0$, and let $c_1 \geq \cdots \geq c_{d_1}$ be its conjugate as in Algorithm H. Prove that $d_1 \ldots d_n$ is graphical if and only if $d_1 + \cdots + d_n$ is even and $d_1 + \cdots + d_k \leq c_1 + \cdots + c_k - k$ for $1 \leq k \leq s$, where s is maximal such that $d_s \geq s$.

106. [20] True or false: If $d_1 = \cdots = d_n = d < n$ and nd is even, Algorithm H constructs a *connected* graph.

107. [M21] Prove that the degree sequence $d_1 \ldots d_n$ of a self-complementary graph satisfies $d_j + d_{n+1-j} = n - 1$ and $d_{2j-1} = d_{2j}$ for $1 \leq j \leq n/2$.

▶ **108.** [M23] Design an algorithm analogous to Algorithm H that constructs a *simple directed graph* on vertices $\{1, \ldots, n\}$, having specified values d_k^- and d_k^+ for the in-degree and out-degree of each vertex k, whenever at least one such graph exists.

109. [M20] Design an algorithm analogous to Algorithm H that constructs a *bipartite graph* on vertices $\{1, \ldots, m + n\}$, having specified degrees d_k for each vertex k when possible; all edges $j \!-\! k$ should have $j \leq m$ and $k > m$.

110. [M22] Without using Algorithm H, show by a direct construction that the sequence $d_1 \ldots d_n$ is graphical when $n > d_1 \geq \cdots \geq d_n \geq d_1 - 1$ and $d_1 + \cdots + d_n$ is even.

▶ **111.** [25] Let G be a graph on vertices $V = \{1, \ldots, n\}$, with d_k the degree of k and $\max(d_1, \ldots, d_n) = d$. Prove that there's an integer N with $n \leq N \leq 2n$ and a graph H on vertices $\{1, \ldots, N\}$, such that H is regular of degree d and $H \,|\, V = G$. Explain how to construct such a regular graph with N as small as possible.

▶ **112.** [*20*] Does the network $miles(128, 0, 0, 0, 0, 127, 0)$ have three equidistant cities? If not, what three cities come closest to an equilateral triangle?

113. [*05*] When H is a hypergraph with m edges and n vertices, how many rows and columns does its incidence matrix have?

114. [*M20*] Suppose the multigraph (26) is regarded as a hypergraph. What is the corresponding incidence matrix? What is the corresponding bipartite graph?

▶ **115.** [*M20*] When B is the incidence matrix of a graph G, explain the significance of the symmetric matrices $B^T B$ and BB^T.

116. [*M17*] Describe the edges of the complete bipartite r-uniform hypergraph $K_{m,n}^{(r)}$.

117. [*M22*] How many nonisomorphic 1-uniform hypergraphs have m edges and n vertices? (Edges may be repeated.) List them all when $m = 4$ and $n = 3$.

118. [*M20*] A "hyperforest" is a hypergraph that contains no cycles. If a hyperforest has m edges, n vertices, and p components, what's the sum of the degrees of its vertices?

119. [*M18*] What hypergraph corresponds to (60) without the final term $(\bar{x}_1 \vee \bar{x}_2 \vee \bar{x}_3)$?

120. [*M20*] Define *directed hypergraphs*, by generalizing the concept of directed graphs.

121. [*M19*] Given a hypergraph $H = (V, E)$, let $I(H) = (V, F)$, where F is the family of all maximal independent sets of H. Express $\chi(H)$ in terms of $|V|$, $|F|$, and $\alpha(I(H)^T)$.

▶ **122.** [*M24*] Find a maximum independent set and a minimum coloring of the following triple systems: (a) the hypergraph (56); (b) the dual of the Petersen graph.

123. [*17*] Show that the optimum colorings of $K_n \square K_n$ are equivalent to the solutions of a famous combinatorial problem.

124. [*M22*] What is the chromatic number of the Chvátal graph, Fig. 2(f)?

125. [*M48*] For what values of g is there a 4-regular, 4-chromatic graph of girth g?

▶ **126.** [*M22*] Find optimum colorings of the "kingwise torus," $C_m \boxtimes C_n$, when $m, n \geq 3$.

127. [*M22*] Prove that (a) $\chi(G) + \chi(\overline{G}) \leq n + 1$ and (b) $\chi(G)\chi(\overline{G}) \geq n$ when G is a graph of order n, and find graphs for which equality holds.

128. [*M18*] Express $\chi(G \square H)$ in terms of $\chi(G)$ and $\chi(H)$, when G and H are graphs.

129. [*23*] Describe the maximal cliques of the 8×8 queen graph (37).

130. [*M20*] How many maximal cliques are in a complete k-partite graph?

131. [*M30*] Let $N(n)$ be the largest number of maximal cliques that an n-vertex graph can have. Prove that $3^{\lfloor n/3 \rfloor} \leq N(n) \leq 3^{\lceil n/3 \rceil}$.

▶ **132.** [*M20*] We call G *tightly colorable* if $\chi(G) = \omega(G)$. Prove that $\chi(G \boxtimes H) = \chi(G)\chi(H)$ whenever G and H are tightly colorable.

133. [*21*] The "musical graph" illustrated here provides a nice way to review numerous definitions that were given in this section, because its properties are easily analyzed. Determine its (a) order; (b) size; (c) girth; (d) diameter; (e) independence number, $\alpha(G)$; (f) chromatic number, $\chi(G)$; (g) edge-chromatic number, $\chi(L(G))$; (h) clique number, $\omega(G)$; (i) algebraic formula as a product of well-known smaller graphs. What is the size of (j) a minimum vertex cover? (k) a maximum matching? Is G (l) regular? (m) planar? (n) connected? (o) directed? (p) a free tree? (q) Hamiltonian?

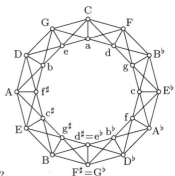

134. [*M22*] How many automorphisms does the musical graph have?

▶ **135.** [*HM26*] Suppose a composer takes a random walk in the musical graph, starting at vertex C and then making five equally likely choices at each step. Show that after an even number of steps, the walk is more likely to end at vertex C than at any other vertex. What is the exact probability of going from C to C in a 12-step walk?

136. [*HM23*] A *Cayley digraph* is a directed graph whose vertices V are the elements of a group and whose arcs are $v \longrightarrow v\alpha_j$ for $1 \le j \le d$ and all vertices v, where $(\alpha_1, \ldots, \alpha_d)$ are fixed elements of the group. A *Cayley graph* is a Cayley digraph that is also a graph. Is the Petersen graph a Cayley graph?

```
 8 11  2  5  8 11  2  5  8 11  2  5            7           7           7
 4  7 10  1  4  7 10  1  4  7 10  1            3           3           3
 0  3  6  9  0  3  6  9  0  3  6  9       8 11  2  5  8 11  2  5  8 11  2  5
 8 11  2  5  8 11  2  5  8 11  2  5       1  4  7 10  1  4  7 10  1  4  7 10
 4  7 10  1  4  7 10  1  4  7 10  1          3  6  9  0  3  6  9  0  3  6  9  0
 0  3  6  9  0  3  6  9  0  3  6  9       8 11  2  5  8 11  2  5  8 11  2  5
 8 11  2  5  8 11  2  5  8 11  2  5       1  4  7 10  1  4  7 10  1  4  7 10
 4  7 10  1  4  7 10  1  4  7 10  1          3  6  9  0  3  6  9  0  3  6  9  0
 0  3  6  9  0  3  6  9  0  3  6  9       8 11  2  5  8 11  2  5  8 11  2  5
                                          1  4        10  1  4       10  1  4       10
                                                 6  9  0        6  9  0        6  9  0
```

▶ **137.** [*M25*] (*Generalized toruses.*) An $m \times n$ torus can be regarded as a tiling of the plane. For example, we can imagine that infinitely many copies of the 3×4 torus in (50) have been placed together gridwise, as indicated in the left-hand illustration above; from each vertex we can move north, south, east, or west to another vertex of the torus. The vertices have been numbered here so that a northward move from v goes to $(v+4) \bmod 12$, and an eastward move to $(v+3) \bmod 12$, etc. The right-hand illustration shows the same torus, but with a differently shaped tile; *any* way to choose twelve cells numbered $\{0, 1, \ldots, 11\}$ will tile the plane, with exactly the same underlying graph.

Shifted copies of a single shape will also tile the plane if they form a *generalized torus*, in which cell (x, y) corresponds to the same vertex as cells $(x + a, y + b)$ and $(x + c, y + d)$, where (a, b) and (c, d) are integer vectors and $n = ad - bc > 0$. The generalized torus will then have n points. These vectors (a, b) and (c, d) are $(4, 0)$ and $(0, 3)$ in the 3×4 example above; and when they are respectively $(5, 2)$ and $(1, 3)$ we get

```
                   9 10 11 12
                4  5  6  7  8  9 10 11 12
          9 10 11 12  0  1  2  3  4  5  6  7  8
          4  5  6  7  8  9 10 11 12  0  1  2  3
          0  1  2  3  4  5  6  7  8  9 10 11 12          .
          9 10 11 12  0  1  2  3  4  5  6  7  8
          4  5  6  7  8  9 10 11 12  0  1  2  3
          0  1  2  3  4  5  6  7  8
                   0  1  2  3
```

Here $n = 13$, and a northward move from v goes to $(v + 4) \bmod 13$; an eastward move goes to $(v + 1) \bmod 13$.

Prove that if $\gcd(a, b, c, d) = 1$, the vertices of such a generalized torus can always be assigned integer labels $\{0, 1, \ldots, n-1\}$ in such a way that the neighbors of v are $(v \pm p) \bmod n$ and $(v \pm q) \bmod n$, for some integers p and q.

138. [*HM27*] Continuing exercise 137, what is a good way to label k-dimensional vertices $x = (x_1, \ldots, x_k)$, when integer vectors α_j are given such that each vector x is equivalent to $x + \alpha_j$ for $1 \le j \le k$? Illustrate your method in the case $k = 3$, $\alpha_1 = (3, 1, 1)$, $\alpha_2 = (1, 3, 1)$, $\alpha_3 = (1, 1, 3)$.

▶ **139.** [*M22*] Let H be a fixed graph of order h, and let $\#(H{:}G)$ be the number of times that H occurs as an induced subgraph of a given graph G. If G is chosen at random from the set of all $2^{n(n-1)/2}$ graphs on the vertices $V = \{1, 2, \ldots, n\}$, what is the average value of $\#(H{:}G)$ when H is (a) K_h; (b) P_h, for $h > 1$; (c) C_h, for $h > 2$; (d) arbitrary?

140. [*M30*] A graph G is called *proportional* if its induced subgraph counts $\#(K_3{:}G)$, $\#(\overline{K_3}{:}G)$, and $\#(P_3{:}G)$ each agree with the expected values derived in exercise 139.

a) Show that the wheel graph W_8 of exercise 88 is proportional in this sense.

b) Prove that G is proportional if and only if $\#(K_3{:}G) = \frac{1}{8}\binom{n}{3}$ and the degree sequence $d_1 \ldots d_n$ of its vertices satisfies the identities

$$d_1 + \cdots + d_n = \binom{n}{2}, \qquad d_1^2 + \cdots + d_n^2 = \frac{n}{2}\binom{n}{2}. \qquad (*)$$

141. [*26*] The conditions of exercise 140(b) can hold only if $n \bmod 16 \in \{0, 1, 8\}$. Write a program to find all of the proportional graphs that have $n = 8$ vertices.

142. [*M30*] (S. Janson and J. Kratochvíl, 1991.) Prove that no graph G on 4 or more vertices can be "extraproportional," in the sense that its subgraph counts $\#(H{:}G)$ agree with the expected values in exercise 139 for each of the eleven nonisomorphic graphs H of order 4. *Hint:* $(n - 3)\#(K_3{:}G) = 4\#(K_4{:}G) + 2\#(K_{1,1,2}{:}G) + \#(K_1 \oplus K_3{:}G)$.

▶ **143.** [*M25*] Let A be any matrix with $m > 1$ distinct rows, and $n \ge m$ columns. Prove that at least one column of A can be deleted, without making any two rows equal.

▶ **144.** [*21*] Let X be an $m \times n$ matrix whose entries x_{ij} are either 0, 1, or $*$. A "completion" of X is a matrix X^* in which every $*$ has been replaced by either 0 or 1. Show that the problem of finding a completion with fewest distinct rows is equivalent to the problem of finding the chromatic number of a graph.

▶ **145.** [*25*] (R. S. Boyer and J. S. Moore, 1980.) Suppose the array $a_1 \ldots a_n$ contains a *majority element*, namely a value that occurs more than $n/2$ times. Design an algorithm that finds it after making fewer than n comparisons. *Hint:* If $n \ge 3$ and $a_{n-1} \ne a_n$, the majority element of $a_1 \ldots a_n$ is also the majority element of $a_1 \ldots a_{n-2}$.

Yet now and then your men of wit
Will condescend to take a bit.

— JONATHAN SWIFT, *Cadenus and Vanessa* (1713)

If the base 2 is used the resulting units may be called binary digits,
or more briefly bits, *a word suggested by J. W. Tukey.*

— CLAUDE E. SHANNON, in *Bell System Technical Journal* (1948)

bit (bit), n ... *[A] boring tool ...*
— *Random House Dictionary of the English Language* (1987)

7.1. ZEROS AND ONES

COMBINATORIAL ALGORITHMS often require special attention to efficiency, and the proper representation of data is an important way to gain the necessary speed. It is therefore wise to beef up our knowledge of elementary representation techniques before we set out to study combinatorial algorithms in detail.

Most of today's computers are based on the binary number system, instead of working directly with the decimal numbers that human beings prefer, because machines are especially good at dealing with the two-state on-off quantities that we usually denote by the digits 0 and 1. But in Chapters 1 to 6 we haven't made much use of the fact that binary computers can do several things quickly that decimal computers cannot. A binary machine can usually perform "logical" or "bitwise" operations just as easily as it can add or subtract; yet we have seldom capitalized on that capability. We've seen that binary and decimal computers are not significantly different, for many purposes, but in a sense we've been asking a binary computer to operate with one hand tied behind its back.

The amazing ability of 0s and 1s to encode information as well as to encode the logical relations between items, and even to encode algorithms for processing information, makes the study of binary digits especially rich. Indeed, we not only use bitwise operations to enhance combinatorial algorithms, we also find that the properties of binary logic lead naturally to new combinatorial problems that are of great interest in their own right.

Computer scientists have gradually become better and better at taming the wild 0s and 1s of the universe and making them do useful tricks. But as bit players on the world's stage, we'd better have a thorough understanding of the low-level properties of binary quantities before we launch into a study of higher-level concepts and techniques. Therefore we shall start by investigating basic ways to combine individual bits and sequences of bits.

7.1.1. Boolean Basics

There are 16 possible functions $f(x, y)$ that transform two given bits x and y into a third bit $z = f(x, y)$, since there are two choices for each of $f(0, 0)$, $f(0, 1)$, $f(1, 0)$, and $f(1, 1)$. Table 1 indicates the names and notations that have traditionally been associated with these functions in studies of formal logic, assuming that 1 corresponds to "true" and 0 to "false." The sequence of four values $f(0, 0)f(0, 1)f(1, 0)f(1, 1)$ is customarily called the *truth table* of the function f.

Let us conceive, then, of an Algebra
in which the symbols x, y, z, &c. admit indifferently of
the values 0 and 1, and of these values alone.
— GEORGE BOOLE, *An Investigation of the Laws of Thought* (1854)

'Contrariwise,' continued Tweedledee, 'if it was so, it might be;
and if it were so, it would be;
but as it isn't, it ain't. That's logic.'
— LEWIS CARROLL, *Through the Looking Glass* (1871)

Such functions are often called "Boolean operations" in honor of George Boole, who first discovered that algebraic operations on 0s and 1s could be used to construct a calculus for logical reasoning [*The Mathematical Analysis of Logic* (Cambridge: 1847); *An Investigation of the Laws of Thought* (London: 1854)]. But Boole never actually dealt with the "logical or" operation ∨; he confined himself strictly to ordinary arithmetic operations on 0s and 1s. Thus he would write $x + y$ to stand for disjunction, but he took pains never to use this notation unless x and y were mutually exclusive (not both 1). If necessary, he wrote $x + (1-x)y$ to ensure that the result of a disjunction would never be equal to 2.

When rendering the + operation in English, Boole sometimes called it "and," sometimes "or." This practice may seem strange to modern mathematicians until we realize that his usage was in fact normal English; we say, for example, that "boys and girls are children," but "children are boys or girls."

Boole's calculus was extended to include the unconventional rule $x + x = x$ by W. Stanley Jevons [*Pure Logic* (London: Edward Stanford, 1864), §69], who pointed out that $(x + y)z$ was equal to $xz + yz$ using his new + operation. But Jevons did not know the other distributive law $xy+z = (x+z)(y+z)$. Presumably he missed this because of the notation he was using, since the second distributive law has no familiar counterpart in arithmetic; the more symmetrical notations $x \wedge y$, $x \vee y$ in Table 1 make it easier for us to remember both distributive laws

$$(x \vee y) \wedge z = (x \wedge z) \vee (y \wedge z); \tag{1}$$

$$(x \wedge y) \vee z = (x \vee z) \wedge (y \vee z). \tag{2}$$

The second law (2) was introduced by C. S. Peirce, who had discovered independently how to extend Boole's calculus [*Proc. Amer. Acad. Arts and Sciences* **7** (1867), 250–261]. Incidentally, when Peirce discussed these early developments several years later [*Amer. J. Math.* **3** (1880), 32], he referred to "the Boolian algebra, with Jevons's addition"; his now-unfamiliar spelling of "Boolean" was in use for many years, appearing in the Funk and Wagnalls unabridged dictionary as late as 1963.

The notion of truth-value combination is actually much older than Boolean algebra. Indeed, propositional logic had been developed by Greek philosophers already in the fourth century B.C. There was considerable debate in those days about how to assign an appropriate true-or-false value to the proposition "if x then y" when x and y are propositions; Philo of Megara, about 300 B.C., defined

Table 1

THE SIXTEEN LOGICAL OPERATIONS ON TWO VARIABLES

Truth table	Notation(s)	Operator symbol ∘	Name(s)
0000	0	$\perp$	Contradiction; falsehood; antilogy; constant 0
0001	$xy,\ x \wedge y,\ x \,\&\, y$	$\wedge$	Conjunction; and
0010	$x \wedge \bar{y},\ x \not\supset y,\ [x > y],\ x \mathbin{\dot-} y$	$\bar\supset$	Nonimplication; difference; but not
0011	x	L	Left projection
0100	$\bar{x} \wedge y,\ x \not\subset y,\ [x < y],\ y \mathbin{\dot-} x$	$\bar\subset$	Converse nonimplication; not ... but
0101	y	R	Right projection
0110	$x \oplus y,\ x \not\equiv y,\ x {}^{\wedge} y$	$\oplus$	Exclusive disjunction; nonequivalence; "xor"
0111	$x \vee y,\ x \mid y$	$\vee$	(Inclusive) disjunction; or; and/or
1000	$\bar{x} \wedge \bar{y},\ \overline{x \vee y},\ x \,\bar\vee\, y,\ x \downarrow y$	$\bar\vee$	Nondisjunction; joint denial; neither ... nor
1001	$x \equiv y,\ x \leftrightarrow y,\ x \Leftrightarrow y$	$\equiv$	Equivalence; if and only if; "iff"
1010	$\bar{y},\ \neg y,\ !y,\ \sim y$	$\bar{\mathsf{R}}$	Right complementation
1011	$x \vee \bar{y},\ x \subset y,\ x \Leftarrow y,\ [x \geq y],\ x^{y}$	$\subset$	Converse implication; if
1100	$\bar{x},\ \neg x,\ !x,\ \sim x$	$\bar{\mathsf{L}}$	Left complementation
1101	$\bar{x} \vee y,\ x \supset y,\ x \Rightarrow y,\ [x \leq y],\ y^{x}$	$\supset$	Implication; only if; if ... then
1110	$\bar{x} \vee \bar{y},\ \overline{x \wedge y},\ x \,\bar\wedge\, y,\ x \mid y$	$\bar\wedge$	Nonconjunction; not both ... and; "nand"
1111	1	$\top$	Affirmation; validity; tautology; constant 1

it by the truth table shown in Table 1, which states in particular that the implication is true when both x and y are false. Much of this early work has been lost, but there are passages in the works of Galen (2nd century A.D.) that refer to both inclusive and exclusive disjunction of propositions. [See I. M. Bocheński, *Formale Logik* (1956), English translation by Ivo Thomas (1961), for an excellent survey of the development of logic from ancient times up to the 20th century.]

A function of two variables is often written $x \circ y$ instead of $f(x, y)$, using some appropriate operator symbol $\circ$. Table 1 shows the sixteen operator symbols that we shall adopt for Boolean functions of two variables; for example, $\perp$ symbolizes the function whose truth table is 0000, $\wedge$ is the symbol for 0001, $\bar\supset$ is the symbol for 0010, and so on. We have $x \perp y = 0$, $x \wedge y = xy$, $x \bar\supset y = x \mathbin{\dot-} y$, $x \mathsf{L} y = x$, $\ldots$, $x \bar\wedge y = \bar{x} \vee \bar{y}$, $x \top y = 1$.

Of course the operations in Table 1 aren't all of equal importance. For example, the first and last cases are trivial, since they have a constant value independent of x and y. Four of them are functions of x alone or y alone. We write $\bar{x}$ for $1 - x$, the *complement* of x.

The four operations whose truth table contains just a single 1 are easily expressed in terms of the AND operator $\wedge$, namely $x \wedge y$, $x \wedge \bar{y}$, $\bar{x} \wedge y$, $\bar{x} \wedge \bar{y}$. Those with three 1s are easily written in terms of the OR operator $\vee$, namely $x \vee y$, $x \vee \bar{y}$, $\bar{x} \vee y$, $\bar{x} \vee \bar{y}$. The basic functions $x \wedge y$ and $x \vee y$ have proved to be more useful in practice than their complemented or half-complemented cousins, although the NOR and NAND operations $x \bar\vee y = \bar{x} \wedge \bar{y}$ and $x \bar\wedge y = \bar{x} \vee \bar{y}$ are also of interest because they are easily implemented in transistor circuits.

In 1913, H. M. Sheffer showed that all 16 of the functions can be expressed in terms of just one, starting with either $\bar{\vee}$ or $\bar{\wedge}$ as the given operation (see exercise 4). Actually C. S. Peirce had made the same discovery about 1880, but his work on the subject remained unpublished until after his death [*Collected Papers of Charles Sanders Peirce* **4** (1933), §§12–20, 264]. Table 1 indicates that NAND and NOR have occasionally been written $x \mid y$ and $x \downarrow y$; sometimes they have been called "Sheffer's stroke" and the "Peirce arrow." Nowadays it is best *not* to use Sheffer's vertical line for NAND, because $x \mid y$ denotes bitwise $x \vee y$ in programming languages like C.

So far we have discussed all but two of the functions in Table 1. The remaining two are $x \equiv y$ and $x \oplus y$, "equivalence" and "exclusive-or," which are related by the identities

$$x \equiv y \;=\; \bar{x} \oplus y \;=\; x \oplus \bar{y} \;=\; 1 \oplus x \oplus y; \tag{3}$$

$$x \oplus y \;=\; \bar{x} \equiv y \;=\; x \equiv \bar{y} \;=\; 0 \equiv x \equiv y. \tag{4}$$

Both operations are associative (see exercise 6). In propositional logic, the notion of equivalence is more important than the notion of exclusive-or, which means inequivalence; but when we consider bitwise operations on full computer words, we shall see in Section 7.1.3 that the situation is reversed: Exclusive-or turns out to be more useful than equivalence, in typical programs. The chief reason why $x \oplus y$ has significant applications, even in the one-bit case, is the fact that

$$x \oplus y \;=\; (x + y) \bmod 2. \tag{5}$$

Therefore $x \oplus y$ and $x \wedge y$ denote addition and multiplication in the field of two elements (see Section 4.6), and $x \oplus y$ naturally inherits many "clean" mathematical properties.

Basic identities. Now let's take a look at interactions between the fundamental operators $\wedge$, $\vee$, $\oplus$, and $\bar{}$, since the other operations are easily expressed in terms of these four. Each of $\wedge$, $\vee$, $\oplus$ is associative and commutative. Besides the distributive laws (1) and (2), we also have

$$(x \oplus y) \wedge z \;=\; (x \wedge z) \oplus (y \wedge z), \tag{6}$$

as well as the *absorption laws*

$$(x \wedge y) \vee x \;=\; (x \vee y) \wedge x \;=\; x. \tag{7}$$

One of the simplest, yet most useful, identities is

$$x \oplus x \;=\; 0, \tag{8}$$

since it implies among other things that

$$(x \oplus y) \oplus x \;=\; y, \qquad (x \oplus y) \oplus y \;=\; x, \tag{9}$$

when we use the obvious fact that $x \oplus 0 = x$. In other words, given $x \oplus y$ and either x or y, it is easy to determine the other. And let us not overlook the simple *complementation law*

$$\bar{x} \;=\; x \oplus 1. \tag{10}$$

Another important pair of identities is known as *De Morgan's laws* in honor of Augustus De Morgan, who stated that "The contrary of an aggregate is the compound of the contraries of the aggregants; the contrary of a compound is the aggregate of the contraries of the components. Thus (A, B) and AB have ab and (a, b) for contraries." [*Trans. Cambridge Philos. Soc.* **10** (1858), 208.] In more modern notation, these are the rules we have implicitly derived via truth tables in connection with the operations NAND and NOR in Table 1, namely

$$\overline{x \wedge y} = \bar{x} \vee \bar{y}; \tag{11}$$

$$\overline{x \vee y} = \bar{x} \wedge \bar{y}. \tag{12}$$

Incidentally, W. S. Jevons knew (12) but not (11); he consistently wrote $\bar{A}B + \bar{B}A + \bar{A}\bar{B}$ instead of $\bar{A} + \bar{B}$ for the complement of AB. Yet De Morgan was not the first Englishman who enunciated the laws above. Both (11) and (12) can be found in the early 14th century writings of two scholastic philosophers, William of Ockham [*Summa Logicæ* **2** (1323)] and Walter Burley [*De Puritate Artis Logicæ* (c. 1330)].

De Morgan's laws and a few other identities can be used to express $\wedge$, $\vee$, and $\oplus$ in terms of each other:

$$x \wedge y = \overline{\bar{x} \vee \bar{y}} = x \oplus y \oplus (x \vee y); \tag{13}$$

$$x \vee y = \overline{\bar{x} \wedge \bar{y}} = x \oplus y \oplus (x \wedge y); \tag{14}$$

$$x \oplus y = (x \vee y) \wedge \overline{x \wedge y} = (x \wedge \bar{y}) \vee (\bar{x} \wedge y). \tag{15}$$

According to exercise 7.1.2–77, all computations of $x_1 \oplus x_2 \oplus \cdots \oplus x_n$ that use only the operations $\wedge$, $\vee$, and $^-$ must be at least $4(n - 1)$ steps long; thus, the other three operations are not an especially good substitute for $\oplus$.

Functions of n variables. A Boolean function $f(x, y, z)$ of three Boolean variables x, y, z can be defined by its 8-bit truth table $f(0, 0, 0)f(0, 0, 1) \ldots f(1, 1, 1)$; and in general, every n-ary Boolean function $f(x_1, \ldots, x_n)$ corresponds to a 2^n-bit truth table that lists the successive values of $f(0, \ldots, 0, 0)$, $f(0, \ldots, 0, 1)$, $f(0, \ldots, 1, 0)$, $\ldots$, $f(1, \ldots, 1, 1)$.

We needn't devise special names and notations for all these functions, since they can all be expressed in terms of the binary functions that we've already learned. For example, as observed by I. I. Zhegalkin [*Matematicheskiĭ Sbornik* **35** (1928), 311–369], we can always write

$$f(x_1, \ldots, x_n) = g(x_1, \ldots, x_{n-1}) \oplus h(x_1, \ldots, x_{n-1}) \wedge x_n \tag{16}$$

when $n > 0$, for appropriate functions g and h, by letting

$$\begin{aligned} g(x_1, \ldots, x_{n-1}) &= f(x_1, \ldots, x_{n-1}, 0); \\ h(x_1, \ldots, x_{n-1}) &= f(x_1, \ldots, x_{n-1}, 0) \oplus f(x_1, \ldots, x_{n-1}, 1). \end{aligned} \tag{17}$$

(The operation $\wedge$ conventionally takes precedence over $\oplus$, so we need not use parentheses to enclose the subformula '$h(x_1, \ldots, x_{n-1}) \wedge x_n$' on the right-hand side of (16).) Repeating this process recursively on g and h until we're down to

0-ary functions leaves us with an expression that involves only the operators $\oplus$, $\wedge$, and a sequence of 2^n constants. Furthermore, those constants can usually be simplified away, because we have

$$x \wedge 0 = 0 \qquad \text{and} \qquad x \wedge 1 = x \oplus 0 = x. \qquad (18)$$

After applying the associative and distributive laws, we end up needing the constant 0 only if $f(x_1, \ldots, x_n)$ is identically zero, and the constant 1 only if $f(0, \ldots, 0) = 1$.

We might have, for instance,

$$\begin{aligned}
f(x, y, z) &= \big((1 \oplus 0 \wedge x) \oplus (0 \oplus 1 \wedge x) \wedge y\big) \oplus \big((0 \oplus 1 \wedge x) \oplus (1 \oplus 1 \wedge x) \wedge y\big) \wedge z \\
&= (1 \oplus x \wedge y) \oplus (x \oplus y \oplus x \wedge y) \wedge z \\
&= 1 \oplus x \wedge y \oplus x \wedge z \oplus y \wedge z \oplus x \wedge y \wedge z.
\end{aligned}$$

And by rule (5), we see that we're simply left with the polynomial

$$f(x, y, z) = (1 + xy + xz + yz + xyz) \bmod 2, \qquad (19)$$

because $x \wedge y = xy$. Notice that this polynomial is linear (of degree ≤ 1) in each of its variables. In general, a similar calculation will show that *any* Boolean function $f(x_1, \ldots, x_n)$ has a unique representation such as this, called its *multilinear representation*, which is a sum (modulo 2) of zero or more of the 2^n possible terms 1, x_1, x_2, $x_1 x_2$, x_3, $x_1 x_3$, $x_2 x_3$, $x_1 x_2 x_3$, $\ldots$, $x_1 x_2 \ldots x_n$.

George Boole decomposed Boolean functions in a different way, which is often simpler for the kinds of functions that arise in practice. Instead of (16), he essentially wrote

$$f(x_1, \ldots, x_n) = \big(g(x_1, \ldots, x_{n-1}) \wedge \bar{x}_n\big) \vee \big(h(x_1, \ldots, x_{n-1}) \wedge x_n\big) \qquad (20)$$

and called it the "law of development," where we now have simply

$$\begin{aligned}
g(x_1, \ldots, x_{n-1}) &= f(x_1, \ldots, x_{n-1}, 0), \\
h(x_1, \ldots, x_{n-1}) &= f(x_1, \ldots, x_{n-1}, 1),
\end{aligned} \qquad (21)$$

instead of (17). Repeatedly iterating Boole's procedure, using the distributive law (1), and eliminating constants, leaves us with a formula that is a disjunction of zero or more *minterms*, where each minterm is a conjunction such as $x_1 \wedge \bar{x}_2 \wedge \bar{x}_3 \wedge x_4 \wedge x_5$ in which every variable or its complement is present. Notice that a minterm is a Boolean function that is true at exactly one point.

For example, let's consider the more-or-less random function $f(w, x, y, z)$ whose truth table is

$$1100\ 1001\ 0000\ 1111. \qquad (22)$$

When this function is expanded by repeatedly applying Boole's law (20), we get a disjunction of eight minterms, one for each of the 1s in the truth table:

$$\begin{aligned}
f(w, x, y, z) = {} &(\bar{w} \wedge \bar{x} \wedge \bar{y} \wedge \bar{z}) \vee (\bar{w} \wedge \bar{x} \wedge \bar{y} \wedge z) \vee (\bar{w} \wedge x \wedge \bar{y} \wedge \bar{z}) \vee (\bar{w} \wedge x \wedge y \wedge z) \\
&\vee (w \wedge x \wedge \bar{y} \wedge \bar{z}) \vee (w \wedge x \wedge \bar{y} \wedge z) \vee (w \wedge x \wedge y \wedge \bar{z}) \vee (w \wedge x \wedge y \wedge z). \quad (23)
\end{aligned}$$

In general, a disjunction of minterms is called a *full disjunctive normal form*. Every Boolean function can be expressed in this way, and the result is unique — except, of course, for the order of the minterms. *Nitpick:* A special case arises when $f(x_1, \ldots, x_n)$ is identically zero. We consider '0' to be an empty disjunction, with no terms, and we also consider '1' to be an empty conjunction, for the same reasons as we defined $\sum_{k=1}^{0} a_k = 0$ and $\prod_{k=1}^{0} a_k = 1$ in Section 1.2.3.

C. S. Peirce observed, in *Amer. J. Math.* **3** (1880), 37–39, that every Boolean function also has a *full conjunctive normal form*, which is a conjunction of "min-clauses" like $\bar{x}_1 \vee x_2 \vee \bar{x}_3 \vee \bar{x}_4 \vee x_5$. A minclause is 0 at only one point; so each clause in such a conjunction accounts for a place where the truth table has a 0. For example, the full conjunctive normal form of our function in (22) and (23) is

$$f(w,x,y,z) \;=\; (w \vee x \vee \bar{y} \vee z) \wedge (w \vee x \vee \bar{y} \vee \bar{z}) \wedge (w \vee \bar{x} \vee y \vee \bar{z}) \wedge (w \vee \bar{x} \vee \bar{y} \vee z)$$

$$\wedge \, (\bar{w} \vee x \vee y \vee z) \wedge (\bar{w} \vee x \vee y \vee \bar{z}) \wedge (\bar{w} \vee x \vee \bar{y} \vee z) \wedge (\bar{w} \vee x \vee \bar{y} \vee \bar{z}). \quad (24)$$

Not surprisingly, however, we often want to work with disjunctions and conjunctions that *don't* necessarily involve full minterms or minclauses. Therefore, following nomenclature introduced by Paul Bernays in his *Habilitationsschrift* (1918), we speak in general of a *disjunctive normal form* or "DNF" as *any* disjunction of conjunctions,

$$\bigvee_{j=1}^{m} \bigwedge_{k=1}^{s_j} u_{jk} \;=\; (u_{11} \wedge \cdots \wedge u_{1s_1}) \vee \cdots \vee (u_{m1} \wedge \cdots \wedge u_{ms_m}), \quad (25)$$

where each u_{jk} is a *literal*, namely a variable x_i or its complement. Similarly, any conjunction of disjunctions of literals,

$$\bigwedge_{j=1}^{m} \bigvee_{k=1}^{s_j} u_{jk} \;=\; (u_{11} \vee \cdots \vee u_{1s_1}) \wedge \cdots \wedge (u_{m1} \vee \cdots \vee u_{ms_m}), \quad (26)$$

is called a *conjunctive normal form*, or "CNF" for short.

A great many electrical circuits embedded inside today's computer chips are composed of "programmable logic arrays" (PLAs), which are ORs of ANDs of possibly complemented input signals. In other words, a PLA basically computes one or more disjunctive normal forms. Such building blocks are fast, versatile, and relatively inexpensive; and indeed, DNFs have played a prominent role in electrical engineering ever since the 1950s, when switching circuits were implemented with comparatively old-fashioned devices like relays or vacuum tubes. Therefore people have long been interested in finding the simplest DNFs for classes of Boolean functions, and we can expect that an understanding of disjunctive normal forms will continue to be important as technology continues to evolve.

The terms of a DNF are often called *implicants*, because the truth of any term in a disjunction implies the truth of the whole formula. In a formula like

$$f(x,y,z) \;=\; (x \wedge \bar{y} \wedge z) \vee (y \wedge z) \vee (\bar{x} \wedge y \wedge \bar{z}),$$

for example, we know that f is true when $x \wedge \bar{y} \wedge z$ is true, namely when $(x, y, z) = (1, 0, 1)$. But notice that in this example the shorter term $x \wedge z$ also turns out to be an implicant of f, even though not written explicitly, because the additional term $y \wedge z$ makes the function true whenever $x = z = 1$, regardless of the value of y. Similarly, $\bar{x} \wedge y$ is an implicant of this particular function. So we might as well work with the simpler formula

$$f(x, y, z) = (x \wedge z) \vee (y \wedge z) \vee (\bar{x} \wedge y). \tag{27}$$

At this point no more deletions are possible within the implicants, because neither x nor y nor z nor $\bar{x}$ is a strong enough condition to imply the truth of f.

An implicant that can't be factored further by removing any of its literals without making it too weak is called a *prime implicant*, following the terminology of W. V. Quine in *AMM* **59** (1952), 521–531.

These basic concepts can perhaps be understood most easily if we simplify the notation and adopt a more geometric viewpoint. We can write simply '$f(x)$' instead of $f(x_1, \ldots, x_n)$, and regard x as a vector, or as a binary string $x_1 \ldots x_n$ of length n. For example, the strings $wxyz$ where the function of (22) is true are

$$\{0000, 0001, 0100, 0111, 1100, 1101, 1110, 1111\}, \tag{28}$$

and we can think of them as eight points in the 4-dimensional hypercube $2 \times 2 \times 2 \times 2$. The eight points in (28) correspond to the minterm implicants that are explicitly present in the full disjunctive normal form (23); but none of those implicants is actually prime. For example, the first two points of (28) make the subcube 000∗, and the last four points constitute the subcube 11∗∗, if we use asterisks to denote "wild cards" as we did when discussing database queries in Section 6.5; therefore $\bar{w} \wedge \bar{x} \wedge \bar{y}$ is an implicant of f, and so is $w \wedge x$. Similarly, we can see that the subcube 0∗00 accounts for two of the eight points in (28), making $\bar{w} \wedge \bar{y} \wedge \bar{z}$ an implicant.

In general, each prime implicant corresponds in this way to a *maximal* subcube that stays within the set of points that make f true. (The subcube is maximal in the sense that it isn't contained in any larger subcube with the same property; we can't replace any of its explicit bits by an asterisk. A maximal subcube has a maximal number of asterisks, hence a minimal number of constrained coordinates, hence a minimal number of variables in the corresponding implicant.) The maximal subcubes of the eight points in (28) are

$$000∗, 0∗00, ∗100, ∗111, 11∗∗; \tag{29}$$

so the prime implicants of the function $f(w, x, y, z)$ in (23) are

$$(\bar{w} \wedge \bar{x} \wedge \bar{y}) \vee (\bar{w} \wedge \bar{y} \wedge \bar{z}) \vee (x \wedge \bar{y} \wedge \bar{z}) \vee (x \wedge y \wedge z) \vee (w \wedge x). \tag{30}$$

The *disjunctive prime form* of a Boolean function is the disjunction of all its prime implicants. Exercise 30 contains an algorithm to find all the prime implicants of a given function, based on a list of the points where the function is true.

We can define a *prime clause* in an exactly similar way: It is a disjunctive clause that is implied by f, having no subclause with the same property. And the *conjunctive prime form* of f is the conjunction of all its prime clauses. (An example appears in exercise 19.)

In many simple cases, the disjunctive prime form is the shortest possible disjunctive normal form that a function can have. But we can often do better, because we might be able to cover all the necessary points with only a few of the maximal subcubes. For example, the prime implicant $(y \wedge z)$ is unnecessary in (27). And in expression (30) we don't need both $(\bar{w} \wedge \bar{y} \wedge \bar{z})$ and $(x \wedge \bar{y} \wedge \bar{z})$; either one is sufficient, in the presence of the other terms.

Unfortunately, we will see in Section 7.9 that the task of finding a best disjunctive normal form is NP-complete, thus quite difficult in general. But many useful shortcuts have been developed for sufficiently small problems, and they are well explained in the book *Introduction to the Theory of Switching Circuits* by E. J. McCluskey (New York: McGraw–Hill, 1965). For later developments, see Petr Fišer and Jan Hlavička, *Computing and Informatics* **22** (2003), 19–51.

There's an important special case for which the shortest DNF is, however, easily characterized. A Boolean function is said to be *monotone* or *positive* if its value does not change from 1 to 0 when any of its variables changes from 0 to 1. In other words, f is monotone if and only if $f(x) \le f(y)$ whenever $x \subseteq y$, where the bit string $x = x_1 \ldots x_n$ is regarded as contained in or equal to the bit string $y = y_1 \ldots y_n$ if and only if $x_j \le y_j$ for all j. An equivalent condition (see exercise 21) is that the function f either is constant or can be expressed entirely in terms of $\wedge$ and $\vee$, without complementation.

Theorem Q. *The shortest disjunctive normal form of a monotone Boolean function is its disjunctive prime form.*

Proof. [W. V. Quine, *Boletín de la Sociedad Matemática Mexicana* **10** (1953), 64–70.] Let $f(x_1, \ldots, x_n)$ be monotone, and let $u_1 \wedge \cdots \wedge u_s$ be one of its prime implicants. We cannot have, say, $u_1 = \bar{x}_i$, because in that case the shorter term $u_2 \wedge \cdots \wedge u_s$ would also be an implicant, by monotonicity. Therefore no prime implicant has a complemented literal.

Now if we set $u_1 \leftarrow \cdots \leftarrow u_s \leftarrow 1$ and all other variables to 0, the value of f will be 1, but all of f's other prime implicants will vanish. Thus $u_1 \wedge \cdots \wedge u_s$ must be in every shortest DNF, because every implicant of a shortest DNF is clearly prime. ∎

Corollary Q. *A disjunctive normal form is the disjunctive prime form of a monotone Boolean function if and only if it has no complemented literals and none of its implicants is contained in another.* ∎

Satisfiability. A Boolean function is said to be *satisfiable* if it is not identically zero — that is, if it has at least one implicant. The most famous unsolved problem in all of computer science is to find an efficient way to decide whether a given Boolean function is satisfiable or unsatisfiable. More precisely, we ask: Is there an algorithm that inputs a Boolean formula of length N and tests it for satisfiability, always giving the correct answer after performing at most $N^{O(1)}$ steps?

When you hear about this problem for the first time, you might be tempted to ask a question of your own in return: "What? Are you serious that computer scientists still haven't figured out how to do such a simple thing?"

Well, if you think satisfiability testing is trivial, please tell us your method. We agree that the problem isn't always difficult; if, for example, the given formula involves only 30 Boolean variables, a brute-force trial of 2^{30} cases — that's about a billion — will indeed settle the matter. But an enormous number of practical problems that still await solution can be formulated as Boolean functions with, say, 100 variables, because mathematical logic is a very powerful way to express concepts. And the solutions to those problems correspond to the vectors $x = x_1 \ldots x_{100}$ for which $f(x) = 1$. So a truly efficient solution to the satisfiability problem would be a wonderful achievement.

There is at least one sense in which satisfiability testing is a no-brainer: If the function $f(x_1, \ldots, x_n)$ has been chosen at random, so that all 2^n truth tables are equally likely, then f is almost surely satisfiable, and we can find an x with $f(x) = 1$ after making fewer than 2 trials (on the average). It's like flipping a coin until it comes up heads; we rarely need to wait long. But the catch, of course, is that practical problems do not have random truth tables.

Okay, let's grant that satisfiability testing does seem to be tough, in general. In fact, satisfiability turns out to be difficult even when we try to simplify it by requiring that the Boolean function be presented as a "formula in 3CNF" — namely as a conjunctive normal form that has only *three* literals in each clause:

$$f(x_1, \ldots, x_n) = (t_1 \vee u_1 \vee v_1) \wedge (t_2 \vee u_2 \vee v_2) \wedge \cdots \wedge (t_m \vee u_m \vee v_m). \quad (31)$$

Here each t_j, u_j, and v_j is x_k or $\bar{x}_k$ for some k. The problem of deciding satisfiability for formulas in 3CNF is called "3SAT," and exercise 39 explains why it is not really easier than satisfiability in general.

We will be seeing many examples of hard-to-crack 3SAT problems, especially in Section 7.9, where satisfiability testing will be discussed in great detail. The situation is a little peculiar, however, because a formula needs to be fairly long before we need to think twice about its satisfiability. For example, the shortest unsatisfiable formula in 3CNF is $(x \vee x \vee x) \wedge (\bar{x} \vee \bar{x} \vee \bar{x})$; but it is obviously no challenge to the intellect. We don't get into rough waters unless the three literals t_j, u_j, v_j of a clause correspond to three different variables. And in that case, each clause rules out exactly 1/8 of the possibilities, because seven different settings of (t_j, u_j, v_j) will make it true. Consequently every such 3CNF with at most seven clauses is automatically satisfiable, and a random setting of its variables will succeed with probability $\geq 1 - 7/8 = 1/8$.

The shortest interesting formula in 3CNF therefore has at least eight clauses. And in fact, an interesting 8-clause formula does exist, based on the associative block design by R. L. Rivest that we considered in 6.5–(13):

$$(x_2 \vee x_3 \vee \bar{x}_4) \wedge (x_1 \vee x_3 \vee x_4) \wedge (\bar{x}_1 \vee x_2 \vee x_4) \wedge (\bar{x}_1 \vee \bar{x}_2 \vee x_3)$$
$$\wedge (\bar{x}_2 \vee \bar{x}_3 \vee x_4) \wedge (\bar{x}_1 \vee \bar{x}_3 \vee \bar{x}_4) \wedge (x_1 \vee \bar{x}_2 \vee \bar{x}_4) \wedge (x_1 \vee x_2 \vee \bar{x}_3). \quad (32)$$

Any seven of these eight clauses are satisfiable, in exactly two ways, and they force the values of three variables; for example, the first seven imply that we have $x_1 x_2 x_3 = 001$. But the complete set of eight cannot be satisfied simultaneously.

Simple special cases. Two important classes of Boolean formulas have been identified for which the satisfiability problem does turn out to be pretty easy. These special cases arise when the conjunctive normal form being tested consists entirely of "Horn clauses" or entirely of "Krom clauses." A *Horn clause* is an OR of literals in which all or nearly all of the literals are complemented — at most one of its literals is a pure, unbarred variable. A *Krom clause* is an OR of exactly two literals. Thus, for example,

$$\bar{x} \vee \bar{y}, \qquad w \vee \bar{y} \vee \bar{z}, \qquad \bar{u} \vee \bar{v} \vee \bar{w} \vee \bar{x} \vee \bar{y} \vee z, \qquad \text{and} \quad x$$

are examples of Horn clauses; and

$$x \vee x, \qquad \bar{x} \vee \bar{x}, \qquad \bar{x} \vee \bar{y}, \qquad x \vee \bar{y}, \qquad \bar{x} \vee y, \qquad \text{and} \quad x \vee y$$

are examples of Krom clauses, only the last of which is not also a Horn clause. (The first example qualifies because $x \vee x = x$.) Notice that a Horn clause is allowed to contain any number of literals, but when we restrict ourselves to Krom clauses we are essentially considering the 2SAT problem. In both cases we will see that satisfiability can be decided in linear time — that is, by carrying out only $O(N)$ simple steps, when given a formula of length N.

Let's consider Horn clauses first. Why are they so easy to handle? The main reason is that a clause like $\bar{u} \vee \bar{v} \vee \bar{w} \vee \bar{x} \vee \bar{y} \vee z$ can be recast in the form $\neg(u \wedge v \wedge w \wedge x \wedge y) \vee z$, which is the same as

$$u \wedge v \wedge w \wedge x \wedge y \;\Rightarrow\; z.$$

In other words, if u, v, w, x, and y are all true, then z must also be true. For this reason, parameterized Horn clauses were chosen to be the basic underlying mechanism of the programming language called Prolog. Furthermore there is an easy way to characterize exactly which Boolean functions can be represented entirely with Horn clauses:

Theorem H. *The Boolean function $f(x_1, \ldots, x_n)$ is expressible as a conjunction of Horn clauses if and only if*

$$f(x_1, \ldots, x_n) = f(y_1, \ldots, y_n) = 1 \quad \text{implies} \quad f(x_1 \wedge y_1, \ldots, x_n \wedge y_n) = 1 \quad (33)$$

for all Boolean values x_j and y_j.

Proof. [Alfred Horn, *J. Symbolic Logic* **16** (1951), 14–21, Lemma 7.] If we have $x_0 \vee \bar{x}_1 \vee \cdots \vee \bar{x}_k = 1$ and $y_0 \vee \bar{y}_1 \vee \cdots \vee \bar{y}_k = 1$, then

$$(x_0 \wedge y_0) \vee \overline{x_1 \wedge y_1} \vee \cdots \vee \overline{x_k \wedge y_k}$$
$$= (x_0 \vee \bar{x}_1 \vee \bar{y}_1 \vee \cdots \vee \bar{x}_k \vee \bar{y}_k) \wedge (y_0 \vee \bar{x}_1 \vee \bar{y}_1 \vee \cdots \vee \bar{x}_k \vee \bar{y}_k)$$
$$\geq (x_0 \vee \bar{x}_1 \vee \cdots \vee \bar{x}_k) \wedge (y_0 \vee \bar{y}_1 \vee \cdots \vee \bar{y}_k) \;=\; 1;$$

and a similar (but simpler) calculation applies when the unbarred literals x_0 and y_0 are not present. Therefore every conjunction of Horn clauses satisfies (33).

Conversely, condition (33) implies that every prime clause of f is a Horn clause (see exercise 44). ∎

Let's say that a *Horn function* is a Boolean function that satisfies condition (33), and let's also call it *definite* if it satisfies the further condition $f(1, \ldots, 1) = 1$. It's easy to see that a conjunction of Horn clauses is definite if and only if each clause has *exactly* one unbarred literal, because only an entirely negative clause like $\bar{x} \vee \bar{y}$ will fail if all variables are true. Definite Horn functions are slightly simpler to work with than Horn functions in general, because they are obviously always satisfiable. Thus, by Theorem H, they have a unique least vector x such that $f(x) = 1$, namely the bitwise AND of all vectors that satisfy all clauses. The *core* of a definite Horn function is the set of all variables x_j that are true in this minimum vector x. Notice that the variables in the core must be true whenever f is true, so we can essentially factor them out.

Definite Horn functions arise in many ways, for example in the analysis of games (see exercises 51 and 52). Another nice example comes from compiler technology. Consider the following typical (but simplified) grammar for algebraic expressions in a programming language:

$$
\begin{aligned}
&\langle\,\text{expression}\,\rangle \to \langle\,\text{term}\,\rangle \mid \langle\,\text{expression}\,\rangle + \langle\,\text{term}\,\rangle \mid \langle\,\text{expression}\,\rangle - \langle\,\text{term}\,\rangle \\
&\langle\,\text{term}\,\rangle \to \langle\,\text{factor}\,\rangle \mid -\langle\,\text{factor}\,\rangle \mid \langle\,\text{term}\,\rangle * \langle\,\text{factor}\,\rangle \mid \langle\,\text{term}\,\rangle / \langle\,\text{factor}\,\rangle \\
&\langle\,\text{factor}\,\rangle \to \langle\,\text{variable}\,\rangle \mid \langle\,\text{constant}\,\rangle \mid (\langle\,\text{expression}\,\rangle) \\
&\langle\,\text{variable}\,\rangle \to \langle\,\text{letter}\,\rangle \mid \langle\,\text{variable}\,\rangle\langle\,\text{letter}\,\rangle \mid \langle\,\text{variable}\,\rangle\langle\,\text{digit}\,\rangle \quad\quad (34) \\
&\langle\,\text{letter}\,\rangle \to \text{a} \mid \text{b} \mid \text{c} \\
&\langle\,\text{constant}\,\rangle \to \langle\,\text{digit}\,\rangle \mid \langle\,\text{constant}\,\rangle\langle\,\text{digit}\,\rangle \\
&\langle\,\text{digit}\,\rangle \to \text{0} \mid \text{1}
\end{aligned}
$$

For example, the string a/(-b0-10)+cc*cc meets the syntax for $\langle\,\text{expression}\,\rangle$ and uses each of the grammatical rules at least once.

Suppose we want to know what pairs of characters can appear next to each other in such expressions. Definite Horn clauses provide the answer, because we can set the problem up as follows: Let the quantities Xx, xX, and xy denote Boolean "propositions," where X is one of the symbols $\{\text{E}, \text{T}, \text{F}, \text{V}, \text{L}, \text{C}, \text{D}\}$ standing respectively for $\langle\,\text{expression}\,\rangle$, $\langle\,\text{term}\,\rangle$, $\ldots$, $\langle\,\text{digit}\,\rangle$, and where x and y are symbols in the set $\{+, -, *, /, (,), \text{a}, \text{b}, \text{c}, \text{0}, \text{1}\}$. The proposition Xx means, "X can end with x"; similarly, xX means, "X can start with x"; and xy means, "The character x can be followed immediately by y in an expression." (There are $7 \times 11 + 11 \times 7 + 11 \times 11 = 275$ propositions altogether.) Then we can write

$$
\begin{array}{llllll}
\text{xT} \Rightarrow \text{xE} & \Rightarrow \text{-T} & \text{xC} \Rightarrow \text{xF} & \text{Vx} \wedge \text{yL} \Rightarrow \text{xy} & \Rightarrow \text{Lc} \\
\text{Tx} \Rightarrow \text{Ex} & \text{xF} \Rightarrow \text{-x} & \text{Cx} \Rightarrow \text{Fx} & \text{Vx} \wedge \text{yD} \Rightarrow \text{xy} & \text{xD} \Rightarrow \text{xC} \\
\text{Ex} \Rightarrow \text{x+} & \text{Tx} \Rightarrow \text{x*} & \Rightarrow \text{(F} & \text{Dx} \Rightarrow \text{Vx} & \text{Dx} \Rightarrow \text{Cx} \\
\text{xT} \Rightarrow \text{+x} & \text{xF} \Rightarrow \text{*x} & \text{xE} \Rightarrow \text{(x} & \Rightarrow \text{aL} & \text{Cx} \wedge \text{yD} \Rightarrow \text{xy} \\
\text{Ex} \Rightarrow \text{x-} & \text{Tx} \Rightarrow \text{x/} & \text{Ex} \Rightarrow \text{x)} & \Rightarrow \text{La} & \Rightarrow \text{0D} \\
\text{xT} \Rightarrow \text{-x} & \text{xF} \Rightarrow \text{/x} & \Rightarrow \text{F)} & \Rightarrow \text{bL} & \Rightarrow \text{D0} \\
\text{xF} \Rightarrow \text{xT} & \text{xV} \Rightarrow \text{xF} & \text{xL} \Rightarrow \text{xV} & \Rightarrow \text{Lb} & \Rightarrow \text{1D} \\
\text{Fx} \Rightarrow \text{Tx} & \text{Vx} \Rightarrow \text{Fx} & \text{Lx} \Rightarrow \text{Vx} & \Rightarrow \text{cL} & \Rightarrow \text{D1}
\end{array} \quad (35)
$$

where x and y run through the eleven terminal symbols $\{+, \ldots, \text{1}\}$. This schematic specification gives us a total of $24 \times 11 + 3 \times 11 \times 11 + 13 \times 1 = 640$ definite

Horn clauses, which we could write out formally as

$$\left(\overline{+T} \vee +E\right) \wedge \left(\overline{-T} \vee -E\right) \wedge \cdots \wedge \left(\overline{V+} \vee \overline{OL} \vee +0\right) \wedge \cdots \wedge \left(D1\right)$$

if we prefer the cryptic notation of Boolean algebra to the $\Rightarrow$ convention of (35).

Why did we do this? Because *the core of all these clauses is the set of all propositions that are true in this particular grammar.* For example, one can verify that $-E$ is true, hence the symbols $(-$ can occur next to each other within an expression; but the symbol pairs $++$ and $*-$ cannot (see exercise 46).

Furthermore, we can find the core of any given set of definite Horn clauses without great difficulty. We just start out with the propositions that appear alone, on the right-hand side of $\Rightarrow$ when the left-hand side is empty; thirteen clauses of that kind appear in (35). And once we assert the truth of those propositions, we might find one or more clauses whose left-hand sides are now known to be true. Hence their right-hand sides also belong to the core, and we can keep going in the same way. The whole procedure is pretty much like letting water run downhill until it has found its proper level. In fact, when we choose appropriate data structures, this downhill process goes quite fast, requiring only $O(N+n)$ steps, when N denotes the total length of the clauses and n is the number of propositional variables. (We assume here that all clauses have been expanded out, not abbreviated in terms of parameters like x and y above. More sophisticated techniques of theorem proving are available to deal with parameterized clauses, but they are beyond the scope of our present discussion.)

Algorithm C (*Core computation for definite Horn clauses*). Given a set P of propositional variables and a set C of clauses, each having the form

$$u_1 \wedge \cdots \wedge u_k \Rightarrow v \qquad \text{where } k \geq 0 \text{ and } \{u_1, \ldots, u_k, v\} \subseteq P, \qquad (36)$$

this algorithm finds the set $Q \subseteq P$ of all propositional variables that are necessarily true whenever all of the clauses are true.

We use the following data structures for clauses c, propositions p, and hypotheses h, where a "hypothesis" is the appearance of a proposition on the left-hand side of a clause:

CONCLUSION(c) is the proposition on the right of clause c;

COUNT(c) is the number of hypotheses of c not yet asserted;

TRUTH(p) is 1 if p is known to be true, otherwise 0;

LAST(p) is the last hypothesis in which p appears;

CLAUSE(h) is the clause for which h appears on the left;

PREV(h) is the previous hypothesis containing the proposition of h.

We also maintain a stack $S_0, S_1, \ldots, S_{s-1}$ of all propositions that are known to be true but not yet asserted.

C1. [Initialize.] Set LAST$(p) \leftarrow \Lambda$ and TRUTH$(p) \leftarrow 0$ for each proposition p. Also set $s \leftarrow 0$, so that the stack is empty. Then for each clause c, having the form (36), set CONCLUSION$(c) \leftarrow v$ and COUNT$(c) \leftarrow k$. If $k = 0$ and

TRUTH$(v) = 0$, set TRUTH$(v) \leftarrow 1$, $S_s \leftarrow v$, and $s \leftarrow s + 1$. Otherwise, for $1 \leq j \leq k$, create a hypothesis record h and set CLAUSE$(h) \leftarrow c$, PREV$(h) \leftarrow$ LAST(u_j), LAST$(u_j) \leftarrow h$.

C2. [Prepare to assert p.] Terminate the algorithm if $s = 0$; the desired core now consists of all propositions whose TRUTH has been set to 1. Otherwise set $s \leftarrow s - 1$, $p \leftarrow S_s$, and $h \leftarrow$ LAST(p).

C3. [Done with hypotheses?] If $h = \Lambda$, return to C2.

C4. [Validate h.] Set $c \leftarrow$ CLAUSE(h) and COUNT$(c) \leftarrow$ COUNT$(c) - 1$. If the new value of COUNT(c) is still nonzero, go to step C6.

C5. [Deduce CONCLUSION(c).] Set $p \leftarrow$ CONCLUSION(c). If TRUTH$(p) = 0$, set TRUTH$(p) \leftarrow 1$, $S_s \leftarrow p$, $s \leftarrow s + 1$.

C6. [Loop on h.] Set $h \leftarrow$ PREV(h) and return to C3. ∎

Notice how smoothly the data structures work together, avoiding any need to search for a place to make progress in the calculation. Algorithm C is similar in many respects to Algorithm 2.2.3T (topological sorting), which was the first example of multilinked data structures that we discussed long ago in Chapter 2; in fact, we can regard Algorithm 2.2.3T as the special case of Algorithm C in which every proposition appears on the right-hand side of exactly one clause. (See exercise 47.)

Exercise 48 shows that a slight modification of Algorithm C solves the satisfiability problem for Horn clauses in general. Further discussion can be found in a paper by W. F. Dowling and J. H. Gallier, *J. Logic Programming* **1** (1984), 267–284.

We turn now to Krom functions and the 2SAT problem. Again there's a linear-time algorithm; but again, we can probably appreciate it best if we look first at a simplified-but-practical application. Let's suppose that seven comedians have each agreed to do one-night standup gigs at two of five hotels during a three-day festival, but each of them is available for only two of those days because of other commitments:

> Tomlin should do Aladdin and Caesars on days 1 and 2;   Unwin should do Bellagio and Excalibur on days 1 and 2;   Vegas should do Desert and Excalibur on days 2 and 3;   Williams should do Aladdin and Desert on days 1 and 3;   (37)   Xie should do Caesars and Excalibur on days 1 and 3;   Yankovic should do Bellagio and Desert on days 2 and 3;   Zany should do Bellagio and Caesars on days 1 and 2.

Is it possible to schedule them all without conflict?

To solve this problem, we can introduce seven Boolean variables $\{t, u, v, w, x, y, z\}$, where t (for example) means that Tomlin does Aladdin on day 1 and Caesars on day 2 while $\bar{t}$ means that the days booked for those hotels occur in the opposite order. Then we can set up constraints to ensure that no two comedians are booked in the same hotel on the same day:

$$
\begin{array}{llll}
\neg(t \wedge w) \ [\text{A1}] & \neg(y \wedge \bar{z}) \ [\text{B2}] & \neg(t \wedge z) \ [\text{C2}] & \neg(w \wedge y) \ [\text{D3}] \\
\neg(u \wedge z) \ [\text{B1}] & \neg(\bar{t} \wedge x) \ [\text{C1}] & \neg(v \wedge \bar{y}) \ [\text{D2}] & \neg(\bar{u} \wedge \bar{x}) \ [\text{E1}] \\
\neg(\bar{u} \wedge y) \ [\text{B2}] & \neg(\bar{t} \wedge \bar{z}) \ [\text{C1}] & \neg(\bar{v} \wedge w) \ [\text{D3}] & \neg(u \wedge \bar{v}) \ [\text{E2}] \\
\neg(\bar{u} \wedge \bar{z}) \ [\text{B2}] & \neg(x \wedge \bar{z}) \ [\text{C1}] & \neg(\bar{v} \wedge y) \ [\text{D3}] & \neg(v \wedge x) \ [\text{E3}]
\end{array}
\tag{38}
$$

Each of these constraints is, of course, a Krom clause; we must satisfy

$$(\bar{t} \vee \bar{w}) \wedge (\bar{u} \vee \bar{z}) \wedge (u \vee \bar{y}) \wedge (u \vee z) \wedge (\bar{y} \vee z) \wedge (t \vee \bar{x}) \wedge (t \vee z) \wedge (\bar{x} \vee z)$$
$$\wedge\ (\bar{t} \vee \bar{z}) \wedge (\bar{v} \vee y) \wedge (v \vee \bar{w}) \wedge (v \vee \bar{y}) \wedge (\bar{w} \vee \bar{y}) \wedge (u \vee x) \wedge (\bar{u} \vee v) \wedge (\bar{v} \vee \bar{x}). \tag{39}$$

Furthermore, Krom clauses (like Horn clauses) can be written as implications:

$$t \Rightarrow \bar{w}, \quad u \Rightarrow \bar{z}, \quad \bar{u} \Rightarrow \bar{y}, \quad \bar{u} \Rightarrow z, \quad y \Rightarrow z, \quad \bar{t} \Rightarrow \bar{x}, \quad \bar{t} \Rightarrow z, \quad x \Rightarrow z,$$
$$t \Rightarrow \bar{z}, \quad v \Rightarrow y, \quad \bar{v} \Rightarrow \bar{w}, \quad \bar{v} \Rightarrow \bar{y}, \quad w \Rightarrow \bar{y}, \quad \bar{u} \Rightarrow x, \quad u \Rightarrow v, \quad v \Rightarrow \bar{x}. \tag{40}$$

And every such implication also has an alternative, "contrapositive" form:

$$w \Rightarrow \bar{t}, \quad z \Rightarrow \bar{u}, \quad y \Rightarrow u, \quad \bar{z} \Rightarrow u, \quad \bar{z} \Rightarrow \bar{y}, \quad x \Rightarrow t, \quad \bar{z} \Rightarrow t, \quad \bar{z} \Rightarrow \bar{x},$$
$$z \Rightarrow \bar{t}, \quad \bar{y} \Rightarrow \bar{v}, \quad w \Rightarrow v, \quad y \Rightarrow v, \quad y \Rightarrow \bar{w}, \quad \bar{x} \Rightarrow u, \quad \bar{v} \Rightarrow \bar{u}, \quad x \Rightarrow \bar{v}. \tag{41}$$

But oops — alas — there is a vicious cycle,

$$
\begin{array}{ccccccccccccccc}
u & \Rightarrow & \bar{z} & \Rightarrow & \bar{y} & \Rightarrow & \bar{v} & \Rightarrow & \bar{u} & \Rightarrow & z & \Rightarrow & \bar{t} & \Rightarrow & \bar{x} & \Rightarrow & u \\
 & [\text{B1}] & & [\text{B2}] & & [\text{D2}] & & [\text{E2}] & & [\text{B2}] & & [\text{C2}] & & [\text{C1}] & & [\text{E1}] &
\end{array}
\tag{42}
$$

This cycle tells that u and $\bar{u}$ must both have the same value; so there is no way to accommodate all of the conditions in (37). The festival organizers will have to renegotiate their agreement with at least one of the six comedians $\{t, u, v, x, y, z\}$, if a viable schedule is to be achieved. (See exercise 53.)

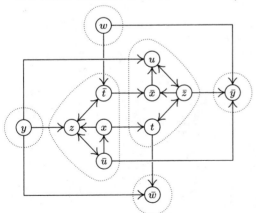

Fig. 6. The digraph corresponding to all implications of (40) and (41) that do not involve either v or $\bar{v}$. Assigning appropriate values to the literals in each strong component will solve a binary scheduling problem that is an instance of 2SAT.

The organizers might, for instance, try to leave v out of the picture temporarily. Then five of the sixteen constraints in (38) would go away and only 22 of the implications from (40) and (41) would remain, leaving the directed graph illustrated in Fig. 6. This digraph does contain cycles, like $z \Rightarrow \bar{u} \Rightarrow x \Rightarrow z$ and $t \Rightarrow \bar{z} \Rightarrow t$; but no cycle contains both a variable and its complement. Indeed, we can see from Fig. 6 that the values $tuwxyz = 110000$ do satisfy every clause of (39) that doesn't involve v or $\bar{v}$. These values give us a schedule that satisfies six of the seven original stipulations in (37), starting with (Tomlin, Unwin, Zany, Williams, Xie) at the (Aladdin, Bellagio, Caesars, Desert, Excalibur) on day 1.

In general, given any 2SAT problem with m Krom clauses that involve n Boolean variables, we can form a directed graph in the same way. There are $2n$ vertices $\{x_1, \bar{x}_1, \ldots, x_n, \bar{x}_n\}$, one for each possible literal; and there are $2m$ arcs of the form $\bar{u} \to v$ and $\bar{v} \to u$, two for each clause $u \vee v$. Two literals u and v belong to the same *strong component* of this digraph if and only if there are oriented paths from u to v and from v to u. For example, the six strong components of the digraph in Fig. 6 are indicated by dotted contours. All literals in a strong component must have the same Boolean value, in any solution to the corresponding 2SAT problem.

Theorem K. *A conjunctive normal form with two literals per clause is satisfiable if and only if no strong component of the associated digraph contains both a variable and its complement.*

Proof. [Melven Krom, *Zeitschrift für mathematische Logik und Grundlagen der Mathematik* **13** (1967), 15–20, Corollary 2.2.] If there are paths from x to $\bar{x}$ and from $\bar{x}$ to x, the formula is certainly unsatisfiable.

Conversely, assume that no such paths exist. Any digraph has at least one strong component S that is a "source," having no incoming arcs from vertices in any other strong component. Moreover, our digraph always has an attractive antisymmetry, illustrated in Fig. 6: We have $u \to v$ if and only if $\bar{v} \to \bar{u}$. Therefore the complements of the literals in S form another strong component $\overline{S} \neq S$ that is a "sink," having no *outgoing* arcs to other strong components. Hence we can assign the value 0 to all literals in S and 1 to all literals in $\overline{S}$, then remove them from the digraph and proceed in the same way until all literals have received a value. The resulting values satisfy $u \leq v$ whenever $u \to v$ in the digraph; hence they satisfy $\bar{u} \vee v$ whenever $\bar{u} \vee v$ is a clause of the formula. ∎

Theorem K leads immediately to an efficient solution of the 2SAT problem, thanks to an algorithm by R. E. Tarjan that finds strong components in linear time. [See *SICOMP* **1** (1972), 146–160; D. E. Knuth, *The Stanford GraphBase* (1993), 512–519.] We shall study Tarjan's algorithm in detail in Section 7.4.1. Exercise 54 shows that the condition of Theorem K is readily checked whenever the algorithm detects a new strong component. Furthermore, the algorithm detects "sinks" first; thus, as a simple byproduct of Tarjan's procedure, we can assign values that establish satisfiability by choosing the value 1 for each literal in a strong component that occurs before its complement.

Medians. We've been focusing on Boolean binary operations like $x \vee y$ or $x \oplus y$. But there's also a significant *ternary* operation $\langle xyz \rangle$, called the *median* of x, y, and z:

$$\langle xyz \rangle = (x \wedge y) \vee (y \wedge z) \vee (x \wedge z) = (x \vee y) \wedge (y \vee z) \wedge (x \vee z). \tag{43}$$

In fact, $\langle xyz \rangle$ is probably the most important ternary operation in the entire universe, because it has amazing properties that are continually being discovered and rediscovered.

In the first place, we can see easily that this formula for $\langle xyz \rangle$ describes the *majority* value of any three Boolean quantities x, y, and z: $\langle 000 \rangle = \langle 001 \rangle = 0$ and $\langle 011 \rangle = \langle 111 \rangle = 1$. We call $\langle xyz \rangle$ the "median" instead of the "majority" because, if x, y, and z are arbitrary *real* numbers, and if the operations $\wedge$ and $\vee$ denote min and max, then

$$\langle xyz \rangle \; = \; y \qquad \text{when } x \le y \le z. \tag{44}$$

Secondly, the basic binary operations $\wedge$ and $\vee$ are special cases of medians:

$$x \wedge y \; = \; \langle x0y \rangle; \qquad\qquad x \vee y \; = \; \langle x1y \rangle. \tag{45}$$

Thus *any* monotone Boolean function can be expressed entirely in terms of the ternary median operator and the constants 0 and 1. In fact, if we lived in a median-only world, we could let $\wedge$ stand for falsehood and $\vee$ for truth; then $x \wedge y = \langle x \wedge y \rangle$ and $x \vee y = \langle x \vee y \rangle$ would be perfectly natural expressions, and we could even use Polish notation like $\langle \wedge xy \rangle$ and $\langle \vee xy \rangle$ if that was our preference! The same idea applies to extended real numbers under the min-max interpretation of $\wedge$ and $\vee$, if we take medians with respect to the constants $\wedge = -\infty$ and $\vee = +\infty$.

A Boolean function $f(x_1, x_2, \ldots, x_n)$ is called *self-dual* when it satisfies

$$\overline{f(x_1, x_2, \ldots, x_n)} \; = \; f(\bar{x}_1, \bar{x}_2, \ldots, \bar{x}_n). \tag{46}$$

We've noted that a Boolean function is monotone if and only if it can be expressed in terms of $\wedge$ and $\vee$; by De Morgan's laws (11) and (12), a monotone formula is self-dual if and only if the symbols $\wedge$ and $\vee$ can be interchanged without changing the formula's value. Thus the median operation defined in (43) is both monotone and self-dual. In fact, it is the simplest nontrivial function of that kind, since none of the binary operations in Table 1 are both monotone and self-dual except the projections $\llcorner$ and $\lrcorner$.

Furthermore, *any* expression that has been formed entirely with the median operator, without using constants, is both monotone and self-dual. For example, the function $\langle w \langle xyz \rangle \langle w \langle uvw \rangle x \rangle \rangle$ is self-dual because

$$\overline{\langle w \langle xyz \rangle \langle w \langle uvw \rangle x \rangle \rangle} \; = \; \langle \bar{w} \, \overline{\langle xyz \rangle} \, \overline{\langle w \langle uvw \rangle x \rangle} \rangle$$
$$= \; \langle \bar{w} \langle \bar{x}\bar{y}\bar{z} \rangle \langle \bar{w} \overline{\langle uvw \rangle} \bar{x} \rangle \rangle \; = \; \langle \bar{w} \langle \bar{x}\bar{y}\bar{z} \rangle \langle \bar{w} \langle \bar{u}\bar{v}\bar{w} \rangle \bar{x} \rangle \rangle.$$

Emil Post, while working on his Ph.D. thesis (Columbia University, 1920), proved that the converse statement is also true:

Theorem P. *Every monotone, self-dual Boolean function $f(x_1, \ldots, x_n)$ can be expressed entirely in terms of the median operation $\langle xyz \rangle$.*

Proof. [*Annals of Mathematics Studies* **5** (1941), 74–75.] Observe first that

$$\langle x_1 y \langle x_2 y \dots y \langle x_{s-1} y x_s \rangle \dots \rangle \rangle$$
$$= ((x_1 \vee x_2 \vee \cdots \vee x_{s-1} \vee x_s) \wedge y) \vee (x_1 \wedge x_2 \wedge \cdots \wedge x_{s-1} \wedge x_s); \qquad (47)$$

this formula for repeated medianing is easily proved by induction on s.

Now suppose $f(x_1, \dots, x_n)$ is monotone, self-dual, and has the disjunctive prime form

$$f(x_1, \dots, x_n) = t_1 \vee \cdots \vee t_m, \qquad t_j = x_{j1} \wedge \cdots \wedge x_{js_j},$$

where no prime implicant t_j is contained in another (Corollary Q). Any two prime implicants must have at least one variable in common. For if we had, say, $t_1 = x \wedge y$ and $t_2 = u \wedge v \wedge w$, the value of f would be 1 when $x = y = 1$ and $u = v = w = 0$, as well as when $x = y = 0$ and $u = v = w = 1$, contradicting self-duality. Therefore if any t_j consists of a single variable x, it must be the only prime implicant — in which case f is the trivial function $f(x_1, \dots, x_n) = x = \langle xxx \rangle$.

Define the functions $g_0, g_1, \dots, g_m$ by composing medians as follows:

$$g_0(x_1, \dots, x_n) = x_1;$$
$$g_j(x_1, \dots, x_n) = h(x_{j1}, \dots, x_{js_j}; g_{j-1}(x_1, \dots, x_n)), \text{ for } 1 \le j \le m; \qquad (48)$$

here $h(x_1, \dots, x_s; y)$ denotes the function on the top line of (47). By induction on j, we can prove from (47) and (48) that $g_j(x_1, \dots, x_n) = 1$ whenever we have $t_1 \vee \cdots \vee t_j = 1$, because $(x_{j1} \vee \cdots \vee x_{js_j}) \wedge t_k = t_k$ when $k < j$.

Finally, $f(x_1, \dots, x_n)$ must equal $g_m(x_1, \dots, x_n)$, because both functions are monotone and self-dual, and we have shown that $f(x_1, \dots, x_n) \le g_m(x_1, \dots, x_n)$ for all combinations of 0s and 1s. This inequality suffices to prove equality, because a self-dual function equals 1 in exactly half of the 2^n possible cases. ∎

One consequence of Theorem P is that we can express the median of five elements via medians of three, because the median of any odd number of Boolean variables is obviously a monotone and self-dual Boolean function. Let's write $\langle x_1 \dots x_{2k-1} \rangle$ for such a median. Then the disjunctive prime form of $\langle vwxyz \rangle$ is

$$(v \wedge w \wedge x) \vee (v \wedge w \wedge y) \vee (v \wedge w \wedge z) \vee (v \wedge x \wedge y) \vee (v \wedge x \wedge z)$$
$$\vee (v \wedge y \wedge z) \vee (w \wedge x \wedge y) \vee (w \wedge x \wedge z) \vee (w \wedge y \wedge z) \vee (x \wedge y \wedge z);$$

so the construction in the proof of Theorem P expresses $\langle vwxyz \rangle$ as a huge formula $g_{10}(v, w, x, y, z)$ involving 2,046 median-of-3 operations. Of course this expression isn't the shortest possible one; we actually have

$$\langle vwxyz \rangle = \langle v \langle xyz \rangle \langle wx \langle wyz \rangle \rangle \rangle. \qquad (49)$$

[See H. S. Miiller and R. O. Winder, *IRE Transactions* **EC-11** (1962), 89–90.]

*Median algebras and median graphs. We noted earlier that the ternary operation $\langle xyz \rangle$ is useful when x, y, and z belong to any ordered set like the real numbers, when $\wedge$ and $\vee$ are regarded as the operators min and max. In fact, the operation $\langle xyz \rangle$ also plays a useful role in far more general circumstances.

A *median algebra* is any set M on which a ternary operation $\langle xyz \rangle$ is defined that takes elements of M into elements of M and obeys the following three axioms:

$$\langle xxy \rangle = x \quad \text{(majority law)}; \tag{50}$$

$$\langle xyz \rangle = \langle xzy \rangle = \langle yxz \rangle = \langle yzx \rangle = \langle zxy \rangle = \langle zyx \rangle \quad \text{(commutative law)}; \tag{51}$$

$$\langle xw\langle ywz \rangle \rangle = \langle\langle xwy \rangle wz \rangle \quad \text{(associative law)}. \tag{52}$$

In the Boolean case, for example, the associative law (52) holds for $w = 0$ and $w = 1$ because $\wedge$ and $\vee$ are associative. Exercises 75 and 76 prove that these three axioms imply also a *distributive law* for medians, which has both a short form

$$\langle\langle xyz \rangle uv \rangle = \langle x\langle yuv \rangle\langle zuv \rangle\rangle \tag{53}$$

and a more symmetrical long form

$$\langle\langle xyz \rangle uv \rangle = \langle\langle xuv \rangle\langle yuv \rangle\langle zuv \rangle\rangle. \tag{54}$$

No simple proof of this fact is known, but we can at least verify the special case of (53) and (54) when $y = u$ and $z = v$: We have

$$\langle\langle xyz \rangle yz \rangle = \langle xyz \rangle \tag{55}$$

because both sides equal $\langle xy\langle zyz \rangle\rangle$. In fact, the associative law (52) is just the special case $y = u$ of (53). And with (55) and (52) we can also verify the case $x = u$: $\langle\langle uyz \rangle uv \rangle = \langle vu\langle yuz \rangle\rangle = \langle\langle vuy \rangle uz \rangle = \langle\langle yuv \rangle uz \rangle = \langle\langle\langle yuv \rangle uv \rangle uz \rangle = \langle\langle yuv \rangle u\langle vuz \rangle\rangle = \langle u\langle yuv \rangle\langle zuv \rangle\rangle$.

An *ideal* in a median algebra M is a set $C \subseteq M$ for which we have

$$\langle xyz \rangle \in C \quad \text{whenever } x \in C, \ y \in C, \text{ and } z \in M. \tag{56}$$

If u and v are any elements of M, the *interval* $[u \mathbin{..} v]$ is defined as follows:

$$[u \mathbin{..} v] = \{ \langle xuv \rangle \mid x \in M \}. \tag{57}$$

We say that "x is between u and v" if and only if $x \in [u \mathbin{..} v]$. According to these definitions, u and v themselves always belong to the interval $[u \mathbin{..} v]$.

Lemma M. *Every interval $[u \mathbin{..} v]$ is an ideal, and $x \in [u \mathbin{..} v] \iff x = \langle uxv \rangle$.*

Proof. Let $\langle xuv \rangle$ and $\langle yuv \rangle$ be arbitrary elements of $[u \mathbin{..} v]$. Then

$$\langle\langle xuv \rangle\langle yuv \rangle z \rangle = \langle\langle xyz \rangle uv \rangle \in [u \mathbin{..} v]$$

for all $z \in M$, by (51) and (53), so $[u \mathbin{..} v]$ is an ideal. Furthermore every element $\langle xuv \rangle \in [u \mathbin{..} v]$ satisfies $\langle xuv \rangle = \langle u\langle xuv \rangle v \rangle$ by (51) and (55). ∎

Our intervals $[u \mathbin{..} v]$ have nice properties, because of the median laws:

$$v \in [u \mathbin{..} u] \implies u = v; \tag{58}$$

$$x \in [u \mathbin{..} v] \text{ and } y \in [u \mathbin{..} x] \implies y \in [u \mathbin{..} v]; \tag{59}$$

$$x \in [u \mathbin{..} v] \text{ and } y \in [u \mathbin{..} z] \text{ and } y \in [v \mathbin{..} z] \implies y \in [x \mathbin{..} z]. \tag{60}$$

Equivalently, $[u \mathbin{..} u] = \{u\}$; if $x \in [u \mathbin{..} v]$ then $[u \mathbin{..} x] \subseteq [u \mathbin{..} v]$; and $x \in [u \mathbin{..} v]$ also implies that $[u \mathbin{..} z] \cap [v \mathbin{..} z] \subseteq [x \mathbin{..} z]$ for all z. (See exercise 72.)

Now let's define a graph on the vertex set M, with the following edges:

$$u \!-\! v \quad \Longleftrightarrow \quad u \neq v \text{ and } \langle xuv \rangle \in \{u, v\} \text{ for all } x \in M. \tag{61}$$

In other words, u and v are adjacent if and only if the interval $[u .. v]$ consists of just the two points u and v.

Theorem G. *If M is any finite median algebra, the graph defined by (61) is connected. Moreover, vertex x belongs to the interval $[u .. v]$ if and only if x lies on a shortest path from u to v.*

Proof. If M isn't connected, choose u and v so that there is no path from u to v and the interval $[u .. v]$ has as few elements as possible. Let $x \in [u .. v]$ be distinct from u and v. Then $\langle xuv \rangle = x \neq v$, so $v \notin [u .. x]$; similarly $u \notin [x .. v]$. But $[u .. x]$ and $[x .. v]$ are contained in $[u .. v]$, by (59). So they are smaller intervals, and there must be a path from u to x and from x to v. Contradiction.

The other half of the theorem is proved in exercise 73. ∎

Our definition of intervals implies that $\langle xyz \rangle \in [x .. y] \cap [x .. z] \cap [y .. z]$, because $\langle xyz \rangle = \langle \langle xyz \rangle xy \rangle = \langle \langle xyz \rangle xz \rangle = \langle \langle xyz \rangle yz \rangle$ by (55). Conversely, if $w \in [x .. y] \cap [x .. z] \cap [y .. z]$, exercise 74 proves that $w = \langle xyz \rangle$. In other words, *the intersection $[x .. y] \cap [x .. z] \cap [y .. z]$ always contains exactly one point*, whenever x, y, and z are points of M.

Figure 7 illustrates this principle in a $4 \times 4 \times 4$ cube, where each point x has coordinates (x_1, x_2, x_3) with $0 \leq x_1, x_2, x_3 < 4$. The vertices of this cube form a median algebra because $\langle xyz \rangle = (\langle x_1 y_1 z_1 \rangle, \langle x_2 y_2 z_2 \rangle, \langle x_3 y_3 z_3 \rangle)$; furthermore, the edges of the graph in Fig. 7 are those defined in (61), running between vertices whose coordinates agree except that one coordinate changes by ± 1. Three typical intervals $[x .. y]$, $[x .. z]$, and $[y .. z]$ are shown; the only point common to all three intervals is the vertex $\langle xyz \rangle = (2, 2, 1)$.

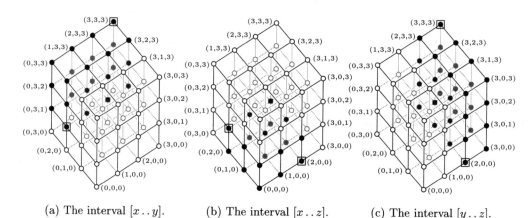

(a) The interval $[x .. y]$.   (b) The interval $[x .. z]$.   (c) The interval $[y .. z]$.

Fig. 7. Intervals between the vertices $x = (0, 2, 1)$,
$y = (3, 3, 3)$, and $z = (2, 0, 0)$ in a $4 \times 4 \times 4$ cube.

So far we've started with a median algebra and used it to define a graph with certain properties. But we can also start with a graph that has those properties and use it to define a median algebra. If u and v are vertices of *any* graph, let us define the interval $[u .. v]$ to be the set of all points on shortest paths between u and v. A finite graph is said to be a *median graph* if exactly one vertex lies in the intersection $[x .. y] \cap [x .. z] \cap [y .. z]$ of the three intervals that tie any three given vertices x, y, and z together; and we denote that vertex by $\langle xyz \rangle$. Exercise 75 proves that the resulting ternary operation satisfies the median axioms.

Many important graphs turn out to be median graphs according to this definition. For example, any free tree is easily seen to be a median graph; and a graph like the $n_1 \times n_2 \times \cdots \times n_m$ hyperrectangle provides another simple example. Cartesian products of arbitrary median graphs also satisfy the required condition.

*Median labels. If u and v are any elements of a median algebra, the mapping $f(x)$ that takes $x \mapsto \langle xuv \rangle$ is a *homomorphism*; that is, it satisfies

$$f(\langle xyz \rangle) = \langle f(x)f(y)f(z) \rangle, \tag{62}$$

because of the long distributive law (54). This function $\langle xuv \rangle$ "projects" any given point x into the interval $[u .. v]$, by (57). And it is particularly interesting in the case when $u - v$ is an edge of the corresponding graph, because $f(x)$ is then two-valued, essentially a Boolean mapping.

For example, consider the typical free tree shown below, with eight vertices and seven edges. We can project each vertex x onto each of the edge intervals $[u .. v]$ by deciding whether x is closer to u or to v:

	ac	bc	cd	de	ef	eg	dh		
$a \mapsto$	a	c	c	d	e	e	d	0000000	
$b \mapsto$	c	b	c	d	e	e	d	1100000	
$c \mapsto$	c	c	c	d	e	e	d	1000000	
$d \mapsto$	c	c	d	d	e	e	d	1010000	(63)
$e \mapsto$	c	c	d	e	e	e	d	1011000	
$f \mapsto$	c	c	d	e	f	e	d	1011100	
$g \mapsto$	c	c	d	e	e	g	d	1011010	
$h \mapsto$	c	c	d	d	e	e	h	1010001	

On the right we've reduced the projections to 0s and 1s, arbitrarily deciding that $a \mapsto 0000000$. The resulting bit strings are called *labels* of the vertices, and we write, for example, $l(b) = 1100000$. Since each projection is a homomorphism, we can calculate the median of any three points by simply taking Boolean medians in each component of their labels. For example, to compute $\langle bgh \rangle$ we find the bitwise median of $l(b) = 1100000$, $l(g) = 1011010$, and $l(h) = 1010001$, namely $1010000 = l(d)$.

When we project onto all the edges of a median graph, we might find that two columns of the binary labels are identical. This situation cannot occur with a free tree, but let's consider what would happen if the edge $g - h$ were added to the tree in (63): The resulting graph would still be a median graph, but the columns for eg and dh would become identical (except with $e \leftrightarrow d$ and $g \leftrightarrow h$). Furthermore, the new column for gh would turn out to be equivalent to the column for de. Redundant components should be omitted from the labels in such cases; therefore the vertices of the augmented graph would have six-bit labels, like $l(g) = 101101$ and $l(h) = 101001$, instead of seven-bit labels.

The elements of any median algebra can always be represented by labels in this way. Therefore *any identity that holds in the Boolean case will be true in all median algebras.* This "zero-one principle" makes it possible to test whether any two given expressions built from the ternary operation $\langle xyz \rangle$ can be shown to be equal as a consequence of axioms (50), (51), and (52) — although we do have to check $2^{n-1} - 1$ cases when we test n-variable expressions by this method.

For example, the associative law $\langle xw\langle ywz\rangle\rangle = \langle\langle xwy\rangle wz\rangle$ suggests that there should be a symmetrical interpretation of both sides that does not involve nested brackets. And indeed, there is such a formula:

$$\langle xw\langle ywz\rangle\rangle = \langle\langle xwy\rangle wz\rangle = \langle xwywz\rangle, \tag{64}$$

where $\langle xwywz \rangle$ denotes the median of the five-element multiset $\{x, w, y, w, z\} = \{w, w, x, y, z\}$. We can prove this formula by using the zero-one principle, noting also that median is the same thing as majority in the Boolean case. In a similar way we can prove (49), and we can show that the function used by Post in (47) can be simplified to

$$\langle x_1 y\langle x_2 y \ldots y\langle x_{s-1} y x_s\rangle \ldots\rangle\rangle = \langle x_1 y x_2 y \ldots y x_{s-1} y x_s\rangle; \tag{65}$$

it's a median of $2s - 1$ quantities, where nearly half of them are equal to y.

A set C of vertices in a graph is called *convex* if $[u \mathbin{..} v] \subseteq C$ whenever $u \in C$ and $v \in C$. In other words, whenever the endpoints of a shortest path belong to C, all vertices of that path must also be present in C. (A convex set is therefore identical to what we called an "ideal," a few pages ago; now our language has become geometric instead of algebraic.) The *convex hull* of $\{v_1, \ldots, v_m\}$ is defined to be the smallest convex set that contains each of the vertices $v_1, \ldots, v_m$. Our theoretical results above have shown that every interval $[u \mathbin{..} v]$ is convex; hence $[u \mathbin{..} v]$ is the convex hull of the two-point set $\{u, v\}$. But in fact much more is true:

Theorem C. *The convex hull of $\{v_1, v_2, \ldots, v_m\}$ in a median graph is the set of all points*

$$C = \{\langle v_1 x v_2 x \ldots x v_m\rangle \mid x \in M\}. \tag{66}$$

Furthermore, x is in C if and only if $x = \langle v_1 x v_2 x \ldots x v_m\rangle$.

Proof. Clearly $v_j \in C$ for $1 \le j \le m$. Every point of C must belong to the convex hull, because the point $x' = \langle v_2 x \ldots x v_m\rangle$ is in the hull (by induction on m), and because $\langle v_1 x \ldots x v_m\rangle \in [v_1 \mathbin{..} x']$. The zero-one principle proves that

$$\langle x\langle v_1 y v_2 y \ldots y v_m\rangle\langle v_1 z v_2 z \ldots z v_m\rangle\rangle = \langle v_1\langle xyz\rangle v_2\langle xyz\rangle \ldots \langle xyz\rangle v_m\rangle; \tag{67}$$

hence C is convex. Setting $x = y$ in this formula proves that $\langle v_1 x v_2 x \ldots x v_m\rangle$ is the closest point of C to x, and that $\langle v_1 x v_2 x \ldots x v_m\rangle \in [x \mathbin{..} z]$ for all $z \in C$. ∎

Corollary C. *Let the label of v_j be $v_{j1} \ldots v_{jt}$ for $1 \le j \le m$. Then the convex hull of $\{v_1, \ldots, v_m\}$ is the set of all $x \in M$ whose label $x_1 \ldots x_t$ satisfies $x_j = c_j$ whenever $v_{1j} = v_{2j} = \cdots = v_{mj} = c_j$.* ∎

For example, the convex hull of $\{c, g, h\}$ in (63) consists of all elements whose label matches the pattern $10**0**$, namely $\{c, d, e, g, h\}$.

When a median graph contains a 4-cycle $u \relbar x \relbar v \relbar y \relbar u$, the edges $u \relbar x$ and $v \relbar y$ are equivalent, in the sense that projection onto $[u \mathinner{.\,.} x]$ and projection onto $[v \mathinner{.\,.} y]$ both yield the same label coordinates. The reason is that, for any z with $\langle zux \rangle = u$, we have

$$
\begin{aligned}
y = \langle uvy \rangle &= \langle \langle zux \rangle vy \rangle \\
&= \langle \langle zvy \rangle \langle uvy \rangle \langle xvy \rangle \rangle \\
&= \langle \langle zvy \rangle yv \rangle,
\end{aligned}
$$

hence $\langle zvy \rangle = y$; similarly $\langle zux \rangle = x$ implies $\langle zvy \rangle = v$. The edges $x \relbar v$ and $y \relbar u$ are equivalent for the same reasons. Exercise 77 shows, among other things, that two edges yield equivalent projections if and only if they can be proved equivalent by a chain of equivalences obtained from 4-cycles in this way. Therefore the number of bits in each vertex label is the number of equivalence classes of edges induced by the 4-cycles; and it follows that the reduced labels for vertices are uniquely determined, once we specify a vertex whose label is $00 \ldots 0$.

A nice way to find the vertex labels of any median graph was discovered by P. K. Jha and G. Slutzki [*Ars Combin.* **34** (1992), 75–92] and improved by J. Hagauer, W. Imrich, and S. Klavžar [*Theor. Comp. Sci.* **215** (1999), 123–136]:

Algorithm H (*Median labels*). Given a median graph G and a source vertex a, this algorithm determines the equivalence classes defined by the 4-cycles of G, and computes the labels $l(v) = v_1 \ldots v_t$ of each vertex, where t is the number of classes and $l(a) = 0 \ldots 0$.

H1. [Initialize.] Preprocess G by visiting all vertices in order of their distance from a. For each edge $u \relbar v$, we say that u is an *early neighbor* of v if a is closer to u than to v, otherwise u is a *late neighbor*; in other words, the early neighbors of v will already have been visited when v is encountered, but the late neighbors will still be awaiting their turn. Rearrange all adjacency lists so that early neighbors are listed first. Place each edge initially in its own equivalence class; a "union-find algorithm" like Algorithm 2.3.3E will be used to merge classes when the algorithm learns that they're equivalent.

H2. [Call the subroutine.] Set $j \leftarrow 0$ and invoke Subroutine I with parameter a. (Subroutine I appears below. The global variable j will be used to create a master list of edges $r_j \relbar s_j$ for $1 \le j < n$, where n is the total number of vertices; there will be one entry with $s_j = v$, for each vertex $v \ne a$.)

H3. [Assign the labels.] Number the equivalence classes from 1 to t. Then set $l(a)$ to the t-bit string $0 \ldots 0$. For $j = 1, 2, \ldots, n - 1$ (in this order), set $l(s_j)$ to $l(r_j)$ with bit k changed from 0 to 1, where k is the equivalence class of edge $r_j \relbar s_j$. ∎

Subroutine I (*Process descendants of r*). This recursive subroutine, with parameter r and global variable j, does the main work of Algorithm H on the graph of all vertices currently reachable from vertex r. In the course of processing, all such vertices will be recorded on the master list, except r itself, and all edges between them will be removed from the current graph. Each vertex has four fields called its LINK, MARK, RANK, and MATE, initially null.

I1. [Loop over s.] Choose a vertex s with $r \text{---} s$. If there is no such vertex, return from the subroutine.

I2. [Record the edge.] Set $j \leftarrow j + 1$, $r_j \leftarrow r$, and $s_j \leftarrow s$.

I3. [Begin breadth-first search.] (Now we want to find and delete all edges of the current graph that are equivalent to $r \text{---} s$.) Set MARK$(s) \leftarrow s$, RANK$(s) \leftarrow 1$, LINK$(s) \leftarrow \Lambda$, and $v \leftarrow q \leftarrow s$.

I4. [Find the mate of v.] Find the early neighbor u of v for which MARK$(u) \neq s$. (There will be exactly one such vertex u. Recall that early neighbors have been placed first, in step H1.) Set MATE$(v) \leftarrow u$.

I5. [Delete $u \text{---} v$.] Make the edges $u \text{---} v$ and $r \text{---} s$ equivalent by merging their equivalence classes. Remove u and v from each other's adjacency lists.

I6. [Classify the neighbors of v.] For each early neighbor u of v, do step I7; for each late neighbor u of v, do step I8. Then go to step I9.

I7. [Note a possible equivalence.] If MARK$(u) = s$ and RANK$(u) = 1$, make the edge $u \text{---} v$ equivalent to the edge MATE$(u) \text{---}$ MATE(v). Return to I6.

I8. [Rank u.] If MARK$(u) = s$ and RANK$(u) = 1$, return to I6. Otherwise set MARK$(u) \leftarrow s$ and RANK$(u) \leftarrow 2$. Set w to the first neighbor of u (it will be early). If $w = v$, reset w to u's second early neighbor; but return to I6 if u has only one early neighbor. If MARK$(w) \neq s$ or RANK$(w) \neq 2$, set RANK$(u) \leftarrow 1$, LINK$(u) \leftarrow \Lambda$, LINK$(q) \leftarrow u$, and $q \leftarrow u$. Return to I6.

I9. [Continue breadth-first search.] Set $v \leftarrow$ LINK(v). Return to I4 if $v \neq \Lambda$.

I10. [Process subgraph s.] Call Subroutine I recursively with parameter s. Then return to I1. ∎

This algorithm and subroutine have been described in terms of relatively high-level data structures; further details are left to the reader. For example, adjacency lists should be doubly linked, so that edges can readily be deleted in step I5. Any convenient method for merging equivalence classes can be used in that step.

Exercise 77 explains the theory that makes this algorithm work, and exercise 78 proves that each vertex is encountered at most $\lg n$ times in step I4. Furthermore, exercise 79 shows that a median graph has at most $O(n \log n)$ edges. Therefore the total running time of Algorithm H is $O(n(\log n)^2)$, except perhaps for the bit-setting in step H3.

The reader may wish to play through Algorithm H by hand on the median graph in Table 2, whose vertices represent the twelve monotone self-dual Boolean functions of four variables $\{w, x, y, z\}$. All such functions that actually involve all four variables can be expressed as a median of five things, like (64). With

Table 2
LABELS FOR THE FREE MEDIAN ALGEBRA ON FOUR GENERATORS

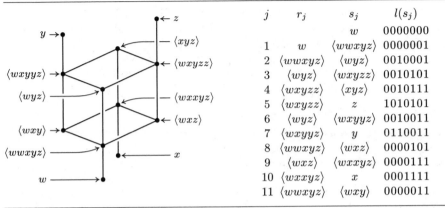

j	r_j	s_j	$l(s_j)$
		w	0000000
1	w	$\langle wwxyz \rangle$	0000001
2	$\langle wwxyz \rangle$	$\langle wyz \rangle$	0010001
3	$\langle wyz \rangle$	$\langle wxyzz \rangle$	0010101
4	$\langle wxyzz \rangle$	$\langle xyz \rangle$	0010111
5	$\langle wxyzz \rangle$	z	1010101
6	$\langle wyz \rangle$	$\langle wxyyz \rangle$	0010011
7	$\langle wxyyz \rangle$	y	0110011
8	$\langle wwxyz \rangle$	$\langle wxz \rangle$	0000101
9	$\langle wxz \rangle$	$\langle wxxyz \rangle$	0000111
10	$\langle wxxyz \rangle$	x	0001111
11	$\langle wwxyz \rangle$	$\langle wxy \rangle$	0000011

starting vertex $a = w$, the algorithm computes the master list of edges $r_j - s_j$ and the binary labels shown in the table. (The actual order of processing depends on the order in which vertices appear in adjacency lists. But the final labels will be the same under any ordering, except for permutations of the columns.)

Notice that the number of 1-bits in each label $l(v)$ is the distance of v from the starting vertex a. In fact, the uniqueness of labels tells us that *the distance between any two vertices is the number of bit positions in which their labels differ*, because we could have started at any particular vertex.

The special median graph in Table 2 could actually have been handled in a completely different way, without using Algorithm H at all, because the labels in this case are essentially the same as the *truth tables* of the corresponding functions. Here's why: We can say that the simple functions w, x, y, z have the respective truth tables $t(w) = 0000000011111111$, $t(x) = 0000111100001111$, $t(y) = 0011001100110011$, $t(z) = 0101010101010101$. Then the truth table of $\langle wwxyz \rangle$ is the bitwise majority function $\langle t(w)t(w)t(x)t(y)t(z) \rangle$, namely the string 0000000101111111; and a similar computation gives the truth tables of all the other vertices.

The last half of any self-dual function's truth table is the same as the first half, but complemented and reversed, so we can eliminate it. Furthermore the leftmost bit in each of our truth tables is always zero. We are left with the seven-bit labels shown in Table 2; and the uniqueness property guarantees that Algorithm H will produce the same result, except for possible permutation of columns, when it is presented with this particular graph.

This reasoning tells us that the edges of the graph in Table 2 correspond to pairs of functions whose truth tables are almost the same. We move between neighboring vertices by switching only two complementary bits of their truth tables. In fact, the degree of each vertex turns out to be exactly the number of prime implicants in the disjunctive prime form of the monotone self-dual function represented by that vertex (see exercises 70 and 84).

*Median sets.** A *median set* is a collection X of binary vectors with the property that $\langle xyz \rangle \in X$ whenever $x \in X$, $y \in X$, and $z \in X$, where the medians are computed componentwise as we've done with median labels. Thomas Schaefer noticed in 1978 that median sets provide us with an attractive counterpoint to the characterization of Horn functions in Theorem H:

Theorem S. *The Boolean function* $f(x_1, \ldots, x_n)$ *is expressible as a conjunction of Krom clauses if and only if*

$$f(x_1, \ldots, x_n) = f(y_1, \ldots, y_n) = f(z_1, \ldots, z_n) = 1$$
$$\text{implies} \quad f(\langle x_1 y_1 z_1 \rangle, \ldots, \langle x_n y_n z_n \rangle) = 1 \qquad (68)$$

for all Boolean values x_j, y_j, *and* z_j.

Proof. [*STOC* **10** (1978), 216–226, Lemma 3.1B.] If we have $x_1 \vee x_2 = y_1 \vee y_2 = z_1 \vee z_2 = 1$, say, with $x_1 \leq y_1 \leq z_1$, then $\langle x_1 y_1 z_1 \rangle \vee \langle x_2 y_2 z_2 \rangle = y_1 \vee \langle x_2 y_2 z_2 \rangle = 1$, since $y_1 = 0$ implies that $x_2 = y_2 = 1$. Thus (68) is necessary.

Conversely, if (68) holds, let $u_1 \vee \cdots \vee u_k$ be a prime clause of f, where each u_j is a literal. Then, for $1 \leq j \leq k$, the clause $u_1 \vee \cdots \vee u_{j-1} \vee u_{j+1} \vee \cdots \vee u_k$ is not a clause of f; so there's a vector $x^{(j)}$ with $f(x^{(j)}) = 1$ but with $u_i^{(j)} = 0$ for all $i \neq j$. If $k \geq 3$, the median $\langle x^{(1)} x^{(2)} x^{(3)} \rangle$ has $u_i = 0$ for $1 \leq i \leq k$; but that's impossible, because $u_1 \vee \cdots \vee u_k$ was supposedly a clause. Hence $k \leq 2$. ∎

Thus median sets are the same as "2SAT instances," the sets of points that satisfy some formula f in 2CNF.

A median set is said to be *reduced* if its vectors $x = x_1 \ldots x_t$ contain no redundant components. In other words, for each coordinate position k, a reduced median set has at least two vectors $x^{(k)}$ and $y^{(k)}$ with the property that $x_k^{(k)} = 0$ and $y_k^{(k)} = 1$ but $x_i^{(k)} = y_i^{(k)}$ for all $i \neq k$. We've seen that the labels of a median graph satisfy this condition; in fact, if coordinate k corresponds to the edge $u - v$ in the graph, we can let $x^{(k)}$ and $y^{(k)}$ be the labels of u and v. Conversely, any reduced median set X defines a median graph, with one vertex for each element of X and with adjacency defined by all-but-one equality of coordinates. The median labels of these vertices must be identical to the original vectors in X, because we know that median labels are essentially unique.

Median labels and reduced median sets can also be characterized in yet another instructive way, which harks back to the networks of *comparator modules* that we studied in Section 5.3.4. We noted in that section that such networks are useful for "oblivious sorting" of numbers, and we noted in Theorem 5.3.4Z that a network of comparators will sort all $n!$ possible input permutations if and only if it correctly sorts all 2^n combinations of 0s and 1s. When a comparator module is attached to two horizontal lines, with inputs x and y entering from the left, it outputs the same two values on the right, but with $\min(x, y) = x \wedge y$ on the upper line and $\max(x, y) = x \vee y$ on the lower line. Let's now extend the concept slightly by also allowing *inverter modules*, which change 0 to 1 and vice versa. Here, for example, is a comparator-inverter network (or CI-net, for short), which transforms the binary value 0010 into 0111:

$$(69)$$

(A single dot denotes an inverter.) Indeed, this network transforms

$0000 \mapsto 0110$;	$0100 \mapsto 0111$;	$1000 \mapsto 0111$;	$1100 \mapsto 0110$;
$0001 \mapsto 0111$;	$0101 \mapsto 1111$;	$1001 \mapsto 0101$;	$1101 \mapsto 0111$;
$0010 \mapsto 0111$;	$0110 \mapsto 1111$;	$1010 \mapsto 0101$;	$1110 \mapsto 0111$;
$0011 \mapsto 0110$;	$0111 \mapsto 0111$;	$1011 \mapsto 0111$;	$1111 \mapsto 0110$.

$$(70)$$

Suppose a CI-net transforms the bit string $x = x_1 \ldots x_t$ into the bit string $x'_1 \ldots x'_t = f(x)$. This function f, which maps the t-cube into itself, is in fact a *graph homomorphism.* In other words, we have $f(x) - f(y)$ whenever $x - y$ in the t-cube: Changing one bit of x always causes exactly one bit of $f(x)$ to change, because every module in the network has this behavior. Moreover, CI-nets have a remarkable connection with median labels:

Theorem F. *Every set X of t-bit median labels can be represented by a comparator-inverter network that computes a Boolean function $f(x)$ with the property that $f(x) \in X$ for all bit vectors $x_1 \ldots x_t$, and $f(x) = x$ for all $x \in X$.*

Proof. [Tomás Feder, *Memoirs Amer. Math. Soc.* **555** (1995), 1–223, Lemma 3.37; see also the Ph. D. thesis of D. H. Wiedemann (University of Waterloo, 1986).] Consider columns i and j of the median labels, where $1 \le i < j \le t$. Any such pair of columns contains at least three of the four possibilities $\{00, 01, 10, 11\}$, if we look through the entire set of labels, because median labels have no redundant columns. Let us write $\bar{j} \to i$, $j \to i$, $i \to j$, or $i \to \bar{j}$ if the value 00, 01, 10, or 11 (respectively) is missing from those two columns; we can also note the equivalent relations $\bar{i} \to j$, $\bar{i} \to \bar{j}$, $\bar{j} \to \bar{i}$, or $j \to \bar{i}$, respectively, which involve $\bar{i}$ instead of i. For example, the labels in Table 2 give us the relations

$$
\begin{array}{ll}
1 \to \bar{2}, 3, \bar{4}, 5, \bar{6}, 7 & 2, \bar{3}, 4, \bar{5}, \bar{6}, \bar{7} \to \bar{1}; \\
2 \to 3, \bar{4}, \bar{5}, 6, 7 & \bar{3}, 4, 5, \bar{6}, \bar{7} \to \bar{2}; \\
3 \to \bar{4}, 7 & 4, \bar{7} \to \bar{3}; \\
4 \to 5, 6, 7 & \bar{5}, \bar{6}, \bar{7} \to \bar{4}; \\
5 \to 7 & \bar{7} \to \bar{5}; \\
6 \to 7 & \bar{7} \to \bar{6}.
\end{array}
$$

$$(71)$$

(There is no relation between 3 and 5 because all four possibilities occur in those columns. But we have $3 \to \bar{4}$ because 11 doesn't appear in columns 3 and 4. The vertices whose label has a 1 in column 3 are those closer to $\langle wyz \rangle$ than to $\langle wwxyz \rangle$ in Table 2; they form a convex set in which column 4 of the labels is always 0, because they are also closer to $\langle wxxyz \rangle$ than to x.)

These relations between the literals $\{1, \bar{1}, 2, \bar{2}, \ldots, t, \bar{t}\}$ contain no cycles, so they can always be topologically sorted into an anti-symmetrical sequence

$u_1 u_2 \ldots u_{2t}$ in which u_j is the complement of u_{2t+1-j}. For example,

$$1\ \bar{7}\ 4\ 2\ \bar{3}\ \bar{5}\ \bar{6}\ 6\ 5\ 3\ \bar{2}\ \bar{4}\ 7\ \bar{1} \tag{72}$$

is one such way to sort the relations in (71) topologically.

Now we proceed to construct the network, by starting with t empty lines and successively examining elements u_k and u_{k+d} in the topological sequence, for $d = 2t - 2,\ 2t - 3,\ \ldots,\ 1$ (in this order), and for $k = 1, 2, \ldots, t - \lceil d/2 \rceil$. If $u_k \le u_{k+d}$ is a relation between columns i and j, where $i < j$, we append new modules to lines i and j of the network as follows:

$$\text{If } i \to j \qquad \text{If } i \to \bar{j} \qquad \text{If } \bar{i} \to j \qquad \text{If } \bar{i} \to \bar{j} \tag{73}$$

For example, from (71) and (72) we first enforce $1 \to 7$, then $1 \to \bar{4}$, then $1 \to \bar{2}$, then $\bar{7} \to \bar{4}$ (that is, $4 \to 7$), etc., obtaining the following network:

$$\tag{74}$$

(Go figure. No modules are contributed when, say, u_k is $\bar{7}$ and u_{k+d} is 3, because the relation $\bar{3} \to 7$ does not appear in (71).)

Exercise 89 proves that each new cluster of modules (73) preserves all of the previous inequalities and enforces a new one. Therefore, if x is any input vector, $f(x)$ satisfies all of the inequalities; so $f(x) \in X$ by Theorem S. Conversely, if $x \in X$, every cluster of modules in the network leaves x unchanged. ∎

Corollary F. *Suppose the median labels in Theorem F are closed under the operations of bitwise AND and OR, so that $x \,\&\, y \in X$ and $x \mid y \in X$ whenever $x \in X$ and $y \in X$. Then there is a permutation of coordinates under which the labels are representable by a network of comparator modules only.*

Proof. The bitwise AND of all labels is $0 \ldots 0$, and the bitwise OR is $1 \ldots 1$. So the only possible relations between columns are $i \to j$ and $j \to i$. By topologically sorting and renaming the columns, we can ensure that only $i \to j$ occurs when $i < j$; and in this case the construction in the proof never uses an inverter. ∎

In general, if G is any graph, a homomorphism f that maps the vertices of G onto a subset X of those vertices is called a *retraction* if it satisfies $f(x) = x$ for all $x \in X$; and we call X a *retract* of G when such an f exists. The importance of this concept in the theory of graphs was first pointed out by Pavol Hell [see *Lecture Notes in Math.* **406** (1974), 291–301]. One consequence, for example, is that the distance between vertices in X—the number of edges on a shortest path— remains the same even if we restrict consideration to paths that lie entirely in X. (See exercise 93.)

Theorem F demonstrates that every t-dimensional set of median labels is a retract of the t-dimensional hypercube. Conversely, exercise 94 shows that hypercube retracts are always median graphs.

Threshold functions. A particularly appealing and important class of Boolean functions $f(x_1, x_2, \ldots, x_n)$ arises when f can be defined by the formula

$$f(x_1, x_2, \ldots, x_n) = [w_1x_1 + w_2x_2 + \cdots + w_nx_n \geq t], \qquad (75)$$

where the constants w_1, w_2, $\ldots$, w_n are integer "weights" and t is an integer "threshold" value. For example, threshold functions are important even when all the weights are unity: We have

$$x_1 \wedge x_2 \wedge \cdots \wedge x_n = [x_1 + x_2 + \cdots + x_n \geq n]; \qquad (76)$$

$$x_1 \vee x_2 \vee \cdots \vee x_n = [x_1 + x_2 + \cdots + x_n \geq 1]; \qquad (77)$$

$$\text{and} \qquad \langle x_1 x_2 \ldots x_{2t-1} \rangle = [x_1 + x_2 + \cdots + x_{2t-1} \geq t], \qquad (78)$$

where $\langle x_1 x_2 \ldots x_{2t-1} \rangle$ stands for the median (or majority) value of a multiset that consists of any odd number of Boolean values $\{x_1, x_2, \ldots, x_{2t-1}\}$. In particular, the basic mappings $x \wedge y$, $x \vee y$, and $\langle xyz \rangle$ are all threshold functions, and so is

$$\bar{x} = [-x \geq 0]. \qquad (79)$$

With more general weights we get many other functions of interest, such as

$$[2^{n-1}x_1 + 2^{n-2}x_2 + \cdots + x_n \geq (t_1 t_2 \ldots t_n)_2], \qquad (80)$$

which is true if and only if the binary string $x_1 x_2 \ldots x_n$ is lexicographically greater than or equal to a given binary string $t_1 t_2 \ldots t_n$. Given a set of n objects having sizes w_1, w_2, $\ldots$, w_n, a subset of those objects will fit into a knapsack of size $t - 1$ if and only if $f(x_1, x_2, \ldots, x_n) = 0$, where $x_j = 1$ represents the presence of object j in the subset. Simple models of neurons, originally proposed by W. McCullough and W. Pitts in *Bull. Math. Biophysics* **5** (1943), 115–133, have led to thousands of research papers about "neural networks" built from threshold functions.

We can get rid of any negative weight w_j by setting $x_j \leftarrow \bar{x}_j$, $w_j \leftarrow -w_j$, and $t \leftarrow t + |w_j|$. Thus a general threshold function can be reduced to a positive threshold function in which all weights are nonnegative. Furthermore, any positive threshold function (75) can be expressed as a special case of the median/majority-of-odd function, because we have

$$\langle 0^a 1^b x_1^{w_1} x_2^{w_2} \ldots x_n^{w_n} \rangle = [b + w_1 x_1 + w_2 x_2 + \cdots + w_n x_n \geq b + t], \qquad (81)$$

where x^m stands for m copies of x, and where a and b are defined by the rules

$$a = \max(0, 2t - 1 - w), \quad b = \max(0, w + 1 - 2t), \quad w = w_1 + w_2 + \cdots + w_n. \qquad (82)$$

For example, when all weights are 1, we have

$$\langle 0^{n-1} x_1 \ldots x_n \rangle = x_1 \wedge \cdots \wedge x_n \quad \text{and} \quad \langle 1^{n-1} x_1 \ldots x_n \rangle = x_1 \vee \cdots \vee x_n; \qquad (83)$$

we've already seen these formulas in (45) when $n = 2$. In general, either a or b is zero, and the left-hand side of (81) specifies a median of $2T - 1$ elements, where

$$T = b + t = \max(t, w_1 + w_2 + \cdots + w_n + 1 - t). \qquad (84)$$

There would be no point in letting both a and b be greater than zero, because the majority function clearly satisfies the cancellation law

$$\langle 01x_1x_2\ldots x_{2t-1}\rangle = \langle x_1x_2\ldots x_{2t-1}\rangle. \tag{85}$$

One important consequence of (81) is that every positive threshold function comes from the pure majority function

$$g(x_0, x_1, x_2, \ldots, x_n) = \langle x_0^{a+b}x_1^{w_1}x_2^{w_2}\ldots x_n^{w_n}\rangle \tag{86}$$

by setting $x_0 = 0$ or 1. In other words, we know all threshold functions of n variables if and only if we know all of the distinct median-of-odd functions of $n+1$ or fewer variables (containing no constants). Every pure majority function is monotone and self-dual; thus we've seen the pure majority functions of four variables $\{w, x, y, z\}$ in column s_j of Table 2 on page 71, namely $\langle w\rangle$, $\langle wwxyz\rangle$, $\langle wyz\rangle$, $\langle wxyzz\rangle$, $\langle xyz\rangle$, $\langle z\rangle$, $\langle wxyyz\rangle$, $\langle y\rangle$, $\langle wxz\rangle$, $\langle wxxyz\rangle$, $\langle x\rangle$, $\langle wxy\rangle$. By setting $w = 0$ or 1, we obtain all the positive threshold functions $f(x, y, z)$ of three variables:

$$\langle 0\rangle, \langle 1\rangle, \langle 00xyz\rangle, \langle 11xyz\rangle, \langle 0yz\rangle, \langle 1yz\rangle, \langle 0xyzz\rangle, \langle 1xyzz\rangle, \langle xyz\rangle, \langle z\rangle,$$

$$\langle 0xyyz\rangle, \langle 1xyyz\rangle, \langle y\rangle, \langle 0xz\rangle, \langle 1xz\rangle, \langle 0xxyz\rangle, \langle 1xxyz\rangle, \langle x\rangle, \langle 0xy\rangle, \langle 1xy\rangle. \tag{87}$$

All 150 positive threshold functions of four variables can be obtained in a similar fashion from the self-dual majority functions in the answer to exercise 84.

There are infinitely many sequences of weights $(w_1, w_2, \ldots, w_n)$, but only finitely many threshold functions for any given value of n. So it is clear that many different weight sequences are equivalent. For example, consider the pure majority function

$$\langle x_1^2 x_2^3 x_3^5 x_4^7 x_5^{11} x_6^{13}\rangle,$$

in which prime numbers have been used as weights. A brute-force examination of 2^6 cases shows that

$$\langle x_1^2 x_2^3 x_3^5 x_4^7 x_5^{11} x_6^{13}\rangle = \langle x_1 x_2^2 x_3^2 x_4^3 x_5^4 x_6^5\rangle; \tag{88}$$

thus we can express the same function with substantially smaller weights. Similarly, the threshold function

$$[(x_1x_2\ldots x_{20})_2 \geq (01100100100001111110)_2] = \langle 1^{225028} x_1^{524288} x_2^{262144} \ldots x_{20}\rangle,$$

a special case of (80), turns out to be simply

$$\langle 1^{323} x_1^{764} x_2^{323} x_3^{323} x_4^{118} x_5^{118} x_6^{87} x_7^{31} x_8^{31} x_9^{25} x_{10}^6 x_{11}^6 x_{12}^6 x_{13}^6 x_{14}x_{15}x_{16}x_{17}x_{18}x_{19}\rangle. \tag{89}$$

Exercise 103 explains how to find a minimum set of weights without resorting to a huge brute-force search, using linear programming.

A nice indexing scheme by which a unique identifier can be assigned to any threshold function was discovered by C. K. Chow [*FOCS* **2** (1961), 34–38]. Given any Boolean function $f(x_1, \ldots, x_n)$, let $N(f)$ be the number of vectors $x = (x_1, \ldots, x_n)$ for which $f(x) = 1$, and let $\Sigma(f)$ be the sum of all those vectors. For example, if $f(x_1, x_2) = x_1 \vee x_2$, we have $N(f) = 3$ and $\Sigma(f) = (0, 1) + (1, 0) + (1, 1) = (2, 2)$.

Theorem T. *Let $f(x_1,\ldots,x_n)$ and $g(x_1,\ldots,x_n)$ be Boolean functions with $N(f) = N(g)$ and $\Sigma(f) = \Sigma(g)$, where f is a threshold function. Then $f = g$.*

Proof. Suppose there are exactly k vectors $x^{(1)}$, ..., $x^{(k)}$ such that $f(x^{(j)}) = 1$ and $g(x^{(j)}) = 0$. Since $N(f) = N(g)$, there must be exactly k vectors $y^{(1)}$, ..., $y^{(k)}$ such that $f(y^{(j)}) = 0$ and $g(y^{(j)}) = 1$. And since $\Sigma(f) = \Sigma(g)$, we must also have $x^{(1)} + \cdots + x^{(k)} = y^{(1)} + \cdots + y^{(k)}$.

Now suppose f is the threshold function (75); then we have $w \cdot x^{(j)} \geq t$ and $w \cdot y^{(j)} < t$ for $1 \leq j \leq k$. But if $f \neq g$ we have $k > 0$, and $w \cdot (x^{(1)} + \cdots + x^{(k)}) \geq kt > w \cdot (y^{(1)} + \cdots + y^{(k)})$, a contradiction. ∎

Threshold functions have many curious properties, some of which are explored in the exercises below. Their classical theory is well summarized in Saburo Muroga's book *Threshold Logic and its Applications* (Wiley, 1971).

Symmetric Boolean functions. A function $f(x_1,\ldots,x_n)$ is called *symmetric* if $f(x_1,\ldots,x_n)$ is equal to $f(x_{p(1)},\ldots,x_{p(n)})$ for all permutations $p(1)\ldots p(n)$ of $\{1,\ldots,n\}$. When all the x_j are 0 or 1, this condition means that f depends only on the number of 1s that are present in the arguments, namely the "sideways sum" $\nu x = \nu(x_1,\ldots,x_n) = x_1 + \cdots + x_n$. The notation $S_{k_1,k_2,\ldots,k_r}(x_1,\ldots,x_n)$ is commonly used to stand for the Boolean function that is true if and only if νx is either k_1 or k_2 or $\cdots$ or k_r. For example, $S_{1,3,5}(v,w,x,y,z) = v \oplus w \oplus x \oplus y \oplus z$; $S_{3,4,5}(v,w,x,y,z) = \langle vwxyz \rangle$; $S_{4,5}(v,w,x,y,z) = \langle 00vwxyz \rangle$.

Many applications of symmetry involve the basic functions $S_k(x_1,\ldots,x_n)$ that are true only when $\nu x = k$. For example, $S_3(x_1,x_2,x_3,x_4,x_5,x_6)$ is true if and only if exactly half of the arguments $\{x_1,\ldots,x_6\}$ are true and the other half are false. In such cases we obviously have

$$S_k(x_1,\ldots,x_n) = S_{\geq k}(x_1,\ldots,x_n) \wedge \overline{S_{\geq k+1}(x_1,\ldots,x_n)}, \qquad (90)$$

where $S_{\geq k}(x_1,\ldots,x_n)$ is an abbreviation for $S_{k,k+1,\ldots,n}(x_1,\ldots,x_n)$. The functions $S_{\geq k}(x_1,\ldots,x_n)$ are, of course, the threshold functions $[x_1 + \cdots + x_n \geq k]$ that we have already studied.

More complicated cases can be treated as threshold functions of threshold functions. For example, we have

$$S_{2,3,6,8,9}(x_1,\ldots,x_{12}) = \left[\nu x \geq 2 + 4[\nu x \geq 4] + 2[\nu x \geq 7] + 5[\nu x \geq 10]\right]$$
$$= \langle 00x_1\ldots x_{12}\langle 0^5\bar{x}_1\ldots\bar{x}_{12}\rangle^4\langle 1\bar{x}_1\ldots\bar{x}_{12}\rangle^2\langle 1^7\bar{x}_1\ldots\bar{x}_{12}\rangle^5\rangle, \qquad (91)$$

because the number of 1s in the outermost majority-of-25 turns out to be respectively $(11, 12, 13, 14, 11, 12, 13, 12, 13, 14, 10, 11, 12)$ when $x_1 + \cdots + x_{12} = (0, 1, \ldots, 12)$. A similar two-level scheme works in general [R. C. Minnick, *IRE Trans.* **EC-10** (1961), 6–16]; and with three or more levels of logic we can reduce the number of thresholding operations even further. (See exercise 113.)

A variety of ingenious tricks have been discovered for evaluating symmetric Boolean functions. For example, S. Muroga attributes the following remarkable sequence of formulas to F. Sasaki:

$$x_0 \oplus x_1 \oplus \cdots \oplus x_{2m} = \langle \bar{x}_0 s_1 s_2 \ldots s_{2m}\rangle,$$
$$\text{where} \quad s_j = \langle x_0 x_j x_{j+1}\ldots x_{j+m-1}\bar{x}_{j+m}\bar{x}_{j+m+1}\ldots\bar{x}_{j+2m-1}\rangle, \qquad (92)$$

if $m > 0$ and if we consider x_{2m+k} to be the same as x_k for $k \geq 1$. In particular, when $m = 1$ and $m = 2$ we have the identities

$$x_0 \oplus x_1 \oplus x_2 = \langle \bar{x}_0 \langle x_0 x_1 \bar{x}_2 \rangle \langle x_0 x_2 \bar{x}_1 \rangle \rangle; \tag{93}$$

$$x_0 \oplus \cdots \oplus x_4 = \langle \bar{x}_0 \langle x_0 x_1 x_2 \bar{x}_3 \bar{x}_4 \rangle \langle x_0 x_2 x_3 \bar{x}_4 \bar{x}_1 \rangle \langle x_0 x_3 x_4 \bar{x}_1 \bar{x}_2 \rangle \langle x_0 x_4 x_1 \bar{x}_2 \bar{x}_3 \rangle \rangle. \tag{94}$$

The right-hand sides are fully symmetric, but not obviously so! (See exercise 115.)

Canalizing functions. A Boolean function $f(x_1, \ldots, x_n)$ is said to be *canalizing* or "forcing" if we might be able to deduce its value by examining at most one of its variables. More precisely, f is canalizing if $n = 0$ or if there's a subscript j for which $f(x)$ either has a constant value when we set $x_j = 0$ or a constant value when we set $x_j = 1$. For example, $f(x, y, z) = (x \oplus z) \vee \bar{y}$ is canalizing because it always equals 1 when $y = 0$. (When $y = 1$ we don't know the value of f without examining also x and z; but half a loaf is better than none.) Such functions, introduced by Stuart Kauffman [*Lectures on Mathematics in the Life Sciences* **3** (1972), 63–116; *J. Theoretical Biology* **44** (1974), 167–190], have proved to be important in many applications, especially in chemistry and biology. Some of their properties are examined in exercises 125–129.

Quantitative considerations. We've been studying many different kinds of Boolean functions, so it's natural to ask: How many n-variable functions of each type actually exist? Tables 3, 4, and 5 provide the answers, at least for small values of n.

All functions are counted in Table 3. There are 2^{2^n} possibilities for each n, since there are 2^{2^n} possible truth tables. Some of these functions are self-dual, some are monotone; some are both monotone and self-dual, as in Theorem P. Some are Horn functions as in Theorem H; some are Krom functions as in Theorem S; and so on.

But in Table 4, two functions are considered identical if they differ only because the names of variables have changed. Thus only 12 different cases arise when $n = 2$, because (for example) $x \vee \bar{y}$ and $\bar{x} \vee y$ are essentially the same.

Table 5 goes a step further: It allows us to complement individual variables, and even to complement the entire function, without essentially changing it. From this perspective the 256 Boolean functions of (x, y, z) fall into only 14 different equivalence classes:

Representative	Class size	Representative	Class size
0	2	$x \wedge (y \oplus z)$	24
x	6	$x \oplus (y \wedge z)$	24
$x \wedge y$	24	$(x \wedge y) \vee (\bar{x} \wedge z)$	24
$x \oplus y$	6	$(x \vee y) \wedge (x \oplus z)$	48
$x \wedge y \wedge z$	16	$(x \oplus y) \vee (x \oplus z)$	8
$x \oplus y \oplus z$	2	$\langle xyz \rangle$	8
$x \wedge (y \vee z)$	48	$S_1(x, y, z)$	16

$$(95)$$

We shall study ways to count and to list inequivalent combinatorial objects in Section 7.2.3.

Table 3

BOOLEAN FUNCTIONS OF n VARIABLES

	$n=0$	$n=1$	$n=2$	$n=3$	$n=4$	$n=5$	$n=6$
arbitrary	2	4	16	256	65,536	4,294,967,296	18,446,744,073,709,551,616
self-dual	0	2	4	16	256	65,536	4,294,967,296
monotone	2	3	6	20	168	7,581	7,828,354
both	0	1	2	4	12	81	2,646
Horn	2	4	14	122	4,960	2,771,104	151,947,502,948
Krom	2	4	16	166	4,170	224,716	24,445,368
threshold	2	4	14	104	1,882	94,572	15,028,134
symmetric	2	4	8	16	32	64	128
canalizing	2	4	14	120	3,514	1,292,276	103,071,426,294

Table 4

BOOLEAN FUNCTIONS DISTINCT UNDER PERMUTATION OF VARIABLES

	$n=0$	$n=1$	$n=2$	$n=3$	$n=4$	$n=5$	$n=6$
arbitrary	2	4	12	80	3,984	37,333,248	25,626,412,338,274,304
self-dual	0	2	2	8	32	1,088	6,385,408
monotone	2	3	5	10	30	210	16,353
both	0	1	1	2	3	7	30
Horn	2	4	10	38	368	29,328	216,591,692
Krom	2	4	12	48	308	3,028	49,490
threshold	2	4	10	34	178	1,720	590,440
canalizing	2	4	10	38	294	15,774	149,325,022

Table 5

BOOLEAN FUNCTIONS DISTINCT UNDER COMPLEMENTATION/PERMUTATION

	$n=0$	$n=1$	$n=2$	$n=3$	$n=4$	$n=5$	$n=6$
arbitrary	1	2	4	14	222	616,126	200,253,952,527,184
self-dual	0	1	1	3	7	83	109,950
threshold	1	2	3	6	15	63	567
both	0	1	1	2	3	7	21
canalizing	1	2	3	6	22	402	1,228,158

EXERCISES

1. [*15*] (Lewis Carroll.) Make sense of Tweedledee's comment, quoted near the beginning of this section. [*Hint:* See Table 1.]

2. [*17*] Logicians on the remote planet Pincus use the symbol 1 to represent "false" and 0 to represent "true." Thus, for example, they have a binary operation called "or" whose properties

$$1 \text{ or } 1 = 1, \qquad 1 \text{ or } 0 = 0, \qquad 0 \text{ or } 1 = 0, \qquad 0 \text{ or } 0 = 0$$

we associate with $\wedge$. What operations would we associate with the 16 logical operators that Pincusians respectively call "falsehood," "and," ..., "nand," "validity" (see Table 1)?

▶ **3.** [*13*] Suppose logical values were respectively -1 for falsehood and $+1$ for truth, instead of 0 and 1. What operations $\circ$ in Table 1 would then correspond to (a) $\max(x, y)$? (b) $\min(x, y)$? (c) $-x$? (d) $x \cdot y$?

4. [*24*] (H. M. Sheffer.) The purpose of this exercise is to show that all of the operations in Table 1 can be expressed in terms of NAND. (a) For each of the 16 operators $\circ$ in that table, find a formula equivalent to $x \circ y$ that uses only $\bar{\wedge}$ as an operator. Your formula should be as short as possible. For example, the answer for operation $\llcorner$ is simply "x", but the answer for $\bar{\llcorner}$ is "$x \bar{\wedge} x$". Do not use the constants 0 or 1 in your formulas. (b) Similarly, find 16 short formulas when constants *are* allowed. For example, $x \bar{\llcorner} y$ can now be expressed also as "$x \bar{\wedge} 1$".

5. [*24*] Consider exercise 4 with $\bar{\sqsubset}$ as the basic operation instead of $\bar{\wedge}$.

6. [*21*] (E. Schröder.) (a) Which of the 16 operations in Table 1 are associative — in other words, which of them satisfy $x \circ (y \circ z) = (x \circ y) \circ z$? (b) Which of them satisfy the identity $(x \circ y) \circ (y \circ z) = x \circ z$?

7. [*20*] Which operations in Table 1 have the property that $x \circ y = z$ if and only if $y \circ z = x$?

8. [*24*] Which of the 16^2 pairs of operations $(\circ, \square)$ satisfy the left-distributive law $x \circ (y \square z) = (x \circ y) \square (x \circ z)$?

9. [*16*] True or false? (a) $(x \oplus y) \vee z = (x \vee z) \oplus (y \vee z)$; (b) $(w \oplus x \oplus y) \vee z = (w \vee z) \oplus (x \vee z) \oplus (y \vee z)$; (c) $(x \oplus y) \vee (y \oplus z) = (x \oplus z) \vee (y \oplus z)$.

10. [*17*] What is the multilinear representation of the "random" function (22)?

11. [*M25*] Is there an intuitive way to understand exactly when the multilinear representation of $f(x_1, \ldots, x_n)$ contains, say, the term $x_2 x_3 x_6 x_8$? (See (19).)

▶ **12.** [*M23*] The *integer multilinear representation* of a Boolean function extends representations like (19) to a polynomial $f(x_1, \ldots, x_n)$ with integer coefficients, in such a way that $f(x_1, \ldots, x_n)$ has the correct value (0 or 1) for all 2^n possible 0–1 vectors $(x_1, \ldots, x_n)$, *without* taking a remainder mod 2. For example, the integer multilinear representation corresponding to (19) is $1 - xy - xz - yz + 3xyz$.
   a) What is the integer multilinear representation of the "random" function (22)?
   b) How large can the coefficients of such a representation $f(x_1, \ldots, x_n)$ be?
   c) Show that, in every integer multilinear representation, $0 \le f(x_1, \ldots, x_n) \le 1$ whenever $x_1, \ldots, x_n$ are real numbers with $0 \le x_1, \ldots, x_n \le 1$.
   d) Similarly, if $f(x_1, \ldots, x_n) \le g(x_1, \ldots, x_n)$ whenever $\{x_1, \ldots, x_n\} \subseteq \{0, 1\}$, then $f(x_1, \ldots, x_n) \le g(x_1, \ldots, x_n)$ whenever $\{x_1, \ldots, x_n\} \subseteq [0 \mathinner{.\,.} 1]$.
   e) If f is monotone and $0 \le x_j \le y_j \le 1$ for $1 \le j \le n$, prove that $f(x) \le f(y)$.

▶ **13.** [*20*] Consider a system that consists of n units, each of which may be "working" or "failing." If x_j represents the condition "unit j is working," then a Boolean function like $x_1 \wedge (\bar{x}_2 \vee \bar{x}_3)$ represents the statement "unit 1 is working, but either unit 2 or unit 3 is failing"; and $S_3(x_1, \ldots, x_n)$ means "exactly three units are working."

Suppose each unit j is in working order with probability p_j, independent of the other units. Show that the Boolean function $f(x_1, \ldots, x_n)$ is true with probability $F(p_1, \ldots, p_n)$, where F is a polynomial in the variables $p_1, \ldots, p_n$.

14. [*20*] The probability function $F(p_1, \ldots, p_n)$ in exercise 13 is often called the *availability* of the system. Find the self-dual function $f(x_1, x_2, x_3)$ of maximum availability when the probabilities (p_1, p_2, p_3) are (a) $(.9, .8, .7)$; (b) $(.8, .6, .4)$; (c) $(.8, .6, .1)$.

▶ **15.** [*M20*] If $f(x_1, \ldots, x_n)$ is any Boolean function, show that there is a polynomial $F(x)$ with the property that $F(x)$ is an integer when x is an integer, and $f(x_1, \ldots, x_n) = F((x_n \ldots x_1)_2) \bmod 2$. *Hint:* Consider $\binom{x}{k} \bmod 2$.

16. [*13*] Can we replace each $\vee$ by $\oplus$ in a full disjunctive normal form?

17. [*10*] By De Morgan's laws, a general disjunctive normal form such as (25) is not only an OR of ANDs, it is a NAND of NANDs:

$$\overline{\overline{(u_{11} \wedge \cdots \wedge u_{1s_1})} \wedge \cdots \wedge \overline{(u_{m1} \wedge \cdots \wedge u_{ms_m})}}.$$

Both levels of logic can therefore be considered to be identical.

A student named J. H. Quick rewrote this expression in the form

$$(u_{11} \overline{\wedge} \cdots \overline{\wedge} u_{1s_1}) \overline{\wedge} \cdots \overline{\wedge} (u_{m1} \overline{\wedge} \cdots \overline{\wedge} u_{ms_m}).$$

Was that a good idea?

▶ **18.** [*20*] Let $u_1 \wedge \cdots \wedge u_s$ be an implicant in a disjunctive normal form for a Boolean function f, and let $v_1 \vee \cdots \vee v_t$ be a clause in a conjunctive normal form for the same function. Prove that $u_i = v_j$ for some i and j.

19. [*20*] What is the conjunctive prime form of the "random" function in (22)?

20. [*M21*] True or false: Every prime implicant of $f \wedge g$ can be written $f' \wedge g'$, where f' is a prime implicant of f and g' is a prime implicant of g.

21. [*M20*] Prove that a nonconstant Boolean function is monotone if and only if it can be expressed entirely in terms of the operations $\wedge$ and $\vee$.

22. [*20*] Suppose $f(x_1, \ldots, x_n) = g(x_1, \ldots, x_{n-1}) \oplus h(x_1, \ldots, x_{n-1}) \wedge x_n$ as in (16). What conditions on the functions g and h are necessary and sufficient for f to be monotone?

23. [*15*] What is the conjunctive prime form of $(v \wedge w \wedge x) \vee (v \wedge x \wedge z) \vee (x \wedge y \wedge z)$?

24. [*M20*] Consider the complete binary tree with 2^k leaves, illustrated here for $k = 3$. Operate alternately with $\wedge$ or $\vee$ on each level, using $\wedge$ at the root, obtaining for example $((x_0 \wedge x_1) \vee (x_2 \wedge x_3)) \wedge$  $((x_4 \wedge x_5) \vee (x_6 \wedge x_7))$. How many prime implicants does the resulting function contain?

25. [*M21*] How many prime implicants does $(x_1 \vee x_2) \wedge (x_2 \vee x_3) \wedge \cdots \wedge (x_{n-1} \vee x_n)$ have?

26. [*M23*] Let $\mathcal{F}$ and $\mathcal{G}$ be the families of index sets for the prime clauses and the prime implicants of a monotone CNF and a monotone DNF:

$$f(x) = \bigwedge_{I \in \mathcal{F}} \bigvee_{i \in I} x_i; \qquad g(x) = \bigvee_{J \in \mathcal{G}} \bigwedge_{j \in J} x_j.$$

Exhibit an x such that $f(x) \neq g(x)$ if any of the following conditions hold:
  a) There is an $I \in \mathcal{F}$ and a $J \in \mathcal{G}$ with $I \cap J = \emptyset$.
  b) $\bigcup_{I \in \mathcal{F}} I \neq \bigcup_{J \in \mathcal{G}} J$.
  c) There's an $I \in \mathcal{F}$ with $|I| > |\mathcal{G}|$, or a $J \in \mathcal{G}$ with $|J| > |\mathcal{F}|$.
  d) $\sum_{I \in \mathcal{F}} 2^{n-|I|} + \sum_{J \in \mathcal{G}} 2^{n-|J|} < 2^n$, where $n = |\bigcup_{I \in \mathcal{F}} I|$.

27. [*M31*] Continuing the previous exercise, consider the following algorithm X($\mathcal{F}, \mathcal{G}$), which either returns a vector x with $f(x) \neq g(x)$, or returns Λ if $f = g$:

X1. [Check necessary conditions.] Return an appropriate value x if condition (a), (b), (c), or (d) in exercise 26 applies.

X2. [Done?] If $|\mathcal{F}||\mathcal{G}| \leq 1$, return Λ.

X3. [Recurse.] Compute the following reduced families, for a "best" index k:

$$\mathcal{F}_1 = \{I \mid I \in \mathcal{F}, \ k \notin I\}, \qquad \mathcal{F}_0 = \mathcal{F}_1 \cup \{I \mid k \notin I, \ I \cup \{k\} \in \mathcal{F}\};$$
$$\mathcal{G}_0 = \{J \mid J \in \mathcal{G}, \ k \notin J\}, \qquad \mathcal{G}_1 = \mathcal{G}_0 \cup \{J \mid k \notin J, \ J \cup \{k\} \in \mathcal{G}\}.$$

Delete any member of $\mathcal{F}_0$ or $\mathcal{G}_1$ that contains another member of the same family. The index k should be chosen so that the ratio $\rho = \min(|\mathcal{F}_1|/|\mathcal{F}|, |\mathcal{G}_0|/|\mathcal{G}|)$ is as small as possible. If $\mathrm{X}(\mathcal{F}_0, \mathcal{G}_0)$ returns a vector x, return the same vector extended with $x_k = 0$. Otherwise if $\mathrm{X}(\mathcal{F}_1, \mathcal{G}_1)$ returns a vector x, return the same vector extended with $x_k = 1$. Otherwise return Λ. ▮

If $N = |\mathcal{F}| + |\mathcal{G}|$, prove that step X1 is executed at most $N^{O(\log N)^2}$ times. *Hint:* Show that we always have $\rho \leq 1 - 1/\lg N$ in step X3.

28. [*21*] (W. V. Quine, 1952.) If $f(x_1, \ldots, x_n)$ is a Boolean function with prime implicants $p_1, \ldots, p_q$, let $g(y_1, \ldots, y_q) = \bigwedge_{f(x)=1} \bigvee \{y_j \mid p_j(x) = 1\}$. For example, the "random" function (22) is true at the eight points (28), and it has five prime implicants given by (29) and (30); so $g(y_1, \ldots, y_5)$ is

$$(y_1 \vee y_2) \wedge (y_1) \wedge (y_2 \vee y_3) \wedge (y_4) \wedge (y_3 \vee y_5) \wedge (y_5) \wedge (y_5) \wedge (y_4 \vee y_5)$$
$$= (y_1 \wedge y_2 \wedge y_4 \wedge y_5) \vee (y_1 \wedge y_3 \wedge y_4 \wedge y_5)$$

in this case. Prove that every shortest DNF expression for f corresponds to a prime implicant of the monotone function g.

29. [*22*] (The next several exercises are devoted to algorithms that deal with the implicants of Boolean functions by representing points of the n-cube as n-bit numbers $(b_{n-1} \ldots b_1 b_0)_2$, rather than as bit strings $x_1 \ldots x_n$.) Given a bit position j, and given n-bit values $v_0 < v_1 < \cdots < v_{m-1}$, explain how to find all pairs (k, k') such that $0 \leq k < k' < m$ and $v_{k'} = v_k \oplus 2^j$, in increasing order of k. The running time of your procedure should be $O(m)$, if bitwise operations on n-bit words take constant time.

▶ **30.** [*27*] The text points out that an implicant of a Boolean function can be regarded as a subcube such as $01*0*$, contained in the set V of all points for which the function is true. Every subcube can be represented as a pair of binary numbers $a = (a_{n-1} \ldots a_0)_2$ and $b = (b_{n-1} \ldots b_0)_2$, where a records the positions of the asterisks and b records the bits in non-$*$ positions. For example, the numbers $a = (00101)_2$ and $b = (01000)_2$ represent the subcube $c = 01*0*$. We always have $a \ \& \ b = 0$.

The "j-buddy" of a subcube is defined whenever $a_j = 0$, by changing b to $b \oplus 2^j$. For example, $01*0*$ has three buddies, namely its 4-buddy $11*0*$, its 3-buddy $00*0*$, and its 1-buddy $01*1*$. Every subcube $c \subseteq V$ can be assigned a tag value $(t_{n-1} \ldots t_0)_2$, where $t_j = 1$ if and only if the j-buddy of c is defined and contained in V. With this definition, c represents a maximal subcube (hence a prime implicant) if and only if its tag is zero.

Use these concepts to design an algorithm that finds all maximal subcubes (a, b) of a given set V, where V is represented by the n-bit numbers $v_0 < v_1 < \cdots < v_{m-1}$.

▶ **31.** [*28*] The algorithm in exercise 30 requires a complete list of all points where a Boolean function is true, and that list may be quite long. Therefore we may prefer to work directly with subcubes, never going down to the level of explicit n-tuples unless necessary. The key to such higher-level methods is the notion of *consensus* between subcubes c and c', denoted by $c \sqcup c'$ and defined to be the largest subcube c'' such that

$$c'' \subseteq c \cup c', \qquad c'' \not\subseteq c, \quad \text{and} \quad c'' \not\subseteq c'.$$

Such a c'' does not always exist. For example, if $c = 000*$ and $c' = *111$, every subcube contained in $c \cup c'$ is contained either in c or in c'.

a) Prove that the consensus, when it exists, can be computed componentwise using the following formulas in each coordinate position:

$$x \sqcup x = x \sqcup * = *\sqcup x = x \quad \text{and} \quad x \sqcup \bar{x} = *\sqcup * = *, \qquad \text{for } x = 0 \text{ and } x = 1.$$

Furthermore, $c \sqcup c'$ exists if and only if the rule $x \sqcup \bar{x} = *$ has been used in exactly one component.

b) A subcube with k asterisks is called a k-cube. Show that, if c is a k-cube and c' is a k'-cube, and if the consensus $c'' = c \sqcup c'$ exists, then c'' is a k''-cube where $1 \le k'' \le \min(k, k') + 1$.

c) If C and C' are families of subcubes, let

$$C \sqcup C' = \{\, c \sqcup c' \mid c \in C,\ c' \in C',\ \text{and } c \sqcup c' \text{ exists}\,\}.$$

Explain why the following algorithm works.

Algorithm E (*Find maximal subcubes*). Given a family C of subcubes of the n-cube, this algorithm outputs the maximal subcubes of $V = \bigcup_{c \in C} c$, without actually computing the set V itself.

E1. [Initialize.] Set $j \leftarrow 0$. Delete any subcube c of C that is contained in another.

E2. [Done?] (At this point, every j-cube $\subseteq V$ is contained in some element of C, and C contains no k-cubes with $k < j$.) If C is empty, the algorithm terminates.

E3. [Take consensuses.] Set $C' \leftarrow C \sqcup C$, and remove all subcubes from C' that are k-cubes for $k \le j$. While performing this computation, also output any j-cube $c \in C$ for which $c \sqcup C$ does not produce a $(j+1)$-cube of C'.

E4. [Advance.] Set $C \leftarrow C \cup C'$, but delete all j-cubes from this union. Then delete any subcube $c \in C$ that is contained in another. Set $j \leftarrow j+1$ and go to E2. ∎

(See exercise 7.1.3–142 for an efficient way to perform these computations.)

▶ **32.** [*M29*] Let $c_1, \ldots, c_m$ be subcubes of the n-cube.

a) Prove that $c_1 \cup \cdots \cup c_m$ contains at most one maximal subcube c that is not contained in $c_1 \cup \cdots \cup c_{j-1} \cup c_{j+1} \cup \cdots \cup c_m$ for any $j \in \{1, \ldots, m\}$. (If c exists, we call it the *generalized consensus* of $c_1, \ldots, c_m$, because $c = c_1 \sqcup c_2$ in the notation of exercise 31 when $m = 2$.)

b) Find a set of m subcubes for which each of the $2^m - 1$ nonempty subsets of $\{c_1, \ldots, c_m\}$ has a generalized consensus.

c) Prove that a DNF with m implicants has at most $2^m - 1$ prime implicants.

d) Find a DNF that has m implicants and $2^m - 1$ prime implicants.

33. [*M21*] Let $f(x_1, \ldots, x_n)$ be one of the $\binom{2^n}{m}$ Boolean functions that are true at exactly m points. If f is chosen at random, what is the probability that $x_1 \wedge \cdots \wedge x_k$ is (a) an implicant of f? (b) a prime implicant of f? [Give the answer to part (b) as a sum; but evaluate it in closed form when $k = n$.]

▶ **34.** [*HM37*] Continuing exercise 33, let $c(m, n)$ be the average total number of implicants, and let $p(m, n)$ be the average total number of prime implicants.

  a) If $0 \leq m \leq 2^n/n$, show that $m \leq c(m, n) \leq \frac{3}{2}m + O(m/n)$ and $p(m, n) \geq me^{-1} + O(m/n)$; hence $p(m, n) = \Theta(c(m, n))$ in this range.

  b) Now let $2^n/n \leq m \leq (1 - \epsilon)2^n$, where ϵ is a fixed positive constant. Define the numbers t and α_{mn} by the relations

$$n^{-4/3} \leq \left(\frac{m}{2^n}\right)^{2^t} = \alpha_{mn} < n^{-2/3}, \qquad \text{integer } t.$$

    Express the asymptotic values of $c(m, n)$ and $p(m, n)$ in terms of n, t, and α_{mn}. [*Hint:* Show that almost all of the implicants have exactly $n - t$ or $n - t - 1$ literals.]

  c) Estimate $c(m, n)/p(m, n)$ when $m = 2^{n-1}$ and $n = \lfloor (\ln t - \ln \ln t)2^{2^t} \rfloor$, integer t.

  d) Prove that $c(m, n)/p(m, n) = O(\log \log n / \log \log \log n)$ when $m \leq (1 - \epsilon)2^n$.

▶ **35.** [*M25*] A DNF is called *orthogonal* if its implicants correspond to disjoint subcubes. Orthogonal disjunctive normal forms are particularly useful when the reliability polynomial of exercise 13 is being calculated or estimated.

    The full DNF of every function is obviously orthogonal, because its subcubes are single points. But we can often find an orthogonal DNF that has significantly fewer implicants, especially when the function is monotone. For example, the function $(x_1 \wedge x_2) \vee (x_2 \wedge x_3) \vee (x_3 \wedge x_4)$ is true at eight points, and it has the orthogonal DNF

$$(x_1 \wedge x_2) \vee (\bar{x}_1 \wedge x_2 \wedge x_3) \vee (\bar{x}_2 \wedge x_3 \wedge x_4).$$

In other words, the overlapping subcubes 11∗∗, ∗11∗, ∗∗11 can be replaced by the disjoint subcubes 11∗∗, 011∗, ∗011. Using the binary notation for subcubes in exercise 30, these subcubes have asterisk codes 0011, 0001, 1000 and bit codes 1100, 0110, 0011.

    Every monotone function can be defined by a list of bit codes $B_1, \ldots, B_p$, when the asterisk codes are respectively $\bar{B}_1, \ldots, \bar{B}_p$. Given such a list, let the "shadow" S_k of B_k be the bitwise OR of $B_j \,\&\, \bar{B}_k$, for all $1 \leq j < k$ such that $\nu(B_j \,\&\, \bar{B}_k) = 1$:

$$S_k = \beta_{1k} \mid \cdots \mid \beta_{(k-1)k}, \qquad \beta_{jk} = ((B_j \,\&\, \bar{B}_k) \oplus ((B_j \,\&\, \bar{B}_k) - 1)) \div ((B_j \,\&\, \bar{B}_k) - 1).$$

For example, when the bit codes are $(B_1, B_2, B_3) = (1100, 0110, 0011)$, we get the shadow codes $(S_1, S_2, S_3) = (0000, 1000, 0100)$.

  a) Show that the asterisk codes $A'_j = \bar{B}_j - S_j$ and bit codes B_j define subcubes that cover the same points as the subcubes with asterisk codes $A_j = \bar{B}_j$.

  b) A list of bit codes $B_1, \ldots, B_p$ is called a *shelling* if $B_j \,\&\, S_k$ is nonzero for all $1 \leq j < k \leq p$. For example, $(1100, 0110, 0011)$ is a shelling; but if we arrange those bit codes in the order $(1100, 0011, 0110)$ the shelling condition fails when $j = 1$ and $k = 2$, although we do have $S_3 = 1001$. Prove that the subcubes in part (a) are disjoint if and only if the list of bit codes is a shelling.

  c) According to Theorem Q, every prime implicant must appear among the B's when we represent a monotone Boolean function in this way. But sometimes we need to add additional implicants if we want the subcubes to be disjoint. For example, there is no shelling for the bit codes 1100 and 0011. Show that we can, however, obtain a shelling for this function $(x_1 \wedge x_2) \vee (x_3 \wedge x_4)$ by adding one more bit code. What is the resulting orthogonal DNF?

  d) Permute the bit codes $\{11000, 01100, 00110, 00011, 11010\}$ to obtain a shelling.

  e) Add two bit codes to the set $\{110000, 011000, 001100, 000110, 000011\}$ in order to make a shellable list.

36. [*M21*] Continuing exercise 35, let f be any monotone function, not identically 1. Show that the set of bit vectors

$$B = \{\, x \mid f(x) = 1 \text{ and } f(x') = 0 \,\}, \qquad x' = x \mathbin{\&} (x-1),$$

is always shellable when listed in decreasing lexicographic order. (The vector x' is obtained from x by zeroing out the rightmost 1.) For example, this method produces an orthogonal DNF for $(x_1 \wedge x_2) \vee (x_3 \wedge x_4)$ from the list $(1100, 1011, 0111, 0011)$.

▶ **37.** [*M31*] Find a shellable DNF for $(x_1 \wedge x_2) \vee (x_3 \wedge x_4) \vee \cdots \vee (x_{2n-1} \wedge x_{2n})$ that has $2^n - 1$ implicants, and prove that no orthogonal DNF for this function has fewer.

38. [*05*] Is it hard to test the satisfiability of functions in *disjunctive* normal form?

▶ **39.** [*25*] Let $f(x_1, \ldots, x_n)$ be a Boolean formula represented as an extended binary tree with N internal nodes and $N + 1$ leaves. Each leaf is labeled with a variable x_k, and each internal node is labeled with one of the sixteen binary operators in Table 1; applying the operators from bottom to top yields $f(x_1, \ldots, x_n)$ as the value of the root.

Explain how to construct a formula $F(x_1, \ldots, x_n, y_1, \ldots, y_N)$ in 3CNF, having exactly $4N + 1$ clauses, such that $f(x_1, \ldots, x_n) = \exists y_1 \ldots \exists y_N F(x_1, \ldots, x_n, y_1, \ldots, y_N)$. (Thus f is satisfiable if and only if F is satisfiable.)

40. [*23*] Given an undirected graph G, construct the following clauses on the Boolean variables $\{\, p_{uv} \mid u \neq v \,\} \cup \{\, q_{uvw} \mid u \neq v, u \neq w, v \neq w, u \not\!\!-\!\!w \,\}$, where u, v, and w denote vertices of G:

$$A = \bigwedge \{\, (p_{uv} \vee p_{vu}) \wedge (\bar{p}_{uv} \vee \bar{p}_{vu}) \mid u \neq v \,\};$$
$$B = \bigwedge \{\, (\bar{p}_{uv} \vee \bar{p}_{vw} \vee p_{uw}) \mid u \neq v, u \neq w, v \neq w \,\};$$
$$C = \bigwedge \{\, (\bar{q}_{uvw} \vee p_{uv}) \wedge (\bar{q}_{uvw} \vee p_{vw}) \wedge (q_{uvw} \vee \bar{p}_{uv} \vee \bar{p}_{vw}) \mid u \neq v, u \neq w, v \neq w, u \not\!\!-\!\!w \,\};$$
$$D = \bigwedge \{\, (\bigvee_{v \notin \{u,w\}} (q_{uvw} \vee q_{wvu})) \mid u \neq w, u \not\!\!-\!\!w \,\}.$$

Prove that the formula $A \wedge B \wedge C \wedge D$ is satisfiable if and only if G has a Hamiltonian path. *Hint:* Think of p_{uv} as the statement '$u < v$'.

41. [*20*] (*The pigeonhole principle.*) The island of San Serriffe contains m pigeons and n holes. Find a conjunctive normal form that is satisfiable if and only if each pigeon can be the sole occupant of at least one hole.

42. [*20*] Find a short, unsatisfiable CNF that is not totally trivial, although it consists entirely of Horn clauses that are also Krom clauses.

43. [*20*] Is there an efficient way to decide satisfiability of a conjunctive normal form that consists entirely of Horn clauses and/or Krom clauses (possibly mixed)?

44. [*M23*] Complete the proof of Theorem H by studying the implications of (33).

45. [*M20*] (a) Show that exactly half of the Horn functions of n variables are definite. (b) Also show that there are more Horn functions of n variables than monotone functions of n variables (unless $n = 0$).

46. [*20*] Which of the 11×11 character pairs xy can occur next to each other in the context-free grammar (34)?

47. [*20*] Given a sequence of relations $j \prec k$ with $1 \leq j, k \leq n$ as in Algorithm 2.2.3T (topological sorting), consider the clauses

$$x_{j_1} \wedge \cdots \wedge x_{j_t} \Rightarrow x_k \qquad \text{for } 1 \leq k \leq n,$$

where $\{j_1, \ldots, j_t\}$ is the set of elements such that $j_i \prec k$. Compare the behavior of Algorithm C on these clauses to the behavior of Algorithm 2.2.3T.

▸ **48.** [*21*] What's a good way to test a set of Horn clauses for satisfiability?

49. [*22*] Show that, if $f(x_1, \ldots, x_n)$ and $g(x_1, \ldots, x_n)$ are both defined by Horn clauses in CNF, there is an easy way to test if $f(x_1, \ldots, x_n) \le g(x_1, \ldots, x_n)$ for all $x_1, \ldots, x_n$.

50. [*HM42*] There are $(n+2)2^{n-1}$ possible Horn clauses on n variables. Select $c \cdot 2^n$ of them at random, with repetition permitted, where $c > 0$; and let $P_n(c)$ be the probability that all of the selected clauses are simultaneously satisfiable. Prove that

$$\lim_{n \to \infty} P_n(c) = 1 - (1 - e^{-c})(1 - e^{-2c})(1 - e^{-4c})(1 - e^{-8c}) \ldots.$$

▸ **51.** [*22*] A great many two-player games can be defined by specifying a directed graph in which each vertex represents a game position. There are two players, Alice and Bob, who construct an oriented path by starting at a particular vertex and taking turns to extend the path, one arc at a time. Before the game starts, each vertex has either been marked A (meaning that Alice wins), or marked B (meaning that Bob wins), or marked C (meaning that the cat wins), or left unmarked.

When the path reaches a vertex v marked A or B, that player wins. The game stops without a winner if v has been visited before, with the same player to move. If v is marked C, the currently active player has the option of accepting a draw; otherwise he or she must choose an outgoing arc to extend the path, and the other player becomes active. (If v is an unmarked vertex with out-degree zero, the active player loses.)

Associating four propositional variables $A^+(v)$, $A^-(v)$, $B^+(v)$, and $B^-(v)$ with every vertex v of the graph, explain how to construct a set of definite Horn clauses such that $A^+(v)$ is in the core if and only if Alice can force a win when the path starts at v and she moves first; $A^-(v)$ is in the core if and only if Bob can force her to lose in that game; $B^+(v)$ and $B^-(v)$ are similar to $A^+(v)$ and $A^-(v)$, but with roles reversed.

52. [*25*] (*Boolean games.*) Any Boolean function $f(x_1, \ldots, x_n)$ leads to a game called "two steps forward or one step back," in the following way: There are two players, 0 and 1, who repeatedly assign values to the variables x_j; player y tries to make $f(x_1, \ldots, x_n)$ equal to y. Initially all variables are unassigned, and the position marker m is zero. Players take turns, and the currently active player either sets $m \leftarrow m + 2$ (if $m + 2 \le n$) or $m \leftarrow m - 1$ (if $m - 1 \ge 1$), then sets

$$\begin{cases} x_m \leftarrow 0 \text{ or } 1, & \text{if } x_m \text{ was not previously assigned;} \\ x_m \leftarrow \bar{x}_m, & \text{if } x_m \text{ was previously assigned.} \end{cases}$$

The game is over as soon as a value has been assigned to all variables; then $f(x_1, \ldots, x_n)$ is the winner. A draw is declared if the same state (including the value of m) is reached twice. Notice that at most four moves are possible at any time.

Study examples of this game when $2 \le n \le 9$, in the following four cases:
a) $f(x_1, \ldots, x_n) = [x_1 \ldots x_n < x_n \ldots x_1]$ (in lexicographic order);
b) $f(x_1, \ldots, x_n) = x_1 \oplus \cdots \oplus x_n$;
c) $f(x_1, \ldots, x_n) = [x_1 \ldots x_n \text{ contains no two consecutive 1s}]$;
d) $f(x_1, \ldots, x_n) = [(x_1 \ldots x_n)_2 \text{ is prime}]$.

53. [*23*] Show that the impossible comedy festival of (37) *can* be scheduled if a change is made to the requirements of only (a) Tomlin; (b) Unwin; (c) Vegas; (d) Xie; (e) Yankovic; (f) Zany.

54. [*20*] Let $S = \{u_1, u_2, \ldots, u_k\}$ be the set of literals in some strong component of a digraph that corresponds to a 2CNF formula as in Fig. 6. Show that S contains both a variable and its complement if and only if $u_j = \bar{u}_1$ for some j with $2 \le j \le k$.

▶ **55.** [*30*] Call $f(x_1, \ldots, x_n)$ a *renamed Horn function* if there are Boolean constants $y_1, \ldots, y_n$ such that $f(x_1 \oplus y_1, \ldots, x_n \oplus y_n)$ is a Horn function.

　　a) Given $f(x_1, \ldots, x_n)$ in CNF, explain how to construct $g(y_1, \ldots, y_n)$ in 2CNF so that the clauses of $f(x_1 \oplus y_1, \ldots, x_n \oplus y_n)$ are Horn clauses if and only if $g(y_1, \ldots, y_n) = 1$.

　　b) Design an algorithm that decides in $O(m)$ steps whether or not all clauses of a given CNF of length m can be converted into Horn clauses by complementing some subset of the variables.

▶ **56.** [*20*] The satisfiability problem for a Boolean function $f(x_1, x_2, \ldots, x_n)$ can be stated formally as the question of whether or not the quantified formula

$$\exists x_1 \, \exists x_2 \, \ldots \, \exists x_n \, f(x_1, x_2, \ldots, x_n)$$

is true; here '$\exists x_j \, \alpha$' means, "there exists a Boolean value x_j such that α holds."

　　A much more general evaluation problem arises when we replace one or more of the existential quantifiers $\exists x_j$ by the universal quantifier $\forall x_j$, where '$\forall x_j \, \alpha$' means, "for all Boolean values x_j, α holds."

　　Which of the eight quantified formulas $\exists x \, \exists y \, \exists z \, f(x, y, z)$, $\exists x \, \exists y \, \forall z \, f(x, y, z)$, $\ldots$, $\forall x \, \forall y \, \forall z \, f(x, y, z)$ are true when $f(x, y, z) = (x \vee y) \wedge (\bar{x} \vee z) \wedge (y \vee \bar{z})$?

▶ **57.** [*30*] (B. Aspvall, M. F. Plass, and R. E. Tarjan.) Continuing exercise 56, design an algorithm that decides in linear time whether or not a given fully quantified formula $f(x_1, \ldots, x_n)$ is true, when f is any formula in 2CNF (any conjunction of Krom clauses).

▶ **58.** [*37*] Continuing exercise 57, design an efficient algorithm that decides whether or not a given fully quantified conjunction of *Horn* clauses is true.

▶ **59.** [*M20*] (D. Pehoushek and R. Fraer, 1997.) If the truth table for $f(x_1, x_2, \ldots, x_n)$ has a 1 in exactly k places, show that exactly k of the fully quantified formulas $Qx_1 \, Qx_2 \, \ldots Qx_n \, f(x_1, x_2, \ldots, x_n)$ are true, when each Q is either $\exists$ or $\forall$.

60. [*12*] Which of the following expressions yield the median $\langle xyz \rangle$, as defined in (43)? (a) $(x \wedge y) \oplus (y \wedge z) \oplus (x \wedge z)$. (b) $(x \vee y) \oplus (y \vee z) \oplus (x \vee z)$. (c) $(x \oplus y) \wedge (y \oplus z) \wedge (x \oplus z)$. (d) $(x \equiv y) \oplus (y \equiv z) \oplus (x \equiv z)$. (e) $(x \bar{\wedge} y) \wedge (y \bar{\wedge} z) \wedge (x \bar{\wedge} z)$. (f) $(x \bar{\wedge} y) \vee (y \bar{\wedge} z) \vee (x \bar{\wedge} z)$.

61. [*13*] True or false: If $\circ$ is any one of the Boolean binary operations in Table 1, we have the distributive law $w \circ \langle xyz \rangle = \langle (w \circ x)(w \circ y)(w \circ z) \rangle$.

62. [*25*] (C. Schensted.) If $f(x_1, \ldots, x_n)$ is a monotone Boolean function and $n \geq 3$, prove the median expansion formula

$$f(x_1, \ldots, x_n) = \langle f(x_1, x_1, x_3, x_4, \ldots, x_n) f(x_1, x_2, x_2, x_4, \ldots, x_n) f(x_3, x_2, x_3, x_4, \ldots, x_n) \rangle.$$

63. [*20*] Equation (49) shows how to compute the median of five elements via medians of three. Conversely, can we compute $\langle xyz \rangle$ with a subroutine for medians of five?

64. [*23*] (S. B. Akers, Jr.) (a) Prove that a Boolean function $f(x_1, \ldots, x_n)$ is monotone and self-dual if and only if it satisfies the following condition:

For all $x = x_1 \ldots x_n$ and $y = y_1 \ldots y_n$ there exists k such that $f(x) = x_k$ and $f(y) = y_k$.

(b) Suppose f is undefined for certain values, but the stated condition holds whenever both $f(x)$ and $f(y)$ are defined. Show that there is a monotone self-dual Boolean function g for which $g(x) = f(x)$ whenever $f(x)$ is defined.

▶ **65.** [*M21*] Any subset X of $\{1, 2, \ldots, n\}$ corresponds to a binary vector $x = x_1 x_2 \ldots x_n$ via the rule $x_j = [j \in X]$. And any family $\mathcal{F}$ of such subsets corresponds to a Boolean function $f(x) = f(x_1, x_2, \ldots, x_n)$ of n variables, via the rule $f(x) = [X \in \mathcal{F}]$. Therefore every statement about families of subsets corresponds to a statement about Boolean functions, and vice versa.

A family $\mathcal{F}$ is called *intersecting* if $X \cap Y \neq \emptyset$ whenever $X, Y \in \mathcal{F}$. An intersecting family that loses this property whenever we try to add another subset is said to be *maximal*. Prove that $\mathcal{F}$ is a maximal intersecting family if and only if the corresponding Boolean function f is monotone and self-dual.

▶ **66.** [*M25*] A *coterie* of $\{1, \ldots, n\}$ is a family $\mathcal{C}$ of subsets called *quorums*, which have the following properties whenever $Q \in \mathcal{C}$ and $Q' \in \mathcal{C}$: (i) $Q \cap Q' \neq \emptyset$; (ii) $Q \subseteq Q'$ implies $Q = Q'$. Coterie $\mathcal{C}$ *dominates* coterie $\mathcal{C}'$ if $\mathcal{C} \neq \mathcal{C}'$ and if, for every $Q' \in \mathcal{C}'$, there is a $Q \in \mathcal{C}$ with $Q \subseteq Q'$. For example, the coterie $\{\{1,2\},\{2,3\}\}$ is dominated by $\{\{1,2\},\{1,3\},\{2,3\}\}$ and also by $\{\{2\}\}$. [Coteries were introduced in classic papers by L. Lamport, *CACM* **21** (1978), 558–565; H. Garcia-Molina and D. Barbara, *JACM* **32** (1985), 841–860. They have numerous applications to distributed system protocols, including mutual exclusion, data replication, and name servers. In these applications $\mathcal{C}$ is preferred to any coterie that it dominates.]

Prove that $\mathcal{C}$ is a nondominated coterie if and only if its quorums are the index sets of variables in the prime implicants of a monotone self-dual Boolean function $f(x_1, \ldots, x_n)$. (Thus Table 2 illustrates the nondominated coteries on $\{1, 2, 3, 4\}$.)

▶ **67.** [*M30*] (J. W. Milnor and C. Schensted.) A triangular grid of order n, illustrated here for $n = 3$, contains $(n+2)(n+1)/2$ points with nonnegative "barycentric coordinates" xyz, where $x+y+z = n$. Two points are adjacent if they differ by ± 1 in exactly two coordinate positions. A point is said to lie on the x side if its x coordinate is zero, on the y side if its y coordinate is zero, or on the z side if its z coordinate is zero; thus each side contains $n+1$ points. If $n > 0$, a point lies on two different sides if and only if it occupies one of the three corner positions.

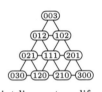

A "Y" is a connected set of points with at least one point on each side. Suppose each vertex of a triangular grid is covered with a white stone or a black stone. For example, the 52 black stones in

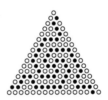

contain a (somewhat distorted) Y; but if any of them is changed from black to white, there is a white Y instead. A moment's thought makes it intuitively clear that, in any placement, the black stones contain a Y if and only if the white stones do not.

We can represent the color of each stone by a Boolean variable, with 0 for white and 1 for black. Let $Y(t) = 1$ if and only if there's a black Y, where t is a triangular grid comprising all the Boolean variables. This function Y is clearly monotone; and the intuitive claim made in the preceding paragraph is equivalent to saying that Y is also self-dual. The purpose of this exercise is to prove the claim rigorously, using median algebra.

Given $a, b, c \geq 0$, let t_{abc} be the triangular subgrid containing all points whose coordinates xyz satisfy $x \geq a$, $y \geq b$, $z \geq c$. For example, t_{001} denotes all points except those on the z side (the bottom row). Notice that, if $a + b + c = n$, t_{abc} is the single point with coordinates abc; and in general, t_{abc} is a triangular grid of order $n - a - b - c$.

a) Prove that, if $n > 0$, $Y(t) = \langle Y(t_{100})Y(t_{010})Y(t_{001})\rangle$.

b) If $n > 0$, let t^* be the triangular grid of order $n - 1$ defined by the rule

$$t^*_{xyz} = \langle t_{(x+1)yz} t_{x(y+1)z} t_{xy(z+1)}\rangle, \qquad \text{for } x + y + z = n - 1.$$

Prove that $Y(t) = Y(t^*)$. [In other words, t^* condenses each small triangle of stones by taking the median of their colors. Repeating this process defines a *pyramid* of stones, with the top stone black if and only if there is a black Y at the bottom. It's fun to apply this condensation principle to the twisted Y above.]

68. [*46*] The just-barely-Y configuration shown in the previous exercise has 52 black stones. What is the largest number of black stones possible in such a configuration? (That is, how many variables can there be in a prime implicant of the function $Y(t)$?)

▶ **69.** [*M26*] (C. Schensted.) Exercise 67 expresses the Y function in terms of medians. Conversely, let $f(x_1, \ldots, x_n)$ be any monotone self-dual Boolean function with $m + 1$ prime implicants $p_0, p_1, \ldots, p_m$. Prove that $f(x_1, \ldots, x_n) = Y(T)$, where T is any triangular grid of order $m - 1$ in which T_{abc} is a variable common to p_a and p_{a+b+1}, for $a + b + c = m - 1$. For example, when $f(w, x, y, z) = \langle xwywz\rangle$ we have $m = 3$ and

$$f(w, x, y, z) = (w \wedge x) \vee (w \wedge y) \vee (w \wedge z) \vee (x \wedge y \wedge z) = Y\left(\begin{smallmatrix} & & w & \\ & w & & w \\ x & & y & & z\end{smallmatrix}\right).$$

▶ **70.** [*M20*] (A. Meyerowitz, 1989.) Given any monotone self-dual Boolean function $f(x) = f(x_1, \ldots, x_n)$, choose any prime implicant $x_{j_1} \wedge \cdots \wedge x_{j_s}$ and let

$$g(x) = (f(x) \wedge [x \neq t]) \vee [x = \bar{t}],$$

where $t = t_1 \ldots t_n$ is the bit vector that has 1s in positions $\{j_1, \ldots, j_s\}$. Prove that $g(x)$ is also monotone and self-dual. (Notice that $g(x)$ is equal to $f(x)$ except at the two points t and $\bar{t}$.)

▶ **71.** [*M21*] Given the axioms (50), (51), and (52) of a median algebra, prove that the long distributive law (54) is a consequence of the shorter law (53).

72. [*M22*] Derive (58), (59), and (60) from the median laws (50)–(53).

73. [*M32*] (S. P. Avann.) Given a median algebra M, whose intervals are defined by (57) and whose corresponding median graph is defined by (61), let $d(u, v)$ denote the distance from u to v. Also let '$[uxv]$' stand for the statement "x lies on a shortest path from u to v."

a) Prove that $[uxv]$ holds if and only if $d(u, v) = d(u, x) + d(x, v)$.

b) Suppose $x \in [u \,..\, v]$ and $u \in [x \,..\, y]$, where $x \neq u$ and $y \,—\, v$ is an edge of the graph. Show that $x \,—\, u$ is also an edge.

c) If $x \in [u \,..\, v]$, prove $[uxv]$, by induction on $d(u, v)$.

d) Conversely, prove that $[uxv]$ implies $x \in [u \,..\, v]$.

74. [*M21*] In a median algebra, show that $w = \langle xyz\rangle$ whenever we have $w \in [x \,..\, y]$, $w \in [x \,..\, z]$, and $w \in [y \,..\, z]$ according to definition (57).

▶ **75.** [*M36*] (M. Sholander, 1954.) Suppose M is a set of points with a betweenness relation "x lies between u and v," symbolized by $[uxv]$, which satisfies the following three axioms:

i) If $[uvu]$ then $u = v$.

ii) If $[uxv]$ and $[xyu]$ then $[vyu]$.

iii) Given x, y, and z, exactly one point $w = \langle xyz\rangle$ satisfies $[xwy]$, $[xwz]$, and $[ywz]$.

The object of this exercise is to prove that M is a median algebra.

a) Prove the majority law $\langle xxy\rangle = x$, Eq. (50).

b) Prove the commutative law $\langle xyz \rangle = \langle xzy \rangle = \cdots = \langle zyx \rangle$, Eq. (51).

c) Prove that $[uxv]$ if and only if $x = \langle uxv \rangle$.

d) If $[uxy]$ and $[uyv]$, prove that $[xyv]$.

e) If $[uxv]$ and $[uyz]$ and $[vyz]$, prove that $[xyz]$. *Hint:* Construct the points $w = \langle yuv \rangle$, $p = \langle wux \rangle$, $q = \langle wvx \rangle$, $r = \langle pxz \rangle$, $s = \langle qxz \rangle$, and $t = \langle rsz \rangle$.

f) Finally, deduce the short distributive law, Eq. (53): $\langle\langle xyz \rangle uv \rangle = \langle x \langle yuv \rangle \langle zuv \rangle\rangle$.

76. [*M33*] Derive the betweenness axioms (i), (ii), and (iii) of exercise 75, starting from the three median axioms (50), (51), and (52), letting $[uxv]$ be an abbreviation for "$x = \langle uxv \rangle$." Do not use the distributive law (53). *Hint:* See exercise 74.

77. [*M28*] Let G be a median graph containing the edge $r - s$. For each edge $u - v$, call u an *early neighbor* of v if and only if r is closer to u than to v. Partition the vertices into "left" and "right" parts, where left vertices are closer to r than to s and right vertices are closer to s than to r. Each right vertex v has a *rank*, which is the shortest distance from v to a left vertex. Similarly, each left vertex u has rank $1 - d$, where d is the shortest distance from u to a right vertex. Thus u has rank zero if it is adjacent to a right vertex, otherwise its rank is negative. Vertex r clearly has rank 0, and s has rank 1.

a) Show that every vertex of rank 1 is adjacent to exactly one vertex of rank 0.

b) Show that the set of all right vertices is convex.

c) Show that the set of all vertices with rank 1 is convex.

d) Prove that steps I3–I9 of Subroutine I correctly mark all vertices of ranks 1 and 2.

e) Prove that Algorithm H is correct.

▶ **78.** [*M26*] If the vertex v is examined k times in step I4 during the execution of Algorithm H, prove that the graph has at least 2^k vertices. *Hint:* There are k ways to start a shortest path from v to a; thus at least k 1s appear in $l(v)$.

▶ **79.** [*M27*] (R. L. Graham.) A *subgraph of a hypercube* is a graph whose vertices v can be labeled with bit strings $l(v)$ in such a way that $u - v$ if and only if $l(u)$ and $l(v)$ differ in exactly one bit position. (Each label has the same length.)

a) One way to define an n-vertex subgraph of a hypercube is to let $l(v)$ be the binary representation of v, for $0 \le v < n$. Show that this subgraph has exactly $f(n) = \sum_{k=0}^{n-1} \nu(k)$ edges, where $\nu(k)$ is the sideways addition function.

b) Prove that $f(n) \le n\lceil \lg n \rceil / 2$.

c) Prove that no n-vertex subgraph of a hypercube has more than $f(n)$ edges.

80. [*27*] A *partial cube* is an "isometric" subgraph of a hypercube, namely a subgraph in which the distances between vertices are the same as they are in the full graph. The vertices of a partial cube can therefore be labeled in such a way that the distance from u to v is the "Hamming distance" between $l(u)$ and $l(v)$, namely $\nu(l(u) \oplus l(v))$. Algorithm H shows that every median graph is a partial cube.

a) Find a subgraph of the 4-cube that isn't a partial cube.

b) Give an example of a partial cube that isn't a median graph.

81. [*16*] Is every median graph bipartite?

82. [*25*] (*Incremental changes in service.*) Given a sequence of vertices $(v_0, v_1, \ldots, v_t)$ in a graph G, consider the problem of finding another sequence $(u_0, u_1, \ldots, u_t)$ for which $u_0 = v_0$ and the sum

$$\big(d(u_0, u_1) + d(u_1, u_2) + \cdots + d(u_{t-1}, u_t)\big) + \big(d(u_1, v_1) + d(u_2, v_2) + \cdots + d(u_t, v_t)\big)$$

is minimized, where $d(u, v)$ denotes the distance from u to v. (Each v_k can be regarded as a request for a resource needed at that vertex; a server moves to u_k as those requests are handled in sequence.) Prove that if G is a median graph, we get an optimum solution by choosing $u_k = \langle u_{k-1} v_k v_{k+1} \rangle$ for $0 < k < t$, and $u_t = v_t$.

▶ **83.** [*28*] Generalizing exercise 82, find an efficient way to minimize

$$\big(d(u_0, u_1) + d(u_1, u_2) + \cdots + d(u_{t-1}, u_t)\big) \;+\; \rho\big(d(u_1, v_1) + d(u_2, v_2) + \cdots + d(u_t, v_t)\big)$$

in a median graph, given any positive ratio ρ.

84. [*30*] Write a program to find all monotone self-dual Boolean functions of five variables. What are the edges of the corresponding median graph? (Table 2 illustrates the four-variable case.)

▶ **85.** [*M22*] Theorem S tells us that every formula in 2CNF corresponds to a median set; therefore every antisymmetric digraph such as Fig. 6 also corresponds to a median set. Precisely which of those digraphs correspond to *reduced* median sets?

86. [*15*] If v, w, x, y, and z belong to a median set X, does their five-element median $\langle vwxyz \rangle$, computed componentwise, always belong to X?

87. [*24*] What CI-net does the proof of Theorem F construct for the free tree (63)?

88. [*M21*] We can use parallel computation to condense the network (74) into

by letting each module act at the earliest possible time. Prove that, although the network constructed in the proof of Theorem F may contain $\Omega(t^2)$ modules, it always requires at most $O(t \log t)$ levels of delay.

89. [*24*] When the construction (73) appends a new cluster of modules to enforce the condition $u \to v$, for some literals u and v, prove that it preserves all previously enforced conditions $u' \to v'$.

▶ **90.** [*21*] Construct a CI-net with input bits $x_1 \ldots x_t$ and output bits $y_1 \ldots y_t$, where $y_1 = \cdots = y_{t-1} = 0$ and $y_t = x_1 \oplus \cdots \oplus x_t$. Try for only $O(\log t)$ levels of delay.

91. [*46*] Can a retraction mapping for the labels of every median graph of dimension t be computed by a CI-net that has only $O(\log t)$ levels of delay? [This question is motivated by the existence of asymptotically optimum networks for the analogous problem of sorting; see M. Ajtai, J. Komlós, and E. Szemerédi, *Combinatorica* **3** (1983), 1–19.]

92. [*46*] Can a CI-net sort n Boolean inputs with fewer modules than a "pure" sorting network that has no inverters?

93. [*M20*] Prove that every retract X of a graph G is an isometric subgraph of G. (In other words, distances in X are the same as in G; see exercise 80.)

94. [*M21*] Prove that every retract X of a hypercube is a set of median labels, if we suppress coordinates that are constant for all $x \in X$.

95. [*M25*] True or false: The set of all outputs produced by a comparator-inverter network, when the inputs range over all possible bit strings, is always a median set.

96. [*HM25*] Instead of insisting that the constants w_1, w_2, $\ldots$, w_n, and t in (75) must be integers, we could allow them to be arbitrary real numbers. Would that increase the number of threshold functions?

97. [*10*] What median/majority functions arise in (8₁) when $n = 2$, $w_1 = w_2 = 1$, and $t = -1$, 0, 1, 2, 3, or 4?

98. [*M23*] Prove that any self-dual threshold function can be expressed in the form

$$f(x_1, x_2, \ldots, x_n) = [v_1 y_1 + \cdots + v_n y_n > 0],$$

where each y_j is either x_j or $\bar{x}_j$. For example, $2x_1 + 3x_2 + 5x_3 + 7x_4 + 11x_5 + 13x_6 \geq 21$ if and only if $2x_1 + 3x_2 + 5x_3 - 7\bar{x}_4 + 11x_5 - 13\bar{x}_6 > 0$.

▶ **99.** [*20*] (J. E. Mezei, 1961.) Prove that

$$\langle\langle x_1 \ldots x_{2s-1}\rangle y_1 \ldots y_{2t-2}\rangle = \langle x_1 \ldots x_{2s-1} y_1^s \ldots y_{2t-2}^s\rangle.$$

100. [*20*] True or false: If $f(x_1, \ldots, x_n)$ is a threshold function, so are the functions $f(x_1, \ldots, x_n) \wedge x_{n+1}$ and $f(x_1, \ldots, x_n) \vee x_{n+1}$.

101. [*M23*] The *Fibonacci threshold function* $F_n(x_1, \ldots, x_n)$ is defined by the formula $\langle x_1^{F_1} x_2^{F_2} \cdots x_{n-1}^{F_{n-1}} x_n^{F_{n-2}}\rangle$ when $n \geq 3$; for example, $F_7(x_1, \ldots, x_7) = \langle x_1 x_2 x_3^2 x_4^3 x_5^5 x_6^8 x_7^5\rangle$.
   a) What are the prime implicants of $F_n(x_1, \ldots, x_n)$?
   b) Find an orthogonal DNF for $F_n(x_1, \ldots, x_n)$ (see exercise 35).
   c) Express $F_n(x_1, \ldots, x_n)$ in terms of the Y function (see exercises 67 and 69).

102. [*M21*] The *self-dualization* of a Boolean function is defined by the formulas

$$\hat{f}(x_0, x_1, \ldots, x_n) = (x_0 \wedge f(x_1, \ldots, x_n)) \vee (\bar{x}_0 \wedge \overline{f(\bar{x}_1, \ldots, \bar{x}_n)})$$
$$= (\bar{x}_0 \vee f(x_1, \ldots, x_n)) \wedge (x_0 \vee \overline{f(\bar{x}_1, \ldots, \bar{x}_n)}).$$

   a) If $f(x_1, \ldots, x_n)$ is any Boolean function, prove that $\hat{f}$ is self-dual.
   b) Prove that $\hat{f}$ is a threshold function if and only if f is a threshold function.

103. [*HM25*] Explain how to use linear programming to test whether or not a monotone, self-dual Boolean function is a threshold function, given a list of its prime implicants. Also, if it is a threshold function, explain how to minimize the size of its representation as a majority function $\langle x_1^{w_1} \ldots x_n^{w_n}\rangle$.

104. [*25*] Apply the method of exercise 103 to find the shortest representations of the following threshold functions as majority functions: (a) $\langle x_1^2 x_2^3 x_3^5 x_4^7 x_5^{11} x_6^{13} x_7^{17} x_8^{19}\rangle$; (b) $[(x_1 x_2 x_3 x_4)_2 \geq t]$, for $0 \leq t \leq 16$ (17 cases); (c) $\langle x_1^{29} x_2^{25} x_3^{19} x_4^{15} x_5^{12} x_6^8 x_7^8 x_8^3 x_9^3 x_{10}\rangle$.

105. [*M25*] Show that the Fibonacci threshold function in exercise 101 has no shorter representation as a majority function than the one used to define it.

▶ **106.** [*M25*] The median-of-three operation $\langle x\bar{y}\bar{z}\rangle$ is true if and only if $x \geq y + z$.
   a) Generalizing, show that we can test the condition $(x_1 x_2 \ldots x_n)_2 \geq (y_1 y_2 \ldots y_n)_2 + z$ by performing a median of $2^{n+1} - 1$ Boolean variables.
   b) Prove that no median of fewer than $2^{n+1} - 1$ will suffice for this problem.

107. [*17*] Calculate $N(f)$ and $\Sigma(f)$ for the 16 functions in Table 1. (See Theorem T.)

108. [*M21*] Let $g(x_0, x_1, \ldots, x_n)$ be a self-dual function; thus $N(g) = 2^n$ in the notation of Theorem T. Express $N(f)$ and $\Sigma(f)$ in terms of $\Sigma(g)$, when $f(x_1, \ldots, x_n)$ is (a) $g(0, x_1, \ldots, x_n)$; (b) $g(1, x_1, \ldots, x_n)$.

109. [*M25*] The binary string $\alpha = a_1 \ldots a_n$ is said to *majorize* the binary string $\beta = b_1 \ldots b_n$, written $\alpha \succeq \beta$ or $\beta \preceq \alpha$, if $a_1 + \cdots + a_k \geq b_1 + \cdots + b_k$ for all $k \geq 0$.
   a) Let $\bar{\alpha} = \bar{a}_1 \ldots \bar{a}_n$. Show that $\alpha \succeq \beta$ if and only if $\bar{\beta} \succeq \bar{\alpha}$.

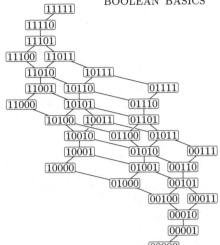

Fig. 8. The binary majorization lattice for strings of length 5. (See exercise 109.)

b) Show that any two binary strings of length n have a greatest lower bound $\alpha \wedge \beta$, which has the property that $\alpha \succeq \gamma$ and $\beta \succeq \gamma$ if and only if $\alpha \wedge \beta \succeq \gamma$. Explain how to compute $\alpha \wedge \beta$, given α and β.

c) Similarly, explain how to compute a least upper bound $\alpha \vee \beta$, with the property that $\gamma \succeq \alpha$ and $\gamma \succeq \beta$ if and only if $\gamma \succeq \alpha \vee \beta$.

d) True or false: $\alpha \wedge (\beta \vee \gamma) = (\alpha \wedge \beta) \vee (\alpha \wedge \gamma); \ \alpha \vee (\beta \wedge \gamma) = (\alpha \vee \beta) \wedge (\alpha \vee \gamma)$.

e) Say that α *covers* β if $\alpha \succeq \beta$ and $\alpha \neq \beta$, and if $\alpha \succeq \gamma \succeq \beta$ implies that we have either $\gamma = \alpha$ or $\gamma = \beta$. For example, Fig. 8 illustrates the covering relations between binary strings of length 5. Find a simple way to describe the strings that are covered by a given binary string.

f) Show that every path $\alpha = \alpha_0, \alpha_1, \ldots, \alpha_r = 0 \ldots 0$ from a given string α to $0 \ldots 0$, where α_{j-1} covers α_j for $1 \leq j \leq r$, has the same length $r = r(\alpha)$.

g) Let $m(\alpha)$ be the number of binary strings β with $\beta \succeq \alpha$. Prove that $m(1\alpha) = m(\alpha)$ and $m(0\alpha) = m(\alpha) + m(\alpha')$, where α' is α with its leftmost 1 (if any) changed to 0.

h) How many strings α of length n satisfy $\bar{\alpha} \succeq \alpha$?

110. [*M23*] A Boolean function is called *regular* if $x \preceq y$ implies that $f(x) \leq f(y)$ for all vectors x and y, where $\preceq$ is the majorization relation in exercise 109. Prove or disprove the following statements:

a) Every regular function is monotone.

b) If f is a threshold function (75) for which $w_1 \geq w_2 \geq \cdots \geq w_n$, f is regular.

c) If f is as in (b) and $\Sigma(f) = (s_1, \ldots, s_n)$, then $s_1 \geq s_2 \geq \cdots \geq s_n$.

d) If f is a threshold function (75) with $s_1 \geq s_2 \geq \cdots \geq s_n$, then $w_1 \geq w_2 \geq \cdots \geq w_n$.

111. [*M36*] An *optimum coterie* for a system with working probabilities $(p_1, \ldots, p_n)$ is a coterie that corresponds to a monotone self-dual function with maximum availability, among all monotone self-dual functions with n variables. (See exercises 14 and 66.)

a) Prove that if $1 \geq p_1 \geq \cdots \geq p_n \geq \frac{1}{2}$, at least one self-dual function with maximum availability is a regular function. Describe such a function.

b) Furthermore, it suffices to test the optimality of a regular self-dual function f at points y of the binary majorization lattice for which $f(y) = 1$ but $f(x) = 0$ for all x covered by y.

c) What coterie is optimum when some probabilities are $< \frac{1}{2}$?

▶ **112.** [*M37*] (J. Håstad.) If $f(x_1, x_2, \ldots, x_m)$ is a Boolean function, let $M(f)$ be its representation as a multilinear polynomial with integer coefficients (see exercise 12). Arrange the terms in this polynomial by using Chase's sequence $\alpha_0 = 00\ldots0$, $\alpha_1 = 10\ldots0$, $\ldots$, $\alpha_{2^m-1} = 11\ldots1$ to order the exponents; Chase's sequence, obtained by concatenating the sequences A_{n0}, $A_{(n-1)1}$, $\ldots$, A_{0n} of 7.2.1.3–(35), has the nice property that α_j is identical to α_{j+1} except for a slight change, either $0 \to 1$ or $01 \to 10$ or $001 \to 100$ or $10 \to 01$ or $100 \to 001$. For example, Chase's sequence is

$$0000, 1000, 0010, 0001, 0100, 1100, 1010, 1001, 0011, 0101, 0110, 1110, 1101, 1011, 0111, 1111$$

when $m = 4$, corresponding to the respective terms $1, x_1, x_3, x_4, x_2, x_1x_2, \ldots, x_2x_3x_4$, $x_1x_2x_3x_4$; so the relevant representation of, say, $((x_1 \oplus \bar{x}_2) \wedge x_3) \vee (x_1 \wedge \bar{x}_3 \wedge x_4)$ is

$$x_3 - x_1x_3 + x_1x_4 - x_2x_3 + 2x_1x_2x_3 - x_1x_3x_4$$

when the terms have been arranged in this order. Now let

$$F(f) = [\text{the most significant coefficient of } M(f) \text{ is positive}].$$

For example, the most significant (final) nonzero term of $((x_1 \oplus \bar{x}_2) \wedge x_3) \vee (x_1 \wedge \bar{x}_3 \wedge x_4)$ is $-x_1x_3x_4$ in Chase's ordering, so $F(f) = 0$ in this case.

    a) Determine $F(f)$ for each of the 16 functions in Table 1.

    b) Show that $F(f)$ is a threshold function of the $n = 2^m$ entries $\{f_{0\ldots00}, f_{0\ldots01}, \ldots, f_{1\ldots11}\}$ of the truth table for f. Write this function out explicitly when $m = 2$.

    c) Prove that, when m is large, all the weights in any threshold representation of F must be huge: Their absolute values must all exceed

$$\frac{3^{\binom{m}{3}} 7^{\binom{m}{4}} 15^{\binom{m}{5}} \ldots (2^{m-1}-1)^{\binom{m}{m}}}{n}(1 - O(n^{-1})) = 2^{mn/2 - n - 2(3/2)^m/\ln 2 + O((5/4)^m)}.$$

Hint: Consider discrete Fourier transforms of the truth table entries.

113. [*24*] Show that the following three threshold operations suffice to evaluate the function $S_{2,3,6,8,9}(x_1, \ldots, x_{12})$ in (91):

$$g_1(x_1, \ldots, x_{12}) = [\nu x \geq 6] = \langle 1x_1 \ldots x_{12}\rangle;$$
$$g_2(x_1, \ldots, x_{12}) = [\nu x - 6g_1 \geq 2] = \langle 1^3 x_1 \ldots x_{12}\bar{g}_1^6\rangle;$$
$$g_3(x_1, \ldots, x_{12}) = [-2\nu x + 13g_1 + 7g_2 \geq 1] = \langle 0^5 \bar{x}_1^2 \ldots \bar{x}_{12}^2 g_1^{13} g_2^7\rangle.$$

Also find a four-threshold scheme that evaluates $S_{1,3,5,8}(x_1, \ldots, x_{12})$.

114. [*20*] (D. A. Huffman.) What is the function $S_{3,6}(x, x, x, x, y, y, z)$?

115. [*M22*] Explain why (92) correctly computes the parity function $x_0 \oplus x_1 \oplus \cdots \oplus x_{2m}$.

▶ **116.** [*HM28*] (B. Dunham and R. Fridshal, 1957.) By considering symmetric functions, one can prove that Boolean functions of n variables might have many prime implicants.

    a) Suppose $0 \leq j \leq k \leq n$. For which symmetric functions $f(x_1, \ldots, x_n)$ is the term $x_1 \wedge \cdots \wedge x_j \wedge \bar{x}_{j+1} \wedge \cdots \wedge \bar{x}_k$ a prime implicant?

    b) How many prime implicants does the function $S_{3,4,5,6}(x_1, \ldots, x_9)$ have?

    c) Let $\hat{b}(n)$ be the maximum number of prime implicants, over all symmetric Boolean functions of n variables. Find a recurrence formula for $\hat{b}(n)$, and compute $\hat{b}(9)$.

    d) Prove that $\hat{b}(n) = \Theta(3^n/n)$.

    e) Show that, furthermore, there are symmetric functions $f(x_1, \ldots, x_n)$ for which both f and $\bar{f}$ have $\Theta(2^{3n/2}/n)$ prime implicants.

117. [*M26*] A disjunctive normal form is called *irredundant* if none of its implicants implies another. Let $b^*(n)$ be the maximum number of implicants in an irredundant

DNF, over all Boolean functions of n variables. Find a simple formula for $b^*(n)$, and determine its asymptotic value.

118. [*29*] How many Boolean functions $f(x_1, x_2, x_3, x_4)$ have exactly m prime implicants, for $m = 0, 1, \ldots$?

119. [*M48*] Continuing the previous exercises, let $b(n)$ be the maximum number of prime implicants in a Boolean function of n variables. Clearly $\hat{b}(n) \le b(n) < b^*(n)$; what is the asymptotic value of $b(n)$?

120. [*23*] What is the shortest DNF for the symmetric functions (a) $x_1 \oplus x_2 \oplus \cdots \oplus x_n$? (b) $S_{0,1,3,4,6,7}(x_1, \ldots, x_7)$? (c) Prove that every Boolean function of n variables can be expressed as a DNF with at most 2^{n-1} prime implicants.

▶ **121.** [*M23*] The function $\langle 1(x_1 \oplus x_2)y_1 y_2 y_3 \rangle$ is partially symmetric, since it is symmetric in $\{x_1, x_2\}$ and in $\{y_1, y_2, y_3\}$, but not in all five variables $\{x_1, x_2, y_1, y_2, y_3\}$.

  a) Exactly how many Boolean functions $f(x_1, \ldots, x_m, y_1, \ldots, y_n)$ are symmetric in $\{x_1, \ldots, x_m\}$ and $\{y_1, \ldots, y_n\}$?
  b) How many of those functions are monotone?
  c) How many of those functions are self-dual?
  d) How many of those functions are monotone and self-dual?

122. [*M25*] Continuing exercises 110 and 121, find all Boolean functions $f(x_1, x_2, x_3, y_1, y_2, y_3, y_4, y_5, y_6)$ that are simultaneously symmetric in $\{x_1, x_2, x_3\}$, symmetric in $\{y_1, y_2, \ldots, y_6\}$, self-dual, and regular. Which of them are threshold functions?

123. [*46*] Determine the exact number of self-dual Boolean functions of ten variables that are threshold functions.

124. [*20*] Find a Boolean function of four variables that is equivalent to 767 other functions, under the ground rules of Table 5.

125. [*18*] Which of the function classes in (95) are canalizing?

126. [*23*] (a) Show that a Boolean function is canalizing if and only if its sets of prime implicants and prime clauses have a certain simple property. (b) Show that a Boolean function is canalizing if and only if its Chow parameters $N(f)$ and $\Sigma(f)$ have a certain simple property (see Theorem T). (c) Define the Boolean vectors

$$\vee(f) = \bigvee\{x \mid f(x) = 1\} \quad \text{and} \quad \wedge(f) = \bigwedge\{x \mid f(x) = 1\};$$

by analogy with the integer vector $\Sigma(f)$. Show that it's possible to decide whether or not f is canalizing, given only the four vectors $\vee(f)$, $\vee(\bar{f})$, $\wedge(f)$, and $\wedge(\bar{f})$.

127. [*M25*] Which canalizing functions are (a) self-dual? (b) definite Horn functions?

▶ **128.** [*20*] Find a noncanalizing $f(x_1, \ldots, x_n)$ that is true at exactly two points.

129. [*M25*] How many different canalizing functions of n variables exist?

130. [*M21*] According to Table 3, there are 168 monotone Boolean functions of four variables. But some of them, like $x \wedge y$, depend on only three variables or fewer.

  a) How many 4-variable monotone Boolean functions actually involve each variable?
  b) How many of those functions are distinct under permutation, as in Table 4?

131. [*HM42*] Table 3 makes it clear that there are many more Horn functions than Krom functions. What is the asymptotic number, as $n \to \infty$?

▶ **132.** [*HM30*] The Boolean function $g(x) = g(x_1, \ldots, x_n)$ is called *affine* if it can be written in the form $y_0 \oplus (x_1 \wedge y_1) \oplus \cdots \oplus (x_n \wedge y_n) = (y_0 + x \cdot y) \bmod 2$ for some Boolean constants $y_0, y_1, \ldots, y_n$.

a) Given any Boolean function $f(x)$, show that some affine function agrees with $f(x)$ at $2^{n-1} + 2^{n/2-1}$ or more points x. *Hint:* Let $s(y) = \sum_x (-1)^{f(x)+x \cdot y}$, and prove that $\sum_y s(y) s(y \oplus z) = 2^{2n}[z = 0 \ldots 0]$ for all vectors z.

b) The Boolean function $f(x)$ is called *bent* if no affine function agrees with it at more than $2^{n-1} + 2^{n/2-1}$ points. Prove that

$$(x_1 \wedge x_2) \oplus (x_3 \wedge x_4) \oplus \cdots \oplus (x_{n-1} \wedge x_n) \oplus h(x_2, x_4, \ldots, x_n)$$

is a bent function, when n is even and $h(y_1, y_2, \ldots, y_{n/2})$ is arbitrary.

c) Prove that $f(x)$ is a bent function if and only if

$$\sum_x (f(x) \oplus f(x \oplus y)) = 2^{n-1} \qquad \text{for all } y \neq 0 \ldots 0.$$

d) If a bent function $f(x_1, \ldots, x_n)$ is represented by a multilinear polynomial mod 2 as in (19), show that it never contains the term $x_1 \ldots x_r$ when $r > n/2 > 1$.

▶ **133.** [*20*] (Mark A. Smith, 1990.) Suppose we flip n independent coins to get n random bits, where the kth coin produces bit 1 with probability p_k. Find a way to choose $(p_1, \ldots, p_n)$ so that $f(x_1, \ldots, x_n) = 1$ with probability $(t_0 t_1 \ldots t_{2^n-1})_2/(2^{2^n}-1)$, where $t_0 t_1 \ldots t_{2^n-1}$ is the truth table of the Boolean function f. (Thus, n suitable random coins can generate a probability with 2^n-bit precision.)

> *By and large the minimization of switching components*
> *outweighs all other engineering considerations*
> *in designing economical logic circuits.*
> — H. A. CURTIS, *A New Approach to the Design of Switching Circuits* (1962)

> *He must be a great calculator indeed who succeeds.*
> *Simplify, simplify.*
> — HENRY D. THOREAU, *Walden; or, Life in the Woods* (1854)

7.1.2. Boolean Evaluation

Our next goal is to study the efficient evaluation of Boolean functions, much as we studied the evaluation of polynomials in Section 4.6.4. One natural way to investigate this topic is to consider chains of basic operations, analogous to the polynomial chains discussed in that section.

A *Boolean chain*, for functions of n variables $(x_1, \ldots, x_n)$, is a sequence $(x_{n+1}, \ldots, x_{n+r})$ with the property that each step combines two of the preceding steps:

$$x_i = x_{j(i)} \circ_i x_{k(i)}, \qquad \text{for } n+1 \leq i \leq n+r, \tag{1}$$

where $1 \leq j(i) < i$ and $1 \leq k(i) < i$, and where $\circ_i$ is one of the sixteen binary operators of Table 7.1.1–1. For example, when $n = 3$ the two chains

$$
\begin{aligned}
x_4 &= x_1 \wedge x_2 \\
x_5 &= \bar{x}_1 \wedge x_3 \\
x_6 &= x_4 \vee x_5
\end{aligned}
\qquad \text{and} \qquad
\begin{aligned}
x_4 &= x_2 \oplus x_3 \\
x_5 &= x_1 \wedge x_4 \\
x_6 &= x_3 \oplus x_5
\end{aligned}
\tag{2}
$$

both evaluate the "mux" or "if-then-else" function $x_6 = (x_1?\ x_2\!:\ x_3)$, which takes the value x_2 or x_3 depending on whether x_1 is 1 (true) or 0 (false).

(Notice that the left-hand example in (2) uses the simplified notation '$x_5 = \bar{x}_1 \wedge x_3$' to specify the NOT-BUT operation, instead of the form '$x_5 = x_1 \bar{\subset} x_3$' that appears in Table 7.1.1–1. The main point is that, regardless of notation, every step of a Boolean chain is a Boolean combination of two prior results.)

Boolean chains correspond naturally to electronic circuits, with each step in the chain corresponding to a "gate" that has two inputs and one output. Electrical engineers traditionally represent the Boolean chains of (2) by circuit diagrams such as

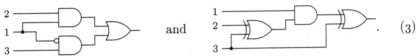

They need to design economical circuits that are subject to various technological constraints; for example, some gates might be more expensive than others, some outputs might need to be amplified if reused, the layout might need to be planar or nearly so, some paths might need to be short. But our chief concern in this book is software, not hardware, so we don't have to worry about such things. For our purposes, all gates have equal cost, and all outputs can be reused as often as desired. (Jargonwise, our Boolean chains boil down to circuits in which all gates have fan-in 2 and unlimited fan-out.)

Furthermore we shall depict Boolean chains as binary trees such as

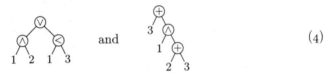

instead of using circuit diagrams like (3). Such binary trees will have overlapping subtrees when intermediate steps of the chain are used more than once. Every internal node is labeled with a binary operator; external nodes are labeled with an integer k, representing the variable x_k. The label '$\bigcirc\!\!\!<$' in the left tree of (4) stands for the NOT-BUT operator, since $\bar{x} \wedge y = [x < y]$; similarly, the BUT-NOT operator, $x \wedge \bar{y}$, can be represented by the node label '$\bigcirc\!\!\!>$'.

Several different Boolean chains might have the same tree diagram. For example, the left-hand tree of (4) also represents the chain

$$x_4 = \bar{x}_1 \wedge x_3, \qquad x_5 = x_1 \wedge x_2, \qquad x_6 = x_5 \vee x_4.$$

Any topological sorting of the tree nodes yields an equivalent chain.

Given a Boolean function f of n variables, we often want to find a Boolean chain such that $x_{n+r} = f(x_1, \ldots, x_n)$, where r is as small as possible. The *combinational complexity* $C(f)$ of a function f is the length of the shortest chain that computes it. To save excess verbiage, we will simply call $C(f)$ the "cost of f." The mux function in our examples above has cost 3, because one can show by exhaustive trials that it can't be produced by any Boolean chain of length 2.

The DNF and CNF representations of f, which we studied in Section 7.1.1, rarely tell us much about $C(f)$, since substantially more efficient schemes of calculation are usually possible. For example, in the discussion following 7.1.1–(30) we found that the more-or-less random function of four variables whose truth table is 1100 1001 0000 1111 has no DNF expression shorter than

$$(\bar{x}_1 \wedge \bar{x}_2 \wedge \bar{x}_3) \vee (\bar{x}_1 \wedge \bar{x}_3 \wedge \bar{x}_4) \vee (x_2 \wedge x_3 \wedge x_4) \vee (x_1 \wedge x_2). \qquad (5)$$

This formula corresponds to a Boolean chain of 10 steps. But that function can also be expressed more cleverly as

$$\big(((x_2 \wedge \bar{x}_4) \oplus \bar{x}_3) \wedge \bar{x}_1\big) \oplus x_2, \qquad (6)$$

so its complexity is at most 4.

How can nonobvious formulas like (6) be discovered? We will see that a computer can find the best chains for functions of four variables without doing an enormous amount of work. Still, the results can be quite startling, even for people who have had considerable experience with Boolean algebra. Typical examples of this phenomenon can be seen in Fig. 9, which illustrates the four-variable functions that are perhaps of greatest general interest, namely the functions that are symmetric under all permutations of their variables.

Consider, for example, the function $S_2(x_1, x_2, x_3, x_4)$, for which we have

$$
\begin{array}{ll}
x_1 & \text{0000 0000 1111 1111} \\
x_2 & \text{0000 1111 0000 1111} \\
x_3 & \text{0011 0011 0011 0011} \\
x_4 & \text{0101 0101 0101 0101} \\
x_5 = x_1 \oplus x_3 & \text{0011 0011 1100 1100} \\
x_6 = x_1 \oplus x_2 & \text{0000 1111 1111 0000} \\
x_7 = x_3 \oplus x_4 & \text{0110 0110 0110 0110} \\
x_8 = x_5 \vee x_6 & \text{0011 1111 1111 1100} \\
x_9 = x_6 \oplus x_7 & \text{0110 1001 1001 0110} \\
x_{10} = x_8 \wedge \bar{x}_9 & \text{0001 0110 0110 1000}
\end{array}
\qquad (7)
$$

according to Fig. 9. Truth tables are shown here so that we can easily verify each step of the calculation. Step x_8 yields a function that is true whenever $x_1 \neq x_2$ or $x_1 \neq x_3$; and $x_9 = x_1 \oplus x_2 \oplus x_3 \oplus x_4$ is the parity function $(x_1 + x_2 + x_3 + x_4) \bmod 2$. Therefore the final result, x_{10}, is true precisely when exactly two of $\{x_1, x_2, x_3, x_4\}$ are 1; these are the cases that satisfy x_8 and have even parity.

Several of the other computational schemes of Fig. 9 can also be justified intuitively. But some of the chains, like the one for $S_{1,4}$, are quite amazing.

Notice that the intermediate result x_6 is used twice in (7). In fact, no six-step chain for the function $S_2(x_1, x_2, x_3, x_4)$ is possible without making double use of some intermediate subexpression; the shortest algebraic formulas for S_2, including nice symmetrical ones like

$$\big((x_1 \wedge x_2) \vee (x_3 \wedge x_4)\big) \oplus \big((x_1 \vee x_2) \wedge (x_3 \vee x_4)\big), \qquad (8)$$

all have cost 7. But Fig. 9 shows that the other symmetric functions of four variables can all be evaluated optimally via "pure" binary trees, without overlapping subtrees except at external nodes (which represent the variables).

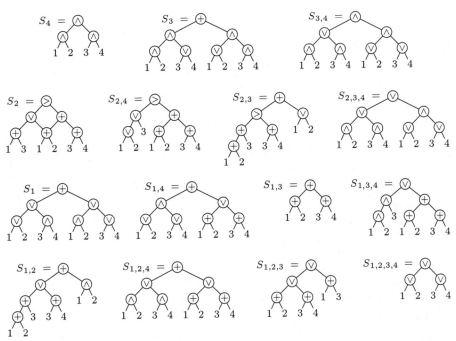

Fig. 9. Optimum Boolean chains for the symmetric functions of four variables.

In general, if $f(x_1, \ldots, x_n)$ is any Boolean function, we say that its *length* $L(f)$ is the number of binary operators in the shortest formula for f. Obviously $L(f) \geq C(f)$; and we can easily verify that $L(f) = C(f)$ whenever $n \leq 3$, by considering the fourteen basic types of 3-variable functions in 7.1.1–(95). But we have just seen that $L(S_2) = 7$ exceeds $C(S_2) = 6$ when $n = 4$, and in fact $L(f)$ is almost always substantially larger than $C(f)$ when n is large (see exercise 49).

The *depth* $D(f)$ of a Boolean function f is another important measure of its inherent complexity: We say that the depth of a Boolean chain is the length of the longest downward path in its tree diagram, and $D(f)$ is the minimum achievable depth when all Boolean chains for f are considered. All of the chains illustrated in Fig. 9 have not only the minimum cost but also the minimum depth — except in the cases $S_{2,3}$ and $S_{1,2}$, where we cannot simultaneously achieve cost 6 and depth 3. The formula

$$S_{2,3}(x_1, x_2, x_3, x_4) = \big((x_1 \wedge x_2) \oplus (x_3 \wedge x_4)\big) \vee \big((x_1 \vee x_2) \wedge (x_3 \oplus x_4)\big) \qquad (9)$$

shows that $D(S_{2,3}) = 3$, and a similar formula works for $S_{1,2}$.

Optimum chains for $n = 4$. Exhaustive computations for 4-variable functions are feasible because such functions have only $2^{16} = 65{,}536$ possible truth tables. In fact we need only consider half of those truth tables, because the complement $\bar{f}$ of any function f has the same cost, length, and depth as f itself.

Let's say that $f(x_1, \ldots, x_n)$ is *normal* if $f(0, \ldots, 0) = 0$, and in general that

$$f(x_1, \ldots, x_n) \oplus f(0, \ldots, 0) \tag{10}$$

is the "normalization" of f. Any Boolean chain can be normalized by normalizing each of its steps and by making appropriate changes to the operators; for if $(\hat{x}_1, \ldots, \hat{x}_{i-1})$ are the normalizations of $(x_1, \ldots, x_{i-1})$ and if $x_i = x_{j(i)} \circ_i x_{k(i)}$ as in (1), then $\hat{x}_i$ is clearly a binary function of $\hat{x}_{j(i)}$ and $\hat{x}_{k(i)}$. (Exercise 7 presents an example.) Therefore we can restrict consideration to normal Boolean chains, without loss of generality.

Notice that a Boolean chain is normal if and only if each of its binary operators $\circ_i$ is normal. And there are only eight normal binary operators — three of which, namely $\perp$, L, and R, are trivial. So we can assume that all Boolean chains of interest are formed from the five operators $\wedge$, $\overline{\subset}$, $\overline{\supset}$, $\vee$, and $\oplus$, which are denoted respectively by $\varwedge$, $\varobslash$, $\varobackslash$, $\varvee$, and $\oplus$ in Fig. 9. Furthermore we can assume that $j(i) < k(i)$ in each step.

There are $2^{15} = 32{,}768$ normal functions of four variables, and we can compute their lengths without difficulty by systematically enumerating all functions of length 0, 1, 2, etc. Indeed, $L(f) = r$ implies that $f = g \circ h$ for some g and h, where $L(g) + L(h) = r - 1$ and $\circ$ is one of the five nontrivial normal operators; so we can proceed as follows:

Algorithm L (*Find normal lengths*). This algorithm determines $L(f)$ for all normal truth tables $0 \leq f < 2^{2^n - 1}$, by building lists of all nonzero normal functions of length r for $r \geq 0$.

L1. [Initialize.] Let $L(0) \leftarrow 0$ and $L(f) \leftarrow \infty$ for $1 \leq f < 2^{2^n - 1}$. Then, for $1 \leq k \leq n$, set $L(x_k) \leftarrow 0$ and put x_k into list 0, where

$$x_k = (2^{2^n} - 1)/(2^{2^{n-k}} + 1) \tag{11}$$

is the truth table for x_k. (See exercise 8.) Finally, set $c \leftarrow 2^{2^n - 1} - n - 1$; c is the number of places where $L(f) = \infty$.

L2. [Loop on r.] Do step L3 for $r = 1, 2, \ldots$; eventually the algorithm will terminate when c becomes 0.

L3. [Loop on j and k.] Do step L4 for $j = 0, 1, \ldots$, and $k = r - 1 - j$, while $j \leq k$.

L4. [Loop on g and h.] Do step L5 for all g in list j and all h in list k. (If $j = k$, it suffices to restrict h to functions that *follow* g in list k.)

L5. [Loop on f.] Do step L6 for $f = g \mathbin{\&} h$, $f = \bar{g} \mathbin{\&} h$, $f = g \mathbin{\&} \bar{h}$, $f = g \mid h$, and $f = g \oplus h$. (Here $g \mathbin{\&} h$ denotes the bitwise AND of the integers g and h; we are representing truth tables by integers in binary notation.)

L6. [Is f new?] If $L(f) = \infty$, set $L(f) \leftarrow r$, $c \leftarrow c - 1$, and put f in list r. Terminate the algorithm if $c = 0$. ∎

Exercise 10 shows that a similar procedure will compute all depths $D(f)$.

With a little more work, we can in fact modify Algorithm L so that it finds better upper bounds on $C(f)$, by computing a heuristic bit vector $\phi(f)$ called

Table 1

THE NUMBER OF FOUR-VARIABLE FUNCTIONS WITH GIVEN COMPLEXITY

$C(f)$	Classes	Functions	$L(f)$	Classes	Functions	$D(f)$	Classes	Functions
0	2	10	0	2	10	0	2	10
1	2	60	1	2	60	1	2	60
2	5	456	2	5	456	2	17	1458
3	20	2474	3	20	2474	3	179	56456
4	34	10624	4	34	10624	4	22	7552
5	75	24184	5	75	24184	5	0	0
6	72	25008	6	68	24640	6	0	0
7	12	2720	7	16	3088	7	0	0

the "footprint" of f. A normal Boolean chain can begin in only $5\binom{n}{2}$ different ways, since the first step x_{n+1} must be either $x_1 \wedge x_2$ or $\bar{x}_1 \wedge x_2$ or $x_1 \wedge \bar{x}_2$ or $x_1 \vee x_2$ or $x_1 \oplus x_2$ or $x_1 \wedge x_3$ or $\cdots$ or $x_{n-1} \oplus x_n$. Suppose $\phi(f)$ is a bit vector of length $5\binom{n}{2}$ and $U(f)$ is an upper bound on $C(f)$, with the following property: Every 1 bit in $\phi(f)$ corresponds to the first step of some Boolean chain that computes f in $U(f)$ steps.

Such pairs $(U(f), \phi(f))$ can be computed by extending the basic strategy of Algorithm L. Initially we set $U(f) \leftarrow 1$ and we set $\phi(f)$ to an appropriate vector $0\ldots010\ldots0$, for all functions f of cost 1. Then, for $r = 2, 3, \ldots$, we proceed to look for functions $f = g \circ h$ where $U(g) + U(h) = r - 1$, as before, but with two changes: (1) If the footprints of g and h have at least one element in common, namely if $\phi(g) \,\&\, \phi(h) \neq 0$, then we know that $C(f) \leq r - 1$, so we can decrease $U(f)$ if it was $\geq r$. (2) If the cost of $g \circ h$ is equal to (but not less than) our current upper bound $U(f)$, we can set $\phi(f) \leftarrow \phi(f) \mid (\phi(g) \mid \phi(h))$ if $U(f) = r$, $\phi(f) \leftarrow \phi(f) \mid (\phi(g) \,\&\, \phi(h))$ if $U(f) = r - 1$. Exercise 11 works out the details.

It turns out that this footprint heuristic is powerful enough to find chains of optimum cost $U(f) = C(f)$ for all functions f, when $n = 4$. Moreover, we'll see later that footprints also help us solve more complicated evaluation problems.

According to Table 7.1.1–5, the $2^{16} = 65{,}536$ functions of four variables belong to only 222 distinct classes when we ignore minor differences due to permutation of variables and/or complementation of values. Algorithm L and its variants lead to the overall statistics shown in Table 1.

*Evaluation with minimum memory. Suppose the Boolean values $x_1, \ldots, x_n$ appear in n registers, and we want to evaluate a function by performing a sequence of operations having the form

$$x_{j(i)} \leftarrow x_{j(i)} \circ_i x_{k(i)}, \qquad \text{for } 1 \leq i \leq r, \tag{12}$$

where $1 \leq j(i) \leq n$ and $1 \leq k(i) \leq n$ and $\circ_i$ is a binary operator. At the end of the computation, the desired function value should appear in one of the registers. When $n = 3$, for example, the four-step sequence

$$
\begin{aligned}
x_1 &\leftarrow x_1 \oplus x_2 \\
x_3 &\leftarrow x_3 \wedge x_1 \\
x_2 &\leftarrow x_2 \wedge \bar{x}_1 \\
x_3 &\leftarrow x_3 \vee x_2
\end{aligned}
\qquad
\begin{aligned}
&(x_1 = 00001111 \quad x_2 = 00110011 \quad x_3 = 01010101) \\
&(x_1 = 00111100 \quad x_2 = 00110011 \quad x_3 = 01010101) \\
&(x_1 = 00111100 \quad x_2 = 00110011 \quad x_3 = 00010100) \\
&(x_1 = 00111100 \quad x_2 = 00000011 \quad x_3 = 00010100) \\
&(x_1 = 00111100 \quad x_2 = 00000011 \quad x_3 = 00010111)
\end{aligned}
\tag{13}
$$

computes the median $\langle x_1 x_2 x_3 \rangle$ and puts it into the original position of x_3. (All eight possibilities for the register contents are shown here as truth tables, before and after each operation.)

In fact we can check the calculation by working with only one truth table at a time, instead of keeping track of all three, if we analyze the situation backwards. Let $f_l(x_1, \ldots, x_n)$ denote the function computed by steps l, $l+1$, $\ldots$, r of the sequence, omitting the first $l-1$ steps; thus, in our example, $f_2(x_1, x_2, x_3)$ would be the result in x_3 after the three steps $x_3 \leftarrow x_3 \wedge x_1$, $x_2 \leftarrow x_2 \wedge \bar{x}_1$, $x_3 \leftarrow x_3 \vee x_2$. Then the function computed in register x_3 by all four steps is

$$f_1(x_1, x_2, x_3) \;=\; f_2(x_1 \oplus x_2, x_2, x_3). \tag{14}$$

Similarly $f_2(x_1, x_2, x_3) = f_3(x_1, x_2, x_3 \wedge x_1)$, $f_3(x_1, x_2, x_3) = f_4(x_1, x_2 \wedge \bar{x}_1, x_3)$, $f_4(x_1, x_2, x_3) = f_5(x_1, x_2, x_3 \vee x_2)$, and $f_5(x_1, x_2, x_3) = x_3$. We can therefore go back from f_5 to f_4 to $\cdots$ to f_1 by operating on truth tables in an appropriate way.

For example, suppose $f(x_1, x_2, x_3)$ is a function whose truth table is

$$t \;=\; a_0 a_1 a_2 a_3 a_4 a_5 a_6 a_7;$$

then the truth table for $g(x_1, x_2, x_3) = f(x_1 \oplus x_2, x_2, x_3)$ is

$$u \;=\; a_0 a_1 a_6 a_7 a_4 a_5 a_2 a_3,$$

obtained by replacing a_x by $a_{x'}$, where

$$x = (x_1 x_2 x_3)_2 \qquad \text{implies} \qquad x' = ((x_1 \oplus x_2) x_2 x_3)_2.$$

Similarly the truth table for, say, $h(x_1, x_2, x_3) = f(x_1, x_2, x_3 \wedge x_1)$ is

$$v \;=\; a_0 a_0 a_2 a_2 a_4 a_5 a_6 a_7.$$

And we can use bitwise operations to compute u and v from t:

$$u = t \oplus \big((t \oplus (t \gg 4)) \oplus (t \ll 4)) \,\&\, (00110011)_2\big), \tag{15}$$

$$v = t \oplus \big((t \oplus (t \gg 1)) \,\&\, (01010000)_2\big). \tag{16}$$

Let $C_m(f)$ be the length of a shortest minimum-memory computation for f. The backward-computation principle tells us that, if we know the truth tables of all functions f with $C_m(f) < r$, we can readily find all the truth tables of functions with $C_m(f) = r$. Namely, we can restrict consideration to normal functions as before. Then, for all normal g such that $C_m(g) = r - 1$, we can construct the $5n(n-1)$ truth tables for

$$g(x_1, \ldots, x_{j-1}, x_j \circ x_k, x_{j+1}, \ldots, x_n) \tag{17}$$

and mark them with cost r if they haven't previously been marked. Exercise 14 shows that those truth tables can all be computed by performing simple bitwise operations on the truth table for g.

When $n = 4$, all but 13 of the 222 basic function types turn out to have $C_m(f) = C(f)$, so they can be evaluated in minimum memory without increasing the cost. In particular, all of the symmetric functions have this property — although that fact is not at all obvious from Fig. 9. Five classes of functions have $C(f) = 5$ but $C_m(f) = 6$; eight classes have $C(f) = 6$ but $C_m(f) = 7$. The most interesting example of the latter type is probably the function $(x_1 \vee x_2) \oplus (x_3 \vee x_4) \oplus (x_1 \wedge x_2 \wedge x_3 \wedge x_4)$, which has cost 6 because of the formula

$$x_1 \oplus (x_3 \vee x_4) \oplus \big(x_2 \wedge (\bar{x}_1 \vee (x_3 \wedge x_4))\big), \tag{18}$$

but it has no minimum-memory chain of length less than 7. (See exercise 15.)

*Determining the minimum cost. The exact value of $C(f)$ can be found by observing that all optimum Boolean chains $(x_{n+1}, \ldots, x_{n+r})$ for f obviously satisfy at least one of three conditions:

i) $x_{n+r} = x_j \circ x_k$, where x_j and x_k use no common intermediate results;

ii) $x_{n+1} = x_j \circ x_k$, where either x_j or x_k is not used in steps $x_{n+2}, \ldots, x_{n+r}$;

iii) Neither of the above, even when the intermediate steps are renumbered.

In case (i) we have $f = g \circ h$, where $C(g) + C(h) = r - 1$, and we can call this a "top-down" construction. In case (ii) we have $f(x_1, \ldots, x_n) = g(x_1, \ldots, x_{j-1}, x_j \circ x_k, x_{j+1}, \ldots, x_n)$, where $C(g) = r - 1$; we call this construction "bottom-up."

The best chains that recursively use only top-down constructions correspond to minimum formula length, $L(f)$. The best chains that recursively use only bottom-up constructions correspond to minimum-memory calculations, of length $C_m(f)$. We can do better yet, by mixing top-down constructions with bottom-up constructions; but we still won't know that we've found $C(f)$, because a special chain belonging to case (iii) might be shorter.

Fortunately such special chains are rare, because they must satisfy rather strong conditions, and they can be exhaustively listed when n and r aren't too large. For example, exercise 19 proves that no special chains exist when $r < n+2$; and when $n = 4$, $r = 6$, there are only 25 essentially different special chains that cannot obviously be shortened:

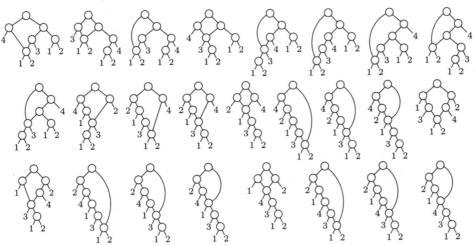

By systematically trying 5^r possibilities in every special chain, one for each way to assign a normal operator to the internal nodes of the tree, we will find at least one function f in every equivalence class for which the minimum cost $C(f)$ is achievable only in case (iii).

In fact, when $n = 4$ and $r = 6$, these $25 \cdot 5^6 = 390{,}625$ trials yield only one class of functions that can't be computed in 6 steps by any top-down-plus-bottom-up chain. The missing class, typified by the partially symmetric function $(\langle x_1 x_2 x_3 \rangle \vee x_4) \oplus (x_1 \wedge x_2 \wedge x_3)$, can be reached in six steps by appropriately specializing any of the first five chains illustrated above; for example, one way is

$$x_5 = x_1 \wedge x_2, \quad x_6 = x_1 \vee x_2, \quad x_7 = x_3 \oplus x_5,$$
$$x_8 = x_4 \wedge \bar{x}_5, \quad x_9 = x_6 \wedge x_7, \quad x_{10} = x_8 \vee x_9, \qquad (19)$$

corresponding to the first special chain. Since all other functions have $L(f) \le 7$, these trial calculations have established the true minimum cost in all cases.

Historical notes: The first concerted attempts to evaluate all Boolean functions $f(w, x, y, z)$ optimally were reported in *Annals of the Computation Laboratory of Harvard University* **27** (1951), where Howard Aiken's staff presented heuristic methods and extensive tables of the best switching circuits they were able to construct. Their cost measure $V(f)$ was different from the cost $C(f)$ that we've been considering, because it was based on "control grids" of vacuum tubes: They had three kinds of gates, NOR, OR, and NAND, each of which could take k inputs with cost k. Every input to such a gate could be either a variable, or the complement of a variable, or the result of a previous gate. Furthermore the function being evaluated was represented at the top level as an AND of any number of gates, with no additional cost.

With those cost criteria, a function might not have the same cost as its complement, because AND gates were possible only at the top level. One could evaluate $x \wedge y$ as $\text{NOR}(\bar{x}, \bar{y})$, with cost 2; but the cost of $\bar{x} \vee (\bar{y} \wedge \bar{z}) = \text{NAND}(x, \text{OR}(y, z))$ was 4 while its complement $x \wedge (y \vee z) = \text{AND}(\text{NOR}(\bar{x}), \text{OR}(y, z))$ cost only 3. Therefore the Harvard researchers needed to consider 402 essentially different classes of 4-variable functions instead of 222 (see the answer to exercise 7.1.1–125). Of course in those days they were working by hand. They found $V(f) < 20$ in all cases, except for the 64 functions equivalent to $S_{0,1}(w, x, y, z) \vee (S_2(w, x, y) \wedge z)$, which they evaluated with 20 control grids as follows:

$$g_1 = \text{NOR}(\bar{w}, \bar{x}), \quad g_2 = \text{NAND}(\bar{y}, z), \quad g_3 = \text{NOR}(w, x),$$
$$f = \text{AND}\big(\text{NAND}(g_1, g_2), \text{NAND}(g_3, \text{NOR}(\bar{y}, \bar{z})),$$
$$\text{NOR}(\text{NOR}(g_3, \bar{y}, z), \text{NOR}(g_1, g_2, g_3))\big). \qquad (20)$$

The first computer program to find provably optimum circuits was written by Leo Hellerman [*IEEE Transactions* **EC-12** (1963), 198–223], who determined the fewest NOR gates needed to evaluate any given function $f(x, y, z)$. He required every input of every gate to be either an uncomplemented variable or the output of a previous gate; fan-in and fan-out were limited to at most 3. When two circuits had the same gate count, he preferred the one with smallest sum-of-inputs. For example, he computed $\bar{x} = \text{NOR}(x)$ with cost 1; $x \vee y \vee z = \text{NOR}(\text{NOR}(x, y, z))$ with cost 2; $\langle xyz \rangle = \text{NOR}(\text{NOR}(x, y), \text{NOR}(x, z), \text{NOR}(y, z))$

Table 2

THE NUMBER OF FIVE-VARIABLE FUNCTIONS WITH GIVEN COMPLEXITY

$C(f)$	Classes	Functions	$L(f)$	Classes	Functions	$D(f)$	Classes	Functions
0	2	12	0	2	12	0	2	12
1	2	100	1	2	100	1	2	100
2	5	1140	2	5	1140	2	17	5350
3	20	11570	3	20	11570	3	1789	6702242
4	93	109826	4	93	109826	4	614316	4288259592
5	389	995240	5	366	936440	5	0	0
6	1988	8430800	6	1730	7236880	6	0	0
7	11382	63401728	7	8782	47739088	7	0	0
8	60713	383877392	8	40297	250674320	8	0	0
9	221541	1519125536	9	141422	955812256	9	0	0
10	293455	2123645248	10	273277	1945383936	10	0	0
11	26535	195366784	11	145707	1055912608	11	0	0
12	1	1920	12	4423	31149120	12	0	0

with cost 4; $S_1(x, y, z) = \text{NOR}\big(\text{NOR}(x, y, z), \langle xyz \rangle\big)$ with cost 6; etc. Since he limited the fan-out to 3, he found that every function of three variables could be evaluated with cost 7 or less, except for the parity function $x \oplus y \oplus z = (x \equiv y) \equiv z$, where $x \equiv y$ has cost 4 because it is $\text{NOR}(\text{NOR}(x, \text{NOR}(x, y)), \text{NOR}(y, \text{NOR}(x, y)))$.

Electrical engineers continued to explore other cost criteria; but four-variable functions seemed out of reach until 1977, when Frank M. Liang established the values of $C(f)$ shown in Table 1. Liang's unpublished derivation was based on a study of all chains that cannot be reduced by the bottom-up construction.

The case $n = 5$. There are 616,126 classes of essentially different functions $f(x_1, x_2, x_3, x_4, x_5)$, according to Table 7.1.1–5. Computers are now fast enough that this number is no longer frightening; so the author decided while writing this section to investigate $C(f)$ for all Boolean functions of five variables. Thanks to a bit of good luck, complete results could indeed be obtained, leading to the statistics shown in Table 2.

For this calculation Algorithm L and its variants were modified to deal with class representatives, instead of with the entire set of 2^{31} normal truth tables. The method of exercise 7.2.1.2–20 made it easy to generate all functions of a class, given any one of them, resulting in a thousand-fold speedup. The bottom-up method was enhanced slightly, allowing it to deduce for example that $f(x_1 \wedge x_2, x_1 \vee x_2, x_3, x_4, x_5)$ has cost $\leq r$ if $C(f) = r - 2$. After all classes of cost 10 had been found, the top-down and bottom-up methods were able to find chains of length ≤ 11 for all but seven classes of functions. Then the time-consuming part of the computation began, in which approximately 53 million special chains with $n = 5$ and $r = 11$ were generated; every such chain led to $5^{11} = 48,828,125$ functions, some of which would hopefully fall into the seven remaining mystery classes. But only six of those classes were found to have 11-step solutions. The lone survivor, whose truth table is **169ae443** in hexadecimal notation, is the unique class for which $C(f) = 12$, and it also has $L(f) = 12$.

The resulting constructions of symmetric functions are shown in Fig. 10. Some of them are astonishingly beautiful; some of them are beautifully simple;

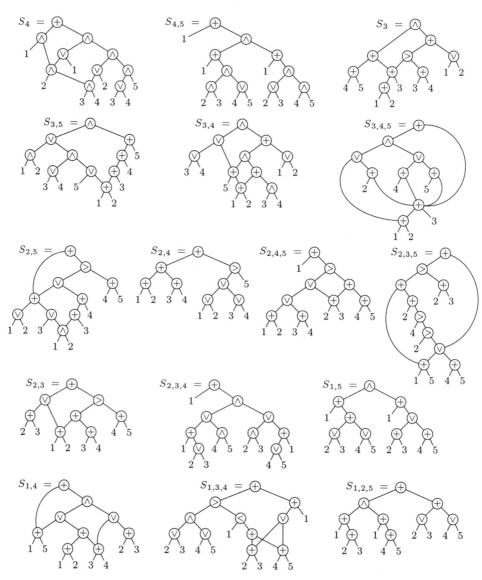

Fig. 10. Boolean chains of minimum cost
for symmetric functions of five variables.

and others are simply astonishing. (Look, for example, at the 8-step computation
of $S_{2,3}(x_1, x_2, x_3, x_4, x_5)$, or the elegant formula for $S_{2,3,4}$, or the nonmonotonic
chains for $S_{4,5}$ and $S_{3,4,5}$.) Incidentally, Table 2 shows that all 5-variable functions have depth ≤ 4, but no attempt to minimize depth has been made in Fig. 10.

It turns out that all of these symmetric functions can be evaluated in
minimum memory without increasing the cost. But no simple proof of that
fact is known.

Multiple outputs. We often want to evaluate several different Boolean functions $f_1(x_1, \ldots, x_n)$, $\ldots$, $f_m(x_1, \ldots, x_n)$ at the same input values x_1, $\ldots$, x_n; in other words, we often want to evaluate a multibit function $y = f(x)$, where $y = f_1 \ldots f_m$ is a binary vector of length m and $x = x_1 \ldots x_n$ is a binary vector of length n. With luck, much of the work involved in the computation of one component value $f_j(x_1, \ldots, x_n)$ can be shared with the operations that are needed to evaluate the other component values $f_k(x_1, \ldots, x_n)$.

Let $C(f) = C(f_1 \ldots f_m)$ be the length of a shortest Boolean chain that computes all of the nontrivial functions f_j. More precisely, the chain $(x_{n+1}, \ldots, x_{n+r})$ should have the property that, for $1 \leq j \leq m$, either $f_j(x_1, \ldots, x_n) = x_{l(j)}$ or $f_j(x_1, \ldots, x_n) = \bar{x}_{l(j)}$, for some $l(j)$ with $0 \leq l(j) \leq n+r$, where $x_0 = 0$. Clearly $C(f) \leq C(f_1) + \cdots + C(f_m)$, but we might be able to do much better.

For example, suppose we want to compute the functions z_1 and z_0 defined by

$$(z_1 z_0)_2 = x_1 + x_2 + x_3, \tag{21}$$

the two-bit binary sum of three Boolean variables. We have

$$z_1 = \langle x_1 x_2 x_3 \rangle \qquad \text{and} \qquad z_0 = x_1 \oplus x_2 \oplus x_3, \tag{22}$$

so the individual costs are $C(z_1) = 4$ and $C(z_0) = 2$. But it's easy to see that the combined cost $C(z_1 z_0)$ is at most 5, because $x_1 \oplus x_2$ is a suitable first step in the evaluation of each bit z_j:

$$x_4 = x_1 \oplus x_2, \quad z_0 = x_5 = x_3 \oplus x_4;$$
$$x_6 = x_3 \wedge x_4, \quad x_7 = x_1 \wedge x_2, \quad z_1 = x_8 = x_6 \vee x_7. \tag{23}$$

Furthermore, exhaustive calculations show that $C(z_1 z_0) > 4$; hence $C(z_1 z_0) = 5$.

Electrical engineers traditionally call a circuit for (21) a *full adder*, because n such building blocks can be hooked together to add two n-bit numbers. The special case of (22) in which $x_3 = 0$ is also important, although it boils down simply to

$$z_1 = x_1 \wedge x_2 \qquad \text{and} \qquad z_0 = x_1 \oplus x_2 \tag{24}$$

and has complexity 2; engineers call it a "half adder" in spite of the fact that the cost of a full adder exceeds the cost of two half adders.

The general problem of radix-2 addition

$$\frac{\begin{array}{c} (x_{n-1} \ldots x_1 x_0)_2 \\ (y_{n-1} \ldots y_1 y_0)_2 \end{array}}{(z_n z_{n-1} \ldots z_1 z_0)_2} \tag{25}$$

is to compute $n + 1$ Boolean outputs $z_n \ldots z_1 z_0$ from the $2n$ Boolean inputs $x_{n-1} \ldots x_1 x_0 y_{n-1} \ldots y_1 y_0$; and it is readily solved by the formulas

$$c_{j+1} = \langle x_j y_j c_j \rangle, \qquad z_j = x_j \oplus y_j \oplus c_j, \qquad \text{for } 0 \leq j < n, \tag{26}$$

where the c_j are "carry bits" and we have $c_0 = 0$, $z_n = c_n$. Therefore we can use a half adder to compute c_1 and z_0, followed by $n - 1$ full adders to compute the other c's and z's, accumulating a total cost of $5n - 3$. And in fact N. P. Red'kin [*Problemy Kibernetiki* **38** (1981), 181–216] has proved that $5n - 3$ steps are actually necessary, by constructing an elaborate 35-page proof by induction, which concludes with Case 2.2.2.3.1.2.3.2.4.3(!). But the depth of this circuit, $2n - 1$, is far too large for practical parallel computation, so a great deal of effort has gone into the task of devising circuits for addition that have depth $O(\log n)$ as well as reasonable cost. (See exercises 41–44.)

Now let's extend (21) and try to compute a general "sideways sum"

$$(z_{\lfloor \lg n \rfloor} \dots z_1 z_0)_2 = x_1 + x_2 + \cdots + x_n. \tag{27}$$

If $n = 2k+1$, we can use k full adders to reduce the sum to $(x_1 + \cdots + x_n) \bmod 2$ plus k bits of weight 2, because each full adder decreases the number of weight-1 bits by 2. For example, if $n = 9$ and $k = 4$ the computation is

$$x_{10} = x_1 \oplus x_2 \oplus x_3, \quad x_{11} = x_4 \oplus x_5 \oplus x_6, \quad x_{12} = x_7 \oplus x_8 \oplus x_9, \quad x_{13} = x_{10} \oplus x_{11} \oplus x_{12},$$
$$y_1 = \langle x_1 x_2 x_3 \rangle, \qquad y_2 = \langle x_4 x_5 x_6 \rangle, \qquad y_3 = \langle x_7 x_8 x_9 \rangle, \qquad y_4 = \langle x_{10} x_{11} x_{12} \rangle,$$

and we have $x_1 + \cdots + x_9 = x_{13} + 2(y_1 + y_2 + y_3 + y_4)$. If $n = 2k$ is even, a similar reduction applies but with a half adder at the end. The bits of weight 2 can then be summed in the same way; so we obtain the recurrence

$$s(n) = 5\lfloor n/2 \rfloor - 3[n \text{ even}] + s(\lfloor n/2 \rfloor), \qquad s(0) = 0, \tag{28}$$

for the total number of gates needed to compute $z_{\lfloor \lg n \rfloor} \dots z_1 z_0$. (A closed formula for $s(n)$ appears in exercise 30.) We have $s(n) < 5n$, and the first values

$$n = 1 \ 2 \ 3 \ 4 \ 5 \ \ 6 \ \ 7 \ \ 8 \ \ 9 \ \ 10 \ \ 11 \ \ 12 \ \ 13 \ \ 14 \ \ 15 \ \ 16 \ \ 17 \ \ 18 \ \ 19 \ \ 20$$
$$s(n) = 0 \ 2 \ 5 \ 9 \ 12 \ 17 \ 20 \ 26 \ 29 \ 34 \ 37 \ 44 \ 47 \ 52 \ 55 \ 63 \ 66 \ 71 \ 74 \ 81$$

show that the method is quite efficient even for small n. For example, when $n = 5$ it produces

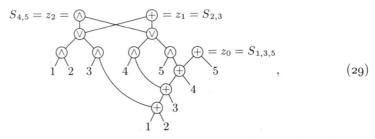

$$\tag{29}$$

which computes three different symmetric functions $z_2 = S_{4,5}(x_1, \dots, x_5)$, $z_1 = S_{2,3}(x_1, \dots, x_5)$, $z_0 = S_{1,3,5}(x_1, \dots, x_5)$ in just 12 steps. The 10-step computation of $S_{4,5}$ is optimum, according to Fig. 10; of course the 4-step computation of $S_{1,3,5}$ is also optimum. Furthermore, although $C(S_{2,3}) = 8$, the function $S_{2,3}$ is computed here in a clever 10-step way that shares all but one gate with $S_{4,5}$.

Notice that we can now compute *any* symmetric function efficiently, because every symmetric function of $\{x_1, \dots, x_n\}$ is a Boolean function of $z_{\lfloor \lg n \rfloor} \dots z_1 z_0$. We know, for example, that any Boolean function of four variables has complexity ≤ 7; therefore any symmetric function $S_{k_1, \dots, k_t}(x_1, \dots, x_{15})$ costs at most $s(15) + 7 = 62$. Surprise: The symmetric functions of n variables were among the hardest of all to evaluate, when n was small, but they're among the easiest when $n \geq 10$.

We can also compute *sets* of symmetric functions efficiently. If we want, say, to evaluate all $n+1$ symmetric functions $S_k(x_1, \ldots, x_n)$ for $0 \le k \le n$ with a single Boolean chain, we simply need to evaluate the first $n+1$ *minterms* of $z_0, z_1, \ldots, z_{\lfloor \lg n \rfloor}$. For example, when $n = 5$ the minterms that give us all functions S_k are respectively $S_0 = \bar{z}_0 \wedge \bar{z}_1 \wedge \bar{z}_2$, $S_1 = \bar{z}_0 \wedge \bar{z}_1 \wedge z_2$, ..., $S_5 = z_0 \wedge \bar{z}_1 \wedge z_2$.

How hard is it to compute all 2^n minterms of n variables? Electrical engineers call this function an n-to-2^n *binary decoder*, because it converts n bits $x_1 \ldots x_n$ into a sequence of 2^n bits $d_0 d_1 \ldots d_{2^n-1}$, exactly one of which is 1. The principle of "divide and conquer" suggests that we first evaluate all minterms on the first $\lceil n/2 \rceil$ variables, as well as all minterms on the last $\lfloor n/2 \rfloor$; then 2^n AND gates will finish the job. The cost of this method is $t(n)$, where

$$t(0) = t(1) = 0; \qquad t(n) = 2^n + t(\lceil n/2 \rceil) + t(\lfloor n/2 \rfloor) \quad \text{for } n \ge 2. \qquad (30)$$

So $t(n) = 2^n + O(2^{n/2})$; there's roughly one gate per minterm. (See exercise 32.)

Functions with multiple outputs often help us build larger functions with single outputs. For example, we've seen that the sideways adder (27) allows us to compute symmetric functions; and an n-to-2^n decoder also has many applications, in spite of the fact that 2^n can be huge when n is large. A case in point is the 2^m-*way multiplexer* $M_m(x_1, \ldots, x_m; y_0, y_1, \ldots, y_{2^m-1})$, also known as the m-bit *storage access function*, which has $n = m + 2^m$ inputs and takes the value y_k when $(x_1 \ldots x_m)_2 = k$. By definition we have

$$M_m(x_1, \ldots, x_m; y_0, y_1, \ldots, y_{2^m-1}) = \bigvee_{k=0}^{2^m-1} (d_k \wedge y_k), \qquad (31)$$

where d_k is the kth output of an m-to-2^m binary decoder; thus, by (30), we can evaluate M_m with $2^m + (2^m-1) + t(m) = 3n + O(\sqrt{n})$ gates. But exercise 39 shows that we can actually reduce the cost to only $2n + O(\sqrt{n})$. (See also exercise 79.)

Asymptotic facts. When the number of variables is small, our exhaustive-search methods have turned up lots of cases where Boolean functions can be evaluated with stunning efficiency. So it's natural to expect that, when more variables are present, even more opportunities for ingenious evaluations will arise. But the truth is exactly the opposite, at least from a statistical standpoint:

Theorem S. *The cost of almost every Boolean function* $f(x_1, \ldots, x_n)$ *exceeds* $2^n/n$. *More precisely, if* $c(n, r)$ *Boolean functions have complexity* $\le r$, *we have*

$$(r-1)! \, c(n, r) \le 2^{2r+1}(n+r-1)^{2r}. \qquad (32)$$

Proof. If a function can be computed in $r-1$ steps, it is also computable by an r-step chain. (This statement is obvious when $r = 1$; otherwise we can let $x_{n+r} = x_{n+r-1} \wedge x_{n+r-1}$.) We will show that there aren't very many r-step chains, hence we can't compute very many different functions with cost $\le r$.

Let π be a permutation of $\{1, \ldots, n+r\}$ that takes $1 \mapsto 1, \ldots, n \mapsto n$, and $n+r \mapsto n+r$; there are $(r-1)!$ such permutations. Suppose $(x_{n+1}, \ldots, x_{n+r})$ is a

Boolean chain in which each of the intermediate steps $x_{n+1}, \ldots, x_{n+r-1}$ is used in at least one subsequent step. Then the permuted chains defined by the rule

$$x_i = x_{j'(i)} \circ'_i x_{k'(i)} = x_{j(i\pi)\pi^-} \circ_{i\pi} x_{k(i\pi)\pi^-}, \qquad \text{for } n < i \le n+r, \qquad (33)$$

are distinct for different π. (If π takes $a \mapsto b$, we write $b = a\pi$ and $a = b\pi^-$.) For example, if π takes $5 \mapsto 6 \mapsto 7 \mapsto 8 \mapsto 9 \mapsto 5$, the chain (7) becomes

Original	Permuted	
$x_5 = x_1 \oplus x_3,$	$x_5 = x_1 \oplus x_2,$	
$x_6 = x_1 \oplus x_2,$	$x_6 = x_3 \oplus x_4,$	
$x_7 = x_3 \oplus x_4,$	$x_7 = x_9 \vee x_5,$	(34)
$x_8 = x_5 \vee x_6,$	$x_8 = x_5 \oplus x_6,$	
$x_9 = x_6 \oplus x_7,$	$x_9 = x_1 \oplus x_3,$	
$x_{10} = x_8 \wedge \bar{x}_9;$	$x_{10} = x_7 \wedge \bar{x}_8.$	

Notice that we might have $j'(i) \ge k'(i)$ or $j'(i) > i$ or $k'(i) > i$, contrary to our usual rules. But the permuted chain computes the same function x_{n+r} as before, and it doesn't have any cycles by which an entry is defined indirectly in terms of itself, because the permuted x_i is the original $x_{i\pi}$.

We can restrict consideration to *normal* Boolean chains, as remarked earlier. So the $c(n,r)/2$ normal Boolean functions of cost $\le r$ lead to $(r-1)! \, c(n,r)/2$ different permuted chains, where the operator $\circ_i$ in each step is either $\wedge$, $\vee$, $\bar{\supset}$, or $\oplus$. And there are at most $4^r(n+r-1)^{2r}$ such chains, because there are four choices for $\circ_i$ and $n+r-1$ choices for each of $j(i)$ and $k(i)$, for $n < i \le n+r$. Equation (32) follows; and we obtain the opening statement of the theorem by setting $r = \lfloor 2^n/n \rfloor$. (See exercise 46.) ∎

On the other hand, there's also good news for infinity-minded people: We can actually evaluate every Boolean function of n variables with only slightly more than $2^n/n$ steps of computation, even if we avoid $\oplus$ and $\equiv$, using a technique devised by C. E. Shannon and improved by O. B. Lupanov [*Bell System Tech. J.* **28** (1949), 59–98, Theorem 6; *Isvestiia VUZov, Radiofizika* **1** (1958), 120–140].

In fact, the Shannon–Lupanov approach leads to useful results even when n is small, so let's get acquainted with it by studying a small example. Consider

$$f(x_1, x_2, x_3, x_4, x_5, x_6) = \big[(x_1 x_2 x_3 x_4 x_5 x_6)_2 \text{ is prime}\big], \qquad (35)$$

a function that identifies all 6-bit prime numbers. Its truth table has $2^6 = 64$ bits, and we can work with it conveniently by using a 4×16 array to look at those bits instead of confining ourselves to one dimension:

$$
\begin{array}{l}
x_3 = 0\ 0\ 0\ 0\ 0\ 0\ 0\ 0\ 1\ 1\ 1\ 1\ 1\ 1\ 1\ 1 \\
x_4 = 0\ 0\ 0\ 0\ 1\ 1\ 1\ 1\ 0\ 0\ 0\ 0\ 1\ 1\ 1\ 1 \\
x_5 = 0\ 0\ 1\ 1\ 0\ 0\ 1\ 1\ 0\ 0\ 1\ 1\ 0\ 0\ 1\ 1 \\
x_6 = 0\ 1\ 0\ 1\ 0\ 1\ 0\ 1\ 0\ 1\ 0\ 1\ 0\ 1\ 0\ 1
\end{array}
$$

$x_1 x_2 = 00$	$0\ 0\ 1\ 1\ 0\ 1\ 0\ 1\ 0\ 0\ 0\ 1\ 0\ 1\ 0\ 0$	⎫ Group 1
$x_1 x_2 = 01$	$0\ 1\ 0\ 1\ 0\ 0\ 0\ 1\ 0\ 0\ 0\ 0\ 0\ 1\ 0\ 1$	⎬ (36)
$x_1 x_2 = 10$	$0\ 0\ 0\ 0\ 0\ 1\ 0\ 0\ 0\ 1\ 0\ 1\ 0\ 0\ 0\ 1$	⎫ Group 2
$x_1 x_2 = 11$	$0\ 0\ 0\ 0\ 0\ 1\ 0\ 0\ 0\ 0\ 0\ 1\ 0\ 1\ 0\ 0$	⎬

The rows have been divided into two groups of two rows each; and each group of rows has 16 columns, which are of four basic types, namely $\substack{0\\0}$, $\substack{0\\1}$, $\substack{1\\0}$, or $\substack{1\\1}$. Thus we see that the function can be expressed as

$$\begin{aligned}
f(x_1,\ldots,x_6) = \ & ([x_1x_2 \in \{00\}] \quad \wedge [x_3x_4x_5x_6 \in \{0010, 0101, 1011\}]) \\
\vee \ & ([x_1x_2 \in \{01\}] \quad \wedge [x_3x_4x_5x_6 \in \{0001, 1111\}]) \\
\vee \ & ([x_1x_2 \in \{00, 01\}] \wedge [x_3x_4x_5x_6 \in \{0011, 0111, 1101\}]) \\
\vee \ & ([x_1x_2 \in \{10\}] \quad \wedge [x_3x_4x_5x_6 \in \{1001, 1111\}]) \\
\vee \ & ([x_1x_2 \in \{11\}] \quad \wedge [x_3x_4x_5x_6 \in \{1101\}]) \\
\vee \ & ([x_1x_2 \in \{10, 11\}] \wedge [x_3x_4x_5x_6 \in \{0101, 1011\}]). \quad (37)
\end{aligned}$$

(The first line corresponds to group 1, type $\substack{1\\0}$, then comes group 1, type $\substack{0\\1}$, etc.; the last line corresponds to group 2 and type $\substack{1\\1}$.) A function like $[x_3x_4x_5x_6 \in \{0010, 0101, 1011\}]$ is the OR of three minterms of $\{x_3, x_4, x_5, x_6\}$.

In general we can view the truth table as a $2^k \times 2^{n-k}$ array, with l groups of rows having either $\lfloor 2^k/l \rfloor$ or $\lceil 2^k/l \rceil$ rows in each group. A group of size m will have columns of 2^m basic types. We form a conjunction $(g_{it}(x_1,\ldots,x_k) \wedge h_{it}(x_{k+1},\ldots,x_n))$ for each group i and each nonzero type t, where g_{it} is the OR of all minterms of $\{x_1,\ldots,x_k\}$ for the rows of the group where t has a 1, while h_{it} is the OR of all minterms of $\{x_{k+1},\ldots,x_n\}$ for the columns having type t in group i. The OR of all these conjunctions $(g_{it} \wedge h_{it})$ gives $f(x_1,\ldots,x_n)$.

Once we've chosen the parameters k and l, with $1 \le k \le n-2$ and $1 \le l \le 2^k$, the computation starts by computing all the minterms of $\{x_1,\ldots,x_k\}$ and all the minterms of $\{x_{k+1},\ldots,x_n\}$, in $t(k) + t(n-k)$ steps (see (30)). Then, for $1 \le i \le l$, we let group i consist of rows for the values of $(x_1,\ldots,x_k)$ such that $(i-1)2^k/l \le (x_1 \ldots x_k)_2 < i2^k/l$; it contains $m_i = \lceil i2^k/l \rceil - \lceil (i-1)2^k/l \rceil$ rows. We form all functions g_{it} for $t \in S_i$, the family of $2^{m_i} - 1$ nonempty subsets of those rows; $2^{m_i} - m_i - 1$ ORs of previously computed minterms will accomplish that task. We also form all functions h_{it} representing columns of nonzero type t; for this purpose we'll need at most 2^{n-k} OR operations in each group i, since we can OR each minterm into the h function of the appropriate type t. Finally we compute $f = \bigvee_{i=1}^{l} \bigvee_{t \in S_i} (g_{it} \wedge h_{it})$; each AND operation is compensated by an unnecessary first OR into h_{it}. So the total cost is at most

$$t(k) + t(n-k) + (l-1) + \sum_{i=1}^{l} \left((2^{m_i} - m_i - 1) + 2^{n-k} + (2^{m_i} - 2)\right); \quad (38)$$

we want to choose k and l so that this upper bound is minimized. Exercise 52 discusses the best choice when n is small. And when n is large, a good choice yields a provably near-optimum chain, at least for most functions:

Theorem L. *Let $C(n)$ denote the cost of the most expensive Boolean functions of n variables. Then as $n \to \infty$ we have*

$$C(n) \ge \frac{2^n}{n}\left(1 + \frac{\lg n}{n} + O\left(\frac{1}{n}\right)\right); \quad (39)$$

$$C(n) \le \frac{2^n}{n}\left(1 + 3\frac{\lg n}{n} + O\left(\frac{1}{n}\right)\right). \quad (40)$$

Proof. Exercise 48 shows that the lower bound (39) is a consequence of Theorem S. For the upper bound, we set $k = \lfloor 2\lg n\rfloor$ and $l = \lceil 2^k/(n - 3\lg n)\rceil$ in Lupanov's method; see exercise 53. ∎

Synthesizing a good chain. Formula (37) isn't the best way to implement a 6-bit prime detector, but it does suggest a decent strategy. For example, we needn't let variables x_1 and x_2 govern the rows: Exercise 51 shows that a better chain results if the rows are based on x_5x_6 while the columns come from $x_1x_2x_3x_4$, and in general there are many ways to partition a truth table by playing k of the variables against the other $n - k$.

Furthermore, we can improve on (37) by using our complete knowledge of all 4-variable functions; there's no need to evaluate a function like $[x_3x_4x_5x_6 \in \{0010, 0101, 1011\}]$ by first computing the minterms of $\{x_3, x_4, x_5, x_6\}$, if we know the best way to evaluate every such function from scratch. On the other hand, we do need to evaluate several 4-variable functions simultaneously, so the minterm approach might not be such a bad idea after all. Can we really improve on it?

Let's try to find a good way to synthesize a Boolean chain that computes a given set of 4-variable functions. The six functions of $x_3x_4x_5x_6$ in (37) are rather tame (see exercise 54), so we'll learn more by considering a more interesting example chosen from everyday life.

A *seven-segment display* is a now-ubiquitous way to represent a 4-bit number $(x_1x_2x_3x_4)_2$ in terms of seven cleverly positioned segments that are either visible or invisible. The segments are traditionally named (a, b, c, d, e, f, g) as shown; we get a '0' by turning on segments (a, b, c, d, e, f), but a '1' uses only segments (b, c). (Incidentally, the idea for such displays was invented by F. W. Wood, *U.S. Patent 974943* (1910), although Wood's original design used eight segments because he thought that a '4' requires a diagonal stroke.) Seven-segment displays usually support only the decimal digits '0', '1', ..., '9'; but of course a computer scientist's digital watch should display also hexadecimal digits. So we shall design seven-segment logic that displays the sixteen digits

$$\textsf{0123456789AbcdEF} \tag{41}$$

when given the respective inputs $x_1x_2x_3x_4 = 0000, 0001, 0010, \ldots, 1111$.

In other words, we want to evaluate seven Boolean functions whose truth tables are respectively

$$
\begin{aligned}
a &= 1011\ 0111\ 1110\ 0011, \\
b &= 1111\ 1001\ 1110\ 0100, \\
c &= 1101\ 1111\ 1111\ 0100, \\
d &= 1011\ 0110\ 1101\ 1110, \\
e &= 1010\ 0010\ 1011\ 1111, \\
f &= 1000\ 1111\ 1111\ 0011, \\
g &= 0011\ 1110\ 1111\ 1111.
\end{aligned}
\tag{42}
$$

If we simply wanted to evaluate each function separately, several methods that we've already discussed would tell us how to do it with minimum costs $C(a) = 5$, $C(b) = C(c) = C(d) = 6$, $C(e) = C(f) = 5$, and $C(g) = 4$; the total cost for all seven functions would then be 37. But we want to find a single Boolean chain that contains them all, and the shortest such chain is presumably much more efficient. How can we discover it?

Well, the task of finding a truly optimum chain for $\{a, b, c, d, e, f, g\}$ is probably infeasible from a computational standpoint. But a surprisingly good solution can be found with the help of the "footprint" idea explained earlier. Namely, we know how to compute not only a function's minimum cost, but also the set of all first steps consistent with that minimum cost in a normal chain. Function e, for example, has cost 5, but only if we evaluate it by starting with one of the instructions

$$x_5 = x_1 \oplus x_4 \quad \text{or} \quad x_5 = x_2 \wedge \bar{x}_3 \quad \text{or} \quad x_5 = x_2 \vee x_3.$$

Fortunately, one of the desirable first steps belongs to four of the seven footprints: Functions c, d, f, and g can all be evaluated optimally by starting with $x_5 = x_2 \oplus x_3$. So that is a natural choice; it essentially saves us three steps, because we know that at most 33 of the original 37 steps will be needed to finish.

Now we can recompute the costs and footprints of all 2^{16} functions, proceeding as before but also initializing the cost of the new function x_5 to zero. The costs of functions c, d, f, and g decrease by 1 as a result, and the footprints change too. For example, function a still has cost 5, but its footprint has increased from $\{x_1 \oplus x_3, x_2 \wedge x_3\}$ to $\{x_1 \oplus x_3, x_1 \wedge x_4, \bar{x}_1 \wedge x_4, x_2 \wedge x_3, \bar{x}_2 \wedge x_4, x_2 \oplus x_4, x_4 \wedge x_5, x_4 \oplus x_5\}$ when the function $x_5 = x_2 \oplus x_3$ is available for free.

In fact, $x_6 = \bar{x}_1 \wedge x_4$ is common to four of the new footprints, so again we have a natural way to proceed. And when everything is recalculated with zero cost given to both x_5 and x_6, the subsequent step $x_7 = x_3 \wedge \bar{x}_6$ turns out to be desirable in five of the newest footprints. Continuing in this "greedy" fashion, we aren't always so lucky, but a remarkable chain of only 22 steps does emerge:

$$
\begin{array}{llr}
x_5 = x_2 \oplus x_3, & x_{13} = x_1 \oplus x_7, & \bar{a} = x_{20} = x_{14} \wedge \bar{x}_{19}, \\
x_6 = \bar{x}_1 \wedge x_4, & x_{14} = x_5 \oplus x_6, & \bar{b} = x_{21} = x_7 \oplus x_{12}, \\
x_7 = x_3 \wedge \bar{x}_6, & x_{15} = x_7 \vee x_{12}, & \bar{c} = x_{22} = \bar{x}_8 \wedge x_{15}, \\
x_8 = x_1 \oplus x_2, & x_{16} = x_1 \vee x_5, & \bar{d} = x_{23} = x_9 \wedge \bar{x}_{13}, \\
x_9 = x_4 \oplus x_5, & x_{17} = x_5 \vee x_6, & \bar{e} = x_{24} = x_6 \vee x_{18}, \\
x_{10} = \bar{x}_7 \wedge x_8, & x_{18} = x_9 \wedge x_{10}, & \bar{f} = x_{25} = \bar{x}_8 \wedge x_{17}, \\
x_{11} = x_9 \oplus x_{10}, & x_{19} = x_3 \wedge x_9, & g = x_{26} = x_7 \vee x_{16}. \\
x_{12} = x_5 \wedge x_{11}, & &
\end{array}
\tag{43}
$$

(This is a *normal* chain, so it contains the normalizations $\{\bar{a}, \bar{b}, \bar{c}, \bar{d}, \bar{e}, \bar{f}, g\}$ instead of $\{a, b, c, d, e, f, g\}$. Simple changes will produce the unnormalized functions without changing the cost.)

Partial functions. In practice the output value of a Boolean function is often specified only at certain inputs $x_1 \ldots x_n$, and the outputs in other cases don't really matter. We might know, for example, that some of the input combinations will never arise. In such cases, we place an asterisk into the corresponding positions of the truth table, instead of specifying 0 or 1 everywhere.

The seven-segment display provides a case in point, because most of its applications involve only the ten binary-coded decimal inputs for which we have $(x_1x_2x_3x_4)_2 \leq 9$. We don't care what segments are visible in the other six cases. So the truth tables of (42) actually become

$$
\begin{aligned}
a &= \text{1011 0111 11** ****}, \\
b &= \text{1111 1001 11** ****}, \\
c &= \text{1101 1111 11** ****}, \\
d &= \text{1011 0110 11** ****}, \\
e &= \text{1010 0010 10** ****}, \\
f &= \text{1000 111* 11** ****}, \\
g &= \text{0011 1110 11** ****}.
\end{aligned}
\qquad (44)
$$

(Function f here has an asterisk also in position $x_1x_2x_3x_4 = 0111$, because a '7' can be displayed as either ⅂ or ⅂. Both of these styles appeared about equally often in the display units available to the author when this section was written. Truncated variants of the 6 and the 9 were sometimes seen in olden days, but they have thankfully disappeared.)

Asterisks in truth tables are generally known as *don't-cares* — a quaint term that could only have been invented by an electrical engineer. Table 3 shows that the freedom to choose arbitrary outputs is advantageous. For example, there are $\binom{16}{3}2^{13} = 4{,}587{,}520$ truth tables with 3 don't-cares; 69% of them cost 4 or less, even though only 21% of the asterisk-free truth tables permit such economy. On the other hand, don't-cares don't save us as much as we might hope; exercise 63 proves that a random function with, say, 30% don't-cares in its truth table tends to save only about 30% of the cost of a fully specified function.

What is the shortest Boolean chain that evaluates the seven partially specified functions in (44)? Our greedy-footprint method adapts itself readily to the presence of don't-cares, because we can OR together the footprints of all 2^d functions that match a pattern with d asterisks. The initial costs to evaluate each function separately are now reduced to $C(a) = 3$, $C(b) = C(c) = 2$, $C(d) = 5$, $C(e) = 2$, $C(f) = 3$, $C(g) = 4$, totalling just 21 instead of 37. Function g hasn't gotten cheaper, but it does have a larger footprint. Proceeding as before, but taking advantage of the don't-cares, we now can find a suitable chain of length only 13 — a chain with fewer than two operations per output(!):

$$
\begin{aligned}
x_5 &= x_1 \oplus x_2, & \bar{e} = x_{10} &= x_4 \vee x_8, & \bar{b} = x_{15} &= x_2 \wedge \bar{x}_{13}, \\
x_6 &= x_3 \wedge \bar{x}_4, & g = x_{11} &= x_7 \oplus x_8, & \bar{c} = x_{16} &= \bar{x}_2 \wedge x_6, \\
x_7 &= x_1 \oplus x_3, & x_{12} &= x_4 \oplus x_{11}, & \bar{f} = x_{17} &= \bar{x}_5 \wedge x_9. \\
x_8 &= x_2 \wedge \bar{x}_6, & \bar{d} = x_{13} &= x_{10} \wedge x_{12}, & & \qquad (45) \\
x_9 &= x_3 \vee x_4, & \bar{a} = x_{14} &= \bar{x}_3 \wedge x_{13},
\end{aligned}
$$

Tic-tac-toe. Let's turn now to a slightly larger problem, based on a popular children's game. Two players take turns filling the cells of a 3×3 grid. One player writes ×'s and the other writes ○'s, continuing until there either are three

Table 3
THE NUMBER OF 4-VARIABLE FUNCTIONS WITH d DON'T-CARES AND COST c

	$c=0$	$c=1$	$c=2$	$c=3$	$c=4$	$c=5$	$c=6$	$c=7$
$d=0$	10	60	456	2474	10624	24184	25008	2720
$d=1$	160	960	7296	35040	131904	227296	119072	2560
$d=2$	1200	7200	52736	221840	700512	816448	166144	
$d=3$	5600	33600	228992	831232	2045952	1381952	60192	
$d=4$	18200	108816	666528	2034408	3505344	1118128	3296	
$d=5$	43680	257472	1367776	3351488	3491648	433568	32	
$d=6$	80080	455616	2015072	3648608	1914800	86016		
$d=7$	114400	606944	2115648	2474688	533568	12032		
$d=8$	128660	604756	1528808	960080	71520	896		
$d=9$	114080	440960	707488	197632	4160			
$d=10$	78960	224144	189248	20160				
$d=11$	41440	72064	25472	800				
$d=12$	15480	12360	1280					
$d=13$	3680	800						
$d=14$	480							
$d=15$	32							
$d=16$	1							

X's or three O's in a straight line (in which case that player wins) or all nine cells are filled without a winner (in which case it's a "cat's game" or tie). For example, the game might proceed thus:

$$\# \quad \# \quad \# \quad \# \quad \# \quad \# \quad \# \quad \# ; \tag{46}$$

X has won. Our goal is to design a machine that plays tic-tac-toe optimally — making a winning move from each position in which a forced victory is possible, and never making a losing move from a position in which defeat is avoidable.

More precisely, we will set things up so that there are 18 Boolean variables $x_1, \ldots, x_9, o_1, \ldots, o_9$, which govern lamps to illuminate cells of the current position. The cells are numbered $\begin{smallmatrix}1&2&3\\4&5&6\\7&8&9\end{smallmatrix}$ as on a telephone dial. Cell j displays an X if $x_j = 1$, an O if $o_j = 1$, or remains blank if $x_j = o_j = 0$.* We never have $x_j = o_j = 1$, because that would display '⊗'. We shall assume that the variables $x_1 \ldots x_9 o_1 \ldots o_9$ have been set to indicate a legal position in which nobody has won; the computer plays the X's, and it is the computer's turn to move. For this purpose we want to define nine functions $y_1, \ldots, y_9$, where y_j means "change x_j from 0 to 1." If the current position is a cat's game, we should make $y_1 = \cdots = y_9 = 0$; otherwise exactly one y_j should be equal to 1, and of course the output value $y_j = 1$ should occur only if $x_j = o_j = 0$.

With 18 variables, each of our nine functions y_j will have a truth table of size $2^{18} = 262{,}144$. It turns out that only 4520 legal inputs $x_1 \ldots x_9 o_1 \ldots o_9$ are

---

* This setup is based on an exhibit from the early 1950s at the Museum of Science and Industry in Chicago, where the author was first introduced to the magic of switching circuits. The machine in Chicago, designed circa 1940 by W. Keister at Bell Telephone Laboratories, allowed me to go first; yet I soon discovered that there was no way to defeat it. Therefore I decided to move as stupidly as possible, hoping that the designer had not anticipated such bizarre behavior. In fact I allowed the machine to reach a position where it had two winning moves; and it seized *both* of them! Moving twice is of course a flagrant violation of the rules, so I had won a moral victory even though the machine announced that I had lost.

I commenced an examination of a game called "tit-tat-to" ...
to ascertain what number of combinations were required
for all the possible variety of moves and situations.
I found this to be comparatively insignificant.
... A difficulty, however, arose of a novel kind.
When the automaton had to move, it might occur that there were
two different moves, each equally conducive to his winning the game.
... Unless, also, some provision were made,
the machine would attempt two contradictory motions.
— CHARLES BABBAGE, *Passages from the Life of a Philosopher* (1864)

possible, so those truth tables are 98.3% filled with don't-cares. Still, 4520 is uncomfortably large if we hope to design and understand a Boolean chain that makes sense intuitively. Section 7.1.4 will discuss alternative ways to represent Boolean functions, by which it is often possible to deal with hundreds of variables even though the associated truth tables are impossibly large.

Most functions of 18 variables require more than $2^{18}/18$ gates, but let's hope we can do better. Indeed, a plausible strategy for making suitable moves in tic-tac-toe suggests itself immediately, in terms of several conditions that aren't hard to recognize:

w_j, an X in cell j will win, completing a line of X's;
b_j, an O in cell j would lose, completing a line of O's;
f_j, an X in cell j will give X two ways to win;
d_j, an O in cell j would give O two ways to win.

For example, X's move to the center in (46) was needed to block O, so it was of type b_5; fortunately it was also of type f_5, forcing a win on the next move.

Let $L = \{\{1,2,3\}, \{4,5,6\}, \{7,8,9\}, \{1,4,7\}, \{2,5,8\}, \{3,6,9\}, \{1,5,9\}, \{3,5,7\}\}$ be the set of winning lines. Then we have

$$m_j = \bar{x}_j \wedge \bar{o}_j; \qquad\qquad\qquad\qquad\quad \text{[moving in cell } j \text{ is legal]} \quad (47)$$

$$w_j = m_j \wedge \bigvee\nolimits_{\{i,j,k\}\in L}(x_i \wedge x_k); \qquad\qquad \text{[moving in cell } j \text{ wins]} \quad (48)$$

$$b_j = m_j \wedge \bigvee\nolimits_{\{i,j,k\}\in L}(o_i \wedge o_k); \qquad\qquad \text{[moving in cell } j \text{ blocks]} \quad (49)$$

$$f_j = m_j \wedge S_2(\{\alpha_{ik} \mid \{i,j,k\} \in L\}); \qquad \text{[moving in cell } j \text{ forks]} \quad (50)$$

$$d_j = m_j \wedge S_2(\{\beta_{ik} \mid \{i,j,k\} \in L\}); \qquad \text{[moving in cell } j \text{ defends]} \quad (51)$$

here α_{ik} and β_{ik} denote a single X or O together with a blank, namely

$$\alpha_{ik} = (x_i \wedge m_k) \vee (m_i \wedge x_k), \qquad \beta_{ik} = (o_i \wedge m_k) \vee (m_i \wedge o_k). \quad (52)$$

For example, $b_1 = m_1 \wedge ((o_2 \wedge o_3) \vee (o_4 \wedge o_7) \vee (o_5 \wedge o_9))$; $f_2 = m_2 \wedge S_2(\alpha_{13}, \alpha_{58}) = m_2 \wedge \alpha_{13} \wedge \alpha_{58}$; $d_5 = m_5 \wedge S_2(\beta_{19}, \beta_{28}, \beta_{37}, \beta_{46})$.

With these definitions we might try rank-ordering our moves thus:

$$\{w_1, \ldots, w_9\} > \{b_1, \ldots, b_9\} > \{f_1, \ldots, f_9\} > \{d_1, \ldots, d_9\} > \{m_1, \ldots, m_9\}. \quad (53)$$

"Win if you can; otherwise block if you can; otherwise fork if you can; otherwise defend if you can; otherwise make a legal move." Furthermore, when choosing between legal moves it seems sensible to use the ordering

$$m_5 > m_1 > m_3 > m_9 > m_7 > m_2 > m_6 > m_8 > m_4, \qquad (54)$$

because 5, the middle cell, occurs in four winning lines, while a corner move to 1, 3, 9, or 7 occurs in three, and a side cell 2, 6, 8, or 4 occurs in only two. We might as well adopt this ordering of subscripts within all five groups of moves $\{w_j\}$, $\{b_j\}$, $\{f_j\}$, $\{d_j\}$, and $\{m_j\}$ in (53).

To ensure that at most one move is chosen, we define w'_j, b'_j, f'_j, d'_j, m'_j to mean "a prior choice is better." Thus, $w'_5 = 0$, $w'_1 = w_5$, $w'_3 = w_1 \vee w'_1$, $\ldots$, $w'_4 = w_8 \vee w'_8$, $b'_5 = w_4 \vee w'_4$, $b'_1 = b_5 \vee b'_5$, $\ldots$, $m'_4 = m_8 \vee m'_8$. Then we can complete the definition of a tic-tac-toe automaton by letting

$$y_j = (w_j \wedge \overline{w'_j}) \vee (b_j \wedge \overline{b'_j}) \vee (f_j \wedge \overline{f'_j}) \vee (d_j \wedge \overline{d'_j}) \vee (m_j \wedge \overline{m'_j}), \quad \text{for } 1 \le j \le 9. \quad (55)$$

So we've constructed 9 gates for the m's, 48 for the w's, 48 for the b's, 144 for the α's and β's, 35 for the f's (with the help of Fig. 9), 35 for the d's, 43 for the primed variables, and 80 for the y's. Furthermore we can use our knowledge of partial 4-variable functions to reduce the six operations in (52) to only four,

$$\alpha_{ik} = (x_i \oplus x_k) \vee \overline{(o_i \oplus o_k)}, \qquad \beta_{ik} = \overline{(x_i \oplus x_k)} \vee (o_i \oplus o_k). \quad (56)$$

This trick saves 48 gates; so our design has cost 396 gates altogether.

The strategy for tic-tac-toe in (47)–(56) works fine in most cases, but it also has some glaring glitches. For example, it loses ignominiously in the game

$\qquad (57)$

the second X move is d_3, defending against a fork by O, yet it actually forces O to fork in the opposite corner! Another failure arises, for example, after position , when move m_5 leads to the cat's game , instead of to the victory for X that appeared in (46). Exercise 65 patches things up and obtains a fully correct Boolean tic-tac-toe player that needs just 445 gates.

*Functional decomposition. If the function $f(x_1, \ldots, x_n)$ can be written in the form $g(x_1, \ldots, x_k, h(x_{k+1}, \ldots, x_n))$, it's usually a good idea to evaluate $y = h(x_{k+1}, \ldots, x_n)$ first and then to compute $g(x_1, \ldots, x_k, y)$. Robert L. Ashenhurst inaugurated the study of such decompositions in 1952 [see *Annals Computation Lab. Harvard University* **29** (1957), 74–116], and observed that there's an easy way to recognize when f has this special property: If we write the truth table for f in a $2^k \times 2^{n-k}$ array as in (36), with rows for each setting of $x_1 \ldots x_k$ and columns for each setting of $x_{k+1} \ldots x_n$, then the desired subfunctions g and h exist if and only if the columns of this array have at most two different values. For example, the truth table for the function $\langle x_1 x_2 \langle x_3 x_4 x_5 \rangle \rangle$ is

$$
\begin{array}{cccccccc}
0 & 0 & 0 & 0 & 0 & 0 & 0 & 0 \\
0 & 0 & 0 & 1 & 0 & 1 & 1 & 1 \\
0 & 0 & 0 & 1 & 0 & 1 & 1 & 1 \\
1 & 1 & 1 & 1 & 1 & 1 & 1 & 1 \\
\end{array}
$$

when expressed in this two-dimensional form. One type of column corresponds to the case $h(x_{k+1}, \ldots, x_n) = 0$; the other corresponds to $h(x_{k+1}, \ldots, x_n) = 1$.

In general the variables $X = \{x_1, \ldots, x_n\}$ might be partitioned into any two disjoint subsets $Y = \{y_1, \ldots, y_k\}$ and $Z = \{z_1, \ldots, z_{n-k}\}$, and we might have $f(x) = g(y, h(z))$. We could test for a (Y, Z) decomposition by looking at the columns of the $2^k \times 2^{n-k}$ truth table whose rows correspond to values of y. But there are 2^n such ways to partition X; and all of them are potential winners, except for trivial cases when $|Y| = 0$ or $|Z| \leq 1$. How can we avoid examining such a humungous number of possibilities?

A practical way to proceed was discovered by V. Y.-S. Shen, A. C. McKellar, and P. Weiner [*IEEE Transactions* **C-20** (1971), 304–309], whose method usually needs only $O(n^2)$ steps to identify any potentially useful partition (Y, Z) that may exist. The basic idea is simple: Suppose $x_i \in Z$, $x_j \in Z$, and $x_m \in Y$. Define eight binary vectors δ_l for $l = (l_1 l_2 l_3)_2$, where δ_l has (l_1, l_2, l_3) respectively in components (i, j, m), and zeros elsewhere. Consider any randomly chosen vector $x = x_1 \ldots x_n$, and evaluate $f_l = f(x \oplus \delta_l)$ for $0 \leq l \leq 7$. Then the four pairs

$$\begin{pmatrix} f_0 \\ f_1 \end{pmatrix} \qquad \begin{pmatrix} f_2 \\ f_3 \end{pmatrix} \qquad \begin{pmatrix} f_4 \\ f_5 \end{pmatrix} \qquad \begin{pmatrix} f_6 \\ f_7 \end{pmatrix} \tag{58}$$

will appear in a 2×4 submatrix of the $2^k \times 2^{n-k}$ truth table. So a decomposition is impossible if these pairs are distinct, or if they contain three different values.

Let's call the pairs "good" if they're all equal, or if they have only two different values. Otherwise they're "bad." If f has essentially random behavior, we'll soon find bad pairs if we do this experiment with several different randomly chosen vectors x, because only 88 of the 256 possibilities for $f_0 f_1 \ldots f_7$ correspond to a good set of pairs; the probability of finding good pairs ten times in a row is only $(\frac{88}{256})^{10} \approx .00002$. And when we do discover bad pairs, we can conclude that

$$x_i \in Z \quad \text{and} \quad x_j \in Z \implies x_m \in Z, \tag{59}$$

because the alternative $x_m \in Y$ is impossible.

Suppose, for example, that $n = 9$ and that f is the function whose truth table $11001001000011 \ldots 00101$ consists of the 512 most significant bits of π, in binary notation. (This is the "more-or-less random function" that we studied for $n = 4$ in (5) and (6) above.) Bad pairs for this π function are quickly found in each of the cases (i, j, m) for which $m \neq i < j \neq m$. Indeed, in the author's experiments, 170 of those 252 cases were decided immediately; the average number of random x vectors per case was only 1.52; and only one case needed as many as eight x's before bad pairs appeared. Thus (59) holds for all relevant (i, j, m), and the function is clearly indecomposable. In fact, exercise 73 points out that we needn't make 252 tests to establish the indecomposability of this π function; only $\binom{n}{2} = 36$ of them would have been sufficient.

Turning to a less random function, let $f(x_1, \ldots, x_9) = (\det X) \bmod 2$, where

$$X = \begin{pmatrix} x_1 & x_2 & x_3 \\ x_4 & x_5 & x_6 \\ x_7 & x_8 & x_9 \end{pmatrix}. \tag{60}$$

This function does not satisfy condition (59) when $i = 1$, $j = 2$, and $m = 3$, because there are no bad pairs in that case. But it does satisfy (59) for $4 \le m \le 9$ when $\{i, j\} = \{1, 2\}$. We can denote this behavior by the convenient abbreviation '12⇒456789'; the full set of implications, for all pairs $\{i, j\}$, is

12⇒456789	18⇒34569	27⇒34569	37⇒24568	48⇒12369	67⇒12358
13⇒456789	19⇒24568	28⇒134679	38⇒14567	49⇒12358	68⇒12347
14⇒235689	23⇒456789	29⇒14567	39⇒124578	56⇒123789	69⇒124578
15⇒36789	24⇒36789	34⇒25789	45⇒123789	57⇒12369	78⇒123456
16⇒25789	25⇒134679	35⇒14789	46⇒123789	58⇒134679	79⇒123456
17⇒235689	26⇒14789	36⇒124578	47⇒235689	59⇒12347	89⇒123456

(see exercise 69). Bad pairs are a little more difficult to find when we probe this function at random: The average number of x's needed in the author's experiments rose to about 3.6, when bad pairs did exist. And of course there was a need to limit the testing, by choosing a tolerance threshold t and then giving up when t consecutive trials failed to find any bad pairs. Choosing $t = 10$ would have found all but 8 of the 198 implications listed above.

Implications like (59) are Horn clauses, and we know from Section 7.1.1 that it's easy to make further deductions from Horn clauses. Indeed, the method of exercise 74 will deduce that the only possible partition with $|Z| > 1$ is the trivial one ($Y = \emptyset$, $Z = \{x_1, \ldots, x_9\}$), after looking at fewer than 50 cases (i, j, m).

Similar results occur when $f(x_1, \ldots, x_9) = [\text{per } X > 0]$, where per denotes the *permanent* function. (In this case f tells us if there is a matching in the bipartite subgraph of $K_{3,3}$ whose edges are specified by the variables $x_1 \ldots x_9$.) Now there are just 180 implications,

12⇒456789	18⇒3459	27⇒3459	37⇒2468	48⇒1269	67⇒1358
13⇒456789	19⇒2468	28⇒134679	38⇒1567	49⇒1358	68⇒2347
14⇒235689	23⇒456789	29⇒1567	39⇒124578	56⇒123789	69⇒124578
15⇒3678	24⇒3678	34⇒2579	45⇒123789	57⇒1269	78⇒123456
16⇒2579	25⇒134679	35⇒1489	46⇒123789	58⇒134679	79⇒123456
17⇒235689	26⇒1489	36⇒124578	47⇒235689	59⇒2347	89⇒123456,

only 122 of which would have been discovered with $t = 10$ as the cutoff threshold. (The best choice of t is not clear; perhaps it should vary dynamically.) Still, those 122 Horn clauses were more than enough to establish indecomposability.

What about a decomposable function? With $f = \langle x_2 x_3 x_6 x_9 \langle x_1 x_4 x_5 x_7 x_8 \rangle \rangle$ we get $i \wedge j \Rightarrow m$ for all $m \notin \{i, j\}$, except when $\{i, j\} \subseteq \{1, 4, 5, 7, 8\}$; in the latter case, m must also belong to $\{1, 4, 5, 7, 8\}$. Although only 185 of these 212 implications were discovered with tolerance $t = 10$, the partition $Y = \{x_2, x_3, x_6, x_9\}$, $Z = \{x_1, x_4, x_5, x_7, x_8\}$ emerged quickly as a strong possibility.

Whenever a potential decomposition is supported by the evidence, we need to verify that the corresponding $2^k \times 2^{n-k}$ truth table does indeed have only one or two distinct columns. But we're happy to spend 2^n units of time on that verification, because we've greatly simplified the evaluation of f.

The comparison function $f = \left[(x_1x_2x_3x_4)_2 \geq (x_5x_6x_7x_8)_2 + x_9\right]$ is another interesting case. Its 184 potentially deducible implications are

12⇒3456789	18⇒2345679	27⇒34689	37⇒489	48⇒9	67⇒23489
13⇒2456789	19⇒2345678	28⇒34679	38⇒479	49⇒8	68⇒23479
14⇒2356789	23⇒46789	29⇒34678	39⇒478	56⇒1234789	69⇒23478
15⇒2346789	24⇒36789	34⇒789	45⇒1236789	57⇒1234689	78⇒349
16⇒2345789	25⇒1346789	35⇒1246789	46⇒23789	58⇒1234679	79⇒348
17⇒2345689	26⇒34789	36⇒24789	47⇒389	59⇒1234678	89⇒4,

and 145 of them were found when $t = 10$. Three decompositions reveal themselves in this case, having $Z = \{x_4, x_8, x_9\}$, $Z = \{x_3, x_4, x_7, x_8, x_9\}$, and $Z = \{x_2, x_3, x_4, x_6, x_7, x_8, x_9\}$, respectively. Ashenhurst proved that we can reduce f immediately as soon as we find a nontrivial decomposition; the other decompositions will show up later, when we try to reduce the simpler functions g and h.

*Decomposition of partial functions. When the function f is only partially specified, a decomposition with partition (Y, Z) hinges on being able to assign values to the don't-cares so that at most two different columns appear in the corresponding $2^k \times 2^{n-k}$ truth table.

Two vectors $u_1 \ldots u_m$ and $v_1 \ldots v_m$ consisting of 0s, 1s, and *s are said to be *incompatible* if either $u_j = 0$ and $v_j = 1$ or $u_j = 1$ and $v_j = 0$, for some j — equivalently, if the subcubes of the m-cube specified by u and v have no points in common. Consider the graph whose vertices are the columns of a truth table with don't-cares, where $u — v$ if and only if u and v are incompatible. We can assign values to the *s to achieve at most two distinct columns if and only if this graph is *bipartite*. For if $u_1, \ldots, u_l$ are mutually compatible, their generalized consensus $u_1 \sqcup \cdots \sqcup u_l$, defined in exercise 7.1.1–32, is compatible with all of them. [See S. L. Hight, *IEEE Trans.* **C-22** (1973), 103–110; E. Boros, V. Gurvich, P. L. Hammer, T. Ibaraki, and A. Kogan, *Discrete Applied Math.* **62** (1995), 51–75.] Since a graph is bipartite if and only if it contains no odd cycles, we can easily test this condition with a depth-first search (see Section 7.4.1).

Consequently the method of Shen, McKellar, and Weiner works also when don't-cares are present: The four pairs in (58) are considered bad if and only if three of them are mutually incompatible. We can operate almost as before, although bad pairs will naturally be harder to find when there are lots of *s (see exercise 72). However, Ashenhurst's theorem no longer applies. When several decompositions exist, they all should be explored further, because they might use different settings of the don't-cares, and some might be better than the others.

Although most functions $f(x)$ have no simple decomposition $g(y, h(z))$, we needn't give up hope too quickly, because other forms like $g(y, h_1(z), h_2(z))$ might well lead to an efficient chain. If, for example, f is symmetric in three of its variables $\{z_1, z_2, z_3\}$, we can always write $f(x) = g\big(y, S_{1,2}(z_1, z_2, z_3), S_{1,3}(z_1, z_2, z_3)\big)$, since $S_{1,2}(z_1, z_2, z_3)$ and $S_{1,3}(z_1, z_2, z_3)$ characterize the value of $z_1 + z_2 + z_3$. (Notice that just four steps will suffice to compute both $S_{1,2}$ and $S_{1,3}$.)

In general, as observed by H. A. Curtis [*JACM* **8** (1961), 484–496], $f(x)$ can be expressed in the form $g(y, h_1(z), \ldots, h_r(z))$ if and only if the $2^k \times 2^{n-k}$ truth table corresponding to Y and Z has at most 2^r different columns. And when don't-cares are present, the same result holds if and only if the incompatibility graph for Y and Z can be colored with at most 2^r colors.

For example, the function $f(x) = (\det X) \bmod 2$ considered above turns out to have eight distinct columns when $Z = \{x_4, x_5, x_6, x_7, x_8, x_9\}$; that's a surprisingly small number, considering that the truth table has 8 rows and 64 columns. From this fact we might be led to discover how to expand a determinant by cofactors of the first row,

$$f(x) = x_1 \wedge h_1(x_4, \ldots, x_9) \oplus x_2 \wedge h_2(x_4, \ldots, x_9) \oplus x_3 \wedge h_3(x_4, \ldots, x_9),$$

if we didn't already know such a rule.

When there are $d \le 2^r$ different columns, we can think of $f(x)$ as a function of y and $h(z)$, where h takes each binary vector $z_1 \ldots z_{n-k}$ into one of the values $\{0, 1, \ldots, d-1\}$. Thus $(h_1, \ldots, h_r)$ is essentially an encoding of the different column types, and we hope to find very simple functions $h_1, \ldots, h_r$ that provide such an encoding. Moreover, if d is strictly less than 2^r, the function $g(y, h_1, \ldots, h_r)$ will have many don't-cares that may well decrease its cost.

The distinct columns might also suggest a function g for which the h's have don't-cares. For example, we can use $g(y_1, y_2, h_1, h_2) = (y_1 \oplus (h_1 \wedge y_2)) \wedge h_2$ when all columns are either $(0, 0, 0, 0)^T$ or $(0, 0, 1, 1)^T$ or $(0, 1, 1, 0)^T$; then the value of $h_1(z)$ is arbitrary when z corresponds to an all-zero column. H. A. Curtis has explained how to exploit this idea when $|Y| = 1$ and $|Z| = n - 1$ [see *IEEE Transactions* **C-25** (1976), 1033–1044].

For a comprehensive discussion of decomposition techniques, see Richard M. Karp, *J. Society for Industrial and Applied Math.* **11** (1963), 291–335.

Larger values of n. We've been considering only rather tiny examples of Boolean functions. Theorem S tells us that large, random examples are inherently difficult; but practical examples might well be highly nonrandom. So it makes sense to search for simplifications using heuristic methods.

When n grows, the best ways currently known for dealing with Boolean functions generally start with a Boolean chain — not with a huge truth table — and they try to improve that chain via "local changes." The chain can be specified by a set of equations. Then, if an intermediate result is used in comparatively few subsequent steps, we can try to eliminate it, temporarily making those subsequent steps into functions of three variables, and reformulating those functions in order to make a better chain when possible.

For example, suppose the gate $x_i = x_j \circ x_k$ is used only once, in the gate $x_l = x_i \,\square\, x_m$, so that $x_l = (x_j \circ x_k) \,\square\, x_m$. Other gates might already exist, by which we have computed other functions of x_j, x_k, and x_m; and the definitions of x_j, x_k, and x_m may imply that some of the joint values of (x_j, x_k, x_m) are impossible. Thus we might be able to compute x_l from other gates by doing just one further operation. For example, if $x_i = x_j \wedge x_k$ and $x_l = x_i \vee x_m$, and if the values $x_j \vee x_m$ and $x_k \vee x_m$ appear elsewhere in the chain, we can set $x_l = (x_j \vee x_m) \wedge (x_k \vee x_m)$; this eliminates x_i and reduces the cost by 1. Or if, say, $x_j \wedge (x_k \oplus x_m)$ appears elsewhere and we know that $x_j x_k x_m \neq 101$, we can set $x_l = x_m \oplus (x_j \wedge (x_k \oplus x_m))$.

If x_i is used only in x_l and x_l is used only in x_p, then gate x_p depends on four variables, and we might be able to reduce the cost by using our total knowledge of four-variable functions, obtaining x_p in a better way while eliminating x_i and x_l. Similarly, if x_i appears only in x_l and x_p, we can eliminate x_i if we find a better way to evaluate two different functions of four variables, possibly with don't-cares and with other functions of those four variables available for free. Again, we know how to solve such problems, using the footprint method discussed above.

When no local changes are able to decrease the cost, we can also try local changes that preserve or even increase the cost, in order to discover different kinds of chains that might simplify in other ways. We shall discuss such local search methods extensively in Section 7.10.

Excellent surveys of techniques for Boolean optimization, which electrical engineers call the problem of "multilevel logic synthesis," have been published by R. K. Brayton, G. D. Hachtel, and A. L. Sangiovanni-Vincentelli, *Proceedings of the IEEE* **78** (1990), 264–300, and in the book *Synthesis and Optimization of Digital Circuits* by G. De Micheli (McGraw–Hill, 1994).

Lower bounds. Theorem S tells us that nearly every Boolean function of $n \geq 12$ variables is hard to evaluate, requiring a chain whose length exceeds $2^n/n$. Yet modern computers, which are built from logic circuits involving electric signals that represent thousands of Boolean variables, happily evaluate zillions of Boolean functions every microsecond. Evidently there are plenty of important functions that can be evaluated quickly, in spite of Theorem S. Indeed, the proof of that theorem was indirect; we simply counted the cases of low cost, so we learned absolutely nothing about any particular examples that might arise in practice. When we want to compute a given function and we can only think of a laborious way to do the job, how can we be sure that there's no tricky shortcut?

The answer to that question is almost scandalous: After decades of concentrated research, computer scientists have been unable to find *any* explicit family of functions $f(x_1, \ldots, x_n)$ whose cost is inherently nonlinear, as n increases. The true behavior is $2^n/n$, but no lower bound as strong as $n \log \log \log n$ has yet been proved! Of course we could rig up artificial examples, such as "the lexicographically smallest truth table of length 2^n that isn't achievable by any Boolean chain of length $\lfloor 2^n/n \rfloor - 1$"; but such functions are surely not explicit. The truth table of an explicit function $f(x_1, \ldots, x_n)$ should be computable in at most, say, 2^{cn} units of time for some constant c; that is, the time needed to specify all of the function values should be polynomial in the length of the truth table. Under those ground rules, no family of single-output functions is currently known to have a combinational complexity that exceeds $3n + O(1)$ as $n \to \infty$. [See N. Blum, *Theoretical Computer Science* **28** (1984), 337–345.]

The picture is not totally bleak, because several interesting *linear* lower bounds have been proved for functions of practical importance. A basic way to obtain such results was introduced by N. P. Red'kin in 1970: Suppose we have an optimum chain of cost r for $f(x_1, \ldots, x_n)$. By setting $x_n \leftarrow 0$ or $x_n \leftarrow 1$, we obtain reduced chains for the functions $g(x_1, \ldots, x_{n-1}) = f(x_1, \ldots, x_{n-1}, 0)$ and $h(x_1, \ldots, x_{n-1}) = f(x_1, \ldots, x_{n-1}, 1)$, having cost $r - u$ if x_n was used as an input to u different gates. Moreover, if x_n is used in a "canalizing" gate $x_i = x_n \circ x_k$, where the operator $\circ$ is neither $\oplus$ nor $\equiv$, some setting of x_n will force x_i to be constant, thereby further reducing the chain for g or h. Lower bounds on g and/or h therefore lead to a lower bound on f. (See exercises 77–81.)

But where are the proofs of nonlinear lower bounds? Almost every problem with a yes-no answer can be formulated as a Boolean function, so there's no shortage of explicit functions that we don't know how to evaluate in linear time, or even in polynomial time. For example, any directed graph G with vertices $\{v_1, \ldots, v_m\}$ can be represented by its adjacency matrix X, where $x_{ij} = [v_i \rightarrow v_j]$; then

$$f(x_{12}, \ldots, x_{1m}, \ldots, x_{m1}, \ldots, x_{m(m-1)}) = [G \text{ has a Hamiltonian path}] \quad (61)$$

is a Boolean function of $n = m(m - 1)$ variables. We would dearly love to be able to evaluate this function in, say, n^4 steps. We do know how to compute the truth table for f in $O(m!\, 2^n) = 2^{n+O(\sqrt{n}\,\log n)}$ steps, since only $m!$ potential Hamiltonian paths exist; thus f is indeed "explicit." But nobody knows how to evaluate f in polynomial time, or how to prove that there isn't a $4n$-step chain.

For all we know, short Boolean chains for f might exist, for each n. After all, Figs. 9 and 10 reveal the existence of fiendishly clever chains even in the cases of 4 and 5 variables. Efficient chains for all of the larger problems that we ever will need to solve might well be "out there" — yet totally beyond our grasp, because we don't have time to find them. Even if an omniscient being revealed the simple chains to us, we might find them incomprehensible, because the shortest proof of their correctness might be longer than the number of cells in our brains.

Theorem S rules out such a scenario for most Boolean functions. But fewer than 2^{100} Boolean functions will ever be of practical importance in the entire history of the world, and Theorem S tells us zilch about them.

In 1974, Larry Stockmeyer and Albert Meyer were, however, able to construct a Boolean function f whose complexity is provably huge. Their f isn't "explicit," in the precise sense described above, but it isn't artificial either; it arises naturally in mathematical logic. Consider symbolic statements such as

$$048+1015\neq1063\,; \tag{62}$$
$$\forall m\exists n\,(m<n+1)\,; \tag{63}$$
$$\forall n\exists m\,(m+1<n)\,; \tag{64}$$
$$\forall a\forall b\,(b\geq a+2\Rightarrow\exists ab\,(a<ab\wedge ab<b))\,; \tag{65}$$
$$\forall A\forall B\,(A\equiv B\Leftrightarrow\neg\exists n\,(n\in A\wedge n\notin B\vee n\in B\wedge n\notin A))\,; \tag{66}$$
$$\forall A\,(\exists n\,(n\in A)\Rightarrow\exists m\,(m\in A\wedge\forall n\,(n\in A\Rightarrow m\leq n)))\,; \tag{67}$$
$$\forall A\,(\exists n\,(n\in A)\Rightarrow\exists m\,(m\in A\wedge\forall n\,(n\in A\Rightarrow m\geq n)))\,; \tag{68}$$
$$\exists P\forall a\,((a\in P\Leftrightarrow a+3\notin P)\Leftrightarrow a<1000)\,; \tag{69}$$
$$\forall A\forall B\,(\forall C\forall c\,(C\equiv A\wedge c=1\vee C\equiv B\wedge c=0\Rightarrow(\forall n\,(n\in C\Leftrightarrow n+1\in C)\Leftrightarrow c=1))\Rightarrow\neg A\equiv B)\,. \tag{70}$$

Stockmeyer and Meyer defined a language L by using the 63-character alphabet

∀∃¬()≡∈∉+∧∨⇸⇹<≤=≠≥>abcdefghijklmnopqABCDEFGHIJKLMNOPQ0123456789

and giving conventional meanings to these symbols. Strings of lowercase letters within the sentences of L, like 'ab' in (65), represent numeric variables, restricted to nonnegative integers; strings of uppercase letters represent set variables, restricted to finite sets of such numbers. For example, (66) means, "For all finite sets A and B, we have $A = B$ if and only if there doesn't exist a number n that is in A but not in B, or in B but not in A." Some of these statements are true; others are false. (See exercise 82.)

All of the strings (62)–(70) belong to L, but the language is actually quite restricted: The only arithmetic operation allowed on a number is to add a constant; we can write 'a+13' but not 'a+b'. The only relation allowed between a number and a set is elementhood ($\in$ or $\notin$). The only relation allowed between sets is equality ($\equiv$). Furthermore all variables must be quantified by $\exists$ or $\forall$.*

Every sentence of L that has length $k \leq n$ can be represented by a binary vector of length $6n$, with zeros in the last $6(n-k)$ bits. Let $f(x)$ be a Boolean function of $6n$ variables such that $f(x) = 1$ whenever x represents a true sentence of L, and $f(x) = 0$ whenever x represents a sentence that is false; the value of $f(x)$ is unspecified when x doesn't represent a meaningful sentence. The truth table for such a function f can be constructed in a finite number of steps, according to theorems of Büchi and Elgot [*Zeitschrift für math. Logik und Grundlagen der Math.* **6** (1960), 66–92; *Transactions of the Amer. Math. Soc.* **98** (1961), 21–51]. But "finite" does not mean "feasible": Stockmeyer and Meyer proved that

$$C(f) > 2^{r-5} \qquad \text{whenever } n \geq 460 + .302r + 5.08\ln r \text{ and } r > 36. \qquad (71)$$

In particular, we have $C(f) > 2^{426} > 10^{128}$ when $n = 621$. A Boolean chain with that many gates could never be built, since 10^{128} is a generous upper bound on the number of protons in the universe. So this is a fairly small, finite problem that will never be solved.

Details of Stockmeyer and Meyer's proof appear in *JACM* **49** (2002), 753–784. The basic idea is that the language L, though limited, is rich enough to describe truth tables and the complexity of Boolean chains, using fairly short sentences; hence f has to deal with inputs that essentially refer to themselves.

*For further reading. Thousands of significant papers have been written about networks of Boolean gates, because such networks underlie so many aspects of theory and practice. We have focused in this section chiefly on topics that are relevant to computer programming for sequential machines. But other topics have also been extensively investigated, of primary relevance to parallel computation, such as the study of small-depth circuits in which gates can have any number of inputs ("unlimited fan-in"). Ingo Wegener's book *The Complexity of*

---

* Technically speaking, the sentences of L belong to "weak second-order monadic logic with one successor." Weak second-order logic allows quantification over finite sets; monadic logic with k successors is the theory of unlabeled k-ary trees.

Boolean Functions (Teubner and Wiley, 1987) provides a good introduction to the entire subject.

We have mostly considered Boolean chains in which all binary operators have equal importance. For our purposes, gates such as $\oplus$ or $\bar{\subset}$ are neither more nor less desirable than gates such as $\wedge$ or $\vee$. But it's natural to wonder if we can get by with only the monotone operators $\wedge$ and $\vee$ when we are computing a monotone function. Alexander Razborov has developed striking proof techniques to show that, in fact, monotone operators by themselves have inherently limited capabilities. He proved, for example, that all AND-OR chains to determine whether the permanent of an $n \times n$ matrix of 0s and 1s is zero or nonzero must have cost $n^{\Omega(\log n)}$. [See *Doklady Akademii Nauk SSSR* **281** (1985), 798–801; *Matematicheskie Zametki* **37** (1985), 887–900.] By contrast, we will see in Section 7.5.1 that this problem, equivalent to "bipartite matching," is solvable in only $O(n^{2.5})$ steps. Furthermore, the efficient methods in that section can be implemented as Boolean chains of only slightly larger cost, when we allow negation or other Boolean operations in addition to $\wedge$ and $\vee$. (Vaughan Pratt has called this "the power of negative thinking.") An introduction to Razborov's methods appears in exercises 85 and 86.

EXERCISES

1. [*24*] The "random" function in formula (6) corresponds to a Boolean chain of cost 4 and depth 4. Find a formula of depth 3 that has the same cost.

2. [*21*] Show how to compute (a) $w \oplus \langle xyz \rangle$ and (b) $w \wedge \langle xyz \rangle$ with formulas that have depth 3 and cost 5.

3. [*M23*] (B. I. Finikov, 1957.) If the Boolean function $f(x_1, \ldots, x_n)$ is true at exactly k points, prove that $L(f) < 2n + (k-2)2^{k-1}$. *Hint:* Think of $k = 3$ and $n = 10^6$.

4. [*M26*] (P. M. Spira, 1971.) Prove that the minimum depth and formula length of a Boolean function satisfy $\lg L(f) < D(f) \leq \alpha \lg L(f) + 1$, where $\alpha = 2/\lg(\frac{3}{2}) \approx 3.419$. *Hint:* Every binary tree with $r \geq 3$ internal nodes contains a subtree with s internal nodes, where $\frac{1}{3}r \leq s < \frac{2}{3}r$.

▶ **5.** [*21*] The Fibonacci threshold function $F_n(x_1, \ldots, x_n) = \langle x_1^{F_1} x_2^{F_2} \ldots x_{n-1}^{F_{n-1}} x_n^{F_{n-2}} \rangle$ was analyzed in exercise 7.1.1–101, when $n \geq 3$. Is there an efficient way to evaluate it?

6. [*20*] True or false: A Boolean function $f(x_1, \ldots, x_n)$ is normal if and only if it satisfies the general distributive law $f(x_1, \ldots, x_n) \wedge y = f(x_1 \wedge y, \ldots, x_n \wedge y)$.

7. [*20*] Convert the Boolean chain '$x_5 = x_1 \,\bar{\vee}\, x_4$, $x_6 = \bar{x}_2 \vee x_5$, $x_7 = \bar{x}_1 \wedge \bar{x}_3$, $x_8 = x_6 \equiv x_7$' to an equivalent chain $(\hat{x}_5, \hat{x}_6, \hat{x}_7, \hat{x}_8)$ in which every step is normal.

▶ **8.** [*20*] Explain why (11) is the truth table of variable x_k.

9. [*20*] Algorithm L determines the lengths of shortest formulas for all functions f, but it gives no further information. Extend the algorithm so that it also provides actual minimum-length formulas like (6).

▶ **10.** [*20*] Modify Algorithm L so that it computes $D(f)$ instead of $L(f)$.

▶ **11.** [*22*] Modify Algorithm L so that, instead of lengths $L(f)$, it computes upper bounds $U(f)$ and footprints $\phi(f)$ as described in the text.

12. [*15*] What Boolean chain is equivalent to the minimum-memory scheme (13)?

13. [*16*] What are the truth tables of f_1, f_2, f_3, f_4, and f_5 in example (13)?

14. [*22*] What's a convenient way to compute the $5n(n-1)$ truth tables of (17), given the truth table of g? (Use bitwise operations as in (15) and (16).)

15. [*28*] Find short-as-possible ways to evaluate the following functions using minimum memory: (a) $S_2(x_1, x_2, x_3, x_4)$; (b) $S_1(x_1, x_2, x_3, x_4)$; (c) the function in (18).

16. [*HM33*] Prove that fewer than 2^{118} of the 2^{128} Boolean functions $f(x_1, \ldots, x_7)$ are computable in minimum memory.

▸ **17.** [*25*] (M. S. Paterson, 1977.) Although Boolean functions $f(x_1, \ldots, x_n)$ cannot always be evaluated in n registers, prove that $n + 1$ registers are always sufficient. In other words, show that there is always a sequence of operations like (13) to compute $f(x_1, \ldots, x_n)$ if we allow $0 \le j(i), k(i) \le n$.

▸ **18.** [*35*] Investigate optimum minimum-memory computations for $f(x_1, x_2, x_3, x_4, x_5)$: How many classes of five-variable functions have $C_m(f) = r$, for $r = 0, 1, 2, \ldots$?

19. [*M22*] If a Boolean chain uses n variables and has length $r < n + 2$, prove that it must be either a "top-down" or a "bottom-up" construction.

▸ **20.** [*40*] (R. Schroeppel, 2004.) A Boolean chain is *canalizing* if it does not use the operators $\oplus$ or $\equiv$. Find the optimum cost, length, and depth of all 4-variable functions under this constraint. Does the footprint heuristic still give optimum results?

21. [*46*] For how many four-variable functions did the Harvard researchers discover an optimum vacuum-tube circuit in 1951?

22. [*21*] Explain the chain for S_3 in Fig. 10, by noting that it incorporates the chain for $S_{2,3}$ in Fig. 9. Find a similar chain for $S_2(x_1, x_2, x_3, x_4, x_5)$.

▸ **23.** [*23*] Figure 10 illustrates only 16 of the 64 symmetric functions on five elements. Explain how to write down optimum chains for the others.

24. [*47*] Does every symmetric function f have $C_m(f) = C(f)$?

▸ **25.** [*17*] Suppose we want a Boolean chain that includes *all* functions of n variables: Let $f_k(x_1, \ldots, x_n)$ be the function whose truth table is the binary representation of k, for $0 \le k < m = 2^{2^n}$. What is $C(f_0 f_1 \ldots f_{m-1})$?

26. [*25*] True or false: If $f(x_0, \ldots, x_n) = (x_0 \wedge g(x_1, \ldots, x_n)) \oplus h(x_1, \ldots, x_n)$, where g and h are nontrivial Boolean functions whose joint cost is $C(gh)$, then $C(f) = 2 + C(gh)$.

▸ **27.** [*23*] Can a full adder (22) be implemented in five steps using only minimum memory (that is, completely inside three one-bit registers)?

28. [*26*] Prove that $C(u'v') = C(u''v'') = 5$ for the two-output functions defined by

$$(u'v')_2 = (x + y - (uv)_2) \bmod 4, \qquad (u''v'')_2 = (-x - y - (uv)_2) \bmod 4.$$

Use these functions to evaluate $[(x_1 + \cdots + x_n) \bmod 4 = 0]$ in fewer than $2.5n$ steps.

29. [*M28*] Prove that the text's circuit for sideways addition (27) has depth $O(\log n)$.

30. [*M25*] Solve the binary recurrence (28) for the cost $s(n)$ of sideways addition.

31. [*21*] If $f(x_1, \ldots, x_n)$ is symmetric, prove that $C(f) \le 5n + O(n/\log n)$.

32. [*HM16*] Why does the solution to (30) satisfy $t(n) = 2^n + O(2^{n/2})$?

33. [*HM22*] True or false: If $1 \le N \le 2^n$, the first N minterms of $\{x_1, \ldots, x_n\}$ can all be evaluated in $N + O(\sqrt{N})$ steps, as $n \to \infty$ and $N \to \infty$.

▶ **34.** [*22*] A *priority encoder* has $n = 2^m - 1$ inputs $x_1 \ldots x_n$ and m outputs $y_1 \ldots y_m$, where $(y_1 \ldots y_m)_2 = k$ if and only if $k = \max\{j \mid j = 0 \text{ or } x_j = 1\}$. Design a priority encoder that has cost $O(n)$ and depth $O(m)$.

35. [*23*] If $n > 1$, show that the conjunctions $x_1 \wedge \cdots \wedge x_{k-1} \wedge x_{k+1} \wedge \cdots \wedge x_n$ for $1 \le k \le n$ can all be computed from $(x_1, \ldots, x_n)$ with total cost $\le 3n - 6$.

▶ **36.** [*M28*] (R. E. Ladner and M. J. Fischer, 1980.) Let y_k be the "prefix" $x_1 \wedge \cdots \wedge x_k$ for $1 \le k \le n$. Clearly $C(y_1 \ldots y_n) = n - 1$ and $D(y_1 \ldots y_n) = \lceil \lg n \rceil$; but we can't simultaneously minimize both cost and depth. Find a chain of optimum depth $\lceil \lg n \rceil$ that has cost $< 4n$.

37. [*M28*] (Marc Snir, 1986.) Given $n \ge m \ge 1$, consider the following algorithm:

S1. [Upward loop.] For $t \leftarrow 1, 2, \ldots, \lceil \lg m \rceil$, set $x_{\min(m, 2^t k)} \leftarrow x_{2^t(k-1/2)} \wedge x_{\min(m, 2^t k)}$ for $k \ge 1$ and $2^t(k - 1/2) < m$.

S2. [Downward loop.] For $t \leftarrow \lceil \lg m \rceil - 1, \lceil \lg m \rceil - 2, \ldots, 1$, set $x_{2^t(k+1/2)} \leftarrow x_{2^t k} \wedge x_{2^t(k+1/2)}$ for $k \ge 1$ and $2^t(k + 1/2) < m$.

S3. [Extension.] For $k \leftarrow m + 1, m + 2, \ldots, n$, set $x_k \leftarrow x_{k-1} \wedge x_k$. ∎

  a) Prove that this algorithm solves the prefix problem of exercise 36: It transforms $(x_1, x_2, \ldots, x_n)$ into $(x_1, x_1 \wedge x_2, \ldots, x_1 \wedge x_2 \wedge \cdots \wedge x_n)$.
  b) Let $c(m, n)$ and $d(m, n)$ be the cost and depth of the corresponding Boolean chain. Prove that, if n is sufficiently large, $c(m, n) + d(m, n) = 2n - 2$.
  c) Given n, what is $d(n) = \min_{1 \le m \le n} d(m, n)$? Show that $d(n) < 2 \lg n$.
  d) Prove that there's a Boolean chain of cost $2n - 2 - d$ and depth d for the prefix problem whenever $d(n) \le d < n$. (This cost is optimum, by exercise 81.)

38. [*25*] In Section 5.3.4 we studied *sorting networks*, by which $\hat{S}(n)$ comparator modules are able to sort n numbers $(x_1, x_2, \ldots, x_n)$ into ascending order. If the inputs x_j are 0s and 1s, each comparator module is equivalent to two gates $(x \wedge y, x \vee y)$; so a sorting network corresponds to a certain kind of Boolean chain, which evaluates n particular functions of $(x_1, x_2, \ldots, x_n)$.

  a) What are the n functions $f_1 f_2 \ldots f_n$ that a sorting network computes?
  b) Show that those functions $\{f_1, f_2, \ldots, f_n\}$ can be computed in $O(n)$ steps with a chain of depth $O(\log n)$. (Hence sorting networks aren't asymptotically optimal, Booleanwise.)

▶ **39.** [*M21*] (M. S. Paterson and P. Klein, 1980.) Implement the 2^m-way multiplexer $M_m(x_1, \ldots, x_m; y_0, y_1, \ldots, y_{2^m-1})$ of (31) with an efficient chain that simultaneously establishes the upper bounds $C(M_m) \le 2n + O(\sqrt{n})$ and $D(M_m) \le m + O(\log m)$.

40. [*25*] If $n \ge k \ge 1$, let $f_{nk}(x_1, \ldots, x_n)$ be the "k in a row" function,

$$(x_1 \wedge \cdots \wedge x_k) \vee (x_2 \wedge \cdots \wedge x_{k+1}) \vee \cdots \vee (x_{n+1-k} \wedge \cdots \wedge x_n).$$

Show that the cost $C(f_{nk})$ of this function is less than $4n - 3k$.

41. [*M23*] (*Conditional-sum adders.*) One way to accomplish binary addition (25) with depth $O(\log n)$ is based on the multiplexer trick of exercise 4: If $(xx')_2 + (yy')_2 = (zz')_2$, where $|x'| = |y'| = |z'|$, we have either $(x)_2 + (y)_2 = (z)_2$ and $(x')_2 + (y')_2 = (z')_2$, or $(x)_2 + (y)_2 + 1 = (z)_2$ and $(x')_2 + (y')_2 = (1z')_2$. To save time, we can compute *both* $(x)_2 + (y)_2$ and $(x)_2 + (y)_2 + 1$ simultaneously as we compute $(x')_2 + (y')_2$. Afterwards, when we know whether or not the less significant part $(x')_2 + (y')_2$ produces a carry, we can use multiplexers to select the correct bits for the most significant part.

If this method is used recursively to build $2n$-bit adders from n-bit adders, how many gates are needed when $n = 2^m$? What is the corresponding depth?

42. [*25*] In the binary addition (25), let $u_k = x_k \wedge y_k$ and $v_k = x_k \oplus y_k$ for $0 \le k < n$.

a) Show that $z_k = v_k \oplus c_k$, where the carry bits c_k satisfy

$$c_k = u_{k-1} \vee (v_{k-1} \wedge (u_{k-2} \vee (v_{k-2} \wedge (\cdots (u_1 \wedge v_0) \cdots)))).$$

b) Let $U_k^k = 0$, $V_k^k = 1$, and $U_j^{k+1} = u_k \vee (v_k \wedge U_j^k)$, $V_j^{k+1} = v_k \wedge V_j^k$, for $k \ge j$. Prove that $c_k = U_0^k$, and that $U_i^k = U_j^k \vee (V_j^k \wedge U_i^j)$, $V_i^k = V_j^k \wedge V_i^j$ for $i \le j \le k$.

c) Let $h(m) = 2^{m(m-1)/2}$. Show that when $n = h(m)$, the carries $c_1, \ldots, c_n$ can all be evaluated with depth $(m+1)m/2 \approx \lg n + \sqrt{2\lg n}$ and with total cost $O(2^m n)$.

▶ **43.** [*28*] A *finite state transducer* is an abstract machine with a finite input alphabet A, a finite output alphabet B, and a finite set of internal states Q. One of those states, q_0, is called the "initial state." Given a string $\alpha = a_1 \ldots a_n$, where each $a_j \in A$, the machine computes a string $\beta = b_1 \ldots b_n$, where each $b_j \in B$, as follows:

T1. [Initialize.] Set $j \leftarrow 1$ and $q \leftarrow q_0$.

T2. [Done?] Terminate the algorithm if $j > n$.

T3. [Output b_j.] Set $b_j \leftarrow c(q, a_j)$.

T4. [Advance j.] Set $q \leftarrow d(q, a_j)$, $j \leftarrow j + 1$, and return to step T2. ∎

The machine has built-in instructions that specify $c(q, a) \in B$ and $d(q, a) \in Q$ for every state $q \in Q$ and every character $a \in A$. The purpose of this exercise is to show that, if the alphabets A and B of any finite state transducer are encoded in binary, the string β can be computed from α by a Boolean chain of size $O(n)$ and depth $O(\log n)$.

a) Consider the problem of changing a binary vector $a_1 \ldots a_n$ to $b_1 \ldots b_n$ by setting

$$b_j \leftarrow a_j \oplus [a_j = a_{j-1} = \cdots = a_{j-k} = 1 \text{ and } a_{j-k-1} = 0], \text{ where } k \text{ is odd}],$$

assuming that $a_0 = 0$. For example, $\alpha = 1100100100011111101101010 \mapsto \beta = 1000100100010101001001010$. Prove that this transformation can be carried out by a finite state transducer with $|A| = |B| = |Q| = 2$.

b) Suppose a finite state transducer is in state q_j after reading $a_1 \ldots a_{j-1}$. Explain how to compute the sequence $q_1 \ldots q_n$ with a Boolean chain of cost $O(n)$ and depth $O(\log n)$, using the construction of Ladner and Fischer in exercise 36. (From this sequence $q_1 \ldots q_n$ it is easy to compute $b_1 \ldots b_n$, since $b_j = c(q_j, a_j)$.)

c) Apply the method of (b) to the problem in (a).

▶ **44.** [*26*] (R. E. Ladner and M. J. Fischer, 1980.) Show that the problem of binary addition (25) can be viewed as a finite state transduction. Describe the Boolean chain that results from the construction of exercise 43 when $n = 2^m$, and compare it to the conditional-sum adder of exercise 41.

45. [*HM20*] Why doesn't the proof of Theorem S simply argue that the number of ways to choose $j(i)$ and $k(i)$ so that $1 \le j(i), k(i) < i$ is $n^2(n+1)^2 \ldots (n+r-1)^2$?

▶ **46.** [*HM21*] Let $\alpha(n) = c(n, \lfloor 2^n/n \rfloor)/2^{2^n}$ be the fraction of n-variable Boolean functions $f(x_1, \ldots, x_n)$ for which $C(f) \le 2^n/n$. Prove that $\alpha(n) \to 0$ rapidly as $n \to \infty$.

47. [*M23*] Extend Theorem S to functions with n inputs and m outputs.

48. [*HM23*] Find the smallest integer $r = r(n)$ such that $(r-1)! \, 2^{2^n} \le 2^{2r+1}(n+r-1)^{2r}$, (a) exactly when $1 \le n \le 16$; (b) asymptotically when $n \to \infty$.

49. [*HM25*] Prove that, as $n \to \infty$, almost all Boolean functions $f(x_1, \ldots, x_n)$ have minimum formula length $L(f) > 2^n/\lg n - 2^{n+2}/(\lg n)^2$.

50. [*24*] What are the prime implicants and prime clauses of the prime-number function (35)? Express that function in (a) DNF (b) CNF of minimum length.

51. [*20*] What representation of the prime-number detector replaces (37), if rows of the truth table are based on $x_5 x_6$ instead of $x_1 x_2$?

52. [*23*] What choices of k and l minimize the upper bound (38) when $5 \le n \le 16$?

53. [*HM22*] Estimate (38) when $k = \lfloor 2 \lg n \rfloor$ and $l = \lceil 2^k/(n - 3 \lg n) \rceil$ and $n \to \infty$.

54. [*29*] Find a short Boolean chain to evaluate all six of the functions $f_j(x) = [x_1 x_2 x_3 x_4 \in A_j]$, where $A_1 = \{0010, 0101, 1011\}$, $A_2 = \{0001, 1111\}$, $A_3 = \{0011, 0111, 1101\}$, $A_4 = \{1001, 1111\}$, $A_5 = \{1101\}$, $A_6 = \{0101, 1011\}$. (These six functions appear in the prime-number detector (37).) Compare your chain to the minterm-first evaluation scheme of Lupanov's general method.

55. [*34*] Show that the cost of the 6-bit prime-detecting function is at most 14.

▸ **56.** [*16*] Explain why all functions with 14 or more don't-cares in Table 3 have cost 0.

57. [*19*] What seven-segment "digits" are displayed when $(x_1 x_2 x_3 x_4)_2 > 9$ in (45)?

▸ **58.** [*30*] A 4×4-bit *S-box* is a permutation of the 4-bit vectors $\{0000, 0001, \ldots, 1111\}$; such permutations are used as components of well-known cryptographic systems such as the Russian standard GOST 28147 (1989). Every 4×4-bit S-box corresponds to a sequence of four functions $f_1(x_1, x_2, x_3, x_4), \ldots, f_4(x_1, x_2, x_3, x_4)$, which transform $x_1 x_2 x_3 x_4 \mapsto f_1 f_2 f_3 f_4$.

Find all 4×4-bit S-boxes for which $C(f_1) = C(f_2) = C(f_3) = C(f_4) = 7$.

59. [*29*] One of the S-boxes satisfying the conditions of exercise 58 takes $(0, \ldots, \mathsf{f}) \mapsto (0, 6, 5, \mathsf{b}, 3, 9, \mathsf{f}, \mathsf{e}, \mathsf{c}, 4, 7, 8, \mathsf{d}, 2, \mathsf{a}, 1)$; in other words, the truth tables of (f_1, f_2, f_3, f_4) are respectively $(\mathsf{179a}, \mathsf{63e8}, \mathsf{5b26}, \mathsf{3e29})$. Find a Boolean chain that evaluates these four "maximally difficult" functions in fewer than 20 steps.

60. [*23*] (Frank Ruskey.) Suppose $z = (x + y) \bmod 3$, where $x = (x_1 x_2)_2$, $y = (y_1 y_2)_2$, $z = (z_1 z_2)_2$, and each two-bit value is required to be either 00, 01, or 10. Compute z_1 and z_2 from x_1, x_2, y_1, and y_2 in six Boolean steps.

61. [*34*] Continuing exercise 60, find a good way to compute $z = (x + y) \bmod 5$, using the three-bit values 000, 001, 010, 011, 100.

62. [*HM23*] Consider a random Boolean partial function of n variables that has $2^n c$ "cares" and $2^n d$ "don't-cares," where $c + d = 1$. Prove that the cost of almost all such partial functions exceeds $2^n c/n$.

63. [*HM35*] (L. A. Sholomov, 1969.) Continuing exercise 62, prove that all such functions have cost $\le 2^n c/n(1 + O(n^{-1} \log n))$. *Hint:* There is a set of $2^m(1 + k)$ vectors $x_1 \ldots x_k$ that intersects every $(k - m)$-dimensional subcube of the k-cube.

64. [*25*] (*Magic Fifteen.*) Two players alternately select digits from 1 to 9, using no digit twice; the winner, if any, is the first to get three digits that sum to 15. What's a good strategy for playing this game?

▸ **65.** [*35*] Modify the tic-tac-toe strategy of (47)–(56) so that it always plays correctly.

66. [*20*] Criticize the moves chosen in exercise 65. Are they always optimum?

▶ **67.** [*40*] Instead of simply finding one correct move for each position in tic-tac-toe, we might prefer to find them all. In other words, given $x_1 \ldots x_9 o_1 \ldots o_9$, we could try to compute nine outputs $g_1 \ldots g_9$, where $g_j = 1$ if and only if a move into cell j is among X's best. For example, exclamation marks indicate all of the right moves for X in the following typical positions:

[tic-tac-toe position diagrams]

A machine that chooses randomly among these possibilities is more fun to play against than a machine that has only one fixed strategy.

One attractive way to solve the all-good-moves problem is to use the fact that tic-tac-toe has eight symmetries. Imagine a chip that has 18 inputs $x_1 \ldots x_9 o_1 \ldots o_9$ and three outputs (c, s, m), for "corner," "side," and "middle," with the property that the desired functions g_j can be computed by hooking together eight of the chips appropriately:

$$g_1 = c(x_1x_2x_3x_4x_5x_6x_7x_8x_9o_1o_2o_3o_4o_5o_6o_7o_8o_9)$$
$$\qquad \vee\, c(x_1x_4x_7x_2x_5x_8x_3x_6x_9o_1o_4o_7o_2o_5o_8o_3o_6o_9),$$

$$g_2 = s(x_1x_2x_3x_4x_5x_6x_7x_8x_9o_1o_2o_3o_4o_5o_6o_7o_8o_9)$$
$$\qquad \vee\, s(x_3x_2x_1x_6x_5x_4x_9x_8x_7o_3o_2o_1o_6o_5o_4o_9o_8o_7),$$

$$g_3 = c(x_3x_2x_1x_6x_5x_4x_9x_8x_7o_3o_2o_1o_6o_5o_4o_9o_8o_7)$$
$$\qquad \vee\, c(x_3x_6x_9x_2x_5x_8x_1x_4x_7o_3o_6o_9o_2o_5o_8o_1o_4o_7),$$

$$g_4 = s(x_1x_4x_7x_2x_5x_8x_3x_6x_9o_1o_4o_7o_2o_5o_8o_3o_6o_9)$$
$$\qquad \vee\, s(x_7x_4x_1x_8x_5x_2x_9x_6x_3o_7o_4o_1o_8o_5o_2o_9o_6o_3), \qquad \ldots$$

$$g_9 = c(x_9x_8x_7x_6x_5x_4x_3x_2x_1o_9o_8o_7o_6o_5o_4o_3o_2o_1)$$
$$\qquad \vee\, c(x_9x_6x_3x_8x_5x_2x_7x_4x_1o_9o_6o_3o_8o_5o_2o_7o_4o_1),$$

and g_5 is the OR of the m outputs from all eight chips.

Design such a chip, using fewer than 2000 gates.

68. [*M25*] Consider the n-bit π function $\pi_n(x_1 \ldots x_n)$, whose value is the $(x_1 \ldots x_n)_2$th bit to the right of the most significant bit in the binary representation of π. Does the method of exercise 4.3.1–39, which describes an efficient way to compute arbitrary bits of π, prove that $C(\pi_n) < 2^n/n$ for sufficiently large n?

69. [*M24*] Let the multilinear representation of f be

$$\alpha_{000} \oplus \alpha_{001}x_m \oplus \alpha_{010}x_j \oplus \alpha_{011}x_jx_m \oplus \alpha_{100}x_i \oplus \alpha_{101}x_ix_m \oplus \alpha_{110}x_ix_j \oplus \alpha_{111}x_ix_jx_m,$$

where each coefficient α_l is a function of the variables $\{x_1, \ldots, x_n\} \setminus \{x_i, x_j, x_m\}$.

a) Prove that the pairs (58) are "good" if and only if the coefficients satisfy

$$\alpha_{010}\alpha_{101} = \alpha_{011}\alpha_{100}, \quad \alpha_{101}\alpha_{110} = \alpha_{100}\alpha_{111}, \quad \text{and} \quad \alpha_{110}\alpha_{011} = \alpha_{111}\alpha_{010}.$$

b) For which values (i, j, m) are the pairs bad, when $f = (\det X) \bmod 2$? (See (60).)

▶ **70.** [*M27*] Let X be the 3×3 Boolean matrix (60). Find efficient chains for the Boolean functions (a) $(\det X) \bmod 2$; (b) [per $X > 0$]; (c) [$\det X > 0$].

▶ **71.** [*M26*] Suppose $f(x)$ is equal to 0 with probability p at each point $x = x_1 \ldots x_n$, independent of its value at other points.

a) What is the probability that the pairs (58) are good?

b) What is the probability that bad pairs (58) exist?

c) What is the probability that bad pairs (58) are found in at most t random trials?

d) What is the expected time to test case (i, j, m), as a function of p, t, and n?

72. [*M24*] Extend the previous exercise to the case of partial functions, where $f(x) = 0$ with probability p, $f(x) = 1$ with probability q, and $f(x) = *$ with probability r.

▶ **73.** [*20*] If bad pairs (58) exist for all (i, j, m) with $m \neq i \neq j \neq m$, show that the indecomposability of f can be deduced after testing only $\binom{n}{2}$ well-chosen triples (i, j, m).

74. [*25*] Extend the idea in the previous exercise, suggesting a strategy for choosing successive triples (i, j, m) when using the method of Shen, McKellar, and Weiner.

75. [*20*] What happens when the text's decomposition procedure is applied to the "all-equal" function $S_{0,n}(x_1, \ldots, x_n)$?

▶ **76.** [*M25*] (D. Uhlig, 1974.) The purpose of this exercise is to prove the amazing fact that, for certain functions f, the best chain to evaluate the Boolean function

$$F(u_1, \ldots, u_n, v_1, \ldots, v_n) = f(u_1, \ldots, u_n) \vee f(v_1, \ldots, v_n)$$

costs *less* than $2C(f)$; hence functional decomposition is *not* always a good idea.

We let $n = m + 2^m$ and write $f(i_1, \ldots, i_m, x_0, \ldots, x_{2^m-1}) = f_i(x)$, where i is regarded as the number $(i_1 \ldots i_m)_2$. Then $(u_1, \ldots, u_n) = (i_1, \ldots, i_m, x_0, \ldots, x_{2^m-1})$, $(v_1, \ldots, v_n) = (j_1, \ldots, j_m, y_0, \ldots, y_{2^m-1})$, and $F(u, v) = f_i(x) \vee f_j(y)$.

a) Prove that a chain of cost $O(n/\log n)^2$ suffices to evaluate the $2^m + 1$ functions

$$z_l = x \oplus \left(([l \leq i] \oplus [i \leq j]) \wedge (x \oplus y)\right), \qquad 0 \leq l \leq 2^m,$$

from given vectors i, j, x, and y; each z_l is a vector of length 2^m.

b) Let $g_i(x) = f_i(x) \oplus f_{i-1}(x)$ for $0 \leq i \leq 2^m$, where $f_{-1}(x) = f_{2^m}(x) = 0$. Estimate the cost of computing the $2^m + 1$ values $c_l = g_l(z_l)$, given the vectors z_l, for $0 \leq l \leq 2^m$.

c) Let $c'_l = c_l \wedge ([i \leq j] \equiv [l \leq i])$ and $c''_l = c_l \wedge ([i \leq j] \equiv [j > l])$. Prove that

$$f_i(x) = c'_0 \oplus c'_1 \oplus \cdots \oplus c'_{2^m}, \qquad f_j(y) = c''_0 \oplus c''_1 \oplus \cdots \oplus c''_{2^m}.$$

d) Conclude that $C(F) \leq 2^n/n + O(2^n(\log n)/n^2)$. (When n is sufficiently large, this cost is definitely less than $2^{n+1}/n$, but functions f exist with $C(f) > 2^n/n$.)

e) For clarity, write out the chain for F when $m = 1$ and $f(i, x_0, x_1) = (i \wedge x_0) \vee x_1$.

▶ **77.** [*35*] (N. P. Red'kin, 1970.) Suppose a Boolean chain uses only the operations AND, OR, or NOT; thus, every step is either $x_i = x_{j(i)} \wedge x_{k(i)}$ or $x_i = x_{j(i)} \vee x_{k(i)}$ or $x_i = \bar{x}_{j(i)}$. Prove that if such a chain computes either the "odd parity" function $f_n(x_1, \ldots, x_n) = x_1 \oplus \cdots \oplus x_n$ or the "even parity" function $\bar{f}_n(x_1, \ldots, x_n) = 1 \oplus x_1 \oplus \cdots \oplus x_n$, where $n \geq 2$, the length of the chain is at least $4(n-1)$.

78. [*26*] (W. J. Paul, 1977.) Let $f(x_1, \ldots, x_m, y_0, \ldots, y_{2^m-1})$ be any Boolean function that equals y_k whenever $(x_1 \ldots x_m)_2 = k \in S$, for some given set $S \subseteq \{0, 1, \ldots, 2^m - 1\}$; we don't care about the value of f at other points. Show that $C(f) \geq 2\|S\| - 2$ whenever S is nonempty. (In particular, when $S = \{0, 1, \ldots, 2^m - 1\}$, the multiplexer chain of exercise 39 is asymptotically optimum.)

79. [*32*] (C. P. Schnorr, 1976.) Say that variables u and v are "mates" in a Boolean chain if there is exactly one simple path between them in the corresponding binary tree diagram. Two variables can be mates only if they are each used only once in the chain; but this necessary condition is not sufficient. For example, variables 2 and 4 are mates in the chain for $S_{1,2,3}$ in Fig. 9, but they are not mates in the chain for S_2.

a) Prove that a Boolean chain on n variables with no mates has cost $\geq 2n - 2$.

b) Prove that $C(f) = 2n - 3$ when f is the all-equal function $S_{0,n}(x_1, \ldots, x_n)$.

▶ **80.** [*M27*] (L. J. Stockmeyer, 1977.) Another notation for symmetric functions is sometimes convenient: If $\alpha = a_0 a_1 \ldots a_n$ is any binary string, let $S_\alpha(x) = a_{\nu x}$. For example, $\langle x_1 x_2 x_3 \rangle = S_{0011}$ and $x_1 \oplus x_2 \oplus x_3 = S_{0101}$ in this notation. Notice that $S_\alpha(0, x_2, \ldots, x_n) = S_{\alpha'}(x_2, \ldots, x_n)$ and $S_\alpha(1, x_2, \ldots, x_n) = S_{'\alpha}(x_2, \ldots, x_n)$, where α' and $'\alpha$ stand respectively for α with its last or first element deleted. Also,

$$S_\alpha\big(f(x_3, \ldots, x_n), \bar{f}(x_3, \ldots, x_n), x_3, \ldots, x_n\big) = S_{'\alpha'}(x_3, \ldots, x_n)$$

when f is any Boolean function of $n - 2$ variables.

    a) A parity function has $a_0 \neq a_1 \neq a_2 \neq \cdots \neq a_n$. Assume that $n \geq 2$. Prove that if S_α is not a parity function and $S_{'\alpha'}$ isn't constant, then

$$C(S_\alpha) \geq \max\big(C(S_{\alpha'})+2,\, C(S_{'\alpha})+2,\, \min(C(S_{\alpha'})+3,\, C(S_{'\alpha})+3,\, C(S_{'\alpha'})+5)\big).$$

    b) What lower bounds on $C(S_k)$ and $C(S_{\geq k})$ follow from this result, when $0 \leq k \leq n$?

81. [*23*] (M. Snir, 1986.) Show that any chain of cost c and depth d for the prefix problem of exercise 36 has $c + d \geq 2n - 2$.

▶ **82.** [*M23*] Explain the logical sentences (62)–(70). Which of them are true?

83. [*21*] If there's a Boolean chain for $f(x_1, \ldots, x_n)$ that contains p canalizing operations, show that $C(f) < (p + 1)(n + p/2)$.

84. [*M20*] A *monotone Boolean chain* is a Boolean chain in which every operator $\circ_i$ is monotone. The length of a shortest monotone chain for f is denoted by $C^+(f)$. If there's a monotone Boolean chain for $f(x_1, \ldots, x_n)$ that contains p occurrences of $\wedge$ and q occurrences of $\vee$, show that $C^+(f) < \min\big((p + 1)(n + p/2), (q + 1)(n + q/2)\big)$.

▶ **85.** [*M28*] Let M_n be the set of all monotone functions of n variables. If L is a family of functions contained in M_n, let

$$x \sqcup y = \bigwedge \{z \in L \mid z \supseteq x \vee y\} \qquad \text{and} \qquad x \sqcap y = \bigvee \{z \in L \mid z \subseteq x \wedge y\}.$$

We call L "legitimate" if it includes the constant functions 0 and 1 as well as the projection functions x_j for $1 \leq j \leq n$, and if $x \sqcup y \in L$, $x \sqcap y \in L$ whenever $x, y \in L$.

    a) When $n = 3$ we can write $M_3 = \{\texttt{00, 01, 03, 05, 11, 07, 13, 15, 0f, 33, 55, 17, 1f,}$ $\texttt{37, 57, 3f, 5f, 77, 7f, ff}\}$, representing each function by its hexadecimal truth table. There are 2^{15} families L such that $\{\texttt{00, 0f, 33, 55, ff}\} \subseteq L \subseteq M_3$; how many of them are legitimate?

    b) If A is a subset of $\{1, \ldots, n\}$, let $\lceil A \rceil = \bigvee_{a \in A} x_a$; also let $\lceil \infty \rceil = 1$. Suppose $\mathcal{A}$ is a family of subsets of $\{1, \ldots, n\}$ that contains all sets of size ≤ 1 and is closed under intersection; in other words, $A \cap B \in \mathcal{A}$ whenever $A \in \mathcal{A}$ and $B \in \mathcal{A}$. Prove that the family $L = \{\lceil A \rceil \mid A \in \mathcal{A} \cup \{\infty\}\}$ is legitimate.

    c) Let $(x_{n+1}, \ldots, x_{n+r})$ be a monotone Boolean chain (1). Suppose $(\hat{x}_{n+1}, \ldots, \hat{x}_{n+r})$ is obtained from the same Boolean chain, but with every operator $\wedge$ changed to $\sqcap$ and with every operator $\vee$ changed to $\sqcup$, with respect to some legitimate family L. Prove that, for $n + 1 \leq l \leq n + r$, we must have

$$\hat{x}_l \subseteq x_l \vee \bigvee_{i=n+1}^{l} \{\hat{x}_i \oplus (\hat{x}_{j(i)} \vee \hat{x}_{k(i)}) \mid \circ_i = \vee\};$$

$$x_l \subseteq \hat{x}_l \vee \bigvee_{i=n+1}^{l} \{\hat{x}_i \oplus (\hat{x}_{j(i)} \wedge \hat{x}_{k(i)}) \mid \circ_i = \wedge\}.$$

86. [*HM37*] A graph G on vertices $\{1, \ldots, n\}$ can be defined by $N = \binom{n}{2}$ Boolean variables x_{uv} for $1 \le u < v \le n$, where $x_{uv} = [u\!-\!v \text{ in } G]$. Let f be the function $f(x) = [G \text{ contains a triangle}]$; for example, when $n = 4$, $f(x_{12}, x_{13}, x_{14}, x_{23}, x_{24}, x_{34}) = (x_{12} \wedge x_{13} \wedge x_{23}) \vee (x_{12} \wedge x_{14} \wedge x_{24}) \vee (x_{13} \wedge x_{14} \wedge x_{34}) \vee (x_{23} \wedge x_{24} \wedge x_{34})$. The purpose of this exercise is to prove that the monotone complexity $C^+(f)$ is $\Omega(n/\log n)^3$.

a) If $u_j \!-\! v_j$ for $1 \le j \le r$ in a graph G, call $S = \{\{u_1, v_1\}, \ldots, \{u_r, v_r\}\}$ an r-*family*, and let $\Delta(S) = \bigcup_{1 \le i < j \le r}(\{u_i, v_i\} \cap \{u_j, v_j\})$ be the elements of its pairwise intersections. Say that G is r-*closed* if we have $u \!-\! v$ whenever $\Delta(S) \subseteq \{u, v\}$ for some r-family S. It is *strongly r-closed* if, in addition, we have $|\Delta(S)| \ge 2$ for all r-families S. Prove that a strongly r-closed graph is also strongly $(r + 1)$-closed.

b) Prove that the complete bigraph $K_{m,n}$ is strongly r-closed when $r > \max(m, n)$.

c) Prove that a strongly r-closed graph has at most $(r - 1)^2$ edges.

d) Let L be the family of functions $\{1\} \cup \{\lceil G \rceil \mid G \text{ is a strongly } r\text{-closed graph on } \{1, \ldots, n\}\}$. (See exercise 85(b); we regard G as a set of edges. For example, when the edges are $1\!-\!3$, $1\!-\!4$, $2\!-\!3$, $2\!-\!4$, we have $\lceil G \rceil = x_{13} \vee x_{14} \vee x_{23} \vee x_{24}$.) Is L legitimate?

e) Let $x_{N+1}, \ldots, x_{N+p+q} = f$ be a monotone Boolean chain with p $\wedge$-steps and q $\vee$-steps, and consider the modified chain $\hat{x}_{N+1}, \ldots, \hat{x}_{N+p+q} = \hat{f}$ based on the family L in (d). If $\hat{f} \ne 1$, show that $2(r - 1)^3 p + (r - 1)^2 (n - 2) \ge \binom{n}{3}$. *Hint:* Use the second formula in exercise 85(c).

f) Furthermore, if $\hat{f} = 1$ we must have $r^2 q \ge 2^{r-1}$.

g) Therefore $p = \Omega(n/\log n)^3$. *Hint:* Let $r \approx 6 \lg n$ and apply exercise 84.

87. [*M20*] Show that when nonmonotonic operations are permitted, the triangle function of exercise 86 has cost $C(f) = O(n^{\lg 7}(\log n)^2) = O(n^{2.81})$. *Hint:* A graph has a triangle if and only if the cube of its adjacency matrix has a nonzero diagonal.

88. [*40*] A *median chain* is analogous to a Boolean chain, but it uses median-of-three steps $x_i = \langle x_{j(i)} x_{k(i)} x_{l(i)} \rangle$ for $n+1 \le i \le n+r$, instead of the binary operations in (1).

Study the optimum length, depth, and cost of median chains, for all self-dual monotone Boolean functions of 7 variables. What is the shortest chain for $\langle x_1 x_2 x_3 x_4 x_5 x_6 x_7 \rangle$?

ANSWERS TO EXERCISES

SECTION 7

1. Following the hint, we'll want the second '$4m-4$' to be immediately followed by the first '$2m-1$'. The desired arrangements can be deduced from the first four examples, given in hexadecimal notation: `231213`, `46171435623725`, `86a31b1368597a425b2479`, `ca8e531f1358ac7db9e6427f2469bd`. [R. O. Davies, *Math. Gazette* **43** (1959), 253–255.]

2. Such arrangements exist if and only if $n \bmod 4 = 0$ or 1. This condition is necessary because there must be an even number of odd items. And it is sufficient because we can place '00' in front of the solutions in the previous exercise.

Notes: This question was first raised by Marshall Hall in 1951, and solved the following year by F. T. Leahy, Jr., in unpublished work [Armed Forces Security Agency report 343 (28 January 1952)]. It was independently posed and resolved by T. Skolem and T. Bang, *Math. Scandinavica* **5** (1957), 57–58. For other intervals of numbers, see the complete solution by J. E. Simpson, *Discrete Math.* **44** (1983), 97–104.

3. Yes. For example, the cycle (0072362435714165) can't be broken up.

4. The kth occurrence of b is in position $\lfloor k\phi \rfloor$ from the left, and the kth occurrence of a is in position $\lfloor k\phi^2 \rfloor$. Clearly $\lfloor k\phi^2 \rfloor - \lfloor k\phi \rfloor = k$, because $\phi^2 = \phi + 1$. (The integers $\lfloor k\phi \rfloor$ form the "spectrum" of ϕ; see exercise 3.13 of *CMath*.)

5. $2n - k - 1$ of the $\binom{2n}{2}$ equally likely pairs of positions satisfy the stated condition. If these probabilities were independent (but they aren't), the value of $2L_n$ would be

$$\binom{2n}{2,2,\ldots,2} \prod_{k=1}^{n} ((2n-1-k)/\binom{2n}{2}) = \frac{(2n)!^2 n(n-1)}{n!(2n)^{n+1}(2n-1)^{n+1}}$$

$$= \exp\left(n \ln \frac{4n}{e^3} + \ln \sqrt{\frac{\pi e n}{2}} + O(n^{-1}) \right).$$

6. (a) When the products are expanded, we obtain a polynomial of $(2n-2)!/(n-2)!$ terms, each of degree $4n$. There's a term $x_1^2 \ldots x_{2n}^2$ for each Langford pairing; every other term has at least one variable of degree 1. Summing over $x_1, \ldots, x_{2n} \in \{-1, +1\}$ therefore cancels out all the bad terms, but gives 2^{2n} for the good terms. An extra factor of 2 arises because there are $2L_n$ Langford pairings (including left-right reversals).

134

(b) Let $f_k = \sum_{j=1}^{2n-k-1} x_j x_{j+k+1}$ be the main part of the kth factor. We can run through all 4^n cases $x_1, \ldots, x_{2n} \in \{-1, +1\}$ in Gray-code order (Algorithm 7.2.1.1L), negating only one of the x_j each time. A change in x_j causes at most two adjustments to each f_k; so each Gray-code step costs $O(n)$.

We needn't compute the sum exactly; it suffices to work mod 2^N, where 2^N comfortably exceeds $2^{2n+1} L_n$. Even better, when $n = 24$, would be to do the computations mod $2^{60} - 1$, or mod both $2^{30} - 1$ and $2^{30} + 1$. One can also save $\lceil n/2 \rceil$ bits of precision by exploiting the fact that $f_k \equiv k + 1$ (modulo 2).

(c) The third equality is actually valid only when $n \bmod 4 = 0$ or 3; but those are the interesting n's. The sum can be carried out in n phases, where phase p for $p < n$ involves the cases where $x_{n-1} = x_{n+2}$, $x_{n-2} = x_{n+3}$, $\ldots$, $x_{n-p+1} = x_{n+p}$, $x_{n-p} = x_n = x_{n+1} = +1$, and $x_{n+p+1} = -1$; it has an outer loop that chooses $(x_{n-p+1}, \ldots, x_{n-1})$ in all 2^{p-1} ways, and an inner loop that chooses $(x_1, \ldots, x_{n-p-1}, x_{n+p+2}, \ldots, x_{2n})$ in all $2^{2n-2p-2}$ ways. (The inner loop uses Gray binary code, preferably with "organ-pipe order" to prioritize the subscripts so that x_1 and x_{2n} vary most rapidly. The outer loop need not be especially efficient.) Phase n covers the 2^{n-1} palindromic cases with $x_j = x_{2n+1-j}$ for $1 \le j < n$ and $x_n = x_{n+1} = +1$. If s_p denotes the sum in phase p, then $s_1 + \cdots + s_{n-1} + \frac{1}{2} s_n = 2^{2n-2} L_n$.

A substantial fraction of the terms turn out be zero. For example, when $n = 16$, zeros appear about 76% of the time (in 408,838,754 cases out of $2^{29} + 2^{14}$). This fact can be used to avoid many multiplications in the inner loop. (Only $f_1, f_3, \ldots$ can be zero.)

7. Let d_k be the number of incomplete pairs after k characters have been read; thus $d_0 = d_{2n} = 0$, and $d_k = d_{k-1} \pm 1$ for $1 \le k \le 2n$. The largest such sequence in which d_k never exceeds 6 is $(0, 1, 2, 3, 4, 5, 6, 5, 6, \ldots, 5, 6, 5, 4, 3, 2, 1, 0)$. This sequence has $\sum_{k=1}^{2n} d_k = 11n - 30$. But $\sum_{k=1}^{2n} d_k = \sum_{k=1}^{n} (k+1) = \binom{n+1}{2} + n$ in any Langford pairing. Hence $\binom{n+1}{2} + n \le 11n - 30$, and $n \le 15$. (In fact, width 6 is also impossible when $n = 15$. The largest and smallest possible width are unknown in general.)

8. There are no solutions when $n = 4$ or $n = 7$. When $n = 8$ there are four:

1317538642572468; 1418634753268257; 4275248635713168; 5286235743681417.

(This problem makes a pleasant mechanical puzzle, using gadgets of width $k + 1$ and height $\lceil k/2 \rceil$ for piece k. In his original note [*Math. Gazette* **42** (1958), 228], C. Dudley Langford illustrated similar pieces, and exhibited a planar solution for $n = 12$. The question can be cast as an exact cover problem, with nonprimary columns representing places where two gadgets are not allowed to intersect; see exercise 7.2.2.1–00. Jean Brette has devised a somewhat similar puzzle, based on Skolem's variant of the problem and using width instead of planarity; he gave a copy to David Singmaster in 1992.)

9. Just three ways: 18191526728529647538463974, 19121824627945863475396857, 19161825726925847635493874 (and their reversals). [First found in 1969 by G. Baron; see *Combinatorial Theory and Its Applications* (Budapest: 1970), 81–92. The "dancing links" method of Section 7.2.2.1 resolves this question by traversing a search tree that has only 360 nodes, given an exact cover problem with 132 rows.]

10. For example, let A = 12, K = 8, Q = 4, J = 0, ♠ = 4, ♡ = 3, ◇ = 2, ♣ = 1; add.

[In this connection, orthogonal latin squares equivalent to Fig. 1 were implicitly present already in medieval Islamic talismans illustrated by Ibn al-Hajj in his *Kitab Shumus al-Anwar* (Cairo: 1322); he also gave a 5×5 example. See E. Doutté, *Magie et Religion dans l'Afrique du Nord* (Algiers: 1909), 193–194, 214, 247; W. Ahrens, *Der Islam* **7** (1917), 228–238. See also an article on the history of latin squares being prepared by Lars D. Andersen.]

11. $\begin{pmatrix} d\gamma\aleph & a\delta\beth & b\beta\lambda & c\alpha\daleth \\ c\beta\beth & b\alpha\aleph & a\gamma\daleth & d\delta\lambda \\ a\alpha\lambda & d\beta\daleth & c\delta\aleph & b\gamma\beth \\ b\delta\daleth & c\gamma\lambda & d\alpha\beth & a\beta\aleph \end{pmatrix}$. [Joseph Sauveur presented the earliest known example of such squares in *Mémoires de l'Académie Royale des Sciences* (Paris, 1710), 92–138, §83.]

12. If n is odd, we can let $M_{ij} = (i - j) \bmod n$. But if n is even, there are no transversals: For if $\{(t_0+0) \bmod n, \ldots, (t_{n-1}+n-1) \bmod n\}$ is a transversal, we have $\sum_{k=0}^{n-1} t_k \equiv \sum_{k=0}^{n-1} (t_k + k)$ (modulo n), hence $\sum_{k=0}^{n-1} k = \frac{1}{2}n(n-1)$ is a multiple of n.

13. Replace each element l by $\lfloor l/5 \rfloor$ to get a matrix of 0s and 1s. Let the four quarters be named $\begin{pmatrix} A & B \\ C & D \end{pmatrix}$; then A and D each contain exactly k 1s, while B and C each contain exactly k 0s. Suppose the original matrix has ten disjoint transversals. If $k \le 2$, at most four of them go through a 1 in A or D, and at most four go through a 0 in B or C. Thus at least two of them hit only 0s in A and D, only 1s in B and C. But such a transversal has an even number of 0s (not five), because it intersects A and D equally often.

Similarly, a latin square of order $4m + 2$ with an orthogonal mate must have more than m intruders in each of its $(2m + 1) \times (2m + 1)$ submatrices, under all renamings of the elements. [H. B. Mann, *Bull. Amer. Math. Soc.* (2) **50** (1944), 249–257.]

14. Cases (b) and (d) have no mates. Cases (a), (c), and (e) have respectively 2, 6, and 12265168(!), of which the lexicographically first and last are

(a)	(a)	(c)	(c)	(e)	(e)
0456987213	0691534782	0362498571	0986271435	0214365897	0987645321
1305629847	1308257964	1408327695	1354068792	1025973468	1795402638
2043798165	2169340578	2673519408	2741853960	2690587143	2506913874
3289176504	3250879416	3521970846	3572690814	3857694201	3154067289
4518263790	4587902631	4890253167	4630789251	4168730925	4231850967
5167432089	5412763890	5736841920	5218947306	5473829016	5348276190
6894015372	6945081327	6259784013	6095324178	6942158730	6820394715
7920341658	7836425109	7915602384	7869512043	7309216584	7069128543
8731504926	8723196045	8147036259	8407136529	8531402679	8412739056
9672850431	9074618253	9084165732	9123405687	9786041352	9673581402

Notes: Squares (a), (b), (c), and (d) were obtained from the decimal digits of π, e, γ, and ϕ, by discarding each digit that is inconsistent with a completed latin square. Although they aren't truly random, they're probably typical of 10×10 latin squares in general, roughly half of which appear to have orthogonal mates. Parker constructed square (e) in order to obtain an unusually large number of transversals; it has 5504 of them. (Euler had studied a similar example of order 6, therefore "just missing" the discovery of a 10×10 pair.)

15. Parker was dismayed to discover that none of the mates of square 14(e) are orthogonal to each other. With J. W. Brown and A. S. Hedayat [*J. Combinatorics, Inf. and System Sci.* **18** (1993), 113–115], he later found two 10×10s that have four disjoint common transversals (but not ten). [See also B. Ganter, R. Mathon, and A. Rosa, *Congressus Numerantium* **20** (1978), 383–398; **22** (1979), 181–204.] While pursuing an idea of L. Weisner [*Canadian Math. Bull.* **6** (1963), 61–63], the author accidentally noticed some squares that come even closer to a mutually orthogonal trio: The square below is orthogonal to its transpose; and it has five diagonally symmetric transversals, in cells $(0, p_0), \ldots, (9, p_9)$ for $p_0 \ldots p_9 = 0132674598, 2301457689, 3210896745,$

4897065312, and 6528410937, which are *almost* disjoint: They cover 49 cells.

$$
L \;=\; \begin{pmatrix} 0234567891 \\ 3192708546 \\ 6528139407 \\ 8753241960 \\ 1689473025 \\ 4970852613 \\ 5047986132 \\ 9416320758 \\ 7361095284 \\ 2805614379 \end{pmatrix} \quad \perp \quad \begin{pmatrix} 0368145972 \\ 2157690438 \\ 3925874160 \\ 4283907615 \\ 5712489306 \\ 6034758291 \\ 7891326054 \\ 8549061723 \\ 9406213587 \\ 1670532849 \end{pmatrix} \;=\; L^T .
$$

Extensive computations by B. D. McKay, A. Meynert, and W. Myrvold [*J. Comb. Designs* **15** (2007), 98–119] prove that no 10×10 latin square with nontrivial symmetry has two mates orthogonal to each other. Three mutually orthogonal latin squares are known to exist for all orders $n > 10$ [see S. M. P. Wang and R. M. Wilson, *Congressus Numerantium* **21** (1978), 688; D. T. Todorov, *Ars Combinatoria* **20** (1985), 45–47].

16. See R. A. Brualdi and H. J. Ryser, *Combinatorial Matrix Theory* (Cambridge University Press, 1991), §8.2.

17. (a) Let there be $3n$ columns r_j, c_j, v_j for $0 \le j < n$, and n^2 rows; row (i,j) has 1 in columns r_i, c_j, and v_l, where $l = L_{ij}$, for $0 \le i, j < n$.

(b) Let there be $4n^2$ columns r_{ij}, c_{ij}, x_{ij}, y_{ij} for $0 \le i,j < n$, and $n^3 - n^2 + n$ rows; row (i,j,k) has 1 in columns r_{ik}, c_{jk}, x_{ij}, and y_{lk}, where $l = L_{ij}$, for $0 \le i,j,k < n$ and $(i = k$ or $j > 0)$.

18. Given an orthogonal array A with rows A_i for $1 \le i \le m$, define latin square $L_i = (L_{ijk})$ for $1 \le i \le m - 2$ by setting $L_{ijk} = A_{iq}$ when $A_{(m-1)q} = j$ and $A_{mq} = k$, for $0 \le j, k < n$. (The value of q is uniquely determined by the values of j and k.) Permuting the columns of the array does not change the corresponding latin squares.

This construction can also be reversed, to produce orthogonal arrays of order n from mutually orthogonal latin squares of order n. In exercise 11, for example, we can let $a = \alpha = \aleph = 0$, $b = \beta = \beth = 1$, $c = \gamma = \gimel = 2$, and $d = \delta = \daleth = 3$, obtaining

$$
A = \begin{pmatrix} 3012210303211230 \\ 2310102301323201 \\ 0123103223013210 \\ 0000111122223333 \\ 0123012301230123 \end{pmatrix} .
$$

(The concept of an orthogonal array is mathematically "cleaner" than the concept of orthogonal latin squares, because it accounts better for the underlying symmetries. Notice, for example, that an $n \times n$ matrix L is a latin square if and only if it is orthogonal to two particular non-latin squares, namely

$$
L \perp \begin{pmatrix} 1 & 1 & \cdots & 1 \\ 2 & 2 & \cdots & 2 \\ \vdots & \vdots & \ddots & \vdots \\ n & n & \cdots & n \end{pmatrix} \quad \text{and} \quad L \perp \begin{pmatrix} 1 & 2 & \cdots & n \\ 1 & 2 & \cdots & n \\ \vdots & \vdots & \ddots & \vdots \\ 1 & 2 & \cdots & n \end{pmatrix} .
$$

Therefore Latin squares, Græco-Latin squares, Hebraic-Græco-Latin squares, etc., are equivalent to orthogonal arrays of depth 3, 4, 5, ... Moreover, the orthogonal arrays considered here are merely the special case $t = 2$ and $\lambda = 1$ of a more general concept of n-ary $m \times \lambda n^t$ arrays having "strength t" and "index λ," introduced by C. R. Rao in *Proc. Edinburgh Math. Soc.* **8** (1949), 119–125; see the book *Orthogonal Arrays* by A. S. Hedayat, N. J. A. Sloane, and J. Stufken (Springer, 1999).)

19. We can rearrange the columns so that the first row is $0^n 1^n \ldots (n-1)^n$. Then we can renumber the elements of the other rows so that they begin with $01 \ldots (n-1)$. The elements in each remaining column must then be distinct, in all rows but the first.

   To achieve the upper bound when $n = p$, let each column be indexed by two numbers x and y, where $0 \le x, y < p$, and put the numbers y, x, $(x + y) \bmod p$, $(x + 2y) \bmod p$, $\ldots$, $(x + (p-1)y) \bmod p$ into that column. For example, when $p = 5$ we get the following orthogonal array, equivalent to four mutually orthogonal latin squares:

$$\begin{pmatrix} 0\,0\,0\,0\,0\,1\,1\,1\,1\,1\,2\,2\,2\,2\,2\,3\,3\,3\,3\,3\,4\,4\,4\,4\,4 \\ 0\,1\,2\,3\,4\,0\,1\,2\,3\,4\,0\,1\,2\,3\,4\,0\,1\,2\,3\,4\,0\,1\,2\,3\,4 \\ 0\,1\,2\,3\,4\,1\,2\,3\,4\,0\,2\,3\,4\,0\,1\,3\,4\,0\,1\,2\,4\,0\,1\,2\,3 \\ 0\,1\,2\,3\,4\,2\,3\,4\,0\,1\,4\,0\,1\,2\,3\,1\,2\,3\,4\,0\,3\,4\,0\,1\,2 \\ 0\,1\,2\,3\,4\,3\,4\,0\,1\,2\,1\,2\,3\,4\,0\,4\,0\,1\,2\,3\,2\,3\,4\,0\,1 \\ 0\,1\,2\,3\,4\,4\,0\,1\,2\,3\,3\,4\,0\,1\,2\,2\,3\,4\,0\,1\,1\,2\,3\,4\,0 \end{pmatrix}.$$

[Essentially the same idea works when n is a prime power, using the finite field $\mathrm{GF}(p^e)$; see E. H. Moore, *American Journal of Mathematics* **18** (1896), 264–303, §15(1). These arrays are equivalent to finite *projective planes*; see Marshall Hall, Jr., *Combinatorial Theory* (Blaisdell, 1967), Chapters 12 and 13.]

20. Let $\omega = e^{2\pi i/n}$, and suppose $a_1 \ldots a_{n^2}$ and $b_1 \ldots b_{n^2}$ are the vectors in different rows. Then $a_1 b_1 + \cdots + a_{n^2} b_{n^2} = \sum_{0 \le j,k < n} \omega^{j+k} = 0$ because $\sum_{k=0}^{n-1} \omega^k = 0$.

21. (a) To show that equality-or-parallelism is an equivalence relation, we need to verify the transitive law: If $L \parallel M$ and $M \parallel N$ and $L \ne N$, then we must have $L \parallel N$. Otherwise there would be a point p with $L \cap N = \{p\}$, by (ii); and p would lie on two different lines parallel to M, contradicting (iii).

   (b) Let $\{L_1, \ldots, L_n\}$ be a class of parallel lines, and assume that M is a line of another class. Then each L_j intersects M in a unique point p_j; and every point of M is encountered in this way, because every point of the geometry lies on exactly one line of each class, by (iii). Thus M contains exactly n points.

   (c) We've already observed that every point belongs to m lines when there are m classes. If lines L, M, and N belong to three different classes, then M and N have the same number of points as the number of lines in L's class. So there's a common line size n, and in fact the total number of points is n^2. (Of course n might be infinite.)

22. Given an orthogonal array A of order n and depth m, define a geometric net with n^2 points and m classes of parallel lines by regarding the columns of A as points; line j of class k is the set of columns where symbol j appears in row k of A.

   All finite geometric nets with $m \ge 3$ classes arise in this way. But a geometric net with only one class is trivially a partition of the points into disjoint subsets. A geometric net with $m = 2$ classes has nn' points (x, x'), where there are n lines '$x = $ constant' in one class and n' lines '$x' = $ constant' in the other. [For further information, see R. H. Bruck, *Canadian J. Math.* **3** (1951), 94–107; *Pacific J. Math.* **13** (1963), 421–457.]

23. (a) If $d(x, y) \le t$ and $d(x', y) \le t$ and $x \ne x'$, then $d(x, x') \le 2t$. Thus a code with distance $> 2t$ between codewords allows the correction of up to t errors — at least in principle, although the computations might be complex. Conversely, if $d(x, x') \le 2t$ and $x \ne x'$, there's an element y with $d(x, y) \le t$ and $d(x', y) \le t$; hence we can't reconstruct x uniquely when y is received.

   (b,c) Let $m = r + 2$, and observe that a set of b^2 b-ary m-tuples has Hamming distance $\ge m - 1$ between all pairs of elements if and only if it forms the columns of a

b-ary orthogonal array of depth m. [See S. W. Golomb and E. C. Posner, *IEEE Trans.* **IT-10** (1964), 196–208. The literature of coding theory often denotes a code $C(b, n, r)$ of distance d by the symbol $(n + r, b^n, d)_b$. Thus, a b-ary orthogonal array of depth m is essentially an $(m, b^2, m - 1)_b$ code.]

24. (a) Suppose $x_j \neq x'_j$ for $1 \leq j \leq l$ and $x_j = x'_j$ for $l < j \leq N$. We have $x = x'$ if $l = 0$. Otherwise consider the parity bits that correspond to the m lines through point 1. At most $l - 1$ of those bits correspond to lines that touch the points $\{2, \ldots, l\}$. Hence x' has at least $m - (l-1)$ parity changes, and $d(x, x') \geq l + (m - (l-1)) = m + 1$.

(b) Let $l_{p1}, \ldots, l_{pm}$ be the index numbers of the lines through point p. After receiving a message $y_1 \ldots y_{N+R}$, compute x_p for $1 \leq p \leq N$ by taking the majority value of the $m + 1$ "witness bits" $\{y_{p0}, \ldots, y_{pm}\}$, where $y_{p0} = y_p$ and

$$y_{pk} = \left(y_{N+l_{pk}} + \sum\{y_j \mid j \neq p \text{ and point } j \text{ lies on line } l_{pk}\}\right) \bmod 2, \quad \text{for } 1 \leq k \leq m.$$

This method works because each received bit y_j affects at most one of the witness bits.

For example, in the 25-point geometry of exercise 19, suppose the parity bit $x_{26+5i+j}$ of each codeword corresponds to line j of row i, for $0 \leq i \leq 5$ and $0 \leq j < 5$; thus $x_{26} = x_1 \oplus x_2 \oplus x_3 \oplus x_4 \oplus x_5$, $x_{27} = x_6 \oplus x_7 \oplus x_8 \oplus x_9 \oplus x_{10}$, ..., $x_{55} = x_5 \oplus x_6 \oplus x_{12} \oplus x_{18} \oplus x_{24}$. Given message $y_1 \ldots y_{55}$, we decode bit x_1 (say) by computing the majority of the seven bits y_1, $y_{26} \oplus y_2 \oplus y_3 \oplus y_4 \oplus y_5$, $y_{31} \oplus y_6 \oplus y_{11} \oplus y_{16} \oplus y_{21}$, $y_{36} \oplus y_{10} \oplus y_{14} \oplus y_{18} \oplus y_{22}$, $y_{41} \oplus y_9 \oplus y_{12} \oplus y_{20} \oplus y_{23}$, $y_{46} \oplus y_8 \oplus y_{15} \oplus y_{17} \oplus y_{24}$, $y_{51} \oplus y_7 \oplus y_{13} \oplus y_{19} \oplus y_{25}$. [Section 7.1.2 explains how to calculate majority functions efficiently. Notice that we can eliminate the last 10 bits if we only wish to correct up to two errors, and the last 20 if single-error correction is sufficient. See M. Y. Hsiao, D. C. Bossen, and R. T. Chien, *IBM J. Research and Development* **14** (1970), 390–394.]

25. By considering anagrams of $\{1, e, a, s, t\}$ (see exercise 5–21), we're led to the square

```
stela
telas
elast ,
laste
astel
```

and the cyclic rotations of its rows. Here `telas` are Spanish fabrics; `elast` is a prefix meaning flexible; and `laste` is an imperative Chaucerian verb. (Of course just about every pronounceable combination of five letters has been used to spell or misspell something somewhere, at some point in history.)

26. "`every night, young video buffs catch rerun fever forty years after those great shows first aired.`" [Robert Leighton, *GAMES* **16**, 6 (December 1992), 34, 47.]

27. $(0, 4, 163, 1756, 3834)$ for $k = (1, 2, 3, 4, 5)$; `mamma` and `esses` give a "full house."

28. Yes, 38 pairs altogether. The "most common" solution is `needs` (rank 180) and `offer` (rank 384). Only three cases differ consistently by $+1$ (`adder beefs`, `sheer tiffs`, `sneer toffs`). Other memorable examples are `ghost hints` and `strut rusts`. One word of the pair ends with the letter s except in four cases, such as `robed spade`. [See Leonard J. Gordon, *Word Ways* **23** (1990), 59–61.]

29. There are 18 palindromes, from `level` (rank 184) to `dewed` (rank 5688). Some of the 34 mirror pairs are '`devil lived`', '`knits stink`', '`smart trams`', '`faced decaf`'.

30. Among 105 such words in the SGB, `first`, `below`, `floor`, `begin`, `cells`, `empty`, and `hills` are the most common; `abbey` and `pssst` are lexicographically first and last. (If you don't like `pssst`, the next-to-last is `mossy`.) Only 37 words, from `mecca` to `zoned`, have their letters in *reverse* order; but they are, of course, **wrong** answers.

31. The middle word is the average of the other two, so the extreme words must be congruent mod 2; this observation reduces the number of dictionary lookups by a factor of about 32. There are 119 such triples in WORDS(5757), but only two in WORDS(2000): marry, photo, solve; risky, tempo, vague. [*Word Ways* **25** (1992), 13–15.]

32. The only reasonably common example seems to be peopleless.

33. chief, fight, right, which, ouija, jokes, ankle, films, hymns, known, crops, pique, quart, first, first, study, mauve, vowel, waxes, proxy, crazy, pizza. (The idea is to find the most common word in which x is followed by $(x + 1)$ mod 26, for $x = $ a (0), $x = $ b (1), $\ldots$, $x = $ z (25). We also minimize the intervening distance, thus preferring bacon to the more common word black. In the one case where no such word exists, crazy seems most rational. See *OMNI* **16**, 8 (May 1994), 94.)

34. The top two (and total number) in each category are: pssst and pffft (2), schwa and schmo (2), threw and throw (36), three and spree (5), which and think (709), there and these (234), their and great (291), whooo and wheee (3), words and first (628), large and since (376), water and never (1313), value and radio (84), would and could (460), house and voice (101), quiet and queen (25), queue only (1), ahhhh and ankhs (4), angle and extra (20), other and after (227), agree and issue (20), along and using (124), above and alone (92), about and again (58), adieu and aquae (2), earth and eight (16), eagle and ounce (8), outer and eaten (42), eerie and audio (4), (0), ouija and aioli (2), (0), (0); years and every are the most common of the 868 omitted words. [To fill the three holes, Internet usage suggests ooops, ooooh, and ooooo. See P. M. Cohen, *Word Ways* **10** (1977), 221–223.]

35. Consider the collection WORDS(n) for $n = 1, 2, \ldots, 5757$. The illustrated trie, rooted at s, first becomes possible when n reaches 978 (the rank of stalk). The next root letter to support such a trie is c, which acquires enough branching in its descendants when $n = 2503$ (the rank of craze). Subsequent breakthroughs occur when $n = 2730$ (bulks), 3999 (ducky), 4230 (panty), 4459 (minis), 4709 (whooo), 4782 (lardy), 4824 (herem), 4840 (firma), 4924 (ridgy), 5343 (taxol).

(A breakthrough occurs when a top-level trie acquires Horton–Strahler number 4; see exercise 7.2.1.6–124. Amusing sets of words, suggestive of a new kind of poetry, arise also when the branching is right-to-left instead of left-to-right: black, slack, crack, track, click, slick, brick, trick, blank, plank, crank, drank, blink, clink, brink, drink. In fact, right-to-left branching yields a complete *ternary* trie with 81 leaves: males, sales, tales, files, miles, piles, holes, $\ldots$, tests, costs, hosts, posts.)

36. Denoting the elements of the cube by a_{ijk} for $1 \leq i, j, k \leq 5$, the symmetry condition is $a_{ijk} = a_{ikj} = a_{jik} = a_{jki} = a_{kij} = a_{kji}$. In general an $n \times n \times n$ cube has $3n^2$ words, obtained by fixing two coordinates and letting the third range from 1 to n; but the symmetry condition means that we need only $\binom{n+1}{2}$ words. Hence when $n = 5$ the number of necessary words is reduced from 75 to 15. [Jeff Grant was able to find 75 suitable words in the *Oxford English Dictionary*; see *Word Ways* **11** (1978), 156–157.]

Changing (stove, event) to (store, erect) or (stole, elect) gives two more.

37. The densest part of the graph, which we might call its "bare core," contains the vertices named bares and cores, which each have degree 25.

38. tears $\rightarrow$ raise $\rightarrow$ aisle $\rightarrow$ smile; the second word might also be reals. [Going from tears to smile as in (11) was one of Lewis Carroll's first five-letter examples. He would have been delighted to learn that the directed rule makes it more difficult to go from smile to tears, because *four* steps are needed in that direction.]

39. Always spanning, never induced.

40. (a) 2^e, (b) 2^n, one for each subset of E or V.

41. (a) $n = 1$ and $n = 2$; P_0 is undefined. (b) $n = 0$ and $n = 3$.

42. G has $65/2$ edges (hence it doesn't exist).

43. Yes: The first three are isomorphic to Fig. 2(e). [The left-hand diagram is, in fact, identical to the earliest known appearance of the Petersen graph in print: See A. B. Kempe, *Philosophical Transactions* **177** (1886), 1–70, especially Fig. 13 in §59.] But the right-hand graph is definitely different; it is planar, Hamiltonian, and has girth 4.

44. Any automorphism must take a corner point into a corner point, because three distinct paths of length 2 can be found only between certain pairs of non-corner points. Therefore the graph has only the eight symmetries of C_4.

45. All edges of this graph connect vertices of the same row or adjacent rows. Therefore we can use the colors 0 and 2 alternately in even-numbered rows, 1 and 3 alternately in odd-numbered rows. The neighbors of NV form a 5-cycle, hence four colors are necessary.

46. (a) Every vertex has degree ≥ 2, and its neighbors have a well-defined cyclic order corresponding to the incoming lines. If $u \longrightarrow v$ and $u \longrightarrow w$, where v and w are cyclically consecutive neighbors of u, we must have $v \longrightarrow w$. Thus all points in the vicinity of any vertex u belong to a unique triangular region.

(b) The formula holds when $n = 3$. If $n > 3$, shrink any edge to a point; this transformation removes one vertex and three edges. (If $u \longrightarrow v$ shrinks, suppose it was part of the triangles $x \longrightarrow u \longrightarrow v \longrightarrow x$ and $y \longrightarrow u \longrightarrow v \longrightarrow y$. We lose vertex v and edges $\{x \longrightarrow v, u \longrightarrow v, y \longrightarrow v\}$; all other edges of the form $w \longrightarrow v$ become $w \longrightarrow u$.)

47. A planar diagram would divide the plane into regions, with either 4 or 6 vertices in the boundary of each region (because $K_{3,3}$ has no odd cycles). If there are f_4 and f_6 of each kind, we must have $4f_4 + 6f_6 = 18$, since there are 9 edges; hence $(f_4, f_6) = (3, 1)$ or $(0, 3)$. We could also triangulate the graph by adding $f_4 + 3f_6$ more edges; but then it would have at least 15 edges, contradicting exercise 46.

[The fact that $K_{3,3}$ is nonplanar goes back to a puzzle about connecting three houses to three utilities (water, gas, and electricity), without crossing pipes. Its origin is unknown; H. E. Dudeney called it "ancient" in *Strand* **46** (1913), 110.]

48. If u, v, w are vertices and $u \longrightarrow v$, we must have $d(w, u) \not\equiv d(w, v)$ (modulo 2); otherwise shortest paths from w to u and from w to v would yield an odd cycle. After w is colored 0, the procedure therefore assigns the color $d(w, v) \bmod 2$ to each new uncolored vertex v that is adjacent to a colored vertex u; and every vertex v with $d(w, v) < \infty$ is colored before a new w is chosen.

49. There are only three: K_4, $K_{3,3}$, and $\boxed{}$ (which is $\overline{C_6}$).

50. The graph must be connected, because the number of 3-colorings is divisible by 3^r when there are r components. It must also be contained in a complete bipartite graph $K_{m,n}$, which can be 3-colored in $3(2^m + 2^n - 2)$ ways. Deleting edges from $K_{m,n}$ does not decrease the number of colorings; hence $2^m + 2^n - 2 \leq 8$, and we have $\{m, n\} = \{1, 1\}$, $\{1, 2\}$, $\{1, 3\}$, or $\{2, 2\}$. So the only possibilities are the claw $K_{1,3}$ and the path P_4.

51. A 4-cycle $p_1 \longrightarrow L_1 \longrightarrow p_2 \longrightarrow L_2 \longrightarrow p_1$ would correspond to two distinct lines $\{L_1, L_2\}$ with two common points $\{p_1, p_2\}$, contradicting (ii). So the girth is at least 6.

If there's only one class of parallel lines, the girth is ∞; if there are two classes, with $n \leq n'$ members, it is 8, or ∞ if $n = 1$. (See answer 22.) Otherwise we can find a 6-cycle by making a triangle from three lines that are chosen from different classes.

52. If the diameter is d and the girth is g, then $d \geq \lfloor g/2 \rfloor$, unless $g = \infty$.

53. happy (which is connected to tears and sweat, but not to world).

54. (a) It's a single, highly connected component. (Incidentally, this graph is the *line graph* of the bipartite graph in which one part corresponds to the initial letters $\{A, C, D, F, G, \ldots, W\}$ and the other to the final letters $\{A, C, D, E, H, \ldots, Z\}$.)

(b) Vertex WY is isolated. The other vertices with in-degree zero, namely FL, GA, PA, UT, WA, WI, and WV, form strong components by themselves; they all precede a giant strong component, which is followed by each of the remaining single-vertex strong components with out-degree zero: AZ, DE, KY, ME, NE, NH, NJ, NY, OH, TX.

(c) Now the strong component $\{GU\}$ precedes $\{UT\}$; NH, OH, PA, WA, WI, and WV join the giant strong component; $\{FM\}$ precedes it; $\{AE\}$ and $\{WY\}$ follow it.

55. $\binom{N}{2} - \binom{n_1}{2} - \cdots - \binom{n_k}{2}$, where $N = n_1 + \cdots + n_k$.

56. True. Note that J_n is simple, but it doesn't correspond to any multigraph.

57. False, in the connected digraph $u \longrightarrow w \longleftarrow v$. (But u and v are in the same *strongly connected* component if and only if $d(u, v) < \infty$ and $d(v, u) < \infty$; see Section 2.3.4.2.)

58. Each component is a cycle whose order is at least (a) 3 (b) 1.

59. (a) By induction on n, we can use straight insertion sorting: Suppose $v_1 \longrightarrow \cdots \longrightarrow v_{n-1}$. Then either $v_n \longrightarrow v_1$ or $v_{n-1} \longrightarrow v_n$ or $v_{k-1} \longrightarrow v_n \longrightarrow v_k$, where k is minimum such that $v_n \longrightarrow v_k$. [L. Rédei, *Acta litterarum ac scientiarum* **7** (Szeged, 1934), 39–43.]

(b) 15: 01234, 02341, 02413, and their cyclic shifts. [The number of such oriented paths is always odd; see T. Szele, *Matematikai és Fizikai Lapok* **50** (1943), 223–256.]

(c) Yes. (By induction: If there's only one place to insert v_n as in part (a), the tournament is transitive.)

60. Set $A = \{x \mid u \longrightarrow x\}$, $B = \{x \mid x \longrightarrow v\}$, $C = \{x \mid v \longrightarrow x\}$. If $v \notin A$ and $A \cap B = \emptyset$ we have $|A| + |B| = |A \cup B| \leq n - 2$, because $u \notin A \cup B$ and $v \notin A \cup B$. But $|B| + |C| = n - 1$; hence $|A| < |C|$. [H. G. Landau, *Bull. Math. Biophysics* **15** (1953), 148.]

61. $1 \longrightarrow 1$, $1 \longrightarrow 2$, $2 \longrightarrow 2$; then $A = \left(\begin{smallmatrix} 1 & 1 \\ 0 & 1 \end{smallmatrix}\right)$ and $A^k = \left(\begin{smallmatrix} 1 & k \\ 0 & 1 \end{smallmatrix}\right)$ for all integers k.

62. (a) Suppose the vertices are $\{1, \ldots, n\}$. Each of the $n!$ terms $a_{1p_1} \ldots a_{np_n}$ in the expansion of the permanent is the number of spanning permutation digraphs that have arcs $j \longrightarrow p_j$. (b) A similar argument shows that $\det A$ is the number of even spanning permutation digraphs minus the number of odd ones. [See F. Harary, *SIAM Review* **4** (1962), 202–210, where permutation digraphs are called "linear subgraphs."]

63. Let v be any vertex. If $g = 2t+1$, at least $d(d-1)^{k-1}$ vertices x satisfy $d(v, x) = k$, for $1 \leq k < t$. If $g = 2t + 2$ and v' is any neighbor of v, there also are at least $(d-1)^t$ vertices x for which $d(v, x) = t + 1$ and $d(v', x) = t$.

64. To achieve the lower bound in answer 63, *every* vertex v must have degree d, and the d neighbors of v must all be adjacent to the remaining $d - 1$ vertices. This graph is, in fact, $K_{d,d}$.

65. (a) By answer 63, G must be regular of degree d, and there must be exactly one path of length ≤ 2 between any two distinct vertices.

(b) We may take $\lambda_1 = d$, with $x_1 = (1 \ldots 1)^T$. All other eigenvectors satisfy $Jx_j = (0 \ldots 0)^T$; hence $\lambda_j^2 + \lambda_j = d - 1$ for $1 < j \leq N$.

(c) If $\lambda_2 = \cdots = \lambda_m = (-1+\sqrt{4d-3})/2$ and $\lambda_{m+1} = \cdots = \lambda_N = (-1-\sqrt{4d-3})/2$, we must have $m - 1 = N - m$. With this value we find $\lambda_1 + \cdots + \lambda_N = d - d^2/2$.

(d) If $4d - 3 = s^2$ and m is as in (c), the eigenvalues sum to

$$\frac{s^2 + 3}{4} + (m-1)\frac{s-1}{2} - \left(\frac{(s^2+3)^2}{16} + 1 - m\right)\frac{s+1}{2},$$

which is 15/32 plus a multiple of s. Hence s must be a divisor of 15.

[These results are due to A. J. Hoffman and R. R. Singleton, *IBM J. Research and Development* **4** (1960), 497–504, who also proved that the graph for $d = 7$ is unique.]

66. Denote the 50 vertices by $[a, b]$ and (a, b) for $0 \le a, b < 5$, and define three kinds of edges, using arithmetic mod 5:

$$[a, b] \!-\! [a + 1, b]; \qquad (a, b) \!-\! (a + 2, b); \qquad (a, b) \!-\! [a + bc, c] \quad \text{for } 0 \le a, b, c < 5.$$

[See W. G. Brown, *Canadian J. Math.* **19** (1967), 644–648; *J. London Math. Soc.* **42** (1967), 514–520. Without the edges of the first two kinds, the graph has girth 6 and corresponds to a geometric net as in exercise 51, using the orthogonal array in answer 19.]

67. Certain possibilities have been ruled out by Michael Aschbacher in *Journal of Algebra* **19** (1971), 538–540.

68. If G has s automorphisms, it has $n!/s$ adjacency matrices, because there are s permutation matrices P such that $P^- AP = A$.

69. First set $\texttt{IDEG}(v) \leftarrow 0$ for all vertices v. Then perform (31) for all v, also setting $u \leftarrow \texttt{TIP}(a)$ and $\texttt{IDEG}(u) \leftarrow \texttt{IDEG}(u) + 1$ in the second line of that mini-algorithm.

To do something "for all v" using the SGB format, first set $v \leftarrow \texttt{VERTICES}(g)$; then while $v < \texttt{VERTICES}(g) + \texttt{N}(g)$, do the operation and set $v \leftarrow v + 1$.

70. Step B1 is performed once (but it takes $O(n)$ units of time). Steps (B2, B3, ..., B8) are performed respectively $(n + 1, n, n, m + n, m, m, n)$ times, each with $O(1)$ cost.

71. Many choices are possible. Here we use 32-bit pointers, all relative to a symbolic address `Pool`, which lies in the `Data_Segment`. The following declarations provide one way to establish conventions for dealing with basic SGB data structures.

```
VSIZE IS 32 ;ASIZE IS 24            Node sizes
ARCS IS 0 ;COLOR IS 8 ;LINK IS 12   Offsets of vertex fields
TIP IS 0 ;NEXT IS 4                 Offsets of arc fields

arcs GREG Pool+ARCS ;color GREG Pool+COLOR ;link GREG Pool+LINK
tip GREG Pool+TIP ;next GREG Pool+NEXT
u GREG ;v GREG ;w GREG ;s GREG ;a GREG ;mone GREG -1
```

AlgB	BZ	n,Success	Exit if the graph is null.
	MUL	$0,n,VSIZE	*B1. Initialize.*
	ADDU	v,v0,$0	$v \leftarrow v_0 + n$.
	SET	w,v0	$w \leftarrow v_0$.
1H	STT	mone,color,w	$\texttt{COLOR}(w) \leftarrow -1$.
	ADDU	w,w,VSIZE	$w \leftarrow w + 1$.
	CMP	$0,w,v	
	PBNZ	$0,1B	Repeat until $w = v$.
0H	SUBU	w,w,VSIZE	$w \leftarrow w - 1$.
3H	LDT	$0,color,w	*B3. Color w if necessary.*
	PBNN	$0,2F	To B2 if $\texttt{COLOR}(w) \ge 0$.
	STCO	0,link,w	$\texttt{COLOR}(w) \leftarrow 0$, $\texttt{LINK}(w) \leftarrow \Lambda$.
	SET	s,w	$s \leftarrow w$.
4H	SET	u,s	*B4. Stack $\Rightarrow u$.* Set $u \leftarrow s$.

	LDTU	s,link,s	$s \leftarrow$ LINK(s).
	LDT	\$1,color,u	
	NEG	\$1,1,\$1	$\$1 \leftarrow 1 -$ COLOR(u).
	LDTU	a,arcs,u	$a \leftarrow$ ARCS(u).
5H	BZ	a,8F	*B5. Done with u?* To B8 if $a = \Lambda$.
5H	LDTU	v,tip,a	$v \leftarrow$ TIP(a).
6H	LDT	\$0,color,v	*B6. Process v.*
	CMP	\$2,\$0,\$1	(Here the program is slightly clever)
	PBZ	\$2,7F	To B7 if COLOR$(v) = 1 -$ COLOR(u).
	BNN	\$0,Failure	Fail if COLOR$(v) =$ COLOR(u).
	STT	\$1,color,v	COLOR$(v) \leftarrow 1 -$ COLOR(u).
	STTU	s,link,v	LINK$(v) \leftarrow s$.
	SET	s,v	$s \leftarrow v$.
7H	LDTU	a,next,a	*B7. Loop on a.* Set $a \leftarrow$ NEXT(a).
	PBNZ	a,5B	To B5 if $a \neq \Lambda$.
8H	PBNZ	s,4B	*B8. Stack nonempty?* To B4 if $s \neq \Lambda$.
2H	CMP	\$0,w,v0	*B2. Done?*
	PBNZ	\$0,0B	If $w \neq v_0$, decrease w and go to B3.
Success	LOC	@	(Successful termination) ▮

72. (a) This condition clearly remains invariant as vertices enter or leave the stack.

(b) Vertex v has been colored but not yet explored, because the neighbors of every explored vertex have the proper color.

(c) Just before setting $s \leftarrow v$ in step B6, set PARENT$(v) \leftarrow u$, where PARENT is a new utility field. And just before terminating unsuccessfully in that step, do the following: "Repeatedly output NAME(u) and set $u \leftarrow$ PARENT(u), until $u =$ PARENT(v); then output NAME(u) and NAME(v)."

73. K_{10}. (And *random_graph*$(10, 100, 0, 1, 1, 0, 0, 0, 0, 0)$ is J_{10}.)

74. **badness** has out-degree 22; no other vertices have out-degree > 20.

75. Let the parameters $(n_1, n_2, n_3, n_4, p, w, o)$ be respectively (a) $(n, 0, 0, 0, -1, 0, 0)$; (b) $(n, 0, 0, 0, 1, 0, 0)$; (c) $(n, 0, 0, 0, 1, 1, 0)$; (d) $(n, 0, 0, 0, -1, 0, 1)$; (e) $(n, 0, 0, 0, 1, 0, 1)$; (f) $(n, 0, 0, 0, 1, 1, 1)$; (g) $(m, n, 0, 0, 1, 0, 0)$; (h) $(m, n, 0, 0, 1, 2, 0)$; (i) $(m, n, 0, 0, 1, 3, 0)$; (j) $(m, n, 0, 0, -1, 0, 0)$; (k) $(m, n, 0, 0, 1, 3, 1)$; (l) $(n, 0, 0, 0, 2, 0, 0)$; (m) $(2, -n, 0, 0, 1, 0, 0)$.

76. Yes, for example from C_1 and C_2 in answer 75(c). (But no self-loops can occur when $p < 0$, because arcs $x \longrightarrow y = x + k\delta$ are generated for $k = 1, 2, \ldots$ until y is out of range or $y = x$.)

77. Suppose x and y are vertices with $d(x, y) > 2$. Thus $x \not\!\!\!- y$; and if v is any other vertex we must have either $v \not\!\!\!- x$ or $v \not\!\!\!- y$. These facts yield a path of length at most 3 in $\overline{G}$ between any two vertices u and v.

78. (a) The number of edges, $\binom{n}{2}/2$, must be an integer. The smallest examples are K_0, K_1, P_4, C_5, and $\mathcal{W}$.

(b) If q is any odd number, we have $u \!-\! v$ if and only if $\varphi^q(u) \not\!\!\!- \varphi^q(v)$. Therefore φ^q cannot have two fixed points, nor can it contain a 2-cycle.

(c) Such a permutation of V also defines a permutation $\widehat{\varphi}$ of the edges of K_n, taking $\{u, v\} \mapsto \widehat{\varphi}(\{u, v\}) = \{\varphi(u), \varphi(v)\}$, and it's easy to see that the cycle lengths of $\widehat{\varphi}$ are all multiples of 4. If $\widehat{\varphi}$ has t cycles, we obtain 2^t self-complementary graphs by painting the edges of each cycle with alternating colors.

(d) In this case φ has a unique fixed point v, and $G' = G \setminus v$ is self-complementary. Suppose φ has r cycles in addition to (v); then $\widehat{\varphi}$ has r cycles involving the edges that touch vertex v, and there are 2^r ways to extend G' to a graph G.

[*References:* H. Sachs, *Publicationes Mathematicæ* **9** (Debrecen, 1962), 270–288; G. Ringel, *Archiv der Mathematik* **14** (1963), 354–358.]

79. Solution 1, by H. Sachs, with $\varphi = (1\,2\,\dots\,4k)$: Let $u \mathbin{\text{—}} v$ when $u > v > 0$ and $u + v \bmod 4 \le 1$; also $0 \mathbin{\text{—}} v$ when $v \bmod 2 = 0$.

Solution 2, with $\varphi = (a_1\,b_1\,c_1\,d_1)\dots(a_k\,b_k\,c_k\,d_k)$, where $a_j = 4j - 3$, $b_j = 4j - 2$, $c_j = 4j - 1$, and $d_j = 4j$: Let $0 \mathbin{\text{—}} b_j \mathbin{\text{—}} a_j \mathbin{\text{—}} c_j \mathbin{\text{—}} d_j \mathbin{\text{—}} 0$ for $1 \le j \le k$, and $a_i \mathbin{\text{—}} a_j \mathbin{\text{—}} b_i \mathbin{\text{—}} d_j \mathbin{\text{—}} c_i \mathbin{\text{—}} c_j \mathbin{\text{—}} d_i \mathbin{\text{—}} b_j \mathbin{\text{—}} a_i$, for $1 \le i < j \le k$.

80. (Solution by G. Ringel.) Let φ be as in answer 79, solution 2. Let E_0 be the $3k$ edges $b_j \mathbin{\text{—}} a_j \mathbin{\text{—}} c_j \mathbin{\text{—}} d_j$ for $1 \le j \le k$; let E_1 be the $8\binom{k}{2}$ edges between $\{a_i, b_i, c_i, d_i\}$ and $\{b_j, d_j\}$ for $1 \le i < j \le k$; let E_2 be the $8\binom{k}{2}$ edges between $\{a_i, b_i, c_i, d_i\}$ and $\{a_j, c_j\}$ for $1 \le i < j \le k$. In case (a), $E_0 \cup E_1$ gives diameter 2; $E_0 \cup E_2$ gives diameter 3. Case (b) is similar, but we add $2k$ edges $b_j \mathbin{\text{—}} 0 \mathbin{\text{—}} d_j$ to E_1, $a_j \mathbin{\text{—}} 0 \mathbin{\text{—}} c_j$ to E_2.

81. $\vec{C_3}$, $\vec{K_3}$, $D = \text{o}\!\!\longrightarrow\!\!\text{o}\!\!\curvearrowright\!\!\text{o}$, and $D^T = \text{o}\!\!\longleftarrow\!\!\text{o}\!\!\curvearrowleft\!\!\text{o}$. (The *converse* D^T of a digraph D is obtained by reversing the direction of its arcs. There are 16 nonisomorphic simple digraphs of order 3 without loops, 10 of which are self-converse, including $\vec{C_3}$ and $\vec{K_3}$.)

82. (a) True, by definition. (b) True: If every vertex has d neighbors, every edge $u \mathbin{\text{—}} v$ has $d - 1$ neighbors $u \mathbin{\text{—}} w$ and $d - 1$ neighbors $w \mathbin{\text{—}} v$. (c) True: $\{a_i, b_j\}$ has $m + n - 2$ neighbors, for $0 \le i < m$ and $0 \le j < n$. (d) False: $L(K_{1,1,2})$ has 5 vertices and 8 edges. (e) True. (f) True: The only nonadjacent edges are $\{0,1\} \not\mathbin{\text{—}} \{2,3\}$, $\{0,2\} \not\mathbin{\text{—}} \{1,3\}$, $\{0,3\} \not\mathbin{\text{—}} \{1,2\}$. (g) True, for all $n > 0$. (h) False, unless G has no isolated vertices.

83. It is the Petersen graph. [A. Kowalewski, *Sitzungsberichte der Akademie der Wissenschaften in Wien*, Mathematisch-Nat. Klasse, Abteilung IIa, **126** (1917), 67–90.]

84. Yes: Let $\varphi(\{a_u, b_v\}) = \{a_{(u+v) \bmod 3}, b_{(u-v) \bmod 3}\}$ for $0 \le u, v < 3$.

85. Let the vertex degrees be $\{d_1, \dots, d_n\}$. Then G has $\frac{1}{2}(d_1 + \dots + d_n)$ edges, and $L(G)$ has $\frac{1}{2}(d_1(d_1 - 1) + \dots + d_n(d_n - 1))$. Thus G and $L(G)$ both have exactly n edges if and only if $(d_1 - 2)^2 + \dots + (d_n - 2)^2 = 0$. Consequently exercise 58 gives the answer. [See V. V. Menon, *Canadian Math. Bull.* **8** (1965), 7–15.]

86. If $G = \text{⟨graph⟩}$ then $\overline{G} = \text{⟨graph⟩} = L(G)$.

87. (a) Yes, easily. [In fact, R. L. Brooks has proved that *every* connected graph with maximum vertex degree $d > 2$ is d-colorable, except for the complete graph K_{d+1}; see *Proc. Cambridge Phil. Soc.* **37** (1941), 194–197.]

(b) No. There's essentially only one way to 3-color the edges of the outer 5-cycle in Fig. 2(e); this forces a conflict on the inner 5-cycle. [Petersen proved this in 1898.]

88. One cycle doesn't use the center vertex, and there are $(n-1)(n-2)$ cycles that do (namely, one for every ordered pair of distinct vertices on the rim). We don't count C_0.

89. Both sides equal $\begin{pmatrix} A & O & O \\ O & B & O \\ O & O & C \end{pmatrix}$, $\begin{pmatrix} A & J & J \\ J & B & J \\ J & J & C \end{pmatrix}$, $\begin{pmatrix} A & J & J \\ O & B & J \\ O & O & C \end{pmatrix}$, $\begin{pmatrix} A & O & O \\ J & B & O \\ J & J & C \end{pmatrix}$, respectively.

90. K_4 and $\overline{K_4}$; $K_{1,1,2}$ and $\overline{K_{1,1,2}}$; $K_{2,2} = C_4$ and $\overline{K_{2,2}}$; $K_{1,3}$ and $\overline{K_{1,3}}$; $K_1 \oplus K_{1,2}$ and its complement; all graphs K_α are cographs by (47). Missing is $P_4 = \overline{P_4}$. (All connected subgraphs of a cograph have diameter ≤ 2; W_5 is a cograph, but not W_6.)

91. (a) ⬜; (b) ✕; (c) ⊠; (d) ⬜; (e) ⊠; (f) ⎮ ⎮; (g) ⧖. (In general we have $K_2 \triangle H = (K_2 \,\square\, H) \cup (K_2 \otimes \overline{H})$, and $K_2 \circ H = H \,$—$\, H$. Thus the coincidences $K_2 \triangle H = K_2 \,\square\, H$ and $K_2 \circ H = K_2 \boxtimes H$ occur if and only if H is a complete graph.)

   Mnemonics: Our notations $G \,\square\, H$ and $G \boxtimes H$ nicely match diagrams (a) and (c), as suggested by J. Nešetřil, *Lecture Notes in Comp. Sci.* **118** (1981), 94–102. His analogous recommendation to write $G \times H$ for (b) is also tempting; but it wasn't adopted here, because hundreds of authors have used $G \times H$ to denote $G \,\square\, H$.

92. (a) ⬡; (b) ⬦; (c) ⬕; (d) ⬔; (e) ⊠.

93. $K_m \boxtimes K_n = K_m \circ K_n \cong K_{mn}$.

94. No; they're induced subgraphs of $K_{26} \,\square\, K_{26} \,\square\, K_{26} \,\square\, K_{26} \,\square\, K_{26}$.

95. (a) $d_u + d_v$. (b) $d_u d_v$. (c) $d_u d_v + d_u + d_v$. (d) $d_u(n - d_v) + (m - d_u)d_v$. (e) $d_u n + d_v$.

96. (a) $A \,\square\, B = A \otimes I + I \otimes B$. (b) $A \boxtimes B = A \,\square\, B + A \otimes B$. (c) $A \triangle B = A \otimes J + J \otimes B - 2A \otimes B$. (d) $A \circ B = A \otimes J + I \otimes B$. (Formulas (a), (b), and (d) define graph products of arbitrary digraphs and multigraphs. Formula (c) is valid in general for simple digraphs; but negative entries can occur when A and B contain values > 1.)

   Historical notes: The direct product of matrices is often called the Kronecker product, because K. Hensel [*Crelle* **105** (1889), 329–344] said he had heard it in Kronecker's lectures; however, Kronecker never actually published anything about it. Its first known appearance was in a paper by J. G. Zehfuss [*Zeitschrift für Math. und Physik* **3** (1858), 298–301], who proved that $\det(A \otimes B) = (\det A)^n (\det B)^m$ when $m = m'$ and $n = n'$. The basic formulas $(A \otimes B)^T = A^T \otimes B^T$, $(A \otimes B)(A' \otimes B') = AA' \otimes BB'$, and $(A \otimes B)^{-1} = A^{-1} \otimes B^{-1}$ are due to A. Hurwitz [*Math. Annalen* **45** (1894), 381–404].

97. Operations on adjacency matrices prove that $(G \oplus G') \,\square\, H = (G \,\square\, H) \oplus (G' \,\square\, H)$; $(G \oplus G') \boxtimes H = (G \boxtimes H) \oplus (G' \boxtimes H)$; $(G \oplus G') \circ H = (G \circ H) \oplus (G' \circ H)$. Since $G \,\square\, H \cong H \,\square\, G$, $G \otimes H \cong H \otimes G$, and $G \boxtimes H \cong H \boxtimes G$, we also have right-distributive laws $G \,\square\, (H \oplus H') \cong (G \,\square\, H) \oplus (G \,\square\, H')$; $G \otimes (H \oplus H') \cong (G \otimes H) \oplus (G \otimes H')$; $G \boxtimes (H \oplus H') \cong (G \boxtimes H) \oplus (G \boxtimes H')$. The lexicographic product satisfies $\overline{G \circ H} = \overline{G} \circ \overline{H}$; also $K_m \circ H = H \,$—$ \cdots$—$\, H$, hence $K_m \circ \overline{K}_n = K_{n,\dots,n}$. Furthermore $G \circ K_n = G \boxtimes K_n$; $K_m \otimes K_n = \overline{K_m \,\square\, K_n} = L(K_{m,n})$.

98. There are kl components (because of the distributive laws in the previous exercise, and the facts that $G \,\square\, H$ and $G \boxtimes H$ are connected when G and H are connected).

99. Every path from (u, v) to (u', v') in $G \,\square\, H$ must use at least $d_G(u, u')$ "G-steps" and at least $d_H(v, v')$ "H-steps"; and that minimum is achievable. Similar reasoning shows that $d_{G \boxtimes H}((u, v), (u', v')) = \max(d_G(u, u'), d_H(v, v'))$.

100. If G and H are connected, and if each of them has at least two vertices, $G \otimes H$ is disconnected if and only if G and H are bipartite. The "if" part is easy; conversely, if there's an odd cycle in G, we can get from (u, v) to (u', v') as follows: First go to (u'', v'), where u'' is any vertex of G that happens to be expedient. Then walk an even number of steps in G from u'' to u', while alternating in H between v' and one of its neighbors. [P. M. Weichsel, *Proc. Amer. Math. Soc.* **13** (1962), 47–52.]

101. Choose vertices u and v with maximum degree. Then $d_u + d_v = d_u d_v$ by exercise 95; so either $G = H = K_1$, or $d_u = d_v = 2$. In the latter case, $G = P_m$ or C_m, and $H = P_n$ or C_n. But $G \,\square\, H$ is connected, so G or H must be nonbipartite, say G. Then $G \,\square\, H$ is nonbipartite, so H must also be nonbipartite; thus $G = C_m$ and $H = C_n$, with m and n both odd. The shortest cycle in $C_m \,\square\, C_n$ has length $\min(m, n)$; in $C_m \otimes C_n$ it has length $\max(m, n)$; hence $m = n$. Conversely, if $n \geq 3$

is odd, we have $C_n \square C_n \cong C_n \otimes C_n$, under the isomorphism that takes $(u, v) \mapsto$ $((u + v) \bmod n, (u - v) \bmod n)$ for $0 \le u, v < n$. [D. J. Miller, *Canadian J. Math.* **20** (1968), 1511–1521.]

102. $P_m \boxtimes P_n$. (It is planar only when $\min(m, n) \le 2$ or $m = n = 3$.)

103.

1	2	3	4	5	7
2	1	3	4	6	8
3	1	2	5	6	8
4	1	2	5	6	
5	3	4	1	7	
6	2	3	4		
7	5	1			
8	2	3			

1	2	3	4	5	6	7	8	9
2	1	3	4	6	8	9		
3	1	2	5	6	8	9		
4	1	2	5	7				
5	3	4	1	7				
6	2	3	1	7				
7	4	5	6	1				
8	2	3	1	9				
9	8	2	3	1				

104. Edges must be created in a somewhat circuitous order, to maintain the tableau shape. Variables r and i mark the starting and ending row in column t. For example, the second part of exercise 103 begins with $i \leftarrow 1$, $t \leftarrow 8$, $r \leftarrow 1$; then $9 \mathbin{\text{—}} 1$, $i \leftarrow 2$, $t \leftarrow 6$, $r \leftarrow 3$; then $9 \mathbin{\text{—}} 3$, $9 \mathbin{\text{—}} 2$, $i \leftarrow 4$, $t \leftarrow 4$, $r \leftarrow 8$; then $9 \mathbin{\text{—}} 8$.

105. Notice that $d_k \ge k$ if and only if $c_k \ge k$. When $d_k \ge k$ we have

$$c_1 + \cdots + c_k = k^2 + \min(k, d_{k+1}) + \min(k, d_{k+2}) + \cdots + \min(k, d_n);$$

therefore the condition $d_1 + \cdots + d_k \le c_1 + \cdots + c_k - k$ is equivalent to

$$d_1 + \cdots + d_k \le f(k), \quad \text{where } f(k) = k(k-1) + \min(k, d_{k+1}) + \cdots + \min(k, d_n). \quad (*)$$

If $k \ge s$ we have $f(k + 1) - f(k) = 2k - d_{k+1} \ge d_{k+1}$; hence $(*)$ holds for $1 \le k \le n$ if and only if it holds for $1 \le k \le s$. Condition $(*)$ was discovered by P. Erdős and T. Gallai [*Matematikai Lapok* **11** (1960), 264–274]. It is obviously necessary, if we consider the edges between $\{1, \ldots, k\}$ and $\{k+1, \ldots, n\}$.

Let $a_k = d_1 + \cdots + d_k - c_1 - \cdots - c_k + k$, and suppose that $a_k > 0$ for some $k \le s$ after steps H3 and H4 have acted. Let A_j, C_j, D_j, N, and S be the numbers that correspond to a_j, c_j, d_j, n, and s *before* steps H3 and H4; thus $N = n + 1$, $D_j = d_j + (0 \text{ or } 1)$, etc. We want to prove that $A_K > 0$ for some $K \le S$.

Steps H3 and H4 have removed the bottommost q cells in column t, for some $t \ge S$, together with the rightmost cells in rows 1 through p, where $q + p = D_N$. Thus $A_j = a_j$ for $1 \le j \le p$; furthermore $A_j = a_j$ when $j \ge C_t$.

Let k be minimal with $a_k > 0$, and let $d_k = d$; notice that $c_k \le d$. If $d > t$ we have $k \le p$, hence $A_k = a_k > 0$. Therefore we may assume that $d = t - (0 \text{ or } 1)$, and $D_k = t$. If $k < j \le C_t$ we have $d_j \ge D_j - 1 = t - 1 \ge d - 1 \ge c_k - 1 \ge c_j - 1$. Therefore $A_K = a_K \ge a_k$ when $K = C_t$; we may assume that $C_t > S$.

Now $D_S = D_{S+1} = t$, so $S = t$. Also $k = t$; otherwise $c_k \ge S + 1 > t \ge d$. Therefore $s = S$ and $d = t = c_t$. Further analysis shows that the only possibility with $A_t \le 0$ is $D_j = t + [j \ge t]$ for $1 \le j \le N = t + 2$. Algorithm H does indeed change this "good" sequence into a "bad" one; but $D_1 + \cdots + D_N = t^2 + 3t - 1$ is odd.

106. False in the trivial cases when $d \le 1$ and $n \ge d + 2$. Otherwise true: In fact, the first $n - 1$ edges generated in step H4 contain no cycles, so they form a spanning tree.

107. The permutation φ of exercise 78 takes a vertex of degree d into a vertex of degree $n - 1 - d$. And φ^2 is an automorphism that pairs up two vertices of equal degree, except for a possible fixed point of degree $(n - 1)/2$.

(Conversely, a somewhat intricate extension of Algorithm H will construct a self-complementary graph from every graphical sequence that satisfies these conditions, provided that $d_{(n-1)/2} = (n-1)/2$ when n is odd. See C. R. J. Clapham and D. J. Kleitman, *J. Combinatorial Theory* **B20** (1976), 67–74.)

108. We may assume that $d_1^+ \geq \cdots \geq d_n^+$; the in-degrees d_k^- need not be in any particular order. Apply Algorithm H to the sequence $d_1 \ldots d_n = d_1^+ \ldots d_n^+$, but with the following changes: Step H2 becomes "[Done?] Terminate successfully if $d_1 = n = 0$; terminate unsuccessfully if $d_1 > n$." After setting i, t, and r in step H3, terminate unsuccessfully if $d_n^- > c_1$; otherwise do step H4 for $1 \leq j \leq d_n^-$, then set $n \leftarrow n-1$ and return to H2. In step H5, omit "$c_j \leftarrow c_j - 1$," and create the arc $k \longrightarrow n$ instead of the edge $k \text{---} n$. An argument like Lemma M and Corollary H justifies this approach.

(Exercise 7.2.1.4–57 proves that such digraphs exist if and only if $d_1^- + \cdots + d_n^- = d_1^+ + \cdots + d_n^+$ and $d_1^- \ldots d_n^- = \{d_1', \ldots, d_n'\}$, where $d_1' \geq \cdots \geq d_n'$ and $d_1' \ldots d_n'$ is majorized by the conjugate partition $c_1 \ldots c_n = (d_1^+ \ldots d_n^+)^T$. The variant where loops $v \longrightarrow v$ are forbidden is harder; see D. R. Fulkerson, *Pacific J. Math.* **10** (1960), 831–836.)

109. It's the same as exercise 108, if we put $d_k^+ = d_k[k \leq m]$ and $d_k^- = d_k[k > m]$.

110. There are p vertices of degree $d = d_1$ and q vertices of degree $d-1$, where $p+q = n$.

Case 1, $d = 2k+1$. Make $u \text{---} v$ whenever $(u - v) \bmod n \in \{2, 3, \ldots, k+1, n-k-1, \ldots, n-3, n-2\}$; also add the $p/2$ edges $1 \text{---} 2$, $3 \text{---} 4$, $\ldots$, $(p-1) \text{---} p$.

Case 2, $d = 2k$. Make $u \text{---} v$ whenever $(u - v) \bmod n \in \{2, 3, \ldots, k, n-k, \ldots, n-3, n-2\}$; also add the edges $1 \text{---} 2$, $\ldots$, $(q-1) \text{---} q$, as well as the path or cycle $(q = 0? \ n: q) \text{---} (q+1) \text{---} \cdots \text{---} (n-1) \text{---} n$. [D. L. Wang and D. J. Kleitman, in *Networks* **3** (1973), 225–239, have proved that such graphs are highly connected.]

111. Suppose $N = n + n'$ and $V' = \{n+1, \ldots, N\}$. We want to construct $e_k = d - d_k$ edges between k and V', and additional edges within V', so that each vertex of V' has degree d. Let $s = e_1 + \cdots + e_n$. This task is possible only if (i) $n' \geq \max(e_1, \ldots, e_n)$; (ii) $n'd \geq s$; (iii) $n'd \leq s + n'(n'-1)$; and (iv) $(n+n')d$ is even.

Such edges do exist whenever n' satisfies (i)–(iv): First, s suitable edges between V and V' can be created by cyclically choosing endpoints $(n+1, n+2, \ldots, n+n', n+1, \ldots)$, because of (i). This process assigns either $\lfloor s/n' \rfloor$ or $\lceil s/n' \rceil$ edges to each vertex of V'; we have $\lceil s/n' \rceil \leq d$ by (ii), and $d - \lfloor s/n' \rfloor \leq n' - 1$ by (iii). Therefore the additional edges needed inside V' are constructible by exercise 110 and (iv).

The choice $n' = n$ always works. Conversely, if $G = K_n(V) \setminus \{1 \text{---} 2\}$, condition (iii) requires $n' \geq n$ when $n \geq 4$. [P. Erdős and P. Kelly, *AMM* **70** (1963), 1074–1075.]

112. The uniquely best triangle in the *miles* data is

Saint Louis, MO $\overset{748}{\text{---}}$ Toronto, ON $\overset{746}{\text{---}}$ Winston-Salem, NC $\overset{748}{\text{---}}$ Saint Louis, MO.

113. By Murphy's Law, it has n rows and m columns; so it's $n \times m$, not $m \times n$.

114. A loop in a multigraph is an edge $\{a, a\}$ with repeated vertices, and a multigraph is a 2-uniform hypergraph. Thus we should allow the incidence matrix of a general hypergraph to have entries greater than 1 when an edge contains a vertex more than once. (A pedant would probably call this a "multihypergraph.") With these considerations in mind, the incidence matrix and bipartite graph corresponding to (26) are

$$\begin{pmatrix} 210000 \\ 011100 \\ 001122 \end{pmatrix};$$

115. The element in row e and column f of $B^T B$ is $\sum_v b_{ve} b_{vf}$; so $B^T B$ is $2I$ plus the adjacency matrix of $L(G)$. Similarly, BB^T is D plus the adjacency matrix of G, where D is the diagonal matrix with $d_{vv} = $ degree of v. (See exercises 2.3.4.2–18, 19, and 20.)

116. $\overline{K_{m,n}^{(r)}} = K_m^{(r)} \oplus K_n^{(r)}$, generalizing (38), for all $r \geq 1$.

117. The nonisomorphic multisets of singleton edges for $m = 4$ and $V = \{0, 1, 2\}$ are $\{\{0\}, \{0\}, \{0\}, \{0\}\}$, $\{\{0\}, \{0\}, \{0\}, \{1\}\}$, $\{\{0\}, \{0\}, \{1\}, \{1\}\}$, and $\{\{0\}, \{0\}, \{1\}, \{2\}\}$. The answer in general is the number of partitions of m into at most n parts, namely $\left|\begin{smallmatrix} m+n \\ n \end{smallmatrix}\right|$, using the notation explained in Section 7.2.1.4. (Of course, there's little reason to think of partitions as 1-uniform hypergraphs, except when answering strange exercises.)

118. Let d be the sum of the vertex degrees. The corresponding bipartite graph is a forest with $m + n$ vertices, d edges, and p components. Hence $d = m + n - p$, by Theorem 2.3.4.1A.

119. Then there's an additional edge, containing all seven vertices.

120. We could say that (hyper)arcs are arbitrary sequences of vertices, or sequences of distinct vertices. But most authors seem to define hyperarcs to be $A \longrightarrow v$, where A is an unordered set of vertices. When the best definition is found, it will probably be the one that has the most important practical applications.

121. $\chi(H) = |F| - \alpha(I(H)^T)$ is the size of a minimum cover of V by sets of F.

122. (a) One can verify that there are just seven 3-element covers, namely the vertices of an edge; so there are seven 4-element independent sets, namely the complements of an edge. We can't two-color the hypergraph, because one color would need to be used 4 times and the other three colors would be an edge. (Hypergraph (56) is essentially the projective plane with seven points and seven lines.)

(b) Since we're dualizing, let's call the vertices and edges of the Petersen graph "points" and "lines"; then the vertices and edges of the dual are lines and points, respectively. Color red the five lines that join an outer point to an inner point. The other ten lines are independent (they don't contain all three of the lines touching any point); so they can be colored green. No set of eleven lines can be independent, because no four lines can touch all ten points. (Thus the Petersen dual is a bipartite hypergraph, in spite of the fact that it contains cycles of length 5.)

123. They correspond to $n \times n$ latin squares, whose entries are the vertex colors.

124. Four colors easily suffice. If it were 3-colorable, there must be four vertices of each color, since no five vertices are independent. Then two opposite corners must have the same color, and a contradiction arises quickly.

125. The Chvátal graph is the smallest such graph with $g = 4$. G. Brinkmann found the smallest with $g = 5$: It has 21 vertices a_j, b_j, c_j for $0 \leq j < 7$, with edges $a_j \,\text{---}\, a_{j+2}$, $a_j \,\text{---}\, b_j$, $a_j \,\text{---}\, b_{j+1}$, $b_j \,\text{---}\, c_j$, $b_j \,\text{---}\, c_{j+2}$, $c_j \,\text{---}\, c_{j+3}$ and subscripts mod 7. M. Meringer showed that there must be at least 35 vertices if $g > 5$. B. Grünbaum conjectured that g can be arbitrarily large; but no further constructions are known. [See *AMM* **77** (1970), 1088–1092; *Graph Theory Notes of New York* **32** (1997), 40–41.]

126. When m and n are even, both C_m and C_n are bipartite, and 4-coloring is easy. Otherwise a 4-coloring is impossible. When $m = n = 3$, a 9-coloring is optimum by exercise 93. When $m = 3$ and $n = 4$ or 5, at most two vertices are independent; it's easy to find an optimum 6- or 8-coloring. Otherwise we obtain a 5-coloring by painting vertex (j, k) with $(a_j + 2b_k) \bmod 5$, where periodic sequences $\langle a_j \rangle$ and $\langle b_k \rangle$ exist with period lengths m and n, respectively, such that $a_j - a_{j+1} \equiv \pm 1$ and $b_k - b_{k+1} \equiv \pm 1$ for all j and k. [K. Vesztergombi, *Acta Cybernetica* **4** (1978), 207–212.]

127. (a) The result is true when $n = 1$. Otherwise let $H = G \setminus v$, where v is any vertex. Then $\overline{H} = \overline{G} \setminus v$, and we have $\chi(H) + \chi(\overline{H}) \leq n$ by induction. Clearly $\chi(G) \leq \chi(H) + 1$

and $\chi(\overline{G}) \leq \chi(\overline{H}) + 1$; so there's no problem unless equality holds in all three cases. But that can't happen; it implies that $\chi(H) \leq d$ and $\chi(\overline{H}) \leq n - 1 - d$, where d is the degree of v in G. [E. A. Nordhaus and J. W. Gaddum, *AMM* **63** (1956), 175–177.]

To get equality, let $G = K_a \oplus \overline{K_b}$, where $ab > 0$ and $a + b = n$. Then we have $\overline{G} = \overline{K_a} \!-\! K_b$, $\chi(G) = a$, and $\chi(\overline{G}) = b + 1$. [All graphs for which equality holds have been found by H.-J. Finck, *Wiss. Zeit. der Tech. Hochschule Ilmenau* **12** (1966), 243–246.]

(b) A k-coloring of G has at least $\lceil n/k \rceil$ vertices of some color; those vertices form a clique in $\overline{G}$. Hence $\chi(G)\chi(\overline{G}) \geq \chi(G)\lceil n/\chi(G)\rceil \geq n$. Equality holds when $G = K_n$.

(From (a) and (b) we deduce that $\chi(G)+\chi(\overline{G}) \geq 2\sqrt{n}$ and $\chi(G)\chi(\overline{G}) \leq \frac{1}{4}(n+1)^2$.)

128. $\chi(G \,\square\, H) = \max(\chi(G), \chi(H))$. This many colors is clearly necessary. And if the functions $a(u)$ and $b(v)$ color G and H with the colors $\{0, 1, \ldots, k - 1\}$, we can color $G \,\square\, H$ with $c(u, v) = (a(u) + b(v)) \bmod k$.

129. A complete row or column (16 cases); a complete diagonal of length 4 or more (18 cases); a 5-cell pattern $\{(x,y), (x\!-\!a, y\!-\!a), (x\!-\!a, y\!+\!a), (x\!+\!a, y\!-\!a), (x\!+\!a, y\!+\!a)\}$ for $a \in \{1,2,3\}$ $(36 + 16 + 4$ cases$)$; a 5-cell pattern $\{(x,y), (x\!-\!a, y), (x\!+\!a, y), (x, y\!-\!a),$ $(x, y\!+\!a)\}$ for $a \in \{1,2,3\}$ $(36 + 16 + 4$ cases$)$; a pattern containing four of those five cells, when the fifth lies off the board $(24 + 32 + 24$ cases$)$; or a 4-cell pattern $\{(x,y), (x\!+\!a, y), (x, y\!+\!a), (x\!+\!a, y\!+\!a)\}$ for $a \in \{1,3,5,7\}$ $(49 + 25 + 9 + 1$ cases$)$. Altogether 310 maximal cliques, with respectively $(168, 116, 4, 4, 18)$ of size $(4, 5, 6, 7, 8)$.

130. If graph G has p maximal cliques and graph H has q, then the join $G \!-\! H$ has pq, because the cliques of $G \!-\! H$ are simply the unions of cliques from G and H. Furthermore, the empty graph $\overline{K_n}$ has n maximal cliques (namely its singleton sets).

Thus the complete k-partite graph with part sizes $\{n_1, \ldots, n_k\}$, being the join of empty graphs of those sizes, has $n_1 \ldots n_k$ maximal cliques.

131. Assume that $n > 1$. In a complete k-partite graph, the number $n_1 \ldots n_k$ is maximized when each part has size 3, except perhaps for one or two parts of size 2. (See exercise 7.2.1.4–68(a).) So we must prove that $N(n)$ cannot be larger than this in *any* graph.

Let $m(v)$ be the number of maximal cliques that contain vertex v. If $u \not\!\!-\!\!\!\!- v$ and $m(u) \leq m(v)$, construct the graph G' that is like G except that u is now adjacent to all the neighbors of v instead of to its former neighbors. Every maximal clique U in either graph belongs to one of three classes:

   i) $u \in U$; there are $m(u)$ of these in G and $m(v)$ of them in G'.

   ii) $v \in U$; there are $m(v)$ of these in G and also in G'.

   iii) $u \notin U$ and $v \notin U$; such maximal cliques in G are also maximal in G'.

Therefore G' has at least as many maximal cliques as G. And we can obtain a complete k-partite graph by appropriately repeating the process.

[This argument, due to Paul Erdős, was presented by J. W. Moon and L. Moser in *Israel J. Math.* **3** (1965), 23–25.]

132. The strong product of cliques in G and H is a clique in $G \boxtimes H$, by exercise 93; hence $\omega(G \boxtimes H) \geq \omega(G)\omega(H) = \chi(G)\chi(H)$. On the other hand, colorings $a(u)$ and $b(v)$ of G and H lead to the coloring $c(u, v) = (a(u), b(v))$ of $G \boxtimes H$; hence $\chi(G \boxtimes H) \leq \chi(G)\chi(H)$. And $\omega(G \boxtimes H) \leq \chi(G \boxtimes H)$.

133. (a) 24; (b) 60; (c) 3; (d) 6; (e) 6; (f) 4; (g) 5; (h) 4; (i) $K_2 \boxtimes C_{12}$; (j) 18; (k) 12. (l) Yes, of degree 5. (m) No. [Can it be drawn with fewer than 12 crossings?] (n) Yes; in fact, it is 4-connected (see Section 7.4.1). (o) Yes; we consider *every* graph to be directed, with two arcs for each edge. (p) Of course not. (q) Yes, easily.

[The musical graph represents simple modulations between key signatures. It appears on page 73 of *Graphs* by R. J. Wilson and J. J. Watkins (1990).]

134. By rotating and/or swapping the inner and outer vertices, we can find an automorphism that takes any vertex into C. If C is fixed, we can interchange the inner and outer vertices of any subset of the remaining 11 pairs, and/or do a left-right reflection. Therefore there are $24 \times 2^{11} \times 2 = 98,304$ automorphisms altogether.

135. Let $\omega = e^{2\pi i/6}$, and define the matrices $Q = (q_{ij})$, $S = (s_{ij})$, where $q_{ij} = [j = (i+1) \bmod 12]$ and $s_{ij} = \omega^{ij}$, for $0 \le i, j < 12$. By exercise 96(b), the adjacency matrix of the musical graph $K_2 \boxtimes C_{12}$ is $A = \left(\begin{smallmatrix}1&1\\1&1\end{smallmatrix}\right) \otimes (I + Q + Q^-) - I$. Let T be the matrix $\left(\begin{smallmatrix}1&1\\1&-1\end{smallmatrix}\right) \otimes S$; then $T^- AT$ is a diagonal matrix D whose first 12 entries are $1 + 4\cos\frac{j\pi}{6}$ for $0 \le j < 12$, and whose other 12 entries are -1. Therefore $A^{2m} = TD^mT^-$, and it follows that the number of $2m$-step walks from C to (C, G, D, A, E, B, F$^\sharp$) respectively is

$$C_m = \tfrac{1}{24}(25^m + 2(13 + 4\sqrt{3})^m + 3^{2m+1} + 2(13 - 4\sqrt{3})^m + 16);$$
$$G_m = \tfrac{1}{24}(25^m + \sqrt{3}(13 + 4\sqrt{3})^m - \sqrt{3}(13 - 4\sqrt{3})^m - 1);$$
$$D_m = \tfrac{1}{24}(25^m + (13 + 4\sqrt{3})^m + (13 - 4\sqrt{3})^m - 3);$$
$$A_m = \tfrac{1}{24}(25^m - 3^{2m+1} + 2);$$
$$E_m = \tfrac{1}{24}(25^m - (13 + 4\sqrt{3})^m - (13 - 4\sqrt{3})^m + 1);$$
$$B_m = \tfrac{1}{24}(25^m - \sqrt{3}(13 + 4\sqrt{3})^m + \sqrt{3}(13 - 4\sqrt{3})^m - 1);$$
$$F^\sharp_m = \tfrac{1}{24}(25^m - 2(13 + 4\sqrt{3})^m + 3^{2m+1} - 2(13 - 4\sqrt{3})^m);$$

also $a_m = C_m - 1$, $d_m = F_m = e_m = G_m$, etc. In particular, $(C_6, G_6, D_6, A_6, E_6, B_6, F^\sharp_6) = (15462617, 14689116, 12784356, 10106096, 7560696, 5655936, 5015296)$, so the desired probability is $15462617/5^{12} \approx 6.33\%$. As $m \to \infty$, the probabilities are all $\frac{1}{24} + O(0.8^m)$.

136. No. Only two Cayley graphs of order 10 are cubic, namely $K_2 \square C_5$ (whose vertices can be written $\{e, \alpha, \alpha^2, \alpha^3, \alpha^4, \beta, \beta\alpha, \beta\alpha^2, \beta\alpha^3, \beta\alpha^4\}$ where $\alpha^5 = \beta^2 = (\alpha\beta)^2 = e$) and the graph with vertices $\{0, 1, \ldots, 9\}$ and arcs $v \to (v\pm 1) \bmod 10$, $v \to (v+5) \bmod 10$. [See D. A. Holton and J. Sheehan, *The Petersen Graph* (1993), exercise 9.10. Incidentally, the SGB graphs $raman(p, q, t, 0)$ are Cayley graphs.]

137. Let $[x, y]$ denote the label of (x, y); we want $[x, y] = [x + a, y + b] = [x + c, y + d]$ for all x and y. If A is the matrix $\left(\begin{smallmatrix}a&b\\c&d\end{smallmatrix}\right)$, the operation of adding t times the bottom row of A to the top row changes A to the matrix $A' = \left(\begin{smallmatrix}1&t\\0&1\end{smallmatrix}\right)A = \left(\begin{smallmatrix}a'&b'\\c'&d'\end{smallmatrix}\right)$, where $a' = a + tc$, $b' = b + td$, $c' = c$, $d' = d$. The new condition $[x, y] = [x + a', y + b'] = [x + c', y + d']$ is equivalent to the old; and $\gcd(a', b', c', d') = \gcd(a, b, c, d)$. Similarly we can premultiply A by $\left(\begin{smallmatrix}1&0\\t&1\end{smallmatrix}\right)$ without really changing the problem.

We can also operate on columns, replacing A by $A'' = A\left(\begin{smallmatrix}1&t\\0&1\end{smallmatrix}\right) = \left(\begin{smallmatrix}a''&b''\\c''&d''\end{smallmatrix}\right)$, where $a'' = a$, $b'' = ta + b$, $c'' = c$, $d'' = tc + d$. This operation does alter the problem, but only slightly: If we find a labeling that satisfies $[\![x, y]\!] = [\![x + a'', y + b'']\!] = [\![x + c'', y + d'']\!]$ for all x and y, then we'll have $[x, y] = [x + a, y + b] = [x + c, x + d]$ if $[x, y] = [\![x, y + tx]\!]$. Similarly we can postmultiply A by $\left(\begin{smallmatrix}1&0\\t&1\end{smallmatrix}\right)$; the problem remains almost the same.

A series of such row and column operations will reduce A to the simple form $UAV = \left(\begin{smallmatrix}1&0\\0&n\end{smallmatrix}\right)$, where U and V are integer matrices with $\det U = \det V = 1$. And if we have $V = \left(\begin{smallmatrix}\alpha&\beta\\\gamma&\delta\end{smallmatrix}\right)$, a labeling for the reduced problem that satisfies the simple conditions $[\![x, y]\!] = [\![x + 1, y]\!] = [\![x, y + n]\!]$ will provide a solution to the original labeling problem if we define $[x, y] = [\![\alpha x + \gamma y, \beta x + \delta y]\!]$.

Finally, the reduced labeling problem is easy: We let $[\![x, y]\!] = y \bmod n$. Thus the desired answer is to set $p = \beta$, $q = \delta$.

138. Proceeding as before, but with a $k \times k$ matrix A, row and column operations will reduce the problem to a diagonal matrix UAV. The diagonal entries $(d_1, \ldots, d_k)$ are characterized by the condition that $d_1 \ldots d_j$ is the greatest common divisor of the determinants of all $j \times j$ submatrices of A. [This is "Smith normal form"; see H. J. S. Smith, *Philosophical Transactions* **151** (1861), 293–326, §14.] If the labeling $[\![x]\!]$ satisfies the reduced problem, the original problem is satisfied by $[x] = [\![xV]\!]$. The number of elements in the generalized torus is $n = \det A = d_1 \ldots d_k$.

The reduced problem has a simple solution as before if $d_1 = \cdots = d_{k-1} = 1$. But in general the reduced labeling will be an r-dimensional ordinary torus of dimensions $(d_{k-r+1}, \ldots, d_k)$, where $d_{k-r+1} > d_{k-r} = 1$. (Here $d_0 = 1$; we might have $r = k$.)

In the requested example, we find $d_1 = 1$, $d_2 = 2$, $d_3 = 10$, $n = 20$; indeed,

$$UAV = \begin{pmatrix} 1 & -2 & 0 \\ 0 & 1 & -1 \\ -1 & -1 & 4 \end{pmatrix} \begin{pmatrix} 3 & 1 & 1 \\ 1 & 3 & 1 \\ 1 & 1 & 3 \end{pmatrix} \begin{pmatrix} 1 & 5 & 6 \\ 0 & 1 & 1 \\ 0 & 0 & 1 \end{pmatrix} = \begin{pmatrix} 1 & 0 & 0 \\ 0 & 2 & 0 \\ 0 & 0 & 10 \end{pmatrix}.$$

Each point (x, y, z) now receives a two-dimensional label $(u, v) = ((5x + y) \bmod 2, (6x + y + z) \bmod 10)$. The six neighbors of (u, v) are $((u \pm 1) \bmod 2, v)$, $((u \pm 1) \bmod 2, (v \pm 1) \bmod 10)$, $(u, (v \pm 1) \bmod 10)$. It's a multigraph, since the first two neighbors are identical; but it's not the same as the multigraph $C_2 \boxtimes C_{10}$, which has degree 8.

[Generalized toruses are essentially the Cayley graphs of Abelian groups; see exercise 136. They have been proposed as convenient interconnection networks, in which case it is desirable to minimize the diameter when k and n are given. See C. K. Wong and D. Coppersmith, *JACM* **21** (1974), 392–402; C. M. Fiduccia, R. W. Forcade, and J. S. Zito, *SIAM J. Discrete Math.* **11** (1998), 157–167.]

139. (This exercise helps clarify the distinction between labeled graphs G, in which the vertices have definite names, and unlabeled graphs H such as those in Fig. 2.) If N_H is the number of labeled graphs on $\{1, 2, \ldots, h\}$ that are isomorphic to H, and if U is any h-element subset of V, the probability that $G \mid U$ is isomorphic to H is $N_H/2^{h(h-1)/2}$. Therefore the answer is $\binom{n}{h} N_H/2^{h(h-1)/2}$. We need only figure out the value of N_H, which is: (a) 1; (b) $h!/2$; (c) $(h - 1)!/2$; (d) $h!/a$, where H has a automorphisms.

140. (a) $\#(K_3{:}W_n) = n-1$ and $\#(P_3{:}W_n) = \binom{n-1}{2}$ for $n \geq 5$; also $\#(\overline{K_3}{:}W_8) = 7$.

(b) G is proportional if and only if $\#(K_3{:}G) = \#(\overline{K_3}{:}G) = \frac{1}{8}\binom{n}{3}$ and $\#(P_3{:}G) = \#(\overline{P_3}{:}G) = \frac{3}{8}\binom{n}{3}$. If G has e edges, we have $(n-2)e = 3\#(K_3{:}G)+2\#(P_3{:}G)+\#(\overline{P_3}{:}G)$, because every pair of vertices appears in $n-2$ induced subgraphs. If G has degree sequence $d_1 \ldots d_n$, we have $d_1 + \cdots + d_n = 2e$, $\binom{d_1}{2} + \cdots + \binom{d_n}{2} = 3\#(K_3{:}G)+\#(P_3{:}G)$, and $d_1(n-1-d_1)+\cdots+d_n(n-1-d_n) = 2\#(P_3{:}G)+2\#(\overline{P_3}{:}G)$. Therefore a proportional graph satisfies $(*)$ — unless $n = 2$. (The exercise should have excluded that case.)

Conversely, if G satisfies $(*)$ and has the correct $\#(K_3{:}G)$, it also has the correct $\#(P_3{:}G)$, $\#(\overline{P_3}{:}G)$, and $\#(\overline{K_3}{:}G)$.

[*References:* S. Janson and J. Kratochvíl, *Random Structures & Algorithms* **2** (1991), 209–224. In *J. Combinatorial Theory* **B47** (1989), 125–145, A. D. Barbour, M. Karoński, and A. Ruciński had shown that the variance of $\#(H{:}G)$ is proportional to either n^{2h-2}, n^{2h-3}, or n^{2h-4}, where the first case occurs when H does not have $\frac{1}{2}\binom{h}{2}$ edges, and the third case occurs when H is a proportional graph.]

141. Only 8 degree sequences $d_1 \ldots d_8$ satisfy $(*)$: $73333333\,(1/2)$, $65433322\,(26/64)$, $64444222\,(2/10)$, $64443331\,(8/22)$, $55543222\,(8/20)$, $55533331\,(2/10)$, $55444321\,(26/64)$, and 44444440 (1/2). Each degree sequence is shown here with statistics (N_1/N), where N nonisomorphic graphs have that sequence and N_1 of them are proportional. The last three cases are complements of the first three. No graph of order 8 is both proportional and self-complementary. Maximally symmetric examples of the first five cases are W_8,

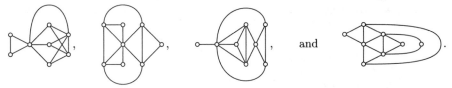

, , , and .

142. The hint follows as in the previous answer; $(n-3)\#(\overline{K_3}{:}G)$ and $(n-3)\#(P_3{:}G)$ can also be expressed in terms of four-vertex counts. Furthermore, a graph with e edges has $\binom{e}{2} = \#(P_3 \subseteq G) + \#(K_2 \oplus K_2 \subseteq G)$, because any two edges form either P_3 or $K_2 \oplus K_2$; in this formula, $\#(P_3 \subseteq G)$ counts not-necessarily-induced subgraphs.

We have $\#(P_3 \subseteq G) = \#(P_3{:}G) + 3\#(K_3{:}G)$, and a similar formula expresses $\#(K_2 \oplus K_2 \subseteq G)$ in terms of induced counts. Thus an extraproportional graph must be proportional and satisfy $e = \frac{1}{2}\binom{n}{2}$, $\#(P_3 \subseteq G) = \frac{3}{4}\binom{n}{3}$, $\#(K_2 \oplus K_2 \subseteq G) = \frac{3}{4}\binom{n}{4}$. But these values contradict the formula for $\binom{e}{2}$.

143. Consider the graph whose vertices are the rows of A, and whose edges $u \,\text{---}\, v$ signify that rows u and v agree except in one column, j. Label such an edge j.

If the graph contains a cycle, delete any edge of the cycle, and repeat the process until no cycles remain. Notice that the label on every deleted edge appears elsewhere in its cycle; hence the deletions don't affect the set of edge labels. But we're left with fewer than $m \le n$ edges, by Theorem 2.3.4.1A; so there are fewer than n different labels. [See J. A. Bondy, *J. Combinatorial Theory* **B12** (1972), 201–202.]

144. Let G be the graph on vertices $\{1, \dots, m\}$, with edges $i \,\text{---}\, j$ if and only if $* \ne x_{il} \ne x_{jl} \ne *$ for some l. This graph is k-colorable if and only if there is a completion with at most k distinct rows. Conversely, if G is a graph on vertices $\{1, \dots, n\}$, with adjacency matrix A, the $n \times n$ matrix $X = A + *(J - I - A)$ has the property that $i \,\text{---}\, j$ if and only if $* \ne x_{il} \ne x_{jl} \ne *$ for some l. [See M. Sauerhoff and I. Wegener, *IEEE Trans.* **CAD-15** (1996), 1435–1437.]

145. Set $c \leftarrow 0$ and repeat the following operations for $1 \le j \le n$: If $c = 0$, set $x \leftarrow a_j$ and $c \leftarrow 1$; otherwise if $x = a_j$, set $c \leftarrow c + 1$; otherwise set $c \leftarrow c - 1$. Then x is the answer. The idea is to keep track of a possible majority element x, which occurs c times in nondiscarded elements; we discard a_j and one x whenever finding $x \ne a_j$. [See *Automated Reasoning* (Kluwer, 1991), 105–117. Extensions to find all elements that occur more than n/k times, in $O(n \log k)$ steps, have been discussed by J. Misra and D. Gries, *Science of Computer Programming* **2** (1982), 143–152.]

SECTION 7.1.1

1. (Solution by C. Sartena.) He was describing the implication $x \Rightarrow y$, with "it" standing respectively for y, x, x, y, y, x. (Other solutions are possible.)

2. The Earth operation corresponding to the Pincusian $x \circ y$ is $\overline{\overline{x} \circ \overline{y}}$; its truth table is therefore the reverse of the complement of the truth table for $\circ$. Hence the respective answers are $\top, \vee, \subset, \mathsf{L}, \supset, \mathsf{R}, \equiv, \wedge, \overline{\wedge}, \oplus, \overline{\mathsf{R}}, \overline{\supset}, \overline{\mathsf{L}}, \overline{\subset}, \overline{\vee}, \bot$. (Any identity involving the 16 operations of Table 1 implies a corresponding dual identity obtained by substituting the Pincusian equivalents. For example, each of De Morgan's laws (11) and (12) is the dual of the other, as are the identities (3), (4) relating $\equiv$ and $\oplus$. In this sense $\equiv$ can be considered to be just as useful as its dual, $\oplus$.)

3. (a) $\vee$; (b) $\wedge$; (c) $\overline{\mathsf{L}}$; (d) $\equiv$. [Many formulas actually work out better if we use -1 for truth and $+1$ for falsehood, even though this convention seems a bit immoral; then $x \cdot y$ corresponds to $\oplus$. Notice that $\langle xyz \rangle = \operatorname{sign}(x + y + z)$, with either convention.]

4. [*Trans. Amer. Math. Soc.* **14** (1913), 481–488.] (a) Start with the truth tables for L and R; then compute truth table $\alpha \overline{\wedge} \beta$ bitwise from each known pair of truth tables α and β, generating the results in order of the length of each formula and writing down a shortest formula that leads to each new 4-bit table:

$\bot$: $(x \overline{\wedge} (x \overline{\wedge} x)) \overline{\wedge} (x \overline{\wedge} (x \overline{\wedge} x))$	$\overline{\vee}$: $(x \overline{\wedge} (x \overline{\wedge} x)) \overline{\wedge} ((y \overline{\wedge} y) \overline{\wedge} (x \overline{\wedge} x))$
$\wedge$: $(x \overline{\wedge} y) \overline{\wedge} (x \overline{\wedge} y)$	$\equiv$: $(x \overline{\wedge} y) \overline{\wedge} ((y \overline{\wedge} y) \overline{\wedge} (x \overline{\wedge} x))$
$\overline{\supset}$: $(x \overline{\wedge} (x \overline{\wedge} y)) \overline{\wedge} (x \overline{\wedge} (x \overline{\wedge} y))$	$\overline{\mathsf{R}}$: $y \overline{\wedge} y$
L: x	$\subset$: $y \overline{\wedge} (x \overline{\wedge} x)$
$\overline{\subset}$: $(y \overline{\wedge} (x \overline{\wedge} x)) \overline{\wedge} (y \overline{\wedge} (x \overline{\wedge} x))$	$\overline{\mathsf{L}}$: $x \overline{\wedge} x$
R: y	$\supset$: $x \overline{\wedge} (x \overline{\wedge} y)$
$\oplus$: $(y \overline{\wedge} (x \overline{\wedge} x)) \overline{\wedge} (x \overline{\wedge} (x \overline{\wedge} y))$	$\overline{\wedge}$: $x \overline{\wedge} y$
$\vee$: $(y \overline{\wedge} y) \overline{\wedge} (x \overline{\wedge} x)$	$\top$: $x \overline{\wedge} (x \overline{\wedge} x)$

(b) In this case we start with four tables $\bot, \top, \mathsf{L}, \mathsf{R}$, and we prefer formulas with fewer occurrences of variables whenever there's a choice between formulas of a given length:

$\bot$: 0	$\overline{\vee}$: $1 \overline{\wedge} ((y \overline{\wedge} 1) \overline{\wedge} (x \overline{\wedge} 1))$
$\wedge$: $(x \overline{\wedge} y) \overline{\wedge} 1$	$\equiv$: $(x \overline{\wedge} y) \overline{\wedge} ((y \overline{\wedge} 1) \overline{\wedge} (x \overline{\wedge} 1))$
$\overline{\supset}$: $((y \overline{\wedge} 1) \overline{\wedge} x) \overline{\wedge} 1$	$\overline{\mathsf{R}}$: $y \overline{\wedge} 1$
L: x	$\subset$: $y \overline{\wedge} (x \overline{\wedge} 1)$
$\overline{\subset}$: $(y \overline{\wedge} (x \overline{\wedge} 1)) \overline{\wedge} 1$	$\overline{\mathsf{L}}$: $x \overline{\wedge} 1$
R: y	$\supset$: $(y \overline{\wedge} 1) \overline{\wedge} x$
$\oplus$: $(y \overline{\wedge} (x \overline{\wedge} 1)) \overline{\wedge} ((y \overline{\wedge} 1) \overline{\wedge} x)$	$\overline{\wedge}$: $x \overline{\wedge} y$
$\vee$: $(y \overline{\wedge} 1) \overline{\wedge} (x \overline{\wedge} 1)$	$\top$: 1

5. (a) $\bot$: $x \overline{\subset} x$; $\wedge$: $(x \overline{\subset} y) \overline{\subset} y$; $\overline{\supset}$: $y \overline{\subset} x$; L: x; $\overline{\subset}$: $x \overline{\subset} y$; R: y;   the other 10 cannot be expressed.   (b) With constants, however, all 16 are possible:

$\bot$: 0	$\overline{\vee}$: $y \overline{\subset} (x \overline{\subset} 1)$
$\wedge$: $(y \overline{\subset} 1) \overline{\subset} x$	$\equiv$: $(y \overline{\subset} x) \overline{\subset} ((x \overline{\subset} y) \overline{\subset} 1)$
$\overline{\supset}$: $y \overline{\subset} x$	$\overline{\mathsf{R}}$: $y \overline{\subset} 1$
L: x	$\subset$: $(x \overline{\subset} y) \overline{\subset} 1$
$\overline{\subset}$: $x \overline{\subset} y$	$\overline{\mathsf{L}}$: $x \overline{\subset} 1$
R: y	$\supset$: $(y \overline{\subset} x) \overline{\subset} 1$
$\oplus$: $((y \overline{\subset} x) \overline{\subset} ((x \overline{\subset} y) \overline{\subset} 1)) \overline{\subset} 1$	$\overline{\wedge}$: $((y \overline{\subset} 1) \overline{\subset} x) \overline{\subset} 1$
$\vee$: $(y \overline{\subset} (x \overline{\subset} 1)) \overline{\subset} 1$	$\top$: 1

[B. A. Bernstein, *University of California Publications in Mathematics* **1** (1914), 87–96.]

6. (a) $\perp, \wedge, \mathsf{L}, \mathsf{R}, \oplus, \vee, \equiv, \top$. (b) $\perp, \mathsf{L}, \mathsf{R}, \oplus, \equiv, \top$. [Notice that all of these operators are associative. In fact, the stated identity implies the associative law in general: First we have (i) $(x \circ y) \circ ((z \circ y) \circ w) = ((x \circ z) \circ (z \circ y)) \circ ((z \circ y) \circ w) = (x \circ z) \circ w$, and similarly (ii) $(x \circ (y \circ z)) \circ (y \circ w) = x \circ (z \circ w)$. Furthermore (iii) $(x \circ y) \circ (z \circ w) = (x \circ y) \circ ((z \circ y) \circ (y \circ w)) = (x \circ z) \circ (y \circ w)$ by (i). Thus $(x \circ z) \circ w = (x \circ z) \circ ((z \circ z) \circ w) = (x \circ (z \circ z)) \circ (z \circ w) = x \circ (z \circ w)$ by (i), (iii), (ii). The free system generated by $\{x_1, \ldots, x_n\}$ has exactly $n + 2^n n^2$ distinct elements, namely $\{x_j \mid 1 \le j \le n\}$ and $\{x_i \circ x_{j_1} \circ \cdots \circ x_{j_r} \circ x_k \mid r \ge 0 \text{ and } 1 \le i, k \le n \text{ and } 1 \le j_1 < \cdots < j_r \le n\}$.]

7. Equivalently, we want the identity $y \circ (x \circ y) = x$, which holds only for $\oplus$ and $\equiv$. [Jevons noticed this property of $\oplus$ in *Pure Logic* §151, but he did not pursue the matter. We will investigate general systems of this nature, called "gropes," in Section 7.2.3.]

8. $(\{\perp, \wedge, \overline{\mathsf{C}}\}, S_0)$, $(\{\top, \vee, \supset\}, S_1)$, $(\{\mathsf{L}, \overline{\mathsf{L}}\}, S_0 \cap S_1)$, $(\{\oplus, \equiv, \overline{\mathsf{R}}\}, S_2)$, $(\{\overline{\supset}, \overline{\vee}\}, S_0 \cap S_2)$, $(\{\mathsf{C}, \overline{\wedge}\}, S_1 \cap S_2)$, and (R, any), where $S_0 = \{\mathbin{\raisebox{0.2ex}{$\scriptstyle\square$}} \mid 0 \mathbin{\raisebox{0.2ex}{$\scriptstyle\square$}} 0 = 0\}$, $S_1 = \{\mathbin{\raisebox{0.2ex}{$\scriptstyle\square$}} \mid 1 \mathbin{\raisebox{0.2ex}{$\scriptstyle\square$}} 1 = 1\}$, and $S_2 = \{\mathbin{\raisebox{0.2ex}{$\scriptstyle\square$}} \mid \bar{x}\mathbin{\raisebox{0.2ex}{$\scriptstyle\square$}}\bar{y} = \overline{x\mathbin{\raisebox{0.2ex}{$\scriptstyle\square$}}y}\} = \{\mathsf{L}, \mathsf{R}, \overline{\mathsf{L}}, \overline{\mathsf{R}}\}$. Thus 92 of the 256 pairs are left-distributive. [This problem and those of exercise 6 were first treated by E. Schröder in §55 of his posthumously published *Vorlesungen über die Algebra der Logik* **2**, 2 (1905). He expressed the answer by saying in essence that the respective truth tables $(pqrs, wxyz)$ of $(\circ, \mathbin{\raisebox{0.2ex}{$\scriptstyle\square$}})$ must satisfy the relation $((pq \vee rs) \wedge \bar{z}) \vee ((\bar{p}\bar{q} \vee \bar{r}\bar{s}) \wedge w) \vee ((p\bar{q} \vee r\bar{s}) \wedge ((w \equiv z) \vee (x \equiv y))) = 0$.]

9. (a) False; $(x \oplus y) \vee z = (x \vee z) \oplus (y \vee z) \oplus z$. (b) True, because the identity obviously holds when $z = 0$ and when $z = 1$. (c) True; it's also $(x \oplus y) \vee (x \oplus z) = 1 - [x = y = z]$.

10. The first stage of decomposition (16) yields the functions with truth tables $g = 10100011$ and $h = 10100011 \oplus 10010011 = 00110000$; and the process continues in a similar way, yielding $1 + y + xz + w + wy + wx + wxz$ (modulo 2).

11. The stated term is present if and only if $f(x_1, \ldots, x_n)$ is true an odd number of times when $x_1 = x_4 = x_5 = x_7 = x_9 = x_{10} = \cdots = 0$. (There are 2^k such cases when we set all but k variables to zero.) In other words the multilinear representation can be expressed in a suggestive notation like

$$f(x, y, z) = (f_{000} + f_{00*}z + f_{0*0}y + f_{0**}yz + f_{*00}x + f_{*0*}xz + f_{**0}xy + f_{***}xyz) \bmod 2$$

illustrated here for $n = 3$, where $f_{**0} = f(1, 1, 0) \oplus f(1, 0, 0) \oplus f(0, 1, 0) \oplus f(0, 0, 0)$, etc.

12. (a) Substitute $1 - w$ for $\bar{w}$, etc., in (23), getting $1 - y - xz + 2xyz - w + wy + wx + wxz - 2wxyz$. [Some authors have called this the "Zhegalkin polynomial"; but I. I. Zhegalkin himself always worked modulo 2. Other names in the literature are "availability polynomial," "reliability polynomial," "characteristic polynomial."]

(b) The corresponding coefficients for an arbitrary n-ary function can be as large as 2^{n-1} in absolute value (and this, by induction, is the maximum). For example, the integer multilinear representation of $x_1 \oplus \cdots \oplus x_n$ over the integers turns out to be $e_1 - 2e_2 + 4e_3 - \cdots + (-2)^{n-1}e_n$, where e_k is the kth elementary symmetric function of $\{x_1, \ldots, x_n\}$. The formula in the previous answer becomes

$$f(x, y, z) = f_{000} + f_{00*}z + f_{0*0}y + f_{0**}yz + f_{*00}x + f_{*0*}xz + f_{**0}xy + f_{***}xyz$$

over the integers, where we now have $f_{**0} = f(1, 1, 0) - f(1, 0, 0) - f(0, 1, 0) + f(0, 0, 0)$, etc. This expansion is a disguised form of the Hadamard transform, Eq. 4.6.4–(38).

(c,d) The polynomial is the sum of its minterms like $x_1(1 - x_2)(1 - x_3)x_4$. Each minterm is nonnegative for $0 \le x_1, \ldots, x_n \le 1$, and the sum of all minterms is 1.

(e) $\partial f / \partial x_j = h(x) - g(x)$, where $h(x) \ge g(x)$ by (d). (See exercise 21.)

13. In fact, F is precisely the integer multilinear representation (see exercise 12).

14. Let $r_j = p_j/(1 - p_j)$. We want $f(0,0,0) = 0$ and $f(1,1,1) = 1 \Leftrightarrow r_1 r_2 r_3 > 1$, $f(0,0,1) = 0$ and $f(1,1,0) = 1 \Leftrightarrow r_1 r_2 > r_3$, $f(0,1,0) = 0$ and $f(1,0,1) = 1 \Leftrightarrow r_1 r_3 > r_2$, $f(0,1,1) = 0$ and $f(1,0,0) = 1 \Leftrightarrow r_1 > r_2 r_3$. So we get (a) $\langle x_1 x_2 x_3 \rangle$; (b) x_1; (c) $\bar{x}_3$.

15. Exercise 1.2.6–10 tells us that $\binom{x}{k} \bmod 2 = [x \,\&\, k = k]$. Hence, for example, $\binom{x}{11} \equiv x_4 \wedge x_2 \wedge x_1$ (modulo 2) when $x = (x_n \ldots x_1)_2$; and we can obtain every term in a multilinear representation like (19) in this way. Moreover, we needn't work mod 2, because the interpolating polynomial $\binom{x}{11}\binom{15-x}{4}$ represents $x_4 \wedge \bar{x}_3 \wedge x_2 \wedge x_1$ exactly.

16. Yes, or even by $+$, because different minterms can't be simultaneously true. (But we can't do that in ordinary disjunctive normal forms like (25). See exercise 35.)

17. The binary operation $\bar{\wedge}$ is not associative, so an expression like $x \,\bar{\wedge}\, y \,\bar{\wedge}\, z$ must be interpreted as a *ternary* operation. Quick's notation is fine if one understands NAND to be an n-ary operation, being careful to note that the NAND of a *single* variable x is $\bar{x}$.

18. If not, we could set $u_1 \leftarrow \cdots \leftarrow u_s \leftarrow 1$ and $v_1 \leftarrow \cdots \leftarrow v_t \leftarrow 0$, making f both true and false. (And if we consider applying the distributive law (2) repeatedly to a DNF until it becomes a CNF, we find that the converse is also true: The disjunction $v_1 \vee \cdots \vee v_t$ is implied by f if and only if it has a literal in common with every implicant of f, if and only if it has a literal in common with every prime implicant of f, if and only if it has a literal in common with every implicant of some DNF for f.)

19. The maximal subcubes contained in 0010, 0011, 0101, 0110, 1000, 1001, 1010, and 1011 are 0∗10, 0101, ∗01∗, and 10∗∗; so the answer is $(w \vee \bar{y} \vee z) \wedge (w \vee \bar{x} \vee y \vee \bar{z}) \wedge (x \vee \bar{y}) \wedge (\bar{w} \vee x)$. (This CNF is also shortest.)

20. True. The corresponding maximal subcube is contained in some maximal subcubes f' and g', and their intersection can't be larger. (This observation is due to Samson and Mills, whose paper is cited in answer 31 below.)

21. By Boole's law (20), we see that an n-ary function f is monotone if and only if its $(n-1)$-ary projections g and h are monotone and satisfy $g \leq h$. Therefore

$$f = (g \wedge \bar{x}_n) \vee (h \wedge x_n) = (g \wedge \bar{x}_n) \vee (g \wedge x_n) \vee (h \wedge x_n) = g \vee (h \wedge x_n),$$

so we can do without complementation. The constants 0 and 1 disappear unless the function is identically constant. Conversely, any expression built up from $\wedge$ and $\vee$ is obviously monotone.

Note on terminology: Strictly speaking, we should say "monotone nondecreasing" instead of simply "monotone," if we want to preserve the language of classical mathematics, because a decreasing function of a real variable is also said to be monotonic. (See, for example, the "run test" in Section 3.3.2G.) But "nondecreasing" is quite a mouthful; so researchers who work extensively on Boolean functions have almost unanimously opted to assume that "monotone" automatically implies nondecreasing, in a Boolean context. Similarly, the mathematical term "positive function" normally refers to a function whose value exceeds zero; but authors who write about "positive Boolean functions" are referring to the functions that we are calling monotone. Since a monotone function is order-preserving, some authors have adopted the term *isotone*; but that word has already been coopted by physicists, chemists, and musicologists.

A Boolean function like $\bar{x} \vee y$, which becomes monotone if some subset of its variables is complemented, is called *unate*. Theorem Q obviously applies to unate functions.

22. Both g and $g \oplus h$ must be monotone, and $g(x) \wedge h(x) = 0$.

23. $x \wedge (v \vee y) \wedge (v \vee z) \wedge (w \vee z)$. (Corollary Q applies also to *conjunctive* prime forms of monotone functions. Therefore, to solve any problem of this kind, we need only apply the distributive law (2) until no $\wedge$ occurs within a $\vee$, then remove any clause that contains all the variables of another.)

24. By induction on k, the similar tree with $\vee$ at the root gives a function with $2^{2^{\lceil k/2 \rceil}-1}$ prime implicants of length $2^{\lfloor k/2 \rfloor}$, while the tree with $\wedge$ gives $4^{2^{\lfloor k/2 \rfloor}-1}$ of length $2^{\lceil k/2 \rceil}$. When $k = 6$, for example, the $4^7 = 2^{14}$ prime implicants in the $\wedge$ case have the form

$$x_{(0t_00t_00t_{000})_2} \wedge x_{(0t_00t_00 1t_{001})_2} \wedge x_{(0t_01t_01 0t_{010})_2} \wedge x_{(0t_01t_01 1t_{011})_2}$$

$$\wedge\, x_{(1t_10t_10 0t_{100})_2} \wedge x_{(1t_10t_10 1t_{101})_2} \wedge x_{(1t_11t_11 0t_{110})_2} \wedge x_{(1t_11t_11 1t_{111})_2},$$

with the t's either 0 or 1. [For further information about such Boolean functions, see D. E. Knuth and R. W. Moore, *Artificial Intelligence* **6** (1975), 293–326; V. Gurvich and L. Khachiyan, *Discrete Mathematics* **169** (1997), 245–248.]

25. Let a_n be the answer. Then $a_2 = a_3 = 2$, $a_4 = 3$, and $a_n = a_{n-2} + a_{n-3}$ for $n > 4$, because the prime implicants when $n > 4$ are either $p_{n-2} \wedge x_{n-1}$ or $p_{n-3} \wedge x_{n-2} \wedge x_n$ for some prime implicant p_k in the k-variable case. (These prime implicants correspond to minimal vertex covers of the path graph P_n. They are *shellable*, in the sense of exercise 35, when listed in lexicographic order. We have $a_n = (7P_n + 10P_{n+1} + P_{n+2})/23$ when P_n is the Perrin number of exercise 7.1.4–15.)

26. (a) Let $x_j = [j \in J]$. Then $f(x) = 0$ and $g(x) = 1$. (This fact was exercise 18.)

(b) Suppose, for example, that $k \in J \in \mathcal{G}$ and $k \notin \bigcup_{I \in \mathcal{F}} I$, and assume that test (a) has been passed. Let $x_j = [j \in J$ and $j \neq k]$. Then $f(x) = 1$; and $g(x) = 0$, because every $J' \in \mathcal{G}$ with $J' \neq J$ contains an element $\notin J$.

(c) Again assume that condition (a) has been ruled out. If, say, $|J| > |\mathcal{F}|$, let $x_j = [j$ is the smallest element of $I \cap J$, for some $I \in \mathcal{F}]$. Then $f(x) = 1$, $g(x) = 0$.

(d) Now we assume that $\bigcup_{I \in \mathcal{F}} I = \bigcup_{J \in \mathcal{G}} J$. Each $I \in \mathcal{F}$ stands for $2^{n-|I|}$ vectors where $f(x) = 0$; similarly, each $J \in \mathcal{G}$ stands for $2^{n-|J|}$ vectors where $g(x) = 1$. If the sum s is less than 2^n, we can compute $s = s_0 + s_1$, where s_0 counts the contributions to s when $x_n = 0$. If $s_0 < 2^{n-1}$, set $x_n \leftarrow 0$; otherwise $s_1 < 2^{n-1}$, so we set $x_n \leftarrow 1$. Then we set $n \leftarrow n - 1$; eventually all x_j are known, and $f(x) = 1$, $g(x) = 0$.

27. Let $m = \min(\{|I| \mid I \in \mathcal{F}\} \cup \{|J| \mid J \in \mathcal{G}\})$ be the length of the shortest prime clause or implicant. Then $N \cdot 2^{n-m} \geq \sum_{I \in \mathcal{F}} 2^{n-|I|} + \sum_{J \in \mathcal{G}} 2^{n-|J|} \geq 2^n$; so we have $m \leq \lg N$. If, say, $|I| = m$, some index k must appear in at least $1/m$ of the members $J \in \mathcal{G}$, because each J intersects I. This observation proves the hint.

Now let $A(0) = A(1) = 1$ and $A(v) = 1 + A(v-1) + A(\lfloor \rho v \rfloor)$ for $v > 1$. Then $A(|\mathcal{F}||\mathcal{G}|)$ is an upper bound on the number of recursive calls (the number of times X1 is performed). Letting $B(v) = A(v) + 1$, we have $B(v) = B(v-1) + B(\lfloor \rho v \rfloor)$ for $v > 1$, hence $B(v) \leq B(v-k) + kB(\lfloor \rho v \rfloor)$ for $v > k$. Taking $k = v - \lfloor \rho v \rfloor$ shows that $B(v) \leq ((1-\rho)v + 2)B(\lfloor \rho v \rfloor)$; hence $B(v) = O(((1-\rho)v + 2)^t)$ when $\rho^t v \leq 1$, namely when $t \geq \ln v / \ln(1/\rho) = \Theta((\log v)(\log N))$. Consequently $A(|\mathcal{F}||\mathcal{G}|) \leq A(N^2/4) = N^{O(\log N)^2}$.

In practice the algorithm will run much faster than the pessimistic bounds just derived. Since the prime clauses of a function are the prime implicants of its dual, this problem is essentially the same as verifying that one given DNF is the dual of another. Moreover, if we start with $f(x) = 0$ and repeatedly find minimal x's where $f(x) = g(\bar{x}) = 0$, we can "grow" f until we've obtained the dual of g.

The ideas presented here are due to M. L. Fredman and L. Khachiyan, *J. Algorithms* **21** (1996), 618–628, who also presented refinements that reduce the running time to $N^{O(\log N/ \log \log N)}$. No polynomial-time algorithm is known; yet the problem is unlikely to be NP-complete, because we can solve it in less-than-exponential time.

28. This result is obvious once understood, but the notations and terminology can make it confusing; so let's consider a concrete example: If, say, $y_1 = y_4 = y_6 = 1$ and the other y_k are zero, the function g is true if and only if the prime implicants p_1, p_4, and p_6 cover all the places where f is true. Thus we see that there is a one-to-one correspondence between every implicant of g and every DNF for f that contains only prime implicants p_j. In this correspondence, the prime implicants of g correspond to the "irredundant" DNFs in which no p_j can be left out.

Numerous refinements of this principle have been discussed by R. B. Cutler and S. Muroga, *IEEE Transactions* **C-36** (1987), 277–292.

29. B1. [Initialize.] Set $k \leftarrow k' \leftarrow 0$. (Similar methods are discussed in exercise 5–19.)

B2. [Find a zero.] Increase k zero or more times, until either $k = m$ (terminate) or $v_k \mathbin{\&} 2^j = 0$.

B3. [Make $k' > k$.] If $k' \leq k$, set $k' \leftarrow k + 1$.

B4. [Advance k'.] Increase k' zero or more times, until either $k' = m$ (terminate) or $v_{k'} \geq v_k + 2^j$.

B5. [Skip past a big mismatch.] If $v_k \oplus v_{k'} \geq 2^{j+1}$, set $k \leftarrow k'$ and return to B2.

B6. [Record a match.] If $v_{k'} = v_k + 2^j$, output (k, k').

B7. [Advance k.] Set $k \leftarrow k + 1$ and return to B2. ∎

(Steps B3 and B5 are optional, but recommended.)

30. The following algorithm keeps variable-length, sorted lists in a stack S whose size will never exceed $2m + n$. When the topmost entry of the stack is $S_t = s$, the topmost list is the ordered set $S_s < S_{s+1} < \cdots < S_{t-1}$. Tag bits are maintained in another stack T, having the same size as S (after the initialization step).

P1. [Initialize.] Set $T_k \leftarrow 0$ for $0 \leq k < m$. Then for $0 \leq j < n$, apply the j-buddy scan algorithm of exercise 29, and set $T_k \leftarrow T_k + 2^j$, $T_{k'} \leftarrow T_{k'} + 2^j$ for all pairs (k, k') found. Then set $s \leftarrow t \leftarrow 0$ and repeat the following operations until $s = m$: If $T_s = 0$, output the subcube $(0, v_s)$ and set $s \leftarrow s+1$; otherwise set $S_t \leftarrow v_s$, $T_t \leftarrow T_s$, $t \leftarrow t + 1$, $s \leftarrow s + 1$. Finally set $A \leftarrow 0$ and $S_t \leftarrow 0$.

P2. [Advance A.] (At this point stack S contains $\nu(A) + 1$ lists of subcubes. Namely, if $A = 2^{e_1} + \cdots + 2^{e_r}$ with $e_1 > \cdots > e_r \geq 0$, the stack contains the b-values of all subcubes $(a, b) \subseteq V$ whose a-values are respectively 0, 2^{e_1}, $2^{e_1} + 2^{e_2}$, ..., A, except that subcubes whose tags are zero do not appear. All of these lists are nonempty, except possibly the last. We will now increase A to the next relevant value.) Set $j \leftarrow 0$. If $S_t = t$ (that is, if the topmost list is empty), increase j zero or more times until $j \geq n$ or $A \mathbin{\&} 2^j \neq 0$. Then while $j < n$ and $A \mathbin{\&} 2^j \neq 0$, set $t \leftarrow S_t - 1$, $A \leftarrow A - 2^j$, and $j \leftarrow j + 1$. Terminate the algorithm if $j \geq n$; otherwise set $A \leftarrow A + 2^j$.

P3. [Generate list A.] Set $r \leftarrow t$, $s \leftarrow S_t$, and apply the j-buddy scan algorithm of exercise 29 to the $r - s$ numbers $S_s < \cdots < S_{r-1}$. For all pairs (k, k') found, set $x \leftarrow (T_k \mathbin{\&} T_{k'}) - 2^j$; and if $x = 0$, output the subcube (A, S_k), otherwise set $t \leftarrow t + 1$, $S_t \leftarrow S_k$, $T_t \leftarrow x$. Finally set $t \leftarrow t + 1$, $S_t \leftarrow r + 1$, and go back to step P2. ∎

This algorithm is based in part on ideas of Eugenio Morreale [*IEEE Trans.* **EC-16** (1967), 611–620; *Proc. ACM Nat. Conf.* **23** (1968), 355–365]. The running time is essentially proportional to mn (for step P1) plus the total number of subcubes contained in V. If $m \leq 2^n(1 - \epsilon)$, and if V is chosen at random with size m, exercise 34 shows that the average total number of subcubes is at most $O(\log \log n / \log \log \log n)$ times the average number of maximal subcubes; hence the average running time in most cases will be nearly proportional to the average amount of output produced. On the other hand, exercises 32 and 116 show that the amount of output might be huge.

31. (a) Let $c = c_{n-1} \ldots c_0$, $c' = c'_{n-1} \ldots c'_0$, $c'' = c''_{n-1} \ldots c''_0$. There must be some j with $c_j \neq *$ and $c_j \neq c''_j$; otherwise $c'' \subseteq c$. Similarly there must be some k with $c'_k \neq *$ and $c'_k \neq c''_k$. If $j \neq k$, there would be a point $x_{n-1} \ldots x_0 \in c''$ that is in neither c nor c', because we could let $x_j = \bar{c}_j$ and $x_k = \bar{c}'_k$. Hence $j = k$, and the value of j is uniquely determined. Furthermore it's easy to see that $c'_j = \bar{c}_j$. And if $i \neq j$, we have either $c_i = *$ or $c_i = c''_i$, and either $c'_i = *$ or $c'_i = c''_i$.

(b) This statement is an obvious consequence of (a).

(c) First we prove that the parenthesized remark in step E2 is true whenever that step is encountered. It's clearly true when $j = 0$. Otherwise, let $c \subseteq V$ be a j-cube, and suppose $c = c_0 \sqcup c_1$ where c_0 and c_1 are $(j-1)$-cubes. On the preceding execution of step E2 we had $c_0 \subseteq c'_0 \in C$ and $c_1 \subseteq c'_1 \in C$ for some c'_0 and c'_1; hence either $c \subseteq c'_0 \sqcup c'_1$ or $c \subseteq c'_0$ or $c \subseteq c'_1$. In each case, c is now contained in some element of C.

Secondly, we prove that the outputs in step E3 are precisely the maximal j-cubes contained in V: Let $c \subseteq V$ be any k-cube. If c is maximal, then c will be in C when we reach step E3 with $j = k$, and it will be output. If c isn't maximal, it has a buddy $c' \subseteq V$, which is a k-cube contained in some subcube $c'' \in C$ when we reach E3. Since $c \not\subseteq c''$, the consensus $c \sqcup c''$ will be a $(j+1)$-cube of C', and c will not be output.

References: The notion of consensus was first defined by Archie Blake in his Ph.D. dissertation at the University of Chicago (1937); see *J. Symbolic Logic* **3** (1938), 93, 112–113. It was independently rediscovered by Edward W. Samson and Burton E. Mills [Air Force Cambridge Research Center Tech. Report 54-21 (Cambridge, Mass.: April 1954), 54 pp.] and by W. V. Quine [*AMM* **62** (1955), 627–631]. The operation is also sometimes called the *resolvent,* since J. A. Robinson used it in a more general form (but with respect to clauses rather than implicants) as the basis of his "resolution principle" for theorem proving [*JACM* **12** (1965), 23–41]. Algorithm E is due to Ann C. Ewing, J. Paul Roth, and Eric G. Wagner, *AIEE Transactions,* Part 1, **80** (1961), 450–458.

32. (a) Change the definition of $\sqcup$ in exercise 31 to the following associative and commutative operation on the four symbols $A = \{0, 1, *, \bullet\}$, for all $a \in A$ and $x \in \{0, 1\}$:

$$* \sqcup a = a \sqcup * = a, \qquad \bullet \sqcup a = a \sqcup \bullet = x \sqcup \bar{x} = \bullet, \qquad \text{and} \qquad x \sqcup x = x.$$

Also let $h(0) = 0$, $h(1) = 1$, $h(*) = *$, and $h(\bullet) = *$. Then $c = h(c_1 \sqcup \cdots \sqcup c_m)$, computed componentwise, is the generalized consensus if and only if this subcube is contained in $c_1 \cup \cdots \cup c_m$. [See P. Tison, *IEEE Transactions* **EC-16** (1967), 446–456.]

(b) For example, let $c_j = *^{j-1}1*^{m-j}1^{j-1}0*^{m-j}$. [The final component is superfluous. All solutions have been characterized by R. H. Sloan, B. Szörényi, and G. Turán, in *Electronic Colloquium on Computational Complexity* (2005), Report 23.]

(c) By (a), every prime implicant corresponds uniquely to the subset of implicants that it "meets." [A. K. Chandra and G. Markowsky, *Discrete Math.* **24** (1978), 7–11.]

(d) For example, $(y_1 \wedge \bar{x}_1) \vee (y_2 \wedge x_1 \wedge \bar{x}_2) \vee \cdots \vee (y_m \wedge x_1 \wedge \cdots \wedge x_{m-1} \wedge \bar{x}_m)$ as in (b). [J.-M. Laborde, *Discrete Math.* **32** (1980), 209–212.]

33. (a) $\binom{2^n - 2^{n-k}}{m - 2^{n-k}} / \binom{2^n}{m}$. (b) We must exclude the cases when $x_1 \wedge \cdots \wedge x_{j-1} \wedge \bar{x}_j \wedge x_{j+1} \wedge \cdots \wedge x_k$ is also an implicant. By the inclusion-exclusion principle, the answer is

$$\sum_l \binom{k}{l} (-1)^l \binom{2^n - (l+1)2^{n-k}}{m - (l+1)2^{n-k}} / \binom{2^n}{m};$$

it simplifies to $\binom{2^n - n - 1}{m - 1} / \binom{2^n}{m}$ when $k = n$.

34. (a) We have $c(m,n) = \sum c_j(m,n)$, where $c_j(m,n) = 2^{n-j}\binom{n}{j}\binom{2^n-2^j}{m-2^j}/\binom{2^n}{m}$ is the average number of implicants with $n - j$ literals (the average number of subcubes of dimension j in the terminology of exercise 30). Clearly $c_0(m,n) = m$, and

$$c_1(m,n) = \frac{nm(m-1)}{2(2^n-1)} \le \frac{mn}{2}\left(\frac{m}{2^n}\right) \le \frac{1}{2}m;$$

similarly $c_j(m,n) \le m/(2^j j! n^{2^j - 1 - j})$. Also $p(m,n) = \sum_j p_j(m,n)$, where we have

$$p_0(m,n) = 2^n \binom{2^n-n-1}{m-1}/\binom{2^n}{m} = m\frac{(2^n-n-1)^{\underline{m-1}}}{(2^n-1)^{\underline{m-1}}} \ge m\frac{(2^n-n-m)^{m-1}}{(2^n-m)^{m-1}}$$

$$\ge m\left(1 - \frac{n}{2^n-m}\right)^m \ge m\left(1 - \frac{n}{2^n - 2^n/n}\right)^{2^n/n} = m\exp\left(\frac{2^n}{n}\ln\left(1 - \frac{n^2}{2^n(n-1)}\right)\right).$$

(b) Notice that $t = \lfloor \lg\lg n - \lg\lg(2^n/m) + \lg(4/3)\rfloor \le \lg\lg n + O(1)$ is quite small. We will repeatedly use the fact that $\binom{2^n-j\cdot 2^t}{m-j\cdot 2^t}/\binom{2^n}{m} < \alpha_{mn}^j$, and indeed that

$$\binom{2^n-j\cdot 2^t}{m-j\cdot 2^t}/\binom{2^n}{m} = \alpha_{mn}^j(1 + O(j^2 2^{2t}/m))$$

is an extremely good approximation when j isn't too large. To establish the hint, note that $\sum_{j<t} c_j(m,n)/c_t(m,n) = O(t c_{t-1}(m,n)/c_t(m,n)) = O(t^2/(n\sqrt{\alpha_{mn}})) = O((\log\log n)^2/n^{1/3})$; and $c_{t+j}(m,n)/c_t(m,n) = O((n/(2t))^j \alpha_{mn}^{2^j-1})$. Consequently we have $c(m,n)/c_t(m,n) \approx 1 + \frac{1}{2}\left(\frac{n-t}{t+1}\right)\alpha_{mn}$, where the second term dominates when α_{mn} is in the upper part of its range. Furthermore

$$\sum_l \binom{n-t}{l}(-1)^l \alpha_{mn}^l\left(1 + O\left(\frac{l^2 2^{2t}}{m}\right)\right) = (1-\alpha_{mn})^{n-t} + O(n^2\alpha_{mn}(1+\alpha_{mn})^n 2^{2t}/m)$$

has an exponentially small error term, because $(1+\alpha_{mn})^n = O(e^{n^{1/3}}) \ll m$. Therefore $p(m,n)/c_t(m,n)$ is asymptotically $e^{-n\alpha_{mn}} + \frac{1}{2}\left(\frac{n-t}{t+1}\right)\alpha_{mn}ne^{-n\alpha_{mn}^2}$.

(c) Here $\alpha_{mn} = 2^{-2^t} \approx n^{-1}\ln(t/\ln t)$; so $c(m,n)/c_t(m,n) = 1 + O(t^{-1}\log t)$, $p(m,n)/c_t(m,n) = t^{-1}\ln t + \frac{1}{2}t^{-1}\ln t + O(t^{-1}\log\log t)$. We conclude that, in this case,

$$\frac{c(m,n)}{p(m,n)} = \frac{2}{3}\frac{\lg\lg n}{\lg\lg\lg n}\left(1 + O\left(\frac{\log\log\log\log n}{\log\log\log n}\right)\right).$$

(d) If $n\alpha_{mn} \le \ln t - \ln\ln t$, we have $p(m,n)/c(m,n) \ge p_t(m,n)/c(m,n) \ge t^{-1}\ln t + O(t^{-1}\log t)^2$. On the other hand if $n\alpha_{mn} \ge \ln t - \ln\ln t$, we have $p(m,n)/c(m,n) \ge p_{t+1}(m,n)/c(m,n) \ge \frac{1}{2}t^{-1}\ln t + O(t^{-1}\log\log t)$.

[The means $c(m,n)$ and $p(m,n)$, and the variance of $c(m,n)$, were first studied by F. Mileto and G. Putzolu, *IEEE Trans.* **EC-13** (1964), 87–92; *JACM* **12** (1965), 364–375. Detailed asymptotic information about implicants, prime implicants, and irredundant DNFs of random Boolean functions, when each value $f(x_1,\ldots,x_n)$ is independently equal to 1 with probability $p(n)$, has been derived by Karl Weber, *Elektronische Informationsverarbeitung und Kybernetik* **19** (1983), 365–374, 449–458, 529–534.]

35. (a) By rearranging coordinates we can assume that the pth subcube is $0^k 1^u *^v$, so that $B_p = 0^k 1^u 0^v$ and $S_p = 1^k 0^{u+v}$. Then all points of $*^k 1^u *^v$ are still covered, by induction on p, because all points of $*^{j-1} 1 *^{k-j} 1^u *^v$ have been covered for $1 \le j \le k$.

(b) The jth and kth subcubes differ in every coordinate position where B_j & S_k is nonzero. On the other hand if B_j & S_k is zero, the point $\bar{S}_k$ of subcube k lies in a previous subcube, by (a), because we have $\bar{S}_k \supseteq B_j$.

(c) From the list 1100, 10̲1̲1̲, 0̲0̲11 (with the bits of each S_k underlined) we obtain the orthogonal DNF $(x_1 \wedge x_2) \vee (x_1 \wedge \bar{x}_2 \wedge x_3 \wedge x_4) \vee (\bar{x}_1 \wedge x_3 \wedge x_4)$.

(d) There are eight solutions; for example, $(01100, 00̲0̲110, 00̲0̲11, 110̲1̲0, 110̲0̲0)$.

(e) $(001100, 011̲0̲00, 000̲1̲10, 110̲0̲10, 110̲0̲00, 0̲1̲0̲011, 000̲0̲11)$ is a symmetrical solution. And there are many more possibilities; for example, 42 permutations of the bit codes $\{110000, 011000, 001100, 000110, 000011, 110010, 011010\}$ are shellings.

[The concept of a shelling for monotone Boolean functions was introduced by Michael O. Ball and J. Scott Provan, *Operations Research* **36** (1988), 703–715, who discussed many significant applications.]

36. If $j < k$ we have $B_j = \alpha 1 \beta$ and $B_k = \alpha 0 \gamma$ for some strings α, β, γ. Form the sequence $x_0 = \alpha 1 \gamma$, $x_1 = x_0'$, ..., $x_l = x_{l-1}'$, where $x_l = \alpha 00^{|\gamma|}$. We have $f(x_0) = 1$ since $x_0 \supseteq B_k$, but $f(x_l) = 0$ since $x_l \subseteq B_j'$. So the string x_i, where $f(x_i) = 1$ and $f(x_{i+1}) = \cdots = f(x_l) = 0$, is in B. It precedes B_k and proves that $B_j \,\&\, S_k \supseteq 0^{|\alpha|} 10^{|\beta|}$.

[This construction and parts of exercise 35 are due to E. Boros, Y. Crama, O. Ekin, P. L. Hammer, T. Ibaraki, and A. Kogan, *SIAM J. Discrete Math.* **13** (2000), 212–226.]

37. The shelling order (000011, 0011̲0̲1, 00110̲0̲, 110̲1̲01, 110̲1̲0̲0, 11000̲1̲, 110000̲) generalizes to all n. There also are interesting solutions not based on shelling, like the cyclically symmetrical (110***, 1110**, **110*, **1110, 0***11, 10**11, 111111).

For the lower bound, assign the weight $w_x = -\prod_{j=1}^{n}(x_{2j-1} + x_{2j} - 3x_{2j-1}x_{2j})$ to each point x, and notice that the sum of w_x over all x in any subcube is 0 or ± 1. (It suffices to verify this curious fact for each of the nine possible subcubes when $n = 1$.) Now choose a set of disjoint subcubes that partition the set $F = \{x \mid f(x) = 1\}$; we have

$$\sum_{C \text{ chosen}} 1 \geq \sum_{C \text{ chosen}} \sum_{x \in C} w_x = \sum_{x \in F} w_x \sum_{C \text{ chosen}} [x \in C] = \sum_{x \in F} w_x.$$

There are $\binom{n}{k} 2^{n-k}$ vectors x with exactly k pairs $x_{2j-1}x_{2j} = 1$ and nonzero weight. Their weight is $(-1)^{k-1}$, and they lie in F except when $k = 0$. Hence $\sum_{x \in F} w_x = \sum_{k>0} \binom{n}{k} 2^{n-k} (-1)^{k-1} = 2^n - (2-1)^n$. [See M. O. Ball and G. L. Nemhauser, *Mathematics of Operations Research* **4** (1979), 132–143.]

38. Certainly not; a DNF is satisfiable if and only if it has at least one implicant. The hard problem for a DNF is to decide whether or not it is a *tautology* (always true).

39. Associate variables $y_1, \ldots, y_N$ with each internal node in preorder, so that every tree node corresponds to exactly one variable of F. For each internal node y, with children (l, r) and labeled with the binary operator $\circ$, construct four 3CNF clauses $c_{00} \wedge c_{01} \wedge c_{10} \wedge c_{11}$, where

$$c_{pq} = (y^{\overline{p \circ q}N} \vee l^{pN} \vee r^{qN})$$

and N denotes complementation (so that $x^{0N} = x$ and $x^{1N} = \bar{x}$). These clauses state in effect that $y = l \circ r$; for example, if $\circ$ is $\wedge$, the four clauses are $(\bar{y} \vee l \vee r) \wedge (\bar{y} \vee l \vee \bar{r}) \wedge (\bar{y} \vee \bar{l} \vee r) \wedge (y \vee \bar{l} \vee \bar{r})$. Finally, add one more clause, $(y_1 \vee y_1 \vee y_1)$, to force $F = 1$.

> *Every higher number can be formed by mere complications of threes.*
> ... *Take the quadruple fact that A sells B to C for the price D.*
> *This is a compound of two facts:*
> *first, that A makes with C a certain transaction, which we may name E;*
> *and second, that this transaction E is a sale of B for the price D.*
> — CHARLES S. PEIRCE, *A Guess at the Riddle* (1887)

40. Following the hint, A says '$u < v \oplus v < u$' and B says '$u < v \wedge v < w \Rightarrow u < w$'. So $A \wedge B$ says that there's a linear ordering of the vertices, $u_1 < u_2 < \cdots < u_n$. (There are $n!$ ways to satisfy $A \wedge B$.) Now C says that q_{uvw} is equivalent to $u < v < w$; so D says that u and w are not consecutive in the ordering, when $u \not\!\!-\, w$. Thus $A \wedge B \wedge C \wedge D$ is satisfiable if and only if there is a linear ordering in which all nonadjacent vertices are nonconsecutive (that is, in which all consecutive vertices are adjacent).

41. Solution 0: '$[m \leq n]$' is such a formula, but it is not in the spirit of this exercise.

Solution 1: Let x_{jk} mean that pigeon j occupies hole k. Then the clauses are $(x_{j1} \vee \cdots \vee x_{jn})$ for $1 \leq j \leq m$ and $(\bar{x}_{ik} \vee \bar{x}_{jk})$ for $1 \leq i < j \leq m$ and $1 \leq k \leq n$. [See S. A. Cook and R. A. Reckhow, *J. Symbolic Logic* **44** (1979), 36–50; A. Haken, *Theoretical Comp. Sci.* **39** (1985), 297–308.]

Solution 2: Assume that $n = 2^t$ and let pigeon j occupy hole $(x_{j1} \ldots x_{jt})_2$. The clauses $((x_{i1} \oplus x_{j1}) \vee \cdots \vee (x_{it} \oplus x_{jt}))$ for $1 \leq i < j \leq m$ can be put into the CNF form $(y_{ij1} \vee \cdots \vee y_{ijt})$ as in exercise 39, by introducing auxiliary clauses $(\bar{y}_{ijk} \vee x_{ik} \vee x_{jk}) \wedge (y_{ijk} \vee x_{ik} \vee \bar{x}_{jk}) \wedge (y_{ijk} \vee \bar{x}_{ik} \vee x_{jk}) \wedge (\bar{y}_{ijk} \vee \bar{x}_{ik} \vee \bar{x}_{jk})$. The total size of this CNF is $\Theta(m^2 \log n)$, compared to $\Theta(m^2 n)$ in Solution 1. If n is not a power of 2, $O(m \log n)$ additional clauses of size $O(\log n)$ will rule out inappropriate values.

42. $(\bar{x} \vee y) \wedge (\bar{z} \vee x) \wedge (\bar{y} \vee \bar{z}) \wedge (z \vee z)$.

43. Probably not, because every 3SAT problem can be converted to this form. For example, the clause $(x_1 \vee x_2 \vee \bar{x}_3)$ can be replaced by $(x_1 \vee \bar{y} \vee \bar{x}_3) \wedge (\bar{y} \vee \bar{x}_2) \wedge (y \vee x_2)$, where y is a new variable (essentially equivalent to $\bar{x}_2$).

44. Suppose $f(x) = f(y) = 1$ implies $f(x \& y) = 1$ and also that, say, $c = x_1 \vee x_2 \vee \bar{x}_3 \vee \bar{x}_4$ is a prime clause of f. Then $c' = \bar{x}_1 \vee x_2 \vee \bar{x}_3 \vee \bar{x}_4$ is *not* a clause; otherwise $c \wedge c' = x_2 \vee \bar{x}_3 \vee \bar{x}_4$ would also be a clause, contradicting primality. So there's a vector y with $f(y) = 1$ and $y_1 = 1$, $y_2 = 0$, $y_3 = y_4 = 1$. Similarly, there's a z with $f(z) = 1$ and $z_1 = 0$, $z_2 = 1$, $z_3 = z_4 = 1$. But then $f(y \& z) = 1$, and c isn't a clause. The same argument works for a clause c that has a different number of literals, as long as at least two of the literals aren't complemented.

45. (a) A Horn function $f(x_1, \ldots, x_n)$ is indefinite if and only if it is unequal to the definite Horn function $g(x_1, \ldots, x_n) = f(x_1, \ldots, x_n) \vee (x_1 \wedge \cdots \wedge x_n)$. So $f \leftrightarrow g$ is a one-to-one correspondence between indefinite and definite Horn functions. (b) If f is monotone, its complement $\bar{f}$ is either identically 1 or an indefinite Horn function.

46. Algorithm C puts 88 pairs xy in the core: When x = a, b, c, 0, or 1, the following character y can be anything but (. When x = (, *, /, +, -, we can have y = (, a, b, c, 0, 1; also y = - when x = (, +, or -. Finally, the legitimate pairs beginning with x =) are)+,)-,)*,)/,)).

47. The order in which Algorithm C brings vertices into the core is a topological sort, since all predecessors of k are asserted before the algorithm sets TRUTH(x_k) ← 1. But Algorithm 2.2.3T uses a queue instead of a stack, so the ordering it actually produces is usually different from that of Algorithm C.

48. Let $\perp$ be a new variable, and change every indefinite Horn clause to a definite one by ORing in this new variable. (For example, '$\bar{w} \vee \bar{y}$' becomes '$\bar{w} \vee \bar{y} \vee \perp$', namely '$w \wedge y \Rightarrow \perp$'; definite Horn clauses stay unchanged.) Then apply Algorithm C. The original clauses are unsatisfiable if and only if $\perp$ is in the core of the new clauses. The algorithm can therefore be terminated as soon as it is about to set TRUTH($\perp$) ← 1.

(J. H. Quick thought of another solution: We could apply Algorithm C to the function g constructed in the answer to exercise 45(a), because f is unsatisfiable if and only if *every* variable x_j is in the core of g. However, indefinite clauses of f such as $\bar{w} \vee \bar{y}$ become many different clauses $(\bar{w} \vee \bar{y} \vee z) \wedge (\bar{w} \vee \bar{y} \vee x) \wedge (\bar{w} \vee \bar{y} \vee v) \wedge (\bar{w} \vee \bar{y} \vee u) \wedge \cdots$ of g, one for each variable not in the original clause. So Quick's suggestion, which might sound elegant at first blush, could increase the number of clauses by a factor of $\Omega(n)$.)

49. We have $f \leq g$ if and only if $f \wedge \bar{g}$ is unsatisfiable, if and only if $f \wedge \bar{c}$ is unsatisfiable for every clause c of g. But $\bar{c}$ is an AND of literals, so we can apply exercise 48. [See H. Kleine Büning and T. Lettmann, *Aussagenlogik: Deduktion und Algorithmen* (1994), §5.6, for further results including an efficient way to test if g is a "renaming" of f, namely to determine whether or not there exist constants $(y_1, \ldots, y_n)$ such that $f(x_1, \ldots, x_n) = g(x_1 \oplus y_1, \ldots, x_n \oplus y_n)$.]

50. See Gabriel Istrate, *Random Structures & Algorithms* **20** (2002), 483–506.

51. If vertex v is marked A, introduce the clauses $\Rightarrow A^+(v)$ and $\Rightarrow B^-(v)$; if it is marked B, introduce $\Rightarrow A^-(v)$ and $\Rightarrow B^+(v)$. Otherwise let v have k outgoing arcs $v \rightarrow u_1, \ldots, v \rightarrow u_k$. Introduce the clauses $A^-(u_j) \Rightarrow B^+(v)$ and $B^-(u_j) \Rightarrow A^+(v)$ for $1 \leq j \leq k$. Also, if v is not marked C, introduce the clauses $A^+(u_1) \wedge \cdots \wedge A^+(u_k) \Rightarrow B^-(v)$ and $B^+(u_1) \wedge \cdots \wedge B^+(u_k) \Rightarrow A^-(v)$. All forcing strategies are consequences of these clauses. Exercise 2.2.3–28 and its answer provide further information.

    Notice that, in principle, Algorithm C can therefore be used to decide whether or not the game of chess is a forced victory for the white pieces — except for the annoying detail that the corresponding digraph is larger than the physical universe.

52. With best play, the results (see exercise 51) are:

n	(a)	(b)	(c)	(d)
2	0 wins	second player wins	1 wins	second player wins
3	0 wins	first player wins	first player wins	first player wins
4	first player wins	first player wins	first player wins	first player wins
5	second player wins	draw	draw	1 loses if first
6	second player wins	second player wins	1 loses if first	1 loses if first
7	1 loses if first	second player wins	1 loses if first	1 loses if first
8	draw	draw	draw	1 loses if first
9	draw	draw	draw	1 loses if first

(Here "1 loses if first" means that the game is a draw if player 0 plays first, otherwise 0 can win.) *Comments:* In (a), player 1 has a slight disadvantage, because $f(x) = 0$ when $x_1 \ldots x_n$ is a palindrome. This small difference affects the result even when $n = 7$. Although player 1 would seem to be better off playing 0s in the left half of the board, it turns out that his/her first move when $n = 4$ must be to $*1**$; the alternative, $*0**$, draws. Game (b) is essentially a race to see who can eliminate the last $*$. In game (c), a random choice of $x_1 \ldots x_n$ makes $f(x) = 1$ with probability $F_{n+2}/2^n = \Theta((\phi/2)^n)$; in game (d), this probability approaches zero more slowly, as $\Theta(1/\log n)$. Still, player 1 does better in (c) than in (d) when $n = 2, 5, 8,$ and 9; no worse in the other cases.

53. (a) She should switch either day 1 or day 2 to day 3. (b, f) Several possibilities; for example, change day 2 to day 3. (c) This case is illustrated in Fig. 6; change either Desert or Excalibur to Aladdin. (d) Change either Caesars or Excalibur to Aladdin. (e) Change either Bellagio or Desert to Aladdin. Of course Williams, who doesn't appear in the cycle (42), bears no responsibility whatever for the conflicts.

54. If x and $\bar{x}$ are both in S, then $u \in S \iff \bar{u} \in S$, because the existence of paths from x to $\bar{x}$ and $\bar{x}$ to x and x to u and u to x implies the existence of paths from $\bar{u}$ to $\bar{x}$ and $\bar{x}$ to $\bar{u}$, hence from u to $\bar{u}$ and $\bar{u}$ to u.

55. (a) Necessary and sufficient conditions for successfully renaming a clause such as $x_1 \vee \bar{x}_2 \vee x_3 \vee \bar{x}_4$ are $(y_1 \vee \bar{y}_2) \wedge (y_1 \vee y_3) \wedge (y_1 \vee \bar{y}_4) \wedge (\bar{y}_2 \vee y_3) \wedge (\bar{y}_2 \vee \bar{y}_4) \wedge (y_3 \vee \bar{y}_4)$. A similar set of $\binom{k}{2}$ clauses of length 2 in the variables $\{y_1, \ldots, y_n\}$ corresponds to any clause of length k in $\{x_1, \ldots, x_n\}$. [H. R. Lewis, *JACM* **25** (1978), 134–135.]

(b) A given clause of length $k > 3$ in $\{x_1, \ldots, x_n\}$ can be converted into $3(k-2)$ clauses of length 2, instead of the $\binom{k}{2}$ clauses above, by introducing $k-3$ new variables $\{t_2, \ldots, t_{k-2}\}$, illustrated here for the clause $x_1 \vee x_2 \vee x_3 \vee x_4 \vee x_5$:

$$(y_1 \vee y_2) \wedge (y_1 \vee t_2) \wedge (y_2 \vee t_2) \wedge (\bar{t}_2 \vee y_3) \wedge (\bar{t}_2 \vee t_3) \wedge (y_3 \vee t_3) \wedge (\bar{t}_3 \vee y_4) \wedge (\bar{t}_3 \vee y_5) \wedge (y_4 \vee y_5).$$

In general, the clauses from $x_1 \vee \cdots \vee x_k$ are $(\bar{t}_{j-1} \vee y_j) \wedge (\bar{t}_{j-1} \vee t_j) \wedge (y_j \vee t_j)$ for $1 < j < k$, but with t_1 replaced by $\bar{y}_1$ and t_{k-1} replaced by y_k; change y_j to $\bar{y}_j$ if $\bar{x}_j$ appears instead of x_j. Do this for each given clause, using different auxiliary variables t_j for different clauses; the result is a formula in 2CNF that has length $< 3m$ and is satisfiable if and only if Horn renaming is possible. Now apply Theorem K.

[See B. Aspvall, *J. Algorithms* **1** (1980), 97–103. One consequence, noted by H. Kleine Büning and T. Lettmann in *Aussagenlogik: Deduktion und Algorithmen* (1994), Theorem 5.24, is that any satisfiable formula in 2CNF can be renamed to Horn clauses. Notice that two CNFs for the same function may give different outcomes; for example, $(x \vee y \vee z) \wedge (\bar{x} \vee \bar{y} \vee \bar{z}) \wedge (\bar{x} \vee z) \wedge (\bar{y} \vee z)$ is actually a Horn function, but the clauses in this representation cannot be converted to Horn form by complementation.]

56. Here $f(x, y, z)$ corresponds to the digraph shown below (analogous to Fig. 6), and it can also be simplified to $y \wedge (\bar{x} \vee z)$. Each vertex is a strong component. So the formula is true with respect to the quantifiers $\exists\exists\exists$, $\exists\exists\forall$, $\forall\exists\exists$; false in the other cases $\forall\exists\forall$, (any)$\forall$(any). In general the eight possibilities can be arranged at the corners of a cube, with each change from $\exists$ to $\forall$ making the formula more likely to be false.

57. Forming the digraph as in Theorem K, we can prove that the quantified formula holds if and only if (i) no strong component contains both x and $\bar{x}$; (ii) there is no path from one universal variable x to another universal variable y or to its complement $\bar{y}$; (iii) no strong component containing a universal variable x also contains an existential variable v or its complement $\bar{v}$, when '$\exists v$' appears to the left of '$\forall x$'. These three conditions are clearly necessary, and they are readily tested as the strong components are being found.

To show that they are sufficient, notice first that if S is a strong component with only existential literals, condition (i) allows us to set them all equal as in Theorem K. Otherwise S has exactly one universal literal, $u_j = x_j$ or $u_j = \bar{x}_j$; all other literals in S are existential and declared to the right of x_j, so we can equate them to u_j. And all paths into S in such a case come from purely existential strong components, whose value can be set to 0 because the complements of such strong components cannot also lead into S; for if v and $\bar{v}$ imply u_j, then $\bar{u}_j$ implies $\bar{v}$ and v.

[*Information Proc. Letters* **8** (1979), 121–123. By contrast, M. Krom had proved in *J. Symbolic Logic* **35** (1970), 210–216, that an analogous problem in first-order predicate calculus (where parameterized predicates take the place of simple Boolean variables, and quantification is over the parameters) is actually unsolvable in general.]

58. We can assume that each clause is definite, by introducing '$\perp$' as in exercise 48 and placing '$\forall\perp$' at the left. Call the universal variables $x_0, x_1, \ldots, x_m$ (where x_0 is $\perp$) and call the existential variables $y_1, \ldots, y_n$. Let '$u \prec v$' mean that variable u appears to the left of variable v in the list of quantifiers. Remove $\bar{x}_j$ from any clause whose unbarred literal is y_k when $y_k \prec x_j$. Then, for $0 \le j \le m$, let C_j be the core of the Horn clauses when the additional clauses $(x_0) \wedge \cdots \wedge (x_{j-1}) \wedge (x_{j+1}) \wedge \cdots \wedge (x_m) \wedge \bigwedge \{(y_k) \mid y_k \prec x_j$ and $y_k \in C_0\}$ are appended. (In other words, C_j tells us what can be deduced when all the x's except x_j are assumed to be true.) We claim that the given formula is true if and only if $x_j \notin C_j$, for $0 \le j \le m$.

To prove this claim, note first that the formula is certainly false if $x_j \in C_j$ for some j. (When $y_k \in C_0$ and $y_k \prec x_j$ and $x_i = 1$ for $i \ne j$ we must set $y_k \leftarrow 1$.) Otherwise we can choose each y_k to make the formula true, as follows: If $y_k \notin C_0$, set $y_k \leftarrow 0$; otherwise set $y_k \leftarrow \bigwedge \{x_j \mid y_k \notin C_j\}$. Notice that y_k depends on x_j only when $x_j \prec y_k$. Each clause c with unbarred literal x_j is now true: For if $x_j = 0$, some $\bar{y}_k$ appears in c for which $y_k \notin C_j$, because $x_j \notin C_j$; hence $y_k = 0$. And each clause c with unbarred literal y_k is also true: If $y_k = 0$, we either have $y_k \notin C_0$, in which case some $\bar{y}_l$ in c is $\notin C_0$, hence $y_l = 0$; or $y_k \in C_0 \setminus C_j$ for some j, in which case some $x_j = 0$ and either $\bar{x}_j$ appears in c or some $\bar{y}_l$ appears in c where $y_l \notin C_j$, making $y_l = 0$.

[This solution is due to T. Dahlheimer. See M. Karpinski, H. Kleine Büning, and P. H. Schmitt, *Lecture Notes in Comp. Sci.* **329** (1988), 129–137; H. Kleine Büning, K. Subramani, and X. Zhao, *Lecture Notes in Comp. Sci.* **2919** (2004), 93–104.]

59. By induction on n: Suppose $f(0, x_2, \ldots, x_n)$ leads to the quantified results $y_1, \ldots, y_{2^{n-1}}$, while $f(1, x_2, \ldots, x_n)$ leads similarly to $z_1, \ldots, z_{2^{n-1}}$. Then $\exists x_1 f(x_1, x_2, \ldots, x_n)$ leads to $y_1 \vee z_1, \ldots, y_{2^{n-1}} \vee z_{2^{n-1}}$, and $\forall x_1 f(x_1, x_2, \ldots, x_n)$ leads to $y_1 \wedge z_1, \ldots, y_{2^{n-1}} \wedge z_{2^{n-1}}$. Now use the fact that $(y \vee z) + (y \wedge z) = y + z$. [See *Proc. Mini-Workshop on Quantified Boolean Formulas* **2** (QBF-02) (Cincinnati: May 2002), 1–16.]

60. Both (a) and (b). But (c) is always 0; (d) is always 1; (e) is $\langle xyz \rangle$; (f) is $\bar{x} \vee \bar{y} \vee \bar{z}$.

61. True — indeed obviously so, when $w = 0$, and when $w = 1$.

62. Since $\{x_1, x_2, x_3\} \subseteq \{0, 1\}$, we can assume by symmetry that x_1 equals x_2. Then either $f(x_1, x_1, x_3, x_4, \ldots, x_n) = f(x_1, x_1, x_1, x_4, \ldots, x_n)$ or $f(x_1, x_1, x_3, x_4, \ldots, x_n) = f(x_3, x_1, x_3, x_4, \ldots, x_n)$, assuming only that f is monotone in its first three variables.

63. $\langle xyz \rangle = \langle xxyyz \rangle$. *Note:* Emil Post proved, in fact, that a single subroutine for *any* nontrivial monotone self-dual function will suffice to compute them all. (By induction on n, at least one appropriate way to call such an n-ary subroutine will yield $\langle xyz \rangle$.)

64. [*FOCS* **3** (1962), 149–157.] (a) If f is monotone and self-dual, Theorem P says that $f(x) = x_k$ or $f(x) = \langle f_1(x) f_2(x) f_3(x) \rangle$. The condition therefore holds either immediately or by induction. Conversely, if the condition holds it implies that f is monotone (when x and y differ in just one bit) and self-dual (when they differ in all bits).

(b) We merely need to show that it is possible to define f at one new point without introducing a conflict. Let x be the lexicographically smallest point where $f(x)$ is undefined. If $f(\bar{x})$ is defined, set $f(x) = \overline{f(\bar{x})}$. Otherwise if $f(x') = 1$ for some $x' \subseteq x$, set $f(x) = 1$; otherwise set $f(x) = 0$. Then the condition still holds.

65. If $\mathcal{F}$ is maximal intersecting, we have (i) $X \in \mathcal{F} \implies \overline{X} \notin \mathcal{F}$, where $\overline{X}$ is the complementary set $\{1, 2, \ldots, n\} \setminus X$; (ii) $X \in \mathcal{F}$ and $X \subseteq Y \implies Y \in \mathcal{F}$, because $\mathcal{F} \cup \{Y\}$ is intersecting; and (iii) $X \notin \mathcal{F} \implies \overline{X} \in \mathcal{F}$, because $\mathcal{F} \cup \{X\}$ must contain an element $Y \subseteq \overline{X}$. Conversely, one can prove without difficulty that any family $\mathcal{F}$ satisfying (i) and (ii) is intersecting, and maximal if it also satisfies (iii).

Punch line: All three statements are simple, in the language of Boolean functions: (i) $f(x) = 1 \implies f(\bar{x}) = 0$; (ii) $x \subseteq y \implies f(x) \le f(y)$; (iii) $f(x) = 0 \implies f(\bar{x}) = 1$.

66. [T. Ibaraki and T. Kameda, *IEEE Transactions on Parallel and Distributed Systems* **4** (1993), 779–794.] Every family with the property that $Q \subseteq Q'$ implies $Q = Q'$

clearly corresponds to the prime implicants of a monotone Boolean function f. The further condition that $Q \cap Q' \neq \emptyset$ corresponds to the further relation $f(\bar{x}) \leq \overline{f(x)}$, because $f(\bar{x}) = f(x) = 1$ holds if and only if x and $\bar{x}$ both make prime implicants true.

If coteries $\mathcal{C}$ and $\mathcal{C}'$ correspond in this way to functions f and f', then $\mathcal{C}$ dominates $\mathcal{C}'$ if and only if $f \neq f'$ and $f'(x) \leq f(x)$ for all x. Then f' is not self-dual, because there is an x with $f'(\bar{x}) = 0$, $f(\bar{x}) = 1$; and we have $f(x) = 0$, hence $f'(x) = 0$.

Conversely, if f' is not self-dual, there's a y with $f'(y) = f'(\bar{y}) = 0$. If $y = 0 \ldots 0$, coterie $\mathcal{C}'$ is empty, and dominated by every other coterie. Otherwise define $f(x) = f'(x) \vee [x \supseteq y]$. Then f is monotone, and $f(\bar{x}) \leq \overline{f(x)}$ for all x; so it corresponds to a coterie that dominates $\mathcal{C}'$.

67. (a) By induction, if $Y(t_{100}) = Y(t_{010}) = 1$ we have a Y of 1s, because the Ys in t_{100} and t_{010} either intersect or are adjacent. Similarly, if $Y(t_{100}) = Y(t_{010}) = 0$ we do not have a Y of 1s, because there is a Y of 0s.

(b) This formula follows from (a) and the fact that $(t_{abc})_{def} = t_{(a+d)(b+e)(c+f)} = (t_{def})_{abc}$. [Schensted stated the results of this exercise, and those of exercises 62 and 69, in a 28-page letter sent to Martin Gardner on 21 January 1979. Milnor had written to Gardner on 26 March 1957 about a corresponding game called "Triangle."]

68. When $n = 15$, the author's best attempt so far has 59 black stones: (The answers for $1 \leq n \leq 10$ are respectively 2, 3, 4, 6, 8, 11, 14, 18, 23, 27. The prime implicants for these functions can be represented by fairly small ZDDs; see Section 7.1.4.)

69. The proof of Theorem P shows that we need only prove $Y(T) \leq f(x)$. A Y in T means that we've got at least one variable in each p_j. Therefore $f(\bar{x}_1, \ldots, \bar{x}_n) = 0$, and $f(x_1, \ldots, x_n) = 1$.

70. Self-duality of g is obvious for arbitrary t when f is self-dual: $\overline{g(\bar{x})} = \overline{(\overline{f(\bar{x})} \vee [\bar{x} = t])} \wedge [\bar{x} \neq \bar{t}] = (f(x) \vee [x = \bar{t}]) \wedge [x \neq t] = (f(x) \wedge [x \neq t]) \vee ([x = \bar{t}] \wedge [x \neq t]) = g(x)$.

Let $x = x_1 \ldots x_{j-1} 0 x_{j+1} \ldots x_n$ and $y = x_1 \ldots x_{j-1} 1 x_{j+1} \ldots x_n$; for monotonicity we must prove that $g(x) \leq g(y)$. If $x = t$ or $y = t$, we have $g(x) = 0$; if $x = \bar{t}$ or $y = \bar{t}$, we have $g(y) = 1$; otherwise $g(x) = f(x) \leq f(y) = g(y)$. [*European J. Combinatorics* **16** (1995), 491–501; discovered independently by J. C. Bioch and T. Ibaraki, *IEEE Transactions on Parallel and Distributed Systems* **6** (1995), 905–914.]

71. $\langle\langle xyz\rangle uv\rangle = \langle\langle\langle xyz\rangle uv\rangle uv\rangle = \langle\langle\langle yuv\rangle x\langle zuv\rangle\rangle uv\rangle = \langle\langle yuv\rangle\langle xuv\rangle\langle\langle zuv\rangle uv\rangle\rangle = \langle\langle xuv\rangle\langle yuv\rangle\langle zuv\rangle\rangle$.

72. For (58), $v = \langle uvu\rangle = u$. For (59), $\langle uyv\rangle = \langle vu\langle xuy\rangle\rangle = \langle\langle vux\rangle uy\rangle = \langle xuy\rangle = y$. And for (60), $\langle xyz\rangle = \langle\langle xuv\rangle yz\rangle = \langle x\langle uyz\rangle\langle vyz\rangle\rangle = \langle xyy\rangle = y$.

73. (a) If $d(u, v) = d(u, x) + d(x, v)$, we obviously obtain a shortest path of the form u — $\cdots$ — x — $\cdots$ — v. Conversely, if $[uxv]$, let u — $\cdots$ — x — $\cdots$ — v be a shortest path, with l steps to x followed by m steps to v. Then $d(u, v) = l + m \geq d(u, x) + d(x, v) \geq d(u, v)$.

(b) For all z, $\langle zxu\rangle = \langle z\langle vux\rangle\langle yux\rangle\rangle \in \{\langle yux\rangle, \langle vux\rangle\} = \{u, x\}$.

(c) We can assume that $d(x, u) \geq d(x, v) > 0$. Let u — $\cdots$ — y — v be a shortest path, and let $w = \langle xuy\rangle$. Then $\langle vxw\rangle = \langle v\langle vux\rangle\langle wux\rangle\rangle = \langle\langle vvw\rangle ux\rangle = \langle vux\rangle = x$, so $x \in [w \ldots v]$. We have $[uwy]$, because $d(u, y) < d(u, v)$ and $w \in [u \ldots y]$. If $w \neq u$ we have $d(w, v) < d(u, v)$; hence $[wxv]$, hence $[uxv]$. If $w = u$ we have x — u by (b). But $d(x, u) \geq d(x, v)$; therefore x — v, and $[uxv]$.

(d) Let $y = \langle uxv \rangle$. Since $y \in [u \mathinner{.\,.} x]$, we have $d(u, x) = d(u, y) + d(y, x)$ by (a) and (c). Similarly, $d(u, v) = d(u, y) + d(y, v)$ and $d(x, v) = d(x, y) + d(y, v)$. But these three equations, together with $d(u, v) = d(u, x) + d(x, v)$, yield $d(x, y) = 0$. [*Proc. Amer. Math. Soc.* **12** (1961), 407–414.]

74. $w = \langle yxw \rangle = \langle yx \langle zxw \rangle \rangle = \langle yx \langle zx \langle yzw \rangle \rangle \rangle = \langle \langle yxz \rangle x \langle yzw \rangle \rangle = \langle x \langle xyz \rangle \langle wyz \rangle \rangle = \langle \langle xxw \rangle yz \rangle = \langle xyz \rangle$ by (55), (55), (55), (52), (51), (53), and (50).

75. (a) If $w = \langle xxy \rangle$ we have $[xwx]$ by (iii), hence $w = x$ by (i).

(b) Axiom (iii) and part (a) tell us that $[xxy]$ is always true. So we can set $x = y$ in (ii) to conclude that $[uxv] \iff [vxu]$. The definition of $\langle xyz \rangle$ in (iii) is therefore perfectly symmetrical between x, y, and z.

(c) By the definition of $\langle uxv \rangle$ in (iii), we have $x = \langle uxv \rangle$ if and only if $[uxx]$, $[uxv]$, and $[xxv]$. But we know that $[uxx]$ and $[xxv]$ are always true.

(d) In this step and subsequent steps, we will construct one or more auxiliary points of M and then use Algorithm C to derive every consequence of the betweenness relations that are known. (The axioms have the convenient form of Horn clauses.) For example, here we define $z = \langle xyv \rangle$, so that we know $[uxy]$, $[uyv]$, $[xzy]$, $[xzv]$, and $[yzv]$. From these hypotheses we deduce $[uzy]$ and $[uzv]$. So $z = \langle uyv \rangle = y$.

(e) The hinted construction implies, among other things, $[utv]$, $[utz]$, $[vtz]$, $[uwv]$, $[uwz]$, $[vwz]$; hence $t = w$. (A computer program is helpful here.) Adding the hypotheses $[rws]$, $[rwz]$, $[swz]$ now yields $[xyz]$ as desired; it also turns out that $r = p$ and $s = q$.

(f) Let $r = \langle yuv \rangle$, $s = \langle zuv \rangle$, $t = \langle xyz \rangle$, $p = \langle xrs \rangle$, $q = \langle tuv \rangle$; then $[pqp]$ flows out. [*Proc. Amer. Math. Soc.* **5** (1954), 801–807. For early studies of betweenness axioms, see E. V. Huntington and J. R. Kline, *Trans. Amer. Math. Soc.* **18** (1917), 301–325.]

76. Axiom (i) obviously holds, and axiom (ii) follows from commutativity and (52). The answer to exercise 74 derives (iii) from the identity $\langle xyz \rangle = \langle x \langle xyz \rangle \langle wyz \rangle \rangle$; so we need only verify that formula: $\langle x \langle xyz \rangle \langle wyz \rangle \rangle = \langle \langle yxz \rangle x \langle wyz \rangle \rangle = \langle \langle \langle yxz \rangle xz \rangle x \langle wyz \rangle \rangle = \langle \langle yxz \rangle x \langle zx \langle wyz \rangle \rangle \rangle = \langle x \langle xyz \rangle \langle z \langle xyz \rangle w \rangle \rangle = \langle \langle x \langle xyz \rangle z \rangle \langle xyz \rangle w \rangle = \langle \langle xyz \rangle \langle xyz \rangle w \rangle$.

Notes: The original treatment of median algebra by Birkhoff and Kiss in *Bull. Amer. Math. Soc.* **53** (1947), 749–752, assumed (50), (51), and the short distributive law (53). The fact that associativity (52) actually implies distributivity was not realized until many years later; M. Kolibiar and T. Marcisová, *Matematický Časopis* **24** (1974), 179–185, proved it via Sholander's axioms as in this exercise. A mechanical derivation of (53) from (50)–(52) was found in 2005 by R. Veroff and W. McCune, using an extension of the Otter theorem prover.

77. (a) In coordinate $r \relbar s$ of the labels, suppose $l(r)$ has a 0 and $l(s)$ has a 1; then the left vertices have 0 in that coordinate. If $u \relbar v \relbar u'$, where u and u' are on the left but v is on the right, $\langle uu'v \rangle$ lies on the left. But $[u \mathinner{.\,.} v] \cap [u' \mathinner{.\,.} v] = \{v\}$, unless $u = u'$.

(b) This statement is obvious, by Corollary C.

(c) Suppose $u \relbar v$ and $u' \relbar v'$, where u and u' are on the left, v and v' are on the right. Let $v = v_0 \relbar \cdots \relbar v_k = v'$ be a shortest path, and let $u_0 = u$, $u_k = u'$. All vertices v_j lie on the right, by (b). The left vertex $u_1 = \langle u_0 v_1 u_k \rangle$ must be a common neighbor of u_0 and v_1, since the distance $d(u_0, v_1) = 2$. (We cannot have $u_1 = u_0$, because that would imply the existence of a shortest path from v to v' going through the left vertex u.) Therefore v_1 has rank 1; and so do v_2, ..., v_{k-1}, by the same argument. [L. Nebeský, *Commentationes Mathematicæ Universitatis Carolinæ* **12** (1971), 317–325; M. Mulder, *Discrete Math.* **24** (1978), 197–204.]

(d) These steps visit all vertices v of rank 1 in order of their distance $d(v, s)$ from s. If such a v has a late neighbor u not yet seen, the rank of u must be 1 or 2. If the rank is 1, u will have at least two early neighbors, namely v and the future MATE(u). Step I8 bases its decision on an arbitrary early neighbor w of u such that $w \neq v$. Since $d(w, v) = 2$, the vertex $x = \langle svw \rangle$ has rank 1 by (c). If w has rank 0, then $x = v$; so u has rank 1. Otherwise $d(x, s) < d(v, s)$, and the rank of w was correctly determined when x was visited. If w has rank 1, u lies on a shortest path from v to w; if w has rank 2, w lies on a shortest path from u to s. In both cases u and w have the same rank, by (c).

(e) The algorithm removes all edges equivalent to $r \mathbin{\rule[0.5ex]{1em}{0.4pt}} s$, by (a) and (d). Their removal clearly disconnects the graph; the two pieces that remain are convex by (b), so they are connected and in fact they are median graphs. Step I7 records all of the relevant relations between the two pieces, because all 4-cycles that disappear are examined there. By induction on the number of vertices, each piece is properly labeled.

78. Every time v appears in step I4, it loses one of its neighbors u_j. Each of these edges $v \mathbin{\rule[0.5ex]{1em}{0.4pt}} u_j$ corresponds to a different coordinate of the labels, so we can assume that $l(v)$ has the form $\alpha 1^k$ for some binary string α. The labels for $u_1, u_2, \ldots, u_k$ are then $\alpha 01^{k-1}$, $\alpha 101^{k-2}$, $\ldots$, $\alpha 1^{k-1}0$. By taking componentwise medians, we can now prove that all 2^k labels of the form $\alpha\beta$ occur for vertices in the graph, since $\langle (\alpha\beta)(\alpha\beta')(0\ldots0) \rangle$ is the bit string $\alpha(\beta \mathbin{\&} \beta')$.

79. (a) If $l(v) = k$, exactly $\nu(k)$ smaller vertices are neighbors of v.

(b) At most $\lfloor n/2 \rfloor$ 1s appear in bit position j, for $0 \leq j < \lceil \lg n \rceil$.

(c) Suppose exactly k vertices have labels beginning with 0. At most $\min(k, n-k)$ edges correspond to that bit position, and at most $f(k) + f(n - k)$ other edges are present. But

$$f(n) = \max_{0 \leq k \leq n} \big(\min(k, n - k) + f(k) + f(n - k) \big),$$

because the function $g(m, n) = f(m + n) - m - f(m) - f(n)$ satisfies the recurrence

$$g(2m + a, 2n + b) = ab + g(m + a, n) + g(m, n + b) \qquad \text{for } 0 \leq a, b \leq 1.$$

It follows by induction that $g(m, m) = g(m, m + 1) = 0$, and that $g(m, n) \geq 0$ when $m \leq n$. [*Annals of the New York Academy of Sciences* **175** (1970), 170–186; D. E. Knuth, *Proc. IFIP Congress 1971* (1972), 24.]

80. (a) (Solution by W. Imrich.) The graph with vertex labels 0000, 0001, 0010, 0011, 0100, 0110, 0111, 1100, 1101, 1110, 1111 cannot be labeled in any essentially different way; but the distance from 0001 to 1101 is 4, not 2.

(b) The cycle C_{2m} is a partial cube, because its vertices can be labeled $l(k) = 1^k 0^{m-k}$, $l(m + k) = 0^k 1^{m-k}$ for $0 \leq k < m$. But the bitwise median of $l(0)$, $l(m - 1)$, and $l(m + 1)$ is $01^{m-2}0$; and indeed those vertices don't have a median, when $m > 2$.

81. Yes. A median graph is a subgraph of a hypercube, which is bipartite.

82. The general case reduces to the simple case where G has only two vertices $\{0, 1\}$, because we can operate componentwise on the median labels, and because $d(u, v)$ is the Hamming distance between $l(u)$ and $l(v)$.

In the simple case, the stated rule sets $u_k \leftarrow v_k$ except when $u_{k-1} = v_{k-1} = v_{k+1} \neq v_k$, and it is readily proved optimum. (Other optimum possibilities do exist, however; for example, if $v_0 v_1 v_2 v_3 = 0110$, we could set $u_0 u_1 u_2 u_3 = 0000$.)

[This problem was motivated by the study of self-organizing data structures. F. R. K. Chung, R. L. Graham, and M. E. Saks, in *Discrete Algorithms and Complexity* (Academic Press, 1987), 351–387, have proved that median graphs are the *only* graphs for which u_k can always be chosen optimally as a function of $(v_0, v_1, \ldots, v_{k+1})$, regardless of the subsequent values $(v_{k+2}, \ldots, v_t)$. They have also characterized all cases for which a given finite amount of lookahead will suffice, in *Combinatorica* **9** (1989), 111–131.]

83. Again it suffices to consider the simple two-vertex case. An optimum solution in that case can never have $u_{k-1} \neq u_k$ except when $u_{k-1} = v_{k-1} \neq v_k = u_k$. Therefore we must only decide which runs of consecutive 0s or 1s in $v_0 v_1 \ldots v_t$ should induce matching runs in $u_0 u_1 \ldots u_t$.

Suppose $v_{k-1} v_k \ldots v_{k+r} = 01^r 0$ and $u_{k-1} = 0$. The cost of $u_{k-1} u_k \ldots u_{k+r} = 00 \ldots 0$ is $r\rho$, compared to a cost of 2 if $u_{k-1} u_k \ldots u_{k+r} = 01^r 0$; so we must choose the former if $\rho < 2/r$ and the latter if $\rho > 2/r$. This policy can be expressed in terms of medians, if we set $u_k = \langle u_{k-1} \ldots u_{k-1} v_k \ldots v_{k+r} \rangle$ when $2/(r+1) \leq \rho < 2/r$ for $r \geq 0$, where there are r occurrences of u_{k-1}. (This median-of-$(2r+1)$ gives correct results in a general median graph, since it will produce valid median labels; see exercise 86.)

But we must change this rule when we get near the end, because it eventually asks for the values of v_j with $j > t$. The endgame is tricky; for if $v_{k-1} v_k \ldots v_t = 01^r$ and $u_{k-1} = 0$, with $r = t + 1 - k$, the choice $u_{k-1} u_k \ldots u_t = 00 \ldots 0$ is now preferable only if $\rho < 1/r$. For example, if $2/4 < \rho < 2/3$ and $v_0 v_1 = 01$ and $t = 1$, we want to choose $u_0 u_1 = 00$; but if $v_0 v_1 v_2 = 011$ and $t = 2$ we want $u_0 u_1 u_2 = 011$. One solution is to set $v_{t+j} \leftarrow v_t$ for $1 \leq j \leq \lceil r/2 \rceil$ and $v_{t+j} \leftarrow v_0$ for $\lceil r/2 \rceil < j \leq r$.

84. There are 81 such functions, each of which can be represented as the median of an odd number of elements. Seven types of vertices occur:

Type	Typical vertex	Cases	Adjacent to	Degree
1	$\langle z \rangle$	5	$\langle vwxyzzz \rangle$	1
2	$\langle vwxyzzz \rangle$	5	$\langle z \rangle, \langle wxyzz \rangle$	5
3	$\langle wxyzz \rangle$	20	$\langle vwxyzzz \rangle, \langle vwxxyyzzz \rangle$	4
4	$\langle vwxxyyzzz \rangle$	30	$\langle xyz \rangle, \langle wxyzz \rangle, \langle vwxyyzz \rangle$	5
5	$\langle vwxyyzz \rangle$	10	$\langle vwxxyyzzz \rangle, \langle vwxyz \rangle$	7
6	$\langle vwxyz \rangle$	1	$\langle vwxyyzz \rangle$	10
7	$\langle xyz \rangle$	10	$\langle vwxxyyzzz \rangle$	3

[Von Neumann and Morgenstern enumerated these seven types in their book *Theory of Games and Economic Behavior* (1944), §52.5, in connection with the study of an equivalent problem about systems of winning coalitions that they called *simple games*. The graph for six-variable functions, which has 2646 vertices of 30 types, appears in the paper by Meyerowitz cited in exercise 70. Only 21 of those types can be represented as a simple median-of-odd; a vertex like $\langle \langle abd \rangle \langle ace \rangle \langle bcf \rangle \rangle$, for example, has no such representation. Let the corresponding graph for n variables have M_n vertices; P. Erdős and N. Hindman, in *Discrete Math.* **48** (1984), 61–65, showed that $\lg M_n$ is asymptotic to $\binom{n-1}{\lfloor n/2 \rfloor}$. D. Kleitman, in *J. Combin. Theory* **1** (1966), 153–155, showed that the vertices for distinct projection functions like x and y are always furthest apart in this graph.]

85. Every strong component must consist of a single vertex; otherwise two coordinates would always be equal, or always complementary. Thus the digraph must be acyclic.

Furthermore, there must be no path from a vertex to its complement; otherwise a coordinate would be constant.

When these two conditions are satisfied, we can prove that no vertex x is redundant, by assigning the value 0 to all vertices that precede x or $\bar{x}$, assigning 1 to all vertices that follow, and giving appropriate values to all other vertices.

(Consequently we obtain a completely different way to represent a median graph. For example, the digraph shown corresponds to the median graph whose labels are $\{0000, 0001, 0010, 0011, 0111, 1010\}$.)

86. Yes. By Theorem P, *any* monotone self-dual function maps elements of X into X.

87. Here the topological ordering $7\,6\,5\,4\,3\,2\,1\,\bar{1}\,\bar{2}\,\bar{3}\,\bar{4}\,\bar{5}\,\bar{6}\,\bar{7}$ can replace (72); we get

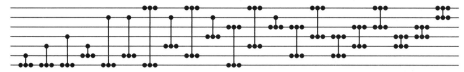

(Consecutive inverters on the same line can, of course, be canceled out.)

88. A given value of d contributes at most $6\lceil t/d\rceil$ units of delay (for $2\lceil t/d\rceil$ clusters).

89. Suppose first that the new condition is $i \to j$ while the old was $i' \to j'$, where $i < j$ and $i' < j'$ and there are no complemented literals. The new module changes $x_1\ldots x_t$ to $y_1\ldots y_t$, where $y_i = x_i \wedge x_j$, $y_j = x_i \vee x_j$, and $y_k = x_k$ otherwise. We certainly have $y_{i'} \le y_{j'}$ when $\{i',j'\} \cap \{i,j\} = \emptyset$. And there is no problem if $i = i'$, since $y_{i'} = y_i \le x_i = x_{i'} \le x_{j'} = y_{j'}$. But the case $i = j'$ is trickier: Here the relations $i' \to i$ and $i \to j$ imply also $i' \to j$; and this relation has been enforced by *previous* modules, because modules have been appended in order of decreasing distance d in the topological ordering $u_1\ldots u_{2t}$. Therefore $y_{i'} = x_{i'} \le x_j$ and $y_{i'} \le x_{j'} = x_i$, hence $y_{i'} \le x_i \wedge x_j = y_i = y_{j'}$. A similar proof works when $j = i'$ or $j = j'$.

Finally, with complemented literals, the construction cleverly reduces the general case to the uncomplemented case by inverting and un-inverting the bits.

90. When $t = 2$, $\underset{\bullet\,\bullet}{\boxed{}}$ does the job. The general case follows recursively from this building block by reducing t to $\lceil t/2\rceil$.

[The study of CI-nets, and other networks of greater generality, was initiated by E. W. Mayr and A. Subramanian, *J. Computer and System Sci.* **44** (1992), 302–323.]

91. The answer does not yet seem to be known even in the special case when the median graph is a free tree (with $t + 1$ vertices), or in the monotone case when it is a distributive lattice as in Corollary F. In the latter case, inverters may be unnecessary.

93. Let $d_X(u,v)$ be the number of edges on a shortest path between u and v, when the path lies entirely within X. Clearly $d_X(u,v) \ge d_G(u,v)$. And if $u = u_0 \,\text{—}\, u_1 \,\text{—}\, \cdots \,\text{—}\, u_k = v$ is a shortest path in G, the path $u = f(u_0) \,\text{—}\, f(u_1) \,\text{—}\, \cdots \,\text{—}\, f(u_k) = v$ lies in X when f is a retraction from G to X; hence $d_X(u,v) \le d_G(u,v)$.

94. If f is a retraction of the t-cube onto X, two different coordinate positions cannot always be equal or always complementary for all $x \in X$, unless they are constant. For if, say, all elements of X have the forms $00*\ldots*$ or $11*\ldots*$, there would be no path between vertices of those two types, contradicting the fact that X is an isometric subgraph (hence connected).

Given $x, y, z \in X$, let $w = \langle xyz\rangle$ be their median in the t-cube. Then $f(w) \in [x..y] \cap [x..z] \cap [y..z]$, because (for example) $f(w)$ lies on a shortest path from x to y in X. So $f(w) = w$, and we have proved that $w \in X$. [This result and its considerably more subtle converse are due to H. J. Bandelt, *J. Graph Theory* **8** (1984), 501–510.]

95. False (although the author was hoping otherwise); the network at the right takes $0001 \mapsto 0000$, $0010 \mapsto 0011$, $1101 \mapsto 0110$, but nothing $\mapsto 0010$.

(The set of all possible outputs appears to have no easy characterization, even when no inverters are used. For example, the pure-comparator network at the left, constructed by Tomás Feder, takes $000000 \mapsto 000000$, $010101 \mapsto 010101$, and $101010 \mapsto 011001$, but nothing $\mapsto 010001$. See also exercises 5.3.4–50, 5.3.4–52.)

96. No. If f is a threshold function based on real parameters $w = (w_1, \ldots, w_n)$ and t, let $\max\{w \cdot x \mid f(x) = 0\} = t - \epsilon$. Then $\epsilon > 0$, and f is defined by the 2^n inequalities $w \cdot x - t \geq 0$ when $f(x) = 1$, $t - w \cdot x - \epsilon \geq 0$ when $f(x) = 0$. If A is any $M \times N$ matrix of integers for which the system of linear inequalities $Av \geq (0, \ldots, 0)^T$ has a real-valued solution $v = (v_1, \ldots, v_N)^T$ with $v_N > 0$, there also is such a solution in integers. (Proof by induction on N.) So we can assume that w_1, $\ldots$, w_n, t, and ϵ are integers.

[A closer analysis using Hadamard's inequality (see Eq. 4.6.1–(25)) proves in fact that integer weights of magnitude at most $(n + 1)^{(n+1)/2}/2^n$ will suffice; see S. Muroga, I. Toda, and S. Takasu, *J. Franklin Inst.* **271** (1961), 376–418, Theorem 16. Furthermore, exercise 112 shows that weights nearly that large are sometimes needed.]

97. $\langle 11111x_1x_2\rangle$, $\langle 111x_1x_2\rangle$, $\langle 1x_1x_2\rangle$, $\langle 0x_1x_2\rangle$, $\langle 000x_1x_2\rangle$, $\langle 00000x_1x_2\rangle$.

98. We may assume that $f(x_1, \ldots, x_n) = \langle y_1^{w_1} \ldots y_n^{w_n}\rangle$, with positive integer weights w_j and with $w_1 + \cdots + w_n$ odd. Let δ be the minimum positive value of the 2^n sums $\pm w_1 \pm \cdots \pm w_n$, with n independently varying signs. Renumber all subscripts so that $w_1 + \cdots + w_k - w_{k+1} - \cdots - w_n = \delta$. Then $w_1y_1 + \cdots + w_ny_n > \frac{1}{2}(w_1 + \cdots + w_n) \iff$ $w_1(y_1 - \frac{1}{2}) + \cdots + w_n(y_n - \frac{1}{2}) > 0 \iff w_1(y_1 - \frac{1}{2}) + \cdots + w_n(y_n - \frac{1}{2}) > -\delta/2 \iff$ $w_1y_1 + \cdots + w_ny_n > \frac{1}{2}(w_1 + \cdots + w_n - (w_1 + \cdots + w_k - w_{k+1} - \cdots - w_n)) = w_{k+1} + \cdots + w_n \iff w_1y_1 + \cdots + w_ky_k - w_{k+1}\bar{y}_{k+1} - \cdots - w_n\bar{y}_n > 0$.

99. We have $[x_1 + \cdots + x_{2s-1} + s(y_1 + \cdots + y_{2t-2}) \geq st] = [\lfloor(x_1 + \cdots + x_{2s-1})/s\rfloor + y_1 + \cdots + y_{2t-2} \geq t]$; and $\lfloor(x_1 + \cdots + x_{2s-1})/s\rfloor = [x_1 + \cdots + x_{2s-1} \geq s]$.

(For example, $\langle\langle xyz\rangle uv\rangle = \langle xyzu^2v^2\rangle$, a quantity that we also know is equal to $\langle x\langle yuv\rangle\langle zuv\rangle\rangle$ and $\langle\langle xuv\rangle\langle yuv\rangle\langle zuv\rangle\rangle$ by Eqs. (53) and (54). *Reference:* C. C. Elgot, *FOCS* **2** (1961), 238.)

100. True, because of the preceding exercise and (45).

101. (a) When $n = 7$ they are $x_7 \wedge x_6$, $x_6 \wedge x_5$, $x_7 \wedge x_5 \wedge x_4$, $x_6 \wedge x_4 \wedge x_3$, $x_7 \wedge x_5 \wedge x_3 \wedge x_2$, $x_6 \wedge x_4 \wedge x_2 \wedge x_1$, $x_7 \wedge x_5 \wedge x_3 \wedge x_1$; and in general there are n prime implicants, forming a similar pattern. (We have either $x_n = x_{n-1}$ or $x_n = \bar{x}_{n-1}$. In the first case, $x_n \wedge x_{n-1}$ is obviously a prime implicant. In the second case, $F_n(x_1, \ldots, x_{n-1}, \bar{x}_{n-1}) = F_{n-1}(x_1, \ldots, x_{n-1})$; so we use the prime implicants of the latter, and insert x_n when x_{n-1} does not appear.)

(b) The shelling pattern (0000011, 0000110, 0001101, 0011010, 0110101, 1101010, 1010101) for $n = 7$ works for all n.

(c) Two of several possibilities for $n = 7$ illustrate the general case:

$$F_7(x_1, \ldots, x_7) = Y\begin{pmatrix} x_6 \\ x_7\ x_5 \\ x_6\ x_6\ x_4 \\ x_7\ x_5\ x_7\ x_3 \\ x_6\ x_6\ x_4\ x_6\ x_2 \\ x_7\ x_5\ x_7\ x_3\ x_7\ x_1 \end{pmatrix} = Y\begin{pmatrix} x_6 \\ x_7\ x_5 \\ x_6\ x_6\ x_4 \\ x_7\ x_5\ x_5\ x_3 \\ x_6\ x_6\ x_4\ x_4\ x_2 \\ x_7\ x_5\ x_5\ x_3\ x_3\ x_1 \end{pmatrix}.$$

[The Fibonacci threshold functions were introduced by S. Muroga, who also discovered the optimality result in exercise 105; see *IEEE Transactions* **EC-14** (1965), 136–148.]

102. (a) By (1) and (2), $\hat{f}(\bar{x}_0, \bar{x}_1, \ldots, \bar{x}_n)$ is the complement of $\hat{f}(x_0, x_1, \ldots, x_n)$.

(b) If f is given by (75), $\hat{f}$ is $[(w + 1 - 2t)x_0 + w_1x_1 + \cdots + w_nx_n \geq w + 1 - t]$, where $w = w_1 + \cdots + w_n$. Conversely, if $\hat{f}$ is a threshold function, so is $f(x_1, \ldots, x_n) = \hat{f}(1, x_1, \ldots, x_n)$. [E. Goto and H. Takahasi, *Proc. IFIP Congress* (1962), 747–752.]

103. [See R. C. Minnick, *IRE Transactions* **EC-10** (1961), 6–16.] We want to minimize $w_1 + \cdots + w_n$ subject to the constraints $w_j \geq 0$ for $1 \leq j \leq n$ and $(2e_1 - 1)w_1 + \cdots + (2e_n-1)w_n \geq 1$ for each prime implicant $x_1^{e_1} \wedge \cdots \wedge x_n^{e_n}$. For example, if $n = 6$, the prime implicant $x_2 \wedge x_5 \wedge x_6$ would lead to the constraint $-w_1 + w_2 - w_3 - w_4 + w_5 + w_6 \geq 1$. If the minimum is $+\infty$, the given function is not a threshold function. (The answer to exercise 84 gives one of the simplest examples of such a case.) Otherwise, if the solution $(w_1, \ldots, w_n)$ involves only integers, it minimizes the desired size. When noninteger solutions arise, additional constraints must be added until the best solution is found, as in part (c) of the following exercise.

104. First we need an algorithm to generate the prime implicants $x_1^{e_1} \wedge \cdots \wedge x_n^{e_n}$ of a given majority function $\langle x_1^{w_1} \ldots x_n^{w_n} \rangle$, when $w_1 \geq \cdots \geq w_n$ and $w_1 + \cdots + w_n$ is odd:

K1. [Initialize.] Set $t \leftarrow 0$. Then for $j = n, n - 1, \ldots, 1$ (in this order), set $a_j \leftarrow t$, $t \leftarrow t + w_j$, $e_j \leftarrow 0$. Finally set $t \leftarrow (t + 1)/2$, $s_1 \leftarrow 0$, and $l \leftarrow 0$.

K2. [Enter level l.] Set $l \leftarrow l + 1$, $e_l \leftarrow 1$, $s_{l+1} \leftarrow s_l + w_l$.

K3. [Below threshold?] If $s_{l+1} < t$, return to K2.

K4. [Visit a prime implicant.] Visit the exponents $(e_1, \ldots, e_n)$.

K5. [Downsize.] Set $e_l \leftarrow 0$. Then if $s_l + a_l \geq t$, set $s_{l+1} \leftarrow s_l$ and go to K2.

K6. [Backtrack.] Set $l \leftarrow l - 1$. Terminate if $l = 0$; otherwise go to K5 if $e_l = 1$; otherwise repeat this step. ∎

(a) $\langle x_1 x_2^2 x_3^3 x_4^5 x_5^6 x_6^8 x_7^{10} x_8^{12} \rangle$ (21 prime implicants).

(b) The optimum weights for $\langle x_0^{16-2t} x_1^8 x_2^4 x_3^2 x_4 \rangle$ are $w_0 w_1 w_2 w_3 w_4 = 10000, 31111, 21110, 32211, 11100, 23211, 12110, 13111, 01000$, for $0 \leq t \leq 8$; the other cases are dual.

(c) Here the optimum weights $(w_1, \ldots, w_{10})$ are $(29, 25, 19, 15, 12, 8, 8, 3, 3, 0)/2$; so we learn that x_{10} is irrelevant, and we must deal with fractional weights. Constraining $w_8 \geq 2$ gives integer weights $(15, 13, 10, 8, 6, 4, 4, 2, 1, 0)$, which must be optimum because their sum exceeds the previous sum by 2. (Only two of the 175,428 self-dual threshold functions on nine variables have nonintegral weights minimizing $w_1 + \cdots + w_n$; the other one is $\langle x_1^{17} x_2^{15} x_3^{11} x_4^9 x_5^7 x_6^5 x_7^4 x_8^2 x_9 \rangle$. The largest w_1 in a minimum representation occurs in $\langle x_1^{42} x_2^{22} x_3^{18} x_4^{15} x_5^{13} x_6^{10} x_7^8 x_8^4 x_9^3 \rangle$; the largest $w_1 + \cdots + w_9$ occurs uniquely in $\langle x_1^{34} x_2^{32} x_3^{28} x_4^{27} x_5^{24} x_6^{20} x_7^{18} x_8^{15} x_9^{11} \rangle$, which is also an example of the largest w_9. See S. Muroga, T. Tsuboi, and C. R. Baugh, *IEEE Transactions* **C-19** (1970), 818–825.)

105. When $n = 7$, the inequalities generated in exercise 103 are $w_7 + w_6 - w_5 - w_4 - w_3 - w_2 - w_1 \geq 1$, $-w_7 + w_6 + w_5 - w_4 - w_3 - w_2 - w_1 \geq 1$, $w_7 - w_6 + w_5 + w_4 - w_3 - w_2 - w_1 \geq 1$, $-w_7 + w_6 - w_5 + w_4 + w_3 - w_2 - w_1 \geq 1$, $w_7 - w_6 + w_5 - w_4 + w_3 + w_2 - w_1 \geq 1$, $-w_7 + w_6 - w_5 + w_4 - w_3 + w_2 + w_1 \geq 1$, $w_7 - w_6 + w_5 - w_4 + w_3 - w_2 + w_1 \geq 1$. Multiply them respectively by 1, 1, 2, 3, 5, 8, 5 to get $w_1 + \cdots + w_7 \geq 1 + 1 + 2 + 3 + 5 + 8 + 5$. The same idea works for all $n \geq 3$.

106. (a) $\langle x_1^{2^{n-1}} x_2^{2^{n-2}} \ldots x_n \bar{y}_1^{2^{n-1}} \bar{y}_2^{2^{n-2}} \ldots \bar{y}_n \bar{z} \rangle$. (By exercise 99, we could also perform n medians-of-three: $\langle \langle \ldots \langle x_n \bar{y}_n \bar{z} \rangle \ldots x_2 \bar{y}_2 \rangle x_1 \bar{y}_1 \rangle$.)

(b) If $\langle x_1^{u_1} x_2^{u_2} \ldots x_n^{u_n} \bar{y}_1^{v_1} \bar{y}_2^{v_2} \ldots \bar{y}_n^{v_n} \bar{z}^w \rangle$ solves the problem, $2^{n+1} - 1$ basic inequalities need to hold; for example, when $n = 2$ they are $u_1 + u_2 - v_1 + v_2 - w \geq 1$, $u_1 + u_2 - v_1 - v_2 + w \geq 1$, $u_1 - u_2 + v_1 - v_2 - w \geq 1$, $u_1 - u_2 - v_1 + v_2 + w \geq 1$, $-u_1 + u_2 + v_1 + v_2 - w \geq 1$, $-u_1 + u_2 + v_1 - v_2 + w \geq 1$, $-u_1 - u_2 + v_1 + v_2 + w \geq 1$. Add them all up to get $u_1 + u_2 + \cdots + u_n + v_1 + v_2 + \cdots + v_n + w \geq 2^{n+1} - 1$.

107.

f	$N(f)$	$\Sigma(f)$	f	$N(f)$	$\Sigma(f)$	f	$N(f)$	$\Sigma(f)$	f	$N(f)$	$\Sigma(f)$
$\bot$	0	$(0,0)$	$\bar{\subset}$	1	$(0,1)$	$\bar{\vee}$	1	$(0,0)$	$\llcorner$	2	$(0,1)$
$\wedge$	1	$(1,1)$	R	2	$(1,2)$	$\equiv$	2	$(1,1)$	$\supset$	3	$(1,2)$
$\bar{\supset}$	1	$(1,0)$	$\oplus$	2	$(1,1)$	$\bar{\mathsf{R}}$	2	$(1,0)$	$\overline{\wedge}$	3	$(1,1)$
$\llcorner$	2	$(2,1)$	$\vee$	3	$(2,2)$	$\subset$	3	$(2,1)$	$\top$	4	$(2,2)$

Notice that $\oplus$ and $\equiv$ have the same parameters $N(f)$ and $\Sigma(f)$; they are the only Boolean binary operations that aren't threshold functions.

108. If $\Sigma(g) = (s_0, s_1, \ldots, s_n)$, the value of g is 1 in s_0 cases when $x_0 = 1$ and in $2^n - s_0$ cases when $x_0 = 0$. We also have $\Sigma(f_0) + \Sigma(f_1) = (s_1, \ldots, s_n)$, and

$$\Sigma(f_0) = \sum_{x_1=0}^{1} \cdots \sum_{x_n=0}^{1} (\bar{x}_1, \ldots, \bar{x}_n) g(0, \bar{x}_1, \ldots, \bar{x}_n)$$

$$= \sum_{x_1=0}^{1} \cdots \sum_{x_n=0}^{1} \big((1, \ldots, 1) - (x_1, \ldots, x_n)\big)\big(1 - g(1, x_1, \ldots, x_n)\big)$$

$$= (2^{n-1} - s_0, \ldots, 2^{n-1} - s_0) + \Sigma(f_1).$$

So the answers, for $n > 0$, are (a) $N(f_0) = 2^n - s_0$, $\Sigma(f_0) = \frac{1}{2}(s_1 - s_0 + 2^{n-1}, \ldots, s_n - s_0 + 2^{n-1})$; (b) $N(f_1) = s_0$, $\Sigma(f_1) = \frac{1}{2}(s_1 + s_0 - 2^{n-1}, \ldots, s_n + s_0 - 2^{n-1})$. [Equivalent results were presented by E. Goto in lectures at MIT in 1963.]

109. (a) $a_1 + \cdots + a_k \geq b_1 + \cdots + b_k$ if and only if $k - a_1 - \cdots - a_k \leq k - b_1 - \cdots - b_k$.

(b) Let $\alpha^+ = (a_1, a_1 + a_2, \ldots, a_1 + \cdots + a_n)$. Then the vector $(c_1, \ldots, c_n)$ obtained by componentwise minimization of α^+ and β^+ is $(\alpha \wedge \beta)^+$. (Clearly $c_j = c_{j-1} + a_j$ or b_j.)

(c) Proceed as in (b) but with componentwise *maximization*; or take $\overline{\bar{\alpha} \wedge \bar{\beta}}$.

(d) True, because max and min satisfy these distributive laws. (In fact, we obtain a distributive *mixed-radix majorization lattice* in a similar way from the set of all n-tuples $a_1 \ldots a_n$ such that $0 \leq a_j < m_j$ for $1 \leq j \leq n$.)

(e) $\alpha 1$ covers $\alpha 0$ and $\alpha 10 \beta$ covers $\alpha 01 \beta$. [This characterization is due to R. O. Winder, *IEEE Trans.* **EC-14** (1965), 315–325, but he didn't prove the lattice property. The lattice is often called $M(n)$; see B. Lindström, *Nordisk Mat. Tidskrift* **17** (1969), 61–70; R. P. Stanley, *SIAM J. Algebraic and Discrete Methods* **1** (1980), 177–179.]

(f) Because of (e) we have $r(\alpha) = na_1 + (n-1)a_2 + \cdots + a_n$.

(g) The point is that $0\beta \succeq 0\alpha$ if and only if $\beta \succeq \alpha$ and that $1\beta \succeq 0\alpha$ if and only if $1\beta \succeq 10\ldots0 \vee 0\alpha = 1\alpha'$.

(h) That is, how many $a_1 \ldots a_n$ have the property that $a_1 \ldots a_k$ contains no more 1s than 0s? The answer is $\binom{n}{\lfloor n/2 \rfloor}$; see, for example, exercise 2.2.1–4 or 7.2.1.6–42(a).

110. (a) If $x \subseteq y$ then $x \preceq y$, hence $f(x) \leq f(y)$; QED.

(b) No; a threshold function need not be monotone (see (79)). But we *can* show that f is regular if we also require $w_n \geq 0$: For if $f(x) = 1$ and y covers x we then have $w \cdot y \geq w \cdot x$.

(c) Whenever $f(x) = 1$ and $x_j < x_{j+1}$, we have $f(y) = 1$ when y covers x with $x_j \leftrightarrow x_{j+1}$; hence $s_j \geq s_{j+1}$. (This argument holds even when $w_n < 0$.)

(d) No; consider, for example, $\langle x_1 x_2^2 x_3^2 \rangle$, which equals $\langle x_1 x_2 x_3 \rangle$. Counterexamples can arise even when the weights minimize $w_1 + \cdots + w_n$, because the solution to the linear program in exercise 103 is not always unique. One such case, found by Muroga, Tsuboi, and Baugh, is $\langle x_1^{17} x_2^9 x_3^8 x_4^6 x_5^7 x_6^5 x_7^3 x_8^2 x_9^2 \rangle$, a function that is actually symmetric in x_4 and x_5. But if $s_j > s_{j+1}$ we must have $w_j > w_{j+1}$, because of (c).

111. (a) Find an optimum self-dual function f pointwise as in exercise 14; in case of ties, set $f(x_1, \ldots, x_n) = x_1$. Then $f(x_1, \ldots, x_n) = [r_1^{x_1} \ldots r_n^{x_n} \geq \sqrt{r_1 \ldots r_n}]$, except that '$\geq$' becomes '$>$' when $x_1 = 0$. This function is regular when $r_1 \geq \cdots \geq r_n \geq 1$.

(b) Let g be the regular, self-dual function constructed in (a). If f is a given regular, self-dual function, we want to verify that $f(x) \leq g(x)$ for all vectors x; this will imply that $f = g$, because both functions are self-dual.

Suppose $f(x) = 1$, and let $y \preceq x$ be minimal such that $f(y) = 1$. If we have verified that $g(y) = 1$, then indeed $g(x) = 1$, as desired. [See K. Makino and T. Kameda, *SIAM Journal on Discrete Mathematics* **14** (2001), 381–407.]

For example, there are only seven self-dual regular Boolean functions when $n = 5$, generated by the following minimal elements in Fig. 8: 10000; 01111, 10001; 01110, 10010; 01101, 10011, 10100; 01100; 01011, 11000; 00111. So an optimum coterie can be found by examining only a few function values.

(c) Suppose $1 > p_1 \geq \cdots \geq p_r \geq \frac{1}{2} > p_{r+1} \geq \cdots \geq p_n > 0$. Let $f_k(x_1, \ldots, x_n)$ be the kth monotone, self-dual function and $F_k(x_1, \ldots, x_n)$ its integer multilinear representation. We want to find the optimum availability $G(p_1, \ldots, p_n) = \max_k F_k(p_1, \ldots, p_n)$. If $p_1 \leq p_1'$, $\ldots$, $p_n \leq p_n'$, we have $F_k(p_1, \ldots, p_n) \leq F_k(p_1', \ldots, p_n')$ by exercise 12(e); hence $G(p_1, \ldots, p_n) \leq G(p_1', \ldots, p_n')$.

Therefore if $0 < r < n$ we have $G(p_1, \ldots, p_n) \leq G(p_1, \ldots, p_r, \frac{1}{2}, \ldots, \frac{1}{2})$. And the latter is $F(p_1, \ldots, p_r, \frac{1}{2}, \ldots, \frac{1}{2})$, where f is the function derived in part (a). This function does not depend on $(x_{r+1}, \ldots, x_n)$, so it gives the optimum.

If $r = 0$ the problem seems to be deeper. We have $G(p_1, \ldots, p_n) \leq G(p_1, \ldots, p_1)$; so we can conclude that the optimum coterie is $f(x_1, \ldots, x_n) = x_1$ if we can show that $F_k(p, \ldots, p) \leq p$ for all k whenever $p < \frac{1}{2}$. In general $F_k(p \ldots, p) = \sum_m c_m p^m (1 - p)^{n-m}$, where c_m is the number of vectors x such that $f_k(x) = 1$ and $\nu x = m$. Exercise 70 tells us that $c_m + c_{n-m} = \binom{n}{m}$, for all k. And the Erdős–Ko–Rado theorem (exercise 7.2.1.3–111) tells us that $c_m \leq \binom{n-1}{m-1}$ for any intersecting family of m-sets when $m \leq n/2$. The result follows.

[See Y. Amir and A. Wool, *Information Processing Letters* **65** (1998), 223–228.]

112. (a) The leading terms are respectively 0, $+xy$, $-xy$, $+x$, $-xy$, $+y$, $-2xy$, $-xy$, $+xy$, $+2xy$, $-y$, $+xy$, $-x$, $+xy$, $-xy$, 1; so $F(f) = 1$ when f is $\wedge$, L, R, $\bar{\vee}$, $\equiv$, C, D, T.

(b) The coefficient corresponding to exponents 01101, say, is f_{0**0*} in the notation of answer 12; it is a linear combination of truth table entries, always lying in the range $\lceil -2^{k-1} \rceil \leq f_{0**0*} \leq \lceil 2^{k-1} \rceil$ when there are k asterisks. Thus the leading coefficient is positive if and only if the mixed-radix number

$$\begin{bmatrix} f_{**\ldots*}, & f_{0*\ldots*}, & \ldots, & f_{*0\ldots0}, & f_{00\ldots0} \\ 2^m+1, & 2^{m-1}+1, & \ldots, & 2^1+1, & 2^0+1 \end{bmatrix}$$

is positive, where the f's are arranged in reverse order of Chase's sequence and the radix $2^k + 1$ corresponds to an f with k asterisks. For example, when $m = 2$ we have $F(f) = 1$ if and only if the sum $18f_{**} + 6f_{0*} + 2f_{*0} + f_{00} = 18(f_{11} - f_{01} - f_{10} + f_{00}) + 6(f_{01} - f_{00}) + 2(f_{10} - f_{00}) + f_{00} = 18f_{11} - 12f_{01} - 16f_{10} + 11f_{00}$ is positive; so the threshold function can be written $\langle f_{11}^{18} \bar{f}_{01}^{12} \bar{f}_{10}^{16} f_{00}^{11} \rangle$.

(In this particular case the much simpler expression $\langle f_{11}f_{11}\bar{f}_{01}\bar{f}_{10}f_{00} \rangle$ is actually valid. But part (c) will show that when m is large we can't do a great deal better.)

(c) Suppose $F(f) = [\sum_\alpha v_\alpha(f_\alpha - \frac{1}{2}) > 0]$, where the sum is over all 2^m binary strings α of length m and where each v_α is an integer weight. Define

$$w_\alpha = \sum_\beta (-1)^{\nu(\alpha \dot- \beta)} v_\beta \quad \text{and} \quad F_\alpha = \sum_\beta (-1)^{\nu(\alpha \dot- \beta)} f_\beta - 2^{m-1}[\alpha = 00 \ldots 0];$$

thus, for example, $w_{01} = -v_{00} + v_{01} - v_{10} + v_{11}$ and $F_{11} = f_{00} - f_{01} - f_{10} + f_{11}$. One can show that $F_{1^k0^l} = 2^l f_{*^k0^l}$, if $F_\alpha = 0$ whenever $\nu(\alpha) > k > 0$; therefore the signs of the transformed truth coefficients F_α determine the sign of the leading coefficient in the multilinear representation. Furthermore, we now have $F(f) = [\sum_\alpha w_\alpha F_\alpha > 0]$.

The general idea of the proof is to choose test functions f from which we can derive properties of the transformed weights w_α. For example, if $f(x_1, \ldots, x_m) = x_1 \oplus \cdots \oplus x_k$, we find $F_\alpha = 0$ for all α except that $F_{1^k0^{m-k}} = (-1)^{k-1}2^{m-1}$. The multilinear representation of $x_1 \oplus \cdots \oplus x_k$ has leading term $\lceil(-2)^{k-1}\rceil x_1 \ldots x_k$; hence we can conclude that $w_{1^k0^{m-k}} > 0$, and in a similar way that $w_\alpha > 0$ for all α. In general if m changes to $m+1$ but f does not depend on x_{m+1}, we have $F_{\alpha 0} = 2F_\alpha$ and $F_{\alpha 1} = 0$.

The test function $x_2 \oplus \cdots \oplus x_m \oplus x_1 \bar{x}_2 \ldots \bar{x}_m$ proves that

$$w_{1^m} > (2^{m-1}-1)w_{01^{m-1}} + \sum_{k=1}^{m-1} w_{1^k01^{m-1-k}} + \text{smaller terms,}$$

where the smaller terms involve only w_α with $\nu(\alpha) \leq m - 2$. In particular, $w_{11} > w_{01} + w_{10} + w_{00}$. The test function $x_1 \oplus \cdots \oplus x_{m-1} \oplus \bar{x}_1 \ldots \bar{x}_{m-2}(x_{m-1} \oplus \bar{x}_m)$ proves

$$w_{1^{m-2}01} > (2^{m-2}-1)w_{1^{m-2}10} + \sum_{k=0}^{m-3}(w_{1^k01^{m-3-k}10} + w_{1^k01^{m-3-k}01}) + \text{smaller terms,}$$

where the smaller terms this time have $\nu(\alpha) \leq m - 3$. In particular, $w_{101} > w_{110} + w_{010} + w_{001}$. By permuting subscripts, we obtain similar inequalities leading to

$$w_{\alpha_j} > (2^{\nu(\alpha_j)-1} - 1)w_{\alpha_{j-1}} \qquad \text{for } 0 < j < 2^m,$$

because the w's begin to grow rapidly. But we have $v_\alpha = \sum_\beta (-1)^{\nu(\beta \dot{-} \alpha)} w_\beta/n$; hence $|v_\alpha| = w_{11\ldots1}/n + O(w_{11\ldots1}/n^2)$. [*SIAM J. Discrete Math.* **7** (1994), 484–492. Important generalizations of this result have been obtained by N. Alon and V. H. Vŭ, *J. Combinatorial Theory* **A79** (1997), 133–160.]

113. The stated g_3 is $S_{2,3,6,8,9}$ because the stated g_2 is $S_{2,3,4,5,8,9,10,11,12}$.

For the more difficult function $S_{1,3,5,8}$, let $g_1 = [\nu x \geq 6]$; $g_2 = [\nu x \geq 3]$; $g_3 = [\nu x - 5g_1 - 2g_2 \geq 2] = S_{2,4,5,9,10,11,12}$; $g_4 = [2\nu x - 15g_1 - 9g_3 \geq 1] = S_{1,3,5,8}$. [See M. A. Fischler and M. Tannenbaum, *IEEE Transactions* **C-17** (1968), 273–279.]

114. $[4x + 2y + z \in \{3,6\}] = (\bar{x} \wedge y \wedge z) \vee (x \wedge y \wedge \bar{z})$. In the same way, *any* Boolean function of n variables is a special case of a symmetric function of $2^n - 1$ variables. [See W. H. Kautz, *IRE Transactions* **EC-10** (1961), 378.]

115. Both sides are self-dual, so we may assume that $x_0 = 0$. Then

$$s_j = [x_j + \cdots + x_{j+m-1} > x_{j+m} + \cdots + x_{j+2m-1}].$$

If $x_1 + \cdots + x_{2m}$ is odd, we have $s_j = \bar{s}_{j+m}$; hence $s_1 + \cdots + s_{2m} = m$ and the result is 1. But if $x_1 + \cdots + x_{2m}$ is even, the difference $x_j + \cdots + x_{j+m-1} - x_{j+m} - \cdots - x_{j+2m-1}$ will be zero for at least one $j \leq m$; that makes $s_j = s_{j+m} = 0$, so we will have $s_1 + \cdots + s_{2m} < m$.

116. (a) It's an implicant if and only if $f(x) = 1$ whenever $j \leq \nu x \leq n - k + j$. It's a prime implicant if and only if we also have $f(x) = 0$ when $\nu x = j-1$ or $\nu x = n-k+j+1$.

(b) Consider the string $v = v_0 v_1 \ldots v_n$ such that $f(x) = v_{\nu x}$. By part (a), there are $\binom{a+b+c}{a,b,c}$ prime implicants when $v = 0^a 1^{b+1} 0^c$. In the stated case, $a = b = c = 3$, so there are 1680 prime implicants.

(c) For a general symmetric function, we add together the prime implicants for each run of 1s in v. Clearly there are more for $v = 0^{a+1}1^{b+1}0^{c-1}$ than for $v = 0^a1^{b+1}0^c$ when $a < c - 1$; so v contains no two consecutive 0s when the maximum is reached.

Let $\hat{b}(m, n)$ be the maximum number of prime implicants possible when $v_m = 1$ and $v_j = 0$ for $m < j \leq n$. Then when $m \leq \frac{1}{2}n$ we have

$$\hat{b}(m, n) = \max_{0 \leq k \leq m} \left(\binom{n}{k, m-k, n-m} + \hat{b}(k - 2, n) \right)$$

$$= \binom{n}{\lceil m/2 \rceil, \lfloor m/2 \rfloor, n-m} + \hat{b}(\lceil m/2 \rceil - 2, n),$$

with $\hat{b}(-2, n) = \hat{b}(-1, n) = 0$. And the overall maximum is

$$\hat{b}(n) = \binom{n}{n_0, n_1, n_2} + \hat{b}(n_1 - 2, n) + \hat{b}(n_2 - 2, n), \qquad n_j = \left\lfloor \frac{n+j}{3} \right\rfloor.$$

In particular we have $\hat{b}(9) = 1698$, with the maximum occurring for $v = 1101111011$.

(d) By Stirling's approximation, $\hat{b}(n) = 3^{n+3/2}/(2\pi n) + O(3^n/n^2)$.

(e) In this case the appropriate recurrence for $m < \lceil n/2 \rceil$ is

$$\tilde{b}(m, n) = \max_{0 \leq k \leq m} \left(\binom{n}{k, m-k, n-m} + \binom{n}{k-1, 0, n-k+1} + \tilde{b}(k-2, n) \right)$$

$$= \binom{n}{\lceil m/2 \rceil, \lfloor m/2 \rfloor, n-m} + \binom{n}{\lceil m/2 \rceil - 1} + \tilde{b}(\lceil m/2 \rceil - 2, n)$$

and $\tilde{b}(n) = \tilde{b}(\lceil n/2 \rceil - 1, n)$ maximizes $\min(\text{prime implicants}(f), \text{prime implicants}(\bar{f}))$. We have $(\tilde{b}(1), \tilde{b}(2), \dots) = (1, 1, 4, 5, 21, 31, 113, 177, 766, 1271, 4687, 7999, 34412, \dots)$; for example, $\tilde{b}(9) = 766$ corresponds to $S_{0,2,3,4,8}(x_1, \dots, x_9)$. Asymptotically, $\tilde{b}(n) = 2^{(3n+3+(n \bmod 2))/2}/(2\pi n) + O(2^{3n/2}/n^2)$.

References: Summaries, Summer Inst. for Symbolic Logic (Dept. of Math., Cornell Univ., 1957), 211–212; B. Dunham and R. Fridshal, *J. Symbolic Logic* **24** (1959), 17–19; A. P. Vikulin, *Problemy Kibernetiki* **29** (1974), 151–166, which reports on work done in 1960; Y. Igarashi, *Transactions of the IEICE of Japan* **E62** (1979), 389–394.

117. The maximum number of subcubes of the n-cube, with none contained in another, is obtained when we choose all subcubes of dimension $\lfloor n/3 \rfloor$. (It is also obtained by choosing all subcubes of dimension $\lfloor (n + 1)/3 \rfloor$; for example, when $n = 2$ we can choose either $\{0*, 1*, *0, *1\}$ or $\{00, 01, 10, 11\}$.) Hence $b^*(n) = \binom{n}{\lfloor n/3 \rfloor}2^{n-\lfloor n/3 \rfloor} = 3^{n+1}/\sqrt{4\pi n} + O(3^n/n^{3/2})$. [See the paper of Vikulin in the previous answer, pages 164–166; A. K. Chandra and G. Markowsky, *Discrete Math.* **24** (1978), 7–11; N. Metropolis and G. C. Rota, *SIAM J. Applied Math.* **35** (1978), 689–694.]

118. Consider two functions equivalent if we can obtain one from the other by complementing and/or permuting variables, but not complementing the function value itself. Such functions clearly have the same number of prime implicants; this equivalence relation is studied further in answer 125 below. A computer program based on exercise 30 produces the following results:

m	Classes	Functions	m	Classes	Functions	m	Classes	Functions
0	1	1	5	87	17472	10	7	632
1	5	81	6	70	12696	11	1	96
2	18	1324	7	43	7408	12	2	24
3	46	6608	8	24	3346	13	1	16
4	87	14536	9	10	1296	14	0	0

And here are the corresponding statistics for functions of five variables:

m	Classes	Functions	m	Classes	Functions	m	Classes	Functions
0	1	1	11	186447	666555696	22	338	608240
1	6	243	12	165460	590192224	23	130	197440
2	37	14516	13	129381	459299440	24	71	75720
3	244	318520	14	91026	319496560	25	37	28800
4	1527	3319580	15	57612	199792832	26	15	10560
5	6997	19627904	16	33590	113183894	27	6	2880
6	23434	73795768	17	17948	58653984	28	4	1040
7	57048	190814016	18	8880	27429320	29	2	640
8	105207	362973410	19	3986	11597760	30	2	48
9	152763	538238660	20	1795	4548568	31	2	64
10	183441	652555480	21	720	1633472	32	1	16

119. Several authors have conjectured that $b(n) = \hat{b}(n)$; M. M. Gadzhiev has proved that equality holds for $n \le 6$ [*Diskretnyĭ Analiz* **18** (1971), 3–24].

120. (a) Every prime implicant is a minterm, since no adjacent points of the n-cube have the same parity. So the full disjunctive form is the only decent DNF in this case.

(b) Now all prime implicants consist of two adjacent points. We must include the 14 subcubes 0^j*0^{6-j} and 1^j*1^{6-j} for $0 \le j \le 6$, in order to cover the points with $\nu x = 1$ and $\nu x = 6$. The other $\binom{7}{3} + \binom{7}{4} = 70$ points can be covered by 35 well-chosen prime implicants (see, for example, exercise 6.5–1, or the "Christmas tree pattern" in Section 7.2.1.6). Thus the shortest DNF has length 49. [An ingeniously plausible but fallacious argument that 70 prime implicants are necessary was presented by S. B. Yablonsky in *Problemy Kibernetiki* **7** (1962), 229–230.]

(c) For each of 2^{n-1} choices of $(x_1, \ldots, x_{n-1})$ we need at most one implicant to account for the behavior of the function with respect to x_n.

[Asymptotically, almost all Boolean functions of n variables have a shortest DNF with $\Theta(2^n/(\log n \log \log n))$ prime implicants. See R. G. Nigmatullin, *Diskretnyĭ Analiz* **10** (1967), 69–89; V. V. Glagolev, *Problemy Kibernetiki* **19** (1967), 75–94; A. D. Korshunov, *Metody Diskretnogo Analiza* **37** (1981), 9–41; N. Pippenger, *Random Structures & Algorithms* **22** (2003), 161–186.]

121. (a) Let $x = x_1 \ldots x_m$ and $y = y_1 \ldots y_n$. Since f is a function of $(\nu x, \nu y)$, there are altogether $2^{(m+1)(n+1)}$ possibilities.

(b) In this case $\nu x \le \nu x'$ and $\nu y \le \nu y'$ implies $f(x, y) \le f(x', y')$. Every such function corresponds to a zigzag path from $a_0 = (-\frac{1}{2}, n + \frac{1}{2})$ to $a_{m+n+2} = (m + \frac{1}{2}, -\frac{1}{2})$, with $a_j = a_{j-1} + (1, 0)$ or $a_j = a_{j-1} - (0, 1)$ for $1 \le j \le m + n + 2$; we have $f(x, y) = 1$ if and only if the point $(\nu x, \nu y)$ lies above the path. So the number of possibilities is the number of such paths, namely $\binom{m+n+2}{m+1}$.

(c) Complementing x and y changes νx to $m - \nu x$ and νy to $n - \nu y$. So there are no such functions when m and n are both even; otherwise there are $2^{(m+1)(n+1)/2}$.

(d) The path in (b) must now satisfy $a_j + a_{m+n+2-j} = (m, n)$ for $0 \le j \le m+n+2$. Hence there are $\binom{\lceil m/2 \rceil + \lceil n/2 \rceil}{\lceil m/2 \rceil}$ [m odd or n odd] such functions. For example, the ten cases when $m = 3$ and $n = 6$ are

122. A function of this kind is regular with the x's to the left of the y's if and only if the zigzag path does not contain two points (x, y) and $(x + 2, y)$ with $0 < y < n$; it is regular with the y's left of the x's if and only if the zigzag path does not contain both $(x, y + 2)$ and (x, y) with $0 < x < m$. It is a threshold function if and only if there is a straight line through the point $(m/2, n/2)$ with the property that (s, t) is above the line if and only if (s, t) is above the path, for $0 \le s \le m$ and $0 \le t \le n$. So cases 5 and 8, illustrated in the previous answer, fail to be regular; cases 1, 2, 3, 7, 9, and 10 are threshold functions. The regular non-threshold functions that remain can also be expressed as follows: $((x_1 \lor x_2 \lor x_3) \land \langle x_1 x_2 x_3 y_1 y_2 y_3 y_4 y_5 y_6 \rangle) \lor (x_1 \land x_2 \land x_3)$ (case 4); $\langle 00 x_1 x_2 x_3 y_1 y_2 y_3 y_4 y_5 y_6 \rangle \lor (\langle x_1 x_2 x_3 \rangle \land \langle 11 x_1 x_2 x_3 y_1 y_2 y_3 y_4 y_5 y_6 \rangle)$ (case 6).

123. Self-dual *regular* functions are relatively easy to list, for small n, but the numbers grow rapidly: When $n = 9$ there are 319,124 of them, found by Muroga, Tsuboi, and Baugh in 1967, and when $n = 10$ there are 1,214,554,343 (see exercise 7.1.4–00). The corresponding numbers for $n \le 6$ appear in Table 5, because all such functions are threshold functions when $n < 9$; there are 135 when $n = 7$, and 2470 when $n = 8$.

The threshold condition can be tested quickly for any such function by improving on the method of exercise 103, because constraints are needed only for the *minimal* vectors x (with respect to majorization) such that $f(x) = 1$.

The number θ_n of n-variable threshold functions is known to satisfy $\lg \theta_n = n^2 - O(n^2/\log n)$; see Yu. A. Zuev, *Matematicheskie Voprosy Kibernetiki* **5** (1994), 5–61.

124. The 222 equivalence classes listed in Table 5 include 24 classes of size $2^{n+1} n! = 768$; so there are $24 \times 768 = 18432$ answers to this problem. One of them is the function $(w \land (x \lor (y \land z))) \oplus z$.

125. 0; x; $x \land y$; $x \land y \land z$; $x \land (y \lor z)$; $x \land (y \oplus z)$. (These functions are $x \land f(y, z)$, where f runs through the equivalence classes of two-variable functions under permutation and/or complementation of variables but *not* of the function values. In general, let $f \simeq g$ mean that f is equivalent to g in that weaker sense, but write $f \cong g$ if they are equivalent in the sense of Table 5. Then $x \land f \cong x \land g$ if and only if $f \simeq g$, assuming that f and g are independent of the variable x. For it's easy to see that $(x \land f) \simeq (\bar{x} \lor \bar{g})$ is impossible. And if $(x \land f) \simeq (x \land g)$, we can prove that $f \simeq g$ by showing that, if σ is a signed permutation of $\{x_0, \ldots, x_n\}$ and if $x = x_1 \ldots x_n$, then the identity $x_0 \land f(x) = (x_0\sigma) \land g(x\sigma)$ implies $f(x) = g(x\sigma\tau)$, where τ interchanges $x_0 \leftrightarrow x_0\sigma$. Consequently the bottom line of Table 5 enumerates equivalence classes under $\simeq$, but with n increased by 1; there are, for example, 402 such classes of 4-variable functions.)

126. (a) The function is canalizing if and only if it has a prime implicant with at most one literal, or a prime clause with at most one literal.

(b) The function is canalizing if and only if at least one of the components of $\Sigma(f)$ is equal to 0, 2^{n-1}, $N(f)$, or $N(f) - 2^{n-1}$. [See I. Shmulevich, H. Lähdesmäki, and K. Egiazarian, *IEEE Signal Processing Letters* **11** (2004), 289–292, Proposition 6.]

(c) If, say, $\lor(f) = y_1 \ldots y_n$ with $y_j = 0$, then $f(x) = 0$ whenever $x_j = 1$. Therefore f is canalizing if and only if we don't have $\lor(f) = \lor(\bar{f}) = 1 \ldots 1$ and $\land(f) = \land(\bar{f}) = 0 \ldots 0$. With this test one can prove that many functions are noncanalizing when their value is known at only a few points.

127. (a) Since a self-dual function $f(x_1, \ldots, x_n)$ is true at exactly 2^{n-1} points, it is canalizing with respect to the variable x_j if and only if $f(x_1, \ldots, x_n) = x_j$.

(b) A definite Horn function is clearly canalizing if (i) it contains any clause with a single literal, or (ii) some literal occurs in every clause. Otherwise it is not canalizing. For we have $f(0, \ldots, 0) = f(1, \ldots, 1) = 1$, because (i) is false; and if x_j is any variable, there is a clause C_0 not containing $\bar{x}_j$ and a clause C_1 not containing x_j, because (ii) is false. By choosing appropriate values of the other variables, we can make $C_0 \wedge C_1$ false when $x_j = 0$ and also when $x_j = 1$.

128. For example, $(x_1 \wedge \cdots \wedge x_n) \vee (\bar{x}_1 \wedge \cdots \wedge \bar{x}_n)$.

129. $\sum_{k=1}^{n} (-1)^{k+1} \binom{n}{k} 2^{2^{n-k}+k+1} - 2(n-1) - 4(n \bmod 2) = n 2^{2^{n-1}+2} + O(n^2 2^{2^{n-2}})$. [See W. Just, I. Shmulevich, and J. Konvalina, *Physica* **D197** (2004), 211–221.]

130. (a) If there are a_n functions of n or fewer variables, but b_n functions of exactly n variables, we have $a_n = \sum_k \binom{n}{k} b_k$. Therefore $b_n = \sum_k (-1)^{n-k} \binom{n}{k} a_k$. (This rule, noted by C. E. Shannon in *Trans. Amer. Inst. Electrical Engineers* **57** (1938), 713–723, §4, applies to all rows of Table 3, *except* for the case of symmetric functions.) In particular, the answer sought here is $168 - 4 \cdot 20 + 6 \cdot 6 - 4 \cdot 3 + 2 = 114$.

(b) If there are a'_n essentially distinct functions of n or fewer variables, and b'_n of exactly n variables, we have $a'_n = \sum_{k=0}^{n} b'_k$. Hence $b'_n = a'_n - a'_{n-1}$, and the answer in this case is $30 - 10 = 20$.

131. Let there be $h(n)$ Horn functions and $k(n)$ Krom functions. Clearly $\lg h(n) \geq \binom{n}{\lfloor n/2 \rfloor}$ and $\lg k(n) \geq \binom{n}{2}$. V. B. Alekseyev [*Diskretnaĭa Matematika* **1** (1989), 129–136] has proved that $\lg h(n) = \binom{n}{\lfloor n/2 \rfloor}(1 + O(n^{-1/4} \log n))$. B. Bollobás, G. Brightwell, and I. Leader [*Israel J. Math.* **133** (2003), 45–60] have proved that $\lg k(n) \sim \frac{1}{2} n^2$.

132. (a) The hint is true because $\sum_y s(y) s(y \oplus z) = \sum_{w,x,y} (-1)^{f(w)+w \cdot y + f(x) + x \cdot (y+z)} = 2^n \sum_{w,x} (-1)^{f(w)+f(x)+x \cdot z} [x = w]$. Now suppose that $f(x) = g(x)$ for $2^{n-1} + k$ values of x; then $f(x) = g(x) \oplus 1$ for $2^{n-1} - k$ values of x. But if $|k| < 2^{n/2-1}$ for all affine g, we would have $|s(y)| < 2^{n/2}$ for all y, contradicting the hint when $z = 0$.

(b) Given $y = y_1 \ldots y_n$, there are exactly $2^{n/2}((y_1 y_2 + y_3 y_4 + \cdots + y_{n-1} y_n + 1 + h(y_1, y_3, \ldots, y_{n-1})) \bmod 2)$ solutions to $f(x) = x \cdot y \bmod 2$ when $x_{2k} = y_{2k-1}$ for $1 \leq k \leq n/2$, and there are $2^{n/2-1}$ solutions for each of the other $2^{n/2} - 1$ values of $(x_2, x_4, \ldots, x_n)$. So there are $2^{n-1} \pm 2^{n/2-1}$ solutions altogether. (This argument proves, in fact, that $(g(x_1, x_3, \ldots, x_{2n-1}) \cdot (x_2, x_4, \ldots, x_{2n}) + h(x_2, x_4, \ldots, x_{2n})) \bmod 2$ is bent whenever $g(x_1, x_3, \ldots, x_{2n-1})$ is a permutation of all $2^{n/2}$-bit vectors.)

(c) If $f(x)$ is bent, the argument in part (a) proves that $s(y) = 2^{n/2}(-1)^{g(y)}$ for some Boolean function $g(y)$. This function is also bent, because $\sum_y (-1)^{g(y)+w \cdot y} = 2^{-n/2} \sum_{x,y} (-1)^{f(x)+x \cdot y + w \cdot y} = 2^{n/2} \sum_x (-1)^{f(x)} [x = w] = 2^{n/2} (-1)^{f(w)}$ for all w. Consequently the hint tells us that we have $\sum_x (-1)^{f(x)+f(x \oplus z)} = 0$ for all nonzero z.

Conversely, assume that $f(x)$ satisfies the stated condition, and that $f(x) = 1$ for exactly k values of x. If y is any Boolean vector, the function $g(x) = (f(x)+x \cdot y) \bmod 2$ also satisfies the condition; therefore we need only prove that $k = 2^{n-1} \pm 2^{n/2-1}$.

Let A be the $2^n \times 2^n$ matrix with $f(x \oplus y)$ in row x and column y, and let J be the $2^n \times 2^n$ matrix of all 1s. Then we have $J^2 = 2^n J$ and $JA = AJ = kJ$, hence

$$2^n I = (J - 2A)^2 = 2^n J - 4kJ + 4A^2;$$

and it follows, when $y \neq 0 \ldots 0$, that the number of x such that $f(x) = 1$ and $f(x \oplus y) = 1$ is $k - 2^{n-2}$. In other words, there are exactly $k - 2^{n-2}$ ordered pairs of vectors (w, x) such that $f(w) = f(x) = 1$ and $w \oplus x = y$. Summing over all y gives $(2^n - 1)(k - 2^{n-2}) = k(k-1)$, and the solutions to this quadratic equation are $k = 2^{n-1} \pm 2^{n/2-1}$.

(d) By exercise 11, the term $x_1 \ldots x_r$ is present if and only if the equation $f(x_1, \ldots, x_r, 0, \ldots, 0) = 1$ has an odd number of solutions, and an equivalent condition is $\left(\sum_{x_1,\dots,x_r}(-1)^{f(x_1,\dots,x_r,0,\dots,0)}\right) \bmod 4 = 2$. We've seen in part (c) that this sum is

$$2^{-n} \sum_{x_1,\dots,x_r,y} s(y)(-1)^{x_1 y_1 + \dots + x_r y_r} = 2^{r-n} \sum_{y_{r+1},\dots,y_n} s(0,\dots,0,y_{r+1},\dots,y_n).$$

If $r = n$, the latter sum is $\pm 2^{n/2}$; otherwise it contains an even number of summands, each of which is $\pm 2^{r-n/2}$. So the result is a multiple of 4.

[Bent functions were introduced by O. S. Rothaus in 1966; his privately circulated paper was eventually published in *J. Combinatorial Theory* **A20** (1976), 300–305. J. F. Dillon, *Congressus Numerantium* **14** (1975), 237–249, discovered additional families of bent functions, and many other examples have subsequently been found when $n \geq 8$ and n is even. Bent functions don't exist when n is odd, but a function like $g(x_1,\dots,x_{n-1}) \oplus x_n \wedge h(x_1,\dots,x_{n-1})$ has distance $2^{n-1} - 2^{(n-3)/2}$ from all affine functions when g and h are bent. A better construction for the case $n = 15$ was found by N. J. Patterson and D. H. Wiedemann, *IEEE Transactions* **IT-29** (1983), 354–356, **IT-36** (1990), 443, achieving distance $2^{14} - 108$.]

133. Let $p_k = 1/(2^{2^{n-k}}+1)$, so that $\bar{p}_k = 2^{2^{n-k}}/(2^{2^{n-k}}+1)$. [Ph.D. thesis (MIT, 1994).]

SECTION 7.1.2

1. $((x_1 \vee x_4) \wedge x_2) \equiv (x_1 \vee x_3)$.

2. (a) $(w \oplus (x \wedge y)) \oplus ((x \oplus y) \wedge z)$; (b) $(w \wedge (x \vee y)) \wedge ((x \wedge y) \vee z)$.

3. [*Doklady Akademii Nauk SSSR* **115** (1957), 247–248.] Construct a $k \times n$ matrix whose rows are the vectors x where $f(x) = 1$. By permuting and/or complementing variables, we may assume that the top row is $1 \ldots 1$ and that the columns are sorted. Suppose there are l distinct columns. Then $f = g \wedge h$, where g is the AND of the expressions $(x_{j-1} \equiv x_j)$ over all $1 < j \leq n$ such that column $j - 1$ equals column j, and h is the OR of k minterms of length l, using one variable from each group of equal columns. For example, if $n = 8$ and if f is 1 at the $k = 3$ points 11111111, 00001111, 00110111, then $l = 4$ and $f(x)$ equals $(x_1 \equiv x_2) \wedge (x_3 \equiv x_4) \wedge (x_6 \equiv x_7) \wedge (x_7 \equiv x_8) \wedge ((x_1 \wedge x_3 \wedge x_5 \wedge x_6) \vee (\bar{x}_1 \wedge \bar{x}_3 \wedge x_5 \wedge x_6) \vee (\bar{x}_1 \wedge x_3 \wedge \bar{x}_5 \wedge x_6))$. The length of this formula in general is $2n + (k - 2)l - 1$, and we have $l \leq 2^{k-1}$.

Notice that, if k is large, we get shorter formulas by writing $f(x)$ as a disjunction $f_1(x) \vee \cdots \vee f_r(x)$, where each f_j has at most $\lceil k/r \rceil$ 1s. Thus

$$L(f) \leq \min_{r \geq 1} (r - 1 + (2n + \lceil k/r - 2 \rceil 2^{\lceil k/r - 1 \rceil}) r).$$

4. The first inequality is obvious, because a binary tree of depth d has at most $1 + 2 + \cdots + 2^{d-1} = 2^d - 1$ internal nodes.

The hint follows because we can find a minimal subtree of size $\geq \lfloor r/3 \rfloor$. Its size s is at most $1 + 2(\lfloor r/3 \rfloor - 1)$. Therefore we can write $f = (g? \ f_1 \colon f_0)$, where g is a subformula of size s; f_0 and f_1 are the formulas of size $r - s - 1$ obtained when that subformula is replaced by 0 and 1, respectively.

Let $d(r) = \max\{ D(f) \mid L(f) = r \}$. Since the mux function has depth 2, and since $\max(s, r - s - 1) < \lceil \frac{2r}{3} \rceil$, we have $d(r) \leq 2 + d(\lceil \frac{2r}{3} \rceil - 1)$ for $r \geq 3$, and the result follows by induction on r. [*Hawaii International Conf. System Sci.* **4** (1971), 525–527.]

5. Let $g_0 = 0$, $g_1 = x_1$, and $g_j = x_j \wedge (x_{j-1} \vee g_{j-2})$ for $j \geq 2$. Then $F_n = g_n \vee g_{n-1}$, with cost $2n - 2$ and depth n. [These functions g_j also play a prominent role in binary addition; see exercises 42 and 44 for ways to compute them with depth $O(\log n)$.]

6. True: Consider the cases $y = 0$ and $y = 1$.

7. $\hat{x}_5 = x_1 \vee x_4$, $\hat{x}_6 = x_2 \wedge \hat{x}_5$, $\hat{x}_7 = x_1 \vee x_3$, $\hat{x}_8 = \hat{x}_6 \oplus \hat{x}_7$. (The original chain computes the "random" function (6); see exercise 1. The new chain computes the normalization of that function, namely its complement.)

8. The desired truth table consists of blocks of 2^{n-k} 0s alternating with blocks of 2^{n-k} 1s, as in (7). Therefore, if we multiply by $2^{2^{n-k}} + 1$ we get $x_k + (x_k \ll 2^{n-k})$, which is all 1s.

9. When finding $L(f) = \infty$ in step L6, we can store g and h in a record associated with f. Then a recursive procedure will be able to construct a minimum-length formula for f from the respective formulas for g and h.

10. In step L3, use $k = r - 1$ instead of $k = r - 1 - j$. Also change L to D everywhere.

11. The only subtle point is that j should *decrease* in step U3; then we'll never have $\phi(g) \& \phi(h) \neq 0$ when $j = 0$, so all cases of cost $r - 1$ will be discovered before we begin to look at list $r - 1$.

    U1. [Initialize.] Set $U(0) \leftarrow \phi(0) \leftarrow 0$ and $U(f) \leftarrow \infty$ for $1 \leq f < 2^{2^{n-1}}$. Then set $U(x_k) \leftarrow \phi(x_k) \leftarrow 0$ and put x_k into list 0, as in step L1. Also set

$U(x_j \circ x_k) \leftarrow 1$, set $\phi(x_j \circ x_k)$ to an appropriate bit vector of weight 1, and put $x_j \circ x_k$ into list 1, for $1 \le j < k \le n$ and all five normal operators $\circ$. Finally set $c \leftarrow 2^{2^n-1} - 5\binom{n}{2} - n - 1$.

U2. [Loop on r.] Do step U3 for $r = 2, 3, \ldots$, while $c > 0$.

U3. [Loop on j and k.] Do step U4 for $j = \lfloor (r-1)/2 \rfloor, \lfloor (r-1)/2 \rfloor - 1, \ldots$, and $k = r - 1 - j$, while $j \ge 0$.

U4. [Loop on g and h.] Do step U5 for all g in list j and all h in list k; if $j = k$, restrict h to functions that *follow* g in list k.

U5. [Loop on f.] If $\phi(g) \& \phi(h) \ne 0$, set $u \leftarrow r - 1$ and $v \leftarrow \phi(g) \& \phi(h)$; otherwise set $u \leftarrow r$ and $v \leftarrow \phi(g) \mid \phi(h)$. Then do step U6 for $f = g \& h$, $f = \bar{g} \& h$, $f = g \& \bar{h}$, $f = g \mid h$, and $f = g \oplus h$.

U6. [Update $U(f)$ and $\phi(f)$.] If $U(f) = \infty$, set $c \leftarrow c - 1$, $\phi(f) \leftarrow v$, and put f into list u. Otherwise if $U(f) > u$, set $\phi(f) \leftarrow v$ and move f from list $U(f)$ to list u. Otherwise if $U(f) = u$, set $\phi(f) \leftarrow \phi(f) \mid v$. ∎

12. $x_4 = x_1 \oplus x_2$, $x_5 = x_3 \wedge x_2$, $x_6 = x_2 \wedge \bar{x}_4$, $x_7 = x_5 \vee x_6$.

13. $f_5 = 01010101$ (x_3); $f_4 = 01110111$ $(x_2 \vee x_3)$; $f_3 = 01110101$ $((\bar{x}_1 \wedge x_2) \vee x_3)$; $f_2 = 00110101$ $(x_1?\ x_3\!: x_2)$; $f_1 = 00010111$ $(\langle x_1 x_2 x_3 \rangle)$.

14. For $1 \le j \le n$, first compute $t \leftarrow (g \oplus (g \gg 2^{n-j})) \& x_j$, $t \leftarrow t \oplus (t \ll 2^{n-j})$, where x_j is the truth table (11); then for $1 \le k \le n$ and $k \ne j$, the desired truth table corresponding to $x_j \leftarrow x_j \circ x_k$ is $g \oplus (t \& ((x_j \circ x_k) \oplus x_j))$.

(The $5n(n-1)$ masks $(x_j \circ x_k) \oplus x_j$ are independent of g and can be computed in advance. The same idea applies if we allow more general computations of the form $x_{j(i)} \leftarrow x_{k(i)} \circ_i x_{l(i)}$, with $5n^2(n-1)$ masks $(x_k \circ x_l) \oplus x_j$.)

15. Remarkably asymmetrical ways to compute symmetrical functions:

(a) $x_1 \leftarrow x_1 \oplus x_2$,   (b) $x_1 \leftarrow x_1 \oplus x_2$,   (c) $x_1 \leftarrow x_1 \oplus x_2$,
    $x_3 \leftarrow x_3 \oplus x_4$, $x_2 \leftarrow x_2 \wedge \bar{x}_1$, $x_2 \leftarrow x_2 \oplus x_3$,
    $x_1 \leftarrow x_1 \oplus x_3$, $x_3 \leftarrow x_3 \oplus x_4$, $x_2 \leftarrow x_2 \vee x_1$,
    $x_2 \leftarrow x_2 \oplus x_4$, $x_4 \leftarrow x_4 \wedge x_1$, $x_1 \leftarrow x_1 \oplus x_4$,
    $x_3 \leftarrow x_3 \vee x_2$, $x_2 \leftarrow \bar{x}_2 \wedge x_3$, $x_1 \leftarrow x_1 \wedge x_3$,
    $x_3 \leftarrow x_3 \wedge \bar{x}_1$. $x_2 \leftarrow x_2 \oplus x_1$, $x_2 \leftarrow x_2 \wedge \bar{x}_1$,
                                $x_2 \leftarrow x_2 \wedge \bar{x}_4$. $x_2 \leftarrow x_2 \oplus x_4$.

16. A computation that uses only $\oplus$ and complementation produces nothing but affine functions (see exercise 7.1.1–132). Suppose $f(x) = f(x_1, \ldots, x_n)$ is a non-affine function computable in minimum memory. Then $f(x)$ has the form $g(Ax + c)$ where $g(y_1, y_2, \ldots, y_n) = g(y_1 \wedge y_2, y_2, \ldots, y_n)$, for some nonsingular $n \times n$ matrix A of 0s and 1s, where x and c are column vectors and the vector operations are performed modulo 2; in this formula the matrix A and vector c account for all operations $x_i \leftarrow x_i \oplus x_j$ and/or permutations and complementations of coordinates that occur after the most recent non-affine operation that was performed. We will exploit the fact that $g(0, 0, y_3, \ldots, y_n) = g(1, 0, y_3, \ldots, y_n)$.

Let α and β be the first two rows of A; also let a and b be the first two elements of c. Then if $Ax + c \equiv y$ (modulo 2) we have $y_1 = y_2 = 0$ if and only if $\alpha \cdot x \equiv a$ and $\beta \cdot x \equiv b$. Exactly 2^{n-2} vectors x satisfy this condition, and for all such vectors we have $f(x) = f(x \oplus w)$, where $Aw \equiv (1, 0, \ldots, 0)^T$.

Given α, β, a, b, and w, with $\alpha \ne (0, \ldots, 0)$, $\beta \ne (0, \ldots, 0)$, $\alpha \ne \beta$, and $\alpha \cdot w \equiv 1$ (modulo 2), there are $2^{2^n - 2^{n-2}}$ functions f with the property that $f(x) = f(x \oplus w)$

whenever $\alpha \cdot x \bmod 2 = a$ and $\beta \cdot x \bmod 2 = b$. Therefore the total number of functions computable in minimum memory is at most 2^{n+1} (for affine functions) plus

$$(2^n - 1)(2^n - 2)2^2(2^{n-1})(2^{2^n - 2^{n-2}}) < 2^{2^n - 2^{n-2} + 3n + 1}.$$

17. Let $f(x_1, \ldots, x_n) = g(x_1, \ldots, x_{n-1}) \oplus (h(x_1, \ldots, x_{n-1}) \wedge x_n)$ as in 7.1.1–(16). Representing h in CNF, form the clauses one by one in x_0 and AND them into x_n, obtaining $h \wedge x_n$. Representing g as a sum (mod 2) of conjunctions, form the successive conjunctions in x_0 and XOR them into x_n when ready.

(It appears to be impossible to evaluate all functions inside of $n + 1$ registers if we disallow the non-canalizing operators $\oplus$ and $\equiv$. But $n + 2$ registers clearly do suffice, even if we restrict ourselves to the single operator $\bar{\wedge}$.)

18. As mentioned in answer 14, we should extend the text's definition of minimum-memory computation to allow also steps like $x_{j(i)} \leftarrow x_{k(i)} \circ_i x_{l(i)}$, with $k(i) \neq j(i)$ and $l(i) \neq j(i)$, because that will give better results for certain functions that depend on only four of the five variables. Then we find $C_m(f) = (0, 1, \ldots, 13, 14)$ for respectively $(2, 2, 5, 20, 93, 389, 1960, 10459, 47604, 135990, 198092, 123590, 21540, 472, 0)$ classes of functions ... leaving 75,908 classes (and 575,963,136 functions) for which $C_m(f) = \infty$ because they cannot be evaluated *at all* in minimum memory. The most interesting function of that kind is probably $(x_1 \wedge x_2) \vee (x_2 \wedge x_3) \vee (x_3 \wedge x_4) \vee (x_4 \wedge x_5) \vee (x_5 \wedge x_1)$, which has $C(f) = 7$ but $C_m(f) = \infty$. Another interesting case is $\big(((x_1 \vee x_2) \oplus x_3) \vee ((x_2 \vee \bar{x}_4) \wedge x_5)\big) \wedge ((x_1 \equiv x_2) \vee x_3 \vee x_4)$, for which $C(f) = 8$ and $C_m(f) = 13$. One way to evaluate that function in eight steps is $x_6 = x_1 \vee x_2$, $x_7 = x_1 \vee x_4$, $x_8 = x_2 \oplus x_7$, $x_9 = x_3 \oplus x_6$, $x_{10} = x_4 \oplus x_9$, $x_{11} = x_5 \vee x_9$, $x_{12} = x_8 \wedge x_{10}$, $x_{13} = x_{11} \wedge \bar{x}_{12}$.

19. If not, the left and right subtrees of the root must overlap, since case (i) fails. Each variable must occur at least once as a leaf, by hypothesis. At least two variables must occur at least twice as leaves, since case (ii) fails. But we can't have $n + 2$ leaves with $r \leq n + 1$ internal nodes, unless the subtrees fail to overlap.

20. Now Algorithm L (with '$f = g \oplus h$' omitted in step L5) shows that some formulas must have length 15; and even the footprint method of exercise 11 does no better than 14. To get truly minimum chains, the 25 special chains for $r = 6$ in the text must be supplemented by five others that can no longer be ruled out, namely

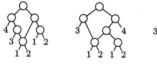

and when $r = (7, 8, 9)$ we must also consider respectively $(653, 12387, 225660)$ additional potential chains that are not special cases of the top-down and bottom-up constructions. Here are the resulting statistics, for comparison with Table 1:

$C_c(f)$	Classes	Functions	$U_c(f)$	Classes	Functions	$L_c(f)$	Classes	Functions	$D_c(f)$	Classes	Functions
0	2	10	0	2	10	0	2	10	0	2	10
1	1	48	1	1	48	1	1	48	1	1	48
2	2	256	2	2	256	2	2	256	2	7	684
3	7	940	3	7	940	3	7	940	3	59	17064
4	9	2336	4	9	2336	4	7	2048	4	151	47634
5	24	6464	5	21	6112	5	20	5248	5	2	96
6	30	10616	6	28	9664	6	23	8672	6	0	0

7	61	18984	7	45	15128	7	37	11768	7	0	0
8	45	17680	8	40	14296	8	27	10592	8	0	0
9	37	7882	9	23	8568	9	33	11536	9	0	0
10	4	320	10	28	5920	10	16	5472	10	0	0
11	0	0	11	6	1504	11	30	6304	11	0	0
12	0	0	12	5	576	12	3	960	12	0	0
13	0	0	13	3	144	13	8	1472	13	0	0
14	0	0	14	2	34	14	2	96	14	0	0
15	0	0	15	0	0	15	4	114	15	0	0

The two function classes of depth 5 are represented by $S_{2,4}(x_1, x_2, x_3, x_4)$ and $x_1 \oplus S_2(x_2, x_3, x_4)$; and those two functions, together with $S_2(x_1, x_2, x_3, x_4)$ and the parity function $S_{1,3}(x_1, x_2, x_3, x_4) = x_1 \oplus x_2 \oplus x_3 \oplus x_4$, have length 15. Also $U_c(S_{2,4}) = U_c(S_{1,3}) = 14$. The four classes of cost 10 are represented by $S_{1,4}(x_1, x_2, x_3, x_4)$, $S_{2,4}(x_1, x_2, x_3, x_4)$, $(x_4? \ x_1 \oplus x_2 \oplus x_3: \langle x_1 x_2 x_3 \rangle)$, and $[(x_1 x_2 x_3 x_4)_2 \in \{0, 1, 4, 7, 10, 13\}]$. (The third of these, incidentally, is the complement of (20), "Harvard's hardest case.")

21. (The authors stated that their table entries "should be regarded only as the most economical operators known to the present writers.")

22. $\nu(x_1 x_2 x_3 x_4 x_5) = 3$ if and only if $\nu(x_1 x_2 x_3 x_4) \in \{2, 3\}$ and $\nu(x_1 x_2 x_3 x_4 x_5)$ is odd. Similarly, $S_2(x_1, x_2, x_3, x_4, x_5) = S_3(\bar{x}_1, \bar{x}_2, \bar{x}_3, \bar{x}_4, \bar{x}_5)$ incorporates $S_{1,2}(x_1, x_2, x_3, x_4)$:

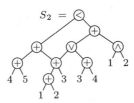

23. We need only consider the 32 normal cases, as in Fig. 9, since the complement of a symmetric function is symmetric. Then we can use reflection, like $S_{1,2}(x) = S_{3,4}(\bar{x})$, possibly together with complementation, like $S_{2,3,4,5}(x) = \bar{S}_{0,1}(x) = \bar{S}_{4,5}(\bar{x})$, to deduce most of the remaining cases. Of course S_1, $S_{1,3,5}$, and $S_{1,2,3,4,5}$ trivially have cost 4. That leaves only $S_{1,2,3,4}(x_1, x_2, x_3, x_4, x_5) = (x_1 \oplus x_2) \vee (x_2 \oplus x_3) \vee (x_3 \oplus x_4) \vee (x_4 \oplus x_5)$, which is discussed for general n in exercise 79.

24. As noted in the text, this conjecture holds for $n \leq 5$.

25. It is $2^{2^n - 1} - n - 1$, the number of nontrivial normal functions. (In any normal chain of length r that doesn't include all of these functions, $x_j \circ x_k$ will be a new function for some j and k in the range $1 \leq j, k \leq n + r$ and some normal binary operator $\circ$; so we can compute a new function with every new step, until we've got them all.)

26. False. For example, if $g = S_{1,3}(x_1, x_2, x_3)$ and $h = S_{2,3}(x_1, x_2, x_3)$, then $C(gh) = 5$ is the cost of a full adder; but $f = S_{2,3}(x_0, x_1, x_2, x_3)$ has cost 6 by Fig. 9.

27. Yes: The operations '$x_2 \leftarrow x_2 \oplus x_1$, $x_1 \leftarrow x_1 \oplus x_3$, $x_1 \leftarrow x_1 \wedge \bar{x}_2$, $x_1 \leftarrow x_1 \oplus x_3$, $x_2 \leftarrow x_2 \oplus x_3$' transform (x_1, x_2, x_3) into (z_1, z_0, x_3).

28. Let $v' = v'' = v \oplus (x \oplus y)$; $u' = ((v \oplus y) \overline{\subset} (x \oplus y)) \oplus u$, $u'' = ((v \oplus y) \vee (x \oplus y)) \oplus u$. Thus we can set $u_0 = 0$, $v_0 = x_1$, $u_j = ((v_{j-1} \oplus x_{2j+1}) \vee (x_{2j} \oplus x_{2j+1})) \oplus u_{j-1}$ if j is odd, $u_j = ((v_{j-1} \oplus x_{2j+1}) \overline{\subset} (x_{2j} \oplus x_{2j+1})) \oplus u_{j-1}$ if j is even, and $v_j = v_{j-1} \oplus (x_{2j} \oplus x_{2j+1})$, obtaining $(u_j v_j)_2 = (x_1 + \cdots + x_{2j+1}) \bmod 4$ for $1 \leq j \leq \lfloor n/2 \rfloor$. Set $x_{n+1} = 0$ if n is even. The function $[(x_1 + \cdots + x_n) \bmod 4 = 0] = \bar{u}_{\lfloor n/2 \rfloor} \wedge \bar{v}_{\lfloor n/2 \rfloor}$ is thereby computed in $\lfloor 5n/2 \rfloor - 2$ steps.

This construction is due to L. J. Stockmeyer, who proved that it is nearly optimal. In fact, the result of exercise 80 together with Figs. 9 and 10 shows that it is at most one step longer than a best possible chain, for all $n \geq 5$.

Incidentally, the analogous formula $u''' = ((v \oplus y) \wedge (x \oplus y)) \oplus u$ yields $(u'''v')_2 = ((uv)_2 + x - y) \bmod 4$. The simpler-looking function $((uv)_2 + x + y) \bmod 4$ costs 6, not 5.

29. To get an upper bound, assume that each full adder or half adder increases the depth by 3. If there are a_{jd} bits of weight 2^j and depth $3d$, we schedule at most $\lceil a_{jd}/3 \rceil$ subsequent bits of weights $\{2^j, 2^{j+1}\}$ and depth $3(d+1)$. It follows by induction that $a_{jd} \leq \binom{d}{j} 3^{-d} n + 4$. Hence $a_{jd} \leq 5$ when $d \geq \log_{3/2} n$, and the overall depth is at most $3 \log_{3/2} n + 3$. (Curiously, the actual depth turns out to be exactly 100 when $n = 10^7$.)

30. As usual, let νn denote the sideways addition of the bits in the binary representation of n itself. Then $s(n) = 5n - 2\nu n - 3\lfloor \lg n \rfloor - 3$.

31. After sideways addition in $s(n) < 5n$ steps, an arbitrary function of $(z_{\lfloor \lg n \rfloor}, \ldots, z_0)$ can be evaluated in $\sim 2n/\lg n$ steps at most, by Theorem L. [See O. B. Lupanov, *Doklady Akademii Nauk SSSR* **140** (1961), 322–325.]

32. Bootstrap: First prove by induction on n that $t(n) \leq 2^{n+1}$.

33. False, on a technicality: If, say, $N = \sqrt{n}$, at least n steps are needed. A correct asymptotic formula $N + O(\sqrt{N}) + O(n)$ can, however, be proved by first noting that the text's method gives $N + O(\sqrt{N})$ when $N \geq 2^{n-1}$; otherwise, if $\lfloor \lg N \rfloor = n - k - 1$, we can use $O(n)$ operations to AND the quantity $\bar{x}_1 \wedge \cdots \wedge \bar{x}_k$ to the other variables $x_{k+1}, \ldots, x_n$, then proceed with n reduced by k.

(One consequence is that we can compute the symmetric functions $\{S_1, S_2, \ldots, S_n\}$ with cost $s(n) + n + O(\sqrt{n}) = 6n + O(\sqrt{n})$ and depth $O(\log n)$.)

34. Say that an *extended* priority encoder has $n + 1 = 2^m$ inputs $x_0 x_1 \ldots x_n$ and $m + 1$ outputs $y_0 y_1 \ldots y_m$, where $y_0 = x_0 \vee x_1 \vee \cdots \vee x_n$. If Q'_m and Q''_m are extended encoders for $x'_0 \ldots x'_n$ and $x''_0 \ldots x''_n$, then Q_{m+1} works for $x'_0 \ldots x'_n x''_0 \ldots x''_n$ if we define $y_0 = y'_0 \vee y''_0$, $y_1 = y''_0$, $y_2 = y_1 ? y''_1 : y'_1, \ldots, y_{m+1} = y_1 ? y''_m : y'_m$. If P'_m is an ordinary priority encoder for $x'_1 \ldots x'_n$, we get P_{m+1} for $x'_1 \ldots x'_n x''_0 \ldots x''_n$ in a similar way.

Starting with $m = 2$ and $y_2 = x_3 \vee (x_1 \wedge \bar{x}_2)$, $y_1 = x_2 \vee x_3$, $y_0 = x_0 \vee x_1 \vee y_1$, this construction yields P_m and Q_m of costs p_m and q_m, where $p_2 = 3$, $q_2 = 5$, and $p_{m+1} = 3m + p_m + q_m$, $q_{m+1} = 3m + 1 + 2q_m$ for $m \geq 2$. Consequently $p_m = q_m - m$ and $q_m = 15 \cdot 2^{m-2} - 3m - 4 \approx 3.75n$.

35. If $n = 2m$, compute $x_1 \wedge x_2, \ldots, x_{n-1} \wedge x_n$, then recursively form $x_1 \wedge \cdots \wedge x_{2k-2} \wedge x_{2k+1} \wedge \cdots \wedge x_n$ for $1 \leq k \leq m$, and finish in n more steps. If $n = 2m - 1$, use this chain for $n + 1$ elements; three steps can be eliminated by setting $x_{n+1} \leftarrow 1$. [I. Wegener, *The Complexity of Boolean Functions* (1987), exercise 3.25. The same idea can be used with *any* associative and commutative operator in place of $\wedge$.]

36. Recursively construct $P_n(x_1, \ldots, x_n)$ and $Q_n(x_1, \ldots, x_n)$ as follows, where P_n has optimum depth and Q_n has depth $\leq \lceil \lg n \rceil + 1$: The case $n = 1$ is trivial; otherwise P_n is obtained from $Q'_r(x_1, \ldots, x_r)$ and $P''_s(x_{r+1}, \ldots, x_n)$, where $r = \lceil n/2 \rceil$ and $s = \lfloor n/2 \rfloor$, by setting $y_j = y'_j$ for $1 \leq j \leq r$, $y_j = y''_r \wedge y''_{j-r}$ for $r < j \leq n$. And Q_n is obtained from either $P'_r(x_1 \wedge x_2, \ldots, x_{n-1} \wedge x_n)$ or $P'_r(x_1 \wedge x_2, \ldots, x_{n-2} \wedge x_{n-1}, x_n)$ by setting $y_1 = x_1$, $y_{2j} = y'_j$, $y_{2j+1} = y'_j \wedge x_{2j+1}$ for $1 \leq j < s$, and $y_{2s} = y'_s$, $y_n = y'_r$.

To prove validity we must show also that output y_n of Q_n has depth $\lceil \lg n \rceil$; notice that Q_{2m+1} would fail if we began it with $P'_m(x_1 \wedge x_2, \ldots, x_{2m-1} \wedge x_{2m})$ instead of with $P'_{m+1}(x_1 \wedge x_2, \ldots, x_{2m-1} \wedge x_{2m}, x_{2m+1})$, *except* when m is a power of 2.

These calculations can be performed in *minimum memory*, setting $x_{k(i)} \leftarrow x_{j(i)} \wedge x_{k(i)}$ at step i for some indices $j(i) < k(i)$. Thus we can illustrate the construction with diagrams analogous to the diagrams for sorting networks. For example,

The costs p_n and q_n satisfy $p_n = \lfloor n/2 \rfloor + q_{\lceil n/2 \rceil} + p_{\lfloor n/2 \rfloor}$, $q_n = 2\lfloor n/2 \rfloor - 1 + p_{\lceil n/2 \rceil}$ when $n > 1$; for example, $(p_1, \ldots, p_7) = (q_1, \ldots, q_7) = (0, 1, 2, 4, 5, 7, 9)$. Setting $\bar{p}_n = 4n - p_n$ and $\bar{q}_n = 3n - q_n$ leads to simpler formulas, which prove that $p_n < 4n$ and $q_n < 3n$: $\bar{q}_n = \bar{p}_{\lceil n/2 \rceil} + [n \text{ even}]$; $\bar{p}_{4n} = \bar{p}_{2n} + \bar{p}_n + 1$, $\bar{p}_{4n+1} = \bar{p}_{2n} + \bar{p}_{n+1} + 1$, $\bar{p}_{4n+2} = \bar{p}_{2n+1} + \bar{p}_{n+1}$, $\bar{p}_{4n+3} = \bar{p}_{4n+2} + 2$. In particular, $1 + \bar{p}_{2^m} = F_{m+5}$ is a Fibonacci number.

[See *JACM* **27** (1980), 831–834. Slightly better chains are obtained if we use the otherwise-forbidden $P'_{\lfloor n/2 \rfloor}$ construction for Q_n when $n = 2^m + 1$, if we replace P_5 and P_6 by Q_5 and Q_6, and if we then replace $(P_9, P_{10}, P_{11}, P_{17})$ by $(Q_9, Q_{10}, Q_{11}, Q_{17})$.]

Notice that this construction works in general if we replace '$\wedge$' by *any* associative operator. In particular, the sequence of prefixes $x_1 \oplus \cdots \oplus x_k$ for $1 \leq k \leq n$ defines the conversion from Gray binary code to radix-2 integers, Eq. 7.2.1.1–(10).

37. The case $m = 15$, $n = 16$ is illustrated at the right.

(a) Let $x_{i..j}$ denote the original value of $x_i \wedge \cdots \wedge x_j$. Whenever the algorithm sets $x_k \leftarrow x_j \wedge x_k$, one can show that the previous value of x_k was $x_{j+1..k}$. After step S1, x_k is $x_{f(k)+1..k}$ where $f(k) = k \,\&\, (k-1)$ for $1 \leq k < m$ and $f(m) = 0$. After step S2, x_k is $x_{1..k}$ for $1 \leq k \leq m$.

(b) The cost of S1 is $m - 1$, the cost of S2 is $m - 1 - \lceil \lg m \rceil$, and the cost of S3 is $n - m$. The final delay of x_k is $\lfloor \lg k \rfloor + \nu k - 1$ for $1 \leq k < m$, and it is $\lceil \lg m \rceil + k - m$ for $m \leq k \leq n$. So the maximum delay for $\{x_1, \ldots, x_{m-1}\}$ turns out to be $g(m) = m - 1$ for $m < 4$, $g(m) = \lfloor \lg m \rfloor + \lfloor \lg \frac{m}{3} \rfloor$ for $m \geq 4$. We have $c(m, n) = m + n - 2 - \lceil \lg m \rceil$, $d(m, n) = \max(g(m), \lceil \lg m \rceil + n - m)$. Hence $c(m, n) + d(m, n) = 2n - 2$ whenever $n \geq m + g(m) - \lceil \lg m \rceil$.

(c) A table of values reveals that $d(n) = \lceil \lg n \rceil$ for $n < 8$, and $d(n) = \lfloor \lg(n - \lfloor \lg n \rfloor + 3) \rfloor + \lfloor \lg \frac{2}{3}(n - \lfloor \lg n \rfloor + 3) \rfloor - 1$ for $n \geq 8$. Stating this another way, we have $d(n) > d(n-1) > 0$ if and only if $n = 2^k + k - 3$ or $2^k + 2^{k-1} + k - 3$ for some $k > 1$. The minimum occurs for $m = n$ when $n < 8$; otherwise it occurs for $m = n - \lfloor \frac{2}{3}(n - \lfloor \lg n \rfloor + 3) \rfloor + 2 - [n = 2^k + k - 3 \text{ for some } k]$.

(d) Set $m \leftarrow m(n, d)$, where $m(n, d(n))$ is defined in the previous sentence and $m(n, d) = m(n - 1, d - 1)$ when $d > d(n)$. [See *J. Algorithms* **7** (1986), 185–201.]

38. (a) From top to bottom, $f_k(x_1, \ldots, x_n)$ is an elementary symmetric function also called the threshold function $S_{\geq k}(x_1, \ldots, x_n)$. (See exercise 5.3.4–28, Eq. 7.1.1–(90).)

(b) After calculating $\{S_1, \ldots, S_n\}$ in $\approx 6n$ steps as in answer 33, we can apply the method of exercise 37 to finish in $2n$ further steps.

But it is more interesting to design a Boolean chain specifically for the computation of the $2^m + 1$ threshold functions $g_k(x_1, \ldots, x_m) = [(x_1 \ldots x_m)_2 \geq k]$ for $0 \leq k \leq 2^m$. Since $[(x'x'')_2 \geq (y'y'')_2] = [(x')_2 \geq (y')_2 + 1] \vee ([(x')_2 \geq (y')_2] \wedge [(x'')_2 \geq (y'')_2])$, a divide-and-conquer construction analogous to a binary decoder solves this problem with a cost at most $2t(m)$.

Furthermore, if $2^{m-1} \le n < 2^m$, the cost $u(n)$ of computing $\{g_1, \ldots, g_n\}$ by this method turns out to be $2n + O(\sqrt{n})$, and it is quite reasonable when n is small:

n =	1	2	3	4	5	6	7	8	9	10	11	12	13	14	15	16	17	18	19	20
$u(n)$ =	0	1	2	4	7	7	8	12	15	17	19	19	20	21	22	27	32	34	36	36

Starting with sideways addition, we can sort n Boolean values in $s(n) + u(n) \approx 7n$ steps. A sorting network, which costs $2\hat{S}(n)$, is better when $n = 4$ but loses when $n \ge 8$. [See 5.3.4–(11); D. E. Muller and F. P. Preparata, *JACM* **22** (1975), 195–201.]

39. [*IEEE Transactions* **C-29** (1980), 737–738.] The identity

$$M_{r+s}(x_1, \ldots, x_r, x_{r+1}, \ldots, x_{r+s}; y_0, \ldots, y_{2^{r+s}-1}) = M_r(x_1, \ldots, x_r; y'_0, \ldots, y'_{2^r-1}),$$

where $y'_j = \bigvee_{k=0}^{2^s-1}(d_k \wedge y_{2^s j + k})$ and d_k is the kth output of an s-to-2^s decoder applied to $(x_{r+1}, \ldots, x_{r+s})$, shows that $C(M_{r+s}) \le C(M_r) + 2^{r+s} + 2^r(2^s - 1) + t(s)$, where $t(s)$ is the cost (30) of the decoder. The depth is $D(M_{r+s}) = \max(D_x(M_{r+s}), D_y(M_{r+s}))$, where D_x and D_y denote the maximum depth of the x and y variables; we have $D_x(M_{r+s}) \le \max(D_x(M_r), 1+s+\lceil\lg s\rceil + D_y(M_r))$ and $D_y(M_{r+s}) \le 1+s+D_y(M_r)$.

Taking $r = \lceil m/2 \rceil$ and $s = \lfloor m/2 \rfloor$ yields $C(M_m) \le 2^{m+1} + O(2^{m/2})$, $D_y(M_m) \le m + 1 + \lceil\lg m\rceil$, and $D_x(M_m) \le D_y(M_m) + \lceil\lg m\rceil$.

40. We can, for example, let $f_{nk}(x) = \bigvee_{j=1}^{n+1-k}(l_j(x) \wedge r_{j+k-1}(x))$, where

$$l_j(x) = \begin{cases} x_j, & \text{if } j \bmod k = 0, \\ x_j \wedge l_{j+1}(x), & \text{if } j \bmod k \ne 0, \end{cases} \quad \text{for } 1 \le j \le n - (n \bmod k);$$

$$r_j(x) = \begin{cases} 1, & \text{if } j \bmod k = 0, \\ x_j \wedge r_{j-1}(x), & \text{if } j \bmod k \ne 0, \end{cases} \quad \text{for } k \le j \le n.$$

The cost is $4n - 3k - 3\lfloor\frac{n}{k}\rfloor - \lfloor\frac{n-1}{k}\rfloor + 2 - (n \bmod k)$.

A recursive solution is preferable when n is small or k is small: Observe that

$$f_{nk}(x) = \begin{cases} x_{n-k+1} \wedge \cdots \wedge x_k \wedge \\ \quad f_{(2n-2k)(n-k)}(x_1, \ldots, x_{n-k}, x_{k+1}, \ldots, x_n), & \text{for } k < n < 2k; \\ f_{\lfloor(n+k)/2\rfloor k}(x_1, \ldots, x_{\lfloor(n+k)/2\rfloor}) \vee \\ \quad f_{\lfloor(n+k-1)/2\rfloor k}(x_{\lfloor(n-k)/2\rfloor+1}, \ldots, x_n), & \text{for } n \ge 2k. \end{cases}$$

The cost of this solution can be shown to equal $n - 1 + \sum_{j=1}^{n-k}\lfloor\lg j\rfloor$ when $k \le n < 2k$, and it lies asymptotically between $(m+\alpha_k-1)n+O(km)$ and $(m+2-2/\alpha_k)n+O(km)$ as $n \to \infty$, where $m = \lfloor\lg k\rfloor$ and $1 < \alpha_k = (k+1)/2^m \le 2$.

A marriage of these methods is better yet; the optimum cost is unknown.

41. Let $c(m)$ be the cost of computing both $(x)_2 + (y)_2$ and $(x)_2 + (y)_2 + 1$ by the conditional-sum method when x and y have $n = 2^m$ bits, and let $c'(m)$ be the cost of the simpler problem of computing just $(x)_2 + (y)_2$. Then $c(m+1) = 2c(m) + 6 \cdot 2^m + 2$, $c'(m+1) = c(m) + c'(m) + 3 \cdot 2^m + 1$. (Bit z_n of the sum costs 1; but bits z_k for $n < k \le 2n+1$ cost 3, because they have the form $c? \, a_k \colon b_k$ where c is a carry bit.) If we start with $n = 1$ and $c(0) = 3$, $c'(0) = 2$, the solution is $c(m) = (3m+5)2^m - 2$, $c'(m) = (3m+2)2^m - m$. But improved constructions for the case $n = 2$ allow us to start with $c(1) = 11$ and $c'(1) = 7$; then the solution is $c(m) = (3m+\frac{7}{2})2^m - 2$, $c'(m) = (3m+\frac{1}{2})2^m - m+1$. In either case the depth is $2m+1$. [See J. Sklansky, *IRE Transactions* **EC-9** (1960), 226–231.]

42. (a) Since $\langle x_k y_k c_k \rangle = u_k \vee (v_k \wedge c_k)$, we can use (26) and induction.

(b) Notice that $U_k^{k+1} = u_k$ and $V_k^{k+1} = v_k$; use induction on $j - i$. [See A. Weinberger and J. L. Smith, *IRE Transactions* **EC-5** (1956), 65–73; R. P. Brent and H. T. Kung, *IEEE Transactions* **C-31** (1982), 260–264.]

(c) First, for $l = 1, 2, \ldots, m - 1$, and for $1 \leq k \leq n$, compute V_i^k for all multiples i of $h(l)$ in the range $k_l \geq i \geq k_{l+1}$, where $k_l = h(l)\lfloor (k-1)/h(l) \rfloor$ denotes the largest multiple of $h(l)$ that is less than k. For example, when $l = 2$ and $k = 99$, we compute V_{96}^{99}, $V_{88}^{99} = V_{96}^{99} \wedge V_{88}^{96}$, $V_{80}^{99} = V_{88}^{99} \wedge V_{80}^{88}$, $\ldots$, $V_{64}^{99} = V_{72}^{99} \wedge V_{64}^{72}$; this is a prefix computation using the values V_{96}^{99}, V_{88}^{96}, V_{80}^{88}, $\ldots$, V_{64}^{72} that were computed when $l = 2$. Using the method of exercise 36, step l adds at most l levels to the depth, and it requires a total of $(p_1 + p_2 + \cdots + p_{2^l}) n/2^l = O(2^l n)$ gates.

Then, again for $l = 1, 2, \ldots, m - 1$, and for $1 \leq k \leq n$, compute U_i^k for $i = k_{l+1}$, using the "unrolled" formula

$$U_{k_{l+1}}^k = U_{k_l}^k \vee \bigvee_{\substack{k_l > j \geq k_{l+1} \\ h(l) \backslash j}} (V_{j+h(l)}^k \wedge U_j^{j+h(l)}).$$

For example, the unrolled formula when $l = 3$ and $k = 99$ is

$$U_{64}^{99} = U_{96}^{99} \vee (V_{96}^{99} \wedge U_{88}^{96}) \vee (V_{88}^{99} \wedge U_{80}^{88}) \vee (V_{80}^{99} \wedge U_{72}^{80}) \vee (V_{72}^{99} \wedge U_{64}^{72}).$$

Every such U_i^k is a union of at most 2^l terms, so it can be computed with depth $\leq l$ in addition to the depth of each term. The total cost of this phase for $1 \leq k \leq n$ is $(0 + 2 + 4 + \cdots + (2^l - 2)) n/2^l = O(2^l n)$.

The overall cost to compute all necessary U's and V's is therefore $\sum_{l=1}^{m-1} O(2^l n) = O(2^m n)$. (Furthermore the quantities V_0^k aren't actually needed, so we save the cost of $\sum_{l=1}^{m-1} h(l) p_{2^l}$ gates.) For example, when $m = (2, 3, 4, 5)$ we obtain Boolean chains for the addition of $(2, 8, 64, 1024)$-bit numbers, respectively, with overall depths $(3, 7, 11, 16)$ and costs $(7, 64, 1254, 48470)$.

[This construction is due to V. M. Khrapchenko, *Problemy Kibernetiki* **19** (1967), 107–122, who also showed how to combine it with other methods so that the overall cost will be $O(n)$ while still achieving depth $\lg n + O(\sqrt{\log n})$. However, his combined method is purely of theoretical interest, because it requires $n > 2^{64}$ before the depth becomes less than $2 \lg n$. Another way to achieve small depth using the recurrences in (b) can be based on the Fibonacci numbers: The Fibonacci method computes the carries with depth $\log_\phi n + O(1) \approx 1.44 \lg n$ and cost $O(n \log n)$. For example, it yields chains for binary addition with the following characteristics:

$n =$	4	8	16	32	64	128	256	512	1024
depth	6	7	9	10	12	13	15	16	18
cost	24	71	186	467	1125	2648	6102	13775	30861

See D. E. Knuth, *The Stanford GraphBase* (1994), 276–279.

Charles Babbage found an ingenious mechanical solution to the analogous problem for addition in radix 10, claiming that his design would be able to add numbers of arbitrary precision in constant time; for this to work he would have needed idealized, rigid components with vanishing clearances. See H. P. Babbage, *Babbage's Calculating Engines* (1889), 334–335. Curiously, an equivalent idea works fine with physical transistors, although it cannot be expressed in terms of Boolean chains; see P. M. Fenwick, *Comp. J.* **30** (1987), 77–79.]

43. (a) Let $A = B = Q = \{0,1\}$ and $q_0 = 0$. Define $c(q,a) = d(q,a) = \bar{q} \wedge a$.

(b) The key idea is to construct the functions $d_1(q) \ldots d_{n-1}(q)$, where $d_1(q) = d(q, a_1)$ and $d_{j+1}(q) = d(d_j(q), a_j)$. In other words, $d_1 = d^{(a_1)}$ and $d_{j+1} = d_j \circ d^{(a_j)}$, where $d^{(a)}$ is the function that takes $q \mapsto d(q,a)$ and where $\circ$ denotes composition of functions. Each function d_j can be encoded in binary notation, and $\circ$ is an associative operation on these binary representations. Hence the functions $d_1 d_2 \ldots d_{n-1}$ are the prefixes $d^{(a_1)}$, $d^{(a_1)} \circ d^{(a_2)}$, ..., $d^{(a_1)} \circ \cdots \circ d^{(a_{n-1})}$; and $q_1 q_2 \ldots q_n = q_0 d_1(q_0) \ldots d_{n-1}(q_0)$.

(c) Represent a function $f(q)$ by its truth table $f_0 f_1$. Then the composition $f_0 f_1 \circ g_0 g_1$ is $h_0 h_1$, where the functions $h_0 = f_0$? g_1: g_0 and $h_1 = f_1$? g_1: g_0 are muxes that can each be computed with cost 3 and depth 2. (The combined cost $C(h_0 h_1)$ is only 5, but we are trying to keep the depth small.) The truth table for $d^{(a)}$ is $a0$. Using exercise 36, we can therefore compute the truth tables $d_{10} d_{11} d_{20} d_{21} \ldots d_{(n-1)0} d_{(n-1)1}$ with cost $\leq 6 p_{n-1} < 24n$ and depth $\leq 2\lceil \lg(n-1) \rceil$; then $b_j = \bar{q}_j \wedge a_j = \bar{d}_{(j-1)0} \wedge a_j$. (These cost estimates are quite conservative; substantial simplifications arise because of the 0s in the initial truth tables of $d^{(a_j)}$ and because many of the intermediate values d_{j1} are never used. For example, when $n = 5$ the actual cost is only 10, not $6 p_4 + 4 = 28$; the actual depth is 4, not $1 + 2\lceil \lg 4 \rceil = 5$.)

44. The inputs may be regarded as the string $x_0 y_0\, x_1 y_1\, \ldots\, x_{n-1} y_{n-1}$ whose elements belong to the four-letter alphabet $A = \{00, 01, 10, 11\}$; there are two states $Q = \{0,1\}$, representing a possible carry bit, with $q_0 = 0$; the output alphabet is $B = \{0,1\}$; and we have $c(q, xy) = q \oplus x \oplus y$, $d(q, xy) = \langle qxy \rangle$. In this case, therefore, the finite state transducer is essentially described by a full adder.

Only three of the four possible functions of q occur when we compose the mappings $d^{(xy)}$. We can encode them as $u \vee (q \wedge v)$. The initial functions $d^{(xy)}$ have $u = x \wedge y$, $v = x \oplus y$; and the composition $(uv) \circ (u'v')$ is $u''v''$, where $u'' = u' \vee (v' \wedge u)$ and $v'' = v \wedge v'$.

When $n = 4$, for example, the chain has the following form, using the notation of exercise 42: $U_k^{k+1} = x_k \wedge y_k$, $V_k^{k+1} = x_k \oplus y_k$, for $0 \leq k < 4$; $U_0^2 = U_1^2 \vee (V_1^2 \wedge U_0^1)$, $U_2^4 = U_3^4 \vee (V_3^4 \wedge U_2^3)$, $V_2^4 = V_2^3 \wedge V_3^4$; $U_0^3 = U_2^3 \vee (V_2^3 \wedge U_0^2)$, $U_0^4 = U_2^4 \vee (V_2^4 \wedge U_0^2)$; $z_0 = V_0^1$, $z_1 = U_0^1 \oplus V_1^2$, $z_2 = U_0^2 \oplus V_2^3$, $z_3 = U_0^3 \oplus V_3^4$, $z_4 = U_0^4$. The total cost is 20, and the maximum depth is 5.

In general the cost will be $2n + 3 p_n$ in the notation of exercise 36, because we need $2n$ gates for the initial u's and v's, then $3 p_n$ gates for the prefix computation; the $n - 1$ additional gates needed to form z_j for $0 < j < n$ are compensated by the fact that we need not compute V_0^j for $1 < j \leq n$. Therefore the total cost is $14 \cdot 2^m - 3 F_{m+5} + 3$, clearly superior to the conditional-sum method (which has the same depth $2m + 1$):

$n =$	2	4	8	16	32	64	128	256	512	1024
cost of conditional-sum chain	7	25	74	197	492	1179	2746	6265	14072	31223
cost of Ladner–Fischer chain	7	20	52	125	286	632	1363	2888	6040	12509

[George Boole introduced his Algebra in order to show that logic can be understood in terms of arithmetic. Eventually logic became so well understood, the situation was reversed: People like Shannon and Zuse began in the 1930s to design circuits for arithmetic in terms of logic, and since then many approaches to the problem of parallel addition have been discovered. The first Boolean chains of cost $O(n)$ and depth $O(\log n)$ were devised by Yu. P. Ofman, *Doklady Akademii Nauk SSSR* **145** (1962), 48–51. His chains were similar to the construction above, but the depth was approximately $4m$.]

45. That argument would indeed be simpler, but it wouldn't be strong enough to prove the desired result. (Many chains with steps of fan-out 0 inflate the simpler estimate.)

The text's permutation-enhanced proof technique was introduced by J. E. Savage in his book *The Complexity of Computing* (New York: Wiley, 1976), Theorem 3.4.1.

46. When $r = 2^n/n + O(1)$ we have $\ln(2^{2r+1}(n+r-1)^{2r}/(r-1)!) = r\ln r + (1+\ln 4)r + O(n) = (2^n/n)(n\ln 2 - \ln n + 1 + \ln 4) + O(n)$. So $\alpha(n) \leq (n/(4e))^{-2^n/n+O(n/\log n)}$, which approaches zero quite rapidly indeed when $n > 4e$.

(In fact, (32) gives $\alpha(11) < 7.6 \times 10^7$, $\alpha(12) < 4.2 \times 10^{-6}$, $\alpha(13) < 1.2 \times 10^{-38}$.)

47. Restrict permutations to the $(r-m)!$ cases where $i\pi = i$ for $1 \leq i \leq n$ and $(n+r+1-k)\pi$ is the kth output. Then we get $(r-m)!\,c(m,n,r) \leq 2^{2r+1}(n+r-1)^{2r}$ in place of (32). Hence, as in exercise 46, almost all such functions have cost exceeding $2^n m/(n + \lg m)$ when $m = O(2^n/n^2)$.

48. (a) Not surprisingly, this lower bound on $C(n)$ is rather crude when n is small:

$n =$	1	2	3	4	5	6	7	8	9	10	11	12	13	14	15	16
$r(n) =$	1	1	2	3	5	9	16	29	54	99	184	343	639	1196	2246	4229

(b) The bootstrap method (see *Concrete Mathematics* §9.4) yields

$$r(n) = \frac{2^n}{n}\left(1 + \frac{\lg n - 2 - 1/\ln 2}{n} + O\left(\frac{\log n}{n^2}\right)\right).$$

49. The number of normal Boolean functions that can be represented by a formula of length $\leq r$ is at most $5^r n^{r+1} g_r$, where g_r is the number of oriented binary trees with r internal nodes. Set $r = 2^n/\lg n - 2^{n+2}/(\lg n)^2$ in this formula and divide by 2^{2^n-1} to get an upper bound on the fraction of functions with $L(f) \leq r$. The result rapidly approaches zero, by exercise 2.3.4.4–7, because it is $O((5\alpha/16)^{2^n/\lg n})$ where $\alpha \approx 2.483$.

[J. Riordan and C. E. Shannon obtained a similar lower bound for series-parallel switching networks in *J. Math. and Physics* **21** (1942), 83–93; such networks are equivalent to formulas in which only canalizing operators are used. R. E. Krichevsky obtained more general results in *Problemy Kibernetiki* **2** (1959), 123–138, and O. B. Lupanov gave an asymptotically matching upper bound in *Prob. Kibernetiki* **3** (1960), 61–80.]

50. (a) Using subcube notation as in exercise 7.1.1–30, the prime implicants are $00001*$, $(0001*1)$, $0100*1$, $0111*1$, $1010*1$, $101*11$, $00*011$, $00*101$, $(01*111)$, $11*101$, $(0*1101)$, $(1*0101)$, $1*1011$, $0*0*11$, $*00101$, $(*01011)$, $(*11101)$, where the parenthesized subcubes are omitted in a shortest DNF. (b) Similarly, the prime clauses and a shortest CNF are given by $00111*$, $01010*$, $10110*$, $0110**$, $00*00*$, $11*00*$, $11*11*$, $(0*100*)$, $(1*00**)$, $1*0*1*$, $(1****0)$, $*0000*$, $(*1100*)$, $*1***0$, $**1**0$, $***1*0$, and $(****00)$. (Thus the CNF is $(x_1 \vee x_2 \vee \bar{x}_3 \vee \bar{x}_4 \vee \bar{x}_5) \wedge (x_1 \vee \bar{x}_2 \vee x_3 \vee \bar{x}_4 \vee x_5) \wedge \cdots \wedge (\bar{x}_4 \vee x_6)$.)

51. $f = ([x_5 x_6 \in \{01\}] \wedge [(x_1 x_2 x_3 x_4)_2 \in \{1, 3, 4, 7, 9, 10, 13, 15\}]) \vee ([x_5 x_6 \in \{10, 11\}] \wedge [x_1 x_2 x_3 x_4 = 0000]) \vee ([x_5 x_6 \in \{11\}] \wedge [(x_1 x_2 x_3 x_4)_2 \in \{1, 2, 4, 5, 7, 10, 11, 14\}])$.

52. The small-n results are quite different from those that work asymptotically:

n	k	l	(38)	n	k	l	(38)	n	k	l	(38)	n	k	l	(38)
5	2	2	39	8	3	2	175	11	4	4	803	14	5	5	4045
6	2	2	67	9	3	2	279	12	4	3	1329	15	5	5	7141
7	2	1	109	10	4	4	471	13	5	6	2355	16	5	4	12431

(Optimizations like the fact that $[x_1 x_2 \in \{00, 01\}] = \bar{x}_1$ usually reduce the cost further.)

53. First note that $2^k/l \leq n - 3\lg n$, hence $m_i \leq n - 3\lg n + 1$ and $2^{m_i} = O(2^n/n^3)$. Also $l = O(n)$ and $t(n-k) = O(2^n/n^2)$. So (38) reduces to $l \cdot 2^{n-k} + O(2^n/n^2) = 2^n/(n - 3\lg n) + O(2^n/n^2)$.

54. The greedy-footprint heuristic gives a chain of length 15:

$$x_5 = x_1 \oplus x_2, \qquad x_{10} = x_4 \oplus x_5, \qquad f_2 = x_{15} = \bar{x}_5 \wedge x_8,$$
$$x_6 = x_2 \oplus x_3, \qquad x_{11} = x_7 \vee x_{10}, \qquad f_3 = x_{16} = x_4 \wedge \bar{x}_{12},$$
$$x_7 = x_1 \wedge \bar{x}_3, \qquad x_{12} = x_6 \oplus x_{11}, \qquad f_4 = x_{17} = x_1 \wedge x_8,$$
$$x_8 = x_4 \wedge \bar{x}_6, \qquad x_{13} = \bar{x}_{10} \wedge x_{12}, \qquad f_5 = x_{18} = x_7 \wedge x_9,$$
$$x_9 = x_4 \wedge \bar{x}_5, \qquad f_1 = x_{14} = x_6 \wedge \bar{x}_{11}, \qquad f_6 = x_{19} = \bar{x}_3 \wedge x_{13}.$$

The minterm-first method corresponds to a chain of length 22, after we remove steps that are never used:

$$x_5 = \bar{x}_1 \wedge \bar{x}_2, \qquad x_{13} = x_5 \wedge x_{10}, \qquad x_{20} = x_8 \wedge x_{11},$$
$$x_6 = \bar{x}_1 \wedge x_2, \qquad x_{14} = x_5 \wedge x_{11}, \qquad f_6 = x_{21} = x_{15} \vee x_{18},$$
$$x_7 = x_1 \wedge \bar{x}_2, \qquad x_{15} = x_6 \wedge x_9, \qquad f_1 = x_{22} = x_{13} \vee x_{21},$$
$$x_8 = x_1 \wedge x_2, \qquad x_{16} = x_6 \wedge x_{11}, \qquad f_2 = x_{23} = x_{12} \vee x_{20},$$
$$x_9 = \bar{x}_3 \wedge x_4, \qquad x_{17} = x_7 \wedge x_9, \qquad x_{24} = x_{14} \vee x_{16},$$
$$x_{10} = x_3 \wedge \bar{x}_4, \qquad x_{18} = x_7 \wedge x_{11}, \qquad f_3 = x_{25} = x_{24} \vee x_{19},$$
$$x_{11} = x_3 \wedge x_4, \qquad f_5 = x_{19} = x_8 \wedge x_9, \qquad f_4 = x_{26} = x_{17} \vee x_{20}.$$
$$x_{12} = x_5 \wedge x_9,$$

(The distributive law could replace the computation of x_{14}, x_{16}, and x_{24} by two steps.)

Incidentally, the three functions in the answer to exercise 51 can be computed in only ten steps:

$$x_5 = x_2 \vee x_4, \qquad f_3 = x_9 = x_6 \oplus x_8, \qquad x_{12} = x_2 \oplus x_3,$$
$$x_6 = \bar{x}_1 \wedge x_5, \qquad x_{10} = x_1 \oplus x_8, \qquad x_{13} = \bar{x}_{10} \wedge x_{12},$$
$$x_7 = x_2 \wedge x_4, \qquad \bar{f}_2 = x_{11} = x_9 \vee x_{10}, \qquad f_1 = x_{14} = x_4 \oplus x_{13}.$$
$$x_8 = x_3 \wedge \bar{x}_7,$$

55. The optimum two-level DNF and CNF representations in answer 50 cost 53 and 43, respectively. Formula (37) costs 30, when optimized as in exercise 54. The alternative in exercise 51 costs only 17. But the catalog of optimum five-variable chains suggests

$$x_7 = \bar{x}_1 \wedge x_2, \qquad x_{11} = x_5 \wedge x_{10}, \qquad x_{15} = x_{13} \oplus x_{14}, \qquad x_{18} = \bar{x}_4 \wedge x_{17},$$
$$x_8 = x_3 \oplus x_7, \qquad x_{12} = x_5 \vee x_{10}, \qquad x_{16} = x_5 \wedge \bar{x}_{10}, \qquad x_{19} = x_6 \wedge x_{15},$$
$$x_9 = x_2 \wedge x_8, \qquad x_{13} = x_4 \wedge \bar{x}_{11}, \qquad x_{17} = \bar{x}_3 \wedge x_{16}, \qquad x_{20} = x_{18} \vee x_{19},$$
$$x_{10} = x_1 \oplus x_9, \qquad x_{14} = x_7 \wedge x_{12},$$

for this six-variable function. Is there a better way?

56. If we care about at most two values, the function can be either constant or x_j or $\bar{x}_j$.

57. The truth tables for x_5 through x_{17}, in hexadecimal notation, are respectively 0ff0, 2222, 33cc, 0d0d, 7777, 5d5d, 3ec1, 6b94, 4914, 4804, 060b, 2020, 7007. So we get

$$1010 = \text{Γ}, \quad 1011 = \text{η}, \quad 1012 = \text{5}, \quad 1013 = \text{I}, \quad 1014 = \text{u}, \quad 1015 = \text{З}.$$

58. The truth tables of all cost-7 functions with exactly eight 1s in their truth tables are equivalent to either 0779, 169b, or 179a. Combining these in all possible ways yields 9656 solutions that are distinct under permutation and/or complementation of $\{x_1, x_2, x_3, x_4\}$ as well as under permutation and/or complementation of $\{f_1, f_2, f_3, f_4\}$.

59. The greedy-footprint heuristic produces the following 17-step chain:

$$x_5 = x_1 \vee x_4, \qquad x_{11} = x_8 \vee x_9, \qquad x_{17} = \bar{x}_2 \wedge x_3,$$
$$x_6 = x_1 \oplus x_3, \qquad x_{12} = x_1 \oplus x_{11}, \qquad f_1 = x_{18} = x_{13} \oplus x_{15},$$
$$x_7 = x_2 \oplus x_4, \qquad x_{13} = x_5 \wedge \bar{x}_9, \qquad f_2 = x_{19} = x_{11} \wedge \bar{x}_{16},$$
$$x_8 = \bar{x}_4 \wedge x_6, \qquad x_{14} = x_5 \wedge x_{12}, \qquad f_3 = x_{20} = x_{12} \oplus x_{17},$$
$$x_9 = x_3 \oplus x_7, \qquad x_{15} = x_2 \wedge x_6, \qquad f_4 = x_{21} = x_{10} \wedge \bar{x}_{14}.$$
$$x_{10} = x_2 \vee x_3, \qquad x_{16} = x_2 \wedge \bar{x}_6,$$

The initial functions all have large footprints, so we can't achieve $C(f_1 f_2 f_3 f_4) = 28$; but a slightly more difficult S-box probably does exist.

60. One way is $u_1 = x_1 \oplus y_1$, $u_2 = x_2 \oplus y_2$, $v_1 = y_2 \oplus u_1$, $v_2 = y_1 \oplus u_2$, $z_1 = v_1 \wedge \bar{u}_2$, $z_2 = v_2 \wedge \bar{u}_1$.

61. Viewing these partial functions of six variables as 4×16 truth tables, with rows governed by $x_1 y_1$, our knowledge of 4-bit functions suggests good ways to compute the rows and leads to the following 25-step solution: $t_1 = x_2 \wedge y_2$, $t_2 = x_3 \wedge y_3$, $t_3 = x_2 \vee y_2$, $t_4 = x_3 \vee y_3$, $t_5 = t_1 \oplus t_2$, $t_6 = t_1 \vee t_2$, $t_7 = t_4 \wedge \bar{t}_5$, $t_8 = t_3 \oplus t_6$, $t_9 = x_2 \oplus y_2$, $t_{10} = t_4 \oplus t_9$, $t_{11} = t_5 \wedge \bar{t}_{10}$, $t_{12} = t_3 \oplus t_4$, $t_{13} = x_1 \vee y_1$, $t_{14} = t_8 \oplus t_{12}$, $t_{15} = t_{13} \wedge \bar{t}_{14}$, $t_{16} = t_4 \oplus t_7$, $t_{17} = t_{13} \wedge \bar{t}_{16}$, $t_{18} = t_3 \vee t_4$, $t_{19} = x_1 \oplus y_1$, $t_{20} = t_{19} \wedge \bar{t}_{18}$, $t_{21} = t_8 \oplus t_{15}$, $t_{22} = t_7 \oplus t_{17}$, $z_1 = t_{11} \vee t_{20}$, $z_2 = t_{21} \wedge \bar{t}_{20}$, $z_3 = t_{22} \wedge \bar{t}_{20}$. (Is there a better way? Gilbert Lee has found a 17-step solution if the inputs are represented by 000, 001, 011, 101, and 111.)

62. There are $\binom{2^n}{2^n d} 2^{2^n c}$ such functions, at most $\binom{2^n}{2^n d} t(n, r)$ of which have cost $\leq r$. So we can argue as in exercise 46 to conclude from (32) that the fraction with cost $\leq r = \lfloor 2^n c/n \rfloor$ is at most $2^{2r+1-2^n c} (n + r - 1)^{2r}/(r - 1)! = 2^{-r \lg n + O(r)}$.

63. [*Problemy Kibernetiki* **21** (1969), 215–226.] Put the truth table in a $2^k \times 2^{n-k}$ array as in Lupanov's method, and suppose there are c_j cares in column j, for $0 \leq j < 2^{n-k}$. Break that column into $\lfloor c_j/m \rfloor$ subcolumns that each have m cares, plus a possibly empty subcolumn at the bottom that contains fewer than m of them. The hint tells us that at most 2^{m+k} column vectors suffice to match the 0s and 1s of every subcolumn that has a specified top row i_0 and bottom row i_1. With $O(m2^{m+3k})$ operations we can therefore construct $O(2^{m+3k})$ functions $g_t(x_1, \ldots, x_k)$ from the minterms of $\{x_1, \ldots, x_k\}$, so that every subcolumn matches some type t. And for every type t we can construct functions $h_t(x_{k+1}, \ldots, x_n)$ from the minterms of $\{x_{k+1}, \ldots, x_n\}$, specifying the columns that match t; the cost is at most $\sum_j (\lfloor c_j/m \rfloor + 1) \leq 2^n c/m + 2^{n-k}$. Finally, $f = \bigvee_t (g_t \wedge h_t)$ requires $O(2^{m+3k})$ additional steps. Choosing $k = \lfloor 2 \lg n \rfloor$ and $m = \lceil n - 9 \lg n \rceil$ makes the total cost at most $(2^n c/n)(1 + 9n^{-1} \lg n + O(n^{-1}))$.

Of course we need to prove the hint, which is due to E. I. Nechiporuk [*Doklady Akad. Nauk SSSR* **163** (1965), 40–42]. In fact, $2^m(1 + \lceil k \ln 2 \rceil)$ vectors suffice (see S. K. Stein, *J. Combinatorial Theory* **A16** (1974), 391–397): If we choose $q = 2^m \lceil k \ln 2 \rceil$ vectors at random, not necessarily distinct, the expected number of untouched subcubes is $\binom{k}{m} 2^m (1 - 2^{-m})^q < \binom{k}{m} 2^m e^{-q 2^{-m}} < 2^m$. (An explicit construction would be nicer.)

For extensive generalizations — tolerating a percentage of errors and specifying the density of 1s — see N. Pippenger, *Mathematical Systems Theory* **10** (1977), 129–167.

64. It's exactly the game of tic-tac-toe, if we number the cells ⊞ as in an ancient Chinese magic square. [Berlekamp, Conway, and Guy use this numbering scheme to present a complete analysis of tic-tac-toe in their book *Winning Ways* **3** (2003), 732–736.]

65. One solution is to replace the "defending" moves d_j by "attacking" moves a_j and "counterattacking" moves c_j, and to include them only for corner cells $j \in \{1, 3, 9, 7\}$.

Let $j \cdot k = (jk) \bmod 10$; then

$$
\begin{array}{ccc}
j \cdot 1 & j \cdot 2 & j \cdot 3 \\
j \cdot 4 & j \cdot 5 & j \cdot 6 \\
j \cdot 7 & j \cdot 8 & j \cdot 9
\end{array}
$$

gives us another way to look at the tic-tac-toe diagram, when j is a corner, because $j \perp 10$. The precise definition of a_j and c_j is then

$$a_j = m_j \wedge \big((x_{j \cdot 3} \wedge \beta_{(j \cdot 8)(j \cdot 9)} \wedge (o_{j \cdot 4} \oplus o_{j \cdot 6})) \vee (x_{j \cdot 7} \wedge \beta_{(j \cdot 6)(j \cdot 9)} \wedge (o_{j \cdot 2} \oplus o_{j \cdot 8}))$$

$$\vee \big(m_{j \cdot 9} \wedge \big((m_{j \cdot 8} \wedge x_{j \cdot 2} \wedge \overline{(o_{j \cdot 3} \oplus o_{j \cdot 6})}) \vee (m_{j \cdot 6} \wedge x_{j \cdot 4} \wedge \overline{(o_{j \cdot 7} \oplus o_{j \cdot 8})}))\big)\big));$$

$$c_j = d_j \wedge \overline{(x_{j \cdot 6} \wedge o_{j \cdot 7})} \wedge \overline{(x_{j \cdot 8} \wedge o_{j \cdot 3})} \wedge \bar{d}_{j \cdot 9};$$

here $d_j = m_j \wedge \beta_{(j \cdot 2)(j \cdot 3)} \wedge \beta_{(j \cdot 4)(j \cdot 7)}$ takes the place of (51). We also define

$$
\begin{aligned}
u &= (x_1 \oplus x_3) \oplus (x_7 \oplus x_9), \\
v &= (o_1 \oplus o_3) \oplus (o_7 \oplus o_9), \\
t &= m_2 \wedge m_6 \wedge m_8 \wedge m_4 \wedge (u \vee \bar{v}),
\end{aligned}
\qquad
z_j = \begin{cases}
m_j \wedge \bar{t}, & \text{if } j = 5, \\
m_j \wedge \bar{d}_{j \cdot 9}, & \text{if } j \in \{1,3,9,7\}, \\
m_j, & \text{if } j \in \{2,6,8,4\},
\end{cases}
$$

in order to cover a few more exceptional cases. Finally the sequence of rank-ordered moves $d_5 d_1 d_3 d_9 d_7 d_2 d_6 d_8 d_4 m_5 m_1 m_3 m_9 m_7 m_2 m_6 m_8 m_4$ in (53) is replaced by the sequence $a_1 a_3 a_9 a_7 c_1 c_3 c_9 c_7 z_5 z_1 z_3 z_9 z_7 z_2 z_6 z_8 z_4$; and we replace $(d_j \wedge \bar{d}'_j) \vee (m_j \wedge \bar{m}'_j)$ in (55) by $(a_j \wedge \bar{a}'_j) \vee (c_j \wedge \bar{c}'_j) \vee (z_j \wedge \bar{z}'_j)$ when j is a corner cell, otherwise simply by $(z_j \wedge \bar{z}'_j)$.

(Notice that this machine is required to move correctly from *all* legal positions, even when those positions couldn't arise after the machine had made X's earlier moves. We essentially allow humans to play the game until they ask the machine for advice. Otherwise great simplifications would be possible. For example, if X always goes first, it could grab the center cell and eliminate a huge number of future possibilities; fewer than $8 \times 6 \times 4 \times 2 = 384$ games could arise. Even if O goes first, there are fewer than $9 \times 7 \times 5 \times 3 = 945$ possible scenarios against a fixed strategy. In fact, the actual number of different games with the strategy defined here turns out to be $76 + 457$, of which $72 + 328$ are won by the machine and the rest belong to the cat.)

66. The Boolean chain in the previous answer fulfills its mission of making correct moves from all 4520 legal positions, where correctness was essentially defined to mean that the worst-case final outcome is maximized. But a truly great tic-tac-toe player would do things differently. For example, from position ⊞ the machine takes the center, and O probably draws by playing in a corner. But moving to would give O only two chances to avoid defeat. [See Martin Gardner, *Hexaflexagons and Other Mathematical Diversions*, Chapter 4.]

Furthermore the best move from a position like is to instead of winning immediately; then if the reply is , move to . That way you still win, but without humiliating your opponent so badly.

Finally, even the concept of a single "best move" is flawed, because a good player will choose different moves in different games (as Babbage observed).

> *It might be thought that programing a digital computer to play ticktacktoe, or designing special circuits for a ticktacktoe machine, would be simple. This is true unless your aim is to construct a master robot that will win the maximum number of games against inexperienced players.*
>
> — MARTIN GARDNER, *The Scientific American Book of Mathematical Puzzles & Diversions* (1959)

67. The author's best effort, with 1734 gates, was constructed by adapting the method of Sholomov in answer 63: First divide the truth tables into 64 rows for $o_5x_5o_2o_6o_8o_4$ and 4096 columns for the other 12 input variables. Then place appropriate 1s into "care" positions, in such a way that the columns have relatively few 1s. Then find a small number of column types that match the cares in all columns; 23 types suffice for the c function, 20 types for s, and 6 for m. We can then compute each output as $\bigvee(g_t \wedge h_t)$, sharing much of the work of the minterm calculations within g_t and h_t.

[This exercise was inspired by a discussion in John Wakerly's book *Digital Design* (Prentice–Hall, 3rd edition, 2000), §6.2.7. Incidentally, Babbage planned to choose among k possible moves by looking at $N \bmod k$, where N was the number of games won so far; he didn't realize that successive moves would tend to be highly correlated until N changed. Much better would have been to let N be the number of *moves made* so far.]

68. No. That method yields a "uniform" chain with a comprehensible structure, but its cost is 2^n times a polynomial in n. A circuit with approximately $2^n/n$ gates, constructed by Theorem L, exists but is more difficult to fabricate. (Incidentally, $C(\pi_5) = 10$.)

69. (a) One can, for example, verify this result by trying all 64 cases.

(b) If x_m lies in the same row or column as x_i, and also in the same row or column as x_j, we have $\alpha_{111} = \alpha_{101} = \alpha_{110} = 0$, so the pairs are good. Otherwise there are essentially three different possibilities, all bad: If $(i,j,m) = (1,2,4)$ then $\alpha_{101} = 0$, $\alpha_{100} = x_5x_9 \oplus x_6x_8$, $\alpha_{011} = x_9$; if $(i,j,m) = (1,2,6)$ then $\alpha_{010} = x_4x_9$, $\alpha_{011} = x_7$, $\alpha_{100} = x_5x_9$, $\alpha_{101} = x_8$; if $(i,j,m) = (1,5,9)$ then $\alpha_{111} = 1$, $\alpha_{110} = 0$, $\alpha_{010} = x_3x_7$.

70. (a) $x_1 \wedge ((x_5 \wedge x_9) \oplus (x_6 \wedge x_8)) \oplus x_2 \wedge ((x_6 \wedge x_7) \oplus (x_4 \wedge x_9)) \oplus x_3 \wedge ((x_4 \wedge x_8) \oplus (x_5 \wedge x_7))$.

(b) $x_1 \wedge ((x_5 \wedge x_9) \vee (x_6 \wedge x_8)) \vee x_2 \wedge ((x_6 \wedge x_7) \vee (x_4 \wedge x_9)) \vee x_3 \wedge ((x_4 \wedge x_8) \vee (x_5 \wedge x_7))$.

(c) Let $y_1 = x_1 \wedge x_5 \wedge x_9$, $y_2 = x_1 \wedge x_6 \wedge x_8$, $y_3 = x_2 \wedge x_6 \wedge x_7$, $y_4 = x_2 \wedge x_4 \wedge x_9$, $y_5 = x_3 \wedge x_4 \wedge x_8$, $y_6 = x_3 \wedge x_5 \wedge x_7$. The function $f(y_1, \ldots, y_6) = [y_1 + y_2 + y_3 > y_4 + y_5 + y_6]$ can be evaluated in 15 further steps with two full adders and a comparator; but there is a 14-step solution: Let $z_1 = (y_1 \oplus y_2) \oplus y_3$, $z_2 = (y_1 \oplus y_2) \vee (y_1 \oplus y_3)$, $z_3 = (y_4 \oplus y_5) \oplus y_6$, $z_4 = (y_4 \oplus y_5) \vee (y_4 \oplus y_6)$. Then $f = (z_1 \oplus (z_2 \wedge (\bar{z}_4 \oplus (z_1 \vee z_3)))) \wedge (\bar{z}_3 \vee z_4)$. Furthermore $y_1y_2y_3 = 111 \iff y_4y_5y_6 = 111$; so there are don't-cares, leading to an 11-step solution: $f = ((\bar{z}_1 \wedge z_3) \vee \bar{z}_4) \wedge z_2$. The total cost is $12 + 11 = 23$.

(The author knows of no way by which a computer could discover such an efficient chain in a reasonable amount of time, given only the truth table of f. But perhaps an even better chain exists.)

71. (a) $P(p) = 1 - 12p^2 + 24p^3 + 12p^4 - 96p^5 + 144p^6 - 96p^7 + 24p^8$, which is $\frac{11}{32} + \frac{9}{2}\epsilon^2 - 3\epsilon^4 - 24\epsilon^6 + 24\epsilon^8$ when $p = \frac{1}{2} + \epsilon$.

(b) There are $N = 2^{n-3}$ sets of eight values $(f_0, \ldots, f_7)$, each of which yields good pairs with probability $P(p)$. So the answer is $1 - P(p)^N$.

(c) The probability is $\binom{N}{r}P(p)^r(1 - P(p))^{N-r}$ that exactly r sets succeed; and in such a case t trials will find good pairs with probability $(r/N)^t$. The answer is therefore $1 - \sum_{r=0}^N \binom{N}{r}P(p)^r(1 - P(p))^{N-r}(r/N)^t = 1 - P(p)^t + O(t^2/N)$.

(d) $\sum_{r=0}^N \binom{N}{r}P(p)^r(1 - P(p))^{N-r}\sum_{j=0}^{t-1}(r/N)^j = (1 - P(p)^t)/(1 - P(p)) + O(t^3/N)$.

72. The probability in exercise 71(a) becomes $P(p) + (72p^3 - 264p^4 + 432p^5 - 336p^6 + 96p^7)r + (60p^2 - 240p^3 + 456p^4 - 432p^5 + 144p^6)r^2 + (-48p^2 + 144p^3 - 216p^4 + 96p^5)r^3 + (-36p^2 + 24p^3 + 12p^4)r^4 + (48p^2 - 24p^3)r^5 - 12p^2r^6$. If $p = q = (1 - r)/2$, this is $(11 + 48r + 36r^2 - 144r^3 - 30r^4 + 336r^5 - 348r^6 + 144r^7 - 21r^8)/32$; for example, it's $7739/8192 \approx 0.94$ when $r = 1/2$.

73. Consider the Horn clauses $1 \wedge 2 \Rightarrow 3$, $1 \wedge 3 \Rightarrow 4$, $\ldots$, $1 \wedge (n-1) \Rightarrow n$, $1 \wedge n \Rightarrow 2$, and $i \wedge j \Rightarrow 1$ for $1 < i < j \le n$. Suppose $|Z| > 1$ in a decomposition, and let i be minimum such that $x_i \in Z$. Also let j be minimum such that $j > i$ and $x_j \in Z$. We cannot have $i > 1$, since $i \wedge j \Rightarrow 1$ in that case. Thus $i = 1$, and $x_j \in Z$ for $2 \le j \le n$.

74. Suppose we know that no nontrivial decomposition exists with $x_1 \in Z$ or $\cdots$ or $x_{i-1} \in Z$; initially $i = 1$. We hope to rule out $x_i \in Z$ too, by choosing j and m cleverly. The Horn clauses $i \wedge j \Rightarrow m$ reduce to Krom clauses $j \Rightarrow m$ when i is asserted. So we essentially want to use Tarjan's depth-first search for strong components, in a digraph with arcs $j \Rightarrow m$ that may or may not exist.

When exploring from vertex j, first try $m = 1$, $\ldots$, $m = i - 1$; if any such implication $i \wedge j \Rightarrow m$ succeeds, we can eliminate j and all its predecessors from the digraph for i. Otherwise, test if $j \Rightarrow m$ for any such eliminated vertex m. Otherwise test unexplored vertices m. Otherwise try vertices m that have already been seen, favoring those near the root of the depth-first tree.

In the example $f(x) = (\det X) \bmod 2$, we would successively find $1 \wedge 2 \not\Rightarrow 3$, $1 \wedge 2 \Rightarrow 4$, $1 \wedge 4 \Rightarrow 3$, $1 \wedge 3 \Rightarrow 5$, $1 \wedge 5 \Rightarrow 6$, $1 \wedge 6 \Rightarrow 7$, $1 \wedge 7 \Rightarrow 8$, $1 \wedge 8 \Rightarrow 9$, $1 \wedge 9 \Rightarrow 2$ (now $i \leftarrow 2$); $2 \wedge 3 \not\Rightarrow 1$, $2 \wedge 3 \Rightarrow 4$, $2 \wedge 4 \not\Rightarrow 1$, $2 \wedge 4 \not\Rightarrow 5$, $2 \wedge 4 \Rightarrow 6$, $2 \wedge 6 \Rightarrow 1$ (now 3, 4, and 6 are eliminated from the digraph for 2), $2 \wedge 5 \Rightarrow 1$ (and 5 is eliminated), $2 \wedge 7 \not\Rightarrow 1$, $2 \wedge 7 \Rightarrow 3$ (7 is eliminated), $2 \wedge 8 \Rightarrow 1$, $2 \wedge 9 \Rightarrow 1$ (now $i \leftarrow 3$); $3 \wedge 4 \not\Rightarrow 1$, $3 \wedge 4 \Rightarrow 2$, $3 \wedge 5 \Rightarrow 1$, etc.

75. This function is 1 at only two points, which are complementary. So it is indecomposable; yet the pairs (58) are *never* bad when $n > 3$. Every partition (Y, Z) will therefore be a candidate for decomposition.

Similarly, if f is decomposable with respect to (Y, Z), the indecomposable function $f(x) \oplus S_{0,n}(x)$ will act essentially like f in the tests. (A method to deal with *approximately decomposable functions* should probably be provided in a general-purpose decomposability tester.)

76. (a) Let $a_l = [i \ge l]$ for $0 \le l \le 2^m$. The cost is $\le 2t(m)$, as observed in answer 38(b); and in fact, the cost can be reduced to $2^{m+1} - 2m - 2$ with $\Theta(m)$ depth. Furthermore the function $[i \le j] = (\bar\imath_1 \wedge j_1) \vee ((i_1 \equiv j_1) \wedge [i_2 \ldots i_m \le j_2 \ldots j_m])$ can be evaluated with $4m - 3$ gates. After computing $x \oplus y$, each z_l costs $2^{m+1} + 1 = O(n/\log n)$.

(b) Here the cost is at most $C(g_0) + \cdots + C(g_{2^m}) \le (2^m + 1)(2^{2^m}/(2^m + O(m)))$ by Theorem L, because each g_l is a function of 2^m inputs.

(c) If $i \le j$ we have $z_l = x$ for $l \le i$ and $z_l = y$ for $l > i$; hence $f_i(x) = c_0 \oplus \cdots \oplus c_i$ and $f_j(y) = c_{j+1} \oplus \cdots \oplus c_{2^m}$. If $i > j$ we have $z_l = y$ for $l \le i$ and $z_l = x$ for $l > i$; hence $f_j(y) = c_0 \oplus \cdots \oplus c_j$ and $f_i(x) = c_{i+1} \oplus \cdots \oplus c_{2^m}$.

(d) The functions $b_l = [j < l]$ can be computed for $0 \le l \le 2^m$ in $O(2^m)$ steps, as in (a). So we can compute F from $(c_0, \ldots, c_{2^m})$ with $O(2^m)$ further gates. Step (b) therefore dominates the cost, for large m.

(e) $a_0 = 1$, $a_1 = i$, $a_2 = 0$; $b_0 = 0$, $b_1 = j$, $b_2 = 1$; $d = [i \le j] = \bar\imath \vee j$; $m_l = a_l \oplus d$, $z_{l0} = x_0 \oplus (m_l \wedge (x_0 \oplus y_0))$, $z_{l1} = x_1 \oplus (m_l \wedge (x_1 \oplus y_1))$, for $l = 0, 1, 2$; $c_0 = z_{01}$; $c_1 = z_{10} \wedge \bar{z}_{11}$; $c_2 = z_{20} \vee z_{21}$; $c'_l = c_l \wedge (d \equiv a_l)$, $c''_l = c_l \wedge (d \equiv b_l)$, for $l = 0, 1, 2$; and finally $F = (c'_0 \oplus c'_1 \oplus c'_2) \vee (c''_0 \oplus c''_1 \oplus c''_2)$.

The net cost (29 after obvious simplifications) is, of course, outrageous in such a small example. But one wonders if a state-of-the-art automatic optimizer would be able to reduce this chain to just 5 gates.

[This result is a special case of more general theorems in *Matematicheskie Zametki* **15** (1974), 937–944; *London Math. Soc. Lecture Note Series* **169** (1992), 165–173.]

77. Given a shortest such chain for f_n or $\bar{f}_n$, let $U_l = \{i \mid l = j(i) \text{ or } l = k(i)\}$ be the "uses" of x_l, and let $u_l = |U_l|$. Let $t_i = 1$ if $x_i = x_{j(i)} \vee x_{k(i)}$, otherwise $t_i = 0$. We will show that there's a chain of length $\leq r - 4$ that computes either f_{n-1} or $\bar{f}_{n-1}$, by using the following idea: If variable x_m is set to 0 or 1, for any m, we can obtain a chain for f_{n-1} or $\bar{f}_{n-1}$ by deleting all steps of U_m and modifying other steps appropriately. Furthermore, if $x_i = x_{j(i)} \circ x_{k(i)}$ and if either $x_{j(i)}$ or $x_{k(i)}$ is known to equal t_i when x_m has been set to 0 or 1, then we can also delete the steps U_i. (Throughout this argument, the letter m will stand for an index in the range $1 \leq m \leq n$.)

Case 1: $u_m = 1$ for some m. This case cannot occur in a shortest chain. For if the only use of x_m is $x_i = \bar{x}_m$, eliminating this step would change $f_n \leftrightarrow \bar{f}_n$; and otherwise we could set the values of $x_1, \ldots, x_{m-1}, x_{m+1}, \ldots, x_n$ to make x_i independent of x_m, contradicting $x_{n+r} = f_n$ or $\bar{f}_n$. Thus every variable must be used at least twice.

Case 2: $x_l = \bar{x}_m$ for some l and m, where $u_m > 1$. Then $x_i = x_l \circ x_k$ for some i and k, and we can set $x_m \leftarrow \bar{t}_i$ to make x_i independent of x_k. Eliminating steps U_m, U_l, and U_i then removes at least 4 steps, except when $u_l = u_i = 1$ and $u_m = 2$ and $x_j = x_m \circ x_i$; but in that case we can also eliminate U_j.

Case 3: $u_m \geq 3$ for some m, and not Case 2. If $i, j, k \in U_m$ and $i < j < k$, set $x_m \leftarrow t_k$ and remove steps i, j, k, U_k.

Case 4: $u_1 = u_2 = \cdots = u_n = 2$, and not Case 2. We may assume that the first step is $x_1 = x_1 \circ x_2$, and that $x_l = x_1 \circ x_k$ for some $k < l$.

Case 4.1: $k > 0$. Then $k > 1$. If $u_k = 1$, set $x_1 \leftarrow t_l$ and remove steps 1, k, l, U_l. Otherwise set $x_2 \leftarrow t_1$; this forces $x_k = \bar{t}_l$, and we can remove steps 1, k, l, U_k.

Case 4.2: $x_l = x_1 \circ x_m$. Then we must have $m = 2$; for if $m > 2$ we could set $x_2 \leftarrow t_1$, $x_m \leftarrow t_l$, and make x_r independent of x_1. Hence we may assume that $x_1 = x_1 \wedge x_2$, $x_2 = x_1 \vee x_2$. Setting $x_1 \leftarrow 0$ allows us to remove U_0 and U_1; setting $x_1 \leftarrow 1$ allows us to remove U_0 and U_2. Thus we're done unless $u_1 = u_2 = 1$.

If $x_p = \bar{x}_1$, set $x_1 \leftarrow 0$ and remove 1, 2, p, U_p; if $x_q = \bar{x}_2$, set $x_1 \leftarrow 1$ and remove 1, 2, q, U_q. Otherwise $x_p = x_1 \circ x_u$ and $x_q = x_2 \circ x_v$, where x_u and x_v do not depend on x_1 or x_2. But that's impossible; it would allow us to set $x_3, \ldots, x_n$ to make $x_u = t_p$, then $x_2 \leftarrow 1$ to make x_r independent of x_1.

[*Problemy Kibernetiki* **23** (1970), 83–101; **28** (1974), 4. With similar proofs, Red'kin showed that the shortest AND-OR-NOT chains for the functions '$x_1 \ldots x_n < y_1 \ldots y_n$' and '$x_1 \ldots x_n = y_1 \ldots y_n$' have lengths $5n - 3$ and $5n - 1$, respectively.]

78. [*SICOMP* **6** (1977), 427–430.] Say that y_k is *active* if $k \in S$. We may assume that the chain is normal and that $\|S\| > 1$; the proof is like Red'kin's in answer 77:

Case 1: Some active y_k is used more than once. Setting $y_k \leftarrow 0$ saves at least two steps and yields a chain for a function with $\|S\| - 1$ active values.

Case 2: Some active y_k appears only in an AND gate. Setting $y_k \leftarrow 0$ eliminates at least two steps, unless this AND is the final step. But it can't be the final step, because $y_k = 0$ makes the result independent of every other active y_j.

Case 3: Like Case 2 but with an OR or NOT-BUT or BUT-NOT gate. Setting $y_k \leftarrow c$ for some appropriate constant c has the desired effect.

Case 4: Like Case 2 but with XOR. The gate can't be final, since the result should be independent of y_k when $(x_1 \ldots x_m)_2$ addresses a different active value y_j. So we can eliminate two steps by setting y_k to the function defined by the *other* input to XOR.

79. (a) Suppose the cost is $r < 2n - 2$; then $n > 1$. If each variable is used exactly once, two leaves must be mates. Therefore some variable is used at least twice. Pruning it away produces a chain of cost $\leq r - 2$ on $n - 1$ variables, having no mates.

(Incidentally, the cost is at least $2n - 1$ if every variable is used at least twice, because at least $2n$ uses of variables must be connected together in the chain.)

(b) Notice that $S_{0,n} = \bigwedge_{u-v}(u \equiv v)$ whenever the edges $u — v$ form a free tree on $\{x_1, \ldots, x_n\}$. So there are many ways to achieve cost $2n - 3$.

Any chain of cost $r < 2n - 3$ must have $n > 2$ and must contain mates u and v. By renaming and possibly complementing intermediate results, we can assume that $u = 1$, $v = 2$, and that $f(x_1, \ldots, x_n) = g(x_1 \circ h(x_3, \ldots, x_n), x_2, \ldots, x_n)$, where $\circ$ is $\wedge$ or $\oplus$.

Case 1: $\circ$ is AND. We must have $h(0, \ldots, 0) = h(1, \ldots, 1) = 1$, for otherwise $f(x_1, x_2, y, \ldots, y)$ wouldn't depend on x_1. Therefore $f(x_1, \ldots, x_n) = h(x_3, \ldots, x_n) \wedge g(x_1, x_2, \ldots, x_n)$ can be computed by a chain of the same cost in which 1 and 2 are mates and in which the path between them has gotten shorter.

Case 2: $\circ$ is XOR. Then $f = f_0 \vee f_1$, where $f_0(x_1, \ldots, x_n) = (x_1 \equiv h(x_3, \ldots, x_n)) \wedge g(0, x_2, \ldots, x_n)$ and $f_1(x_1, \ldots, x_n) = (x_1 \oplus h(x_3, \ldots, x_n)) \wedge g(1, x_2, \ldots, x_n)$. But $f = S_{0,n}$ has only two prime implicants; so there are only four possibilities:

Case 2a: $f_0 = f$. Then we can replace $x_1 \oplus h$ by 0, to get a chain of cost $\leq r - 2$ for the function $g(0, x_2, \ldots, x_n) = S_{0,n-1}(x_2, \ldots, x_n)$.

Case 2b: $f_1 = f$. Similar to Case 2a.

Case 2c: $f_0(x) = x_1 \wedge \cdots \wedge x_n$ and $f_1(x) = \bar{x}_1 \wedge \cdots \wedge \bar{x}_n$. In this case we must have $g(0, x_2, \ldots, x_n) = x_2 \wedge \cdots \wedge x_n$ and $g(1, x_2, \ldots, x_n) = \bar{x}_2 \wedge \cdots \wedge \bar{x}_n$. Replacing h by 1 therefore yields a chain that computes f in $< r$ steps.

Case 2d: $f_0(x) = \bar{x}_1 \wedge \cdots \wedge \bar{x}_n$ and $f_1(x) = x_1 \wedge \cdots \wedge x_n$. Similar to Case 2c.

Applying these reductions repeatedly will lead to a contradiction. Similarly, one can show that $C(S_0S_n) = 2n - 2$. [*Theoretical Computer Science* **1** (1976), 289–295.]

80. [*Mathematical Systems Theory* **10** (1977), 323–336.] Without loss of generality, $a_0 = 0$ and the chain is normal. Define U_l and u_l as in answer 77. We may assume by symmetry that $u_1 = \max(u_1, \ldots, u_n)$.

We must have $u_1 \geq 2$. For if $u_1 = 1$, we could assume further that $x_{n+1} = x_1 \circ x_2$; hence two of the three functions $S_\alpha(0, 0, x_3, \ldots, x_n) = S_{\alpha''}$, $S_\alpha(0, 1, x_3, \ldots, x_n) = S_{'\alpha'}$, $S_\alpha(1, 1, x_3, \ldots, x_n) = S_{''\alpha}$ would be equal. But then S_α would be a parity function, or $S_{'\alpha'}$ would be constant.

Therefore setting $x_1 = 0$ allows us to eliminate the gates of U_1, giving a chain for $S_{\alpha'}$ with at least 2 fewer gates. It follows that $C(S_\alpha) \geq C(S_{\alpha'}) + 2$. Similarly, setting $x_1 = 1$ proves that $C(S_\alpha) \geq C(S_{'\alpha}) + 2$.

Three cases arise when we explore the situation further:

Case 1: $u_1 \geq 3$. Setting $x_1 = 0$ proves that $C(S_\alpha) \geq C(S_{\alpha'}) + 3$.

Case 2: $U_1 = \{i, j\}$ and operator $\circ_j$ is canalizing (namely, AND, BUT-NOT, NOT-BUT, or OR). Setting x_1 to an appropriate constant forces the value of x_j and allows us to eliminate $U_1 \cup U_j$; notice that $i \notin U_j$ in an optimum chain. So either $C(S_\alpha) \geq C(S_{\alpha'}) + 3$ or $C(S_\alpha) \geq C(S_{'\alpha}) + 3$.

Case 3: $U_1 = \{i, j\}$ and $\circ_i = \circ_j = \oplus$. We may assume that $x_i = x_1 \oplus x_2$ and $x_j = x_1 \oplus x_k$. If $u_j = 1$ and $x_l = x_j \oplus x_p$, we can restructure the chain by letting $x_j = x_k \oplus x_p$, $x_l = x_1 \oplus x_j$; therefore we can assume that either $u_j \neq 1$ or $x_l = x_j \circ x_p$ for some canalizing operator $\circ$. If $U_2 = \{i, j'\}$, we can assume similarly that $x_{j'} = x_2 \oplus x_{k'}$ and that either $u_{j'} = 1$ or $x_{l'} = x_{j'} \circ' x_{p'}$ for some canalizing operator $\circ'$. Furthermore we can assume by symmetry that x_j does not depend on $x_{j'}$.

If x_k does not depend on x_i, let $f(x_3, \ldots, x_n) = x_k$; otherwise let $f(x_3, \ldots, x_n)$ be the value of x_k when $x_i = 1$. By setting $x_1 = f(x_3, \ldots, x_n)$ and $x_2 = \bar{f}(x_3, \ldots, x_n)$, or vice versa, we make x_i and x_j constant, and we obtain a chain for the nonconstant function $S_{\alpha'}$. We can, in fact, ensure that x_l is constant in the case $u_j = 1$. We claim that at least five gates of this chain (including x_i and x_j) can be eliminated; hence $C(S_\alpha) \geq C(S_{\alpha'}) + 5$. The claim is clearly true if $|U_i \cup U_j| \geq 3$.

We must have $|U_i \cup U_j| > 1$. Otherwise we'd have $p = i$, and x_k would not depend on x_i, so S_α would be independent of x_1 with our choice of x_2. Therefore $|U_i \cup U_j| = 2$.

Case 3a: $U_j = \{l\}$. Then x_l is constant; we can eliminate x_i, x_j, and $U_i \cup U_j \cup U_l$. If the latter set contains only two elements, then $x_q = x_i \circ x_l$ is also constant and we eliminate U_q. Since $S_{\alpha'}$ isn't constant, we won't eliminate the output gate.

Case 3b: $U_i \subseteq U_j$, $|U_j| = 2$. Then $x_q = x_i \circ x_j$ for some q; we can eliminate x_i, x_j, and $U_j \cup U_q$. The claim has been proved.

(b) By induction, $C(S_k) \geq 2n + \min(k, n - k) - 3 - [n = 2k]$, for $0 < k < n$; $C(S_{\geq k}) \geq 2n + \min(k, n + 1 - k) - 4$, for $1 < k < n$. The easy cases are $C(S_0) = C(S_n) = C(S_{\geq 1}) = C(S_{\geq n}) = n - 1$; $C(S_{\geq 0}) = 0$. (According to Figs. 9 and 10, these bounds are optimum for $k = \lceil n/2 \rceil$ when $n \leq 5$. All known results are consistent with the conjecture that $C(S_k) = C(S_{\geq k})$ for $k \geq n/2$.)

81. If some variable is used more than once, we can set it to a constant, decreasing n by 1 and decreasing c by ≥ 2. Otherwise the first operation must involve x_1, because $y_1 = x_1$ is the only output that doesn't need computation; making x_1 constant decreases n by 1, c by ≥ 1, and d by ≥ 1. [*J. Algorithms* **7** (1986), 185–201.]

82. (62) is false.

(63) reads, "For all numbers m there's a number n such that $m < n + 1$"; it is true because we can take $m = n$.

(64) fails when $n = 0$ or $n = 1$, because the numbers in these formulas are required to be nonnegative integers.

(65) says that, if b exceeds a by 2 or more, there's a number ab between them. Of course it's true, because we can let $ab = a + 1$.

(66) was explained in the text, and it too is true. Notice that '$\wedge$' takes precedence over '$\vee$' and '$\equiv$' takes precedence over '$\Leftrightarrow$', just as '$+$' takes precedence over '$\geq$' and '$<$' over '$\wedge$' in (65); these conventions reduce the need for parentheses in sentences of L.

(67) says that, if A contains at least one element n, it must contain a minimum element m (an element that's less than or equal to all of its elements). True.

(68) is similar, but m is now a maximum element. Again true, because all sets are assumed to be finite.

(69) asks for a set P with the property that $[0 \in P] = [3 \notin P]$, $[1 \in P] = [4 \notin P]$, ..., $[999 \in P] = [1002 \notin P]$, $[1000 \in P] \neq [1003 \notin P]$, $[1001 \in P] \neq [1004 \notin P]$, etc. It's true if (and only if) $P = \{x \mid x \bmod 6 \in \{1, 2, 3\}$ and $0 \leq x < 1000\}$.

Finally, the subformula $\forall n (n \in C \Leftrightarrow n + 1 \in C)$ in (70) is another way of saying that $C = \emptyset$, because C is finite. Hence the parenthesized formula after $\forall A \forall B$ is a tricky way to say that $A = \emptyset$ and $B \neq \emptyset$. (Stockmeyer and Meyer used this trick to abbreviate statements in L that involve long subformulas more than once.) Statement (70) is true because an empty set doesn't equal a nonempty set.

83. We can assume that the chain is normal. Let the canalizing steps be $y_1, \ldots, y_p$. Then $y_k = \alpha_k \circ \beta_k$ and $f = \alpha_{p+1}$, where α_k and β_k are $\oplus$'s of some subsets of $\{x_1, \ldots, x_n, y_1, \ldots, y_{k-1}\}$; at most $n + k - 2$ $\oplus$'s are needed to compute them, combining common terms first. Hence $C(f) \leq p + \sum_{k=1}^{p+1}(n + k - 2) = (p + 1)(n + p/2) - 1$.

84. Argue as in the previous answer, with $\vee$ or $\wedge$ in place of $\oplus$. [N. Alon and R. B. Boppana, *Combinatorica* **7** (1987), 15–16.]

85. (a) A simple computer program shows that 13744 are legitimate and 19024 aren't. (An illegitimate family of this kind has at least 8 members; one such is $\{00, 0f, 33, 55,$ $ff, 15, 3f, 77\}$. Indeed, if the functions $x_1 \vee x_2$ (3f), $x_2 \vee x_3$ (77), and $(x_1 \vee x_2) \wedge x_3$ (15) are present in a legitimate family L, then $x_2 \sqcup 15 = 33 \mid 15 = 37$ must also be in L.)

(b) The projection and constant functions are obviously present. Define $A^* = \bigcap \{B \mid B \supseteq A$ and $B \in \mathcal{A}\}$, or $A^* = \infty$ if no such set B exists. Then we have $\lceil A \rceil \sqcap \lceil B \rceil = \lceil A \cap B \rceil$ and $\lceil A \rceil \sqcup \lceil B \rceil = \lceil (A \cup B)^* \rceil$.

(c) Abbreviate the formulas as $\hat{x}_l \subseteq x_l \vee \bigvee_{i=n+1}^{l} \delta_i$, $x_l \subseteq \hat{x}_l \vee \bigvee_{i=n+1}^{l} \epsilon_i$, and argue by induction: If step l is an AND step, $\hat{x}_l = \hat{x}_j \sqcap \hat{x}_k \subseteq \hat{x}_j \wedge \hat{x}_k \subseteq (x_j \vee \bigvee_{i=n+1}^{l} \delta_i) \wedge (x_k \vee \bigvee_{i=n+1}^{l} \delta_i) = x_l \vee \bigvee_{i=n+1}^{l} \delta_i$; $x_l = x_j \wedge x_k \subseteq (\hat{x}_j \vee \bigvee_{i=n+1}^{l-1} \epsilon_i) \wedge (\hat{x}_k \vee \bigvee_{i=n+1}^{l-1} \epsilon_i) = (\hat{x}_j \wedge \hat{x}_k) \vee \bigvee_{i=n+1}^{l-1} \epsilon_i$, and $\hat{x}_j \wedge \hat{x}_k = \hat{x}_l \vee \epsilon_l$. Argue similarly if step l is an OR step.

86. (a) If S is an r-family contained in the $(r+1)$-family S', clearly $\Delta(S) \subseteq \Delta(S')$.

(b) By the pigeonhole principle, $\Delta(S)$ contains elements u and v of each part, whenever S is an r-family. And if $\Delta(S) = \{u, v\}$, we certainly have $u \text{ --- } v$.

(c) The result is obvious when $r = 1$. There are at most $r - 1$ edges containing any given vertex u, by the "strong" property. And if $u \text{ --- } v$, the edges *disjoint* from $\{u, v\}$ are strongly $(r-1)$-closed; so there are at most $(r-2)^2$ of them, by induction. Thus there are at most $1 + 2(r-2) + (r-2)^2$ edges altogether.

(d) Yes, by exercise 85(b), if $r > 1$, because strongly r-closed graphs are closed under intersection. All graphs with ≤ 1 edges are strongly r-closed when $r > 1$, because they have no r-families containing distinct edges.

(e) There are $\binom{n}{3}$ triangles $x_{ij} \wedge x_{ik} \wedge x_{jk}$, only $n - 2$ of which are contained in any term x_{uv} of $\hat{f}$. Hence the minterms for at most $(r-1)^2(n-2)$ triangles are contained in $\hat{f}$, and the others must be contained in one of the functions $\epsilon_i = \hat{x}_i \oplus (\hat{x}_{j(i)} \wedge x_{k(i)})$. Such a term has the form $T = (\lceil G \rceil \sqcap \lceil H \rceil) \oplus (\lceil G \rceil \wedge \lceil H \rceil) = (\lceil G \rceil \wedge \lceil H \rceil) \wedge \overline{\lceil G \cap H \rceil}$, where G and H are strongly r-closed; we will prove that T contains at most $2(r-1)^3$ triangles.

A triangle $x_{ij} \wedge x_{ik} \wedge x_{jk}$ in T must involve some variable (say x_{ij}) of $\lceil G \rceil$ and some variable (say x_{ik}) of $\lceil H \rceil$, but no variable of $\lceil G \cap H \rceil$. There are at most $(r-1)^2$ choices for ij; and then there are at most $2(r-1)$ choices for k, since H has at most $r - 1$ edges touching i and at most $r - 1$ edges touching j.

(f) There are 2^{n-1} complete bigraphs obtained by coloring 1 red, coloring other vertices either red or blue, and letting $u \text{ --- } v$ if and only if u and v have opposite colors. By the first formula in exercise 85(c), the minterms B for every such graph must be contained in one of the terms $T = \delta_i = \hat{x}_i \oplus (\hat{x}_{j(i)} \vee x_{k(i)}) = \lceil (G \cup H)^* \rceil \wedge \overline{\lceil G \cup H \rceil}$. (For example, if $n = 4$ and vertices $(2, 3, 4)$ are (red, blue, blue), then $B = \bar{x}_{12} \wedge x_{13} \wedge x_{14} \wedge x_{23} \wedge x_{24} \wedge \bar{x}_{34}$.) A minterm B is contained in T if and only if, in the coloring for B, some edge of $(G \cup H)^*$ has vertices of opposite colors, but all edges of $G \cup H$ are monochromatic. We will prove that T includes at most $2^{n-r} r^2$ such B.

Let G be any graph, and $T = \lceil G^* \rceil \wedge \overline{\lceil G \rceil}$. The following (inefficient) algorithm can be used to find G^*: If there's an r-family S with $|\Delta(S)| < 2$, stop with $G^* = \infty$. Otherwise, if $\Delta(S) = \{u, v\}$ and $u \not\!\!- v$, add the edge $u \text{ --- } v$ to G and repeat.

At most 2^{n-r} bipartite minterms B have monochromatic $\{u_j, v_j\}$ for $1 \leq j \leq r$ when $|\Delta(S)| < 2$. And when $\Delta(S) = \{u, v\}$ there are 2^{n-r-1} with monochromatic $\{u_j, v_j\}$ and bichromatic $\{u, v\}$. So we want to show that the algorithm for G takes fewer then $2r^2$ iterations when G is strongly r-closed.

For $k \geq 1$, let $u_k \text{ --- } v_k$ be the first new edge added to G that is disjoint from $\{u_j, v_j\}$ for $1 \leq j < k$. At most r such edges exist, by "strongness"; and each of them is followed by at most $2r - 3$ new edges that touch u_j or v_j. So the total number of steps to find G^* is at most $r(2r - 2) + 1 < 2r^2$.

(g) Exercise 84 tells us that $q < \binom{p}{2} + (p+1)\binom{n}{2}$. Thus we have either $2(r - 1)^3 p \geq \binom{n}{3} - (r - 1)^2(n - 2)$ or $\binom{p}{2} + (p + 1)\binom{n}{2} > 2^{r-1}/r^2$. Both lower bounds for p are

$$\frac{1}{12}\left(\frac{n}{6 \lg n}\right)^3 \left(1 + O\left(\frac{\log \log n}{\log n}\right)\right) \qquad \text{when} \qquad r = \left\lceil \lg\left(\frac{n^6}{186624(\lg n)^4}\right)\right\rceil.$$

[Noga Alon and Ravi B. Boppana, *Combinatorica* **7** (1987), 1–22, proceeded in this way to prove, among other things, the lower bound $\Omega(n/\log n)^s$ for the number of $\wedge$'s in any monotone chain that decides whether or not G has a clique of fixed size $s \geq 3$.]

87. The entries of X^3 are at most n^2 when X is a 0–1 matrix. A Boolean chain with $O(n^{\lg 7}(\log n)^2)$ gates can implement Strassen's matrix multiplication algorithm 4.6.4–(36), on integers modulo $2^{\lfloor \lg n^2 \rfloor +1}$.

88. There are 1,422,564 such functions, in 716 classes with respect to permutation of variables. Algorithm L and the other methods of this section extend readily to ternary operations, and we obtain the following results for optimum median-only computation:

$C(f)$	Classes	Functions	$C_m(f)$	Classes	Functions	$L(f)$	Classes	Functions	$D(f)$	Classes	Functions
0	1	7	0	1	7	0	1	7	0	1	7
1	1	35	1	1	35	1	1	35	1	1	35
2	2	350	2	2	350	2	2	350	2	13	5670
3	9	3885	3	9	3885	3	8	3745	3	700	1416822
4	48	42483	4	48	42483	4	38	35203	4	1	30
5	201	406945	5	188	391384	5	139	270830	5	0	0
6	353	798686	6	253	622909	6	313	699377	6	0	0
7	99	169891	7	69	134337	7	176	367542	7	0	0
8	2	282	8	2	2520	8	34	43135	8	0	0
9	0	0	9	0	0	9	3	2310	9	0	0
10	0	0	10	0	0	10	0	0	10	0	0
11	0	0	∞	143	224654	11	1	30	11	0	0

S. Amarel, G. E. Cooke, and R. O. Winder [*IEEE Trans.* **EC-13** (1964), 4–13, Fig. 5b] conjectured that the 9-operation formula

$$\langle x_1 x_2 x_3 x_4 x_5 x_6 x_7 \rangle = \langle x_1 \langle \langle x_2 x_3 x_5 \rangle \langle x_2 x_4 x_6 \rangle \langle x_3 x_4 x_7 \rangle \rangle \langle \langle x_2 x_5 x_6 \rangle \langle x_3 x_5 x_7 \rangle \langle x_4 x_6 x_7 \rangle \rangle \rangle$$

is the best way to compute medians-of-7 via medians-of-3. But the "magic" formula

$$\langle x_1 \langle x_2 \langle x_3 x_4 x_5 \rangle \langle x_3 x_6 x_7 \rangle \rangle \langle x_4 \langle x_2 x_6 x_7 \rangle \langle x_3 x_5 \langle x_5 x_6 x_7 \rangle \rangle \rangle \rangle$$

needs only 8 operations; and in fact the shortest chain needs just seven steps:

$$\langle x_1 x_2 x_3 x_4 x_5 x_6 x_7 \rangle = \langle x_1 \langle x_2 \langle x_5 x_6 x_7 \rangle \langle x_3 \langle x_5 x_6 x_7 \rangle x_4 \rangle \rangle \langle x_5 \langle x_2 x_3 x_4 \rangle \langle x_6 \langle x_2 x_3 x_4 \rangle x_7 \rangle \rangle \rangle.$$

The interesting function $f(x_1, \ldots, x_7) = (x_1 \wedge x_2 \wedge x_4) \vee (x_2 \wedge x_3 \wedge x_5) \vee (x_3 \wedge x_4 \wedge x_6) \vee (x_4 \wedge x_5 \wedge x_7) \vee (x_5 \wedge x_6 \wedge x_1) \vee (x_6 \wedge x_7 \wedge x_2) \vee (x_7 \wedge x_1 \wedge x_3)$, whose prime implicants correspond to the projective plane with 7 points, is the toughest of all: Its minimum length $L(f) = 11$ and minimum depth $D(f) = 4$ are achieved by the remarkable formula

$$\langle \langle x_1 x_4 \langle x_4 x_5 x_6 \rangle \rangle \langle x_3 x_6 \langle x_1 \langle x_2 x_3 x_7 \rangle \langle x_2 x_5 x_6 \rangle \rangle \rangle \langle x_2 x_7 \langle x_1 \langle x_5 x_2 x_4 \rangle \langle x_5 x_3 x_7 \rangle \rangle \rangle \rangle.$$

And the following even more astonishing chain computes it optimally:

$$x_8 = \langle x_1 x_2 x_3 \rangle, \quad x_9 = \langle x_1 x_4 x_6 \rangle, \quad x_{10} = \langle x_1 x_5 x_8 \rangle, \quad x_{11} = \langle x_2 x_7 x_8 \rangle,$$
$$x_{12} = \langle x_3 x_9 x_{10} \rangle, \quad x_{13} = \langle x_4 x_5 x_{12} \rangle, \quad x_{14} = \langle x_6 x_{11} x_{12} \rangle, \quad x_{15} = \langle x_7 x_{13} x_{14} \rangle.$$

INDEX AND GLOSSARY

When an index entry refers to a page containing a relevant exercise, see also the *answer* to that exercise for further information. An answer page is not indexed here unless it refers to a topic not included in the statement of the exercise.

⌣, *see* smile.
0–1 matrices, 20, 32–35, 44, 46, 125, 130, 179, 200, *see also* Adjacency matrices.
0–1 principle, 68.
0-preserving functions, *see* Normal Boolean functions.
2-coloring, 17, 22–23, 41.
2-monotonic functions, *see* Regular Boolean functions.
2-partite graphs, *see* Bipartite graphs.
2-variable functions, 47–50, 79–80.
  table, 49.
2^m-way multiplexer, 109, 127.
2CNF, 57, 72, 86–87, 91, *see also* Krom functions.
2SAT, 57, 60–62, 72, 86.
2SAT functions, *see* 2CNF.
3-coloring, 39, 42, 149.
3-variable functions, 63, 104–105, 156.
  table, 78.
3CNF, 56.
3SAT, 56, 162.
4-coloring, 17, 39, 149.
4-cycles, 69.
4-variable functions, 98–105, 112–114, 122, 126, 129.
5-variable functions, 105–106, 126, 191.
$\alpha(H)$ (independence number of a graph or hypergraph), 35, 44.
γ (Euler's constant), as source of "random" data, 136.
νx (sideways sum), 77, 90, 108, 126, 158, 185, 187.
π (circle ratio), as source of "random" data, 76, 98, 118, 128, 136, *see also* Pi function.
$\Sigma(f)$ (true-vector sum), 76–77, 92, 95.
ϕ (golden ratio), 134.
  as source of "random" data, 136.
$\chi(H)$ (chromatic number of a graph or hypergraph), 35, 39, 44, 46.
$\omega(G)$ (clique number of a graph), 35, 44.

a-codes, 82, *see* Asterisk codes for subcubes.
Abelian (commutative) groups, 152.
Absorption laws, 50.
Acyclic: Containing no cycles, 15, 31–32.
Acyclic digraphs, 169.
Addition, binary, 107–108, 127–128.
Addition modulo 3 and 5, 129.
Addition modulo 4, 126.
Addition table modulo n, 36.

Adjacency lists, 21–22.
Adjacency matrices, 19–20, 26, 27, 40–41, 43, 123, 133, 148, 153.
Adjacent vertices, 13.
Affine Boolean functions, 95–96, 182–183.
Affirmation (⊤), 49.
Ahrens, Wilhelm Ernst Martin Georg, 136.
Aiken, Howard Hathaway, 104.
Ajtai, Miklós, 91.
Akers, Sheldon Buckingham, Jr., 87.
Alekseyev, Valery Borisovich (Алексеев, Валерий Борисович), 179.
All-0s matrix, 27, 145.
All-1s matrix, 26, 27, 145, 146.
All-equal function ($S_{0,n}$), 131.
Alon, Noga (נגה אלון), 175, 198, 200.
Alphabetic order, 38.
Amarel, Saul, 200.
Amir, Yair (יאיר עמיר), 174.
Anagrams, 139.
Analysis of algorithms, 41, 82–84, 130.
AND (∧), 48–51, 53, 57, 63, 81.
  bitwise (&), 58, 74, 82, 84, 156, 158.
AND operation, bitwise, 22.
AND gates (∧), 32, 33, 97.
  with vacuum tubes, 104.
AND-OR chains, 125, 132–133.
AND-OR–NOT chains, 131, *see also* Canalizing chains.
Andersen, Lars Døvling, 136.
Antisymmetric digraphs, 62, 91.
Appel, Kenneth Ira, 17.
Apportionment, 8.
Approximately decomposable functions, 195.
Arabic mathematics, 135–136.
Arc lists, 21–22.
Arc variables, 21, 23.
Arcs in a graph, 18–23.
  as edges, 18.
ARCS(v) (first arc of a vertex), 21.
Arithmetic progressions, 38.
Aschbacher, Michael George, 143.
Ashenhurst, Robert Lovett, 117, 120.
Aspvall, Bengt Ingemar, 87, 164.
Associative block designs, 56.
Associative laws, 27, 28, 42, 50, 65, 68, 80, 156, 159, 185, 186, 189.
Asterisk codes for subcubes, 82, 84.
Asterisks, 54, 82–84, 155.
Asymptotic methods, 109–112, 128–129, 157, 160, 169, 174, 177–178.
Automated deduction, 167.

Automorphisms, 14–15, 39, 45, 143, 147, 152–153.
Availability polynomials, 80, 81, 84, 93, 155.
Avann, Sherwin Parker, 89.

b-codes, 82, see Bit codes for subcubes.
Babbage, Charles, 116, 188, 193, 194.
Babbage, Henry Provost, 188.
Bach, Johann Sebastian, xii.
Backward-computation principle, 102.
Bad pairs, 118–120, 130–131.
Ball, Michael Owen, 161.
Bandelt, Hans-Jürgen, 170.
Bang, Thøger Sophus Vilhelm, 134.
Barbará Millá, Daniel, 88.
Barbour, Andrew David, 152.
Barnard, Robert, 10.
Baron, Gerd, 135.
Barycentric coordinates, 25, 88.
Bassanio of Venice, 1.
Baugh, Charles Richmond, 172, 173, 178.
Bears, California Golden, 31.
Bell Telephone Laboratories, 115.
Bent functions, 96.
Berge, Claude, 34.
Berlekamp, Elwyn Ralph, 192.
Bernays, Paul Issak, 53.
Bernstein, Benjamin Abram, 154.
Betweenness, 65, 89–90.
bi_book graphs, 23.
bi_lisa graphs, 24.
Biggs, Norman Linstead, 15.
Bigraphs, 17, see Bipartite graphs.
Bijunctive clauses, see Krom clauses.
Binary addition, 107–108, 127–128.
Binary comparison function, 120, 194–196.
Binary decoder, 109, 186.
Binary majorization lattices, 92–93.
Binary number system, 47, 75–76, 80, 82, 90, 92, 175.
Binary operator: A function of two variables, 49.
Binary recurrences, 108, 109, 126, 168, 186.
Binary strings, 54, 67, 90, 92–93.
Binary trees, 85, 97, 98, 190.
    complete, 81.
Binary-coded decimal digits, 114.
Bioch, Jan Corstiaan, 166.
Bipartite graphs, 17, 22–25, 35, 39, 41, 43, 120, 133, 142, 149, 194.
    corresponding to hypergraphs, 33, 44.
Bipartite hypergraphs, 149.
Bipartite matching, 125.
Bipartiteness testing, 22–23.
Birkhoff, Garrett, 167.
Bishop moves on a chessboard, 25, 26, 31.
Bit codes for subcubes, 82, 84–85.
Bitburger Brauerei, x.

Bitwise operations, 47, 74, 82, 100–102, 126, 154, 182, 199.
    AND (&), 22, 58, 74, 82, 84, 156, 158.
    medians, 67, 71, 72, 91, 167, 168.
    OR (|), 50, 74, 84.
    saturating subtraction ($\dot{-}$), 84.
    XOR ($\oplus$), 90, 158.
Blake, Archie, 159.
Block designs, 179.
Blum, Norbert Karl, 122.
$board$ graphs, 25, 26, 31, 41.
Bocheński, Józef (= Innocenty) Maria, 49.
Bollobás, Béla, 179.
Bondy, John Adrian, 14, 153.
$book$ graphs, 23.
Boole, George, 48, 52, 189.
Boolean binary operators, 47–51, 80, 87, 92.
    table, 49.
Boolean chains, 96–133.
    AND-OR, 125, 132–133.
    AND-OR-NOT, 126, 131, 190.
    canalizing, 126, 132, 190.
    definition of, 96.
    monotone, 125, 132–133.
    of 3 variables, 104–105.
    of 4 variables, 98–105, 112–114, 122, 126, 129.
    of 5 variables, 105–106, 126, 191.
    of many variables, 109–112, 117–133.
    optimization of, 121–122, 195.
    with several outputs, 107–109, 112–117, 121–122, 126–130.
Boolean functions, 33, 47–95.
    affine, 95–96, 182–183.
    bent, 96.
    canalizing, 78, 79, 95.
    duals of, 154, 157, 172.
    enumeration of, 79.
    Horn, 58, 79, 95.
    Krom, 60, 72, 79, 81, 95.
    majority, 63, 68, 76, 169, see Medians.
    monotone, 156, see Monotone Boolean functions.
    of 2 variables, 47–50, 79–80.
    of 3 variables, 63, 78, 156.
    random, 56, 83, 160.
    regular, 93, 178.
    self-dual, see Self-dual Boolean functions.
    symmetric, 77–79, 94–95.
    threshold, 75–77, 79, 92–95, 186.
    unate, 156.
Boolean games, 86.
Boolean values, 32.
Bootstrapping, 185, 190.
Boppana, Ravi Babu, 198, 200.
Boros, Endre, 120, 161.
Bose, Raj Chandra (রাজ চন্দ্র বসু), 5.
Bossen, Douglas Craig, 139.
Bottom-up synthesis, 103–105, 126, 183.

Boyer, Robert Stephen, 46.
Brayton, Robert King, 122.
Breadth-first search, 70.
Brent, Richard Peirce, 188.
Brette, Jean, 135.
Brewster, George, 9.
Brightwell, Graham Richard, 179.
Brinkmann, Gunnar, 149.
Brooks, Rowland Leonard, 145.
Brown, John Wesley, 136.
Brown, William Gordon, 143.
Brualdi, Richard Anthony, 137.
Bruck, Richard Hubert, 138.
Büchi, Julius Richard, 124.
Buddies, 82.
Bui, Alain, 2.
Burley (= Burleigh), Walter, 51.
BUT-NOT gates (⊃), 97, 100, 110.

C language, 22, 50.
$C(f)$, 97, 111–112, see Cost of a Boolean
    function.
$C(f_1 \ldots f_m)$, 107.
$C^+(f)$, 132, 133.
$C_m(f)$, 102–103, 126, 200.
C_n (cycle of order n), 13, 28, 39, 41.
$C_n^{\to}$ (oriented cycle of order n), 18, 41.
California Golden Bears, 31.
Canalizing chains, 126, 132, 190.
Canalizing functions, 78, 79, 95.
Canalizing operators, 123, 126, 183, 197.
Cancellation laws, 76, 80.
Canonical forms, see Full conjunction normal
    form, Full disjunctive normal form,
    Integer multilinear representation,
    Multilinear representation of a
    Boolean function.
Cardinal, Stanford, 31.
Cares, 129, 194, see also Don't-cares.
Carroll, Lewis (= Dodgson, Charles
    Lutwidge), 10–12, 48, 79, 140.
Carry bits, 107, 127, 128, 189.
Cartesian product of graphs, 27–28,
    42–44, 67, 146.
Cat's game, 86, 115, 117, 193.
Categorical product of graphs, 28, see
    Direct product of graphs.
Cayley, Arthur, digraphs, 45.
    graphs, 45, 152.
Censorship, 10–11.
Chambers, Ephraim, v.
Chandra, Ashok Kumar (अशोक कुमार
    चन्द्रा), 159, 176.
Characteristic polynomial of a Boolean
    function, 155, see Integer multilinear
    representation.
Chase, Philip John, sequence, 94.
Chaucer, Geoffrey, 139.
Chess, 163.

Chessboard-like graphs,
    bishop moves, 25, 26, 31.
    generalized piece moves, 41.
    king moves, 43.
    knight moves, 15, 25.
    queen moves, 26, 44.
    rook moves, 26, 41.
Chien, Robert Tien Wen (錢天聞), 139.
Christie Mallowan, Agatha Mary Clarissa
    Miller, 18–19.
Chromatic index, see Edge-chromatic
    number.
Chromatic number $\chi(G)$, 35, 39, 44, 46.
Chow, Chaw Kong (周紹康), 76.
    parameters $N(f)$ and $\Sigma(f)$, 76–77, 92, 95.
Christmas tree patterns, 177.
Chung Graham, Fan Rong King
    (鍾金芳蓉), 168.
Chvátal, Václav, 14.
    graph, 14, 39, 44, 149.
CI-nets, 72–74, 91.
Circuits, Boolean, 97, see Boolean chains.
Clapham, Christopher Robert Jasper, 148.
Clause: A disjunction of literals, 54, 81.
Clausen, Thomas, 5.
Claw graph, 141.
Clique covers, 35.
Clique number $\omega(G)$, 35, 44.
Cliques, 35, 44, 200.
Closure under intersections, 57, 132.
Closure under medians, 72.
Clustering, vii.
CMath: Concrete Mathematics, a book
    by R. L. Graham, D. E. Knuth,
    and O. Patashnik.
CNF, 53, see Conjunctive normal form.
Coalitions, 169.
Codewords, b-ary, 38.
Coding theory, 139.
Cographs, 42.
Cohen, Philip Michael, 140.
Coins, biased, 96.
Colleges, 31.
Coloring of graphs, 17, 35, 42, 44,
    46, 120–121.
Coloring of hypergraphs, 32, 35, 44.
Combinational complexity, 97, 111–112, see
    Cost of a Boolean function.
Combinatorial explosion, v.
Combinatorics, 1–7, see also Graphs.
Comedy festival, 60–62, 86.
Commutative laws, 28, 50, 65, 90, 159, 185.
Comparator modules, 72–74, 91, 127, 170.
Comparator-inverter networks, 72–74, 91.
Comparison function, binary, 92, 120,
    194–196.
Compiler technology, 58.

Complement, of a Boolean function, 49, 55, 57, 78–79, 99–100, 107, 154, 184.
of a graph, 26, 27, 35, 41, 42, 146.
of a simple digraph, 42.
of an r-uniform hypergraph, 32.
Complementation laws, 50–51.
Complete bigraphs ($K_{m,n}$), 17, 26, 39, 42, 142.
Complete binary trees, 81.
Complete binary tries, 38–39.
Complete bipartite graphs, 17, 26, 39, 42, 133, 142, 199.
Complete digraphs (J_n), 18, 142, 144.
Complete graphs (K_n), 13, 26–27, 39, 41–43, 145.
Complete k-partite graphs, 17, 26–27, 40, 44.
Complete r-uniform hypergraphs, 32.
bipartite, 44.
Complete ternary tries, 140.
Complete tripartite graphs ($K_{m,n,r}$), 17, 42.
Completion of a matrix, 46.
Components, 16, 18, 26, 40, 42, 43.
Composition of functions, 189.
Composition of graphs, 28, see Lexicographic product of graphs.
Compositions of an integer, 25.
Condensation principle, 89.
Conditional-sum adders, 127–128.
Conjugate of a partition, 29–30, 43, 148.
Conjunction ($\wedge$), 49, see AND.
Conjunction of graphs, 28, see Direct product of graphs.
Conjunctive normal form (CNF), 53, 56–57, 72, 81, 85, 87, 97, 183, 191.
full, 53.
monotone, 81.
Conjunctive prime form, 54, 81.
Connected digraphs, 18.
Connected graphs, 16, 33, 43, 44.
Connectivity of a graph, viii, 150.
Consecutive 1s, 84, 86, 127, 128.
Consecutive arcs, 19.
Consensus, 83.
Consonants, 38.
Context-free grammar, 85.
Contiguous United States of America, 15, 34, 39–40.
Contradiction ($\perp$), 49.
Contrapositive, 61.
Control grids, 104.
Converse implication ($\subset$), 49.
Converse nonimplication ($\overline{\subset}$), 49, 80.
Converse of a digraph, 145.
Convex hull of points, 24, 68–69.
Convex sets, 68–69, 90.
Conway, John Horton, 192.
Cook, Stephen Arthur, 162.
Cooke, George Erskine, 200.

Coppersmith, Don, 152.
Core of a Horn function, 58, 86, 162, 164.
Cost of a Boolean function, 97, 107, 111–112, 126–132.
statistics, 101, 105, 183–184.
Coteries, 88, 93.
Cover, Thomas Merrill, 13.
Covering in a lattice, 93.
Covering problems, 11.
exact, 2, 7, 8, 35, 37, 135.
minimum, 34–35, 44.
Crama, Yves Jean-Marie Mathieu Franz, 161.
Cretté de Palluel, François, 8.
Crossings in a diagram, 14, 150.
Cube graphs (k-cubes), 28, 41.
Cubes, 66, see also Hypercubes, Subcubes.
Cubic graphs, 14, 39, 151.
Curtis, Herbert Allen, 96, 120–121.
Cutler, Robert Brian, 158.
Cycle graph C_n, 13, 28, 39, 41.
Cycles, 13, 28, 39, 41, 42, 44.
in a hypergraph, 33.
of a permutation, 40, 42.
oriented, 18, 19, 32, 40, 41.
Cylinders, 28, 41.

$D(f)$, 99, see Depth of a Boolean function.
$d^+(v)$ (out-degree of v), 18.
$d^-(v)$ (in-degree of v), 18.
$d(u, v)$ (distance in a graph), 16, 43.
directed, 19.
generalized, 16–17.
da Vinci, Leonardo, 9, 24.
Dags (directed acyclic graphs), 31–32.
Dahlheimer, Thorsten, 165.
Dancing links method, 2, 7, 8, 11, 135.
Data replication, 88.
Davies, Roy Osborne, 2, 134.
De Micheli, Giovanni, 122.
De Morgan, Augustus, 51.
laws, 51, 81, 154.
de Palluel, François Cretté, 8.
de Polignac, Camille Armand Jules Marie, 15.
Decoder, binary, 109, 186.
Decomposition of functions, 117–121, 130–131.
Decomposition of partial functions, 120–121.
Decomposition or development laws, 51, 52.
Definite Horn clauses, 58–60, 86.
Definite Horn functions, 58, 85, 95.
Degree of a vertex, 14, 19, 39, 43, 44, 148.
Degree sequences, 29–31, 43, 46, 152–153.
Delaunay, Boris Nikolaevich (Делоне, Борис Николаевич), triangulation, 24.
Depth of a Boolean function, 99, 100, 124–128, 132.
statistics, 101, 105, 183–184.
Depth-first search, 23, 41, 195.

Determinants, 40, 121, 130, 146, 152.
Diagonal matrices, 151, 152.
Diagonalization, 124.
Diagrams for digraphs, 18–19, 42.
Diagrams for graphs, 14–15, 26–28, 39, 42.
Diameter of a free median graph, 169.
Diameter of a graph, 16, 24, 39, 41,
    42, 44, 145.
Dictionaries of English, v, 10, 34, 38,
    47, 48, 140.
Digitized image, 24.
Digraphs, 18, see Directed graphs.
Dillon, John Francis, 180.
Direct product of graphs, 28, 42–43.
Direct product of matrices, 43.
Direct sum of graphs, 26–27, 42, 43.
Direct sum of matrices, 27, 43.
Directed acyclic graphs, 31–32.
Directed distance $d(u, v)$, 19.
Directed graphs, 12, 18–22, 40, 42, 146.
    complete, 18, 142, 144.
    components of, 18.
    converse of, 145.
    random, 25.
    representation of, 19–22.
    strong components of, 40, 61–62, 86,
        142, 164, 195.
Directed hypergraphs, 44.
Directed join of digraphs, 26–27.
Discrete Fourier transforms, 94, 155.
Disjoint decomposition, 117–120.
Disjoint graphs, 26.
Disjoint sets, 25.
Disjunctive normal form (DNF), 53–55,
    81, 85, 97, 191.
    full, 53–54, 81, 84, 176.
    irredundant, 95, 158, 160.
    monotone, 81, 82.
    orthogonal, 84–85, 92.
    shortest, 55, 82, 83, 95.
Disjunctive prime form, 54–55, 64, 71.
Distance $d(u, v)$ in a graph, 16, 43.
    generalized, 16–17.
Distance of a code, 38.
Distinct columns, 33.
Distinct rows, 46.
Distributed systems, 88.
Distributive lattices, 92, 170, 173.
Distributive laws, 43, 48, 50, 80, 87, 93,
    125, 146, 156, 157.
    for medians, 65, 67, 87, 90, 167.
Divide and conquer, 109, 185–188.
DNF, 53, see Disjunctive normal form.
Dodecahedron, 15.
Dodgson, Charles Lutwidge (= Lewis
    Carroll), 10–12, 48, 79, 140.
Dominance order, see Majorization lattices.
Dominated coteries, 88.

Don't-cares, 46, 114, 116, 120–122,
    129, 131, 194.
Dot minus ($\dot{-}$), 49, 84.
Dot product of vectors, 12, 34, 37.
Doublets game, 11.
Doubly linked lists, 70.
Doutté, Edmond, 135.
Dowling, William Francis, 60.
Doyle, Arthur Conan, 1.
Dual identities, 154.
Dual of a Boolean function: $F^D(x) = \bar{F}(\bar{x})$,
    154, 157, 172; see also Self-dual
    Boolean functions.
    computing monotone CNF from DNF, 157.
Dual of a hypergraph, 33, 35, 44.
Dudeney, Henry Ernest, 141.
Dunham, Bradford, 94, 176.
Dynamic programming, 154.

e, as source of "random" data, 136.
Early neighbors, 69, 90.
econ graphs, 31.
Edge-chromatic number $\chi(L(G))$, 44.
Edges in a graph, 11, 13.
    as arcs, 19, 21–22.
Edges in a hypergraph, 32–35.
Egiazarian, Karen, 178.
Eigenvalues of a matrix, 40.
Eigenvectors of a matrix, 40.
Ekin, Oya, 161.
Electoral districts, 8.
Electrical engineers, 96, 97, 105, 107,
    109, 114, 122.
Elementary symmetric functions, 155.
Elgot, Calvin Creston, 124, 171.
Empty graphs ($\overline{K_n}$), 26, 27, 41–43, 46, 150.
English language, v, 9–10.
Enumeration of Boolean functions, 79.
    asymptotic, 177.
Equidistant cities, 44.
Equivalence operator ($\equiv$), 49–50, 154, 172.
Equivalence relations, 45–46, 138.
Equivalence under permutations, 78–79.
    and complementations, 78–79, 178.
Erdős, Pál (= Paul), 147, 148, 150, 169, 174.
Error-correcting codes, 37–38.
Euclidean distance, 10, 12.
Euclidean plane, 17.
Euler, Leonhard (Ейлеръ, Леонардъ =
    Эйлер, Леонард), 3–7, 36, 136.
Evaluation of Boolean functions, 96–133,
    see Boolean chains.
Even permutations, 40.
Evolution of random graphs, 25.
Ewing, Ann Catherine, 159.
Exact cover problems, 2, 7, 8, 35, 37, 135.
Exclusive disjunction ($\oplus$), 49, see XOR.
Existential quantifiers, 85, 87.
Expander graphs, 24.

Exponential growth: $2^{\Theta(n)}$.
Exponential time, 157.
Extended real numbers: Real numbers together with $-\infty$ and $+\infty$, 63.

Factorization of a graph, 28.
Failing units, 80.
Falsehood ($\bot$), 49, 63, 79.
Families of sets, 32, see Hypergraphs.
Families of subsets, 87–88.
Fan-in: The number of inputs to a gate, 97, 104, 124.
Fan-out: The number of uses of a gate, 97, 104, 189.
Feder, Tomás, 73, 170.
Fenwick, Peter McAulay, 188.
Fibonacci, Leonardo, of Pisa
    (= Leonardo filio Bonacii Pisano),
    numbers, 186, 188.
    strings, 36.
    threshold functions, 92, 125.
Fiduccia, Charles Michael, 152.
Fields, finite, 50, 138.
Final vertex of an arc, 18.
Finck, Hans-Joachim, 150.
Finikov, Boris Ivanovich (Фиников, Борис Иванович), 125.
Finite fields, 50, 138.
Finite state transducers, 128.
First-order predicate calculus, 164.
Fischer, Michael John, 127, 128.
Fischler, Martin Alvin, 175.
Fišer, Petr, 55.
Five-letter words, 9–12, 16, 38–39, 43.
Five-variable functions, 105–106, 126, 191.
Flows of money, 31.
Floyd, Robert W, iv.
    Lemma, vi.
Folland, Gerald Budge, iii.
Football scores, 31.
Footprints, 100–101, 113, 114, 122, 125, 126, 191–192.
Forcade, Rodney Warring, 152.
Forcing functions, 78.
Formula complexity, see Length of a Boolean function.
Four Color Theorem, 17.
Four-variable functions, 98–105, 112–114, 122, 126, 129.
Fourier, Jean Baptiste Joseph, transform, discrete, 94, 155.
Fraer, Ranan (רענן פרייר), 87.
Fredman, Michael Lawrence, 157.
Free median algebras, 70–71, 91.
Free systems, 155.
Free trees, 17, 44, 67, 91, 197.
Frequency of usage in English, 10.
Fridshal, Richard, 94, 176.
Fulkerson, Delbert Ray, 148.

Full adders, 107–108, 126, 184, 189, 194.
Full conjunctive normal form, 53.
Full disjunctive normal form, 53–54, 81, 84, 177.
Functional decomposition, 117–121, 130–131.
Funk, Isaac Kauffman, 48.

Gaddum, Jerry William, 150.
Gadzhiev, Makhach Mamaevich (Гаджиев, Махач Мамаевич), 177.
Galen, Claudius (Κλαύδιος Γαληνός), 49.
Gallai, Tibor, 147.
Gallier, Jean Henri, 60.
Games, 86, see also Tic-tac-toe.
games graphs, 31.
Ganter, Bernhard, 136.
García-Molina, Héctor, 88.
Gardner, Martin, 9, 11, 166, 193.
Gates, networks of, 32, 97, 104.
Gauß (= Gauss), Johann Friderich Carl (= Carl Friedrich), 5, 17.
Gégalkine (= Zhegalkin), Jean Jean (Жегалкин, Иван Иванович), 51, 155.
Generalized consensus, 83, 120.
Generalized toruses, 45–46.
Generator routines, 23–26, 30–32, 41.
Geometric nets, 37–39.
Gherardini, Lisa, see Mona Lisa.
Giant component of a graph, 16, 25, 39, 142.
Girth of a graph, 15, 24, 39–41, 44.
Glagolev, Valery Vladimirovich (Глаголев, Валерий Владимирович), 177.
Globally optimum solutions, 34–35.
Godfrey, Michael John, 36.
Golden Bears, California, 31.
Golomb, Solomon Wolf, 139.
Good pairs, 118, 130–131.
Gordon, Leonard Joseph, 139.
GOST cipher, 129.
Goto, Eiichi (後藤英一), 171, 173.
Græco-Latin squares, 4–5, 8, 36, 137.
Graham, Ronald Lewis (葛立恆), 90, 168, 203.
Grammar, context-free, 58.
Grant, Jeffrey Lloydd Jagton, 140.
Graph homomorphisms, 73.
Graph-paper graphs, 28.
Graph theory, introduction to, 13–19.
Graphical degree sequences, 29–31, 43, 46, 152–153.
Graphs, 11–35, 39–45.
    algebra of, 26–28, 42–45.
    bipartite, see Bipartite graphs.
    complete, 13, 26–27, 39, 41–43, 145.
    empty (null), 26, 27, 41–43, 46, 150.
    generators for, 23–26, 30–32, 41.
    labeled versus unlabeled, 15, 16, 152.
    of orders 3 and 4, 42, 46.
    products of, 27–28, 42–44, 146.
    random, 25, 41, 46.

regarded as digraphs, 19–22.
  regular, 14, 24–25, 33, 40–44.
  representation of, 19–22.
Gray, Frank, binary code, 135, 186.
Greatest lower bounds, 93.
Greedy algorithm, 113.
Greedy-footprint heuristic, 113–114,
  122, 191–192.
Greek logic, 48–49.
Grid graphs, 28, 41.
  triangular, 25, 145.
Gries, David Joseph, 153.
Gropes, 155.
Groth, Edward John, Jr., 8.
Grünbaum, Branko, 149.
Gualterus Burleus (= Walter Burley), 51.
Guilielmus ab Occam (= William of
  Ockham), 51.
gunion (union of SGB graphs), 26.
Gurvich, Vladimir Alexander (Гурвич,
  Владимир Александрович), 120, 157.
Guthrie, Francis, 17.
Guy, Richard Kenneth, 192.

Hachtel, Gary Deane, 122.
Hadamard, Jacques Salomon
  inequality, 171.
  matrix, 179.
  transform, 155.
Hagauer, Johann (= Hans), 69.
Haken, Armin, 162.
Haken, Wolfgang, 17.
Half adders, 107–108.
Hall, Marshall, Jr., ix, 134, 138.
Hamilton, William Rowan, 15.
  cycles and paths, 15, 85.
Hamiltonian graphs, 15, 44, 141.
Hammer, Péter László (= Peter Leslie =
  Ivănescu, Petru Ladislav), 120, 161.
Hamming, Richard Wesley, distance, 12,
  28, 37–38, 90, 168.
Harary, Frank, x, 18, 142.
Hardware versus software, 97, 188.
Harvard University Computation
  Laboratory, 126, 184.
Håstad, Johan Torkel, 94.
Havel, Václav (mathematician), 29.
Havel, Václav (playwright and statesman),
  8–9.
Hebraic-Græco-Latin squares, 36, 137.
Hebrew letters, 36.
Hedayat, Samad (= Abdossamad,
  عبدالصمد هدايت), 136, 138.
Heinen, Franz, 17.
Hell, Pavol, 74.
Hellerman, Leo, 104–105.
Hensel, Kurt Wilhelm Sebastian, 146.
Hexadecimal notation for truth tables,
  105, 132, 191.

Hight, Stuart Lee, 120.
Highways, 31.
Hindman, Neil Bruce, 169.
Hlavička, Jan, 55.
Hoffman, Alan Jerome, 143.
Holmes, Thomas Sherlock Scott, 1.
Holton, Derek Alan, 151.
Homer (Ὅμηρος), 9.
Homomorphisms in median algebras, 67.
Homomorphisms of graphs, 74.
Horn, Alfred, 57.
  clauses, 57, 85, 86, 119, 167, 195.
  functions, 58, 79, 95.
  functions, renamed, 87.
  satisfiability, 60, 85–87.
Horton, Robert Elmer, 140.
Hotels and comedians, 60–62, 86.
Hsiao, Ben Mu-Yue (蕭慕岳 = 萧慕岳), 139.
Huffman, David Albert, 94.
Hugo, Victor Marie, 23.
Huntington, Edward Vermilye, 167.
Hurwitz, Adolf, 146.
Hyperarcs, 149.
Hypercubes, 54, 74, *see* n-cube.
  retracts of, 74, 91.
  subgraphs of, 90.
Hyperedges, 32.
Hyperforests, 44.
Hypergraphs, 32–35, 44.
Hyperrectangles ($P_{n_1} \square \cdots \square P_{n_m}$), 28, 67.
Hypotheses, 59–60.

I (identity matrix), 26, 146.
Ibaraki, Toshihide (茨木俊秀), 120,
  161, 165, 166.
IBM Type 650 computer, v.
Ibn al-Ḥājj, Muḥammad ibn Muḥammad
  (محمد بن محمد بن الحاج), 135.
id of an SGB graph, 12, 22.
ID(g), 22.
Ideals in a median algebra, 65.
Identity matrix, 26.
IEEE Transactions, ix.
If-then-else function (mux), 96, 181,
  185, 187, 189.
Igarashi, Yoshihide (五十嵐善英), 176.
Image, digitized, 24.
Implicants, 53–54, 81, *see also* Prime
  implicants.
Implication (⊃), 48–49.
Implicit data structure, 21–22.
Imrich, Wilfried, 28, 69, 168.
In-degree of a vertex, 18, 19, 41, 43.
Incidence matrix of a graph or hypergraph,
  33, 35, 44.
Inclusion-exclusion principle, 159.
Inclusive disjunction (∨), 49, *see* OR.
Incremental changes, 90.
Incompatible columns, 120.

Independence number $\alpha(H)$ of a graph or hypergraph, 35, 44.
Independent vertices, 34, 35, 44.
Induced subgraphs, 13, 18, 39, 42, 43, 46.
Induced subhypergraphs, 32.
Infinity, point at, 24.
Initial vertex of an arc, 18.
Integer multilinear representation, 80, 84, 94, 155, 174.
Integer programming, vii.
Internet, ii, iv, viii, ix, 10, 140.
ITE, *see* If-then-else function.
Interpolating polynomials, 156.
Intersecting families of sets, 88, 174.
Intervals in graphs, 66, 67, 89.
Intervals in median algebras, 65–66.
Intruders, 36.
Inverse permutation, 20.
Inverter gates, 32, *see* Complement of a Boolean function.
Inverter modules, 72–74, 91, 170.
Irredundant DNFs, 94–95, 158, 160.
Islamic mathematics, 135–136.
Isolated vertices: Vertices of degree 0, 25, 142, 145.
Isometric: Distance-preserving, 90. subgraphs, 90, 91, 170.
Isomorphic graphs, 13–15, 28, 39, 152–153. directed, 18.
Isotone functions, 156.
Istrate, Gabriel, 163.
Ivănescu, Petru Ladislav (= Hammer, Peter Leslie), 120, 161.

J (all-ones matrix), 26, 27, 145, 146.
J_n (complete digraph of order n), 18, 142, 144.
Jaillet, Christophe André Georges, 2.
Janson, Carl Svante, 46, 152.
Jevons, William Stanley, 48, 51, 155.
Jha, Pranava Kumar (प्रणव कुमार झा), 69.
Johnson, Samuel, v.
Join of graphs, 26–27, 150.
Just, Winfried, 179.
Juxtaposition of graphs, 26, *see* Direct sum of graphs.

k-ary trees, 124.
k-colorable graphs or hypergraphs, 17, 32, 35, 42, 44.
k-edge-colorable graphs, 26, 42, 44.
k-in-a-row function, 127.
k-partite graphs or hypergraphs, 17, 32, 35, 42, 44.
  complete, 17, 26–27, 40, 44.
K_n (complete graph of order n), 13, 26–27, 41–43, 145.
$K_n^{(r)}$ (complete r-uniform hypergraph), 32.

$\vec{K_n}$ (transitive tournament of order n), 18, 27, 40, 41.
$K_{3,3}$ (utilities graph), 17, 39, 42, 138.
$K_{m,n}$ (complete bipartite graph), 17, 26, 39, 42, 142.
$K_{m,n}^{(r)}$ (complete r-uniform bipartite hypergraph), 44.
$K_{n_1,\ldots,n_k}$ (complete k-partite graph), 17, 26, 40, 44.
Kameda, Tiko (= Tsunehiko) (亀田恒彦), 165, 174.
Karoński, Michał, 152.
Karp, Richard Manning, 121.
Karpiński (= Karpinski), Marek Mieczysław, 165.
Kauffman, Stuart Alan, 78.
Kautz, William Hall, 175.
Ke Zhao (= Chao Ko, 柯召), 174.
Keister, William, 115.
Kelly, Paul Joseph, 148.
Kempe, Alfred Bray, 141.
Kernel of a graph, *see* Maximal independent sets.
Khachiyan, Leonid Genrikhovich (Хачиян, Леонид Генрихович), 157.
Khrapchenko, Valerii Mikhailovich (Храпченко, Валерий Михайлович), 188.
King moves on a chessboard, 43.
Kingwise torus, 44.
Kirkman, Thomas Penyngton, 15.
Kiss, Stephen Anthony, 167.
Klavžar, Sandi, 28, 69.
Klein, Peter, 127.
Kleine Büning, Hans Gerhard, 163–165.
Kleitman, Daniel J (Isaiah Solomon), 148, 169.
Kline, John Robert, 167.
Knapsacks, 75.
Knight moves on a chessboard, 15, 25.
Knuth, Donald Ervin (高德纳), i, ii, iv, ix, xii, 7, 9–10, 12, 32, 62, 105, 115, 136, 157, 168, 188, 203.
Knuth, John Martin, *see* Truth.
Ko, Chao (= Ke Zhao, 柯召), 174.
Koch, John Allen, 17.
Kogan, Alexander (Коган, Александр Юрьевич), 120, 161.
Kolibiar, Milan, 167.
Komlós, János, 91.
Kőnig, Dénes, 17.
Konvalina, John, 179.
Korshunov, Aleksey Dmitrievich (Коршунов, Алексей Дмитриевич), 177.
Kowalewski, Arnold, 145.
Krajecki, Michaël, 2.
Kratochvíl, Jan, 46, 152.

Krichevsky, Rafail Evseevich (Кричевский, Рафаил Евсеевич), 190.
Krom, Melven Robert, 62, 164.
  clauses, 57, 72, 85, 87, 195.
  functions, 60, 72, 79, 81, 95, *see also* 2CNF.
  satisfiability, 57, 60–62, 72, 86.
Kronecker, Leopold, product, 146.
Kung, Hsiang Tsung (孔祥重), 188.

$L(f)$, 99, *see* Length of a Boolean function.
$L(G)$ (line graph of G), 26, 42.
Labeled graphs, 15, 152.
Labels of graph vertices, 67–74, 90.
Laborde, Jean-Marie, 159.
LADDERS program, 32.
Ladner, Richard Emil, 127, 128.
Lähdesmäki, Harri, 178.
Lamport, Leslie B., 88.
Landau, Hyman Garshin, 142.
Langford, Charles Dudley, 7, 9, 135.
  pairs, 1–3, 8, 36.
  triples, 36.
Las Vegas hotels, 60–62, 86.
Latch gates, 32.
Late neighbors, 69.
Latin squares, 3–8, 36–38, 136, 137, 149.
Lattices, *see also* Majorization lattices.
  distributive, 92, 170, 173.
Leader, Imre, 179.
Leahy, Francis Theodore, Jr. (= Ted), 134.
Least upper bounds, 93.
Left complementation ($\bar{\mathsf{L}}$), 49, 80.
Left projection (L), 49, 63, 80, 154.
Legitimate lattices of functions, 132, 133.
Lehmer, Derrick Henry, 39.
Leighton, Robert Eric, 139.
Length of a Boolean function, 99, 103, 125, 192.
  statistics, 101, 105, 183–184.
Lenin, Vladimir Ilyich (Ленин, Владимир Ильич), 86.
Leonardo da Vinci, 9, 24.
Lettmann, Theodor August, 163, 164.
Lexicographic order, 3, 38, 41, 75, 85, 86, 165.
Lexicographic product of graphs, 28, 42–43, 146.
Liang, Franklin Mark, 105.
Lillywaite, Peregrine, 10.
Lindström, Bernt Lennart Daniel, 173.
Line graph of a graph, 26, 35, 42, 142, 146, 148.
Linear inequalities, 171–172.
Linear ordering, 161.
Linear polynomials, 52.
Linear programming, vii, 92.
Linear subgraphs, 142.
Linear time, 57, 82.

Linked allocation, 21.
Literals, 53.
Lloyd, Edward Keith, 15.
Lo Shu magic square, 192.
LOC (memory location), 22.
Local optimizations, 121.
Locally optimal solutions, 34–35.
Logic, 48–51, 123–124, 132.
Long distributive law, 65, 67, 89.
Loops from a vertex to itself, 13, 18, 19, 41, 148.
Lower bounds on combinational complexity, 103–104, 109–112, 122–124, 131–132.
Loyd, Walter (= "Sam Loyd, Jr."), 1.
Lupanov, Oleg Borisovich (Лупанов, Олег Борисович), 110, 112, 129, 185, 190, 192.

$m \times n$ cylinders, 28, 41.
$m \times n$ grids, 28, 41.
$m \times n$ rook graphs, 26, 41.
$m \times n$ toruses, 28, 41.
  directed, 41.
$M(g)$ (the number of arcs in an SGB graph), 22.
$M(n)$ (binary majorization lattice), 173.
MacNeish, Harris Franklin, 5.
Magic Fifteen, 129.
Magic squares, 36, 192.
Majority element, 46.
Majority functions, 63, 68, 104, 139, *see* Medians.
Majority law, 65, 89.
Majority of odd, *see* Median of odd.
Majorization lattices, of binary vectors, 92–94.
  of n-tuples, 30, 148, 173.
Makino, Kazuhisa (牧野和久), 174.
Mann, Henry Berthold, 136.
Marcisová, Tamara, 167.
Matching in a graph, 35, 44, 119.
Markowsky, George, 159, 176.
MATE (the converse arc), 21–22.
Mates in a Boolean chain, 131.
Mates of arcs, 21–22.
Mathon, Rudolf Anton, 136.
Matrix multiplication, 20, 146, 200.
max (maximum operator), 63–64.
Maximal cliques, 44.
Maximal independent sets, 34, 44.
Maximal intersecting families, 88.
Maximal planar graphs, 39.
Maximal subcubes, 54–55, 82–83.
Maximal versus maximum, 34–35.
Maximum independent sets, 34–35.
Maximum matchings, 44.
Maxterms, *see* Minclauses.
Mayr, Ernst Wilhelm, 170.
McCluskey, Edward Joseph, Jr., 55.
McCulloch, Warren Sturgis, 75.

McCune, William Walker, Jr., 167.
McKay, Brendan Damien, 137.
McKellar, Archie Charles, 118, 120, 131.
McManus, Christopher DeCormis, 38.
Median algebras, 64–67, 89.
Median chains, 133.
Median expansion formula, 87.
Median graphs, 67–74, 90, 169.
Median labels, 67–74, 168.
Median of odd, 64, 75–76, 91–92, 94.
   of five, 64, 68, 71, 76, 77, 87, 91.
Median of seven, 133.
Median operation, 102, 125, 133.
Median sets, 72–74, 91.
Medians, 62–74, 87–91.
   bitwise, 67, 71, 72, 91, 167, 168.
Mems: Memory accesses, 2, 6.
Menon, Vairelil Vishwanath (വൈരെലിൽ
   വിശ്വനാഥ മേനോൻ), 145.
Meringer, Markus Reinhard, 149.
METAFONT, 12.
Metropolis, Nicholas Constantine
   (Μητρόπολης, Νικόλαος Κωνσταντίνου),
   176.
Meyer, Albert Ronald da Silva, viii,
   123, 124, 198.
Meyerowitz, Aaron David, 89, 169.
Meynert, Alison, 137.
Mezei, Jorge Esteban (= György István), 92.
Miiller, Henry Sedwick, 64.
miles graphs, 31, 44.
Mileto, Franco, 160.
Miller, Donald John, 147.
Mills, Burton E., 156, 159.
Milnor, John Willard, 88, 166.
min (minimum operator), 63–64.
Minclauses, 53.
Minimal versus minimum, 34–35.
Minimal vertex covers, 157.
Minimum-memory evaluation, 101–103,
   106, 125, 126, 186.
Minimum vertex covers, 34–35, 44.
Minnick, Robert Charles, 77, 172.
Minterms, 52–54, 109, 111, 126, 155.
MIP-years, 2.
Mirror pairs, 38.
Misra, Jayadev (ଜୟଦେବ ମିଶ୍ର), 153.
Mixed-radix majorization lattices, 173.
Mixed-radix numbers, 174.
MMIX computer, ii, iv, viii, 41.
MMIXAL assembly language, 41.
Mnemonics, 146.
Mod 2 canonical form, see Multilinear
   representation of a Boolean function.
Modular arithmetic, 135.
Mona Lisa, 9, 24, 31.
Monadic logic: Logic with only unary
   operators, 123–124, 132.
Monotone Boolean chains, 125, 132–133.

Monotone Boolean functions, 55, 63, 79,
   81, 82, 85, 87, 95, 156.
   computing CNF from DNF, 157.
   self-dual, 63–64, 70, 79, 87–89, 92–93, 133.
   shellability of, 84–85, 157, 161, 171.
   threshold, 75–76, 92.
Monotone complexity, 106, 125, 132–133.
Moon, John Wesley, 150.
Moore, Eliakim Hastings, 138.
Moore, J Strother, 46.
Moore, Ronald Williams, 157.
Morgenstern, Oskar, 169.
Morreale, Eugenio, 158.
Morris, Scot Anderson, 38.
Moser, Leo, 150.
Mulder, Henry Martyn, 167.
Muller, David Eugene, 187.
Multilevel logic synthesis, 122.
Multigraphs, 13, 19–21, 40, 41, 44, 146, 152.
Multihypergraphs, 148.
Multilinear representation of a Boolean
   function, 52, 80, 96, 130, 156, 183; see
   also Integer multilinear representation.
Multilinked data structures, 60.
Multipairs, 19.
Multiple outputs, 107–109, 112–117,
   121–122, 126–130.
Multiplexer, 2-way, see Mux.
   2^m-way, 109, 127, 131.
Multiplication, 8.
Multisets, 12, 18, 19.
Muroga, Saburo (室賀三郎), 77, 158,
   171–173, 178.
Murphy's Law, 148.
Museum of Science and Industry, 115.
Musical graph, 44, 45.
Mutual exclusion, 88.
Mutually orthogonal latin squares, 37–38.
Mux (multiplex) operation, 96, 181,
   185, 187, 189.
Myrvold, Wendy Joanne, 137.

n-ary Boolean functions, 51–55.
n-ary strings, 37.
n-cube: The 2^n points $(x_1, \ldots, x_n)$ with
   $x_j = 0$ or $x_j = 1$ in each coordinate
   position, 28, 41, 73, 129.
   subcubes of, 54, 82–84, 155, 160, 161, 176.
N(g) (the number of vertices in an SGB
   graph), 22, 143.
Name servers, 88.
NAME(v) (the name of a vertex), 21.
NAND ($\barwedge$), 49–51, 80–81, 183.
   with vacuum tubes, 104.
Nanocomputer simulation, 32.
Nebeský, Ladislav, 167.
Nechiporuk, Eduard Ivanovich (Нечипорук,
   Эдуард Иванович), 192.
Neighboring vertices, 13.
Nemhauser, George Lann, 161.

Nešetřil, Jaroslav, 146.
Networks: Graphs or digraphs together
    with auxiliary data, 31–32, 44.
Neumann, John von (= Margittai Neumann
    János), 169.
Neural networks, 75.
NEXT(a) (the next arc with the same
    initial vertex), 21.
Nigmatullin, Roshal' Gabdulkhaevich
    (Нигматуллин, Рошаль
    Габдулхаевич), 177.
Nodes in SGB format, 21–23, 143.
Nonconjunction ($\overline{\wedge}$), 49, see NAND.
Nondisjunction ($\overline{\vee}$), 49, see NOR.
Nonimplication ($\overline{\supset}$), 49.
NOR gates ($\overline{\vee}$), 49–51, 104–105.
Nordhaus, Edward Alfred, 150.
Normal Boolean functions, 100, 102, 110,
    113, 125, 184, 196.
Normal forms, see Full conjunction normal
    form, Full disjunctive normal form,
    Integer multilinear representation,
    Multilinear representation of a
    Boolean function.
Normalization, 100, 181.
NOT gates, 32, 33.
NOT-BUT gates ($\overline{\subset}$), 97, 100.
Notation, 26, 132, 146.
Notational conventions, iv.
    for Boolean binary operators, 48–50.
    for symmetric Boolean functions, 77.
    $\overline{G}$ (complementation), 26, 32, 42.
    $G \cong G'$ (isomorphism), 14.
    $G \mid V'$ (induced subgraph), 13.
    $G \setminus e$ (edge removal), 13.
    $G \setminus v$ (vertex removal), 13.
    $[u \mathbin{..} v]$ (closed interval), 65.
    $x \subseteq y$ (componentwise $\leq$), 55.
    $\langle xyz \rangle$ (median), 62–63.
    $\langle x_1 \ldots x_{2k-1} \rangle$ (median), 64.
    $x?\ y\colon z$, 96, see Mux (multiplex)
        operation.
Noughts and crosses, see Tic-tac-toe.
Novels, 9, 23.
NP-complete problems, viii, 35, 55, 157.
Null graphs ($\overline{K_n}$), 26, 27, 41–43, 46, 150.

O (all-zeros matrix), 27.
Oblivious sorting, 72.
Ockham, William of (= Guilielmus
    ab Occam), 51.
Odd permutations, 40.
Odd product of graphs, 28, 42–43, 146.
ODNFs, 84–85, 92.
Ofman, Yuri Petrovich (Офман, Юрий
    Петрович), 189.
Optimal versus optimum, 34–35.
Optimization of Boolean chains,
    121–122, 195.

Optimum Boolean evaluation, 103–105.
Optimum coteries, 93.
OR (inclusive or, $\vee$), 48–51, 53, 63, 81.
    bitwise ($\mid$), 50, 74, 84.
OR gates ($\vee$), 32, 33, 97.
    with vacuum tubes, 104.
Order of a digraph, 18.
Order of a graph, 13, 44.
Order of a latin square, 37.
Order of an orthogonal array, 37.
Ore, Øystein, ix, 42.
Organ-pipe order, 135.
Oriented binary trees, 190.
Oriented cycles, 18, 19, 32, 40, 41.
Oriented paths, 18, 19, 41.
    spanning, 40.
Orthogonal arrays, 37, 139.
    generalized, 137–138.
Orthogonal DNFs, 84–85, 92.
Orthogonal latin squares, 3–8, 36–38.
Orthogonal strings, 37.
Orthogonal vectors, 34, 37.
Otter theorem-proving program, 167.
Out-degree of a vertex, 18, 19, 21,
    40, 41, 43.
Overlapping subtrees, 97.
Ozanam, Jacques, 3, 7, 9.

$P = NP(?)$, 55.
P_n (path of order n), 13, 28, 39.
$P_n^{\rightarrow}$ (oriented path of order n), 18, 41.
Paige, Lowell J., 5–7.
Palindromes, 38, 135, 163.
Palluel, François Cretté de, 8.
Papadimitriou, Christos Harilaos
    (Παπαδημητρίου, Χρίστος Χαριλάου), ix.
Parallel addition, 108, 127–128, 189.
Parallel computation, vii, 91, 108, 124.
Parallel edges of a multigraph, 19, 41.
Parallel lines, 37.
Parity bits, 38.
Parity function, 51, 77, 94–95, 98, 105,
    131, 132, 184.
Parker, Ernest Tilden, 5–7, 136.
Partial cubes, 90.
Partial functions, 113–114, 131.
Partially symmetric functions, 95.
Partitions of an integer, 25, 30, 149.
parts graphs, 25.
Pascal, Blaise, iii.
Patashnik, Oren, 203.
Patents, 112.
Paterson, Michael Stewart, 126, 127.
Path graph P_n, 13, 28, 39, 157.
Paths in a graph, 13, 41.
    oriented, 18, 19, 41.
    shortest, viii, 12, 16, 32, 66.
Patterson, Nicholas James, 180.
Paul, Wolfgang Jakob, 131.
Pehoushek, Joseph Daniel, 87.

Peirce, Charles Santiago Sanders, 48, 50, 53, 161.
Perfect shuffles, 38.
Permanent of a matrix, 40, 119, 125.
Permutation digraphs, 40.
Permutation matrices, 20, 143.
Perrin, François Olivier Raoul, numbers, 157.
Petersen, Julius Peter Christian, 5, 14, 145.
graph, 14, 15, 25, 39, 42, 44, 45, 145.
Phi (ϕ), 134.
as source of "random" data, 136.
Philo of Megara (= Philo the Dialectician, Φίλων ὁ Μεγαρίτης), 48.
Pi (π), as source of "random" data, 76, 98, 118, 128, 136, see also Pi function.
Pi function, 52, 54, 80–82, 118, 125, 130, 181.
Pigeonhole principle, 85, 199.
Pippenger, Nicholas John, 177, 192.
Pitts, Walter Harry, 75.
Pixels, 24, 31.
Planar graphs, 14, 15, 17, 24, 39, 44, 141, 147.
Planar Langford pairings, 36.
plane_lisa graphs, 24, 31.
plane_miles graphs, 24, 31.
PLAs, 53.
Plass, Michael Frederick, 87.
Playing cards, 3–4.
Poetry, 140.
Pohl, Ira Sheldon, 3.
Poirot, Hercule, 18–19.
Polignac, Camille Armand Jules Marie de, 15.
Polish notation, 63.
Pólya, György (= George), 18.
Polyhedral combinatorics, vii.
Polynomials, see Availability polynomials, Integer multilinear representation, Interpolating polynomials, Multilinear representation of a Boolean function.
Portable programs, 22.
Positive Boolean functions, 55, 156, see Monotone Boolean functions.
Positive normal form, see Multilinear representation of a Boolean function.
Positive threshold functions, 75–76, 92.
Posner, Edward Charles, 139.
Post, Emil Leon, 63, 68, 165.
Postal codes, 15, 40.
Pratt, Vaughan Ronald, 125.
Precedence of operators, 51.
Prefix problem, 127–128, 132.
Prefixes of strings, 132.
Preparata, Franco Paolo, 187.
Prime clauses, 54, 95, 129.
Prime forms, 54, 64, 71, 81.
Prime graphs, 28.

Prime implicants, 54, 64, 71, 82, 89, 94, 95, 129, 197, 200.
of a majority function, 92, 172.
Prime-number function, 110, 129.
Priority encoders, 127.
Product-of-sums expression, see Conjunctive normal form.
Products of digraphs and multigraphs, 146.
Products of graphs, 27–28, 42–44.
Programmable logic arrays, 53.
Programming languages, 58.
Projection functions, 49, 63, 80, 154, 169.
Projections in a median algebra, 67.
Projective planes, finite, 138, 149, 200.
Prolog language, 57.
Proportional graphs, 46.
Provan, John Scott, 161.
Pseudorandom numbers, 12, 25.
Pun resisted, 62.
Pure majority functions, 76, 169.
Putzolu, Gianfranco, 160.
Puzzles, 1, 3, 7–9, 15, 135, 141.
Pyramids, tetrahedral, 89.

Quantified formulas, 87, 123–124, 198.
Queen moves on a chessboard, 26, 44.
Queues, 162.
Quick, Jonathan Horatio, 81, 162–163.
Quine, Willard Van Orman, 54, 55, 82, 159.
Quorums, 88.

r-closed graphs, 133.
r-families of edges, 133.
r-uniform hypergraphs, 32.
Rado, Richard, 174.
RainBones puzzle, 135.
raman graphs, 24, 151.
Ramanujan Iyengar, Srinivasa (ஸ்ரீனிவாஸராமானுஜன் ஐயங்கார்), graphs, 24, 151.
Random Boolean functions, 56, 83, 160.
random_graph graphs, 25, 41.
Random graphs, 25, 41, 46.
Random number generation, 96.
Random walks, 45.
Randomization, 118, 130.
Rao, Calyampudi Radhakrishna (సీయంపూడి రాధాకృష్ణ రావు), 137–138.
Razborov, Alexander Alexandrovich (Разборов, Александр Александрович), 125.
Real numbers, 91.
extended, 63.
Reckhow, Robert Allen, 162.
Recreations, 1, 3, 7–9, 15, 135, 141.
Recurrence relations, 71, 157, 185, 187.
binary, 108, 109, 126, 168, 186.
Recursive procedures, 70, 82, 181, 185.

Red'kin, Nikolai Petrovich (Редькин, Николай Петрович), 107, 122, 131, 196.
Rédei, László, 142.
Reduced median sets, 72, 91.
Redundant coordinates, 72.
Redundant implicants, 94, 158, 160.
Registers, 101–103, 126.
Regular Boolean functions, 93, 178.
Regular graphs, 14, 24–25, 33, 40–44.
Reliability polynomials, 80, 81, 84, 93, 155.
Renaming (selectively complementing) Boolean variables, 87, 156, 163.
Representation of graphs and digraphs, 19–22.
Resolution principle, 159.
Resolvents, 159.
Restriction of a graph, 13.
Retracts, 74, 91.
Retraction mappings, 74, 91.
Right complementation ($\bar{\mathsf{R}}$), 49.
Right projection (R), 49, 63, 154.
Ring sum expansion, *see* Multilinear representation of a Boolean function.
Ringel, Gerhard, 145.
Riordan, John, 190.
risc graphs, 31–32.
RISC: Reduced Instruction Set Computer, 32.
Rivest, Ronald Linn, 56.
Robertson, George Neil, 17.
Robinson, John Alan, 159.
roget graphs, 23, 41.
Roget, John Lewis, 23.
Roget, Peter Mark, 9, 23.
Rook moves on a chessboard, 26, 41.
Rookwise connected pixels, 24.
Rosa, Alexander, 136.
Rota, Gian-Carlo, 176.
Roth, John Paul, 159.
Rothaus, Oscar Seymour, 180.
Ruciński, Andrzej, 152.
Runs of 0s or 1s, 169.
Ruskey, Frank, 129.
Ryser, Herbert John, 37, 137.

S-boxes, 129.
$S_{k_1,\ldots,k_t}(x)$ notation, 77, *see* Symmetric functions.
Sachs, Horst, 145.
Saks, Michael Ezra, 168.
Samson, Edward Walter, 156, 159.
Sanders, Daniel Preston, 17.
Sangiovanni-Vincentelli, Alberto Luigi, 122.
Sartena, Christian, 154.
Sasaki, Fukashi (佐々木不可止), 77.
Satisfiability problem, 55–62, 85–87.
    for Horn clauses, 60, 85–86.
    for Krom clauses, 57, 60–62, 72, 85–86.

Satisfiable Boolean formulas, 55.
Saturating subtraction ($\dot{-}$), 49, 84.
Sauerhoff, Martin, 153.
Sauveur, Joseph, 136.
Savage, John Edmund, 190.
Scandalous fact, 26.
Schaefer, Thomas Jerome, 72.
Scheduling, 60–62, 86.
Schensted, Craige Eugene (= Ea Ea), 87–89, 166.
Schmitt, Peter Hans, 165.
Schnorr, Claus-Peter, 131.
Schröder, Friedrich Wilhelm Karl Ernst, 80, 155.
Schroeppel, Richard Crabtree, 126.
Schumacher, Heinrich Christian, 5, 17.
Scrabble®, 10.
Search trees, 6.
Second-order logic, 124.
Seed value for pseudorandom numbers, 12, 25.
Selection function, *see* Mux.
Self-complementary graphs, 42, 43, 153.
Self-converse graphs, 145.
Self-dual Boolean functions, 63, 79, 81, 92, 95.
    monotone, 63–64, 70, 79, 87–89, 92–93, 133.
    threshold, 79, 92.
Self-dualization, 92.
Self-loops, 13, 18, 19, 41, 148.
Self-organizing data structures, 168.
Self-reference, 124, 213.
Semidefinite programming, vii.
Separable functions, *see* Threshold functions.
Sequential algorithms, vii.
Sequential allocation, 21.
Series-parallel switching networks, 190.
Server locations, 91.
Set systems, 32, *see* Hypergraphs.
Seven-segment display, 112–114, 129.
Seymour, Paul Douglas, 17.
SGB, 9, *see* Stanford GraphBase.
Shadows of bit codes, 84.
Shakespeare (= Shakspere), William, 1.
Shannon, Claude Elwood, Jr., 47, 110, 179, 189, 190.
Sheehan, John, 151.
Sheep, 8, 38.
Sheffer, Henry Maurice, 50, 80.
Shelling a monotone Boolean function, 84–85, 157, 161, 171.
Shen, Vincent Yun-Shen (沈運申), 118, 120, 131.
Shmulevich, Ilya Vladimir (Шмулевич, Илья Владимирович), 178, 179.
Sholander, Marlow Canon, 89, 167.
Sholomov, Lev Abramovich (Шоломов, Лев Абрамович), 129, 194.

Shortest normal forms, 55, 82, 83, 95, 156.
Shortest paths in a graph, viii, 12, 16, 32, 66.
Shrikhande, Sharadchandra Shankar (शरदचन्द्र शंकर श्रीखंडे), 5.
Shrinking an edge, 141.
Sideways addition function (νx), 77, 90, 108, 126, 158, 185, 187.
Signed permutations, 178.
Simple digraphs, 18, 19, 40, 43, 145, 146.
Simple games, 169.
Simple graphs, see Graphs.
simplex graphs, 25.
Simpson, James Edward, 134.
Single-faced functions, see Canalizing functions.
Singleton, Robert Richmond, 143.
Singmaster, David Breyer, 135.
Sink vertex, 18.
Sinks, 62.
Size of a digraph, 18.
Size of a graph, 13, 44.
Sklansky, Jack, 187.
Skolem, Albert Thoralf, ix, 8, 36, 134, 135.
Sloan, Robert Hal, 159.
Sloane, Neil James Alexander, 138.
Slutzki, Giora (גיורא סלוצקי), 69.
smile, 11, 16, 24, 39.
Smith, Henry John Stephen, normal form, 152.
Smith, John Lynn, 188.
Smith, Mark Andrew, 96.
Snir, Marc (מרק שניר), 127, 132.
Sorting networks, 91, 127, 186.
Source vertex, 18.
Sources, 62.
Spanning subgraphs, 13, 15, 18, 39.
Sparse graphs, 20, 23.
Spectrum of an irrational number, 134.
Spheres, vii.
Spira, Philip Martin, 125.
Stability number $\alpha(H)$ of a graph or hypergraph, 35.
Stable sets, 34, see Independent vertices.
Stack structures, 23, 41, 59, 158, 162.
Standard fields in SGB format, 21.
Stanford Cardinal, 31.
Stanford GraphBase, ii, iv, viii, 9–12, 20, 23–26, 31, 62, 188.
    complete guide to, 32.
    format for digraphs and graphs, 21–22, 41.
Stanley, Richard Peter, 13, 173.
Star graphs, 17.
Stein, Sherman Kopald, 192.
Steiner, Jacob, 17.
    trees, vii, 17.
    triple systems, 8.
Stockmeyer, Larry Joseph, viii, 123, 124, 132, 185, 198.

Stone representation, 88–89.
Storage access function, 109.
Strahler, Arthur Newell, 140.
Straight insertion sorting, 142.
Straight-line computations, see Boolean chains.
Strassen, Volker, 200.
Strong components: Strongly connected components, 40, 61–62, 86, 142, 164, 195.
Strong product of graphs, 28, 42–44, 146, 151.
Stufken, John, 138.
Subcubes, 54, 82–84, 129, 155, 160, 161, 176, 190.
    maximal, 54–55, 82–83.
Subgraphs, 13, 17.
    of a hypercube, 90.
Subramani, Krishnamurthy (கிருஷ்ணமூர்த்தி சுப்ரமணி), 165.
Subramanian, Ashok, 170.
subsets graphs, 25.
Subwords, 12.
Suffixes of strings, 132.
Sum-of-products expression, see Disjunctive normal form.
SWAC computer, 5–6.
Swift, Jonathan Dean, 47.
Symmetric block designs, 179.
Symmetric Boolean functions, 77–79, 94.
Symmetric functions, 98–99, 104–106, 108, 109, 116, 126, 131, 132, 184, 185.
Symmetric matrices, 40, 44.
Symmetries of a graph, 14–15, 39, 45, 147, 152–153.
Syntax, context-free, 58.
Szele, Tibor, 142.
Szemerédi, Endre, 91.
Szörényi, Balázs, 159.

Tableaux, 29–30, 43.
Tables of Boolean function counts, 79.
Tags, 82.
Takahasi, Hidetosi (高橋秀俊), 171.
Takasu, Satoru (高須達), 171.
TAKE_RISC program, 32.
Tannenbaum, Meyer, 175.
Tarjan, Robert Endre, 1, 62, 87, 195.
Tarry, Gaston, 5.
Tautology ($\top$), 49, 161.
Taylor, Brook, series, 13.
Tensor product of graphs, see Direct product of graphs.
Terminology, 13, 156.
Ternary Boolean functions, 104–105, 200.
Ternary Boolean operations, 63, 156.
    table, 78.
Tetrahedra, 25.
Tetrahedral pyramids, 88–89.
TEX, 12.

Theorem proving, 59, 167.
Theory meets practice, vii, 13.
Thomas, Herbert Christopher (= Ivo), 49.
Thomas, Robin, 17.
Thoreau, David Henry (= Henry David), 96.
Three-variable functions, 63, 104–105, 156.
  table, 78.
Threshold functions, 75–77, 79, 92–95, 186.
  of threshold functions, 77, 92, 172.
Thue, Axel, ix.
Tic-tac-toe, 114–117, 129–130, 192.
Tightly colorable graphs, 44.
Tilings of the plane, 45.
Tip of an arc, 18.
TIP(a) (final vertex), 21.
Tison, Pierre Louis Joseph, 159.
Toda, Iwao (戸田巌), 171.
Todorov, Dobromir Todorov (Тодоров,
  Добромир Тодоров), 137.
Tolstoy, Leo Nikolaevich, (Толстой, Лев
  Николаевич), 9.
Tomlin, Mary Jean (= Lily), 60, 62, 86.
Tompkins, Charles Brown, 5–7.
Top-down synthesis, 103–105, 126, 183.
Topological sorting, 60, 73, 85, 97.
Toruses, 28, 41.
  generalized, 45–46.
  kingwise, 44.
Tournaments, 40.
  transitive, 18, 27, 40, 41.
Transitive laws, 138.
Translation, tiling by, 45–46.
Transposing a matrix, 20, 33, 137.
Transversals of a latin square, 6–7, 37, 136.
Traveling Salesrep Problem, viii.
Trees, 67, 81, 85, 91.
Triangle function, 133.
Triangle inequality, 16, 19.
Triangular grids, 25, 88, 145.
Tries, 38–39.
Triple systems, 8, 32, 44.
Trivalent graphs, 14, 39, 151.
Trivial functions, 49, 63, 64, 184.
Truth, 47, 63, 79.
Truth tables, 47, 49, 51–53, 71, 94–96, 98,
  100, 102, 105, 154, 189.
  in hexadecimal notation, 105, 132, 191.
  of partial functions, 114–116.
  two-dimensional, 110–111, 117–121,
    192, 194.
Tsuboi, Teiichi (坪井禎一), 172, 173, 178.
Tukey, John Wilder, 47.
Turán, György, 159.
Tweedledee, 48, 79.
Two-variable functions, 47–50, 79–80.
  table, 49.

Uhlig, Dietmar, 131.
Ulyanov, Vladimir Ilyich (Ульянов,
  Владимир Ильич), 86.

Unary operator: A function of one variable.
Unate functions, 156.
Union-find algorithm, 69.
Union of graphs, 26, see also Direct
  sum of graphs.
United States of America, contiguous,
  15, 34, 39–40.
UNIVAC 1206 Military Computer, 5.
Universal algebras, 155.
Universal quantifiers, 87.
Universities, 31.
Unlabeled graphs, 14, 152.
Unsolvable problems, 164.
Upper bounds on combinational complexity,
  110–112, 129, see also Footprints.
Utilities, 141.
Utility fields in SGB format, 21, 144.

Vacuum-tube circuits, 104, 126.
Valency, see Degree of a vertex.
Validity (⊤), 49.
Variance, 152.
Vector-valued Boolean functions, 107, 121.
Vectors, 54.
Veroff, Robert Louis, 167.
Vertex connectivity, 148.
Vertex covers, 157.
  minimum, 34–35, 44.
Vertex variables, 21, 23.
VERTICES(g) (the first vertex node), 22, 143.
Vesztergombi, Katalin, 149.
Vikulin, Anatoly Petrovich (Викулин,
  Анатолий Петрович), 176.
Vinci, Leonardo da, 9, 24.
von Neumann, John (= Margittai Neumann
  János), 169.
Vowels, 38.
Vũ, Văn Hà, 175.

W_n (wheel graph of order n), 42, 46,
  145, 153.
Wagnalls, Adam Willis, 48.
Wagner, Eric Gerhardt, 159.
Wakerly, John Francis, 194.
Walks in a graph, 19–20, 40, 45.
Walter of Burley (= Burleigh = Gualterus
  Burleus), 51.
Wang, Da-Lun (王大倫), 148.
Wang, Shinmin Patrick (王新民), 137.
Watkins, John Jaeger, 151.
Weak second-order logic, 123–124, 132.
Weber, Karl, 160.
Wegener, Ingo Werner, 124, 153, 185.
Weichsel, Paul Morris, 146.
Weinberger, Arnold, 188.
Weiner, Peter Gallegos, 118, 120, 131.
Weisner, Louis, 136.
Well-balanced Langford pairings, 2–3, 36.
Wernicke, August Ludwig Paul, 5.

Wheel graphs, 42, 46, 145, 153.
Width of a Langford pairing, 3, 135.
Wiedemann, Douglas Henry, 73, 180.
William of Ockham (= Guilielmus ab
    Occam), 51.
Williams, Robin McLaurim, 60, 62, 163.
Wilson, Richard Michael, 137.
Wilson, Robin James, iv, 15, 42, 151.
Winder, Robert Owen, 64, 173, 200.
Witness bits, 139.
Wood, Frank W., 112.
Wool, Avishai (אבישי וול), 174.
Wong, Chak-Kuen (黃澤權), 152.
Word cubes, 11, 39.
Word ladders, 11–12, 32.
Word problems, 68.
Word squares, 11, 38.
words graphs, 12–13, 31, 39, 42.
WORDS(n), the n most common five-letter
    words of English, 10–12.
Working units, 80.
Wraparound, 41.
WS1S, 124.

XOR (exclusive or, $\oplus$), 49–52, 77, 80,
    81, 154, 172.
  bitwise, 90, 158.
XOR gates ($\oplus$), 32, 33, 97.

Y functions, 88–89, 92.
Yablonsky, Sergei Vsevolodovich (Яблон-
    ский, Сергей Всеволодович), 177.

ZDDs: Zero-suppressed decision
    diagrams, 166.
Zehfuss, Johann Georg, 146.
Zero-one principle, 68.
Zhao, Xishun (赵希顺), 165.
Zhegalkin (= Gégalkine), Ivan Ivanovich
    (Жегалкин, Иван Иванович), 51, 155.
Zigzag paths, 177.
Zito, Jennifer Snyder, 152.
Zuev, Yuri Anatol'evich (Зуев, Юрий
    Анатольевич), 178.
Zuse, Konrad, 189.
Zykov, Aleksander Aleksandrovich (Зыков,
    Александр Александрович), 26.

Also Available from Donald E. Knuth and Addison-Wesley

0-201-48541-9

Fascicles from Volume 4

For more information about these books, visit us online at www.informit.com/aw.

Also Available from Donald E. Knuth and Addison-Wesley

Concrete Mathematics, Second Edition: A Foundation for Computer Science

0-201-55802-5

This book introduces the mathematics that supports advanced computer programming and the analysis of algorithms. It is an indispensable text and reference not only for computer scientists—the authors themselves rely heavily on it!—but for serious users of mathematics in virtually every discipline.

Surreal Numbers

0-201-03812-9

Some years ago John Horton Conway introduced a new way to construct numbers. Donald E. Knuth, in appreciation of this revolutionary system, wrote an introduction to Conway's method. Knuth wrote this introduction as a work of fiction—a novelette. *Surreal Numbers* will appeal to anyone who might enjoy an engaging dialogue on abstract mathematical ideas, and who might wish to experience how new mathematics is created.

Computers & Typesetting, Volumes A-E Boxed Set

0-201-73416-8

Donald E. Knuth's five volumes on *Computers & Typesetting* comprise the definitive user guides and thoroughly documented program code for the TeX and METAFONT systems. This open-source software is widely used around the world by scientists, mathematicians, and others to produce high-quality, aesthetically pleasing text, especially where technical content is included.